SURVEY OF COMMONWEALTH AFFAIRS

Problems of Expansion and Attrition
1953 — 1969

The Royal Institute of International Affairs is an unofficial body which promotes the scientific study of international questions and does not express opinions of its own. The opinions expressed in this publication are the responsibility of the author

The Institute gratefully acknowledges the comments and suggestions made by the Rt. Hon. Patrick Gordon Walker, P.C., and Professor Kenneth Robinson, who read the manuscript on behalf of the Research Committee

SURVEY OF
COMMONWEALTH AFFAIRS

Problems of Expansion and Attrition
1953 — 1969

BY

J. D. B. MILLER

Professor of International Relations
Australian National University

Published for
The Royal Institute of International Affairs
by

OXFORD UNIVERSITY PRESS

LONDON   NEW YORK   TORONTO

1974

Oxford University Press, Ely House, London W.1

GLASGOW   NEW YORK   TORONTO   MELBOURNE   WELLINGTON
CAPE TOWN   IBADAN   NAIROBI   DAR ES SALAAM   LUSAKA   ADDIS ABABA
DELHI   BOMBAY   CALCUTTA   MADRAS   KARACHI   LAHORE   DACCA
KUALA LUMPUR   SINGAPORE   HONG KONG   TOKYO

ISBN 0 19 214999 7

© Royal Institute of International Affairs 1974

*Printed in Great Britain
by W & J Mackay Limited, Chatham*

To

M

again and for ever

CONTENTS

PART V: DIPLOMATIC CHANGES

PART VI: NETWORKS OF CUSTOM AND CONVENIENCE

PART VII

ABBREVIATIONS*

AAPC	All-African People's Conference
ANC	African National Congress
Anzus	Australia–New Zealand–US alliance
Aus. J. Pol. & Hist.	*Australian Journal of Politics and History*
Canada, HC Deb.	Canada, House of Commons Debates
CDC	Colonial Development Corporation
CDFC	Commonwealth Development Finance Corporation
CN	*Current Notes*
CO	Colonial Office
COI	Central Office of Information (UK)
CRO	Commonwealth Relations Office
CS	*Commonwealth Survey*
CSG, *Ann. rep.* &c.	Commonwealth Secretariat, *Annual* etc. *report of Commonwealth Secretary-General*
DT	*Daily Telegraph*
ECSC	European Coal and Steel Community
Efta	European Free Trade Association
FCO	Foreign and Commonwealth Office
FT	*Financial Times*
GAOR	General Assembly Official Records
Gatt	General Agreement on Tariffs and Trade
Hancock, *Survey*	W. K. Hancock, *Survey of British Commonwealth Affairs* (see bibliography)
HC/HL Deb.	House of Commons/House of Lords Debates
Hist. Stud.	*Historical Studies*
ICRC	International Committee of the Red Cross
IMF	International Monetary Fund
Int. Aff.	*International Affairs*
Int. J.	*International Journal*
Int. Org.	*International Organization*
Int. Stud.	*International Studies*
JCPS	*Journal of Commonwealth Political Studies*
Kitzinger, *ECM & C*	Uwe Kitzinger, *The European Common Market and Community* (1967)
l.d.c.s	Less developed countries
Malaya, HR Deb.	Malaya, House of Representatives Debates
Mansergh, *Documents 1931–52 & 1952–62*	Nicholas Mansergh, ed., *Documents on Commonwealth Affairs 1931–52 & 1952–62* (1953 & 1963)
Mansergh, *Survey 1939–52*	Nicholas Mansergh, *Survey of British Commonwealth Affairs 1939–52* (1958)
MCA	Malayan Chinese Association
MIC	Malayan Indian Congress
NDP	National Democratic Party
Nibmar	No independence before majority rule

* This list excludes those in common use and those which are self-explanatory.

ABBREVIATIONS

NLF	National Liberation Front (Vietnam)
Nigeria, HR Deb.	Nigeria, House of Representatives Debates
NOP	National Opinion Poll
NYHT	*New York Herald Tribune*
NYT	*New York Times*
NZ Deb.	New Zealand Parliamentary Debates
OAU	Organization of African Unity
PAC	Pan-African Congress
Pafmec(s)a	Pan-African Movement for East, Central (and Southern) Africa
PAP	People's Action Party
Rajan, *India ...1959–61*	M. S. Rajan, *India in World Affairs 1959–61* (1965)
RF	Rhodesian Front
RIIA, *Documents*	Royal Inst. of International Affairs, *Documents on International Affairs*
RNP	Rhodesian National Party
S. Africa, HA Deb.	S. Africa, House of Assembly Debates
S. Rhod., LA Deb.	S. Rhodesia, Legislative Assembly Debates
SCAAP	Special Commonwealth Aid to Africa Plan
SCOR	Security Council Official Records
Survey B & CA	*Survey of British & Commonwealth Affairs*
UDI	Unilateral Declaration of Independence
UFP	United Federal Party (S. Rhodesia)
Umno	United Malay National Organization
Unctad	UN Conference on Trade and Development
Zanu	Zimbabwe African National Union
Zapu	Zimbabwe African People's Union

PREFACE

ANDREW SHONFIELD asked me to write this book in 1966, when he was Director of Studies at Chatham House. I started work on it in 1969–70, when I was on study leave from my university. At all stages Chatham House has given me unstinted help. I should like to mention especially Sir Kenneth Younger, who was Director when I began work, and James Fawcett, who as Director of Studies has been constantly sympathetic, and has furnished the book with a title and with a note on appeals to the Judicial Committee of the Privy Council. The librarians of the Institute's Library and Press Library also deserve my thanks, as do Eileen Menzies and my editor, Hermia Oliver, who has again shown the care and discrimination that always mark her work.

The book has been written with continual awareness that it is a successor volume to the major Commonwealth Surveys by Sir Keith Hancock and Professor Nicholas Mansergh. To Kenneth Robinson and Patrick Gordon Walker, who read the manuscript for Chatham House, I am much indebted.

It would be hard to overstate my debt to three friends who have read numerous chapters, sometimes in more than one draft, and have enabled me to improve the structure of the work: Lord Garner, David Bensusan-Butt, and Hedley Bull. I have not always done what they suggested, but mostly their criticisms have been so clear and pointed that no writer could withstand them. Their good humour has been unfailing, their patience extreme.

At Chatham House Hamida Agathocleous did intensive research work for me, and I am grateful. In Canberra I have been helped by research assistants of the Department of International Relations at the Australian National University, especially Marion Cooksey. Doreen Gant and Jo Marsh have typed my chapters quickly and cheerfully.

A book of this kind cannot be written without bothering a great many people for information, materials, and comments on synopses or individual chapters. Those who have kindly helped me in these ways include Dennis Austin, Margaret Ball, Andrew Boyd, Mary Burke, Lord Butler, Charles Carrington, John Chadwick, Sir John Crawford, Roger Davis, James Eayrs, Lord Gore-Booth, Ian Grey, William Heseltine, the High Commissioners in London for Trinidad, Lesotho, Jamaica, Kenya, Sierra Leone, Malaysia and Swaziland, Sir Morrice James, Patrick Keatley, Sir Frank Lee, Michael Lee, Colin Legum, Roy Lewis, Merle and Michael Lipton, Peter Lyon, Sir Laurence McIntyre, Christopher McMahon, Harold Macmillan, Tom Millar, Morris Jones, Patrick O'Leary, William Peters, William Pickles, Richard Preston, M. S. Rajan, Trevor Reese, Stanley de Smith, Arnold Smith, Susan Strange, Hugh Tinker, Sir Burke Trend, Robert Wade-Gery, and Sir Geoffrey Wilson.

It is impossible adequately to acknowledge what I owe to my wife and son Toby, for their forbearance and understanding throughout three years of disturbance and confusion; but I can be concrete, and thank her for correcting my English and him for lending me books on cricket and rugby football.

Canberra
April 1973

J.D.B.M.

INTRODUCTION

AT the time of the Coronation of Queen Elizabeth II in 1953, the point at which Professor Mansergh's last volume in this series ended and this one begins, there were eight members of the Commonwealth. By 1969 one of these, South Africa, had dropped out, but twenty-one others had been admitted. At the time of writing another of the eight has withdrawn (Pakistan), but four others have joined, making a total of thirty-two. The Commonwealth is thus a much bigger and more complex body than when the Queen was crowned. My task has been to ask how it has changed, and why.

In this I am following in the footsteps of my two predecessors, Professors Hancock and Mansergh, but it has not been possible for me to consider each member individually, or to give the same attention to domestic politics. From the inception of this volume, it was not the intention that it should deal substantially with the transfer of power, which was felt to demand quite separate treatment. I have therefore touched upon the process of decolonization only where it seemed essential, as in the rapid movement of events in Africa in the early 1960s, and especially the dissolution of the Federation of Rhodesia and Nyasaland. I have also deliberately neglected constitutional change within the member states.

This study is principally concerned with international politics. It is concerned with what happened to a particular body of states within the international system of the 1950s and 1960s. Throughout, the emphasis is upon the sovereign independence of the members of the Commonwealth, and the use they made of this in their relations with one another and with other states. I have at the same time tried to do justice to the Commonwealth as an assembly of peoples as well as an association between governments, and I have kept constantly in mind the special character of this body of states, derived from the fact that all except Britain were former British dependencies. The many surviving connections with Britain are obviously of great importance.

There is a genuine problem about where to end this *Survey*. I originally intended to stop at the end of 1969, confining mention of later events to footnotes, but it has become clear that such matters as Rhodesia, South Africa, Indo-Pakistani relations, and the sterling area require an extension of this dateline, for events since 1969 have given each of them a different complexion. Hence, while the main narrative deals with the period 1953–69, in some cases I have prolonged it to 1971 or even the early months of 1972.

As the Contents show, Part I opens with a perspective of the Commonwealth in 1953 and then glances at the themes which emerge after that date. Parts II and III present an extended treatment of some of the major international questions which affected the Commonwealth: the Suez crisis; the relations between India, Pakistan, and China; developments in Southeast Asia; the issues of apartheid and of UDI in Rhodesia. Part IV devotes special attention to matters in which British policy was a cardinal factor, such as trade, the sterling area, the EEC, and Commonwealth immigration; some consideration is also given to changes in British policy towards the Commonwealth during the 1950s and 1960s, especially in the light of changes in the international system. Part V develops this last theme in terms of the external policies of Commonwealth members and discusses changes in Commonwealth machinery, including the setting up of the Commonwealth secretariat, and in the 'Commonwealth system'. Part VI treats of various unofficial Commonwealth connections, mainly stressing links with Britain in such matters as trade, investment, migration, language, education, sport, the professions, and images of the Commonwealth. The review with which this study ends attempts to indicate why the Commonwealth of 1969 and later differed so greatly from the Commonwealth of 1953.

PART I

PERSPECTIVE VIEW

CHAPTER 1

THE COMMONWEALTH IN 1953

THE Coronation of Queen Elizabeth II on 2 June 1953 was an occasion for rejoicing and self-congratulation in Britain. Everything but the weather seemed fair. The news of the ascent of Everest, made known to the London crowds, many of whom waited all night to watch the procession from Westminster Abbey, seemed emblematic of British enterprise and initiative and of Britain's position in the world. That position, to many, was symbolized by the fact that the Queen was recognized as Head of the Commonwealth by the independent member-states. In editorials and speeches the Commonwealth was acclaimed when the Coronation was being celebrated.

Indeed, the Archbishop of Canterbury, Dr Fisher, laid great stress on the Queen's position in the Commonwealth. Of a Thanksgiving Service in St Paul's Cathedral a week later, attended by the Queen and the royal family, and at which Sir Winston Churchill read the lesson, it was reported:

> Last Tuesday, Dr Fisher said, this country and this Commonwealth were not far from the Kingdom of Heaven. 'All alike, whether in the Abbey or the stands or linked to the Abbey by broadcast or television found themselves—not a few of them entirely beyond their habits or expectations—absorbed in a ceremony, a service, a sacrament of profound religious meaning.' In the glory of that experience, he said, they were there to give thanks to God for His great goodness 'to us in the Commonwealth and in the Queen, its head and Prince'. The whole Commonwealth went to the Coronation in virtue of mutual trust binding all to the Queen—'the only and the all-sufficient cement of the Commonwealth'.[1]

This was probably the loftiest height to which man's utterance had raised the Commonwealth.

The actual ceremony did not reflect this Commonwealth connection, although there had been consultation about it beforehand. It was essentially traditional, emphasizing established British institutions to the extent that the source of actual political power, the Commons, was almost entirely eclipsed by the Lords and the church dignitaries. The Commonwealth as such was not mentioned in the service. The Queen did, however, swear to 'govern the peoples of the United Kingdom of Great Britain and Northern Ireland, Canada, Australia, New Zealand, the Union of South Africa, Pakistan, and Ceylon and of your possessions and the other territories to any of them

[1] *Manchester Guardian*, 10 June 1953.

belonging or pertaining, according to their respective laws and customs'.[1] These countries were her realms, although they did not constitute the whole of the Commonwealth of which she was Head. India, a republic, was not mentioned, not from neglect but because this was India's wish.

Although the Queen swore a common oath as monarch of her realms, she did not have a common style and title for all of them. Earlier in the year each of the realms had enacted its own version, after they had agreed to a clarification of the position that had been requested by Canada.[2] In all but one of these new rubrics, the point was made that Her Majesty was Queen of the particular country concerned (i.e. of Canada, Australia, and so on); but they differed in that, while the Canadian, New Zealand and Australian ones stated first that she was Queen of the United Kingdom, the South African and Ceylonese ones did not mention the United Kingdom at all, while the Pakistani one mentioned the United Kingdom but not Pakistan. In the Australian parliament the prime minister and leader of the Opposition both insisted that the Commonwealth was British. In South Africa a Nationalist prime minister took evident pleasure in pointing out how unBritish the Commonwealth was, and laboured the point further by quoting the minutes of the Prime Ministers' Meeting of 1949, to the effect that the designation of the monarch as Head of the Commonwealth did not imply the discharge of any constitutional function.

Thus at the time of the Coronation the diversity of the Commonwealth was apparent, and this fact was emphasized by some of the arrangements. The prime ministers of each of the independent member countries, including India, took part in the Queen's procession within the Abbey, and each had his own carriage in the procession outside. The premiers of Malta, Southern Rhodesia, and Northern Ireland, none of which was independent, were not included in the Abbey procession, but rode in carriages from the Abbey.[3] There were colonial contingents in the procession as well as troops from each independent country except India.[4] Queen Salote of Tonga, and the sultans of Lahej, Brunei, Perak, Kelantan, Selangor, Johore, and Zanzibar acknowledged the

---

[1] Details of the oath, and of other matters such as the placement of guests in the processions, are taken from *The Coronation 1953*, suppl. to *The Times*, 1 June, and *DT Second Coronation Supplement*, 2 June 1953.

[2] For details of the various forms of the style and titles, and extracts from the parliamentary debates in the various countries involved, see Mansergh, *Documents 1952–62*, pp. 7–35. The point about Canada was revealed by Dr Malan, then prime minister of South Africa (p. 30).

[3] The prime minister of Malta, Dr Borg Olivier, had refused to come because he considered the original arrangements gave Malta the wrong status; in this he was supported by his parliament. After a late intervention by Sir Winston Churchill, it was arranged that Dr Olivier should have his own carriage in the procession. The prime minister of Ceylon, Mr Dudley Senanayake, who was also to have had his own carriage, obligingly shared it with the premier of Southern Rhodesia, Sir Godfrey Huggins. There were then ten prime ministerial carriages instead of nine (*The Times*, 12, 13, 21, & 22 May and *DT*, 2 June 1953).

[4] India and S. Africa showed their governments' reservations about the ceremonies by opposite policies: India sent no troops but was represented at the Spithead naval review; S. Africa sent troops but no ships.

cheering crowds as the procession moved through the rainy streets. Although widely acclaimed as evidence of Britain's Commonwealth connections, the presence of these colonial rulers suggested a backward rather than forward look in Commonwealth terms. Those African movements which were to dominate Commonwealth controversy within a few years, and countries still to win independence, like Ghana, Zambia, Malawi, Tanzania, and Malaysia, necessarily did not participate in the procession. The future shape of the Commonwealth could be glimpsed only dimly in this show of splendour.

One voice, very much out of tune with most of those raised at the time, proved prophetic. On the Sunday before the Coronation, Canon L. J. Collins, preaching at St Paul's, said: 'Our Coronation celebrations will be a mockery if we fail to be penitent for race discrimination and colour prejudice'. He went on:

The vast majority of our Queen's subjects are coloured. Dare we ask her in the Coronation Oath to promise in our name to govern the peoples of South Africa, nearly ten millions of them, in accordance with racial discrimination laws which every church with the exception of the South African Dutch Reformed Church has condemned as unjust and contrary to the Christian conscience?[1]

In some of the colonies there were minor boycotts, arranged by local national- ists.[2] These attracted only slight attention. Like Canon Collins's sermon, and the reluctance of the governments of the Republic of Ireland, Iran, and Nationalist China to join in celebrating the occasion, they were scarcely noticed. Euphoria was the rule, and it included euphoria about the Common- wealth, which was expressed by *The Times* on Coronation Day itself:

Coronation-tide provides many answers [to the question of what bonds held the Commonwealth together], and the first of them was made plain before the whole world last Wednesday. The gathering together, under the high roof of Westminster Hall, of Prime Ministers and representatives from over fifty Parliaments—almost all of them to hail their Queen, every one of them to hail Her Majesty as Head of the Commonwealth—told far more about the nature of the Commonwealth than a hundred treatises. The practice of parliamentary government as the safeguard of freedom is one of the greatest of the unifying links in the Commonwealth as it is one of the proudest memorials of British rule. . . .

Today, after the sacred hour in the Abbey, another of the links of Commonwealth will be manifest as the soldiers of the Queen march ahead of her coach. The men from Canada and all the senior Commonwealth countries . . . stir the heart because of the pledge they carry with them and the pledge which is returned to them no less fully by the soldiers of the United Kingdom. It is the assurance that no single member of the Commonwealth will be left to stand unaided in face of danger. No

---

[1] *Daily Herald*, 1 June 1953.
[2] There were difficulties in Cyprus, Nyasaland, and Nigeria (see *The Times*, 3 & 4 June, DT and *West African Pilot*, 6 May 1953).

military pact, no matter how precise, has stronger force than that abiding assurance. A Commonwealth country is fully independent, but never alone.

Then, after Coronation Day, there appears yet another side to the partnership when the Prime Ministers meet as equals to speak together on all world affairs. No talks are franker, none are better informed. . . .

. . . The only certain threat to Commonwealth unity would arise if a member deliberately pursued a policy, either internal or external, that put her outside the traditions of civilised conduct. Yet of all the links that bind the members together none is more open, more precious or more real than the link with the Crown; and this day that brings its pledges and its fellowship before the Throne is a renewal of the life of the Commonwealth.[1]

Allowing for the excusable inflation of language on a great national occasion, we may regard this editorial as broadly representing the orthodox British view of the Commonwealth in 1953. A similar note was struck by the CRO *List*, which each year attempted to define the Commonwealth and describe its most recent activities. In the 1953 edition the opening article began by equating 'the Commonwealth' with

what was formerly known as 'the British Empire', i.e., comprising not only the United Kingdom and the countries previously known as Dominions, but also the dependencies of those countries . . . Within the Commonwealth as described above there are certain countries possessing a special status, namely that of a sovereign, independent country, recognised as a separate international entity, but associated with other Commonwealth countries of the same status in a relationship differing from that existing between foreign states.[2]

This cautious definition, with its equation between the Commonwealth and 'what was formerly known as the British Empire' and its avoidance of the word 'state' to describe members of the Commonwealth in order to assert between them 'a relationship differing from that existing between foreign states', brings to mind the doctrine of '*inter se*', whereby, in the years immediately after World War I, the British and some dominion governments sought to confine the status of the dominions to something less than that of a fully sovereign state.[3] Elsewhere in the article, there was an echo of *The Times*: the common pattern of official institutions in Commonwealth countries was said to include their parliamentary procedures, the Queen as head of the executive (except in India), their system of law, their law of nationality, and their free co-operation through 'a system of complete and continuous consultation'. All these factors in combination

have resulted in a unity of purpose and action which could not in any other manner have been achieved by an association consisting of elements in many ways so diverse.

[1] Editorial, 'Light as Air, Strong as Iron', 2 June 1953.
[2] 'The Commonwealth' in *CRO List 1953*, p. 7.
[3] For reviews of the fate of '*inter se*', see J. E. S. Fawcett, *The British Commonwealth in international law* (1963), and S. A. de Smith, *The new Commonwealth and its constitutions* (1964).

The Imperial Conference of 1926 expressed its confidence that 'though every Dominion is now, and must always remain, the sole judge of the nature and extent of its co-operation, no common cause will, in our opinion, be thereby imperilled.' Subsequent events have shown the truth of this prophecy, and the sentiments then expressed can be echoed equally today.

Here, then, was the platonic model of the Commonwealth as seen by British publicists who wished to praise and explain it in 1953. How did it correspond with reality?

The answer must be that there was considerable but not complete correspondence. The Commonwealth consisted of Britain, Canada, Australia, South Africa, New Zealand, India, Pakistan, and Ceylon, together with their dependencies.[1] The monarchical element was still strong. The British connection, as expressed in symbols such as flags and anthems, could still arouse controversy in Canada and South Africa, the two realms in which, traditionally, ethnic minorities had disputed the 'British' quality of their country. In Australia and New Zealand the Britishness was still accepted as natural. India, Pakistan, and Ceylon had been independent for six years and India a republic for four; each of these countries was liable to take a different line from Britain in foreign policy, and to do so without qualms, but there was still a good deal of common ground. While the consultation between Commonwealth members was hardly 'complete and continuous', as the CRO *List* claimed, the fact that a generation of civil servants and politicians who had co-operated closely during World War II was still dominant had much effect. Although the constitutional ties had been loosened and some things had changed, there was much justification for the widespread British feeling that the main things were still much as they had been. In terms of institutions, they certainly were. Each of the members was still operating a form of parliamentary government, although in Pakistan this was showing continual strain and had not been reanimated by elections. Each except India was a realm; and this, perhaps more than anything else, enabled many—perhaps most—British people to feel that the Commonwealth was a group of freely co-operating states which retained British institutions because they were best.

The military links to which *The Times* drew attention were not substantial, but they did exist. The independence of India and Pakistan meant that Britain no longer controlled an Indian Army, but the continued presence in the Suez Canal Zone showed the reality of Britain's interest in the Middle East and the

---

[1] There was ambiguity about whether the dependencies were 'in' the Commonwealth and whether they should be called 'Commonwealth countries' or simply 'colonies'. The British tendency, in my experience, was to stress the inclusiveness of the Commonwealth and the emerging status of its own dependencies; the tendency of the other members (with historical precedent in the attitudes of the self-governing colonies in 1907) was to emphasize that a dependency could not be a Commonwealth *member* until it became an independent state, and that Commonwealth membership had then to be specifically requested and specifically granted by agreement amongst the existing members.

Indian Ocean, an interest which was reinforced by a substantial base at Singapore. Australia and New Zealand, while ensuring their security through the Anzus Pact with the US, regarded the British presence in Egypt and Singapore as important to their defence. There was a British naval base at Trincomalee in Ceylon, and another at Simonstown in South Africa. India and Pakistan sheltered no British forces, but both retained long-standing professional links with the British services which had moulded their own. Everywhere British military equipment and British military practices were predominant. While the Korean war armistice was not signed till a month after the Coronation, in this war a Commonwealth Division, consisting of British, Canadian, Australian, and New Zealand troops, and an Indian Field Ambulance, had been part of the UN forces. Its headquarters had also included some South African officers. It was still possible to combine such troops into a single force.[1]

There were also economic links, of which ministers, officials and others throughout the Commonwealth were acutely aware. These were of various kinds and widely misunderstood. If the man in the street had been asked to describe them, he would probably have mentioned Commonwealth (formerly Imperial) preferences first; but as a practical link affecting policy, these were almost certainly less important than British investment in Commonwealth countries, trade conducted outside the preference system, and membership by all Commonwealth members except Canada of the sterling area.

Of Britain's overseas investment at the end of 1953, some 56 per cent was estimated to be in Commonwealth countries, including the dependencies, but the distribution of this investment was unequal. The developed countries scored most heavily: £344 m. in Australia, £160 m. in South Africa, and £156 m. in Canada. Even New Zealand, with a very small population, had £72 m. of British capital. India had £60 m., Ceylon £23 m., and Pakistan a mere £9 m. By contrast, in no European country had Britain more than £40 m. invested, and the figure for the US was only £172 m. The dependencies, so often regarded by radicals as the special preserves of British capital, did not figure so prominently as the developed independent countries, although the figure for Malaya was given as £69 m., and for Rhodesia and Nyasaland £115 m.[2] British investment abroad was largely within the Commonwealth, but this was a result less of deliberate long-term policy than of the special circumstances of World War II, which had closed many countries to British capital and compelled Britain to sell its holdings in others.

In trade something of the same story could be told. Preference was a factor in causing Commonwealth countries to trade with one another, but even more important was their wartime and postwar experience of a shortage of alternative currencies, markets, and sources of supply. In 1953 Britain imported £376 m. worth of goods from the sterling area, as against £460 m. from non-

---

[1] T. B. Millar, *The Commonwealth and the UN* (1967), pp. 58–62.
[2] Figures collected by the Bank of England and published in *CS*, 9 Aug 1955, pp. 689–90.

sterling countries (including Canada). The rest of the sterling area imported £313 m. worth from Britain and £187 m. from other sterling-area sources, as against £397 m. from non-sterling countries.[1]

The sterling area was not conterminous with the Commonwealth since it did not include Canada and did include certain foreign countries such as Iraq, Iceland, and some of the oil states of the Persian Gulf; but Commonwealth countries were foremost in the organization of the sterling area through their central banks and treasuries. It was widely felt that the area's dependence on a common pool of gold and dollars, held by the Bank of England and forming the backing to Britain's currency, constituted one of the principal links binding the Commonwealth. It was at least a tangible link. Overseas sterling countries had an interest in preserving the stability of the pound sterling, and in having recourse to whatever reserves of foreign exchange the area as a whole could earn. Britain had an interest in maintaining a wide area for free movement of its goods. Not through any coercion, but by the exercise of self-interest, overseas Commonwealth countries recognized that their membership of the sterling area gave them access to a wider choice of goods and investment than each could have attained by its own unaided efforts. The concerted policy of discriminating against goods from dollar areas (including Canada) in order to conserve the pool of gold and dollars meant that they traded more with each other, and especially with Britain, than would otherwise have been the case.

The intermittent meetings of prime ministers were the only visible links between Commonwealth members other than the representation of members in one another's capitals by high commissioners. These meetings, which took place every two years or so, were relatively small and intimate in comparison with the meetings of universal international bodies such as the UN. They were much less formal than were the Imperial Conferences held before World War II. There were not the same assumptions about a united policy for a united Empire as the dominions' leaders had wrestled with in 1930 and 1937, but there was a clear line of descent in terms of the conventions of debate and even the topics discussed. World affairs, economic matters (especially balance-of-payments problems and the needs of the overseas countries for development), and occasionally constitutional questions involving terms of membership, were what the prime ministers talked about in the 1950s, as they had in the 1930s, though not in the same language or as part of the same world. R. G. Menzies, the Australian prime minister, who had been a member of the Australian delegation at the 1937 Imperial Conference and had attended all the conferences of the 1950s, in 1960 looked back on these meetings with a sense of pleasure and of continuity:

When we meet, we have no set agenda. We move no resolutions, and we have never cast votes. But we learn a great deal about the world's problems and our relations

[1] Ibid., 6 Apr 1955, pp. 340–1.

to them. The intolerance engendered by long-range and imperfect knowledge is tempered. From time to time, as I well know from experience, we influence each other's thinking, without the discords of public controversy. We have, after all, some community of history and ideas. We no longer aim at producing a common foreign policy, nor do we any longer find ourselves able to envisage the Commonwealth as a 'world power'. But if we can achieve a common philosophical approach to world problems, there is life and virtue in our deliberations . . .

. . . We are brothers in a special international family. We have done well so far because we have nurtured our elements of unity with loving care and have sought to resolve our differences in a friendly and mutually helpful way. There is, in brief, a quality of intimacy about our meetings which relegates the protocol of diplomacy to its proper place, induces personal friendships, and enables us, between conferences, to communicate with each other without hesitation or reserve.[1]

The international, formally bipolar, environment of 1953, in which the atmosphere of the 'Cold War' induced states to declare their adherence to one side or the other, encouraged such sentiments. Britain, Canada, Australia, New Zealand, and South Africa were all hostile to the Soviet Union's position in world politics, and either allied with or sympathetic towards the US. India, Pakistan, and Ceylon had not taken up formal stances of this kind, although Pakistan was soon to do so in its membership of Seato, established in 1954. However, there was no real gulf between the 'old' and 'new' members; although the 'old' members were allied to the US, they did not subscribe to all its policies. Subject to the obligations of their formal alliances (in each case except South Africa, which belonged to none), they sometimes tried to bring pressure to bear upon the US and to moderate what they regarded as possibly dangerous tendencies in its policy. In this they were often at one with India, Ceylon, and Pakistan.

It had been noticeable at the 1951 Prime Ministers' Meeting that all Commonwealth governments feared an extension of the Korean war, and their communiqué reflected this in the Declaration appended to it.[2] Similarly, at the Prime Ministers' Meeting which followed the Coronation there was 'a distinctive Commonwealth attitude towards the abiding problems of the world',[3] expressing itself this time in support of the ideas which Churchill, then prime minister, had recently put forward for 'summit' talks between the two superpowers, and which, it was hoped, he would be able soon to discuss with President Eisenhower at Bermuda.[4] In each of these cases (as again in 1955, when they were to meet in the shadow of a Taiwan crisis and of the hydrogen bomb) it suited both Britain and the 'old' members, and the 'new' members

---

[1] *The changing Commonwealth* (1960) (Mansergh, *Documents 1952–62*, pp. 764–5).

[2] For details of the 1951 meeting, together with references to those of 1953 and 1955, see J. D. B. Miller, 'Commonwealth conferences 1945–55', *Year Book of World Affairs, 1956*, pp. 156–66.

[3] *The Times*, 10 June 1953.

[4] For a vivid account of these circumstances see Harold Macmillan, *Tides of fortune 1945–55* (1969), pp. 510–13.

as well, to adopt a common attitude which did not condemn American policies outright but urged their moderation in veiled terms, and which attempted to encourage the Soviet Union and China to engage in talks rather than war.

In the Commonwealth of 1953, the key position in an important sense was held by India. Its vast size and population and the highly articulate character of its leaders had given India special stature amongst the new nations of Asia after independence in 1947. At the UN and elsewhere, Indian leaders had been foremost in opposing colonialism and in deploring the tendency of military pacts to rigidify the divisions in world politics. Nehru's policy of 'non-alignment' was regarded as distinctive; when he spoke, men listened.[1] Indian diplomacy had been extremely active over the Korean war. If India had refused to work the Commonwealth system as it stood, and had insisted on changing every institution so as to emphasize the anti-colonial character of Indian policy—as Nehru was often urged to do by members of the Indian parliament —it would have been extremely difficult to sustain the sense of continuity with the past[2] and to cultivate common ground between the members.

We may speculate at length, without absolute assurance, about why Nehru and the Indian government showed such deference to the conventions of Commonwealth behaviour in the early 1950s. No doubt India's economic position, the closeness of Indian leaders to established figures of importance in Britain, the equivocal nature of Russian attitudes to India, the influence of ICS-trained officials, and the British idiom of Indian politics, all had a part in the explanation. Similarly, we can find reasons why, after the establishment of Seato and the apparent favouring of Pakistan at India's expense by the US, and, at a hesitant distance, by Britain, India's policy became somewhat less sympathetic towards Britain and its allies. Even so, the course of India's behaviour within the Commonwealth had been set and was not to be altered

[1] See the discussion of Indian policy after independence in Mansergh, *Survey 1939–52*, pp. 357–60.
[2] Some of the farsightedness and good humour of Indian policy in the Commonwealth at this time can be attributed to sentiments such as those of M. J. Desai, Indian Commonwealth secretary, in 1957: 'There is one point, however, which some of us miss while dealing with Commonwealth affairs. After all, the evolution of what you call the current concept of Commonwealth is pretty recent. There are people alive, and people in authority in various parts of the Commonwealth, who have been associated with the concept of the Commonwealth at the first stage, "Imperial Commonwealth". There are also people in authority in various parts of the world who have been associated with the second stage which one may call "British Commonwealth and Empire". What we regard . . . as "Commonwealth of Nations" is a fairly recent concept and human minds being what they are, they are not so quickly adapted to the new changes. While working out things logically and legally, people may concede the new concept but there is always the tendency to harp back to the old. . . . It is not that people in Britain or Australia or Canada have concepts of the Commonwealth of stage one or stage two. It also applies to us in India because the only concept of the Commonwealth we have is the last stage and we cannot understand why there are people in other parts of the Commonwealth who still cling to old ideas. But that is life. That is human existence. Human beings can only evolve over a period, and ten years is not a long period for the evolution of the new concept and its general acceptance in the minds of men' (M. J. Desai, 'Commonwealth relations', *J. United Service Inst. of India*, July–Sept 1957).

until the appearance of African members in the 1960s. India did not, for example, raise at Commonwealth meetings the alleged enormities of South African racial policy which it raised at the UN, although Nehru frequently expressed his views on major issues. Indian agreement with Britain, while intermittent, was sufficient to make plausible Churchill's comment on the 1955 Prime Ministers' Meeting, as reported by Lord Moran:

a hell of a business . . . not at all like the old gatherings of the Dominions . . . I have held my own, and more than held my own . . . I have led the discussions, made little jokes, given them ideas, and engaged in arguments. . . . I get on very well with him [Nehru]. I tell him he has a great role to play as the leader of Free Asia against Communism. . . . Oh, he wants to do it—and I want him to do it. He has a feeling that the Communists are against him, and that is apt to change people's opinions.[1]

Churchill, deeply affected by the dramatic aspects of India's remaining in the Commonwealth, may have exaggerated Nehru's compliance with his own views and the extent to which he could influence Nehru. Yet in 1953 or 1955, in a world of deceptively simple alignments and looming dangers, the lines taken by Nehru and Churchill were reconcilable within a loose structure of co-operation which contained few obligations but preserved traditional niceties. Nehru's presence at the Coronation was a symbol of that structure.

The major point of tension for India was the possibility that Pakistan might persuade other members to make Kashmir a Commonwealth issue rather than a bilateral one, or one to be debated at the UN. Frequent Pakistani suggestions that the Commonwealth should adjudicate or mediate in disputes between its members met with no response, in spite of a strong feeling in Britain (and to some extent in Australia, Canada, and New Zealand) that it was unseemly to have two members in constant dispute. The 1951 Prime Ministers' Meeting had provided informal opportunities for discussions about Kashmir, although these were not technically part of the meeting itself;[2] thereafter the Commonwealth did not enter into the question in any substantive way. India, like South Africa, could proceed throughout the 1950s on the assumption that what it regarded as its domestic affairs would not be questioned at Commonwealth meetings. With Kashmir confined to the UN, there was no reason why India should not continue to operate within the Commonwealth system.

India can be regarded as holding the key position in the Commonwealth in 1953 because it was in the best position to spoil the appearance of agreement, and did not choose to do so. It was a key in the negative sense that things would have been different if it had acted differently. In a larger sense, however, Britain remained the most significant country in the Commonwealth, since without it there would have been no Commonwealth at all.

At this particular stage in history, no other imperial power was on such good

[1] Lord Moran, *Winston Churchill* (1966), pp. 630-1.
[2] Miller, pp. 158-60.

terms with its former colonies as Britain. France was still in deep trouble in Indo-China and North Africa, and had not begun the process of decolonizing its other African territories. The Netherlands-Indonesian Union, which had been intended to bring the Dutch and the Indonesians together in a working partnership, had been a failure. The US had given independence to the Philippines but had set up only treaty relations with it. Neither Spain nor Portugal was concerned to liberate its colonies. Britain, in contrast, had not only granted independence to India, Pakistan, Ceylon, and Burma, but had also invited them to join an association which had previously been the preserve of white settler colonies when they attained complete self-government. Moreover, the process of accepting these Asian states (except Burma, which declined the offer) as members of the former British Commonwealth of Nations had been not only smooth but instant. Once they had attained independence, it was agreed that they should be full members. Despite some cavilling from the Nationalist government of South Africa, other members had agreed that the Commonwealth would be strengthened, not weakened.

The Commonwealth of 1953 is best seen as an association of Britain with its former dependencies, an association in which the British element was strong (whether in terms of British settlement or British institutions or both), and in which the overseas members were glad to retain some formal connection with Britain. Their contacts with one another were unimportant in comparison with the bilateral contacts which each had with Britain. Those of long standing had connections with Britain which they wished to continue or develop; those whose independence was newer had unfinished business which they had no desire to break off. They were not forced to join the Commonwealth by threats that trade preferences or membership of the sterling area would be withdrawn if they did not; Burma and Ireland continued to exercise these privileges although they were not members. The new members, like the old, presumably considered that they obtained some addition to their diplomatic resources by their membership, an addition which came largely, though not entirely, from the continuance of their association with Britain.

The British government took care to stress the independence of the members, but it also emphasized the existence of the Commonwealth, from which it gained stature of its own.[1] When the prime ministers met, they met in London, and the British premier took the chair. The CRO and the Cabinet Office managed the meetings. When the Commonwealth countries held their informal meetings at the UN in New York, the British representative was again in the chair. The sterling area was based on British currency. Britain was

---

[1] It was typical of conventional wisdom of the time that in the Reith Lectures for 1954 Sir Oliver Franks should say: 'Without the Commonwealth we cannot continue as a Great Power. Little argument is needed to show the necessity of the Commonwealth to Britain's continuing greatness. It is a truth which the British people have intuitively perceived: they do not require a demonstration' (*Britain and the tide of world affairs* (1955), p. 14).

the principal military power amongst the members and had special arrangements with several of them. Whichever way the matter was viewed, the Commonwealth looked like a British group. 'Le Commonwealth Derrière Sir Winston'—the headline in *Le Monde* on 10 June 1953, after the Prime Ministers' Meeting which followed the Coronation—summed up not only the dominant view of the Commonwealth held by foreigners and British people alike, but also the practical situation of the overseas members. For a variety of reasons, each found itself not only in accord with British policy for the time being, but also prepared to continue in formal association with Britain. It could be said with some assurance, and certainly with pride, as Nicholas Mansergh said in concluding the previous volume in this series, that 'the Commonwealth, so it seemed to contemporaries, constituted an experiment in international co-operation that was supremely worth undertaking'.[1]

[1] Mansergh, *Survey 1939–52*, p. 421.

CHAPTER 2

EMERGENT THEMES

FIVE broad themes emerge when one looks at the evolution of the Commonwealth after 1953.

The first and most important is that of a more complex international environment in which members of the Commonwealth had more opportunities for the exercise and diversification of national interests than ever before. The world provided an expanding area of international activity for all, including Britain. It may be seen in economic terms, involving greater multilateralism in trade, aid, investment and currencies; or in the change from bipolarity to an increasing degree of multipolarity in world politics; or in the existence of more organizations for states to belong to, including a greater variety of regional associations; or simply in terms of a more widespread diplomacy in which the Commonwealth element mattered less to the older members than in the 1930s and 1940s, and less to the newer ones than they might have expected before independence.

The point is strikingly illustrated in a speech delivered in 1967 by Chief Leabua Jonathan, the prime minister of Lesotho (formerly Basutoland), a year after his little landlocked country of about a million people, surrounded by South Africa, had gained its independence:

... We have found our self-confidence in the international community, and other countries have come to respect us for what we are. If this were not so, would our Ambassador to the UN have been accepted as Chairman of the Afro-Asian Committee earlier this year? Would our special envoy to the OAU Conference of Ministers at Kinshasa have been elected secretary to the meeting? Would you have thought that my recent Policy speech at the UN Assembly would have received the hundred percent support of all member states, and that today the majority of independent African States are prepared to exchange diplomatic relations with us? I personally have been received and honoured in many countries. . . . My trips abroad have not been in vain. Korea is helping us with doctors; the Republic of China will help us agriculturally; Austria will help us with tourism; the USA will help us in a number of fields, including the Peace Corps volunteer service, the Catholic Relief Service, and the Crossroads Africa organization. During my recent visit to the US I had important discussions with high ranking officials of Government, Corporations, and Banking Institutions, and I am confident that they will help us in a variety of fields. . . . Malawi will help us in the training of our youth pioneer corps. The Prime Minister of Israel and his Foreign Minister have offered us the same help and have undertaken to send us an expert in Youth Organizations and to train our boys and girls . . . I should also mention that I have received, and accepted in principle, an invitation from the Prime Minister of Israel to pay a State Visit to that country. The time when this should take place is still under discussion, and might coincide with a similar visit to Canada which our Ambassador is arranging. No doubt this time I shall also want to pay a visit to the Holy See and a courtesy call on the Italian Prime Minister, with whom we have established diplomatic relations. Let us not forget that we are a Christian government.[1]

Here, in engaging detail, are to be seen the lively cocksureness, the strong desire for involvement, the sense of wide horizons, and the awareness of diplomatic opportunities which characterized new states in the 1960s. The Commonwealth was, to Chief Jonathan, only one of the organizations to which his country might belong. His attitude—extreme perhaps, but nonetheless shared by many of the leaders of the new Commonwealth countries—was worlds away from the cautious view of extra-Commonwealth associations (or even those within it) of the leaders of Australia, Canada, and New Zealand in the 1930s.

A second, related, theme is that of a Commonwealth which became, under the stress of events, much less of a unity. It was more varied in membership, more divergent in aims, less intimate and informal in operation, and more obviously a vehicle for the pressure brought to bear by individual members in pursuit of their national interests. Such a Commonwealth remained largely bilateral in that, although some of the members developed close relations between themselves, none rivalled Britain in the extent to which its contacts were Commonwealth-wide, and each overseas member preserved contacts with Britain. The major 'Commonwealth' interests of the members continued to be expressed through these contacts, rather than through either a general Commonwealth consensus or any concerted action of a Commonwealth kind. This second theme provides an answer to a question asked but not fully answered in the previous volume of this *Survey*: 'Did the nations now mean more than the Commonwealth which collectively they comprised?'[2] The answer, if this theme has been correctly discerned, is yes. Apart from anything else, there was more contention between Commonwealth members after 1953 than ever before.

A third theme, which may seem to contradict the second, is that of a steady growth in Commonwealth machinery and in co-operation in the use of that machinery. Besides the setting up of a Commonwealth secretariat, there were a great enlargement of bodies such as the Commonwealth Parliamentary Association and the growth of Commonwealth co-operation in such fields as education, telecommunications, economic discussion, and the professions, as well as the appearance of a Commonwealth Foundation and the continuance

---

[1] From *Address by the Hon. the Prime Minister at the first anniversary Pitso of Lesotho's independence held on the 4th October 1967* (official text supplied by Lesotho High Commission, London).

[2] Mansergh, *Survey 1939–52*, p. 359.

and expansion of a number of miscellaneous Commonwealth bodies which had been in existence before 1953. When Professor Mansergh surveyed the two postwar decades, in which the 'frontier between reality and nothingness was approached [by the Commonwealth] in international and racial policies', he felt that 'paradoxically as it may seem, the Commonwealth idea acquired content and substance in respect of social, economic and educational coopera- tion, such as it has never hitherto possessed'.[1]

This third theme can be linked with the first. The connection lies in the growth of institutional tissue of all international bodies during the period since World War II. All of these were more extensive and significant than their prewar counterparts; they grew steadily even when their prime purposes seemed to be stultified by international rivalries in general and the Cold War in particular. It would have been extraordinary if the Commonwealth, alone amongst international bodies, had not shared this growth of tissue, especially when its membership increased so greatly. Style and fashion operate in international organization as much as in more obvious fields; and the Common- wealth, although more informal and less obligatory than other bodies, was bound to be affected. It was not as if officials connected with Commonwealth affairs decided consciously that the Commonwealth must be kept in step with other bodies to which their countries belonged. It was rather that in such matters as the style of procedure, the preparation of material, the practice of financial contribution, and the calculation of benefits gained, the Common- wealth grew, and was accepted by its members, in much the same way as other international bodies.

The growth of Commonwealth machinery was also a matter of transferring what had previously been colonial institutions to a Commonwealth sphere, as more and more former colonies became independent: the Colonial Develop- ment Corporation became the Commonwealth Development Corporation in 1963; the Imperial Institute became the Commonwealth Institute in 1958. In the main, however, it involved using the resources of Britain to help countries which required continued assistance in ways which would be consonant with their independent status. Especially in the technical, professional, and educa- tional fields, schemes such as the Commonwealth Scholarship and Fellowship Plan were required to continue and expand the services which Britain had traditionally provided in these fields.

Changes in British policy and opinion form a fourth theme in the movement of Commonwealth affairs between 1953 and 1969, changes which occurred fitfully but in a particular direction—that of concentrating less on the Common- wealth and more on Europe. Much of this study is devoted to British reactions to the decline of British power, the pressures of Commonwealth members for further decolonization, and the weaknesses of sterling. As these influences grew stronger, and as the sense of imperial mission waned, the Commonwealth

[1] Mansergh, *The Commonwealth experience* (1969), p. 342.

lost attraction for many British people. One could find, by searching hard, fainter echoes of a similar theme in the policies of some other members, especially the older ones: Canada, Australia, New Zealand, and India would all repay study as examples of how changes in the Commonwealth were received, reflected and reinforced—and sometimes resisted—by other members. But each of these had a much smaller and less comprehensive role in Commonwealth affairs than Britain. None was so deeply involved in public debate on Commonwealth issues, and none had so much either to lose or gain from the changes that took place or might have taken place. Britain's changes of attitude necessarily loom large in any account of Commonwealth change. In the main, this theme is one of disillusionment.

There is also a fifth theme, dependent upon the others for its course and its emphasis, but important for any synoptic understanding: that of changing conceptions of what the Commonwealth stood for, especially in racial terms. During the period with which we are concerned the most important issue was whether the Commonwealth was 'multiracial', although the full implications of this protean term were rarely considered, and even less rarely agreed on by those who discussed it in public. Similarly, there were discussions of the Commonwealth's function as a 'bridge' between the continents, especially between Europe and North America on the one hand and Africa and Asia on the other. There were arguments about whether Commonwealth membership involved adherence to any code of conduct, in regard to consultation of other members, or the retention of parliamentary government, or the observance of certain human rights, or public respect for the monarchy because of the Queen's position as Head of the Commonwealth. As the period wore on, it became harder for those who wished to explain the Commonwealth to say whether it stood for anything at all; but the idea that it ought to do so persisted. This is a theme which begins in comparative harmony, moves to a point of crashing discord, then fades, but is still there at the end. To anyone who has read the opening volume in this series of *Surveys*, it must be a matter of absorbing interest.[1] The Commonwealth had been regarded, by many of those who wrote about it, as something worthy of respect and belief because it was based upon notions of freedom, self-determination, and racial equality. Much of the disappointment felt by its supporters in the 1960s arose from the retreat from these ideals in the face of the national interests of the members, sometimes of Britain and sometimes of the members overseas.

[1] In W. K. Hancock, *Survey*, i: *Problems of nationality 1918–36* (1937) a triad of character-istics—Liberty, Equality, Unity—is seen as the objective of an emerging British Common-wealth; and the theme of that volume is how 'the government of men by themselves' leads to certain variations within this triad.

PART II

SUEZ AND ASIA

CHAPTER 3

THE INTERNATIONAL BACKGROUND

I N this Part we are concerned with the impact upon the Commonwealth of
critical events in the Middle East and Asia between 1953 and 1969—the
Suez crisis of 1956, the clashes between India and China in 1959 and 1962,
the Indo-Pakistani war of 1965 (and that of six years later), the confrontation
of Malaysia by Indonesia between 1963 and 1965, and the Vietnam war, still
unfinished in 1969. Each of these subjected the Commonwealth to strain.
Moreover, each indicated how the Commonwealth was changing under the
stress of an increase in members and an altered world situation: the relatively
small Commonwealth of the Suez crisis was different in tone and temper from
the greatly enlarged body which had to grapple with the events of the 1960s.
Apart from an abortive attempt at mediation in Vietnam in 1965, there was no
distinctive Commonwealth policy on any of the issues considered. Each was an
illustration of the first two themes outlined in the last chapter. In an increasingly
complex world, the Commonwealth could provide neither a full universe of
discourse nor a ready focus of agreed policy for its members. Wider considerations presented them with awkward choices and difficult associations.

These events occurred within the international framework created by the
Cold War, but were also affected by many states' adherence to a policy of non-
alignment between super-power blocs. Both the Cold War and non-alignment
were greatly modified during the period covered by this and the two succeeding Parts, and the outcome was a world in which states could exercise greater
freedom of choice and be less concerned about great-power connections than
in 1953. But the events discussed here had their roots in the Cold War and
were very much shaped by its conditions.

Thus the vehemence of the British government's attitude on Suez was due
not only to its wish to sustain British influence in the Middle East, but also
to its belief that, since Egypt was getting arms and other support from the
Soviet Union, Egyptian success in the nationalization of the Suez Canal might
extend Soviet influence throughout the Arab world. Such reasoning was also
responsible for the mistaken British belief that the use of armed force against
Egypt would meet with American approval.

The disputes between India and Pakistan were not caused by the Cold
War; they were legacies of partition, rendered more extreme, however, by
Pakistan's receiving arms from, and entering into an alliance with, the US.
The result was India's greater distrust of the western powers and a stronger
Indian assertion of the validity of non-alignment not only for India and South

Asia but for other countries and regions as well. When India fell out with China, the support which it obtained from western countries (notably those in the Commonwealth) was inspired in large part by Cold War considerations. China was still closely allied with the Soviet Union in 1959; in 1962, while it had broken away, it was displaying a defiant independence which provoked even stronger verbal attacks on 'American imperialism' than the Soviet Union had been accustomed to make.

In Southeast Asia the form which the Vietnam war took was a clear outcome of the Cold War—although here the metaphorical use of 'cold' is misleading, since the armed conflict was bloody and prolonged. Vietnam was a continual preoccupation of the US government after 1954. Successive South Vietnamese governments were upheld by American money and arms, the North Vietnamese government being regarded as an actual or potential client of communist China. Its success in overcoming or undermining South Vietnam might be followed, it was thought, by similar communist triumphs elsewhere in Southeast Asia. The smouldering conflict flared up from 1961 onwards, with the US and its allies giving increased support to South Vietnam, until American ground troops were committed in force in 1965. Australian and New Zealand troops joined them.

Indonesian confrontation of Malaysia, also a matter of armed conflict, involved neither a clash with a communist state, nor armed intervention by the US. Nevertheless, the response of Britain, Australia, and New Zealand was bound up with their being US allies. All were members of Seato, an alliance set up to prevent communist expansion after the French failure in Vietnam in 1954. It was understood between the British and American governments that responsibility in Southeast Asia was divided: the defence of Malaysia, whether against internal communist subversion or external attack, was a British responsibility, with help from Australia and New Zealand, whereas Vietnam was American. British responsibility for Malaysia was both an assertion of an individual role in Asia affairs, and an acceptable reason for not sending troops to Vietnam. Moreover, the Indonesian government which began confrontation had received substantial arms aid from the Soviet Union, and appeared to have come increasingly under the influence of the Indonesian Communist Party.

To suggest such a context for the events with which this Part is concerned is not to confine those involving the Commonwealth rigidly to the Cold War. In any case, each event developed ramifications which went beyond the obligations that Commonwealth countries had to their allies. The main point is rather that each occurred as part of general world politics, the principal lines of which, at least until the Cuban missile crisis of 1962, were set by the worldwide antagonism of the two great nuclear powers, the US and the Soviet Union. The establishment of a form of détente between these two led, after Cuba, to a more relaxed international atmosphere, except for the major

upheaval in Vietnam and uncertainties about China. It was in this less constrained atmosphere that the newly independent African states came to
prominence in the 1960s. Their impact on the Commonwealth is discussed in
Part III.

The African presence in the Commonwealth was strong enough by 1961 to
force the withdrawal of South Africa because of its policy of white supremacy.
In the preceding decade African nationalism had exerted increasing pressure
on all the colonial powers in Africa, including Britain. Its influence had
intensified the feeling in western countries that colonialism was becoming an
anachronism, and that Britain had shown wisdom in freely granting independence to India, Pakistan, Ceylon, and Burma in 1947, especially in contrast
with the intransigence of France in Indo-China and the Netherlands in
Indonesia. Colonial independence was increasingly regarded as an end in
itself.

Even so, Britain was involved in colonial conflict in Kenya from 1954 to
1959, and in Cyprus from 1955 to 1960, not to speak of its problems in Aden in
1958, a continual state of insurgency in Malaya in the early 1950s, and states
of emergency in British Guiana. Not all the approaches to independence, even
when peaceful, were successful: the Federation of the West Indies, begun in
1958, foundered three years later, and the Federation of Rhodesia and
Nyasaland became such a centre of discontent that it had to be dismembered in
1963. These issues are not dealt with in this volume, where the term 'Commonwealth' refers only to countries which had obtained independence. But it is
important to realize that in the 1950s some of the most contentious matters for
Britain were labelled 'Commonwealth', although they were essentially colonial
problems. Inevitably, some of them affected the course of Commonwealth
relations, for in some instances the division between Commonwealth and
colonial was of little practical effect. For example, British troops remained in
Malaya after independence, for much the same reasons as they had been there
before.

This Part encompasses a movement, in less than ten years, from the small-
scale Commonwealth of the time of Suez, with 8 members, to the larger body
of 1965, with 22, and looks forward to the even larger body of 1969, with 28.
The change in scale of Commonwealth membership was greater than that in
UN membership where, however, the General Assembly, which at the
beginning of the period was still largely susceptible to control by the US,
became dominated by considerations of anti-colonialism, anti-racism, and
economic development for former colonies, and could be controlled by nobody.
The major powers competed for influence with new and inexperienced states.
A variety of Afro-Asian and pan-African bodies, especially the Organization
of African Unity (OAU), arose to complicate diplomacy in and outside the
UN. Their precursor, the 1955 Bandung conference of Asian and African
states, symbolized the start of a new stage in world politics, in which, while the

main lines of force would continue to be set by the major powers, the new states of Asia and Africa would need to be taken into account by those and lesser powers.

The Commonwealth, as a body which had already incorporated such states as members as early as 1947, was involved in this whole movement. Its increase in membership made the older members, especially Britain, increasingly aware of Afro-Asian problems and opinions. Yet it was still a British Commonwealth—not in name, but in the sense that many British people, and people in other countries, still looked on it as a body which followed Britain's lead, or which, if it did not, should have done so. This created a problem for British ministers, who were not always above giving the impression of greater powers of leadership than circumstances allowed them. In a number of the events discussed in Parts II, III, and IV, one of the major political problems was Britain's inability either to provide a lead for other members to follow, or to embody in policy, to the satisfaction of others, the principles said to be inherent in the Commonwealth. Suez, the first of the issues examined, was a case in point.

It may be helpful at this stage to remind the reader of the increases in Commonwealth membership after 1953. Ghana and Malaya were added in 1957; Nigeria and Cyprus in 1960; Sierra Leone and Tanganyika in 1961 (when South Africa withdrew); Jamaica, Trinidad, and Uganda in 1962; Kenya and Zanzibar (which later was merged with Tanganyika to become Tanzania) in 1963; Malawi, Malta, and Zambia in 1964; the Gambia and Singapore (following its withdrawal from Malaysia, an enlarged version of Malaya) in 1965; Guyana, Botswana, Lesotho, and Barbados in 1966; Mauritius and Swaziland in 1968; and Tonga, Fiji, and Western Samoa in 1970.

CHAPTER 4

THE COMMONWEALTH AND SUEZ

Suez has often been called a 'turning-point' or a 'watershed' in Commonwealth affairs. It was certainly traumatic for Britain and brought into question the nature of Commonwealth ties for Canada, Australia, New Zealand, India, and Pakistan. In order to assess its importance, we must ask what happened in the Commonwealth between 1953 and 1956 to influence the attitudes which Commonwealth members took up as the Suez affair progressed. Commonwealth members—notably Canada, Australia, and India—played important parts at each stage. But how they played them depended to a considerable extent on the positions they had taken up beforehand.

I

From 1953 to 1956 there was relative harmony between Britain and the Asian Commonwealth members, especially India. Such harmony was viewed with reserve by South Africa, and sometimes by Australia and New Zealand. It was much to the taste of Canada, however, and contributed to an overall sense of harmony in the Commonwealth at large. It arose largely from the British government's desire to emphasize Britain's stature in the world by reference to a successful Commonwealth relationship, and to show that the weight of Asian Commonwealth opinion could be used to counterbalance certain American policies in Asia. There were various threats to this relative harmony, in particular from Indo-Pakistani hostility over Kashmir, which was a continuation of the quarrel between Congress and the Muslim League in undivided India. Kashmir became the symbol of conflict between the two countries, because it was brought before the UN, first by India and then by Pakistan, and because Pakistan, intent on achieving a national objective, tried to raise it in the other international bodies to which it belonged—including the Commonwealth. Continued conflict of this sort had a governing effect upon the foreign policies of both countries. India's stance in matters concerned with the Middle East, for example, was clearly affected by the need to prevent Pakistan from gaining leverage there by an appeal to common adherence to Islam; Pakistan's connections with the US, and (much later) with China, were induced by calculation of how these might embarrass India. The Commonwealth could not hope to escape the effects of Indo-Pakistani hostility, although other members strove not to choose between the two.

In a similar but less damaging way, Indian and Pakistani policy towards

South Africa disturbed the harmony of the Commonwealth, although this policy was not pursued through Commonwealth agencies but through the UN. Even before India was divided or became independent, it endeavoured to have the UN censure the treatment of Indians in South Africa. From 1952 onwards the attack was widened to include the whole practice of apartheid. Joined in this particular line of policy by Pakistan, India created considerable difficulty at the UN for the older members of the Commonwealth, which, on the whole, tended to support South Africa—less from sympathy with its policies than because its position rested on the principle of domestic jurisdiction, which was fundamental to the policies of Australia, Britain, and New Zealand in other respects, and which usually commended itself to Canada. In Commonwealth meetings, India and Pakistan did not raise the South African issue.

A third source of disharmony was the Indian policy of non-alignment. Up to 1954, however, this had not created much difficulty for the other members, since India had not taken a strong line against Nato (of which Britain and Canada were members) or Anzus (to which Australia and New Zealand belonged), and South Africa was a member of neither. Pakistan and Ceylon were also officially non-aligned, though not with the comprehensive fervour with which the doctrine was often presented by Nehru.

Indeed, one can regard 1954, and especially the Geneva Conference on Korea and Indo-China of that year, as the high-water-mark of agreement between Britain, India, and the Pacific Commonwealth countries; thereafter, with the beginning of American arms assistance to Pakistan and the formation of Seato, Indian remonstrances were directed at the system of American alliances in general, and its Asian aspects in particular. This strained relations with Australia and New Zealand and changed India's attitude towards Britain.

The sort of arrangement which Eden had tried to operate as foreign secretary under Churchill from 1951 onwards, and from 1955 as prime minister, was one in which Britain emphasized the role of India, and, to a lesser extent, of Pakistan, as supporters in any resistance it wished to make to US policies in Asia; in which, moreover, the tendency of Australia and New Zealand to accept American policies because of their dependence under Anzus was, to some extent, modified by appeals to their sense of Commonwealth solidarity.[1] This Eden line was especially noticeable in the negotiations over the ending of the Korean war, over Indo-China generally and especially at Geneva, and over the formation of Seato. Eden also found the Asian members helpful in dealing with some of Britain's difficult problems of colonial self-government.[2] He was assisted, in his general approach, by the fact that the

[1] The evidence for this highly condensed assertion will be found in Anthony Eden, *Full circle* (1960) and in Dwight D. Eisenhower, *Mandate for change 1953–56* (1963), esp. chs. 2, 5, & 6 of Eden and ch. 14 of Eisenhower.

[2] e.g., in 1952 he had arranged, in respect of the coming self-government of the Sudan,

Soviet Union tended to be suspicious of Indian initiatives. From a British point of view, the position was admirable: it meant that Britain retained its close connection with the US in Nato, but that, when the British government regarded American policies elsewhere as unwise, it had support which could not be branded as simply that of clients. From the standpoint of Commonwealth harmony, whatever entailed Indian co-operation with other members added to the all too few international ties which could be identified as specifically Commonwealth ones.

This relatively happy state of affairs was disturbed by President Eisenhower in February 1954, when, following a visit to Washington by Pakistani leaders in the previous November, he informed Nehru that the US proposed to comply with a Pakistani request for arms assistance.[1] Within a year, Pakistan had also joined the Baghdad Pact (of which the US was not a member, but with which it was closely connected) and Seato. The consequences were substantial.

In the past, India had been opposed to . . . pacts and alliances in principle only, since they did not directly affect her (with the exception of her vigorous reaction during 1952–3 against the proposed setting up of a Middle East Defence Organisation in which Pakistan's membership was envisaged), but with US military aid to Pakistan, the creation of the Southeast Asia Treaty Organisation and the Baghdad Pact in the course of 1954 and 1955, her opposition could not be limited to principle, but became a matter of practical policy.[2]

This practical policy involved increased suspicion of American and Pakistani motives, and a more determined opposition to policies with which the US was associated. Nehru would not be mollified; even a visit from Louis St Laurent, the prime minister of Canada, intended to 'reduce the feeling of mistrust', proved abortive.[3]

Because India was not only the biggest and most sophisticated of the Asian-African states, but was also the key member of the new Commonwealth, such a change in Indian attitudes was bound to have repercussions. The change was dramatized at the Bandung conference of 1955, at which Nehru stood forth as a charismatic figure. This conference marked an open clash between non-alignment in its Indian form and alignment as typified by Pakistan's new relationship with the US, Britain, and other western states. It also saw the emergence into the world's view of the communist government of China, in the person of Chou En-lai, and the appearance as a major figure in Afro-Asian affairs of President Nasser of Egypt. It was not by any means a triumph for non-alignment as a doctrine, since there were articulate spokesmen of the

---

two commissions of assistance to the existing government there; one had an Indian as chairman, the other a Pakistani (Eden, pp. 245–6).

[1] Rajan, *India . . . 1954–6* (1964), p. 270.   [2] Ibid., pp. 79–80.
[3] Dale C. Thomson, *Louis St Laurent* (1968), pp. 360–7.

opposing view, and an undercurrent of dissent from the Indian attempt to placate China and other communist powers;[1] but it dramatized the position of former colonies as no previous event had done, and exuded an air of new potentialities and promise. In a sense it was a vindication of the line Eden had constantly taken with John Foster Dulles and Eisenhower, that Asian opinion had to be taken into account, and that the US could not expect to get universal approval for whatever interpretation it gave to the Asian scene at a particular moment. Paradoxically, however, eighteen months later Eden's own government was being attacked at the UN by nearly all Asian states for its Suez policy, while Eisenhower's was winning friends (if only for the time being) through its condemnation of 'colonialism'.

At Bandung, none of the three Asian Commonwealth members put forward the Commonwealth as a solution to international difficulties; all looked for an increase in co-operation between the independent states of Asia and Africa, regardless of the character of their regimes, and all condemned the existence of colonialism in Asia and Africa. India and Pakistan split, however, on the issue of the right of collective self-defence. Nehru strongly opposed the division of the world into blocs, which he believed could lead only to war; he also pointed out how degrading it was for countries with ancient civilizations to become hangers-on of great powers. Mohammed Ali, for Pakistan, spoke of how the realities of the world situation compelled smaller powers to seek the aid of greater ones in military pacts. Eventually the conference achieved a compromise between these two points of view, but Nehru's received more attention from the world's press. Sir John Kotelawala, for Ceylon, asked the conference to condemn Soviet 'colonialism' in Eastern Europe, as well as the colonialism practised by West European powers in Asia and Africa. But there was much in common between the three; only the Indian fear that American arms aid to Pakistan would give Pakistan more leverage in Kashmir, and (presumably) the Pakistani hope that it would, divided those two states at a major level. Ceylon, as before and since, had no wish to take sides in the matter. All three had conferred with Burma and Indonesia at the Southeast Asian conferences at Colombo and Bogor in 1954; Bandung represented a further extension of their Afro-Asian horizon. Both at Colombo and at Bandung, all three had accepted communiqués which, in dealing with the Middle East, took a pro-Arab position, as they did in respect of North Africa.

The co-operation which Eden had achieved with India had not been concerned with the Middle East, but with areas abutting on China. Pakistan had come into British calculations in connection with the 'northern tier' project, designed to link Turkey, Iraq, and Iran in an alliance with Britain against the Soviet Union, and to safeguard Arab states (such as Iraq and Jordan) with which Britain was on close terms. The question of an attitude towards Israel,

[1] See, e.g., ch. 20 of Sir John Kotelawala, *An Asian prime minister's story* (1956). Sir John led the Ceylonese delegation at Bandung. See also Rajan, *India . . . 1954–6*, pp. 201–13.

or of general support for the Arabs against Israel, had not been an issue in relations with either India or Pakistan. The British government's agreement with Egypt in October 1954 to withdraw from the Suez Canal base was popular with the Asian Commonwealth members, as was the independence of the Sudan, arranged in 1955—without, apparently, more than a faint suggestion that it might join the Commonwealth. One could plausibly argue that the antagonisms of the Middle East were not a Commonwealth question, and that the Sudan case had shown that they need not become so.

Nevertheless, Britain, India, and Pakistan clearly had interests in the Middle East. In Britain's case the view taken of these interests was largely a residue from a period when the Middle East was vital to communications with the Indian Empire. However, Britain was still the most active external force in Middle Eastern affairs. In particular, its links with Iraq and Jordan were still close; it had only recently vacated Egypt and the Sudan; it had both producer's and consumer's interests in oil; and the conception of the Commonwealth still held by its leaders made a sea route to Australia, New Zealand, India, and Malaya seem essential to playing a proper British role in world affairs.[1] Britain was directly involved in the politics of the Arab world. Only a decade before, it had given up the mandate for Palestine—an action which had led directly to the creation of Israel as a sovereign state and to continued enmity between Israel and the Arab states. Not only in the eastern Mediterranean, but also in the Persian Gulf, British connections were still significant and British policy was still a source of anger to militant Arab nationalists, especially because of the long-standing British links with the royal houses of Iraq and Jordan.

Since the revolution which had brought General Neguib to power in 1952, British efforts had been directed towards an accommodation with Egypt, but under President Nasser Egypt showed itself unprepared to accept any form of British tutelage. Instead in 1955, when Britain had refused to supply arms,[2] Nasser's government began to procure them from Eastern Europe; from a traditional British standpoint this meant Soviet interference in an area which was traditionally a British preserve, just as Egypt's encouragement to the nationalist forces in France's North African possessions appeared to the French as interference in French domestic affairs. Egypt had become a nuisance to both these major powers.

To India, however, Egypt had become a highly desirable associate after the revolution which overthrew King Farouk; the regimes of Neguib and then Nasser pursued policies of nationalism, anti-colonialism, and non-alignment

[1] In assessing British interests, a sure guide is Elizabeth Monroe, *Britain's moment in the Middle East 1914–56* (1963), chs. 7, 8, & 9 of which bear directly on the Suez affair.

[2] Under a tripartite agreement between the US, Britain, and France, whereby it was hoped to restrain hostilities between Israel and the Arab states by regulating the supply of arms to all of them.

much closer to India's. At Bandung Nasser had proved an agreeable colleague, and in 1956 he, with Nehru and President Tito, held the first of a series of meetings of the leaders of non-aligned states. India had an interest in out-witting the clumsier Pakistani attempts to gain the support of the Arab states on a pan-Islamic basis. Egypt was the biggest and most developed of these states, the traditional leader in culture and the source of much of the conventional wisdom of the Arab intellectuals and revolutionaries. It had presumably been with Egypt most in mind that 'largely in order not to wound the susceptibilities of the Arab nations, India continued not to establish diplomatic relations with Israel'.[1] This attitude, which had marked India's policy since the establishment of Israel, stood it in good stead when the Suez war broke out.

Pakistan, on the other hand, had by the beginning of 1956 abated its attempt to win over Egypt and had concentrated especially on Iraq, its fellow member in the Baghdad Pact and not only the traditional ally of Britain but also unsympathetic towards the Nasser regime in Egypt. The fact that Egypt had rejected participation in a proposed Middle East Defence Organization, under British and American leadership, while Pakistan had afterwards joined the Baghdad Pact, was another issue between the two countries, and a further reason why Egypt and India should come together.

The other members of the Commonwealth had no interests comparable in intensity with those of Britain, India, and Pakistan. Australia and New Zealand had memories of fighting in the Middle East in two world wars; Australia still sent the mass of its exports to Britain by the Suez route; both depended on Middle East oil. Canada had no special interest. South Africa's position was cautious. While opposed to anti-colonialist powers such as Egypt, it was also traditionally opposed to European attempts to change the status quo in Africa by force; it was not interested in the Suez Canal in terms of trade, although its experience qualified it to emphasize the importance of the Cape route if Suez should be put out of action. Ceylon depended upon the Suez route for its trade to and from Europe but was not involved in Middle East politics. However, all these countries had world-wide interests (especially in relations between the US, the Soviet Union, and Britain) which might be brought into play by some crisis in the Middle East.

The crisis which actually arose in 1956 was unexpected. When the Commonwealth prime ministers met in London on 27 June, they discussed the Middle East but contented themselves in their communiqué with re-affirming 'their interest in the peace and stability of this area', and with commending UN efforts to ensure observance of the armistice agreements between Israel and its Arab neighbours.[2] When the New Zealand prime minister, S. G. Holland, reported to his parliament, he said: 'The Suez

[1] Rajan, *India . . . 1954–6*, p. 242.
[2] Mansergh, *Documents 1952–62*, p. 419. The communiqué was issued on 6 July.

Canal . . . was not even a prospective problem. While I was in London not one word was said about it at the conference.'[1]

II

The Suez Canal became a problem because on 26 July 1956 Nasser announced suddenly that the Canal Company had been nationalized, and that its profits would be used to finance the Aswan High Dam, following the US decision, with British concurrence, to withdraw its offer of financial aid for building the dam a week earlier. The course of events which followed lasted for some six months; it is still the subject of intense controversy.[2]

The decision by the US and Britain to withdraw their offer seems to have arisen from a mixture of motives, especially from the impression that Egypt had come under Soviet influence to an extent that would make the expenditure undesirable.[3] However, one British cabinet minister relates that 'although it seems almost incredible, the British decision was reached almost entirely for economic reasons', and did not recall that 'the immense political implications' were brought home to ministers.[4]

Very quickly the leaders of the British government drew these implications. When Robert Murphy arrived in London at the end of July as an emissary of Eisenhower, he was told by Harold Macmillan and Lord Alexander that Nasser would be dislodged from his position in Egypt, that money had already been set aside for the task, and that, if Britain did not accept what was regarded as a challenge from Egypt, it 'would become another Netherlands'.[5] Whether this was a firm statement of policy, or whether, as Professor Hugh Thomas has suggested,[6] the two ministers knew that an attack could not be mounted quickly and were angling for more American pressure on Nasser, this

---

[1] *NZ Deb.*, vol. 309, 7 Aug 1956, p. 889.

[2] The documentation on the Suez affair is enormous. Only a selection can be mentioned here, with particular reference to Commonwealth aspects. One must begin with a tribute to James Eayrs, ed., *The Commonwealth and Suez* (1964), in which will be found not only significant Commonwealth pronouncements at all stages of the affair, but also a series of commentaries by the editor. This book is indispensable. Other documents will be found in three Chatham House publications: Mansergh, *Documents 1952–62*; D. C. Watt, *Documents on the Suez crisis* (1957); and RIIA, *Documents 1956*. The comprehensive work on the crisis is Hugh Thomas, *The Suez affair* (1967); see also Anthony Moncrieff, ed., *Suez ten years after* (1967). Participants who have told their stories include Eden, and Eisenhower in *Waging peace 1956–61* (1965); Anthony Nutting, *No end of a lesson* (1967); R. G. Menzies, *Afternoon light* (1967); and Harold Macmillan, *Riding the storm* (1971). Terence Robertson, *Crisis: the inside story of the Suez conspiracy* (1965), while undocumented, is valuable for insight into the Canadian government's position.

[3] There is a confused account of the American situation in Eisenhower, *Waging peace*, p. 31; see also Robert Bowie in Moncrieff, pp. 39–41.

[4] The Earl of Kilmuir, *Political adventure* (1964), p. 267.

[5] Robert Murphy, *Diplomat among warriors* (1964), pp. 379–80.

[6] Thomas, p. 50. On the whole, this interpretation is supported by Macmillan (*Riding the storm*, pp. 104–6).

conversation set the stage for the whole operation so far as US-British relations were concerned. On 2 August the British government took its crucial decision: that while a negotiated settlement should be sought, force would be used if negotiations failed within a measurable time.[1] Thereafter, the British strategy was to put as much pressure as possible on Egypt, while endeavouring to obtain the concurrence of the US; the American strategy was to deprecate talk of force and to treat the matter as one involving technical questions affecting the Canal, not the general politics of the Middle East.

After visiting London, Secretary of State Dulles told the Canadian ambassador in Washington on 4 August that the British had reached 'the calm and deliberate decision' that they could not submit to a man like Nasser 'even though the calculated risk of their decision is nuclear war', and the ambassador was asked by Murphy if Canada could 'do something to urge caution' on Britain and France.[2] On 4 August Dulles also saw Menzies and again mentioned the possible use of force, though not, according to Sir Robert's account, with the same emphasis. Menzies, after consulting with his government, returned to London to attend a conference of interested states which had been convened on Dulles's initiative.[3]

This conference, beginning on 16 August, marked a further stage in the affair, which had now reached a point at which the British and French government's determination to use force if they thought it necessary to restore the Canal to something like its former international status was widely known to some governments and suspected by others, and at which the American desire to secure some peaceful solution was evident, though not finally stated.[4] Eden and Dulles, who had been at odds for some years, were now opponents, but this time India was not to be found on the British side. Egypt had refused to attend the London conference because it considered that the assumptions underlying its summoning questioned Egyptian sovereignty. The Egyptian case was put by the Indian delegate, Krishna Menon.[5] The Dulles plan stressed the need for an international board to run the Canal; the Menon one, emphasizing Egyptian sovereignty, proposed an advisory body. Eighteen of the twenty-two states at the conference (including Pakistan) approved the Dulles plan, with India and Ceylon in the minority. Menzies was deputed to lead a committee to Cairo to present and explain the plan to Nasser,[6] who, however, refused to accept it.

---

[1] Thomas, p. 55.   [2] Ibid., p. 460.   [3] Menzies, p. 150.

[4] The authoritative statement of American attitudes at this stage would seem to have been Eisenhower's letter of 31 July to Eden, in which, while force is deplored, a reader can detect ambiguities which might have encouraged a British belief that the US would eventually come round to accept it. (For the text, see Eisenhower, *Waging peace*, p. 664.)

[5] Menon's highly personal account of these and other Suez negotiations is in Michael Brecher, *India and world politics* (1968), ch. 6.

[6] Sir Robert's account of this (*Afternoon light*, ch. 8), may be supplemented by Eden's quotations from him (*Full circle*, pp. 470–3).

In September, while a build-up of British and French forces in the Mediterranean continued, British-American discussions resulted in a second London conference to form a Suez Canal Users' Association, which was duly constituted but which lost any credibility on 2 October, when Dulles, refusing to identify himself with the 'colonial powers', indicated clearly that this body would have no 'teeth'.[1] The question reached the UN in September, first by way of a reference to the Security Council by Britain and France, followed by an Egyptian complaint about their troop concentrations. In October there were discussions under UN auspices between the foreign ministers of Britain, France, and Egypt, with Menon in attendance. These went a considerable distance towards agreement, but were unsatisfactory to Britain, according to Eden, because 'the Egyptians accepted no international authority and they offered no effective sanction for any breach of the principle of free navigation'.[2]

Up to this point the British and French build-up of forces had continued, and there were contingency plans for using them to take control of the Canal. There was a difference between France and Britain in the extent to which they were prepared to enlist Israeli support against Egypt. The French had no inhibitions; they worked out joint arrangements quite early. The British, however, seem to have been more reluctant, because of their responsibilities towards the governments of Jordan and Iraq. It has even been suggested that in mid-October the British government was still thinking of possible military action against both Egypt and Israel[3] because of these responsibilities, and it is likely that the wording of the ultimatum which the British cabinet discussed on 25 October,[4] and which was to be extended to both sides if hostilities broke out between Egypt and Israel, was designed to emphasize Britain's non-collusion with Israel. However, at about the time the cabinet was discussing this as an exercise in preventing hostilities between the two countries, the foreign secretary appears to have been at Sèvres discussing with the Israelis and the French how those hostilities should be begun.[5] Neither the US nor the Commonwealth countries was informed about the proposed ultimatum or the Sèvres talks—not a surprising situation in the latter case, since the cabinet was not informed either.

On 29 October Israel attacked Egypt. The Anglo-French ultimatum went to both sides the following day, calling on them to withdraw from the Canal and stop fighting. If either failed to comply, British and French forces would intervene. Israel accepted with qualifications. Egypt rejected the ultimatum. On 31 October Anglo-French air forces attacked Egyptian airfields. On 5 and 6 November, after a week of furious public debate in Britain, during which

[1] *The Times*, 3 Oct 1956.
[2] For a more favourable account of the Egyptian position, see Nutting, ch. 8 & app. VI.
[3] Thomas, p. 103; see also Eden, p. 512.
[4] Eden, p. 523. The ultimatum as finally delivered is in Watt, p. 85.
[5] See Robertson, chs. 7 & 8; Moncrieff, *passim*, esp. ch. 4; Thomas, *passim*; and Geoffrey McDermott, *The Eden legacy and the decline of British diplomacy* (1969), pp. 145 ff.

British and French attacking forces had to cover the distance by sea from
Malta, there were paratroop and sea-borne landings in the Port Said area. A
ceasefire was declared by Britain and France at midnight on 6 November,
somewhat to the surprise of many people (though the action, dictated by
circumstances of the moment, could be squared with the cabinet decision of
25 October). The week saw tumult in parliament in London and at the UN,
and the overthrow of the Hungarian government by Soviet force in Budapest.
From a British standpoint, however, the most disturbing aspect was the strong
objections of the US government to the whole Suez operation, expressed in
UN votes and in acute financial pressure on the pound.

A UN Emergency Force, proposed by Canada and headed by a Canadian,
General Burns, eventually took over in the Canal area. Clearance of the
Canal, which had been blocked by the Egyptians, began under UN auspices
at the end of December. The period of replacement of British and French by
UN forces saw British-American antagonism at the UN at its height. Lester
Pearson, the Canadian external affairs minister, proved again to be not only a
suitable intermediary between the two powers but a skilful moderator at the
General Assembly. It was no surprise when he was awarded the Nobel Peace
Prize in 1957, although by then the government of which he and St Laurent
were members had been replaced by that of John Diefenbaker.[1] Eden had
resigned as British prime minister on 9 January, on doctor's orders. He was
replaced by Harold Macmillan. His departure on a recuperative voyage to
New Zealand was a kind of Commonwealth coda to such a furious passage;
his visit from Nehru on Christmas Eve 1956, when in Eden's words 'inevitably
we were each a little constrained' but 'our friendship was certainly unimpaired',[2] had been an earlier variation of it.

III

The Commonwealth members responded in different ways to the Suez
affair. In intensity, however, their reactions were the strongest and most
variable aroused by an international issue since the 'new Commonwealth' had
come into being in 1947.

Probably the experience was most intense for Canada, because Suez called
into play not only what some people considered Canada's traditional role as
the interpreter of Britain to the US and vice versa, but also its more recent
role as a supporter of the Asian Commonwealth members. 'Canada accepted
with enthusiasm the new perspectives of the Commonwealth after India and
Pakistan joined in 1947', one of its diplomats wrote later:

---

[1] For the US-British situation see Macmillan, *Riding the storm*, ch. 4, and Robertson, ch.
14. For a further description of Canadian efforts see James Eayrs, *Canada in world affairs
Oct 1955 to June 1957*, ch. 6.

[2] Eden, p. 581.

Canada used its influence to see that the Commonwealth's evolution as a multiracial organisation was not frustrated by nostalgic imperialism . . . Although rejecting neutralism for themselves, Canadians accepted sooner than Americans the wisdom of non-alignment for weak countries.[1]

The Canadian government believed that Britain and France were making a double mistake in not heeding either the wish of the US that force should be foresworn, or the message of India that Nasser was not the Hitler he was thought to be and that the Canal question should be settled by negotiation. Pearson later summed up his aims at the UN:

I felt [the Anglo-French action] should be examined in the fullest possible perspective against the situation that had led to the intervention, and against the past records of both countries. It was clear . . . that if they had suffered considerable provocation at the hands of Egypt, they had endured too the frustrating sequels to what undoubtedly comprised the worst chapter in Dulles's diplomatic career. I regretted they thought it necessary to take the keeping of peace into their own hands, but it was equally obvious that the peace needed keeping in the Middle East.[2]

But the excitement of the time made it inevitable that the Pearson–St Laurent policy should be regarded by some Canadians as one of opposition to Britain, since the Canadian government had not given Britain the full-throated support provided by Menzies's government in Australia, or the slightly more modulated support of Holland's government in New Zealand. During the Canadian general election campaign in May and June 1957 the Conservatives strongly attacked the Liberal government for not supporting Britain and St Laurent's objections to the 'supermen' of Europe who wished to continue to decide the fate of the world; but these objections did not have a decisive effect on electoral results.[3] The shift in Commonwealth circumstances was emphasized by the fact that the Liberal government was criticized for failing to support Britain, which in earlier times would have meant that it was not putting Commonwealth ties first; in this instance the government claimed that it was trying to hold the Commonwealth together by its solicitude for the Asian members. 'Our actions at the United Nations, criticize them if you like, did not bring about a division in the commonwealth', claimed Pearson on 29 November 1956. 'Indeed I am compelled to say that our actions and the attitude we adopted did help and are still helping to heal the divisions which are

---

[1] John W. Holmes, 'The relationship in alliance and in world affairs', in John S. Dickey, *The US & Canada* (1964), p. 113.

[2] Robertson, p. 180.

[3] See Eayrs, *Commonwealth & Suez*, pp. 383–6 for this problem. St Laurent's biographer is in two minds. While asserting that 'the "betrayal" of Britain was to cost the Liberal Party many votes, and almost certainly a majority of seats in parliament, in the next election', he also says that 'a post-election survey was to reveal that, of the persons who abandoned the Grits, 5·1 per cent did so because of the Suez crisis, 38·2 per cent because of the pipeline debate, 26·7 per cent because of the inadequate increase in the old-age pension, and 30 per cent because it was "time for a change" ' (Thomson, pp. 477 & 519).

within the commonwealth at this time'.[1] Two modes of thinking about the Commonwealth were at war between him and his critics.

In Australia, while some of Menzies's opponents accused him of ignoring the Asian Commonwealth members' views and so straining the Commonwealth, the major attack upon him, by his opponent Dr H. V. Evatt, was for his scornful approach to the UN.[2] The issue for the Australian government was whether Eden was right in what he did. Ten years later, when he wrote his memoirs, Menzies still thought Eden was right.[3] His views, which rested basically on the importance of decisive action in situations to forestall a probable communist advantage, also included a strong belief that Nasser's original action in nationalizing the Canal had been a breach of international law, and that Britain and France were justified in taking firm action, especially since the UN had shown no corporate capacity to deal with the problem. He does not seem to have been concerned about Indian hostility, or the effects of Afro-Asian opinion generally. He was much more disturbed at the damage to Anglo-American understanding. While it is believed that his external affairs minister, R. G. Casey, was alarmed at the consequences for the Commonwealth of the British action, Menzies prevailed. There was no public division within the Australian cabinet.[4]

The situation in New Zealand was quieter, although New Zealand gave Britain support throughout the crisis, especially at the UN. The Opposition's position was not so extreme as Evatt's, the government's stand being more accommodating than Menzies's. New Zealand proposed a contingent for the UN Emergency Force, clearly wishing to back up the Canadian initiative, and then accepted with good grace the news that such a contingent would not be agreeable to Egypt. Australia made no offer. Yet these were differences of degree. In both Australia and New Zealand, right-wing governments composed largely of anti-communist exservicemen found it natural to follow Britain, natural to believe the worst of Egypt (which had not been popular with the servicemen of either country in both world wars), and natural to think of the Middle East as an area of strategic importance which had traditionally formed an imperial 'life-line'. The more sophisticated position of the Canadians, embracing a world view rather than a regional or traditional one, had little counterpart in Australia or New Zealand.

In India, as might have been expected, there was great indignation at the

---

[1] Mansergh, *Documents 1952–62*, p. 516.

[2] Evatt was a former president of the General Assembly. For an account of the debate in Australia, see W. Macmahon Ball, 'The Australian reaction to the Suez crisis', *Aus. J. Pol. & Hist.*, 2/2.

[3] Menzies, p. 178.

[4] It was often stated at the time that Casey was in disagreement, but that he kept quiet because a public statement would do more harm than good. Thomas (p. 118) says that late in October 1956 Casey, in London, warned the government against the use of force, but that Menzies 'sent a message to the British that they should pay no attention to Casey'.

use of force by Britain and France. A theoretical conviction that imperialism necessarily meant aggression was mingled with a sense of shock that the British had actually done what they did.[1] Throughout the crisis, Indian efforts, through Krishna Menon, were directed towards achieving a negotiated settlement that would be acceptable to Egypt. India often acted as spokesman for Egypt; there may even have been times when the spokesman ran somewhat ahead of his principal. Yet, when the Indian effort is considered in perspective, it is seen to have been reasonable, substantial, and closer to the basic facts of the situation than that of some other countries—except perhaps for Menon's position over the withdrawal of British and French troops in November, which endangered the conciliatory efforts of Pearson.[2] Essentially, the Indian view was that Egypt had sovereignty over the Canal, and that any arrangement which subjected Egypt to surveillance and perhaps discipline by an 'international' authority was undesirable. India was thus opposed to the position consistently taken by the British government and to some of those taken up at times by the American government, though in line with that which the American government adopted in the end. More importantly, it agreed with the general trend of international assumptions, which, as the number of sovereign states grew and the influence of Asian and African states correspondingly grew, was very much towards emphasis on sovereignty and strictures of states which attempted to coerce those less powerful than themselves.

The joint statement by the prime ministers of India, Ceylon, Burma, and Indonesia, issued in New Delhi on 14 November 1956,[3] was an expression of this trend, directed towards the Soviet Union for its treatment of Hungary as well as towards Britain and France for their actions in Egypt. 'Neither peace nor freedom can come if strong nations, trusting to their armed power, seek to compel weaker countries to obey their will', they said; and, even if the actions of some of the four countries did not entirely bear out this principle in the next decade, it was a principle which was particularly damning when applied to Britain and France, since it put their actions on all fours with those of the Soviet Union.

There was, as might have been expected, considerable agitation for India to leave the Commonwealth, which has always been regarded in India as essentially an association between India and Britain, rather than a body with wider membership. Nehru rebuffed these suggestions.[4] As before and later,

[1] According to Krishna Menon, Mr Nehru did not believe the British would invade Egypt. 'He had great faith in British common sense' (Brecher, p. 65).
[2] For an account of the positions taken by India at various stages, see Rajan, *India . . . 1954–6*, pp. 150 ff. The judgements in the sentence above are not to be attributed to Professor Rajan.
[3] RIIA, *Documents 1956*, p. 315.
[4] See Mansergh, *Documents 1952–62*, pp. 521–7, and Eayrs, *Commonwealth & Suez*, pp. 452–5.

he pointed out that India suffered no harm from the Commonwealth association, that the Commonwealth acted as a bridge between states and a means of influence, that it was easy to break things but not so easy to construct them, and that he did not intend to take India out of the Commonwealth. No doubt he felt that the association had been useful. Commonwealth membership had not prevented India from earning the gratitude of Egypt; it had probably assisted Menon in his attempts to arrange a negotiated settlement; it had made Canada a useful ally in this as in earlier issues;[1] and it had preserved connections with Australia and New Zealand, in spite of their support of Britain. If India left, Pakistan would remain, with all the opportunities for influence which Commonwealth membership involved. From Nehru's standpoint, leaving the Commonwealth would have been an act of supererogation.

Much the same may well have been felt by Huseyn Shaheed Suhrawardy, the prime minister of Pakistan, which had found the Suez affair much more embarrassing than had India.[2] As in other matters, it was the situation of India that ultimately determined Pakistan's position; yet in this case the Pakistani government was not applauded by vocal elements in its community for acting differently from India but denounced. Pakistan's policies before Suez had placed it firmly on the side of Nuri's Iraq, and thus in opposition to Nasser's Egypt. Suhrawardy did not attend the Colombo powers' meeting in New Delhi of 14 November 1956 because he had been at a meeting of the Muslim members of the Baghdad Pact. Although the Baghdad Pact powers called upon Britain to cease fire in Egypt, this was not sufficient to satisfy angry Muslim extremist elements in Pakistan itself, or to placate Egypt. Nasser not only refused to meet Suhrawardy later in November; he also refused to accept a Pakistani contingent in the UN force. Suhrawardy, after some hesitation and under some pressure, was prepared to give Britain the benefit of the doubt in terms more generous than those used by his Indian counterpart;[3] but the upshot was that this comparative generosity received little attention in Britain, while it was attacked by Pakistan's opponents in India, Egypt, and elsewhere. If the Pakistani government had acceded to the requests that Pakistan leave the Commonwealth, this would have left the field free for India, which, in spite of its strong opposition to British policy and its assistance to Egypt, was, if anything, more strongly entrenched as a significant Commonwealth member than before.

No such awkward problems assailed the remaining overseas Commonwealth members, Ceylon and South Africa. After receiving an assurance from Britain in September that there would be no use of British bases in Ceylon to attack Egypt,[4] S. W. R. D. Bandaranaike's government modestly took its place

---

[1] It is said that in the US State Dept the Canadian minister for external affairs was known sometimes as 'Swami Pearson' (Holmes, p. 114).

[2] See Eayrs, *Commonwealth & Suez*, pp. 195–200.

[3] Ibid., pp. 260–70, 457, 460.   [4] Mansergh, *Documents 1952–62*, p. 487.

behind Nehru's. Strijdom's in South Africa adhered to its original cautious statement that 'it is best to keep our heads out of the beehive'.[1] Apart from some gentlemanly scuffling with the British government about consultation, which is discussed below, South Africa took no active part. Its government would probably have preferred Britain and France to carry on with their attack once it had begun, but did not say so at the time.[2]

All of these Commonwealth countries responded to the Suez affair in accordance with what their governments regarded as their national interests. The Canadian concept of national interest was the only one to make the preservation of the Commonwealth a prime concern, and only Canada seems to have been concerned about Suez as a specifically Commonwealth issue. This was due in part to the relatively sophisticated Canadian view of the world; but it was helped by Canada's lack of specific interests in the Middle East. Canada did not trade there to any extent, did not rely on the area for oil, had not fought there in either world war, did not need the Canal to get its troops to any place where they might be required, and was not involved in the complex politics of the Arab and Muslim worlds. Britain, India, Pakistan, and Australia could all be said to have more immediate interests in the area, or to be capable of believing that they had. It was perhaps fortunate for the Commonwealth as an institution that the interests of one of its members included the Commonwealth relationship as an essential element.

During the latter part of the Suez crisis there were serious doubts in some minds whether the Commonwealth could survive the divisions which were being revealed. The matter was debated in the British House of Commons on 8 November, on the motion of Kenneth Younger, a Labour spokesman for foreign affairs.[3] The Opposition displayed concern that not only the Asian members, but also Canada, had disagreed with the government's policy, and that even where no governmental opposition had been expressed abroad, as in Australia, there had been local demonstrations of strong disagreement. The government was able to show that no essential links had been broken. There was, however, an underlying feeling that the Commonwealth would never be the same again; and this feeling was shared by many people outside parliament. Yet after Macmillan assumed the premiership there was a cordial meeting between him and Canadian ministers in March 1957, at which the Middle East was frankly and amicably discussed without any plain disagreement.[4] Furthermore, early in July 1957 the Commonwealth prime ministers assembled in London for a meeting about which *The Times* was able to say with relief, 'the clouds of mistrust engendered in some quarters by Suez may have been dispersing of their own accord, but last week has blown them away

[1] Eayrs, *Commonwealth & Suez*, p. 62.
[2] Ibid., p. 394.
[3] See Mansergh, *Documents 1952–62*, pp. 496–510 for the main speeches.
[4] See Eayrs, *Commonwealth & Suez*, pp. 427 ff.

even more swiftly'.[1] What then was the effect of Suez upon the Commonwealth? Was there none at all?

IV

To be answered properly, the question needs to be seen in wider terms than those of Commonwealth relations. Suez was not simply, or even mainly, a Commonwealth event. It was part of world politics; but, because it starkly displayed certain facts about the Commonwealth relationship, it was widely regarded at the time as constituting a problem for the Commonwealth. The underlying significance of Suez in world affairs has been suggested by the American, George Ball:

> Suez was a major turning point not only in colonial policy but in Atlantic relations and the balance of Western influence in the Middle East. Whatever the merits of the narrow issue—Nasser's nationalisation of the canal—they paled in insignificance before events that the world saw as a plot to preserve and even restore old empire and colonial relationships. The Anglo-French failure at Suez accelerated the tempo of decolonisation in Africa and Asia by tearing away for European electorates, as well as for the world, the flimsy facade of power to reveal the relative political weakness and dependence underneath.
>
> The Europeans drew most of the necessary inferences and proceeded to complete their withdrawal from Africa and Asia in the next five years. The overseas springs of empire were running dry. As de Gaulle asked in 1961, 'Why should we cling to costly, bloody and fruitless domination when our country has to undergo complete renovation . . .?'[2]

Much the same conclusion was drawn by Nasser when he looked back a decade later: 'The meaning of Suez is that there is an end to the methods of the nineteenth century. . . . On the other hand, Suez gave confidence to many countries. I think Suez helped many of the African countries to be sure of themselves and insist about their independence.'[3]

To some extent these are not disinterested statements: Ball had been anxious that the European powers should recognize that the 'colonial' period was over, something which Dulles had been implying with some emphasis; and Nasser naturally wished to put his own country's position in the best light. Nevertheless, they expressed a truth which Suez forced many people to face, especially in Britain. It was clear afterwards, though many people denied it beforehand, that Britain was not one of the super-powers; that it could no

[1] Editorial, 'Loose Unity', 6 July 1957. The recollections of Sir Alec Douglas-Home, who, as Lord Home, was secretary of state for Commonwealth relations during the Suez crisis, suggest that 'it was touch-and-go whether India and Pakistan left the Commonwealth, and that he had to do 'a lot of retrieving'. Detail, unfortunately, is lacking (Kenneth Young, *Sir Alec Douglas-Home* (1970), pp. 96–7).

[2] George W. Ball, *The discipline of power* (1968), p. 23.

[3] Nasser, in Moncrieff, p. 58.

longer police the Middle East; that it did not have interests there of sufficient weight to unite the whole country behind a determined effort; that its other interests, especially its relations with the US, were of greater moment; and that any policy which suggested 'the nineteenth century', in the sense of 'gunboat diplomacy', 'pacification', and the other terms which, while caricaturing some aspects of Britain's overseas efforts in that period, were true of other aspects, could no longer be sustained. Britain could not retain either possessions or influence by unilateral effort, if that effort conflicted with the expressed interests of its vital associates. In the Suez context, it was the US which Britain temporarily alienated, but it also became clear that India and other associates in Asia and Africa had an influence which could be exerted against Britain. They would have to be taken into account in future. 'For us,' Professor Thomas has written of his own, the younger, generation in Britain in 1956, 'Suez is an event already in another world, a world certain to disintegrate, Suez or no Suez, a world already based more on prestige than on power, but one to which the previous two or three centuries of imperial history had accustomed us.'[1] It is in this sense that Suez was a watershed.[2]

Suez showed that the opposition of some of Britain's associates, especially Canada and India, could prove damaging because they were members of the Commonwealth, an institution to which the British government had given special prominence and which was normally regarded as enhancing Britain's position in the world. Perhaps it was because the Commonwealth had been so widely publicized as a post-imperial phenomenon, an advance beyond the practice of imperial domination, that the British action at Suez was so often referred to in Commonwealth circles as 'imperialist' or 'colonialist', when it was, in fact, an act motivated by foreign-policy considerations and not an attempt to establish permanent colonial rule over anyone. The recognition that this was the case may have had something to do with the resumption of normality at the Prime Ministers' Meeting of 1957. But the point of substance is that, in Commonwealth terms, Suez convinced many people that Britain could no longer afford colonialism and must continue to give colonies their independence. This meant embracing with extra fervour the notion of the Commonwealth as an expanding fellowship of former colonies, drawn to Britain, of their own free will, by common ties which did not require coercion to make them effective.

Such views were certainly adopted by many officials and observers in Britain. Whether they were also adopted by the Conservative government is harder to judge. Macmillan's actions in the next few years—especially his 'wind of

---

[1] Thomas, p. 2.

[2] Its significance was fully recognized at the time by Sir Walter Monckton, minister of defence when the Suez troubles began. He opposed intervention (the only member of the cabinet to do so openly, he later wrote), but did not resign from the cabinet because he did not wish to bring down the government (see Lord Birkenhead, *Walter Monckton* (1969), pp. 307–10).

change' speech and his emphasis on faster decolonization in Africa—suggest that he had learnt this lesson from Suez, although his memoirs do not. Amongst some members of his party, however, Suez seemed to create an undercurrent of resentment not only against the UN and the US but also against the newer members of the Commonwealth, which led in its turn to greater scepticism about the Commonwealth as an institution. Many conservative-minded people in all parties felt that, with the Suez debacle, something basic had dropped out of Britain's relations with the UN, the US, and the Commonwealth. No doubt it was the sense of world power that had been affected. This feeling was later reinforced when the African states began to demand both UN and Commonwealth action against South Africa and Rhodesia.

In 1956 the Commonwealth question on which most discussions about Suez turned was that of consultation, now seen to have been an echo of the past rather than a portent of the future. The British government did not inform Commonwealth governments what it was going to do ahead of the invasion; the high commissioners in London were informed only after the ultimatum had been handed to Egypt. This meant that some Commonwealth governments first heard the news from the radio. Canada and South Africa, accustomed to the former practice of the Dominions Office, were especially incensed.[1] Eden's explanation, repeated by other defenders of the government, was that there had been no time: 'This situation called for the swiftest possible action and allowed no time to observe the established practice of prior consultation', was the British high commissioner's answer to the South African government.[2] Menzies was in a somewhat embarrassing position because six months earlier he had published an eloquent article on Commonwealth consultation, in which he had asked for it to be as full as possible.[3] Now, however, he saw no reason why Britain should be blamed for not consulting:

Effective consultation . . . would plainly have occupied considerable time and the urgent position might have fallen into irretrievable disaster. In our opinion, therefore, Great Britain, whose canal and other Middle East economic interests are so vast, was correct in proceeding upon her own judgment and accepting her own responsibility. We are not living in an academic world. . . . There are instances like the present one in which events move too fast for normal processes.[4]

[1] See Thomson, p. 464, for St Laurent's reactions, and Eayrs, *Commonwealth & Suez*, p. 190, for the S. African.

[2] Mansergh, *Documents 1952–62*, p. 519.

[3] The key passage read: 'I am no carping critic; but I would courteously suggest that one text might be boldly printed in every Department in London, New Delhi, Canberra, and the other Seats of Government—"Will any decision I am today contemplating affect some other nation of the Commonwealth? If so, have I informed or consulted it?" ' (R. G. Menzies, 'The ever changing Commonwealth, II, Need for new forms of consultation', *The Times*, 12 June 1956).

[4] Mansergh, *Documents 1952–62*, p. 518. Menzies was speaking in the Australian parliament on 1 November 1956.

These contemporary justifications look less convincing now, in the light of Eden's admission that the British cabinet discussed in detail on 25 October the form of the ultimatum it would serve on Egypt and Israel if hostilities broke out between them. The hostilities occurred on the 29th and the ultimatum, with one small change, was served on the 30th, so there was, in fact, ample time to inform Commonwealth members of what sort of ultimatum the government had in mind. Britain did not do so for the same reason as it did not inform Eisenhower or even its own ambassadors in Moscow and the Arab capitals:[1] it did not want them to know, because if they knew they might have objected, or, in some cases, passed on the information to Egypt or its friends. India, a Commonwealth country, was also Egypt's adviser. Had the Indian government known of the ultimatum prepared on the 25th, how would it have seen its duty: to keep silent because it wished to preserve a Commonwealth confidence, or to inform Egypt in the interests of what it regarded as world peace?

The British government may have been wedded to consultation in general terms,[2] but, like any other sovereign state, it was not prepared to preserve the principle where vital interests were involved. In the previous year it had not consulted 'the US or even the old Commonwealth countries' about its decision to occupy the Buraimi oasis by force. In this case another Arab government, that of Saudi Arabia, was demanding an area 'to which they had no real claim but which was vital to our oil interests', according to Macmillan, then foreign secretary, who took the decision.[3] 'Consultation' was, in fact, a practice which the British government had inherited from a time when Commonwealth members were far less active in world politics than they had become in 1956, which it had made no attempt to explain in contemporary terms or define with any precision,[4] but which those in charge had no intention of putting into practice if national interests seemed likely to be endangered. Suez marked the last occasion when consultation was raised as a Commonwealth issue on anything like the same assumptions as before and during World War II.[5]

Suez was a striking example of two major themes of Commonwealth change:

---

[1] The ambassador in Moscow thought he had drunk too much at the Kremlin when he heard the news of the ultimatum (Sir William Hayter, *The Kremlin and the embassy* (1966), p. 142). See *The Times*, 16 Nov 1956 for the situation in the Arab capitals.

[2] On 26 July 1954 Eden, then foreign secretary, had been asked in the House of Commons if it was still official policy to seek 'the direct agreement of Commonwealth Governments on occasions of the highest strategical importance'. He replied that it was, and would continue to be, the policy (531 HC Deb., cols. 21–22).

[3] Macmillan, *Tides of fortune*, p. 641.

[4] Thus deserving the measured rebuke of Professor Mansergh's letter, *The Times*, 15 Nov 1956.

[5] It is perhaps worth putting on record that Sir Eric Harrison, the Australian high commissioner in London, suggested in December 1956 that there should be permanent machinery in London for consultation about critical matters, but wished to see this confined to the 'British Commonwealth', not 'the Commonwealth'; he did not regard India as a member of the *British* Commonwealth (ibid., 6 Dec 1956).

of the expanding international universe to which Commonwealth countries had to become accustomed, and of the increasing complexity of the individual members' interests which determined the positions they would take up in a Commonwealth context. It showed, in addition, a particular variant—or series of variants, if the national debate and not simply government policy is taken into account—of the attitudes which could be taken in Britain towards the place of the Commonwealth in British policy.[1]

In the long run, the effects of Suez on the Commonwealth may well be seen to be more important, though more complex and indirect, than they seemed at the time. One cannot, for example, properly weigh the effects of the intense division that Suez caused in Britain itself—not only between government and opposition, but also within the Foreign and Commonwealth services, and amongst everyone interested in Britain's external position. Although military intervention was not in line with other policies Britain was pursuing, and looks now like the arbitrary act of a feverish man,[2] it affected not only the image which Britain presented to people in other countries—including Commonwealth members—but also the attitudes of British officials and politicians. It had as well a significant impact on British defence policy for, as Phillip Darby points out, it 'brought to an end the government's world of make-believe when the air transport fleet was shown to be but a shadow of the theory'. It revealed too that many foreign bases were inoperable in times of crisis, and the emergence of the 'air barrier' because of the eruption of nationalist sentiment in the wake of the operation. Above all, it produced a mood of disillusionment and frustration; and the feeling that it had been the conventional forces that had failed led to public clamour for defence retrenchment and further emphasis on the nuclear deterrent.[3] There was besides the effect on many British people's consciences: a sense of shock, of moral outrage, of distress that so much goodwill could be thrown away on such flimsy grounds with so little result. It is said also that certain later decisions were coloured by the recollection of how hastily and secretly policy had been made.

[1] Macmillan's memoirs say nothing at all about the problem of Commonwealth consultation. The whole emphasis is laid on the need to keep the US in the picture (*Riding the storm*, ch. 4).

[2] Although Macmillan points out that a not dissimilar action was carried out by British troops in Oman in 1957—but this time with success (ibid., pp. 270–7).

[3] *British defence policy east of Suez 1947–68* (1973), pp. 95, 99–101.

CHAPTER 5

INDIA, PAKISTAN, AND CHINA

ETWEEN 1953 and 1969 there were changes in bilateral relations between
India and Pakistan in their connections with the great powers and the
countries of the Third World,[1] and in their roles within the Commonwealth. In this chapter those changes are approached by way of the continued
hostility between the two countries which led to the war of 1965 and eventually
to the creation of Bangladesh in 1972, and the tensions in the Sino-Indian
relationship which culminated in the fighting of 1962.

It cannot be emphasized too often that relations between India and
Pakistan have a family quality which baffles the outsider, fascinates the participants, and gives an extra edge to all disputes which arise.[2] In 1969 relations
between the two countries were no better than at their establishment in 1947.
Kashmir was still an open sore. Other matters, such as the use of the Indus
waters and the adjustment of refugee property, had been arranged through
negotiation, and there was a modicum of contact, so that there could be some
movement of persons and goods between them. Life in the subcontinent
would otherwise have been intolerable. But Kashmir had become a problem
which, while peculiar to India and Pakistan, involved a great many other
countries. India and Pakistan had absorbed the question into their foreign-
policy structures, and often judged other countries by their attitudes towards
it. The increasing intricacy of the Kashmir situation was remarked on in the
previous volume in this series.[3] The ceasefire lines of 1948 were largely
adhered to, and each country continued to administer the territory which it
had held. Over the years two strategies emerged.

In the 1950s the Pakistani strategy appeared to be that the more the issue
was brought before the UN the better, since, in the Pakistani view, India had
a poor case and Pakistan a good one, and since the plebiscite which Pakistan
demanded and which, at certain times, India had agreed to (but with qualifications on both sides), would be best administered by an international body.
Pakistan wished to appeal to international opinion in general, and the support

[1] The Third World (from the French *tiers monde*) is a cant phrase, loosely applied to those
countries which are non-European, non-communist, and poor, many of which were colonies
until recently. See my Chatham House Essay, *The politics of the third world* (1966), p. xi. The
phrase is not exact.

[2] From the great mass of material produced on either side of the border in English about
Indo-Pakistani relations, two books which can be recommended are, from the Indian side,
Sisir Gupta, *Kashmir* (1966), and, from the Pakistani, G. W. Choudhury, *Pakistan's relations
with India 1947–66* (1968).

[3] Mansergh, *Survey 1939–52*, p. 260.

of its allies and of Muslim states in particular, to secure a satisfactory result. Whenever an international occasion could be found, Pakistan would bring up Kashmir at what seemed an appropriate time;[1] whenever Pakistan joined an alliance, such as Seato and Cento, it did its best to use the alliance to further its aims in Kashmir.[2]

India, on the other hand, which had originally brought the matter before the UN on grounds of Pakistani aggression, tended thereafter to mistrust international mediation or intervention in Kashmir, and to assert Indian sovereignty, which had been gained by the same quite legal means—the accession of the ruler to India—as Indian sovereignty over other former princely states.

To simplify the issue, we may say that Pakistan relied on opinion and international involvement to obtain action, India upon legality to retain its hold. In order to counter Pakistan's attempts to mobilize opinion on its side, India looked for diplomatic support wherever this could be found. After Pakistan seemed to gain the initiative in international terms with its military agreement with the US late in 1953, India grew even warier of international intervention, and tended to see international pressures—especially those of the US and Britain, Pakistan's allies in formal terms—behind every proposal for a settlement. When in 1957 Pakistan brought the matter back to the UN after a lapse of some years, India had managed to secure the support of the Soviet Union, which effectively counterbalanced whatever influence the US might exercise in support of Pakistan.

I

After 1959, with the beginnings of Sino-Indian hostilities and the rise to power in Pakistan of President Ayub Khan, some further progress seemed possible, since India did not wish to face two enemies at the same time, and Pakistan was reassessing the whole basis of its foreign policy.[3] However, none was achieved. India had been affronted in 1959 by a fresh assertion of US military support for Pakistan, in spite of the American assurance that the arms which Pakistan received were not meant to be used against India.[4] Pakistan, on the other hand, was becoming dissatisfied with its inability to get

---

[1] Liaquat Ali Khan refused at first to attend the 1951 Commonwealth Prime Ministers' Meeting unless Kashmir were on the agenda. In the end he agreed to attend, and Kashmir was discussed privately outside the official meetings (see Gupta, pp. 223–9, and Choudhury pp. 118–19).

[2] See S. C. Gangal, 'The Commonwealth and Indo-Pakistani relations', *Int. Stud.*, July–Oct 1966, p. 140, for instances. This is reprinted in Gangal, *India and the Commonwealth* (1970), useful also for its appendices on published work on India's membership, and Nehru's speeches about the Commonwealth.

[3] See Mohammad Ayub Khan, *Friends not masters* (1967), chs. 9 & 10, for Ayub's exposition of what he sought.

[4] See Jawaharlal Nehru, *India's foreign policy* (1961), pp. 472–6.

anything through the UN or to achieve effective American pressure on India. The change in US policy after the election of President Kennedy, whereby India's non-alignment became much less repugnant to the US than in the days of John Foster Dulles, stimulated Pakistani efforts to 'normalize' relations with the Soviet Union and China. In 1962, when India and China clashed again, Pakistan became apprehensive about a further closing of the gap between India and the US. When, in the following year, the US and Britain (together with Canada, Australia, and New Zealand) began to provide India with large quantities of arms and equipment for use against China, Pakistan's apprehensions appeared to be confirmed, since it was a Pakistani belief that Indian weapons were intended primarily for use against Pakistan, and that India and China would not fight a serious war. Under pressure from Britain and the US, India and Pakistan met again in 1963 to consider possible solutions to the Kashmir problem, but no progress was made. Predictably, each blamed the other for the failure of these talks.

Between the end of 1962 and the middle of 1965 relations between them worsened, still with the quarrels of the subcontinent as the focus but with an even wider range of associations to manipulate. Pakistan, having 'normalized' relations with China, and, in particular, having settled the border between its part of Kashmir and China,[1] found opportunities to work against India in association with Indonesia (which, under President Sukarno, was pursuing a militant line very close to that of China) and with China, in various Third World bodies. India, with its own interests in mind, tried on the one hand to involve the Soviet Union (now China's open antagonist) in order to support its own position, and on the other to divert Third World energies into the channels of 'non-alignment'. Neither Pakistan nor China was formally non-aligned, so both might be excluded from any international gathering that bore the non-aligned label.

These efforts by the two states became distressingly evident in the protracted negotiations over a 'second Bandung' conference, which it was hoped to hold at Algiers in 1965, ten years after the first. Pakistan's energies were directed towards excluding the Soviet Union, in order to satisfy China, and Malaysia, in order to satisfy Indonesia. India's were directed towards including both these countries in order to lessen the influence of Pakistan and China. Other Afro-Asian states proved either apprehensive about involving themselves in these quarrels, or happy to do so, provided they could obtain comparable diplomatic benefits for themselves. In the end, the conference did not take place; but the uproar which it had provoked demonstrated the wider

---

[1] It should be noted (a) that India regarded this arrangement as null and void, since it considered the whole of Kashmir Indian territory, whether administered by India or not; and (b) that Pakistan and China took some account of this sensitivity by not describing the territory south of the border as under Pakistani sovereignty, and by describing the agreement as provisional until there was a final determination of the future of Kashmir.

diplomatic resources which India and Pakistan could now bring to bear upon their family quarrel.[1]

The quarrel burst into flames momentarily in May and June 1965 and for longer in September of the same year. The first clash was over the Rann of Kutch, a desolate marshy area on the north-east coast of the subcontinent, which could be plausibly regarded as land by one side and water by the other, with judgements accordingly about which country it belonged to. After initial hostilities, a diplomatic way round was discovered, largely through the good offices of the British prime minister, Harold Wilson, and his high commissioners in India and Pakistan, John Freeman and Sir Morrice James. The decision of an international tribunal, to be nominated by the parties, was to be final, if India and Pakistan could not at first agree about the border. This decision, made long afterwards, was adhered to; but its success was eclipsed by the outbreak of more serious hostilities.[2]

In August 1965 there were disturbances in Kashmir, followed by the movement of armed men across the ceasefire line from Pakistan, and by corresponding Indian action to stop this movement and deter the Pakistani government from giving it support. Pakistan proved obdurate, and used regular forces and tanks. On 6 September India made a countermove, this time in the plains of the Punjab, with the capture of Lahore as its apparent objective. Both sides used their tanks freely over a wide area. The UN Security Council had been very active in trying to stop the fighting—for once the Soviet Union and the US were agreed that their interests might be impaired if it continued—and the secretary-general succeeded in obtaining a ceasefire on the 23rd.

Two further developments, however, emphasized the complexity of the international network in which the two countries were now involved. One was that China made threatening gestures (but no more) suggesting that it might come to Pakistan's assistance. The other was that India and Pakistan agreed to meet at Tashkent in Uzbekistan in January 1966, to make arrangements for withdrawal of troops. It was not lost on the rest of the world that the Soviet Union had, for the first time, played the part of honest broker for these two countries; nor was it lost on some supporters of the Commonwealth that two of its members had had to look outside it in order to restore relations between them.

II

India's relations with China were in some ways more complicated than with Pakistan, since, while those with Pakistan were consistently bad, those with China changed from good to bad, leaving a bitter taste in Indian mouths.

---

[1] See Miller, *Politics of the third world*, ch. 2.

[2] Wilson's account of the settlement process, part of which took place at the Commonwealth Prime Ministers' Meeting of June 1965 (or, rather, unofficially during the intervals of the meeting) is in Harold Wilson, *The Labour government* (1971), pp. 98–9 & 112–13.

Whereas an Indian nationalist is likely to regard Pakistan's behaviour as typical of recalcitrant Muslim separatism, he is likely to regard China's as an act of betrayal.

In pre-independence days the frontier between India and Tibet was governed in the west by custom and in the east by de facto recognition by both sides of the so-called McMahon Line, established in Simla in 1914 at a conference, the decisions of which have been much in dispute. Independent India adhered to the boundaries recognized by the British, and has continued to regard these as legitimate. When the Chinese communists occupied Tibet in 1950 there was anxiety in India about what the attitude of the Chinese would be, and India moved some forces up to the Indian side of the McMahon Line. Nehru discussed the border with Chou En-lai in 1954 and 1956, his concern having been aroused by Chinese maps which suggested wider claims by China than India would agree to. In Sino-Burmese conversations on the border in 1956, at the suggestion of the Burmese premier Chou agreed that in the north the traditional line, including part of the McMahon Line, should be accepted, and this was incorporated in the border agreement of 1960. But in 1956 India appears not to have pressed the point to the extent of formal Chinese acceptance, presumably because it wished to retain Chinese friendship, which had been demonstrated to the world at Bandung in the previous year. 'Hindi Chini Bhaibhai!' (Indians and Chinese are brothers!) was the prevailing cry in Delhi during Chou's 1956 visit. India, in its reaction against American military assistance to Pakistan, had found China, with its basic antagonism to the US, a useful associate. It was also in Nehru's mind that China, a great power of the future, should be encouraged and mollified rather than harried. In any case, it is fairly clear that the Indian government, in its anxiety about the borders, was not prepared to negotiate afresh, but wanted recognition of the boundaries which it regarded as already fixed by custom or previous treaty.

In 1956–7 the Chinese began constructing a road through the desolate plateau of the Aksai Chin, in Ladakh, the north-western portion of Kashmir, where the boundary was a matter of tradition and custom. This area was so remote and unpopulated that the Indian government did not know till the latter part of 1957 that the road was being made, and did not protest until the following year. A number of border incidents had already occurred; more followed. An open breach with China would not, however, have suited India's general policy, and Indian leaders were reluctant to believe that anything more than a misunderstanding was involved. At the same time they held strongly that a clear boundary existed and that the territorial integrity of India, as measured by this boundary, must not be violated.

So matters stood until early 1959, when a rebellion of Khampa tribesmen in Tibet, which had been going on since 1956, became serious and led to Chinese military occupation and the flight of the Dalai Lama to India. These events sharpened Indian criticism of China, and incurred Chinese hostility because India manifestly sided with the Tibetans.[1] In August there were further clashes; and the Indian public began to hear of what had been happening, including the building of the road across the Aksai Chin. From that point onwards, relations between India and China became publicly hostile, with Indian nationalism stiffening to resist any incursion into what was regarded as Indian territory. The 1962 hostilities between India and China, although they involved serious setbacks for Indian forces on the eastern part of the border, were a pendant to the events of 1959, for it was then that Indians realized, in shock and even recrimination, that the supposed friendship with China had no substance.[2]

Nevertheless, the fighting which began in October 1962 was a bitter blow to India. Indian forces were pushed back in vital areas; many were killed and more missing;[3] worst of all, the Chinese were not defeated either militarily or diplomatically.[4] The Chinese stopped when they thought they had taught the Indians a lesson. They then retreated in their own time and at their own pace. Initially, India found no support from the Soviet Union, which advised acceptance of the ceasefire offer which the Chinese made on 24 October.[5] This offer was unacceptable to Nehru. In distress, he made public appeals to the leaders of a number of countries, including those of the Commonwealth.[6]

At the time of the Sino-Indian clash, the world was preoccupied with the nuclear confrontation between the US and the Soviet Union over Cuba, a situation which may help to explain the divergent responses of those countries which had previously had some connection with India. The response from the US, Britain, Canada, Australia, Malaya, and New Zealand was friendly, accepted the Indian case at face value, and promised assistance. The non-aligned states, especially in the Middle East and Africa, were more cautious. The first group may well have been stimulated by the excitement of the Cuba

[1] According to Nehru, 'Mr Khrushchev explained to me how Tibet seems to be linked up with Hungary in the Chinese mind. While they were facing the Tibetan revolt, a similar insurrection broke out in Hungary; and when the Chinese saw the Western Powers not only intervening but making so much political capital out of the Hungarian crisis, they concluded that Tibet, also, would be subjected to a similar showdown. . . . At the back of their minds of course, is this bogey of a Western intervention in the Tibetan crisis, and that, too, from the Indian side! We had assured them how absurd and impossible this is, but what can we do with people who continued to think in terms of non-aligned, independent India being an imperialist lackey and an Anglo-American stooge?' (R. K. Karanjia, *The philosophy of Mr Nehru* (1966), pp. 103–4).

[2] See RIIA, *Documents 1959*, pp. 164–248, for documents on the 1959 events.

[3] The Indian defence minister reported in January 1963 that 322 had been killed, 676 wounded, and 5,490 were missing. Of these latter, 2,140 were still unaccounted for (*CS*, 12 Mar, 1963, p. 255).

[4] The most circumstantial account of the war is in Neville Maxwell, *India's China war* (1970). See also John Dalvi, *Himalayan blunder* (1969) and B. M. Kaul, *The untold story* (1967).

[5] See Theodore C. Sorensen, *Kennedy* (1965), p. 663. See also *CS*, 20 Nov 1962, p. 966, for some Soviet public statements. Clearly the Soviet Union was in more than one mind. It later took the Indian side.

[6] Nehru's letter to the prime minister of Australia, and the reply, are in *CN*, Jan–Feb 1963, pp. 48–50.

struggle to consider that a firm stand should be taken against the Chinese; the second, in contrast, may have been appalled by the possibilities of conflict inherent in both situations, and decided to keep out. India's only assurances of support came from aligned countries. Non-alignment, in a sense, was now being practised against India. Indian apologists would not accept this interpretation. They would say that non-alignment was a commitment specifically to refrain from joining one or other of the super-power blocs, and that, since India was not appealing for support against either of these, the failure of various Asian and African countries to support India was not an affirmation of non-alignment, any more than India's request for 'sympathy and support' against China was a denial of it. This is true; but, in the sense that non-alignment had been seen as not just a universal doctrine but a specific policy to serve India's interests, the failure of other non-aligned states to support the apostle of non-alignment in its hour of need was regarded by many Indians as proof of the inadequacy of the doctrine. Mediation, which other non-aligned states did offer, was not support.

This mediation was initiated by six non-aligned countries (Ceylon, Cambodia, Indonesia, Ghana, Burma, and the United Arab Republic) at a conference in Colombo in December 1963. The proposals made were not revealed until a month later, after they had been taken to Peking and New Delhi by the Ceylonese prime minister, Mrs Bandaranaike. India accepted the proposals, subject to what were called 'clarifications'. China accepted them in principle, but did not agree with the clarifications. In the upshot, forces were removed in a manner something like the non-aligned states' proposals, but not as a direct result of them. These states made no judgement on the rights and wrongs of the matter, but were concerned simply to see that demilitarized zones were established and that provocations from either side were thereby lessened.

At the time, the assistance offered by the US, Britain, Australia, Canada, Malaya, and New Zealand was probably more to Indian tastes than the non-aligned states' contribution to the situation.[1] It was not, however, to the taste of either Pakistan or Ghana, although Britain's aid was presented by Macmillan as very much a Commonwealth matter.[2] The situation might have become a difficult one for the Commonwealth if the Chinese had not withdrawn. The consequences of the clash for India were substantial. China became finally established as an enemy. The US became temporarily a friend. Britain

---

[1] Details will be found in Richard P. Stebbins, *The US in world affairs 1963* (1964), pp. 167–72, for the US; *CS*, 13 Aug 1963, p. 701, for Britain; Peyton V. Lyon, *Canada in world affairs 1961–3* (1968), pp. 488–9, for Canada; Gordon Greenwood & Norman Harper, eds, *Australia in world affairs 1961–65* (1968), pp. 433–4, for Australia.

[2] See Mansergh, *Documents 1952–62*, pp. 620–8, for statements by Macmillan and Sandys, Nkrumah, and the Pakistani minister for external affairs. Nkrumah objected strongly to the use of the Commonwealth in this connection. He may have known that in late November Macmillan had canvassed with at least one other Commonwealth government the possibility of raising a Commonwealth brigade 'to hold the position in Kashmir until a settlement could be worked out'. This proposal came to nothing. (Private information.)

received unwonted praise. The Soviet Union had preserved a watching brief, but, as time went by, relations between it and India became closer. Britain and the US were not to retain the same warmth in Indian hearts for long, despite their military aid in 1963 and 1964. The war of 1965 between India and Pakistan, one result of which was a suspension of British and American arms supplies, led to greater Indian reliance on the Soviet Union for arms and diplomatic support, to a degree which enabled the Soviet Union to continue to normalize its relations with Pakistan while retaining India as an associate. The 1960s ended with India still opposed to both Pakistan and China, and still receiving aid from the US and the Soviet Union in what some people called 'co-alignment', a development from, or obverse of, non-alignment.

III

Before considering how the Indian conflicts with Pakistan and China affected the Commonwealth, we may ask how they affected the policies of India and Pakistan. In 1953–4, while India remained non-aligned, Pakistan chose alignment with the US not so much from hostility to the Soviet Union (although in the 1950s there was some genuine fear of Russia), as because 'the crux of the problem . . . was the Indian attitude of hostility towards us: we had to look for allies to secure our position.'[1] Neither was fully satisfied with the result. From the Indian standpoint, non-alignment was useful because it isolated Pakistan to a certain extent from other Afro-Asian states, because it constituted a sort of ideology to which newer states were prepared to sub-scribe, and because, while it kept India from being bossed by either of the super-powers, it did not prevent it from receiving economic aid from them. It worked well so long as China was either ranged within the Soviet camp or was pursuing an independent policy which did not cut across India's. Once China changed its attitude non-alignment proved to be inadequate, but to those who had regarded it as largely a rationalization of India's national interests, it was not difficult to adapt to so-called 'co-alignment'. India was helped, in its adaptation, by the fact that by 1962 the US and the Soviet Union were ceasing to operate Cold War tactics with full vigour, and were ready (especially after the Cuban crisis) to aid India jointly: neither wished to see China triumph. If India had had to seek this sort of aid while the lines of the cold war were still rigidly drawn, it would have meant a choice between the two, with conse-quential animosity from whichever was not chosen.

Pakistan did not remain content with its early choice, because it did not get the support it wanted against India. 'People in Pakistan were becoming dis-illusioned; a relationship which had been built up after a great deal of hard work during the fifties was ceasing to command respect.'[2] The shift made by Ayub towards reassurance of the Soviet Union and an entente with China

[1] Ayub Khan, p. 154.   [2] Ibid., p. 158.

looked odd if one assumed that Pakistan must adhere to the anti-communism customary in Seato and Cento press releases, but not if one thought of India as Pakistan's constant preoccupation. The events of 1962, especially the flood of military aid promised by Britain and the US to India, confirmed the desire to move away from the US sphere of influence; and 1965 strengthened this confirmation.

Nevertheless, China and the Soviet Union were not easy bed-fellows for any state, whether aligned, non-aligned, new, old, developed, underdeveloped, communist, or capitalist; and it is not surprising that Pakistan did not wish to be itself entirely dependent on the one, or India on the other. Both attempted to keep up their connections elsewhere, which explains in part their efforts amongst the Third World states, and Pakistan's continued formal membership of Seato and Cento. It also helps to explain why both retained fairly close relations with Britain, in spite of mutual disappointment at Britain's failure to support them at crucial times—India over Kashmir, and Pakistan over such matters as American arms supplies to India.

Next we may ask what effect the events already described had upon the Indian and Pakistani positions in Third World affairs. Here an obvious starting point is the Bandung Conference of 1955, at which India stood out as the champion of non-alignment, and Pakistan of the right of states to align themselves as they wished. Both subscribed to the resolutions about anti-colonialism and economic development. From the Indian standpoint it was essential to pursue non-alignment even after the departure of John Foster Dulles. The reason was that first Pakistan, and then China, could be stigmatized as aligned, and excluded from non-aligned meetings. India succeeded in this manoeuvre at the Belgrade and Cairo conferences of non-aligned states of 1961 and 1964, largely because it suited Egypt and Yugoslavia (the two other major sponsors of these conferences) to keep China at arm's length, and to prevent the Soviet Union from being heavily criticized. Pakistan, China, and Indonesia, on the other hand, were anxious to have an Afro-Asian conference (or 'second Bandung') before the Cairo conference, but were prevented by India and its associates, which managed to ensure such a conference would not be held until 1965. These manoeuvres, unimportant as they may seem, were important to the participants, and much diplomatic ingenuity was expended in trying to operate them to suit one or the other party's interests.

A basic instability in the Third World situation tended to work against India and in favour of Pakistan. It arose from the ever increasing numbers of new states, with interests which could not necessarily be satisfied by Indian (or Russian) influence. A few were under obligations to China; a great many were primarily concerned either with the situation between Israel and the Arab states, or with the freedom movements in southern Africa. India could not do much about either of these. Pakistan, while impotent about the second, might hope, in the long run, to gain something from the first because it was a

Muslim state. It was apparent at the meeting of non-aligned countries in Belgrade, held in July 1969 to consider a further major conference, that India was hardly in a position to decide issues, that there were open requests from some Muslim states for the admission of Pakistan, and that, above all, the issues being raised with greatest zest were those in which India did not wish to be directly involved, or did not wish to take an extreme line.[1] On the other hand, it could be argued that Pakistan had not yet gained entry, and that the rival sort of conference, towards which Pakistan and China had been working had not been held. In this sense India had still made the greater gain.

Pakistan, for its part, seemed to cool somewhat towards these arrangements after 1965, and to pay more attention to Muslim meetings of various kinds, and, in particular, to the organization RCD (Regional Co-operation for Development), in which it was joined by Iran and Turkey. Ayub wrote that 'common sense dictates that Pakistan should belong to a major constellation extending from Casablanca to Djakarta'.[2] This he envisaged as not political, but economic and cultural in character. Its geographical limits, however, were set by two Muslim states, with a number of others in between; and it could be expected that India would react adversely to such a non-secular concept, seeking to continue the co-operation which it had pursued for so long with the Arab states, often to Pakistan's mortification.

IV

The implications of the two conflicts we have considered for the Commonwealth can best be sought by looking at India's changing position, bearing in mind that Pakistan remained present as an antiphon, or perhaps an antipole.

Up to 1959 the breach between the two countries was the major split in Commonwealth relations. It was often deplored, and sometimes discussed in terms of whether the Commonwealth, as a body, could do anything to heal it. Nothing came of these speculations, although individual Commonwealth members—especially Canada and Australia—did their best to help. Pakistan had, on the whole, got the worst of the bargain in terms of political influence, in spite of its adherence to the US. While that adherence gave it arms and some diplomatic support (including, at times, some within the Commonwealth), it also operated disadvantageously, in that newer states, suspicious of US influence and concerned to preserve their new-found independence, often suspected Pakistan's motives and preferred India's stance. If Pakistan had been able to enlist the Arab states on its side, its position would have been stronger; but, as we have seen, it was one of the lasting achievements of Indian diplomacy to secure President Nasser's sympathy at an early stage and to

[1] See *Consultative meeting of special government representatives of non-aligned countries, Belgrade July 8–12, 1969* (Belgrade, 1970).
[2] Ayub Khan, p. 181.

retain it, together with that of the other radical regimes in the Middle East. It was symptomatic that the Suez affair of 1956 operated to India's credit and Pakistan's discredit amongst these regimes, in spite of Pakistan's being a Muslim state.

When Ghana, the first of the new African Commonwealth states, became independent in 1957, many people identified it with India's example. There was some expectation that India would 'lead' the newer members of the Commonwealth. Ghana professed non-alignment and the sort of vague socialist reorganization of society that India had already propounded. But although there was no attachment between Ghana and Pakistan, the expected good relations between Ghana and India did not materialize.[1] This was partly because of Nkrumah's concentration on Africa and his desire not to play second fiddle to Nehru, and partly because of India's preoccupation with its own affairs. Largely, however, it was because the international environment had become too complex for India to think of 'leading' Ghana, and other African states, as once it had managed to 'lead' Burma and Indonesia in a newly emergent Asia. Moreover, the continued weakness of India's international economic position prevented it from giving tangible help to those states which it might have wished to influence.

After 1959 India's open breach with China made it a partisan in Afro-Asian affairs and ensured that whatever it did would be judged in terms of its known animosity towards China. The link between Afro-Asian, or Third World, affairs and those of the Commonwealth is that most of the new Commonwealth members of the 1960s, following Ghana's example, actively participated in Afro-Asian gatherings, were embroiled in the politics of these (especially on the African side, where, as we shall see, rival groupings appeared almost immediately), and judged India's participation in them not by India's standards and interests but by their own and by those of their associates for the time being. At the 1961 Cairo conference, for example, Nkrumah was not on the same side as Nehru; after the Sino-Indian clash of 1962 Ghana and also Ceylon joined in the attempts at mediation made by the non-aligned countries. Apart from Malaya, the only Commonwealth support for India came from non-Afro-Asian members.

India's difficulties with the Third World were compounded not only by splits amongst the black African states, but also by rifts between the Arab states on the one hand and certain African states on the other. Adherence to Egypt was basic to Indian foreign policy; whenever Egypt ceased to be popular with any African regime, India suffered. In due course, too, India began to suffer in esteem because of the minorities of Indian origin in many African states, especially in East Africa. In respect of these, and the Indian minority in Malaya, India had always taken the correct view of eschewing protection for those who were not Indian citizens. Even so, as several of the African regimes

---

[1] See W. Scott Thompson, *Ghana's foreign policy 1957–66* (1969), pp. 51–2, 179–80, 280–3.

grew more nationalistic, their discrimination against local people of Indian or Pakistani origin increased, and opinion in India was aroused. India did not find a sympathetic audience, especially when the local regimes—as in Tanzania —had access to China.

Thus, whereas commentators sometimes speculated about whether India could exercise influence over and even leadership of the new Commonwealth African states, this possibility was rendered nugatory, partly by India's single-minded concentration on its own vital interests as it saw them, but also by the constraints imposed by India's need to follow anti-Chinese and anti-Pakistani policies at international gatherings at which the new states were represented. Inevitably, these requirements cut across the interests of the newer states, which were, in any case, supremely preoccupied with Africa, and were only secondarily concerned about Asia. When the African wave struck the Common-wealth, Nehru was in no position to control it. Indeed, India followed, and did not lead, when the decisive issues of South Africa and Rhodesia arose. The contrast between Nehru's gracious welcome to the emerging African states at Bandung in 1955, and India's anxious and intensive diplomacy in getting enough African states to support its line in regard to the expected Algiers conference of 1965, was striking and significant: these ten years had seen a shift in power and influence within the Afro-Asian world, and India's weight was slighter than before. To some extent, where India lost Pakistan gained; but it was only to some extent, since the new states in the Common-wealth judged others by how they served African interests as the new states saw them, and Pakistan was no more successful than India at getting what it wanted, especially in regard to Kashmir.[1]

However, even if India's (and Pakistan's) lack of success in enlisting new Commonwealth states behind its banner is admitted, one may still ask how these two states' connections with the older Commonwealth countries were affected by the Sino-Indian and Indo-Pakistani quarrels. To what extent, for example, could either be said to have 'built bridges' between themselves and the older members, as the Commonwealth was often said to help them to do? Two kinds of 'bridges' can be envisaged: those involving general propositions such as man's obligations to man in terms of their common humanity, or states' duty to one another to secure peace and amity; and those built because of the shared interests of particular states at particular times. The two kinds can, no doubt, be combined, but they are essentially separate. The first leads

---

[1] Ayub asked for a mention of Kashmir in the communiqué of the 1964 Prime Ministers' Meeting, but had to be content with a vague reference of goodwill to both Pakistan and India—although there was also mention of 'a role of conciliation' which Commonwealth countries might play 'towards the settlement of disputes between member nations provided the parties concerned accepted such mediation'. An India House spokesman denied that Kashmir was discussed and was quoted as saying 'I will go further and say that the Commonwealth Relations Office spokesman's suggestion that Kashmir was discussed is deliberate mischief' (*Guardian*, 16 July 1964). CRO officials would strongly deny this.

to a greater understanding and sympathy between peoples, the second to greater convenience for governments.

In terms of the first sort of bridge, both India and Pakistan, but especially India, tried hard to convince the world at large of the purity of their motives and the excellence of their intentions, and both were prominent in UN attempts at defining human rights and the like. In the Commonwealth sphere, however, neither made any special effort of this sort. In the 1950s, when non-European membership of the Commonwealth was confined to them and to Ceylon, they made no attempt to widen the Commonwealth's functions and aims, apart from the abortive efforts of Pakistan to have Kashmir (a matter of dispute between two members) discussed at a Prime Ministers' Meeting. Once this attempt had failed in 1951, no further attempt was made until 1964. Kashmir was, in fact, the symbol of why India and Pakistan made no major impact upon the Commonwealth. It was clear that each was watching the other in order to see if it gained any advantage; clear too that whatever either might claim of universality in what it said about human or state behaviour, the matter often came down, in the end, to the hostility that existed between them. If India and Pakistan had been able to agree to advance broad, almost universal considerations, such as the African states brought forward in the following decade, they might have turned the Commonwealth into something different; but their evident animosity made concerted action impossible. Although one can say that in the 1950s there was some advance in bridge-building through the mere fact that Asian members were part of the Commonwealth, one cannot say that the Commonwealth was significantly changed in any respect which entailed a special Asian contribution. The Indo-Pakistani conflict was a major reason why.

In the other sense of bridge-building, the result was mixed. India's position over Kashmir did not encourage the older Commonwealth countries to cultivate its society (because of resultant complaints from Pakistan), but the symbolic importance of India in the 1950s did. There was, for example, a considerable development of Indo-Canadian relations, and to some extent of those with Australia and New Zealand, despite their adoption of the Dulles line over Seato. The later hostility of India to China made India correspondingly more attractive to Australia and New Zealand. In contrast, Pakistan had been a popular associate with those states when it adhered to Seato (which had only two other Asian members, Thailand and the Philippines), but became less so when, in the 1960s, it abstained from Seato's main activities and cultivated China.

The Commonwealth significance of these events was twofold. First, when the states in question found it desirable to come together (first Pakistan with Australia and New Zealand in Seato, and then India with the same countries in antagonism to China), all were happy to pin the Commonwealth label on what they were doing, even when it was done under another body's auspices, as with Seato: they were glad to stress their common membership of a body which imposed so few conditions and could encompass both agreement and disagreement. Secondly, when these states did *not* coincide in policy (first India disagreeing with the Pacific countries over Seato, and then Pakistan disagreeing with them over China), they were still glad to use the Commonwealth label to stress the fact that, while disagreeing in some matters, they were still like-minded in others.

The Commonwealth was thus a useful, because highly flexible, bridge-building instrument at the level of the convenience of governments. Because it did not impose any rules except those of equality between its members (unless, like South Africa in 1960-1, they continued to implement policies which were repugnant to African members), it could be employed to maintain relations between states which had disagreed about joining an alternative body, and could provide states which had joined such a body with a further link which it was helpful to preserve. This was bridge-building, less between continents and peoples than between governments which wished to keep some of their options open.

Relations with Britain formed, for India and Pakistan, a special, and often dominant, aspect of Commonwealth membership. Indeed, whenever the government of either country was faced with demands in press or parliament that it should leave the Commonwealth, the reason usually lay in some British action held to have been contrary to that country's interests, as over Suez in 1956. Many a British minister and representative must have echoed, about India and Pakistan, what one British minister wrote to another about the US before it entered World War I:

There is no doubt that [their] behaviour is rather singular. They undoubtedly regard us as something quite different from the ordinary foreigner; but this does not the least prevent them making both the most dangerous requests for our assistance and the most offensive remonstrances whenever we do not do exactly what they like.[1]

The Commonwealth played a symbolic part for both India and Pakistan, as a kind of embodiment, in larger form, of the British connection which was still so significant in their cultural and economic lives. This symbolism often entailed a switchback situation: for India, the Commonwealth was *up* when Britain came to India's assistance with weapons for use against China in 1962-3; it was on the way *down* when Britain and the US seemed to be making agreement with Pakistan about Kashmir a condition of that aid; it was *up* again when Wilson helped to settle the Rann of Kutch dispute in 1965; and it was *down* once more when, on 6 September of that year, commenting on the extension of the Indo-Pakistani war, Wilson was so injudicious as to say:

[1] Lord Balfour to Lord Curzon, 12 Jan 1917; quoted in Max Beloff, *Imperial sunset*, i (1969), p. 233.

I am deeply concerned at the increasingly serious fighting now taking place between India and Pakistan and especially at the news that Indian forces have today attacked Pakistan territory across the international frontier in the Punjab. This is a distressing response to the resolution adopted by the Security Council on 4 September calling for cease-fire.[1]

Two days later the British government imposed a ban on the special arms aid to India instituted in 1962. There was no such special aid to Pakistan, so no comparable ban was imposed. Although shipowners proved reluctant to ship arms to Pakistan because of the risk of seizure by India, the effect was very much to anger Indians, since they regarded the British ban as support for Pakistan. It seemed to some in India that Britain's 'political influence in the Indian subcontinent—through the common membership of the Commonwealth along with India and Pakistan, and otherwise—has been destroyed, and for good.'[2]

In fact, British influence in India a year or so after this explosion was probably much the same as it had been a year or so before: not very great. The switchback system, common to both India and Pakistan in discussions of Britain and the Commonwealth, but more obvious in India's case because of the more articulate character of the Indian political system, ensured that things would return to something like normal. For both India and Pakistan, their own sense of national interest remained the touchstone of their opinion of the Commonwealth, as of other international bodies, and that sense was primarily aroused by the effect of any given course in international matters upon their relations with each other. Indo-Pakistani antagonism must be regarded as a constant. Sino-Indian antagonism introduced a fresh element for both parties, but appears, if anything, to have deepened their hostility to one another. It is not surprising that the newer members of the Commonwealth should have been reluctant to burn their fingers in this pot, or that the older members, while prepared to do so when questions involving China arose, were also

[1] *CS*, 9 Nov 1965, p. 1103. In response to a later complaint from Francis Noel-Baker, MP, that a British parliamentary delegation in India had encountered much resentment at the statement, Wilson defended himself on the ground that 'it was important if we were to maintain a balanced position to react publicly to the India attack' (see *The Times*, 6 Jan 1966 & *Dawn*, same date). Wilson (pp. 133–4) maintained in retrospect that he had been misled by certain officials. See, in this respect, Sir Algernon Rumbold's letter to *The Times*, 5 Aug 1971. Wilson later stated on British television that the statement in his book was ill advised.

[2] M. S. Rajan, 'The Tashkent declaration', *Int. Stud.*, July–Oct 1966, p. 24. Professor Rajan went on: 'The United Kingdom's successful mediation in the Indo-Pakistani conflict in the Kutch war is apparently the last flicker of the dying flame of British influence in the Indian subcontinent. The desperate British efforts (quite possibly to recover this lasting influence, at least with Pakistan) by throwing a spanner in the works . . . only had the effect of further scraping off the traditional British influence over India and goodwill in India for Britain. The few friends of Britain still left in India—who also believe in India's continued membership of the Commonwealth, partly because of the value they attach to the maintenance of friendly relations with that country—will long remain puzzled and confounded by the British political and diplomatic suicide in Indo-Pakistani relations.' For a description of the effects in India of 'Wilson's homily', see Gangal, pp. 146–9.

reluctant to become embroiled in this hostility.[1] Effectively, the area of India's Commonwealth concern (and to some extent of Pakistan's—though Pakistan's was never very large) contracted after Nehru's death in 1964, and had, by 1969, become largely a matter of the subcontinent's affairs.

One cannot say that between 1953 and 1969 either India or Pakistan increased in significance within the Commonwealth. Their conflict with one another became accommodated or absorbed within the Commonwealth system largely by being ignored, although, as we have seen, there were some reactions to British attempts at mediation in 1965. But at no stage was the matter allowed to become directly a Commonwealth issue, in the sense, for example, that South African and Rhodesian racial policy became issues. Non-alignment ceased to be a matter of wide consequence. This was largely because of the movement of the world away from the rigid positions of the mid-1950s towards a more flexible system, occasioned by the nuclear stalemate between the super-powers, and strengthened by the growth of multi-polarity. However, the failure of non-alignment to keep its place as a doctrine was affected also by India's own plight when attacked by China; in the longer term it suffered from its adoption by other Third World countries as a synonym not for what the Indians had meant in the early 1950s, but for their own demands in the Middle East and Africa.

The question of Indian influence on decolonization is disputable. There is little evidence that India directly contributed to the British policy of granting independence to colonies. No doubt Indian (and Pakistani, Ceylonese, and Burmese) independence, when enacted in 1947, represented a substantial advance. But it was ten years before any other colonies were accorded independence (Malaya and Ghana in 1957), and it does not seem that pressure from either India or Pakistan was a significant factor in the decisions, in spite of Nehru's keen interest in the principle of decolonization.[2] The flood of African independence between 1960 and 1965 came for African and British reasons, although one of the British reasons was the belief that the grant of independence to India had been a success. India did, it is true, pay particular attention to colonial questions at the UN, and was very much to the fore in exerting anti-colonial pressure. However, this pressure at the UN was directed much more at France, the Netherlands, Portugal, and Belgium than at

---

[1] There were some suggestions of Commonwealth mediation in the Indo-Pakistani war of September 1965. These came from several quarters and might have been taken further if the UN secretary-general had not succeeded in the quest for a ceasefire. Malaysia and some of the African members were in favour of some effort, but the scheme never materialized (see *Guardian*, 14 Sept and *DT*, 16 Sept 1965). The dangers of the Indo-Pakistani conflict for Commonwealth countries, and its connections with wider Third World relationships, were exemplified in the following month, when Pakistan broke off diplomatic relations with Malaysia because of what it regarded as partisan statements by the Malaysian representative at the UN.

[2] According to Sir Alec Douglas-Home, 'he was very much putting the pressure on us all the time to get out of the colonies as quick as he could. He took the lead in that, without really understanding the conditions in Africa' (Young, *Douglas-Home*, p. 88).

Britain.[1] It was not until the mid- and late 1960s that Britain began to experience insistent anti-colonial pressure, but this was about Rhodesia, and came from the African states rather than from India or Pakistan.

V

In 1971–2 a further stage was reached in India's and Pakistan's mutual relations and in their Commonwealth history. Although it falls outside the time-span of this book, it was so momentous that it requires mention.

Ever since independence in 1947, Pakistan's main weakness had been its division into two wings, East and West. West Pakistan was the Pakistani heartland, its Muslim links with the Middle East uninterrupted by non-Muslim lands in between, its sense of Muslim continuity strong. It was the home of the armed forces and the seat of the bureaucracy. However Pakistan's formal political complexion might change, the top posts went to West Pakistanis. East Pakistan, on the other hand, was separated from the West by a hostile India, and its sole links with the West were religious ones. East Pakistan, better described as East Bengal, was the mainstay of Pakistan's export trade and contained the greater part of its population, although it fared poorly in the allocation of government jobs and public expenditure.

In December 1970 the first free Pakistani elections were held. In East Pakistan they resulted in an overwhelming victory for the Awami League, whose programme included autonomy for the East. The Pakistan government under President Yahya Khan (the successor to Ayub) would not accept this. Fighting broke out between government troops and Awami League supporters in March 1971; there was a vast drift of refugees into neighbouring India; and local armed resistance to the Pakistan army grew more marked. By December open war had begun between India and Pakistan in the East. After a fortnight's campaign the Pakistani forces in that area capitulated, and the former East Pakistan emerged as a sovereign state under the name of Bangladesh. Recognition of the new state by several Commonwealth members led the truncated state of Pakistan to withdraw from the Commonwealth. On 18 April 1972 Bangladesh became a member of the Commonwealth in its own right.

To a considerable extent, these events represented India's final triumph over Pakistan in respect of the Commonwealth. Pakistan, a member consistently hostile to India, was replaced by Bangladesh, a state which owed its independence largely to Indian arms, and could be expected to follow an Indian lead on major issues. Yet it would be wrong to assume that India regarded this triumph as primarily a Commonwealth affair; indeed, the Commonwealth

---

[1] See Millar, *Commonwealth & UN*, ch. 3, for an examination of UN pressure upon Britain in respect of the various colonies which gained independence, and T. Ramakrishna Reddy, *India's policy in the UN* (1968), ch. 3, for India's position on colonial questions in general.

figured hardly at all in its thinking. India was concerned first with the balance of forces in the subcontinent, and then with the implications of the situation in great-power terms. In the Bangladesh crisis, India got steady support from the Soviet Union, while the US and China, in unexpected unison, supported Pakistan. India's success lay partly in the extension of its influence in the subcontinent, but also in the discomfiture of those powers which had supported Pakistan, and in the strengthening of its association with the Soviet Union. The Commonwealth aspect was less important, although Indians got some pleasure from seeing Pakistan resign from this association in which it had tried unsuccessfully to indict India over Kashmir.

This crisis does not seem to have been regarded as a major Commonwealth issue by other members, who viewed it as either a domestic affair of the subcontinent, or as an occasion for great-power rivalry. The days of attempted Commonwealth mediation were over. Commonwealth recognition of Bangladesh was of some importance, because the new state needed to establish itself quickly; but Pakistan's departure occasioned little or none of the concern which a Commonwealth resignation had caused in previous years.

India was thus left with the Commonwealth field to itself. This was hardly the triumph it would have seemed two decades, or even one decade earlier. For India, Pakistan, and Bangladesh, a wider world provided the main inducements and deterrents. The Commonwealth had become an adjunct to their principal concerns.

CHAPTER 6

THE COMMONWEALTH AND SOUTHEAST ASIA

A. THE REGIONAL PROBLEM

IN the 1950s and 1960s Southeast Asia was the most disturbed part of the world, the part in which armed conflict was most frequent and severe, and the one in which great-power antagonism was most clearly evident, even though much of this antagonism was expressed through intermediaries. The Commonwealth was not important numerically in the region—by the end of the 1960s only Malaysia and Singapore were member states—but it was involved because some of its members believed that their interests were directly affected by what happened there, and because others were drawn towards consideration of Southeast Asian matters on account of the prominence these had assumed in world politics.

While it is true that actual conflict was greatest in Southeast Asia, its symbolic importance was even greater. Southeast Asia represented a kind of weakness in the crust of European colonialism: the Dutch, French, and British empires there had all failed to withstand the Japanese thrust in World War II; the return of the colonial powers in 1945 had been impeded, in Indonesia and Indo-China particularly, by local nationalist movements in which communists played a part; and even when those powers managed to re-establish themselves for the time being, resistance movements persisted. The Dutch in 1949 were the first to go, retaining only West New Guinea from their pre-war possessions. The French left in 1954. The British remained, having largely quelled the minority resistance movement before granting independence to Malaya in 1957. This exodus left groups of communists in each of the successor states. In Indo-China there was a communist government in North Vietnam, and communists commanded considerable forces in Laos. In Indonesia the Communist Party suffered a reverse in 1948, when an ill-timed rebellion was crushed by the army, but later increased in numbers and organization before its destruction in 1965. In Malaya and Singapore communist strength lay very largely amongst the radical Chinese, and was for that reason unpopular with the Malays; even so, 'the emergency', as it was known, lasted officially from 1948 to 1961. Communism as a local force was of much less significance in Thailand and Cambodia, but continued throughout the period to be a source of local insurgency in Burma and the Philippines. Nowhere else in the world did communist parties present such an active threat to governments or receive such encouragement, in propaganda, personnel, and equipment, from the Soviet Union, and after 1949 from China. The importance of the area arose from this fact, and even more from the reaction to it of the US.

From Truman onwards, all US presidents wanted to contain communism in Southeast Asia and prevent it from subverting and overthrowing the existing governments, unsatisfactory though these often seemed to American opinion. The reasons were summarized by Eisenhower in a news conference in 1954, when the French seemed likely to lose the battle of Dien Bien Phu:

... You have a row of dominoes set up, you knock over the first one, and what will happen to the last one is the certainty that it will go over very quickly. So you could have a beginning of a disintegration that would have the most profound influences ... when we come to the possible sequence of events, the loss of Indochina, of Burma, of Thailand, of the Peninsula and Indonesia following, now you begin to talk about areas that not only multiply the disadvantages that you would suffer through loss of materials, sources of materials, but now you are talking really about millions and millions of people.

Finally, the geographical position achieved thereby does many things. It turns the so-called island defensive chain of Japan, Formosa, of the Philippines, and to the southward it moves in to threaten Australia and New Zealand.[1]

This basic hypothesis lay behind the whole range of operations of the US and its allies in Indo-China after 1954 and in other parts of Southeast Asia. It was expressed in suaver and more sophisticated fashion by the Kennedy administration,[2] and in bolder terms by President Johnson; but the basic attitude remained the same, that American and world interests were threatened by any advance of communist power in a region in which such an advance was most likely to happen.

Throughout the 1950s and most of the 1960s the reality of politics in Southeast Asia was of weak states and foreign interference—exerted by China and the Soviet Union mainly through the local communist parties (though to what extent this involved control of their actions will be eternally argued by historians), and by the US through compliant governments, the pressure of allies, and covert operations such as the creation of special forces in Laos.[3] The thrust of American policy was sustained, at least until 1962, by a reluctance to believe that there could be any great difference of aim between the Soviet Union, China, and local communist parties;[4] the major difference of opinion within the Kennedy administration was not about whether there should be such interference, but what form it should take, especially in Indo-China, if an increase in communist control was to be prevented.

[1] Presidential news conference, 7 Apr 1954; reprinted in Robert L. Branyan & Lawrence H. Larsen, *The Eisenhower administration* (1971), i. 330–1.
[2] See e.g. Arthur M. Schlesinger Jr, *A thousand days* (1965), chs. 13 & 20, and Roger Hilsman, *To move a nation* (1967), pts III, IV, VIII, & IX.
[3] Hilsman, pts III & IV, *passim*.   [4] Ibid., p. 344.

For our purposes, a second thread of importance in the Southeast Asian skein is the rather more complex position taken by the British government. To simplify what should perhaps not be simplified, there was a continual note of British doubt about whether China was as firmly attached to the Soviet Union as American official opinion believed. Britain had to deal with the China that actually existed, because of its responsibility for Hong Kong, its diplomatic recognition of the communist regime, and its specific commitments in Malaya and Singapore. It could not, nor did its government wish, to pretend that Chiang Kai-shek's regime on Formosa (Taiwan) was the real government of China. Britain had not been involved in the 'loss' of China to the communists, as had the US, and suffered no national trauma as a result. There was not the same compulsion to identify China and the Soviet Union, or to believe that all policies were co-ordinated between them. The British government took a firm line against Chinese propaganda when it appeared to lead to violence as in Malaya; but it was generally sceptical of military action against Southeast Asian communists, although Britain was a member of Seato. Yet Britain was dependent on the US for support of Nato in Europe, and sometimes in need of American financial support. British influence on American policy was clearly important in 1954, when Eden managed to dissuade Dulles and Eisenhower from bombing support for the beleaguered French at Dien Bien Phu, but it was less effective by 1965, when the Vietnam war became an international issue again.

Reference has already been made (ch. 4) to Eden's efforts at the Geneva conference of 1954. His own account, which has not been seriously contested, shows that Commonwealth questions were of some importance to both Eden and Dulles, who were at odds over whether France should be encouraged to stay in Indo-China or enabled to leave with some remaining dignity, and whether the sort of body that eventually emerged as Seato should be organized during the conference, to counter any further communist advance. Eden wanted India associated with the negotiations as much as possible, in order to make them more acceptable to Asian opinion; Dulles did not. Eden wanted Australia and New Zealand on his side; Dulles wanted them on his, knowing that their governments valued greatly the American security guarantee which they had obtained in the Anzus Treaty three years before. There was something of a tug-of-war between the two. At one stage before the conference Eden had to object strongly to Dulles's attempt to include Australia and New Zealand, but not India, in a preliminary meeting. Saying Americans might think they no longer need consider the feelings of their allies, Eden added: 'We, at least, have constantly to bear in mind all our Commonwealth partners, even if the United States does not like some of them'.[1]

Australia and New Zealand, now and afterwards, hedged their bets: they were reported to Eisenhower as ready to listen to US proposals for collective

[1] Eden, *Full circle*, p. 99.

action in the Vietnam war, but Eisenhower did not want this unless he could have Britain too;[1] at Geneva Eden got their agreement to stay out of the war and to try to get India to join Seato when it was set up;[2] soon afterwards, however, Eisenhower and Dulles thought Australia and New Zealand might be induced to intervene in Vietnam after all.[3] In the end they were not called upon to do so, and India was made a member of the International Control Commission with their support; but thereafter Australia and New Zealand were drawn more towards the American view on Vietnam.

Seato, set up at a conference in Manila straight after the Geneva conference had left Vietnam divided de facto between a communist state in the north and a US-supported state in the south, was concerned with Indo-China, although none of the Indochinese successor states was a member. A protocol designated South Vietnam, Laos, and Cambodia as needing special protection. The US continued to be heavily involved in the area, providing military training and equipment and considerable financial help. In 1961 an increase in communist strength in Laos nearly led to large-scale American intervention; this problem was temporarily solved by another international agreement at Geneva.[4] But it was succeeded by more serious developments in South Vietnam—increasing communist insurgency and crumbling law and order. American involvement, already substantial, grew steadily as this insurgency became more serious. The results, in a Commonwealth context, are discussed below.

Meanwhile, it is desirable to indicate how Malaya and Indonesia fitted into the regional pattern. The disturbances in Indo-China had made little difference to Britain's military dispositions in the Far East, which were centred on Singapore and largely concerned with the long-drawn-out emergency in Malaya. This situation continued after Malayan independence in 1957. Insurgency in Malaya, and possible communist insurrection in Singapore itself, led not only Britain but also Australia and New Zealand to station troops in the area.

The presence of Australian and New Zealand troops in Malaya was closely linked with the membership of these two countries and Britain in Seato. At the Commonwealth Prime Ministers' Meeting of 1955, it had been announced by the governments concerned that

the opportunity was taken to discuss, as one element in the defence of the Manila Treaty area, the security of Malaya, which is regarded by the United Kingdom, Australia and New Zealand as of vital importance. The strategic position of the area was clarified by these discussions and it was considered that, in future, joint planning among the three Governments and discussions with other participants in the Manila Treaty would go forward more effectively.[5]

In fact, Australia and New Zealand had been associated with military planning

[1] Eisenhower, *Mandate for change*, p. 352.   [2] Eden, p. 114.
[3] Eisenhower, p. 359.   [4] Hilsman, pt IV, is valuable on the Laos episode.
[5] Cmd 9413 (Mansergh, *Documents 1952–62*, p. 417).

for Malaya since 1948, when they and Britain set up a shadowy consultative body known as Anzam, which was still in being in 1969, but about which no authoritative official statement had ever been made.[1] It was not till after the 1955 announcement that their forces were dispatched to Malaya.

Both governments gave great emphasis to 'discussions with other participants in the Manila Treaty', while retaining their close connections with British defence planning. Both wished to be assured that the American protection afforded by the Anzus Treaty of 1951, and which they saw reinforced by Seato, should extend to any operations in Malaya. Unlike Britain, Australia and New Zealand were anchored in the area. Their governments' overall defence plans assumed that US support would be forthcoming if they were engaged in hostilities anywhere in Southeast Asia. Soon after the London meeting, Menzies visited Eisenhower in order to be satisfied on this point, and came away with what he regarded as a clear assurance, which he described as of historic significance.

It contains in careful language and without exaggeration a general assurance which strengthens us in respect of our commitments enormously in the general task of preventing further Communist aggression. The United States considered the defence of Southeast Asia, of which Malaya is an integral part, to be of very great importance. I raised the question as to whether, in the event of Great Britain, Australia and New Zealand undertaking to station substantial forces in Malaya, we could be assured that the United States would be prepared to give us effective co-operation. I was informed that though the tactical employment of forces was a matter which would have to be worked out in detail on the Services level, the United States considered that such effective co-operation was implicit in the Manila Pact . . .[2]

The kind of position taken by Menzies represents a third thread in the skein, since Australian policy—normally echoed by New Zealand—was an extra complication to British policy, and was often regarded by the nonaligned members of the Commonwealth as itself an echo of American policy in Southeast Asia. This was not not always the case: Australian policy had its own nuances (in respect of Cambodia, for example), and was intended, wherever possible, to bridge any gaps between British and American policy, and to ensure that both these external powers retained forces in the area. But on the Vietnamese issue, in particular, Australia and New Zealand were very closely identified with the US.

Australia and New Zealand became formally associated with the defence of independent Malaya in 1957 through letters expressing assent to the AngloMalayan Defence Agreement.[3] This preserved the status quo. The British,

[1] See T. B. Millar, *Australia's defence* (1969), pp. 57–8.
[2] Statement of 20 Apr 1955 (*CS*, 4 May 1955, p. 386).
[3] The relevant portions of the Defence Agreement (Cmnd 263 of 1957) are in Mansergh, *Documents 1952–62*, pp. 571–3; see also Cmnd 264 for details about the use of what were called Overseas Commonwealth Forces in Emergency Operations. See Millar, *Australia's foreign policy* (1968), app. A, for documents on the Australian position.

Australian, and New Zealand forces formed part of a Commonwealth Strategic Reserve (although no general Commonwealth decision had been made about it); they were regarded by their governments as involved with Seato, since Malaya was an important part of the Seato area; but Malaya itself did not join Seato, and was thereby able to claim formal non-alignment.[1] Malaya was often stated to be a 'Commonwealth responsibility' by British leaders, in contra-distinction to Vietnam and Thailand, which were American. The reality of the situation was a massive concentration of British military force in Singapore and Malaya, largely unaffected by either Malaya's independence or Singapore's movement towards self-government.

Indonesia, Malaya's more populous neighbour, had taken an unsteady course since its independence, first asserted in 1945, was confirmed in 1949. Up to 1957, when President Sukarno proclaimed 'guided democracy' under his leadership as a replacement for 'liberal, western-style democracy', the country had been plagued by governmental instability, economic difficulties, separatism in the outer islands, and the continuance of Dutch rule in West New Guinea (West Irian). Sukarno's personal rule (much diluted by the need to pacify factions and the armed forces, playing off one against another) was marked by a swing away from western connections and towards the Soviet Union and China. In regional terms, Sukarno and many others in the govern-ment were incensed by the covert help given to Sumatran separatist forces in a smouldering civil war from 1958 onwards: supplies were dropped from Singa-pore and Manila, and an American bomber pilot was impounded.[2] While Sukarno was a prominent preacher of non-alignment, he interpreted this in a more anti-western form than other national leaders. By a brilliant combination of threats and diplomacy, he managed, in 1962, to obtain de facto control of West New Guinea, and to convert it soon afterwards into de jure sovereignty. Because of the desirability of making amends for earlier anti-Sukarno actions, and detaching Indonesia from communist connections, the US was the main influence in effecting the change, President Kennedy's brother Robert being its emissary.[3] By 1963 Sukarno was presumably somewhat mollified about the US, but still critical of the British military presence so close to his country. The Australian government had been making overtures to him for some time, but had rendered its own position difficult by encouraging the Dutch in their long effort to retain West New Guinea. This was one matter on which Australia had not succeeded in modifying American policy to suit itself. Australian anxiety about Indonesian intentions persisted.

It will be seen that, by 1963, the regional problem in Southeast Asia was

[1] For official Malayan statements on Seato and non-alignment, see Peter Boyce, *Malaysia and Singapore in international diplomacy* (1968), pp. 42–3.

[2] 'Sukarno and the Indonesians . . . had incontrovertible proof that the 1958 rebellion had received air drops of equipment from planes based in Malaya and the Philippines, and that the CIA [Central Intelligence Agency] was behind this support' (Hilsman, p. 364; see also p. 372).

[3] See ibid., ch. 25, for the reasoning behind US policy.

that Vietnam and Laos were active sources of international tension, while Indonesia might quickly become so. In Vietnam, which constituted the more serious problem, communist and western powers were directly opposed. North Vietnam was believed by the US government to be responsible for the growing insurgency in South Vietnam, and to be incited, if not controlled, by China. On the other side, the South Vietnamese government was buttressed by American support in every possible way except the actual conduct of operations. Indonesia, while clearly in sympathy with the communist powers, was still strongly and unpredictably independent. Whatever inspiring slogan Sukarno might turn to next would necessarily cause major concern to the western powers, especially Britain, the US, and Australia.

B. THE VIETNAM WAR

In 1963–4 South Vietnam's situation worsened, first through President Ngo Din Diemh's deposition and murder by some of his generals, then through rapidly increasing control of parts of the country by the NLF (National Liberation Front) or Vietcong. Following incidents between American and North Vietnamese naval vessels in the Gulf of Tonkin in August 1964, the US began bombing North Vietnam; its strategy was essentially that of measured attacks which, it was hoped, would deter North Vietnam from aiding the insurgents in South Vietnam, and bring about some settlement which would safeguard South Vietnam's continued existence. Australia and New Zealand gave strong, and Britain hesitant, support to this American strategy. It proved ineffective. Hence in the early part of 1965 the US government at last decided to commit combat troops to Vietnam, in addition to some thousands of technicians and support troops already there. Australia and New Zealand agreed to send token forces to assist; Britain did not.[1] The US and its allies were now poised for the destructive experience which, in the next three years, would bring half a million American soldiers to Vietnam, open wounds in the American body politic which led to a change of government, and bring about a situation in which a US president was more concerned with getting his forces out of Vietnam than with the aims which had put them there in the first place.[2]

I

In mid-1965, however, the build-up of US combat troops was still in its early stages. Few people can have imagined the lengths to which it would be

[1] Patrick Gordon Walker, *The cabinet* (1970), p. 125. See also Harold Wilson, *Labour government*, pp. 48, 80, 96, & 264 for repeated requests by President Johnson for a token British force—a 'platoon of bagpipers would be sufficient; it was the British flag that was wanted'. For Menzies's explanation of Australia's decision, see *CN*, Apr 1965, p. 178; for Holyoake on the New Zealand decision, see *New Zealand assistance to the republic of Vietnam*, pp. 5–9.

[2] The record of increasing US involvement in Vietnam can be studied in Hilsman, pts IV & IX; Henry Brandon, *Anatomy of error* (1970); and Townsend Hoopes, *The limits of intervention* (1969).

taken. Attention was concentrated on the bombing of North Vietnam, and on the possibility that China might be drawn in, as in the Korean war. America's European allies were, on the whole, dubious about American intervention (France being strongly opposed to it), and Afro-Asian countries were apprehensive that, if the war spread, they might be affected. The US government appears to have been in two minds, wishing to command the situation and deter further communist advance, but not to become too deeply involved. North Vietnam (backed strongly by China, but rather less resolutely by the Soviet Union, which, while not wishing to fail to support a fellow communist state in North Vietnam, did not wish China to have complete influence there) refused to negotiate unless the US withdrew altogether and recognized the NLF as possessing authority in the South. There were, however, indications that the North Vietnamese might move a little from this rigid position if the right conditions where found. With both major participants publicly firm yet privately signalling (or seeming to signal) the possibility that they might negotiate, the way was open for a variety of 'initiatives' designed to bring them together. Two of these were relevant to the later move for a Commonwealth peace mission.

First, the British government sent Patrick Gordon Walker, a former Commonwealth secretary and foreign secretary, to visit capitals in Asia and to explore the possibilities of a negotiated settlement. Gordon Walker made his tour from 14 April to 4 May 1965. China and North Vietnam refused to see him, and the Soviet Union reiterated its agreement with the North Vietnamese demand that US troops should leave Vietnam before any negotiations could start. Gordon Walker had some success in reopening the possibility of a conference on Cambodia, although this did not eventuate. The British government, through dispatching him, had shown its interest in the Vietnam situation, and had demonstrated that the communist states were not interested in negotiation as such.[1] At the same time it set its hand to the communiqué issued by the Seato Council in Bangkok on 5 May, which included the reaffirmation that 'the defeat of [the] Communist campaign [in South Vietnam] is essential not only to the security of the Republic of Vietnam but to that of Southeast Asia, and would provide convincing proof that Communist expansion by such tactics will not be permitted'. The Council expressed 'warm support' for US policy.[2] The Wilson government was thus supporting the US, but also expressing a desire for negotiation if the North Vietnamese would agree without demanding the withdrawal of American forces as a prior condition. Such a position was appropriate to a Labour government with a very small majority, wishing to retain the goodwill of the US administration; but it was not a comfortable one.

The second initiative was taken in March 1965 by a group of seventeen non-aligned states, which included the Commonwealth countries of Ceylon,

[1] CS, 8 June 1965.   [2] Cmnd 2834 (1965), p. 258.

Cyprus, Ghana, India, Kenya, Uganda, and Zambia. India was responsible for the first move by this group, which, from its membership (which included Yugoslavia but not Indonesia), can be regarded, in the circumstances of the time, as being 'non-aligned against China', in the sense that it consisted of India's rather than China's associates amongst the non-aligned states. The 'joint peace appeal' by the heads of the seventeen governments stated that 'the aggravation of the situation in Vietnam was 'the consequence of foreign intervention in various forms'. Saying that 'the only way leading to the termination of the conflict consists in seeking a political solution through negotiations', it called upon 'the parties concerned to start such negotiations, as soon as possible, without posing any preconditions'.[1] In referring to 'the parties concerned', and in sending their appeal to the NLF as well as to the governments of North and South Vietnam, the non-aligned states were running counter to the American orthodoxy of the time, which refused to accept the NLF as a party in its own right; but in saying no preconditions should be posed, they ran counter to the firm position taken by North Vietnam and China, and the initiative was accordingly rejected by both those countries.[2]

II

So matters stood when the Commonwealth prime ministers assembled in London in the middle of June 1965, for the meeting which will be discussed again in the contexts of Malaysia and Rhodesia. In respect of Vietnam, as of these other two matters, the fact that a number of the prime ministers were supposed to proceed from London to the Afro-Asian conference in Algiers, due to start on 29 June, was of considerable importance. Vietnam would undoubtedly be brought up there, probably on Chinese initiative, and from the standpoint of Commonwealth countries allied with the US, it was desirable that that discussion should not be too one-sided. Further, from the standpoint of those which were non-aligned, especially those which, for reasons of their own, did not wish China to dominate the Algiers conference, it was desirable that some new initiatives should be shown. It was also desirable that, if possible, the refusal of the North Vietnamese to negotiate without preconditions should be made at least as clear as the US refusal to withdraw its forces or to stop bombing North Vietnam. To the Labour government in Britain, the meeting was important since it was the first gathering of Commonwealth leaders to be chaired by Wilson after his electoral victory in late 1964. Wilson had campaigned for a more vigorous use of Commonwealth possibilities. Now, given the Rhodesian problem, something dramatic was certainly desirable.

---

[1] The text of the appeal, which was dated 2 April 1965 but had been sent to various governments and the NLF before that date, is in *Foreign Affairs Record* (New Delhi), Apr 1965, p. 83. The claim that India was responsible was made by the Indian minister for external affairs in the Lok Sabha on 1 April (ibid., p. 72).

[2] *CS*, 8 June 1965, p. 551.

Although the actual form taken by the prime ministers' discussion of Vietnam was a matter of Harold Wilson's initiative (the idea came to him 'pacing the terrace at Chequers'),[1] it was clear beforehand that some of them were concerned about the matter, and would welcome anything that might lead to negotiations between the warring parties. In the week before the meeting began, the prime ministers of India and Canada had discussed in Ottawa what was reported to be 'a draft plan for a diplomatic initiative';[2] the prime minister of New Zealand, on arrival, offered to take the lead in attempting to persuade the US to halt the bombing of North Vietnam 'so that peace talks could take place';[3] and he was the first western premier to suggest that the NLF should be a party to negotiations.[4] If New Zealand, which had already promised to commit troops to Vietnam (but had not at that stage sent them) spoke in these terms, it is not surprising that the meeting should have been receptive to Wilson's scheme, although its actual form came as a surprise.

Wilson proposed that the prime ministers appoint a mission which 'should, on their behalf, make contact with the governments principally concerned with the problem of Vietnam in order to ascertain how far there may be common ground about the circumstances in which a conference might be held leading to the establishment of a just and lasting peace in Vietnam'. The mission, it was decided, would consist of himself, Nkrumah (Ghana), Sir Abubakar Tafawa Balewa (Nigeria), Eric Williams (Trinidad), and Dudley Senanayake (Ceylon). The last-named was not in London, but it was hoped that he, as leader of an Asian non-aligned country, would agree to participate. Although the Tanzanian delegation issued a statement dissociating itself from the communiqué in which the prime ministers announced their decision on the first day of the meeting, on the ground that the mission was doomed to failure because of Wilson's commitment to the American side,[5] the immediate effect was favourable. Wilson, accompanied by Menzies, informed the British public on television; he then went to the House of Commons, where his statement was warmly welcomed, with hardly any criticism from the Conservatives and none from his own left wing.[6]

By the following day, however, the arrangement had begun to look less impressive. According to the main Pakistani newspaper, 'sources close to the Pakistani delegation' said that Pakistan was 'highly sceptical' but was supporting the move.[7] The Kenya delegation stated that it was 'opposed to Britain or

---

[1] Wilson, p. 108.

[2] *Guardian*, 17 June 1965. It should be borne in mind that India was chairman of the International Control Commission, the other members being Canada and Poland, of whom it is said that one of their functions from the beginning was to keep their allies informed about developments in Indo-China (see Peyton V. Lyon, p. 317). For the changing Indian role in the ICC, see D. R. Sar Desai, *Indian foreign policy in Cambodia, Laos and Vietnam* (1968).

[3] *DT*, 17 June 1965.   [4] *NYHT*, 17 June 1965.

[5] *Guardian*, 18 June 1965, for the substance of this paragraph. See also Wilson, pp. 109–11 for the Commonwealth leaders' reactions.

[6] *The Times*, 18 June 1965.   [7] *Dawn*, 19 June 1965.

any other country which has committed itself on the issue being a member of the proposed mission'. It insisted that before any investigation was undertaken, 'the view of the contesting parties should be ascertained as to their willingness to give full co-operation and facilities to the proposed mission'; and President Nyerere said in a BBC broadcast that the mission was 'designed to put China in the dock . . . the Commonwealth as a Commonwealth group should not appear to be backing up Wilson or the United States on this issue'.[1] Nkrumah unsuccessfully appealed to Australia to withdraw its military forces from Vietnam. Holyoake, who seems to have been less whole-heartedly committed than Menzies to full support of US intervention, said he was prepared to hold up the dispatch of New Zealand units until the result of the mission was known. Senanayake announced that he was unable, because of illness, to join the mission.[2]

One day later, although the mission was now a four-, not a five-country affair,[3] it issued a further statement broadening its approach somewhat.

In order to create the conditions in which the mission can carry through its work [it said] the mission is appealing to all parties concerned to show the utmost restraint in military operations as a step towards the total cease fire which the mission hopes will be established at the earliest possible opportunity. The Mission would wish to meet all parties concerned.[4]

The repetition of 'all parties', in contrast with the earlier communiqué's 'governments principally concerned', showed that the NLF was now implicitly included as one of the parties to the dispute. This was in line with statements issued by Nkrumah and Shastri, the Indian prime minister, both of whom had pressed for the NLF to be included.[5] President Johnson was said to have welcomed the initiative and to be ready to see the mission;[6] and the same was said to be true of the UN secretary-general, U Thant.[7]

From this point, however, the scheme for the mission began to slide into frustration. The ostensible problem was that of Wilson as leader of the mission, but this was probably an easy way of identifying difficulties which would have arisen in any case because of the Chinese and North Vietnamese refusal to consider negotiations except on the terms which North Vietnam had stated, and which were quite unacceptable to the US and South Vietnam. The first Chinese reactions were that Wilson's was 'the action of a nitwit making trouble

---

[1] DT, 19 June 1965.   [2] The Times, 19 June 1965.

[3] According to President Ayub's most faithful newspaper, he had declined to be an Asian member of the mission, and had told the meeting that 'owing to the military encirclement of Pakistan by India, all our energies are today devoted to this new Vietnam in the making' (Dawn, 19 June 1965).

[4] Sunday Telegraph, 20 June 1965.   [5] Hindu, 19 June 1965.

[6] Sunday Times, 20 June 1965. In fact, Wilson had approached him first, before sounding out Commonwealth leaders (Wilson, p. 108).

[7] The Times, 21 June 1965.

for himself'. The Wilson government's 'peace formula' and the Johnson administration's 'peace fraud' were one and the same.

To give himself an air of greater authority, Wilson is even making the shameless claim that he is expressing the common will of the "British Commonwealth" which embraces one-quarter of the world's population. Here he is using the names of others and is plainly bluffing. . . . Wilson seems to think that the 'British Commonwealth' label will make his formula 'difficult' 'to refuse'. This is fantastic. China has already banged the door in Gordon Walker's face. If the Wilson government wants to have another try with this 'mission' of his, all that awaits it is another slamming of the door.[1]

North Vietnamese comment was similar.

Before this door-slamming from Peking, there had been further thoughts in London. Some prime ministers were said to be trying to replace Wilson by Pearson, of Canada, without avail; Williams said that he had thrice refused to serve but had been 'drafted', and that Pakistan and Tanzania (neither of which would serve) should be members of the mission to give it a real chance of success.[2] Following the adverse Chinese and North Vietnamese reactions, the Soviet Union rejected the idea of receiving the mission, because, it said, it had not been authorized by anybody to conduct talks on a Vietnam settlement.[3] None the less, the members of the mission issued a further statement on 24 June, saying:

The Commonwealth as such is in no way committed to either side of the conflict in Vietnam and has formed no collective view except on the urgency of re-establishing conditions in which the people of Vietnam may be able to live in peace. Although within the Commonwealth there is diversity of opinion on the Vietnam problem, there is complete unanimity as to the need to find a peaceful solution. In the discharge of the task entrusted to it, the Mission will be guided by the views of the Commonwealth as a whole and not by the views of any individual member of the Commonwealth.[4]

On the following day the prime ministers propounded a 'Statement of Guidance' which would 'enable the Mission to approach its assignment meaningfully'. It called for a 'comprehensive ceasefire and a conference of all the parties directly involved in the situation' as an essential precondition, and went on to list certain 'ultimate objectives' which should guide the mission in its consultations. These included a suspension of US air attacks on North Vietnam; a North Vietnamese undertaking to prevent the movement of

---

[1] 'Observer' in *People's Daily*, 21 June 1965 (Hsinhua newsagency).

[2] *Guardian*, 22 June 1965.

[3] *The Times*, 24 June 1965. The British, Nigerian, and Ghanaian ambassadors in Moscow had laid the proposal before Kosygin.

[4] Like other quotations of communiqués on Vietnam, this is incomplete. The full texts of the statements made by the mission on 19 and 24 June, and of the 'Statement of Guidance' by the prime ministers on 25 June, are in the *CRO Year Book 1966*, pp. 23–4.

military forces, assistance, and material to South Vietnam; a total ceasefire; and a conference which would aim at international policing of Vietnam for a period, and eventual unification through 'free and internationally supervised elections'. These guidelines lay much closer to the American than to the North Vietnamese and Chinese preconditions,[1] and no one can have been surprised when, on the same day, the Chinese foreign ministry delivered a reply to the British chargé d'affaires in Peking, rejecting the idea of the mission. The British government, it said,

is actually appropriating the name of the Commonwealth to launch a new "peace talks" plot, thus rendering yet another service to the US aggressors . . . The communiqué of the Commonwealth Prime Ministers conference on the formation of the mission evades the substance of the Vietnam question by making no mention at all of US aggression, and indiscriminately calls for the realisation of "peace" in Vietnam . . .[2]

On the final day of the meeting, Wilson withstood a direct challenge from the foreign minister of Kenya, Joseph Murumbi, to stand down from the leadership of the mission,[3] and the meeting ended with the public assumption that the mission would proceed. In fact it did not. North Vietnam eventually stated officially that it was not interested; it did invite Nkrumah on a personal basis to visit Hanoi.[4] Wilson sent one of his junior ministers, Harold Davies, to visit Hanoi 'to remove certain doubts which appear to have arisen there', but to no avail.[5] Nothing more was heard of the operation, except amongst Wilson's opponents, who continued to cite it as an example of his tendency towards 'instant government' without any result.

III

The abortive peace mission, a bare nine-days' wonder in 1965 but with no further standing in Commonwealth affairs,[6] prompts certain questions about the suitability of the Commonwealth as a vehicle for efforts of this kind, and about the motives of the members who supported it.

Of the effort itself, one can ask whether it was a matter, as the Chinese government said, of 'appropriating the name of the Commonwealth to launch a new "peace talks" plot'; whether it was, as President Nyerere claimed on his

---

[1] Shastri claimed, before he left London, that these guidelines contained 'many of our ideas and our own formulations in this regard' (*Hindu*, 27 June 1965).

[2] *Guardian*, 26 June 1965.   [3] Ibid.   [4] *FT*, 16 July 1965.

[5] Wilson announced Davies's mission to the House of Commons on 8 July (*CN*, July 1965, p. 389 for a summary of the events).

[6] At their meeting in September 1966, the prime ministers gave fitting burial to their effort of 1965: 'They regretted that the Mission which they had appointed at their 1965 Meeting had not been able to undertake its task. Nonetheless they believed that the Commonwealth should continue its efforts to promote peace in Vietnam.' No further efforts were made. (Extract from communiqué in *CO Year Book 1967*, p. 72.)

return to Tanzania, a case in which 'we were being used for British political purposes';[1] or whether, as Wilson claimed in announcing it in the House of Commons, it was 'an important step in the direction of world peace'. His view was that 'we shall have established the united desire of the Commonwealth to secure peace in Vietnam . . . we shall have asserted the role of the Commonwealth in the world by the statements we have made.'[2]

The difficulty in choosing between these descriptions is that, while each clearly contains an element of the truth, we do not yet know which contains most. The circumstances in which the initiative was originally taken, and the resentment expressed by some members of the Prime Ministers' Meeting at the haste with which it was introduced, do suggest that the name of the Commonwealth was being 'appropriated' to serve the interests, both of Wilson's government with its narrow majority and its turbulent left-wing group opposed to American intervention in Vietnam, and of the US government, which was seeking a way to negotiations without surrendering its own basic demands. But this conclusion is compatible with the service of world peace, provided there was some basis, other than sheer opportunism, for expecting that the mission might meet with a response from North Vietnam and China. It is here that lack of knowledge impedes an answer. Quite possibly, the Soviet Union had intimated that it might be able to influence North Vietnam in the direction of some sort of settlement short of the absolutes which constituted North Vietnam's public posture. It may have led Wilson to believe that external pressure which was neither obviously communist nor entirely pro-western might give Russia extra leverage upon North Vietnam. If the Soviet Union did say this, it may have been sincere or it may not: both possibilities can be entertained in the circumstances of the Soviet Union at the time. One can imagine that Wilson, in his own domestic situation and in such delicate relations with Johnson, would have grasped at such a chance. If the mission did succeed, everything would be gained. If it did not, it would still have tried. 'It is better to have loved and lost than never to have loved at all', said Menzies to the British public on television, when agreeing to the initiative; and if this thought commended itself to him, it must have done so with even greater force to Wilson. Thus it is possible that there was a chance of success, of breaking a deadlock which had resisted all other efforts—provided that Wilson had reason to believe that the North Vietnamese position might be relaxed. If that was not the case, then the enterprise was foolish from the start. We do not know whether it was or not; and Wilson's memoirs do not help us.

Assuming, however, that such a chance existed, was the Commonwealth the right sort of body to act upon it? To answer yes, one need not assume that every Commonwealth country thought the same way or had the same motives in supporting the idea of a peace mission. It has sometimes been possible for

[1] *Guardian*, 3 July 1965.   [2] HC Deb., 17 June 1965, col. 1057.

Commonwealth members to join together in order to secure a result which suited their differing interests. In the case of Vietnam, a number of these interests converged. Although Britain, Canada, Australia, and New Zealand were not entirely at one, their position as US allies, concerned to see that the world balance between the communist and anti-communist powers was not too greatly tilted to communist advantage, gave them something of a common point of view. While none of them was prepared to pillory the US, each would gain from helping the US to extricate itself from the morass in which it seemed to be sinking.

To some extent, their policy was that advocated by an anonymous article in *The Times* on the eve of the Prime Ministers' Meeting. It pointed out that at Algiers the Chinese could be expected to lead 'an all-out and murderous attack on "American imperialism"—thereby strengthening in America the more extreme elements on both sides'. The prime ministers, it said, could give 'cool, dispassionate advice', in order to 'strengthen the moderate forces inside the United States and give the President some of the elbow-room he needs'.[1] No doubt there was wishful thinking in such an approach, but it had much to commend it to the allies of the US. In this context, the fact that Wilson outlined his plan beforehand to the prime ministers of Canada, Australia, and New Zealand—and to none of the Africans and Asians—is of some importance.[2] While Britain and the three old dominions did not want the war called off at the expense of vital western interests, they did not want the US to be too deeply involved or too badly frustrated. Negotiations might conceivably occur; if they occurred they might conceivably succeed. In addition, each of the four prime ministers was troubled by elements in his own country which questioned his support for US intervention in Vietnam. A Commonwealth effort might quieten these.

The range of Afro-Asian positions was much wider, but was still compatible in most cases with agreement to support the mission. Pakistan and Tanzania were both in fairly close relations with China, which they did not wish to disturb. It was natural that they should make their doubts or opposition known. At the other end of the scale, Malaysia was understandably apprehensive about either American failure or undue escalation of the Vietnam war, since either might lead to a failure in the American will to resist communist pressure in Southeast Asia, and to encouragement of Indonesian confrontation. Like many people in Australia and New Zealand, the Malaysian government (and that of Singapore, soon to become separate) must have been torn between the desire to retain US involvement and the suspicion that, in Vietnam at least, that involvement had gone too far in the wrong direction. The peace mission could, in these circumstances, be supported, though with some reluctance.

In between these two extremes there were several different positions which

[1] 'Commonwealth and America', by a Correspondent, 16 June 1965.
[2] *Guardian*, 21 June 1965.

the Africans and Asians might take, including active support for the mission (India), active support with extra conditions (Ghana), a cautious support with some scepticism (Trinidad), and public silence allied with private scepticism (several African countries). We may take as an example the attitude of Nkrumah. In a special statement towards the end of the meeting, he said:

I was originally doubtful whether it would be advisable for Mr Wilson to serve; but once we had made a decision I am certain it is essential that we stick to it. Indeed, I think there are great advantages in his heading our team. He has an influence with the US government which no other member of the mission possesses.

He added that he had personally asked the Chinese to receive the mission, and that he thought it might succeed in its purpose if American air attacks were suspended, if Australia withdrew its troops, and if the NLF and the government of South Vietnam were regarded as rival governments, both of which the mission should see.[1] The condition about Australian troops had already been publicly rejected by Menzies five days before.[2]

Nkrumah had his own reasons for wanting to end the Vietnam war.[3] In his determination to make Ghana the torchbearer of African unity he had alienated a good many African states, and brought himself into conflict with others in Africa and Asia through his open support for Chinese positions and for North Vietnam. At the same time he still valued Ghana's membership of the Commonwealth, and was not under the domination of either Russia or China; he believed in his own capacity for independent diplomatic initiative, and for handling not only African issues but also those affecting the whole of the Third World. His enthusiastic support of the Commonwealth mission may well have been based upon the view that, even if it should fail in its original form, it would leave him personally with more opportunity of influencing the outcome in Vietnam than he would otherwise have. In fact, although the mission failed to visit any of the capitals of the countries concerned, Nkrumah undertook a separate Ghanaian initiative as a consequence; and it was in pursuit of this, some six months later, that he visited Peking, to find that he had been deposed in his absence from Ghana. In his case the Commonwealth scheme may well have seemed to offer a chance to distinguish himself. If so, he was mistaken; but it is the kind of mistake on which political leaders often base their support for particular actions and policies, sometimes with success.

It is not necessary to postulate similarly complex motives for each of the other Afro-Asian leaders in order to recognize that they could support the peace mission in its earlier, more hopeful stages, even if they believed—as some evidently did—that Wilson had taken the initiative for his own purposes.

Still, was the Commonwealth the right body for the task? It should be

[1] *The Times*, 25 June 1965.
[2] Press conference in London, 19 June 1965 (*CN*, June 1965, p. 344).
[3] See W. Scott Thompson, esp. pp. 409–13.

remembered that, even though Commonwealth members had been induced on earlier occasions to embrace a common viewpoint, they had not previously set up a committee to travel the world and convince other states that they should alter their policies. The step which Wilson proposed, and which the great majority of the prime ministers supported, was never repeated, a fact which suggests that the Commonwealth was unsuited to this kind of action, and that member governments may have drawn that conclusion. Even if the Vietnam mission had succeeded, to the extent of enabling it to visit some or all of the capitals originally intended, it would probably have soon revealed the divergence between its members' attitudes towards the war. For the prime ministers to say, as they did in their final communiqué, that 'in the discharge of the task entrusted to it, the Mission will be guided by the views of the Commonwealth as a whole, and not by the view of any individual member' was to fly in the face of the known behaviour of states. The British and Ghanaian leaders' positions could not have been accommodated for long, once the declaratory stage had passed. This might not have been a problem if the Commonwealth mission had been quickly able to induce the parties to talk, but it would have become clear if long negotiation had been required before that position was reached.

In the light of hindsight, we can see that the mission had no chance unless either side in the Vietnam war retreated suddenly and decisively from the position it had already taken up. In June 1965 South Vietnam was in turmoil and seemed as if it might collapse: the North Vietnamese were not prepared to give up the chance of such a prize just because there was the possibility of modifying US attitudes. Indeed, the North Vietnamese may have felt that the further the US was drawn into the morass, the sooner it would want to get out, leaving South Vietnam at the mercy of the North. On the other side, the US government may have wanted a chance to talk, but it had shown no public desire to withdraw from the conflict, and the position of South Vietnam was so weak that the main trend in US official opinion was towards counter-attacks upon the forces of the NLF and the North, rather than to surrender responsibility. In private, influences close to Johnson did counsel negotiation, and warned against the consequences of committing further forces to Vietnam; but the main pressures, and his own inclinations, went the other way.[1]

There is thus little reason to think that the Commonwealth could have persuaded the parties to negotiate, except in the remote circumstances of their being eager to meet one another—in which case the Commonwealth would have been as suitable an intermediary as any other but not necessarily any more so. This was not the case, although, at the time, it seemed to be possibly so. The later realization that it was not is probably why this particular initiative remains an isolated happening in Commonwealth affairs.

From a general Commonwealth standpoint, then, the effort was a failure.

[1] See, e.g., Brandon, ch. 3, esp. George Ball's letter to the president, pp. 57–9.

Was this because of the nature of the Commonwealth or the nature of the issue? The answer must be both, but especially the latter. The issue was so divisive, and so directly involved the associations and alignments of member states, that it was bound to cause trouble between them. It proved, in addition, to be an issue in 1965 which the great powers wished to settle for themselves, not through intermediaries, as they had tended to do at Geneva. The issue of Vietnam was, in fact, difficult for any international body to handle. It had not figured prominently on the agenda of the UN, because of the awareness of members that no progress was likely so long as the US and the Soviet Union were at odds about it. The personal good offices of the secretary-general had been of little help. The Commonwealth was not necessarily less appropriate for this mediatory task than other international bodies, given that those others would also reproduce the divisions current in the world.

If it had been a different issue, then the nature of the Commonwealth would not necessarily have worked against its being discussed and even agreed on. At their 1961 and 1962 meetings, for example, the Commonwealth prime ministers had agreed on a 'Statement on Disarmament' and a reiteration of the principles then stated.[1] These represented a consensus of states which differed on many particular issues but agreed that the world was in danger because of the extent of nuclear and other forms of arms. We may conclude that, while the Vietnam issue was too pointed and immediate for effective consensus by Commonwealth members for more than a brief period, the Commonwealth should not therefore be regarded as incapable of pronouncing on major international issues; those issues would, however, need to be broad in scope and long in range before they could be considered appropriate. Differing national interests and those widening opportunities for states to pursue individual policies, which we have seen to be constant themes in the development of the Commonwealth in the 1950s and 1960s, were very much at work in the Vietnam case.

Two of the other themes we have identified—the changing character of British attitudes towards the Commonwealth, and changing conceptions of what the Commonwealth stood for—were also exemplified. When Wilson took his initiative, he had been prime minister for only a short time. He had been elected on a platform which included a vigorous development of Commonwealth relations. His party looked on the Commonwealth as a bridge between the old and new nations. Its disposition was still to try to enlarge Commonwealth institutions and opportunities, though this was not to be the case for long. Although the Conservatives were now inclined to question the value of attempts at Commonwealth action, in the light of the difficulties which the new African members were causing Britain over Rhodesia,[2] Labour was still

---

[1] Mansergh, *Documents 1952–62*, pp. 556–8 & 560.

[2] See, as an example during the 1965 meeting, Nigel Lawson, 'Should there be another Commonwealth meeting?', *FT*, 23 June 1965.

optimistic. In pursuit of this sentiment, it was good policy, from Wilson's point of view, to try to enlarge the boundaries of Commonwealth effort—so long, presumably, as this remained under British leadership. It was not British opinion, but African and Asian opinion, that tried unsuccessfully to replace Wilson by Pearson as leader of the Vietnam mission. The reception of the plan for the mission by the House of Commons showed that Wilson's initiative was widely regarded as a proper exercise of British policy and the Commonwealth as a proper vehicle of that policy; it was only afterwards that doubts crept in, once it was seen that other Commonwealth members were not wholeheartedly behind the proposal. It was still possible in 1965 to view the Commonwealth as an instrument of British foreign policy. When Wilson next tried unsuccessfully to influence the course of the Vietnam war, in 1967, he did so as intermediary between Johnson and Kosygin;[1] in this the Commonwealth played no part. It was because of the peculiar conjunction of circumstances in 1965—Wilson's situation, and the expected Afro-Asian conference in Algiers in particular—that the two were momentarily and unsuccessfully brought together, with no obvious effect upon either.

The Vietnam war was important for certain relationships within the Commonwealth, as distinct from its impact on the Commonwealth as a whole. Because of its long duration and its disturbing effects throughout Southeast Asia, it probably brought Malaysia and Singapore closer to Australia and New Zealand. As India grew closer to the Soviet Union during the war, and became more inclined to support Soviet interpretations of what was going on, its position became less compatible with those taken by Britain, Australia, New Zealand, and, to some extent, Canada.

But the most important effect was probably the divisive impact on relations between Britain and Australia in respect of Southeast Asia. Australia sent troops to Vietnam in spite of also being involved in confrontation; Britain did not, in spite of being a Seato member and so having some responsibility for South Vietnam under the Seato Protocol, and in spite of having substantial forces in the area, especially after confrontation declined. The difference between the two was easily explained (although the superficial explanation that it was due to Britain's having a Labour government will not do: a Conservative government would have had considerable difficulty in persuading public opinion that it should send troops to Vietnam). Australian security was at stake, in the opinion of its government; Britain's was not. Australia, its government felt, needed to send troops to Vietnam in order to show that it was a good ally; Britain, in the judgement of its government, had other ways of doing this.

To the Australian government, the conflicts in Borneo and Vietnam had much in common, since both could lead to an increase in Chinese power and influence if Sukarno's Indonesia and Ho Chih Minh's North Vietnam were not checked; to the British government, the similarity was not obvious, and

[1] Brandon, ch. 5.

the fear of China was not, in any case, so great. Such a difference of views helped to explain the difference between the actions taken by the two countries in Vietnam, Britain's leaning towards conciliation and Australia's towards intervention. There had been Australian doubts about Eden's policy at Geneva in 1954, and a strong tendency for Australia to follow the American rather than the British line on developments in Indo-China since then. This had been especially so in respect of the position in Laos in 1961.[1] The failure of the Wilson initiative in 1965 helped to confirm the Australian government in its view that toughness towards North Vietnam would bring better dividends than further attempts at negotiation. This did not become the British view at any stage. At bottom, the British interest in Southeast Asia was confined, in military terms, to Malaysia and Singapore. When the ability to sustain a major role there was no longer felt, British concern for the area waned. The equivocal position on Vietnam was a foretaste of this.

C. CONFRONTATION AND BRITISH COMMITMENT

President Sukarno's volatile rule in Indonesia expressed itself, late in 1963, in a policy of 'confrontation' of Malaysia, a new Commonwealth state made out of Malaya, Singapore, and British territories in Borneo. The background of this merger is important, not only for an understanding of later diplomatic and military action, but also because the merger was to be broken by the withdrawal under pressure of Singapore.

I

There was always much to be gained by Singapore from some sort of association with Malaya. The Singapore economy, built up through entrepot trade and British military spending, was inextricably linked with that of Malaya. The movement of people between the two was continuous. Singapore even relied for water upon the mainland. Any notion of separate Singapore defence seemed ludicrous. Many institutions were common to the two; what was at variance was the population balance. If merged with Malaya in some sort of federation or confederation which preserved essential local matters in Singapore hands, Singapore could hope to benefit in many ways.

From the standpoint of the Malayan government, an association with Singapore alone, while clearly desirable in macro-economic terms, was undesirable in communal terms. Malaya was governed by an inter-party coalition, the Alliance, consisting of Umno (the United Malay National Organization), the MCA (Malayan Chinese Association), and the MIC (Malayan Indian Congress). In this coalition the dominant position of the Malays was recognized by the other two communal groups, which were given, in return,

[1] See Macmillan, *Pointing the way* (1972), ch. 11, esp. pp. 346–7, for details of how the British government prevented a military intervention in Laos in April 1961, plans for which were supported by Australia and New Zealand.

certain guarantees of relative autonomy and of protection. Roughly speaking, the balance was the same as in the Malayan population at large. If Singapore were added, the overall balance of population would tilt, and this would be bound to affect the position of the MCA, which would either become enlarged to claim equal power with Umno, or (more likely) be displaced in the affections of the Chinese by an extension of Lee Kuan Yew's activist party in Singapore, the PAP (People's Action Party). The nature of communalism in the area dictated such an analysis. It could hardly appeal to the government of Malaya. A possible solution, however, would be an association which included not only Malaya and Singapore, but also the British dependencies in Borneo—Sarawak, Brunei, and British North Borneo. These were not predominantly Malay in population, but the Chinese were a minority in them. If these territories came into the association, the Chinese would be outnumbered in the population as a whole, and Malay rights, as they operated in the existing Federation of Malaya, could presumably be safeguarded.

The British government's standpoint could accommodate both the Singaporean and the Malayan. Malaya and Singapore combined looked stronger than Malaya and Singapore apart. It would be possible to continue defence arrangements with the two together more easily than if they were separate. In any case, British thinking at the time when these matters were being considered (1960–1) was still opposed to the creation of 'mini-states', such as Singapore would have to be on its own. Moreover, the future of the Borneo territories would be a problem if they were left to themselves. Britain was still in its federation-building frame of mind; the federations in the West Indies, Central Africa, and Nigeria had still not suffered the crippling blows they were later to receive. A federation between the territories was a possible solution, but one in which they were joined to the political experience and the wealth of Malaya and Singapore looked much better.

The coincidence of the three standpoints became apparent once Tunku Abdul Rahman declared to foreign press correspondents at Singapore, on 27 May 1961, that 'Malaya today as a nation realises that she cannot stand alone and in isolation. . . . Sooner or later she should have an understanding with Britain and the peoples of the territories of Singapore, Borneo, Brunei and Sarawak.'[1] Progress thereafter was swift. Within a few months Malaya and Singapore had agreed on suitable arrangements for their merger within the new and greater Federation of Malaysia. The Tunku and Macmillan discussed matters in London in November, and announced that they were in favour of the scheme. It would be necessary to consult the people of Sarawak and North Borneo, and the sultan of Brunei; a commission under Lord Cobbold was duly set up to do this. The two prime ministers agreed that the existing defence agreement would be extended to embrace the new territories when Malaysia

---

[1] Quoted in J. M. Gullick, *Malaysia and its neighbours* (1967), a useful collection of documents (p. 28).

was constituted. The Singapore base, which up to this time had remained in British hands, would become subject to Malaysian sovereignty but would not be a Seato base. It could, however, be used for Seato purposes with Malaysian approval.

Throughout 1962 the process of discussion and consultation continued, with further agreement on the details of the new federation, with the Cobbold Commission at work, and with an approving majority in a referendum on merger in Singapore. In North Borneo (from now on called Sabah) and Sarawak embryo political parties developed quickly, with the general trend of opinion favouring the proposed federation. In Brunei, however, the sultan appeared at first to be in two minds. In December a revolt broke out there. It was quickly quelled by British troops, airlifted from Singapore, but some of its leaders sought refuge in Indonesian Borneo and the Philippines. This was the beginning of a troubled period for which 'confrontation' was to be the new defining term. Both Indonesia and the Philippines, for different but compatible reasons, became opposed to the creation of the new state. The Philippine opposition, while diplomatically vexatious to Malaysia, did not lead to open conflict: it was concerned with a claim to parts of North Borneo, based upon whether land had been leased or ceded by a sultan to the British North Borneo Company, and could be argued at leisure. Indonesia, however, had stronger views to express.

II

Sukarno's supremacy depended on manipulation of the armed forces on the one hand and the PKI (the Communist Party) on the other. A man of great personal magnetism and wide-ranging ideas, he had increasingly embraced an adventurist and declamatory line in foreign affairs. In spite of the strong anti-Chinese feeling amongst Indonesians (similar in character and origins to the feeling amongst the Malays), Sukarno had increasingly aligned himself with China's line in world affairs, after a period during which he had obtained military supplies from the Soviet Union. While highly rhetorical in emphasis, and never worked out with much clarity, his ideas on world affairs crystallized into a dichotomy between the New Emerging Forces (the Afro-Asian countries, the communist countries, the countries of Latin America to an imprecise extent, and the freedom fighters in existing colonies, together with progressives in the capitalist world) and the Old Established Forces (essentially the colonial powers, the unprogressive elements in the capitalist world, and especially, but to an undefined extent, the US).[1] The issue between the two was colonialism, whether in its formal guise as colonial rule or in its informal one as 'neo-colonialism', the economic and military domination of newly

---

[1] The Indonesian liking for contractions turned these two into Nefo and Oldefo; when the Games of the New Emerging Forces were held in Djakarta in November 1963 as a rival to the Olympic Games, they were called Ganefo.

independent countries by their old masters, or by other developed capitalist countries.

The formulation was similar to that made by Nkrumah and other Afro-Asian leaders who, while not communist and not desiring to be controlled by either China or the Soviet Union, wished to express a radical attitude and to mobilize local patriotism generally to oppose western influence. It was vague enough, however, to enable full relations to be retained with most western countries, including the US. It was a form of intellectual alignment without the formal ties of military alignment.

Probably Sukarno thought of himself at times as the leader of a nascent world movement; an insatiable traveller, he lost no opportunity to preach his gospel where he thought it would be well received.[1] As the host at Bandung in 1955, he could claim some primacy in the Afro-Asian movement. At the Non-Aligned Conference in Belgrade in September 1961 he had already clashed with Nehru, and had fairly plainly bid for the support of those Afro-Asian countries which were either hostile to India or well disposed towards China. It was generally considered, however, that much of his rhetoric was for domestic consumption even when it was ostensibly concerned with world events. His balancing of political forces at home, whether between personalities in the government and the armed forces, or between one political party and another, or between the armed forces and the communists, demanded a restless style of rule, especially since the Indonesian economy was in decline. For a long time West Irian provided an external issue which could satisfy both radicalism and nationalism; in 1962, however, as we have seen, it came to an end. The pressures upon Sukarno converged to make it necessary for him to find a new slogan: he found it in 'confrontation' of Malaysia.

The reasons given were various. Following the revolt in 1958, the continuance of a British military presence through Malaysia might, in Sukarno's view, mean further assistance to Indonesian rebels. It was, in any case, a reassertion of western power on his country's doorstep, at a time when Sukarno hoped to see Indonesia's influence widen. He was well aware that American, British, and Australian military men were perturbed at the large size and apparently growing influence of the PKI, as they were at his own identification first with the Soviet Union and then with China. He did not want them to have a base and forces lodged nearby in perpetuity. It looked like 'nekolim', and he would indict it as such. This seems to have been the crux of the matter for Sukarno, apart from his need to create military diversions and to concentrate Indonesia patriotism against an external foe. Objections to the way in which opinion about Malaysia was ascertained in the Borneo territories, although these were the main reasons given at the time for regarding Malaysia as unfit to be recognized as a sovereign state, were probably secondary.

[1] George Modelski, ed., *The new emerging forces* (1963) contains a record of President Sukarno's travels, 1959–63, and numerous examples of his oratory.

The details of how confrontation came about are recorded elsewhere.[1] The course of events was briefly as follows. The Cobbold Commission reported that opinion in Sarawak and Sabah was largely in favour of incorporation in Malaysia; the Sultan of Brunei eventually decided to stay out. Arrangements for completing the merger by the end of August 1963 went ahead smoothly in administrative terms, but were complicated by expressions of disapproval from Indonesia and the Philippines. In June the Tunku and Sukarno met privately in Tokyo. Then the foreign ministers of the three countries met in Manila, and issued a 'Manila Accord', which envisaged a closer connection between the three. They proposed that the UN secretary-general ascertain whether the people in the Borneo territories supported the formation of Malaysia. At the beginning of August the Tunku, President Sukarno, and President Macapagal of the Philippines met to issue a 'Manila Declaration', in which the future establishment of 'Maphilindo' (a grouping of the three countries without loss of sovereignty) was acclaimed, 'foreign bases' were condemned, and the secretary-general was requested to proceed.[2] He did so, but the momentum of events was increasing so as to make his task both difficult and embarrassing. There were difficulties with the British government about the observers from Indonesia and the Philippines; in Singapore and Malaya there was a strong wish to assert the formation of Malaysia as an act of will, not dependent on what the UN or anyone else might say. The upshot was that the Tunku announced on 29 August that Malaysia would come into being on 16 September. The UN report, which was favourable, was not made until that date. 'Malaysia Day' was duly celebrated, but Indonesia and the Philippines broke off diplomatic relations the day after.

From now on, Indonesia and the Philippines waged diplomatic and, in the Indonesian case, armed struggle against Malaysia. At the UN Malaysia's position was strong: it was accepted as a member, and, by the fortunes of UN politics, was actually made a member of the Security Council at the beginning of 1965, upon which Indonesia withdrew from the UN and nearly all its specialized agencies. Indonesia was not condemned outright as an aggressor, but, in diplomatic terms, the Malaysian position was reinforced. At the level of Afro-Asian politics, however, the Indonesian position was stronger. Malaysia became caught up in the quadrangular contest between India on the one side, and China, Indonesia, and Pakistan on the other, with the Soviet Union as a highly interested fifth party. While itself strictly anti-communist, Malaysia was in the ironic position that India championed its inclusion in Afro-Asian gatherings alongside the Soviet Union, while Pakistan, Indonesia, and China maintained that neither was fit to be included. Malaysia itself undertook the unaccustomed role of a radical Afro-Asian state—unaccustomed in the sense that its leaders were deeply conservative by nature, and had done

[1] See Richard Allen, *Malaysia* (1968), chs 13–17 for an informed British account.
[2] The Manila Accord and Manila Declaration are in *Current Notes*, August 1963, pp. 5–11.

little to court the other leaders of Afro-Asian countries by exchanging diplomatic missions or even visits with them. It had, however, in its previous incarnation as Malaya, taken care to follow an orthodox anti-colonialist line at the UN wherever this was called for.[1] Now it bestirred itself, sending Lee Kuan Yew and the minister for external affairs, Tun Razak, to visit countries in Africa in order to acquaint them with the state of things in Malaysia.

Confrontation continued for some two years, absorbing very large numbers of British and Malaysian troops. Most of the operations were along the borders of Indonesia in Borneo, but there were also hit-and-run Indonesian attacks on the mainland. Although the operation absorbed so many servicemen, it was hardly a war. On the British side,

strict limits were set on the use of our superior power. Bombing and naval gunfire were kept to a minimum; patrolling in Borneo was meticulously restricted; everything possible was done not merely to safeguard the local population from danger and inconvenience, but to help them in their daily life. . . . It should be noted that at the end of these long drawn out and victorious operations, Indonesian casualties, which were far higher than our own, amounted to no more than 580 dead.[2]

Probably Sukarno wished to avoid outright war because it might bring more powers into the struggle; certainly some of the Indonesian generals were more worried about the foe at their backs (the PKI) than the one they were confronting. After more noise at the diplomatic than at the military level, confrontation was given its quietus by the series of events in Indonesia which began with the attempted coup in Djakarta on 30 September 1965 and went on to include the eclipse of Sukarno by General Suharto, and Indonesia's turn away from radical and adventurist policies. Complaints from the Philippines about Sabah continued, but were not a bar to the eventual restoration of diplomatic relations. By the end of 1966 Malaysia was firmly established as a sovereign state like any other—except that, on 9 August 1965, Singapore was separated from Malaysia and thereafter continued as a sovereign state in its own right.

The reasons for this sudden change lay within the communal and party

[1] For an examination of Malaya's record at the UN between 1957 and 1961, see Peter Boyce, 'Australian diplomacy in Malaya', in *J. Southeast As. Hist.*, Sept 1963, pp. 96–9, where the voting records of Malaya and Australia are compared; ironically, in view of Australia's staunch support for Malaya as a state and a bastion of anti-communism, it appeared that 'in all sessions the Federation and Australia [had] disagreed oftener than they [had] agreed' (see Dato Muhammad Ghazali bin Shafie, *Malaysia in Afro-Asia* (1964) for a strong defence of Malaysia's position in Afro-Asian terms by its permanent secretary for external affairs).

[2] Christopher Mayhew, *Britain's role tomorrow* (1967), p. 23. Mayhew was a British service minister during confrontation. The biographers of Denis Healey, who was minister of defence from October 1964, say that 119 British servicemen were killed in the operation. They also say that there were strong service pressures to 'escalate the conflict until the Indonesians gave in', but that Healey rejected these (Geoffrey Williams & Bruce Reed, *Denis Healey and the policies of power* (1971), pp. 205–7).

balances described above. Tunku Abdul Rahman returned from a lengthy trip abroad to find relations extremely bad between Lee Kuan Yew and his PAP on the one hand, and the MCA and Umno on the other. It had been hoped that Lee would make Singapore his sphere of influence, and not interfere with the mainland. Instead, in the view of what Lee called the Malay 'ultras', he had extended his party's operations to the peninsula, and was striving to reduce Malay control of affairs. In the view of the MCA leaders, he was challenging their leadership of the Chinese community. To the Tunku, it seemed that Lee and Singapore would have to go, or he could not be responsible for the consequences. They went, in distress but not dismay. The change did not affect military arrangements. Britain continued to be in charge of its Singapore bases, and defence against confrontation was not affected. Like a married couple who are neither happy together nor happy apart, but continue to bicker while managing to keep a household going, Malaysia and Singapore continued with their complex politics.

III

Meanwhile, Malaysia had been considered by the Commonwealth prime ministers at their meetings in 1964 and 1965, which resulted, on both occasions, in expressions of support for the new state. The 1964 communiqué assured the Tunku of their 'sympathy and support' (the words, perhaps coincidental, which Nehru had used in his letters of appeal to other heads of government in 1962), 'in his efforts to preserve the sovereign independence and integrity of his country and to promote a peaceful and honourable settlement of current differences between Malaysia and neighbouring countries'. In 1965 the prime ministers recalled this statement and said they

recognized and supported the right of the Government and people of Malaysia to defend their sovereign independence and territorial integrity, and expressed their sympathy to the Prime Minister of Malaysia in his country's efforts to that end.

They added that they 'looked forward to the establishment of peaceful, friendly and mutually advantageous relations between Malaysia and Indonesia on a just and honourable basis'.[1]

Behind these bland statements lay a good many divergent strands of interest, an examination of which will show something of the Commonwealth's character at the time. It should be borne in mind that membership had recently increased. At the 1964 meeting Uganda, Kenya, and Malawi were present for the first time; in 1965 the new members were Zambia, Malta, and the Gambia. Moreover, these were the first two meetings at which the question of Rhodesia dominated proceedings. Other issues tended to be seen, by some at any rate of those attending, as subordinate to Rhodesia.

[1] *CRO Year Book 1966*, pp. 9 & 17.

Tunku Abdul Rahman twice asked for support at the 1964 meeting; he was strongly backed by Menzies and Holyoake, and received rather more measured support from the British prime minister, Sir Alec Douglas-Home (who was in the chair), and the principal representative of India, T. T. Krishnamachari.[1] The difficulty for the Tunku, however, in the words of a Malaysian newspaper, was that 'while all Commonwealth countries seem to appreciate that Malaysia is the injured party, not all of them see in the criminal campaign against our country any confluence of Indonesian expansionist and Communist revolutionary designs'.[2] The African states, inexperienced about Asia and preoccupied with African affairs (a meeting of the OAU in Cairo was to follow immediately upon the London meeting), saw little to be gained from a gratuitous identification of Indonesia as an aggressor; to an even greater extent, they saw no advantage in linking Indonesia with China or indicting China on its own account, as the Indian delegation appears to have wished. Some of the African prime ministers questioned the Tunku's linking of Indonesia with communist penetration of Southeast Asia. He said it was significant that Indonesian hostility had really begun after Malaysia had declared its support for India 'against unprovoked aggression from China', and said he thought Peking exerted pressure on Indonesia through the PKI.[3] His indictment of China brought rebuttals from President Ayub of Pakistan and Mrs Bandaranaike of Ceylon, both of whom opposed the idea of declared opposition to any 'Chinese threat'.[4] Pakistan had already moved closer to sympathy with China, as we saw in Chapter 5, and Mrs Bandaranaike had recently been through a difficult period in trying to arrange an armistice between China and India; in this, China had proved at least as awkward as India, possibly more so.[5] Ghana had similarly been rebuked by China.

The mood of the Africans was that of covert sympathy and, in the case of Nkrumah, an overt eagerness to provide some mediation between Malaysia and Indonesia. There was, however, no move to give Malaysia the degree of eager backing that the Australians wished it to have.[6] Menzies pushed the matter hard, saying there was some difficulty because some of those represented believed that much might be done by negotiation.

What I was emphasizing was that although only some members of the Commonwealth would find it within their power to give military aid to Malaysia, at least everybody should give moral aid to Malaysia, not only within the United Nations but

[1] Nehru had died on 27 May. His successor, Shastri, was unable to attend because of illness.

[2] *Straits Times* (Kuala Lumpur), 13 July 1964. (Unless otherwise indicated, all references to this paper are to the Kuala Lumpur edition.)

[3] *Sunday Times* (Kuala Lumpur), 12 July 1964.

[4] *Observer*, 12 July 1964. The communiqué eventually contained an innocuous reference to talk about China.

[5] G. H. Jansen, *Afro-Asia and non-alignment* (1966), p. 348.

[6] *Sunday Times* (KL), 12 July and *FT*, 10 July 1964.

around the world. Ultimately we got a result on that which I thought pretty good. . . . There was a good deal of discussion about the word "support" to which there was opposition originally in some quarters . . .[1]

The 1965 meeting, like that of 1964, was very much concerned with Rhodesia, since by this time the government of Ian Smith had already begun to talk about UDI (see ch. 10). The Afro-Asian situation had become even more complicated. The Rann of Kutch outbreak had worsened Indo-Pakistani relations. Indonesia was pressing hard for Malaysia's exclusion from the Afro-Asian conference which, after various postponements, it was proposed to hold at Algiers just after the Commonwealth meeting was to finish at the end of June. At a preliminary meeting in Djakarta in April 1964 India had proposed that Malaysia be invited, but Indonesia and China had demurred. It was left for the Algiers Conference to make a final decision.[2] To support admittance openly was to range oneself with India against China, and vice versa.

It was no surprise, therefore, that the Afro-Asian members of the Commonwealth had been largely silent on the matter, or that the Tunku arrived in London with the aim of getting Commonwealth countries 'to insist on our admission to the Afro-Asian conference'. This would be 'tantamount to saying that Indonesia has committed aggression and must now stop aggression'.[3] Senior members of his delegation were reported as saying he 'had come to the conclusion that the racial-political issue in Rhodesia will be, or should be, the dominant issue' at the London meeting.[4] A quid pro quo for the Africans was worth granting, apart altogether from the Tunku's dislike of white racialist policies in southern Africa.

At the meeting itself, in spite of the concentration on Rhodesia, the Tunku got some of what he hoped for. The draft communiqué evidently contained a passage recommending Malaysia's inclusion in the forthcoming Afro-Asian conference, but Pakistan's representative objected, and was supported by others in excising this.[5] As regards confrontation, the final form (quoted above) was, in the words of an Indian correspondent, 'a rather half-hearted attempt to please Pakistan . . . [which] objected in particular to "sympathy and support".'[6] To Menzies,

the end result . . . I thought was not unsatisfactory. The shadow of the Afro-Asian Conference at Algiers has been rather heavily cast upon this conference. It may seem odd because it has nothing to do with the Commonwealth. It is an entirely different

---

[1] *CN*, July 1964, p. 33.   [2] See Jansen, pp. 380–2, and Boyce, pp. 188–9.

[3] From an interview on the eve of the Prime Ministers' Meeting, *Straits Times*, 17 June 1965.

[4] *Guardian*, 17 June 1965.

[5] *Dawn*, 25 June 1965. The Pakistan foreign minister explained that Pakistan wished to mediate between Malaysia and Indonesia (see Boyce, p. 194).

[6] *Hindu*, 27 June 1965. According to Harold Wilson (p. 116), the final form of the communiqué was 'a bitter blow' to the Tunku.

body which has some membership in common. Still, it was very much in evidence and I thought at one stage there was a disposition to go a little cautiously on the subject of Malaysia and the Indonesian confrontation and this might muddy the waters at Algiers and therefore the end result was very satisfactory from our point of view, because they once more quoted what we said last year and added words bringing it up to date. . . .[1]

It is fairly clear that Pakistan was the strongest opponent of Malaysia at this meeting. Some weeks later the Tunku gave his own explanation of why this should be so: 'Mr Bhutto has misconstrued our action in siding with India against China', he said.[2] There was to be further misconstruction of this kind later in the year, when Pakistan objected strongly to the remarks about the Indo-Pakistani war made in the Security Council by Mr Ramani, the Malaysian representative, who was of Indian descent. Pakistan broke off diplomatic relations with Malaysia, which responded with complaints that Pakistan had been taking Indonesia's side.[3]

In the perspective of later years, much of this argument looks like a storm in a teacup. The Algiers conference did not meet, because Ben Bella, the president, was overthrown on the eve of it; the Afro-Asian Commonwealth leaders took advantage of their joint presence in London to decide not to proceed to Algiers, in spite of strenuous efforts by the Chinese and Algerian embassies to persuade them otherwise. The Indo-Pakistan war did not last long. Confrontation faded away after General Suharto took over in Indonesia. By the end of 1965 the fears and anxieties which had agitated India, Pakistan, and Malaysia, and had drawn in others to take sides about them, had largely been stilled, although basic Indo-Pakistani hostility remained.

Yet it ought to be recognized that in June 1965 the fears expressed seemed more substantial than the light of hindsight suggests. They were sufficient to make Malaysia anxious to recruit support wherever it could be found, to deflect Pakistan from friendship towards another Muslim Commonwealth country, and to concentrate the attention of both for the time being upon the will-o'-the-wisp of Afro-Asian solidarity and approval. In fact, a combination of circumstances (including the debacle of Algiers, the generally intransigent attitude of China towards Afro-Asian affairs, and the deposition before the end of 1965 of Nkrumah and Sukarno) ensured that the will-o'-the-wisp was laid to rest, though in another form—that of non-alignment—it retained some

[1] *CN*, June 1965, p. 348.
[2] *Straits Times*, 16 July 1965. See also Boyce, p. 196 for a statement in October 1965 by the Malaysian permanent secretary for external affairs, in which Pakistan's attitude is attributed to pressure from China.
[3] Ramani's speech, made on 18 September, is reprinted in *Straits Times*, 28 Sept 1965, and Pakistan's official protest ibid., 26 Sept 1965. The delicacy of the confrontation issue is also shown by Lee Kuan Yew's comment, when the Indo-Pakistani war was in progress, that the Indians were friends because they had recognized Singapore after its break from Malaysia; Pakistan had not (ibid., 10 Sept 1965). This led to some later coolness with Pakistan in Commonwealth terms.

institutional existence. Only some of these causes and effects could have been discerned in mid-1965.

IV

Confrontation was a Commonwealth problem in the sense that certain Commonwealth members wished to make it so, especially through their insistence at Commonwealth conferences. Australia, New Zealand, and Britain were the main agents in this course.[1] Australia, through Menzies, was the most vocal. The three countries, having decided that it was right to back Malaysia, tried to get as much support as they could, even though they recognized that they would probably be the only Commonwealth members actually to send troops to resist confrontation.[2] They wanted Malaysia not only to be recognized officially by other Commonwealth countries but also to be given moral support. While some of their leaders may have wished to challenge the other members to provide support in the form of troops, this would hardly have been productive: the troops would not have been forthcoming, and the precedent would have been created for a 'Commonwealth' appeal to Australia and New Zealand to participate in military activities with which they did not want to be associated—say between certain African Commonwealth countries and South Africa. It was sufficient that 'sympathy and support' should be expressed. The matter was put as a simple one of mutual respect and support: here was another Commonwealth member in trouble; let us speak up for it, even if we cannot give much of a helping hand.

It was a Commonwealth problem of a different kind for the Afro-Asian members, some of whom resented the bluff assumption that it was a simple matter to speak out for Malaysia. They had already given explicit recognition to Malaysia when it was admitted to the Commonwealth. However, for some of them, other Afro-Asian relationships might make it desirable to support Indonesia, or, at any rate, not to be seen to oppose it. Especially for the Africans, far removed from Asia and preoccupied with their own affairs—amongst which the recent upheaval in the Congo had not served to improve the prestige of the western powers—it was irritating to be called upon to express approval for one side in a quarrel which appeared to be none of their business. In the atmosphere of mid-1965, in which no-one could be sure of how Afro-Asian alignments would develop, it was a big step for the Africans to agree to reiterate support for Malaysia, especially since the Tunku had not

---

[1] In addition to pressing the matter at the 1964 and 1965 meetings of Commonwealth prime ministers, Australia, through the leader of its delegation, Peter Howson, also challenged other Commonwealth countries to support Malaysia at the Commonwealth Parliamentary Association conference in Jamaica in November 1964 (see ibid., 23 Nov 1964).

[2] Canada also gave help, though not troops. Pearson said in London in July 1964 that Canada would give 'support rather than sympathy' (*The Times*, 10 July 1964), and later in the month announced a programme of military aid (ibid., 29 July 1964), following a visit to Canada by the Tunku.

been noticeably strong in supporting African causes. It was, if anything, a distracting and possibly dangerous interruption to their quest for a satisfactory result in Rhodesia.[1]

It was something of a tribute to the Tunku and Lee that they had managed to convince a number of these Third World leaders that they, not President Sukarno, should be listened to. If there was an Afro-Asian orthodoxy, Sukarno was voicing it, even if he was extreme in doing so. Singapore was, after all, a British Seato base, and Malaya, while not a member of Seato, had not appeared at either the 1961 or 1964 non-aligned meetings. The Africans were being asked to take a good deal on trust in subscribing to support for Malaysia. The Commonwealth, as an institution, could claim some credit for giving the Malaysian leaders a platform on which they could hope to get a favourable (at least not a hostile) reception from other Asian and African states—unless those states had, like Pakistan, specific reasons for rejecting the Malaysian case.

For the Australians and New Zealanders too the matter was not so simple as their statements in Commonwealth terms might have suggested.[2] Although both gave verbal support to Malaysia at an early stage,[3] they were being criticized in the British press in December 1963 and January 1964 for their slowness in sending troops to Borneo—especially since some of their troops had been in Malaya since 1955. It was not until February 1965 that their soldiers actually came into contact with Indonesian forces in Borneo. If the matter had been simply a Commonwealth one, they could be criticized for not making their troops available sooner.

For them too the matter was one of world politics: their hesitancy arose from their uncertainty about two non-Commonwealth countries, the US and Indonesia. Just as, in 1955, the Australian government wished to know whether the US would support its commitment of Australian troops to Malaya, so in 1963 it wanted to know whether action against Indonesia would also be approved. As early as July 1963 Menzies was told that the US supported Malaysia 'as a matter of principle; the one reservation being made by the United States to the effect that any defensive arrangement in relation to Malaysia seems to the United States to be essentially a Commonwealth matter at this stage'.[4] It was an axiom with both Australia and New Zealand that no decisive military step should be taken without the acquiescence, and, if possible, the guaranteed support of the US. Some time elapsed before the two governments were satisfied that the American guarantee under Anzus might

---

[1] The desire to stay neutral was not confined to the Africans. Ceylon denied landing rights and berthing facilities to planes and ships bearing arms to both Malaysia and Indonesia, acting against Britain in the first instance and the Soviet Union in the second (*Straits Times*, 6 Aug; *Asian Recorder*, 26 Aug–1 Sept 1964).

[2] See Trevor R. Reese, *Australia, New Zealand, and the US* (1969), ch. 12, for a helpful discussion of the situation of these two countries.

[3] See *CN*, Sept 1963, for the Australian statement, and *NZ Deb.*, 20 Sept 1963, for the New Zealand.

[4] *CN*, July 1963, p. 58.

be applied to conflict in Borneo if the situation there deteriorated.[1] Until then, and until the US was no longer trying to persuade Indonesia by diplomatic pressure, it was not politic to send their troops to fight Indonesians. If President Kennedy had not been assassinated on 22 November 1963, they might never have done so.[2]

The US apart, there was understandable reluctance to send Australian and New Zealand troops, partly because of dislike of being instructed in Commonwealth duty by Britain, but largely because their opponents would be Indonesian, and Indonesia was itself an important preoccupation to Australia, and, to a lesser extent, to New Zealand. Australia shared a frontier with Indonesia in New Guinea; Indonesia was the nearest Asian country to Australia itself; and to try to achieve friendship with Indonesia was an important aim of sections at least of the Australian government, especially after that government's long and unsuccessful intransigence over West New Guinea. Here, as elsewhere, policy was divided. But the wish to avoid alienating Indonesia, even the unpredictable Indonesia of Sukarno's later years, was strong enough to create an Australian interest in combining declamation with delay. Australia thus tried to get as much moral support as possible for Malaysia while delaying its own whole-hearted commitment of armed forces.[3]

This was, in essence, not so different a situation from that of the Afro-Asian members: both had to take into account certain extra-Commonwealth factors. The British situation was easier. Britain had a clear treaty commitment to Malaysia, it had no close or permanent connection with Indonesia, its military presence in Malaysia could be called upon at will, and it had, in its relations with the US, repeatedly emphasized that it would be responsible for defence in the Malaysian area. Britain did not need to proclaim the need for others to support Malaysia; Australia and New Zealand, in a somewhat equivocal situation themselves, did.

v

After the massive British military effort in response to confrontation had been completed (in February 1965 it was costing about £90,000 a week),[4] the Wilson government began to disengage from the area. In July 1967 it announced its intention of having all its troops out by the mid-1970s. A further decision of January 1968 reduced the time to the end of 1971. British forces would no longer be garrisoned east of Suez or elsewhere than in Europe. This meant that, while Britain would retain the capability to move troops in

---

[1] For the ins and outs of this curious situation, see Reese, pp. 220–4, and J. G. Starke, *The ANZUS treaty alliance* (1965), pp. 126–7 & 201–2.

[2] For inferential evidence on this point, see Hilsman, pp. 405–9.

[3] The deteriorating situation in South Vietnam was another reason for Australian caution in committing troops to Borneo.

[4] Darby, p. 255.

an emergency, and while Malaysia and Singapore could look forward to periodic visits from British detachments engaged in jungle training and in local exercises, they could not expect to see a British base maintained at Singapore or elsewhere in Southeast Asia.[1]

The Commonwealth boot was now on the other foot. Whereas Britain had previously been glad to assume defence responsibilities in Malaysia and Singapore, and to give them a Commonwealth label, it was now unwilling to do so, and found itself subject to pressure from Australia and New Zealand, as well as from Malaysia and Singapore, to continue its military presence.[2] It was no longer a matter of Britain's joining with these four to press Commonwealth obligations on other Commonwealth members; those obligations were now being pressed on Britain.

When George Thomson, the British Commonwealth secretary, toured the four countries in January 1968 to prepare them for the British government's plan to withdraw all garrison forces by the end of 1971, he found all four governments opposed to the idea, but expressing themselves, as might have been expected, in ways appropriate to their circumstances. In Singapore Lee prepared the way for Thomson by threatening in the newspapers to withdraw Singapore from the sterling area; after Thomson had gone, Lee flew to London to argue personally with the British prime minister about the proposed withdrawal of British troops.[3] In Kuala Lumpur the Tunku expressed 'grave concern' about the likelihood of a British withdrawal,[4] but later refused to join Lee's mission; he could hardly have put himself in the position of following Lee's lead.

In Australia Thomson struck a new prime minister, John Gorton, whose statement on the matter was harsher than any previously produced by either side in British-Australian relations. A note of cold scepticism was evident. 'The British Cabinet has not yet, *as we are told*, made final decisions', said Gorton, . . . 'we hope that these proposals may be modified in the light of the views expressed by Australia, New Zealand and Singapore'.[5] He expressed the 'keen concern' of Australian ministers, who, he said, 'without in any way becoming involved in rancour or recrimination . . . were not resigned to the proposals and could not accept them without protest'. He even suggested that British forces in Europe were less important than those in Malaysia and Singapore, and, with obvious reference to Europe, that 'it might be preferable

---

[1] This is a brutally brief statement of a set of decisions made for complicated political and economic reasons (see Mayhew, *passim*; Harold Wilson, pp. 376–8, 479–85; Williams & Reed, chs. 9, 10, & 11; and ch. 21 of this volume). Wilson's statement on the 1968 decision is in HC Deb., 16 Jan. 1968, cols. 1577–1620. Gordon Walker, *The cabinet*, ch. 8, has an authoritative account of how cabinet opinion changed.

[2] There were difficulties between Britain and Malaysia over defence aid as early as 1966 (see Boyce, pp. 142–4).

[3] The newspaper record of Lee's visit, with much supporting detail, will be found in Alex Josey, *Lee Kuan Yew in London* (1968).

[4] *Straits Times*, 9 Jan. 1968.   [5] *CN*, Jan. 1968, pp. 29–30. (Emphasis added.)

to make savings in some other area than that of Malaysia and Singapore'. This was harsh medicine. In Wellington Thomson was received gently, as might have been expected; but there again, 'marked concern' was expressed, although Holyoake said New Zealand had no right to oppose the speeding up of the British withdrawal, if Britain had made up its mind.[1] Neither Malaysia, Australia, nor New Zealand sent ministers to support Lee in London, but the latter two made it clear that he went with their support.[2]

When the British government did announce its decision, it recognized those whom Wilson called 'our Commonwealth partners and allies'[3] but adhered to its expected withdrawal of British forces by the end of 1971. In taking this line, actuated more by immediate financial pressures than by anything else, it was nevertheless proceeding with that withdrawal from the open seas which the Macmillan government had already foreshadowed in its attempt to enter the EEC. The British concentration of forces in Europe reflected the precedence of local over world-wide interests. According to Darby, ministers were primarily influenced by general economic and political considerations, the political considerations including the influence of US experience in Vietnam, in terms of its military demands and its political ineffectiveness, which made for 'a decided shift in ministerial opinion about Britain's capacity to maintain a major military role east of Suez and about the extent to which that role accorded with Britain's real interests'.[4] While the government still intended to retain the capacity to move forces across the world if necessary, the occasions on which necessity would be felt would be fewer. Confrontation might prove to be the last occasion when a British commitment to the Commonwealth involved major military activity.

To a considerable degree, the Malaysian and Singaporean governments recognized this. They asked for an extension of time rather than an absolute commitment; and Lee's visit to London was instrumental in adding nine months or so to the British timetable of withdrawal.[5] For Australia and New Zealand, on the other hand, the urge to call for a permanent commitment of British forces was stronger, largely because of the difficulties they expected to encounter if Britain went. They saw that the Malaysian and Singaporean governments wanted an external presence in their midst, yet they were apprehensive of possible quarrels with Indonesia and, to a lesser extent, with the Philippines. They did not wish to get embroiled in these, any more than in disputes between Malaysia and Singapore themselves, based upon the simmering communalism of the area. To Australia and New Zealand, the solution

---

[1] *Straits Times*, 12 Jan 1968.   [2] e.g., Gorton on 11 January 1968 (*CN*, Jan 1968, p. 29).
[3] *Survey B & CA*, 2 Feb 1968, pp. 116–17.   [4] Darby, p. 317.
[5] Pressure for delay was not directed simply at the need to make essential arrangements in Malaysia and Singapore. It was also concerned with British politics. It was known that a British election would be held in 1970 or, at the latest, in 1971, and that a Conservative government, pledged to some permanent presence east of Suez, might be elected—as did occur in June 1970.

was to promise to maintain a small presence of their own, while continuing to call for a British presence. No attempt appears to have been made to muster general Commonwealth approval for what the two countries intended to do, presumably because they knew that others would regard it as essentially an expression of their own regional interests rather than a matter of wider Commonwealth concern. This was very much in line with their general approach to Malaysian questions.[1]

Malaysia and Singapore were certainly unusual Commonwealth members by the end of the 1960s, in that they were the only ones which desired a British military presence in their territory. Cyprus still had one, as a result of the peculiar conditions of settlement of its independence in 1959,[2] but could hardly be said to be actively in favour of it. None of the other new members had wished to retain British troops. The reasons for the special position of Malaysia and Singapore lay partly in the disturbed conditions of Southeast Asia, partly in the desire of their two governments that they should not be isolated (in case communal extremists fomented further trouble between them), and partly in their specially close relations with Britain. These had been prolonged by the existence of the Singapore base and the whole complex of British defence arrangements in the area. While idiosyncratic in terms of the Sukarno type of Afro-Asian orthodoxy, and ambiguous in terms of the obligations and implications which it entailed, their position was understandable. For them, the disentangling of post-colonial ties came later than for many other Commonwealth members, because the ties were especially direct and were so much connected with their security and prosperity.

It was ironic, from a Commonwealth standpoint, that Britain, after having extended itself to give military assistance to Malaysia far beyond anything it had done for any other Commonwealth member (some 50,000 British troops were involved at the height of confrontation), should decide so soon afterwards to remove its forces. The proposals advanced to replace the former British presence were in fact exiguous. The Wilson government's plan was for an intermittent presence which could hardly be tied into any local scheme of strategic co-operation. The Opposition's was for a tiny local force to be reinforced from Britain's European capability if need should arise.[3]

---

[1] An American scholar teaching in Malaysia wrote: 'Australian (and Canadian or New Zealand) publications in Malaysia, both governmental and commercial, do virtually nothing to further the idea of Australian-Malaysian relations as an aspect of a broader Commonwealth tie, but concentrate on the one-to-one relationship between the two nations as sovereign peoples. . . . When a Malaysian thinks of Australia, he thinks of the Commonwealth of Australia, not of the Commonwealth of Nations' (Robin Winks, 'Malaysia and the Commonwealth', in Wang Gungwu, ed., *Malaysia* (1964), p. 385).

[2] See Mansergh, *Documents 1952–62*, pp. 257–77.

[3] Although quite elaborate arrangements were made for a joint Anzuk (Australian, New Zealand, and British) permanent presence in 1971, the size of the British contribution remained very small, in spite of the change to a Conservative government. Ground forces were limited to a battalion group (*Survey of Current Affairs*, May 1971, p. 224).

The reasons given for British withdrawal were normally those of economic stringency, together with the outmoded character of western bases in overseas countries, and the absence of other European countries' military efforts in the area. In the context of the Commonwealth, however, these reasons do not seem to fully explain why a presence which had been labelled 'Commonwealth' for so long could be reduced (and in prospect eliminated) without substantial protest in Britain itself, and without objection from Commonwealth members other than those immediately affected in regional terms. If one went by widely-accepted British assumptions about the Commonwealth in the 1950s, then what Britain proposed was a step of major proportions. Yet there was little objection in Britain at the time; and the Conservative Party's watered-down version of an east of Suez presence, put forward at the 1970 general elections, aroused little enthusiasm from either press or public. Apart from objections by Malaysia and Singapore, and by Australia and New Zealand, no substantial comment or protest came from other parts of the Commonwealth.

Increasingly in Britain it was considered that the British role in the world had changed, and that Britain could no longer police distant parts without suffering unacceptable disadvantages. This view, while fiercely contested by a diminishing few, was tacitly accepted across the British political spectrum. It commended itself to other Commonwealth countries for different reasons. Each was aware of the declining importance of Britain in world strategy in comparison with the US and the Soviet Union, and, in a different context, with China. Only a few—Australia and New Zealand in particular—were disturbed by this knowledge. The others either did not want British protection or did not think it would be satisfactory if they got it. Even Australia and New Zealand wished Britain to stay in Malaysia-Singapore only because of possible awkward developments if Britain left and because of their American connections, not because they believed that Britain had the capacity to deal with any major disturbance. While they, and Malaysia and Singapore, might still use 'Commonwealth' as a label for joint military action, they were nearly as much convinced as the other Commonwealth members that no joint Commonwealth military operations were likely in the future.

PART III

AFRICA

CHAPTER 7

THE AFRICAN TRANSFORMATION

O F all the processes and events dealt with in this book, the transformation of Africa was the greatest single source of change in the Commonwealth. As the 'Asian dimension' declined, the 'African dimension' grew. By 1969 the matters which engrossed and puzzled Commonwealth leaders were very largely African. The communiqué of the Prime Ministers' Meeting in 1957, the first at which a fully independent African member was represented, had mentioned Ghana's presence but said nothing else about Africa;[1] the same would not be true of subsequent communiqués.

I

The African transformation involved not only self-determination, whereby colonies (British, French, and Belgian) became independent, but also the growth of diplomacy. The newly independent states quickly came to use to the full the resources of international pressure, especially upon their former colonial masters. Most of the disturbance which the African transformation caused in the Commonwealth may be attributed to this second aspect. Before independence, British discussion of the future of the colonies had been very largely about their domestic future, especially the working of their political institutions and their economies. Their participation in international relations had been given much less attention. It was therefore something of a shock to the older members when they developed such a vigorous diplomacy so quickly. To many of the leaders of the new Africa, however, the achievement of independence went hand in hand with a vigorous diplomacy. When men like Nkrumah, Nyerere, and Kaunda began to operate as national leaders on the world scene, they saw independence as an aspiration for the whole of Africa. Diplomacy was an instrument in exerting pressure to liberate territories under European or settler control, especially the multilateral diplomacy of the UN and its related bodies, the regional diplomacy of African states, the informal diplomacy of 'freedom movements' seeking support from established states, and the conference diplomacy of the Commonwealth prime ministers.

For most of the leaders of the African states which had become members of the Commonwealth by 1969 such diplomacy had been constantly employed before independence. As soon as meetings of independent African states began at Accra in 1958, they were attended by 'observers' from independence

[1] Mansergh, *Documents 1952–62*, pp. 534–7.

movements in other parts of Africa. These movements predominated in the AAPC (All-African Peoples' Conference), which first met later in the same year, but governments also participated in this organization. Future prime ministers, foreign ministers, and presidents learnt their trade of international pressure and international rhetoric at these meetings, and Pafmec(s)a, a body which included territories mainly under British control, originated at one of them.[1] In such bodies the successful and the unsuccessful mingled, in the sense that some who bulked large in earlier discussions proved less able to gain independence than others, more favoured by fortune;[2] but the aspiration of general liberation was common to all. A Pafmeca resolution carried at its first meeting at Mwanza in Tanganyika in 1958, read:

Independent States to take Positive Action in the United Nations and in all its agencies, the Prime Ministers' Conference of the Commonwealth and in any other place on all matters affecting the freedom of the African people, and in this connection to reject completely such matters as Domestic Affairs of Colonial or Metropolitan country.[3]

The men from Tanganyika, Kenya, Uganda, Zanzibar, and Nyasaland who attended this conference were soon to gain independence in their own countries. They retained both the aim and the strategy after they became ministers.

Independence for the whole of Africa was not, however, the only reason for the vigorous diplomacy of the new African states. Other reasons arose from the problems of independence itself. The management of economies and societies proved more difficult than had been expected: economic growth was hard to attain, capital was short, education and training needed to be extended, exports often proved disappointing, with consequent balance-of-payments difficulties. Tribalism was a stumbling-block to the national unity which leaders proclaimed, corruption flourished, plots and coups increased, and one-party systems soon began to appear necessary to leaders who had started out with a theoretical devotion to the Westminster system.

Such difficulties intensified diplomatic initiatives, especially to secure as much aid as possible. For multilateral aid, the UN and its agencies, together with the Commonwealth, were obvious targets for the new states' persuasion; for bilateral aid they looked to the major powers. On the political side, the effect of the difficulties was rather different. The character of African regimes

---

[1] This body was started in 1958 as the Pan-African Freedom Movement of East and Central Africa, and became in 1962 the Pan-African Freedom Movement of Eastern, Central, and Southern Africa. It was dissolved after the creation of the OAU (see Richard Cox, *Pan-Africanism in practice* (1964)).

[2] For a detailed and penetrating study of the extra-territorial activities of the Southern Rhodesian nationalists, see John Day, *International nationalism* (1967).

[3] Cox, pp. 11–12. Cf. also Kenneth Younger's 'Reflections on Africa and the Commonwealth' (*World Today*, Mar 1962), written after the unofficial Commonwealth conference at Lagos in January 1962, with its theme that 'at the root of the African approach to all current problems is the importance attached to the Pan-African idea' (p. 121).

became a matter of international debate as coups and one-party states grew more numerous in the former British, French, and Belgian colonies. The forebodings which had been expressed earlier in the metropolitan countries, about tribalism, corruption, inefficiency, racism, and the like, were said to be justified. In response, the new regimes felt obliged to justify their claims to represent true African aspirations. In some cases the instability of those regimes—for example, the Congo in the 1960s and later Nigeria—led to complications amongst the African states themselves. In others, disputes between the leaders of different African states led to attempts at subversion of one by another, resulting in an indignant and often intensified intra-African diplomacy.

African political life became, in the 1960s, more eventful and often more unstable than most people had expected. The pace was quicker, the crises were more immediate, the rhetoric was stronger, and the prospect of exhaustion for both participants and onlookers drew much nearer. It is important to remember that only part of the activity occurred within the Commonwealth, and that extra-Commonwealth influences were often at work. But there was symbiosis between action inside and outside the Commonwealth and the effect of one upon the other was continual.

II

While the transformation of Africa affected French and Belgian public opinion as well as British, British opinion was probably most deeply affected. British dependencies in Africa were more populous and dispersed than French or Belgian; they had desired self-government earlier; argument about them had been a more prominent feature of metropolitan politics, although knowledge about them may not have been detailed and widespread. The Commonwealth system, widened to accommodate India, Pakistan, and Ceylon in 1947, seemed a ready-made means of reconciling the African colonies' interests with those of Britain once they became independent.[1] In addition, the British parliamentary system was widely if diffusely regarded as the natural form in which their post-independence politics would operate, and British regard for civil liberties and the rule of law was often considered to have been implanted in them by British administration. For the British public, ignorance about the colonies was accompanied by a sense of pride that these places were British and that they were being led progressively to self-government. To understand later British feelings about the African transformation's effect upon the Commonwealth, it is desirable to consider how attitudes towards African self-government developed.

[1] Within the British governmental structure, no one seems to have questioned the likelihood that African states would conform to the existing Commonwealth system, and work to its rules as the Asian states had done. (A private communication.)

Self-government, rather than independence, was what the British government was promising in 1953. When the Attlee administration was replaced by that of Churchill in 1951, the new colonial secretary, Oliver Lyttelton, had stated that 'certain broad lines of policy are accepted by all sections of the House as being above party politics'. Two of these, he said, were fundamental:

First, we all aim at helping the colonial territories to attain self-government within the British Commonwealth. To that end we are seeking as rapidly as possible to build up in each territory the institutions which its circumstances require. Second, we are all determined to pursue the economic and social development of the colonial territories so that it keeps pace with their political development.

His predecessor, James Griffiths, stressed the view that 'in all multiracial territories [self-government] must include participation of all the people in those territories, irrespective of race, creed or colour'; and Lyttelton replied that in general terms he could accept this.[1] The coupling of political advance with economic and social development was a frequent feature of discussion. Arthur Creech Jones, who had been colonial secretary from 1946 to 1950, was just as convinced as Lyttelton and Griffiths of the link between the two. Describing what his own party's attitude had been, he wrote at the end of the 1950s:

... But if democratic government were not to become dangerous and futile, informed public opinion had to become an essential feature of the system, and that could be secured only by social and economic progress. Democratic government in the hands of ignorant and politically inexperienced people can easily become unworkable. It is exposed to mass emotional appeals; mass ignorance and prejudice can be exploited and the basic requirements of democracy remain unfulfilled. Widespread education, means of information and a critical and responsible press seemed to Labour Ministers to be among the indispensable factors in the working of political democracy.

He said that new economic resources were essential if such conditions were to be obtained and, like so many of his contemporaries in all parties and in the press, stressed the difficulty of the task, the patience required, and the need to move slowly in step with local opinion.[2] Such an attitude was widely representative of opinion in and around 1953, though some people recognized that the first assumption of ministerial office by elected Africans in a British colonial territory, which had occurred in the Gold Coast in 1951, meant 'that Britain is committed in act as well as word to the speedy promotion of self-government in her African colonies'.[3] For the next few years, difficulties rather than opportunities were usually emphasized: a preparatory, gradualist, and 'economic'

[1] Debate of 14 Nov 1951 (Mansergh, *Documents 1931–52*, ii (1953), p. 1286). See also Lyttelton's reflections in *The memoirs of Lord Chandos* (1962), p. 352.

[2] Arthur Creech Jones, 'The Labour party and colonial policy 1945–51', in A. Creech Jones, ed., *New Fabian colonial essays* (1959), pp. 26–7.

[3] From a highly prescient article by Margery Perham, 'The British problem in Africa', *Foreign Affairs*, July 1951, reprinted in her *Colonial sequence* (1970), p. 26.

frame of mind characterized those who were influential in colonial policy. In the Gold Coast six years elapsed between the assumption of ministerial office and the proclamation of independence; this was regarded as a speedy advance, and as setting an example to others.

Throughout the 1950s it was customary in Britain to stress the differences between the three parts of British Africa—West Africa, where there were no white settlers, where African advancement had been considerable, and where local political life was exclusively African; East Africa where, especially in Kenya, whites and Asians controlled substantial elements in the economy and Africans were often backward; and Central Africa, especially Northern and Southern Rhodesia, where whites not only dominated the economy but were also, in Southern Rhodesia, a dominant and obviously permanent element in society, having enjoyed a system of responsible government since 1923. What would do for the west, it was often said, would not do for the east and the centre. While black control might be suitable in the Gold Coast and Nigeria, it might bring ruin on those territories in which the economy rested on local white enterprise. For these, words like 'partnership' and 'trusteeship' became, sometimes for short periods, the currency of conventional wisdom, especially in opposition to 'paramountcy', the official British doctrine of the paramountcy of native interests against those of other racial minorities. 'Independence' was a tougher word which only gradually made its way, elbowing aside the earlier 'self-government within the British Commonwealth'.

The problem of white minorities received considerable attention, not least because these were the best-educated and most vocal elements in such places as Rhodesia, Kenya, and Tanganyika, but also because of the need to remain on good terms with South Africa, which had had a Nationalist government since Smuts's electoral defeat in 1948. In 1953 a parliamentary journalist wrote:

Dr Malan is the key to much that is said and done at Westminster about African affairs. He is also as responsible as anyone else for the British tendency to adopt a pragmatic approach to African problems. If one eye has to be fixed on the problem itself and the other on Dr Malan, wider considerations tend to get left out of the line of vision.[1]

Any attempt at a wider and more consistent African policy was further frustrated by the fragmentary character of British departmental activity. The Colonial Office had the greatest responsibility in Africa, but others were also involved. The CRO was responsible for Southern Rhodesia (which had never been under direct rule), and from 1953 onwards for the Federation of Rhodesia and Nyasaland. It was also responsible for the High Commission Territories of Basutoland, Bechuanaland, and Swaziland, and for relations with South

---

[1] Ian Trethowan, 'Africa in the Commons', *New Commonwealth*, 9 Nov 1953, p. 491. For S. African influence in the case of Seretse Khama in Bechuanaland, see David Goldsworthy, *Colonial issues in British politics* (1971), p. 160.

Africa, which was very much concerned with these territories. The Foreign Office was responsible for the administration of the Sudan up to its independence in 1956, and also conducted Britain's diplomacy at the UN, where African issues became steadily more important. Britain was, in any case, responsible to the UN for the Trust Territories of Tanganyika, British Togoland, and the British Cameroons. Such an issue as South-West Africa, while not directly a matter of British concern, necessarily affected British policy in Africa at large. So also did relations with Belgium, France, and Portugal, the other main colonial powers, and with the US, which, while the ally in Nato of these powers and Britain, maintained in the 1950s a distinctly anti-colonial stance.

The tendency to treat each African colony as separate and to give special attention to the needs of white settlers, the departmental fragmentation which hindered a general approach, and the differing approaches of the right and left wings of the Conservative and Labour parties, were legacies of the past, along with the earlier belief 'that we had infinite time' which Sir Andrew Cohen found typical of British colonial policy in Africa in the years before World War II.[1] The general effect was to encourage particularism and gradualism. There were, of course, influences in the other direction. The growing anti-colonialist campaign at the UN forced British governments to look at colonial policy at large when defending their practices. The writing and urgings of some academics and left-wing organizations called for policy towards Africa as a whole. What were felt to be the lessons of the Indian experience sometimes led ministers and officials to argue that 'independence works' and 'we must not repeat the mistake of being too slow'. Above all, perhaps, disturbances in the colonies, both in Africa and elsewhere, led to impatience with continued colonial responsibility and the reflection that, if Britain had to hang on to colonies against the will of any significant section of their peoples, it would be committed to a series of costly and barren colonial wars. By the end of the 1950s it had become more usual to talk about Africa at large, and for the Colonial Office to adopt the attitude that arguments were needed for delaying independence rather than for granting it. The former quest for 'viability' in colonies—for the development of their economies and stability in their policies—was yielding to the political requirement that colonies should not be an embarrassment to Britain.

Cohen, who had been head of the Africa Division in the Colonial Office and governor of Uganda, thought that no single factor could be held responsible for changes in colonial policy, that constitutional progress was the result of the 'interrelated pressures' exerted on the one hand through the actions and policies of the British government, the governments in the territories, and British public and parliamentary opinion, and on the other through the pressure of nationalist and other opinions and attitudes in the territories. These pressures

---

[1] Andrew Cohen, *British policy in changing Africa* (1959), p. 26.

were not necessarily always exerted against each other, but were often com-plementary. 'Sometimes one or the other is, so to speak, in the ascendant, and it then supplies the motive force. Things work best when they are both operating effectively.' In the early stages the pressure of local opinion tended to be weak and unorganized and if the official attitude was rigid or negative, progress might be slow or non-existent. 'In such cases action by government is often needed to induce movement forward by doing something which primes the political pump.' In the later stages pressure by nationalist forces tended to be strong, and if government was rigid, there might be an explosion, or if it was weak, progress might be too rapid or in the wrong direction.[1]

The career of Sir Andrew Cohen, who had experienced these various pressures at first hand, exemplified the successive stages of British colonial policy. In the Colonial Office in the early 1950s he had done his share of 'priming the political pump', especially in respect of West Africa; however, he had also urged the formation of the Federation of Rhodesia and Nyasaland.[2] Appointed governor of Uganda in 1952, he attempted to 'induce movement forward' by increasing African representation on his executive council and by seeking greater participation in Uganda's institutions by its most advanced portion, the Kingdom of Buganda. Here, however, he encountered tradition-alist attitudes amongst Africans which temporarily prevented him from push-ing ahead with constitutional reform. Indeed, he found himself in considerable political difficulty because of the need, as he saw it, to withdraw recognition from the Kabaka (the ruler) of Buganda and deport him to Britain. Even so, Cohen was able to use this opportunity to persuade Lyttelton, the colonial secretary, to state in parliament that Uganda's future would be as 'primarily an African country, with proper safeguards for minorities'. This statement 'marked the first crucial breach in the "partnership" line which the Colonial Office was seeking to hold in East and Central Africa';[3] it was a turning-point for the time (December 1953) when it was uttered.

Yet the paradox is that Cohen himself had strongly supported the 'partner-ship' concept not long before, in the case of the Federation of Rhodesia and Nyasaland. (Within a few years he was dismayed by the extent of white supremacy in the Federation.) Here, as in the fact that he tried to secure a period of stability when the Ugandan constitution was being reformed in 1954—asking first for ten years' delay before the constitution was amended again, and then, under pressure, for six—is to be witnessed the effect of 'interrelated pressures' in the one man, himself the cause of some of them, but affected by others to an extent that made him appear to back and fill, first looking for movement forward in African self-government, then for stability in case the movement might prove too fast. From 1957 onwards, as British

---

[1] Ibid., pp. 36–7. [2] Goldsworthy, pp. 52 & 216.
[3] D. A. Low, 'The Buganda mission', in *Hist. Stud.*, Oct 1968, p. 364. Much of the material in this paragraph is from Low, the rest from a private source.

representative on the UN Trusteeship Council, he found the pace had to be faster again, because of the pressure of international opinion and the growing strength of African diplomacy exerted through international bodies. By 1959, as his book quoted above shows, he had elected for rapid colonial advance. A friend said he had decided that, of the two ways of falling off a bicycle, it was better to fall off through going too fast than through going too slow. In this he was typical of many of his fellow officials who had begun with the notion of gradual change and had decided, under the pressure of events, that greater speed was inevitable. In the final stage of Cohen's career, when he was in charge of the British programme of technical co-operation, he personified British assistance to former dependencies which still required help to acquire the economic viability which had once been thought necessary to independence itself.

Against the figure of Cohen, the official and pro-consul in whom the urges towards gradual and rapid political advance in Africa were uneasily blended, we may set that of Kwame Nkrumah, the embodiment of that 'pressure by nationalist forces' which Cohen recognized as decisive in the end. Although Nkrumah came from the Gold Coast, which had been the epitome of gradualism, he quickened the whole pace of African advance.

'So many words, so much to do, So little done, such things to be', he had quoted from *In Memoriam* to the Dean of Lincoln University in the US when applying for admission in 1934.[1] Accomplished, ambitious, sopping up ideas like a sponge, putting forth his own notions freely and effectively by means of his talent for political organization, he had spent ten years in the US as a student and had organized an African Students' Association of America and Canada. He had been closely in touch with radical bodies and radical ideas, but had been most affected by the writings of Marcus Garvey, the apostle of 'Africa for the Africans' and 'Back to Africa'. He had written a pamphlet called *Towards Colonial Freedom*, which he managed to publish in London after going there in 1945. He became the guiding spirit of radical West African students in Britain and helped to arrange the fifth Pan-African Congress in Manchester. He also organized a West African National Secretariat, and made contact not only with men from British Africa but with notables from French West Africa such as Senghor and Houphouët-Boigny, before returning to the Gold Coast at the end of 1947 to become general secretary of the United Gold Coast Convention. In spite of what he felt to be his 'revolutionary background and ideas', and the existing state of the UGCC 'backed almost entirely by reactionaries, middle-class lawyers and merchants', he returned determined on 'positive action'.[2] Thereafter, by a mixture of popular

[1] *The autobiography of Kwame Nkrumah* (1957), p. vii.
[2] The details in this paragraph are from ibid., chs. 3–5. Another symbol of anti-gradualism might have been Jomo Kenyatta, who spent much longer in Britain than Nkrumah, and who also attended the Manchester Congress and published a radical pamphlet (*Kenya—land of*

revivalism and careful political management, he made himself master of his country. When it became independent in 1957, he was at its head. From then until his deposition while abroad in February 1966, he ruled with increasing autocracy and an increasing concentration on pan-African and world issues. His character and achievement are still debated.[1]

Nkrumah embodied much of the African transformation as it affected the Commonwealth. He accepted, with some demur, the slight delays which occurred in the Gold Coast's movement towards independence; he accepted British tutelage in various matters, including continued Gold Coast (later Ghanaian) membership of the sterling area; he was normally correct in observing the conventions of the Commonwealth system, and was, in spite of his republicanism, on good terms with the royal family in its contacts with him. He could, indeed, play the part of the model colonial nationalist with what appears to have been some sincerity. But his essential syncretism (he used Kipling's 'Children's Song' as a party hymn)[2] enabled him to combine with this image the contrary one of the supreme revolutionary, the man to whom African unity mattered above all things, who demanded independence first, and who thought of even independent African countries as subject to continual manipulation by the forces of western capitalism. Being in the Commonwealth for Nkrumah was described by one observer as 'rather in the position of being a socialist and yet a member of the Carlton Club: it is convenient and comfortable to be a member although he will scarcely agree with the views of many other members. It makes him more respectable to be a member.'[3] Yet this respectability was insufficient. The respectability which Nkrumah seems to have wanted most was that of the leader of Africa, the man to whom others deferred because of superior wisdom and greater dedication.

It is not suggested that Nkrumah dominated the transformation of Africa, or that colonial nationalists outside his own country took his lead in all things or even agreed with him most of the time. In fact towards the end of his rule

---

conflict) in 1945. For the atmosphere of this band of temporary exiles in London, see the sensitive and unjustly neglected novel, *A wreath for Udomo* (London, 1956) by the S. African Coloured writer Peter Abrahams, who knew both Kenyatta and Nkrumah.

[1] Because Ghana was the first ex-colony in black Africa to become independent, many students of the social sciences converged on it to make their assessments; since Nkrumah gave shelter to many non-African left-wing thinkers and political refugees, and since he had many foreign admirers, much has been written about him by observers from these two groups. The extent to which he wrote his books himself is disputed, but the *Autobiography* and *I speak of freedom* (1961), which consists largely of his speeches, bear the touch of an individual personality. For two contrasting views, see Henry L. Bretton, *The rise and fall of Kwame Nkrumah* (1966) and Geoffrey Bing, *Reap the whirlwind* (1968); and for an unusual treatment from a specialized standpoint, H. T. Alexander, *African tightrope* (1965).

[2] *I speak of freedom*, p. 47. Another African leader, Tom Mboya of Kenya, relates how, at his eve-of poll rally in Nairobi, before the 1961 elections, he 'read out to the great crowd the whole of Rudyard Kipling's poem If' (*Freedom and after*, 1963, p. 114). The persistence of Kipling's appeal in unlikely circumstances calls for study.

[3] Alexander, p. 27.

in Ghana he became increasingly isolated from most of the other independent African regimes, especially those in East Africa. His interference and dogmatism, while at first congenial to independence movements which wanted to gain ground against the Europeans controlling their countries, were troublesome to independent African regimes confronted by the problems of office. His significance lay in four related facts.[1]

First, he signified the revolt against gradualism in colonial policy: by his own encouragement of nationalist leaders in other territories (especially in British colonies), and by his insistence on 'seeking first the political kingdom', he helped to discredit the notion of Africans' unpreparedness for independence. His attitude in this respect became typical of African leaders generally.

Second, he provided a pan-African rhetoric and atmosphere whereby other nationalist leaders were helped to overcome the particularism inherent in colonial policy. This sentiment, which was central to his thinking from an early time, led him to develop pan-African institutions as soon as he had the power to do so, and to popularize the idea that it was a duty of independent African governments to help other territories to gain independence.

Third, he symbolized the rapidly increasing connection between African and world politics, and the growing pressure exerted by independent African states, at the UN and elsewhere, upon the remaining colonial powers, including Britain.

Fourth, as the first black African prime minister to appear in Commonwealth circles, he demonstrated beyond any shadow of doubt that the Commonwealth was not universal enough for the pursuit of African aims. The same point had been demonstrated by Nehru in respect of India's interests, but with rather more delicacy and less emphasis. While Nkrumah was prepared to abide by most of the conventions of the Commonwealth system as those had been established in the 1950s, he insisted that Ghana express itself with determination and often with stridency in the UN and in other forums, whether it was making demands on Britain or stating what Nkrumah regarded as principles of general international validity. In this respect Nkrumah was, if anything, somewhat less vehement than his successors: between 1957 and 1960 there was no meeting of Commonwealth prime ministers, and no opportunity for Nkrumah to express African demands in this particular forum, whether he wanted to or not. By the time such meetings proliferated in the early 1960s, he was joined by other African leaders who, while deferring initially to him, had by then achieved their own success and resolved on their own strategies.

Nkrumah anticipated but did not necessarily either formulate or dictate the demands later to be made through Commonwealth machinery by Nyerere of Tanzania, Kaunda of Zambia, and Banda of Malawi, leaders of greater

[1] Readers may care to compare this assessment with Ali A. Mazrui's in *Towards a pax africana* (1967), ch. 4.

durability who had more awkward problems to solve. His position was showier and more symbolic. He was the forerunner and provider of opportunities, the man who, working from an economic base consolidated by careful British administrators, sounded the tocsin for swifter advance and a stronger concentration on political power. The others profited from the groundwork he had done, but were often not prepared to accept his leadership in the wider issues in which Africa became embroiled.

III

The phenomenon of Nkrumah has been given prominence here because it typifies the reasons why Britain was not permitted to proceed on its gradualist way in Africa in the 1950s and 1960s, but had to adjust to pressures in Africa itself, in addition to those which African issues generated within British politics, and those which anti-colonialist states exerted through international organizations. A sense of gradualism was still justified and necessary for British governments, and was still present in men like Cohen no matter how strong the pressures. It was justified because most British colonies were in no position to govern themselves unaided while preserving the standards which the British had established, and necessary because Conservative Party governments could not abdicate from the colonial task without some rationalization. But the orthodox position of 1953, as expressed by Lyttelton and Griffiths, was steadily eroded by circumstances.

According to one close observer, looking at the erosion in the 1960s, as the pace of constitutional development increased

the British Government seemed to lose control over the situation, to be following a trend rather than initiating and pursuing a definite, properly conceived policy of disengagement. There were several signs of this. For one thing, there was the fundamental change in the accepted criteria for independence. For another, there was an increasing readiness to see the preparations for independence as a paper exercise of Lancaster House conferences, a challenge to chairmanship rather than a duty to find a constitutional framework genuinely acceptable to the people of the country concerned and relevant to their needs and conditions.[1]

While this criticism was not directed specifically to Africa, it mainly applied to Africa, since the African dependencies occupied most of the attention of British ministers concerned with colonial affairs. To a considerable extent, African nationalists made the running; and the biggest colonies were in Africa.

[1] W. P. Kirkman, *Unscrambling an empire* (1966), p. 13. The author was Colonial Correspondent of *The Times* for four years from the end of 1960. One well-placed observer comments on this passage: 'I do not believe that Britain had lost control. It was the British Government who were forcing the pace, and Mr Sandys was firmly in the driving seat.' There is no dispute, however, about the quickening of the pace.

It is usually said that the symbolic turning-point or watershed between gradualism and more rapid advance was provided by Macmillan's 'wind of change' speech to the South African parliament at Cape Town on 3 February 1960.[1] The main aim of this speech seems to have been to serve notice on the South Africans that Britain would no longer support South Africa unreservedly when it was attacked at the UN; but it also stressed 'the strength of this African national consciousness'. 'The wind of change is blowing through this continent', said Macmillan. 'Whether we like it or not, this growth of national consciousness is a political fact. We must all accept it as a fact. Our national policies must take account of it.'

As I see it [he went on] the great issue in this second half of the twentieth century is whether the uncommitted peoples of Asia and Africa will swing to the East or the West. Will they be drawn into the Communist camp? Or will the great experiments in self-government that are now being made in Asia and Africa, especially in the Commonwealth, prove so successful, and by their example so compelling, that the balance will come down in favour of freedom and order and justice?

The answer was clear, so far as current policy was concerned:

what Governments and Parliaments in the United Kingdom *have* done since the last war in according independence to India, Pakistan, Ceylon, Malaya and Ghana, and what they *will* do for Nigeria and other countries now nearing independence—all this . . . we do in the belief that it is the only way to establish the future of the Commonwealth and of the free world on sound foundations.

The speech thus accepted the need for rapid African change, especially in terms of world political strategy, and made it clear that the interests of white settlers in Africa could not be decisive for British policy.

Macmillan's espousal of a change in tempo had been signified by his appointment as colonial secretary in October 1959 of Iain Macleod, who remained in the post for two years, during which preparations were made for a much more widespread transfer of power in Africa than had been envisaged by ministers before. Macleod's actions were brisker and more daring than those of his predecessors, but they cannot be attributed simply to his own strong-mindedness. As with Nkrumah, the occasion assisted, if it did not produce, the man.

Macleod's Conservative predecessors, Lyttelton and Lennox-Boyd, had experienced considerable political turmoil at home, largely because of fierce

---

[1] Extracts are in Mansergh, *Documents 1952–62*, pp. 347–51. Macmillan has himself suggested that 'wind of change' may have been 'an unconscious echo' of words spoken by Stanley Baldwin to a party meeting in December 1934, on the issue of Indian self-government, when Baldwin said: 'There is a wind of nationalism and freedom blowing round the world and blowing as strongly in Asia as anywhere in the world. And are we less true Conservatives because we say "the time has now come"?' (*Tides of fortune*, p. 232). Macmillan used the phrase a few days earlier in a speech in Accra, but it was in Cape Town that interest was aroused.

argument over the racial policies of the Federation of Rhodesia and Nyasaland but also because of partial or total disagreement by the Labour Party with policies adopted in Kenya, British Guiana, and Cyprus.[1] In 1956 Labour had accepted, for the first time, the policy of egalitarian democracy ('one man one vote') in colonies with plural societies. This had been put forward as official policy by Hugh Gaitskell, the Labour leader, at the 1959 elections.[2] The government itself, while disclaiming such extreme policies, had gone ahead with steady constitutional change. The Sudan had become independent in 1956, and Ghana and Malaya in 1957. Nigeria, like these two latter territories an example of gradualism, was to get its independence in 1960; there had also been considerable advance in the West Indies. It was clear, however, that international pressures would soon force independence for British Somaliland and Cyprus, two colonies which no one assumed to be 'ready' for self-government in the terms conceived before.

Such a varied situation indicated to Macleod (as it had to Cohen) that an increase in pace was called for. A difficulty for him, however, was that there was pressure on the British government from the East and Central African dependencies, in which, while Africans predominated, there were also white settlers who had traditionally received special attention in British policy. In the past, British governments had either asserted the paramountcy of African interests without immediately curbing settler power, as in Kenya and Northern Rhodesia, or, as in Southern Rhodesia, had allowed local settlers to decide local conditions. Now the government was faced with circumstances such as the Devlin Commission discovered in Nyasaland, a constituent part of the Federation of Rhodesia and Nyasaland:

> The majority of Nyasas may be incapable of making a reasoned and prudent judgment on any questions of policy, but there is a small but increasing minority which is just as well equipped to do so as the average European and which considers itself as well fitted to direct the Government of Nyasaland as any European. . . . It has been immensely encouraged by recent developments in Ghana, the Sudan, Nigeria and Uganda. We do not pause to enquire what differences there may be between conditions in these countries and in Nyasaland: the fact is that the success of African nationalism there has stimulated Africans elsewhere to believe that self-government is within their grasp and to behave accordingly.[3]

Such attitudes had brought trouble throughout the Federation: when Macleod assumed office at the end of 1959 there had been riots in Nyasaland (leading to the appointment of the Devlin Commission) and the suppression of the African National Congress in Northern Rhodesia, while in Southern Rhodesia, which was not his responsibility, a state of emergency had been declared because of disturbances amongst the Africans.

1960 was the year of the independence and disruption of the Belgian Congo,

[1] See Goldsworthy, *passim*.   [2] Ibid., pp. 335 & 340.   [3] Cmnd 814 (1959), p. 16.

with effects throughout Africa, especially in the Federation. When a telegram stating the Belgian intention to grant independence was handed to Macleod at the Lancaster House Conference on Kenya, he said to one of the settler representatives: 'Look at this. This is a message to say that the Belgians are giving the Congo independence in June this year—1960. Do you know what this means? We are going to be the last in the colonial sphere instead of the first.'[1]

In fact, this did not turn out to be the case. Portugal was to be the last of the European colonial powers to retain substantial possessions in Africa, with France and Spain, as well as Britain, continuing to hold residual areas. In 1960 and 1961 there was evidence of acceleration in British policy. Sierra Leone became independent in 1961, Tanganyika obtained responsible government in 1960 and full independence in 1961, Uganda became independent in 1962, and Kenya was assured of practical African control. The break-up of the Federation of Rhodesia and Nyasaland became daily more likely, following the report of the Monckton Commission on its constitutional condition. The international climate was to be gauged from a resolution of the UN General Assembly on 28 November 1961. The Assembly voted 97 to nil for a speedy end to colonialism. The abstainers were Britain, France, Portugal, South Africa, and Spain. The 'wind of change' speech had been designed to dispense with company like this; but the association was less damaging than it might otherwise have been, given the acceleration which Macleod had applied and Macmillan had sanctioned.

It appears likely that the most pressing reason for the increased tempo was the fear of bloodshed if nationalist demands were not conceded. Macmillan told President Eisenhower in August 1959: 'We have our Algerias coming to us—Kenya and Central Africa'.[2] Macleod, justifying his policy of speeding up independence some years later, wrote:

... In my view any other policy would have led to terrible bloodshed in Africa. . . . Were the countries fully ready for independence? Of course not. Nor was India, and the bloodshed that followed the grant of independence there was incomparably worse than anything that has happened since to any country. Yet the decision of the Attlee Government was the only realistic one. Equally we could not possibly have held by force to our territories in Africa. We could not, with an enormous force engaged, even continue to hold the small island of Cyprus. General de Gaulle could not contain Algeria. The march of men towards their freedom can be guided but not

---

[1] Michael Blundell, *So rough a wind* (1964), p. 271. Blundell, on what appears to be good authority, states that in January 1959, before Macleod replaced Lennox-Boyd and before Macmillan had won the British general election of 1959, 'the official policy was a slow and unspectacular constitutional advance' for Tanganyika, Uganda, and Kenya, with the first two expected to gain independence no sooner than 1970 and Kenya in 1975 (p. 262). It was this informal timetable—if it can be so called—that Macleod upset (see *Welensky's 4000 days* (1964), p. 139, for confirmation of the 1959 intentions).

[2] Macmillan, *Riding the storm*, p. 748.

halted. Of course there were risks in moving quickly. But the risks of moving slowly were far greater.[1]

The references to Algeria by Macmillan and Macleod are significant. The examples of French failure in Algeria and earlier in Vietnam, as well as the Dutch failure in Indonesia, convinced many influential men in Britain that armed resistance to colonial nationalism was wasteful and self-defeating. This was not the same as a conviction that an imperial role could no longer be sustained in Asia or Africa; but it was sometimes thought to be so. A notable case occurred in February 1962 when Duncan Sandys, the Commonwealth secretary, visited Salisbury to discuss the Federation's troubled affairs. According to Sir Roy Welensky, Sandys said, 'We British have lost the will to govern', thereby incurring the contempt of the Federation ministers who heard him. According to the British high commissioner, however, what Sandys said was that Britain was no longer prepared to govern anyone indefinitely *by force*; there was a substantial difference. In Sandys's extended statement lies a key to the change in British policy.[2]

It is important to emphasize the complexity of the situation in which the vital decisions were taken. Although Africa was, by 1960 and 1961, the centre of world attention so far as decolonization was concerned, it was not the only place with British colonies. The British government also had responsibilities in the Caribbean, the Mediterranean, the Pacific, and Southeast Asia, apart from what was left of its former sphere of influence in the Middle East. Events in these areas interacted with those in Africa, to produce an even more complex set of interrelated pressures than those described by Cohen. Not only did the mass of colonial problems provide ample debate at the UN, much of which was directed against British retention of such diverse colonies as Aden, Cyprus, British Guiana, and Rhodesia; there were, in addition, enough examples of violence in these colonies, and in the French and Belgian territories, to reiterate the point that the alternative to rapid independence might be constant danger of guerrilla warfare. Portugal was prepared to face this in its African colonies; Britain was not. The pressure of nationalist demands had overcome the earlier notion that economic and social conditions must be right before independence could be granted. In due course Britain was applying to reluctant and peaceable colonies like the Gambia and Fiji the lessons which

---

[1] *Weekend Telegraph*, 12 Mar 1965.

[2] *Welensky's 4000 days*, p. 319; Lord Alport, *The sudden assignment* (1965), pp. 167–8. It can be argued, as by Sir Keith Hancock in 1956, that 'the greatest leaders of the British people —for example, Queen Elizabeth and William Pitt and Winston Churchill—have been master practitioners of the economy of force', and that 'in the British Imperial tradition the same initial propensity to economise force has been interwoven with a strong propensity towards political decentralisation and local self-government. There is no more extravagant waste of force than the attempt to govern powerful subjects against their will ...' (*Colonial self-government*, 1956, p. 7). The irony is that this argument was highly acceptable to African nationalists when applied to themselves but was rejected by them with contumely when applied by Britain to white Rhodesians from 1965 onwards.

had been learnt from the more truculent apostles of 'positive action' in Africa, and from the apprehensions aroused by terrorism in Cyprus and Aden. The wind of change had taken more than one form.

IV

The verdict of history on the acceleration in British policy in Africa will depend partly upon assessments of the situation at the time, and partly upon what happened in Africa afterwards. The African transformation was more than a matter of decolonization. It also involved two other processes which could be seen in embryo before 1960 but which became more and more important in the 1960s. These were the development of post-independence instability in many African states, shown by the appearance of military and one-party governments; and the growing connection between African and world politics, which helped to bring about the condition which Ali Mazrui described as existing in 1964: 'There had, in fact, developed two centres of influence within the Commonwealth—Britain herself was one centre, the African group of nations was the other.'[1] However, the situation became more complicated. While there was certainly an African bloc in the Commonwealth, and common African policies developed on certain matters, there were also divisions amongst the Africans. In addition, certain aspects of the African situation helped to change British attitudes from those of 1960 to sterner and harsher ones, often unacceptable to many people in Britain and to other members of the Commonwealth, but understandable in the light of the dis-appointments of the later stages of the African transformation.

With increasing independence elsewhere, the continued existence of South Africa and Southern Rhodesia, countries governed by white men on principles which could not be squared with those which Britain had avowed in grant-ing independence to its African colonies, made them stand out as glaring but prosperous anomalies in the transformed African continent. They con-stituted an embarrassment to Britain, South Africa because British trade had created commercial ties which could not be broken without considerable loss, Southern Rhodesia because it remained nominally subject to British sovereignty but was plainly not subject to British direction. As the independent black African states became accustomed to the processes of diplomacy, they exerted more pressure upon Britain. Since the British government was not prepared to use sanctions against South Africa or force against Rhodesia, clashes with African Commonwealth members were inescapable.

These two matters became international issues, on which such countries as Canada, Australia, New Zealand, India, and Malaysia had to declare them-selves. To some extent they created divisions between the newer African members of the Commonwealth and those older ones which did not wish to

[1] *The Anglo-African Commonwealth* (1967), p. 28.

be hurried into policies which did not coincide with their normal interests. In addition, however, South Africa and Rhodesia caused problems for the African states themselves. By the end of the 1960s four Commonwealth members—Malawi, Botswana, Lesotho, and Swaziland—were dependent on South Africa for much of their economic existence, while another—Zambia— was still reluctantly tied to Southern Rhodesia (and to Portugal and South Africa) in respect of certain economic resources. Some of these states were determined to end the dependence which they found so galling; others were prepared to accept it and profit from it. None, however, could ignore it or escape from it easily. There was, of necessity, some estrangement between African members because of differing approaches to the South African and Rhodesian questions. Some people may have thought in 1961 that South Africa's forced departure from the Commonwealth had settled both, or provided a hope of settlement which would maintain harmony amongst the remaining and future Commonwealth members. This was not to be.

A further important development was the discarding of parliamentary democracy by some of the new African states. It could be argued that there was never much likelihood that they would retain it, either on comparative grounds (since new states everywhere, and many old ones too, did not practise it), or on sociological grounds (since it was often said by those in power that African society was not accustomed to formal opposition to authority, but depended on a form of consensus which required authority to be supreme). This, however, was not what the independence movements had said when they were demanding full self-government: they had maintained not only that they were fit to take the reins of power, but also that they would do so along some-thing like the lines familiar at Westminster. It was therefore a shock, and a source of disappointment, to Britain and the older Commonwealth countries when Nkrumah asserted one-party rule in Ghana, and when his example was followed, in varying degrees and with important local variations, in Kenya, Uganda, Tanzania, Malawi, Zambia, Lesotho, and Sierra Leone. The Sudan had been a precursor. Even more dismaying were the violence which occurred in Uganda, the short-lived military coup in Sierra Leone, and, above all, the military coups and civil war in Nigeria in 1968. Commonwealth countries were not, of course, the only African countries to display either one-party or military regimes. By 1969, nearly all independent black African states were in one of these two conditions.

It is true that, while parliaments had ceased to function in the Westminster manner in most of the Commonwealth states (though they were to be re-established as a source of authority in Ghana and Sierra Leone), optimists could point to the fact that other British institutions, in particular the courts and the administration, still functioned in something like a British fashion. In general, however, the African states had proved a disappointment to those outside Africa who had urged on their independence in the late 1950s. Their lack of political stability made their complaints against South Africa and Rhodesia less acceptable than if parliamentary democracy had survived in Africa to the same extent as in the Caribbean Commonwealth countries or in India and Ceylon.

The sober and significant Lusaka Declaration on Southern Africa, issued in April 1969 by representatives from Kenya, Somalia, the Sudan, Tanzania, Uganda, and Zambia, together with Burundi, the Central African Republic, Chad, the two Congos, Ethiopia and Rwanda would have been much more convincing if so many of the signatories had not come from countries which contravened the basic assertion of the Declaration, that 'we do not accept that any individual or group within a society has the right to rule any society without the continuing consent of all the citizens'. They did state that they would not claim 'that within our own States we have achieved that perfect social, economic and political organization which would ensure a reasonable standard of living for all our people and establish individual security against avoidable hardship or miscarriage of justice'. When they said they were not hostile to the administrations of Rhodesia, South Africa, Mozambique, Angola, and South-West Africa because they were manned and controlled by white people, but were hostile to them 'because they are systems of minority control which exist as a result of, and in the pursuance of, doctrines of human inequality', while stressing their own devotion to the principle of equality, they were expressing a view with which many others would agree. But their own practice remained a handicap. Their instability not only reduced their political credit but also compounded their inability to inflict damage on the regimes which they wished to displace. The longer those regimes survived, the less need there seemed to be for states outside Africa to accede to demands for their supersession.[1]

In 1963, when the OAU was set up, largely through the astute diplomacy of the Emperor Haile Selassie of Ethiopia, it was not apparent that there would be growing instability among African states which would prevent them from gaining the ends their leaders regarded as vital. The OAU was the lineal descendant of a conference called by Nkrumah at Accra in 1958, but in the meantime there had been splits between two and sometimes three such bodies, each claiming to stand for African unity. A nucleus of radical states— Ghana, Guinea, Mali, and the UAR—had pressed forward with demands to which the more conservative francophone states, together with Ethiopia, Liberia, and Nigeria, could not agree. However, such competition for recognition as the true representative of pan-Africanism, and the establishment of the OAU against what seemed to be such odds, showed that the sense of African unity was strong, despite acute differences of opinion about what it entailed or could attain. The OAU did not cause substantial changes in African

---

[1] The Lusaka meeting took place on 16 April 1969. The copy of the Declaration quoted here was issued by the government of Tanzania.

affairs; it provided a forum for grievances and a means of mobilizing resources, but could not confine itself to domestic preoccupations. In calling for an end to the Smith regime in Rhodesia, in helping 'freedom fighters' in Angola and Mozambique, and in calling for boycotts of South Africa it was inviting states outside Africa to take sides with or against it.

The same was true of the efforts of the African bloc at the UN, where the machinery of the General Assembly could be brought into play against Portugal, South Africa, and Rhodesia. The communist and Latin American states and most of those in Asia and the Middle East normally voted with the Africans on African issues. Such a situation could give a false impression of the influence wielded by the African states. The US and the major West European powers, while formally in a minority, could still exert pressure when they wished, and could impose vetoes in the Security Council. The efforts of both the UN and the OAU to dislodge the white regimes of Southern Africa were still, by 1969, a failure.

Pan-Africanism was not, of course, the sole element in the foreign policies of independent African states, although it often supplied the occasion and the rhetoric for those policies. A final aspect to be considered is the growth of individual foreign policies amongst the new states, sometimes involving co-operation with others (as in the joint determination of Zambia and Tanzania to build, with Chinese help, the 'Tanzam' railway, thus reducing Zambia's dependence on the Rhodesian and Portuguese railways), sometimes pursued alone, (e.g. Banda's desire to cultivate South Africa), and sometimes both individual and impractical (as in the case of Nkrumah's grandiose schemes of African unity through the establishment of a single government for the whole of the continent). While professing non-alignment as a kind of general creed for international relations, nearly all the African states—certainly all of those in the Commonwealth—interpreted it as meaning that they were free to make whatever arrangements with the great powers seemed most advantageous. Aid was eagerly competed for; concessions were often granted without regard for their effect on non-alignment in the strictest sense. Associations with countries outside Africa were pursued in a non-ideological fashion: a state might have part of its forces trained by Canada and part by China, like Tanzania; Israel and Taiwan jockeyed for the opportunity to render technical assistance and thus gain some recognition. At the UN attitudes towards particular issues were often framed in accordance with the connections that might be made or broken by a vote this way or that.

Such ambitious and sometimes carefree deployment of foreign policy could hardly have occurred in the 1950s, when the Cold War was at its height and the issue of non-alignment was more serious. In the 1960s, when the newly independent African states began their formal diplomacy, the détente between the US and the Soviet Union, arising from a nuclear stalemate, had stabilized the main framework of world conflict, and some small powers could operate with less fear of great power interference. They could not do so in Eastern Europe, the Caribbean, Central America, or Southeast Asia, as the experiences of Czechoslovakia, Cuba, the Dominican Republic, and Vietnam showed; but they could in Africa. Neither the US nor the Soviet Union had made pacts there. They competed for the attachment of African states, especially through economic aid, but did not set up the apparatus of formal alliance. The determination of most African states that Africa should be declared a non-nuclear zone, and their opposition to great-power intervention in the troubled affairs of the Congo after independence, showed that the US and the Soviet Union were wise to confine themselves largely to economic inducements and to selective military aid. The same was true of China, a growing influence in world affairs in the 1960s and clearly desirous of reducing the influence in Africa of both the super-powers. There was undoubtedly some Chinese assistance to 'freedom fighters', as there was Russian; but China, like the super-powers, was far away from Africa, had had little to do with it in former times, and could be successfully held at arm's length by most African states.

Thus, in spite of the instability which dogged them, and their failure to overcome the 'white redoubt' in Southern Africa, the newly independent African states had achieved, by 1969, a place in the world which ensured that they would be listened to, and that, even if their advice and demands were not always followed, their attachment to this or that great power was of some importance to states outside Africa. The fact that France remained influential with the francophone states (which accounted for roughly half of the independent states in the continent), and that France was, throughout the 1960s, dominated by President de Gaulle, was another significant point. De Gaulle wished to steer an independent course, subservient to none of the other nuclear powers. France's clients were given freedom to act as they saw fit, though subject to occasional discipline if they blatantly opposed French policy. This aspect of the African situation reinforced the influence of the super-power relationship: Africa was relatively free, relatively loose to the international system, compared with those areas, such as Europe and Latin America, which retained restrictions from the past. The African states had room to manoeuvre, subject always to the limitations of their own economic and political weakness, and to the obligations which they acquired in trade and aid, including the supply of arms.

V

In Commonwealth terms, the transformation of Africa was a source of surprise and sometimes resentment amongst British people. Looking at the situation in 1963, Margery Perham diagnosed it as follows:

It seems that there are three main obstacles to our understanding of Africa, and here I am thinking in the main of Commonwealth Africa. One of these is [the] continuing expression of anti-colonialism; the second is the apparent African rejection of democracy; the third is the dangerous and seemingly insoluble conflict between white and black in Southern Africa.[1]

The rejection of democracy was certainly a disappointment; but the vigour and what often seemed the unfairness of the anti-colonialist crusade and the attacks on South Africa and Rhodesia were troublesome and unexpected. As we have seen, the nature of the new African states' foreign policies had been very little discussed in advance. Consideration of their economic and constitutional future had obscured it. Those in Britain who thought about it may have considered that they would behave like India, Pakistan, and Ceylon, which, while opposed to colonialism at the UN, had reserved most of their fire for the Dutch, French, and Portuguese, and had caused Britain relatively little embarrassment, in respect of either Asian dependencies such as Malaya, or those colonies, such as Kenya, Tanganyika, Mauritius, and Fiji, in which immigrants from the Indian subcontinent were a significant element. In any case, India was known to be sophisticated, while Africa was not; there was an expectation of vigorous diplomacy from India but not from Africa. In fact, African diplomacy quickly became not only vigorous but embarrassing, since its emphatic claims were supported by the communist states and by a variety of other anti-colonialist states outside Africa.

The fact that the most strident claims were made about South Africa and Rhodesia, which were especially sensitive areas for Britain, emphasized the difficulties for the Commonwealth. It was easy for resentment to develop on both sides: amongst the Africans because of what they regarded as a double standard employed by Britain in regard to the human rights of Africans in different parts of the continent; and amongst the British on the ground that the Africans were ungrateful for what had been done for them, were not prepared to credit Britain with good faith, and did not recognize the difficulties under which Britain laboured. In addition, the British problem (and the problem, in varying degrees, of the other older members of the Commonwealth) was complicated by the African Commonwealth states' disinclination to confine themselves to Commonwealth means when dealing with Southern Africa.[2]

This particular point was emphasized, with characteristic honesty, by Tom Mboya of Kenya, after attending the 1964 Prime Ministers' Meeting:

It is evident that the African States tried to secure agreement on issues which concerned them most and on which they were due to report to the OAU at the Cairo

---

[1] 'Britain and Africa in 1963', in Perham, p. 254 (originally published in *The Listener*, 4 Apr 1963).
[2] There is no suggestion here that *inter se* questions between Commonwealth members should be kept within the Commonwealth: the Irish in the 1920s and the Indians in the 1950s had shown that they need not be. Undoubtedly, however, many British people and others hoped that Rhodesia could be kept within the Commonwealth in the 1960s.

Conference. These included the questions of Southern Rhodesia, South Africa and even the Portuguese territories.

Will the next conference break up on disputes as to what should go into the communiqué? Will the African States demand more than the Western Powers in the club can agree to support and still remain loyal members of their own bloc? These are important points in considering this question.

At the second meeting of the Council of Ministers of the OAU, the African members of the Commonwealth were specifically asked to raise certain matters at the Commonwealth Conference and to use their influence with Britain on the Southern Rhodesia question. The implication here must lead one to ask whether members of the Commonwealth will in future be able to come to OAU to plead for a point of view of the Commonwealth on a particular matter.

Or will they expect to plead only the OAU point of view at Commonwealth conferences? It is difficult at this stage to see the way ahead.

. . . Before there is a continental Government, the OAU remains an association of free and equal Sovereign states. But with the setting up of a permanent secretariat and the specialised commissions, a Development Bank and so on, we are on the way towards not only pan-African co-operation but co-ordination.

Such co-ordination and harmonising of foreign policy and the need for a joint or common African front at international trade and social conferences and at United Nations must mean that we put pan-African relations first and our other relations second.

There will be occasions when this desire or decision may conflict with the bilateral arrangements we make with other countries or with our Commonwealth arrangements. This is a development which we cannot avoid but which should not necessarily require withdrawal from the Commonwealth.[1]

In the next few years the situation became more complex. While the OAU did not prove to command the full African support that had been hoped for and advanced no further towards continental supranationalism, it continued to be the focus of pan-African demands. At the same time, the situation over Rhodesia became more acute following the Unilateral Declaration of Independence by the Smith government in November 1965. It was not so much the weight of the OAU as that of certain Commonwealth states in Africa which was brought to bear on Britain, at the UN and at Commonwealth meetings, after 1965; but any notion that Commonwealth matters could be kept within the Commonwealth was effectively disproved, since the UN quickly became the main arena for the struggle, and the African states' strategy of pressure within the Commonwealth was co-ordinated with their approach at the UN. Moreover, the fact that the African members were campaigning against white regimes increased tension within the Commonwealth. A split between white and coloured members, which the Canadians and others had tried to avoid during the Suez crisis of 1956 and the South African issue in 1960-1, now

---

[1] From 'Pan-Africanism and the Commonwealth: are they in conflict?', an address at Makerere University College, Kampala, 10 Aug 1964 (reprinted in *The Anglo-African Commonwealth*, pp. 151–2).

seemed a more likely possibility. The Commonwealth secretariat spent much time and effort in trying to prevent it.

Africa brought a new dimension to Commonwealth relations. It was not simply a matter of issues; it involved tone, temper, and emotion.

The Africans [said a British civil servant] are by nature aggressive and self-assertive, condemned by history to be inexperienced, in outlook simplistic and idealistic; ambitious, but unsure of themselves and on the defensive; emotional and apt to be bitter; their inferiority complex is easily aroused and they readily see the rest of the world banded against them as it was in the last century. With little training themselves and with little education among the people they represented, African politicians could and did quickly turn into demagogues.[1]

He went on to say that while some of this might be unfair or exaggerated, the point was that none of it applied to Indians, because of Indian education, the gradual growth of Indian self-government, and the strength of Indian administration. This kind of comparison was often in the minds of British civil servants as Africa became more prominent in Commonwealth affairs. It was not that they necessarily approved of all the policies which India espoused: it was rather that they contrasted the sophistication of the Indians with the uncertainty and demagogism of many of the Africans. The relative smoothness of Commonwealth relations in the 1950s, compared with their tumultuous character in the 1960s, owed something to the contrast.

Much of the difference in tone and temper could be attributed, also, to the persistence after independence of the methods of political pressure which the Africans had found so successful before. Indian anti-colonialism had been transferred to the UN after independence, and was stated in terms of broad principle rather than with constant reference to Britain. African anti-colonialism, in contrast, was pursued at least as vigorously within the Commonwealth as within the UN, and was very much a matter of the particular colonial problems of Africa itself (in which, in the view of most African Commonwealth leaders, the problem of white domination in South Africa was included, in spite of South Africa's formal status as a sovereign state). Much of the strategy of gaining independence in Africa was that of real or implied threat: of strikes, boycotts, sit-downs, and in some cases violence, although most independence movements had been too weak to carry out all these threats. It can be argued that this very weakness was a cause of the constant emphasis on threats. Independence movements could not afford to stand still, could not keep their supporters patiently massed in support of a waiting game; they needed colour, excitement, and verbal pugnacity. These tactics persisted after independence, when the strategy was widened to include also the Africans in Rhodesia and South Africa. Tom Mboya's reflections on the methods used by himself and his fellow-Kenyans to obtain independence are apposite:

[1] A private communication.

We learnt during our struggle that the only way to get anywhere with Britain was by being tough, although of course this meant we were usually accused of being intransigent, obdurate and extreme. It was the only language Britain understood, because Britain was being frightened on her other flank by settlers threatening an open clash. I have had the impression about several Colonial Secretaries we have had to deal with, that they would have come forward with more positive programmes, but hesitated because of their own back-benchers. Colonial issues only became hot matters in the House of Commons when settlers went over and spoke to Tory back-benchers, and then the Ministers were subjected to heavy pressure. It became evident that the face of East and Central Africa depended more on the atmosphere inside the Conservative Party than on any logical analysis of the African case as such. . . . The number of contradictions—the way British Somaliland was handed independence almost overnight, the way the Wild Committee provided a liberal franchise for Uganda, a country without settlers—shows that the only consistent factor in the Conservatives' colonial policy was a yielding to the greatest pressure. They would not take the initiative in advancing the colonies: we had to be tough, vary our tactics, pile on the pressure, appeal to international bodies; and only that way did we slowly begin to move forward.[1]

'Piling on the pressure', after independence, included threats to leave the Commonwealth, to break off diplomatic relations with Britain (carried into effect by Ghana and Tanzania in 1965), and to curtail British economic opportunities in trade and investment. While normally not uttered overtly, they formed part of the Commonwealth political climate in the late 1960s, often through 'leaks' to newspapers. The 'appeal to international bodies' included, in respect of Rhodesia, UN General Assembly demands to Britain to use force against the Smith regime, and the support, by some Commonwealth members, of the Spanish demand for the cession of Gibraltar, in spite of a plebiscite in 1967, held in the presence of Commonwealth observers, whereby a clear majority of Gibraltarians expressed their opposition to the idea.[2]

The objective of this support of Spain was presumably to gain Spanish votes in the UN on African matters, and the links between Spain and the Latin American and Arab states were probably also a factor. From a British standpoint, however, few things could appear more deplorable than the spec-tacle of former British colonies either abstaining on such a vote or supporting the transfer of a British colony to foreign sovereignty against the expressed wishes of the inhabitants. To some African Commonwealth members, en-

[1] *Freedom and after*, pp. 129–30.

[2] The referendum, held on 10 September 1967, resulted in a majority of 12,138 votes out of 12,762 in favour of retaining the link with Britain. Four Commonwealth observers, nomin-ated by the Commonwealth secretary-general, declared that it had been conducted in a fair and proper manner (*Survey B & CA*, 1967, pp. 990, 1030). On 17 December the UN General Assembly passed, by 73 votes to 19 with 27 abstentions, a resolution which declared the referendum a contravention of resolutions of the Assembly, and which, in the opinion of Lord Caradon, the British representative, took Spain's side. Commonwealth members amongst the 73 included Pakistan, Tanzania, and Zambia; 7 Commonwealth members abstained. A similar situation arose with a further resolution of 18 December 1968 (ibid., 1969, p. 100).

meshed in the intricacies of UN vote-getting and the complicated alignments of the anti-colonialist coalition, Gibraltar was evidently not the same sort of colonial issue as their own had been. It was, instead, a matter of tactics in a general strategy, the aim of which was the freeing of Rhodesia and the discomfiture of the white regime in South Africa.

There was little doubt that the African Commonwealth states preferred working with and not against Britain, and that they made their more strident criticisms in a mingled context of anti-colonialist belief, opposition to settler states in Southern Africa, and practical recognition of the legacies they had gained from British colonial rule. After all, there had been no armed struggle except in Kenya (a doubtful case). But their tone and tactics were hurtful to British pride, especially, perhaps, to those British officials and politicians who had worked hard for African independence. This sense of pride, buffeted by the African states' tendency to discard British institutions, was further damaged by such events as the bloody Nigerian coup of January 1966 and the destruction of the Kabaka's position in Uganda in the same year. It was more easy to slip into general condemnation of African regimes, and to regard their performances at the UN and at Commonwealth meetings as routine demagoguery, especially when Britain's motives in respect of its remaining colonies were being impugned. The strain and sense of trauma would not have been so marked if the effort to get independence off to a good start had not been so great.

In the 1950s the Colonial Office and colonial governments, under men like Andrew Cohen, had laboured hard to achieve the conditions in which independence might work well. Rightly or wrongly, independence was substituted for self-government as the goal. 'The only justification for our presence in these places' Cohen had said to Hancock in 1954, 'is to train the peoples for self-government'.[1] Inevitably, that sense of paternalism did not vanish with independence but was transferred to those colonies still under tutelage, and after their independence it continued as a vestigial feeling which made its presence known during such shocking post-independence events as the Nigerian civil war. It inspired much post-independence British aid.

With impatient African nationalism pushing and British pride retreating, it is not surprising that in the 1960s the Commonwealth was strained by African issues. In the following chapters, attention is directed towards aspects of the African transformation which profoundly affected the Commonwealth. Two of these, South Africa and Rhodesia, caused deep and continued difficulties between Britain and a number of African members, involving other members too. A third, the civil war in Nigeria, did not involve overt dispute between members of the Commonwealth, but contributed greatly to existing strains in the Commonwealth and in Africa.

[1] Hancock, *Colonial self-government*, p. 4.

CHAPTER 8

THE SOUTH AFRICAN PROBLEM

SOUTH AFRICA's anomalous position in the Commonwealth in the 1950s was not new, but became increasingly anachronistic in the circumstances of the time. Viewing the position between the two wars in an earlier volume of this *Survey*, W. K. Hancock had recognized as early as 1941 that 'in the twentieth century it is not religious sentiment, but nationalist or racial sentiment, that is the cause of strife', and had said of the situation in South Africa:

> The ideal which the British Commonwealth professes, the ideal of "equal rights for diverse communities", implies among other things resolute warfare against the substantial inequalities which separate one community from another. South African policy in the period under review has been dominated by a conception clean contrary to this: the Commonwealth theory comes rather battered out of the South African struggle.

Believing that it was too soon to draw final conclusions from this experience, and that the problems of multi-racial community were far more complex and stubborn than humanitarian or segregationist idealists were willing to admit, he recognized that there were possibilities for either destruction or liberation in South Africa.[1]

What happened in the 1950s and 1960s was that the destructive possibilities became greater under the pressure of the apartheid policy of the Nationalist government elected in 1948; that world attention became focused on South Africa's racial situation to a degree unknown before; and that an increasing African membership of the Commonwealth led to attacks on South Africa there, and to South Africa's withdrawal from membership. However, this formal departure did not end the South African problem for the Commonwealth, since South Africa remained the strongest state in its continent, well able to deal with its internal African opposition and to outface the hostility of other African states (including those belonging to the Commonwealth) so long as the major powers remained reluctant to take harsh action against it on account of its racial policy.

Here the South African problem is regarded specifically as a Commonwealth one, without forgetting that it was also a matter of intense international debate. To round off the story, it is necessary to go a little beyond 1969, the terminal date of this book, but the problem was most acute in the 1950s and 1960s, and was bound up with the rise of independent African states in the Commonwealth and in the UN and OAU.

---

[1] Hancock, *Survey*, ii, pt 2, pp. 320–1.

I

The Nationalist government elected in 1948 under Dr D. F. Malan wished to fulfil three traditional aims of Afrikaner Nationalists: the effective separation of the races in South Africa (not long before termed 'apartheid', or separate development) with the whites in a position of dominance; the establishment of a republic on the Afrikaner model; and, consequential on this, termination of membership of the Commonwealth. By the end of 1961 all three had been achieved, but the third in different circumstances from those originally envisaged. The militant Afrikaners who set these goals in the 1940s had been motivated largely by the wish to cast off any vestige of South Africa's former subjugation by Britain, in particular the legacies of the defeat of the Boer republics in 1902. To them, the monarchy had been the prime symbol of that defeat, and the adherence of English-speaking South Africans to the monarchy evidence of their allegiance to a foreign power. The Commonwealth, while acceptable to some of them (those following Hertzog) so long as it continued to stress the sovereign independence of its members, was still suspected because of the previous insistence of many of the Nationalists' opponents that the monarchy was not divisible, and that South Africa could not secede or become a republic without breaking the law. Some feared that Commonwealth membership might enable anti-Nationalist South Africans to fall back, as a last resort, upon help from Britain. These suspicions derived largely from the hectic arguments about 'status' in the 1920s and 1930s, aggravated by the bitterness of World War II, when the war effort of the Smuts government had been strongly opposed by the great majority of Nationalists. They look odd in the 1970s, and have done so ever since the 1949 decision to continue India's membership of the Commonwealth after it had become a republic. In 1948, however, they still had substance to those who held them, and were still feared by those who opposed them.

In practice, the decision of the 1949 Prime Ministers' Meeting on India's continued membership of the Commonwealth settled the matter for the Nationalists. As Smuts complained to a friend, it gave them 'a tarred road to the Republic'.[1] Before that meeting Malan had said, in a BBC broadcast, that 'so long as there is no infringement of her rights, even her right to become a republic, South Africa has no intention of leaving the Commonwealth'.[2] He made the same point with renewed emphasis after the decision was taken;[3] and South Africa remained a member without much internal discussion of the point, until in 1960 its leaders decided to seek republican status, thereby precipitating the chain of events that led to withdrawal (see pp. 142–59).

[1] Hancock, *Smuts* (1968), p. 521.
[2] Broadcast of 28 Apr 1949, in *Dr Malan defines South Africa's position in the Commonwealth* (S. Africa House, London, 1949).
[3] See ibid., pp. 6–20, for Malan's long statement in parliament on 11 May 1949. Mansergh, *Documents 1931–52*, pp. 859–74, has the speeches of both Malan and Smuts.

Meanwhile, the government proceeded to remove a number of symbols of the British connection: the appeal to the Privy Council, the Union Jack as officially one of South Africa's flags and 'God Save the Queen' as one of its anthems, and—later—the Queen's head from its coins when South Africa changed to decimal coinage.[1]

To make the separation of the races more systematic and far-reaching was a longer and more arduous process. Unlike the movement towards a republic, which was essentially symbolic in character, the movement towards total apartheid involved the South African economy. The rapid development of industrialization during World War II and afterwards had caused a substantial increase in the number of Africans in the main cities, especially in the Western Cape and in Johannesburg; these people could not be sent back to their tribal lands, because of the damage such a move would cause to the white man's economy, and because of the lack of jobs and land in the reserves. More than a decade elapsed before the third Nationalist prime minister, Dr Verwoerd, announced plans for marginally increasing employment opportunities in the African homelands—the Bantustans—and establishing industries with white capital on their borders. In the 1950s the government's emphasis was on social and political apartheid, on preventing racial mixing rather than on providing opportunities for each race to develop.

Beginning with the prohibition of mixed marriages in 1949, it proceeded in 1950 to ban extra-marital sexual relations between whites and non-whites, to register the population in strictly racial terms, and to demarcate separate residential areas for each race, including (as did the other measures) Cape Coloureds and Indians as well as Africans. In 1953 it made law what had previously been custom, the provision of 'separate amenities' in all public places. The Group Areas Act of 1954 resulted in 100,000 Africans being shifted from squatter camps in Johannesburg and resettled in new areas. In the political sphere, the government removed the Coloured voters from the common roll, following a five-year legal battle in which this previously 'entrenched' provision of the constitution was nullified. An Act of 1959, establishing machinery for self-government in Bantu homelands, led to the removal of the former (white) Native representatives from the South African parliament.[2] The separation of the races was further enhanced in 1953 by placing

---

[1] See C. F. J. Muller, ed., *Five hundred years* (1969), p. 393, for these and other like changes.

[2] The Commonwealth was invoked as a model for the new system. A White Paper issued with the Bill in March 1959 said the new units 'will eventually form a South African commonwealth together with White South Africa, which will serve as its core and as guardian of the emerging Bantu states. . . . Representation in the guardian's parliament is not a factor which plays a role in the attainment of self-government by the dependent territory. This appears clearly from the history of the growth of the British Commonwealth, where none of the component territories, which were destined for autonomy, at any time had direct representation in the parliament of the United Kingdom. The Commonwealth system is based on the systematic political emancipation of the dependent national and territorial units, following on

African education under central instead of provincial control and making it distinct in character. Another Act of 1959 prohibited non-whites from entering the 'open' universities (those of Cape Town and the Witwatersrand) and provided for a number of new segregated universities for them.[1]

These apartheid measures excited opposition in South Africa and abroad, as will be described, but first it is desirable to delineate the position which South Africa held in the Commonwealth, since this involved something of a paradox.

The paradox arose because, while South Africa's increasingly harsh racial policy became a matter of shocked concern to many people interested in the Commonwealth, and its government's amendment of the entrenched clauses of the South Africa Act seemed to have more than local significance,[2] its racial policy was not challenged in Commonwealth circles. Commonwealth members —especially India and Pakistan—attacked South Africa's policies in the UN, but not in the Commonwealth. Perhaps Nehru was aware that if he challenged South Africa in the Commonwealth context he would give Pakistan an opportunity to raise the Kashmir issue. Perhaps he felt too that the informal atmosphere of Commonwealth meetings would be disrupted—not necessarily to India's advantage—if he indicted South Africa's racialism. He could have cited precedents from the inter-war period, when India brought the treatment of Indians in South Africa before Imperial conferences,[3] but he chose the UN instead, an attitude maintained throughout the 1950s. None of the other members was inclined to raise the question.

Throughout the 1950s South Africa remained a near associate of Britain's in the economic sense, however the gap may have widened between the political stances of the two countries. The South African economy experienced a continuous boom, helped by its wartime industrialization, the devaluation of

proof being furnished by the different units of their ability to govern themselves in a progressive manner . . .' (*The state of South Africa*, no. 14, S. Africa House, London, Apr 1959.)

[1] Much of the detail in this paragraph is from Muller, pp. 384–7. See Mansergh, *Documents 1952–62*, pp. 306–46, for material on several of the important measures.

[2] For a time the learned discussion of these matters formed an important aspect of Commonwealth studies. See, e.g., Geoffrey Marshall, *Parliamentary sovereignty and the Commonwealth* (1957), and K. C. Wheare, *The constitutional structure of the Commonwealth* (1960), ch. 3. In the 1960s the movement of various Commonwealth members away from recognized constitutional procedures based on those of Britain weakened the comparative significance of these studies.

[3] See Hancock, *Survey*, i, 183–7, and *Smuts*, pp. 147–9. It might be argued that the Indian government did not wish to cite precedents from the period when, although there was a government of India, it was controlled by Britain. But India had not disdained other legacies of this period, including India House in London and India's membership of the UN, which began before independence because India had been a member of the League of Nations, all members of which were automatically founder members of the UN. In any case the original Indian attack on S. Africa at the UN in 1946 was based on the Cape Town agreement of 1927 between S. Africa and India, which the Indians maintained was a treaty and which S. Africa said was not (Hancock, *Smuts*, pp. 456, 468).

sterling in 1949 (which further stimulated the gold mining industry), the development of new goldfields in the Orange Free State and the West Rand, and the discovery of uranium. South Africa was a fertile field for British trade and investment. It also afforded employment for Africans from the British dependencies of Nyasaland and the High Commission Territories of Basutoland, Bechuanaland, and Swaziland. The future of these territories was still unresolved. Malan considered that Britain should redeem the promise, embodied in the South Africa Act, that they should be absorbed into the Union, but the British insisted that their inhabitants should be consulted, and Churchill gave a firm negative reply in 1954. Nevertheless, the South African commission appointed in 1950 to draw up a scheme for the 'rehabilitation of the Native Areas' (the Tomlinson Commission) included the three territories in the seven Bantustans it proposed to establish.

It was significant that in 1958 the British government agreed to give South Africa certain defence planning facilities in the three territories, including over-flying rights, access through Basutoland to a radar site in Union territory, and reconnaissance of an emergency route to South-West Africa across Bechuanaland.[1] During the 1950s there had been considerable British concern about the Middle East and the security of the British lines of communication to sources of oil, and to India, Malaya, and Australia; it was also felt that some arrangement in Africa was needed to complement Nato, Cento, and Seato. South Africa's participation in regional defence would have satisfied both these British aims: the Cape route was the alternative to Suez, and was guarded by South Africa, although the actual naval operations were, on the whole, conducted by the Royal Navy, which still controlled the long-established base at Simonstown. South Africa was, however, not an ideal partner because of its bad reputation in Asia and its refusal to arm its Africans, so that its military effectiveness beyond its own borders was confined to small units such as the air squadron it had contributed to the Korean war. On the other hand Britain was indispensable for South Africa if it was to be a part of the western alliance system. Britain was a traditional connection through which the US and the European members of Nato could be expected to approach any association with South Africa. In the absence of British goodwill, the debits involved in making an ally of South Africa might well be likely to exceed any credit for other western countries.

For South Africa, the Simonstown Agreement of 1955, providing *inter alia* that sea lanes round South Africa needed to be secured against 'external aggression', seemed to herald further association with the Nato powers. This agreement, which had been preceded by conferences at Nairobi in 1951 and Dakar in 1954, would, it was hoped, form part of a general security arrangement for European powers in Africa. The Nairobi conference had been attended by France, Portugal, Italy, Belgium, Ethiopia, Egypt, and Southern

[1] *The Times*, 18 July 1958.

Rhodesia, as well as Britain and South Africa. The US sent an observer. The Dakar conference had been confined to countries with interests in West Africa, but it too had shown that the European powers were interested in joint arrangements for the movement of troops and supplies. South Africa was interested in the defence of both Africa and the Middle East, with a preference for some kind of general European security body which would encompass Africa;[1] according to the defence minister, the absence of formal organization between anti-communist countries interested in defence south of the Sahara 'constituted a serious gap in the anti-communist security network of the Western powers'.[2] However, the projected general security arrangement 'gradually fell to bits as it became clear that South Africa's racial policies would permit of no co-operation with black African nations, as the Central African Federation collapsed, and when South Africa left the Commonwealth in 1961'.[3]

In addition, from 1954 onwards American interest was concentrated on Southeast Asia, and the US had no wish to identify itself with the perpetuation of white rule in Africa, especially since there seemed no prospect of Soviet military involvement. At the same time as western interest in an African security organization was lessening, the international unpopularity of South African apartheid was growing; and the appearance of independent African states from 1957 onwards, with the concomitant reduction of European power and interest, put paid to any South African ideas of alliance. All the same, the closure of the Suez Canal in 1956 underlined the importance of the Cape route. Although South Africa was not to become part of a white man's alliance in Africa, its importance as a way-station on the high seas continued to be stressed.

It was in this context that the Simonstown Agreement of 1955 was concluded; it was not a treaty but an exchange of letters between the British and South African governments.[4] The agreement affirmed joint interest in Southern Africa and the Middle East, and an intention to convene a conference to carry forward the work begun at Nairobi (an aspiration which was not fulfilled); it also dealt with the transfer of the Simonstown naval base to the South African government by the end of March 1957, the purchase of naval vessels by South Africa in Britain, the joint defence of the sea routes around South Africa, and the use of Simonstown by the Royal Navy in both peace and war, even a war in which South Africa was not a co-belligerent. From a South African point of view, the main achievement was the replacement of the Royal Navy by the South African Navy as the custodian of Simonstown; from the British standpoint, it was the guarantee that Simonstown would continue to be available.

[1] Ibid., 12 Aug 1954.   [2] Senate debate, 7 Mar 1955.
[3] Alastair Buchan, 'Commonwealth military relations', in W. B. Hamilton & others, eds, *A decade of the Commonwealth* (1966), p. 196.
[4] See Cmd 9520 (1955). The main letter from the British minister of defence is in Mansergh, *Documents 1952–62*, p. 456.

There was little opposition to the agreement at the time: it was a matter of convenience, well in line with traditional arrangements. In Commonwealth terms, no more was heard of it until late in the 1960s, in circumstances described below. It did, however, constitute a real link between the two governments.

The Commonwealth of the mid-1950s was thus a congenial place for South Africa. It did not bar republics, if South Africa should become one. It provided a possible way in to the western defence system. It was associated with the monarchical symbols which English-speaking South Africans still valued, and so helped to reconcile them to Nationalist rule. It embodied the preference system which enabled South African wine, sugar, and fruits to find markets in Britain. Moreover, while it included India, a traditional bête noir to white South Africans, it evidently constrained the Indians to take a less hostile line towards South Africa than at the UN. Other than the UN, it was the only major international body to which South Africa belonged; and the UN had become so uncongenial a place by the end of 1956 that South Africa decided to continue only token membership of it.[1] The only drawback of the Commonwealth was the possibility that black African states might also become members and attack South Africa's racial policy. What would happen then?

This was part of a general problem about which thinking South Africans had speculated for some time, the problem of South Africa's relations with other African states if the tide of European power should some day ebb. Afrikaner tradition opposed imperialism, especially British imperialism, and South Africa had strongly supported Abyssinia against Italy in 1935, on the ground that there should be no further extension of European imperialism in Africa.[2] It was also widely believed that South Africa, the richest and most developed part of the continent, had a mission to help other parts, especially in technical matters, but also militarily. It was the natural leader of the white regimes. In 1942 Smuts wrote to a friend, after visits from the governor-general of Angola and the prime minister of Southern Rhodesia:

> . . . It seems as if we have now to carry all the smaller fry of Africa on our back. . . . I make a point of it to help as far as we can, and a little farther, mindful of the advice of scripture to cast your bread upon the waters. We are quite popular nowadays, and hope that something greater may be built on these foundations. . . . They may yet be in the net. I am working on some such plan as that of the Pan-American Union of our Yankee friends.[3]

Such views could have been echoed by even the most militant Nationalist. But there was another side to the picture. If the European powers should go, especially from the areas on South Africa's borders, would that not threaten the position of the white man in South Africa? If black governments should

---

[1] For the announcement, see *The Times*, 28 Nov 1956. Full participation in UN activities was resumed in July 1958.

[2] See Mansergh, *Survey 1931–9*, pp. 230–1.   [3] Ibid., p. 411.

come into being in Southern Africa, as well as in East and West Africa, might they not link up with militant Africans in the Union itself? Would such governments accept leadership or help from a white-dominated South Africa, even though it was clearly in their material interests to do so?

The answer of the Nationalist government, after some hesitation, was to choose 'co-operative co-existence' in Africa,[1] while stressing the vital importance of non-interference by states in one another's affairs, an approach embodied in an address at Pretoria University by Eric Louw, the minister for external affairs, in March 1957. South Africa had to accept its future role in Africa as a vocation, he said. It would not only have to co-operate with European states which had interests and responsibilities there, as it was already doing through CCTA,[2] but must also be prepared to co-operate in matters of common concern with all other states which might be established south of the Sahara. Three conditions were necessary. They were the removal of African suspicion about the Union's colour policy—which would be a gradual process; the acceptance of the Union as an African state by other African states; and the willingness of South Africa as a highly developed country to contribute to solving common problems. The national pride of other states should be recognized and honoured. South African policy and conduct must be such that other states and territories of Africa would accept the Union as their link with western countries.[3] These high ambitions were to be pursued by South Africa in spite of disappointments.

In the Commonwealth sphere, the approach was tested first in respect of Ghana, whose relatively slow movement towards independence had allowed time for considerable speculation about what attitude South Africa would take. Malan had demurred about the possibility of Commonwealth membership as early as 1951, asking that no new members be admitted without existing members' approval. The British government hastened to assure him that there would be full consultation.[4] In 1956, when Gold Coast independence was decided on, it was made clear that Commonwealth membership was a separate matter depending on the attitude of the existing members.[5] The Strijdom government had modified Malan's view. In public (though not in private), Ghana was welcomed when it became sovereign in 1957. South Africa sent the head of the Africa Division of its Department of External Affairs to Accra as high commissioner extraordinary for the celebrations. On Ghana radio he said that the two countries shared many interests and Africa

---

[1] The title of a leaflet issued by S. Africa House, London, in February 1956 (*The state of South Africa*, no. 5).

[2] The Commission for Technical Co-operation in Africa south of the Sahara, established in 1950. S. Africa provided much scientific and technical help before being ousted from it in the 1960s.

[3] *Modern South Africa* (S. Africa House, London), Apr 1957.

[4] Mansergh, *Documents 1931–52*, pp. 1287–9 and Wheare, pp. 120–4.

[5] HC Deb., 11 May 1956, col. 1558.

had a great destiny, but it could be achieved only on the basis of reciprocal confidence and co-operation among the nations of Africa. Nkrumah, for his part, told a correspondent of *Die Burger* of Cape Town that he wished to maintain the best possible relations with the Union. He appreciated the scientific and technical contributions South Africans could make to solving Africa's problems. Although he personally detested all forms of apartheid, and would attack it on a political platform, this issue need not necessarily affect state-to-state relations. 'As long as South Africa maintains friendly relations with Ghana we will be friendly towards South Africa', he said. 'The time has come when the states in Africa should enforce their rights as states of Africa and not as appendages of other groups like the Asiatic group.'[1]

Such sentiments, appropriate to the euphoria of independence celebrations, do not necessarily last, any more than a high commissioner extraordinary is easily turned into an ordinary one. The negotiations on diplomatic relations were protracted and led to nothing. As well as the social problems of how to deal with a black envoy, the South African government became increasingly aware of Ghana's anti-colonialist activities.[2] Nkrumah invited South Africa to the first conference of independent African states held in Accra in January 1958, but South Africa declined on the ground that the objectives of the meeting could not be achieved unless the colonial governments with direct responsibility in Africa were also invited.[3] Relations gradually deteriorated, and in 1960, after the Commonwealth Prime Ministers' Meeting discussed below, Nkrumah's agents began to try to set up a South African 'government-in-exile' in Accra, composed of political refugees.[4]

This chain of events illustrates the difficulties of South Africa's position in Africa and in the Commonwealth. The government was not prepared to modify apartheid or to do what it regarded as wrong simply because other states disapproved of what it was doing. It presumably hoped that if it showed friendship and help towards the new states as they appeared, it would have the support of the major colonial powers—Britain, France, Belgium, and Portugal —against any infringement of South African sovereignty. It strongly asserted the same right of domestic jurisdiction as other states. Its difficulties arose when the European powers, moving out of Africa, showed themselves reluctant to be closely associated with South Africa, partly because of active dislike of apartheid and partly because they wished to retain good relations with their former colonies. The new states, for their part, while asserting domestic jurisdiction in their own cases and especially against one another, regarded South

---

[1] *The state of South Africa*, no. 8, Mar 1957.

[2] See W. Scott Thompson, pp. 28 & 42–3.   [3] *Modern South Africa*, Dec 1957.

[4] W. Scott Thompson, pp. 97–8. Thompson comments of these refugees: 'In the end, no groups were to be more disillusioned with Nkrumah. For one thing, they doubted his commitment to their cause owing to his caution in the Commonwealth. For another, these well-educated men were not prepared to pay the price of deference to and praise of Nkrumah which was required to maintain his financial backing.'

African racial policy as affecting the whole of Africa and therefore 'international' rather than 'domestic'.

In the Commonwealth context, South Africa could also plead domestic jurisdiction, especially since such a plea was important to a number of other members, from India to Australia. It could rely on the British government not to fling aside all the economic and strategic advantages of its association with South Africa, in order to please new members. What it could not rely on, however, was active *support* from Britain. This was the lesson of the Prime Ministers' Meetings of 1960 and 1961.

Before describing these meetings it is desirable to indicate the nature and extent of the opposition to apartheid in the Union itself and throughout the world.

II

Within South Africa itself, there was considerable opposition from the start. It was not uniform, and it varied from issue to issue.[1] The United Party, the main parliamentary Opposition, was suspicious of Nationalist intentions even when it had no direct criticism of the measures which came before parliament. It was not in favour of integration or racial equality, but it strongly believed in the constitution as a form of pact between the Afrikaans and English-speaking groups, and feared that if the government were able to act unconstitutionally on one matter—e.g. on the Coloured franchise—it would be able to do so on others, especially the entrenchment of English as an official language. The UP was in any case inclined to identify the Nationalists with totalitarian methods. It was thus at least sympathetic towards protests such as those of the Torch Commando and Black Sash movements, and made an issue of measures which seemed to threaten the rule of law or the liberty of the subject. It was debarred, however, by its own convictions and those of its electorate from attacking apartheid root and branch since much of the new legislation only codified or extended existing practice in all or parts of the Union. Increasingly, it became as much annoyed as the government by the attacks in the UN and the campaigns instigated or encouraged by the OAU.

So far as the white population was concerned, the burden of opposition to apartheid fell on those known in South Africa as 'liberals' who, while not always accepting the idea or the implications of such a slogan as 'one man one vote', wanted an extension of the former Cape ideal of 'equal rights for all civilized men'. These worked first in the United Party, then moved, in some cases, to form new parties (the Liberal and Progressive) in the 1950s. They were also prominent in Church and academic circles, the student bodies of

---

[1] A valuable study is Janet Robertson, *Liberalism in South Africa* (1971). The bibliography is especially helpful.

South Africa's two 'open' universities being especially notable for resistance to apartheid. The difficulties of the liberals arose partly from the growing restrictions placed upon inter-racial political activity by the government, but largely because they were going against the grain of white society in South Africa. At each election the government got a bigger share of the vote.

There was also opposition from African, Indian, and Coloured groups, most notably the ANC (African National Congress), from which the PAC (Pan-African Congress) split off in 1959. These bodies, led by some of the educated Africans and based largely on the shifting African populations of the towns, organized boycotts and protests about such measures as the pass laws and the forcible population transfers. They became more radical and more inclined to violence as their failure to effect peaceful change became more obvious; and their banning by the government in 1960, together with the detention of many of their leaders at various times, rendered them ineffective.

The ineffectiveness of all forms of outright opposition in South Africa arose from the strong grip which the government kept on political activity and from the apathy of the majority. Through the Suppression of Communism Act and a variety of other measures the government clamped down on radical criticism. While the Communist Party of South Africa had always been small, it had been very active in stimulating white and non-white opposition in the 1940s. The government's identification of all radical opposition with communism was highly plausible to the white electorate in the 1950s and 1960s— especially since communist states were amongst South Africa's shrillest international critics. The black opposition movements, racked by internal divisions, depleted of leaders through imprisonments and escapes to foreign countries, and prevented from advancing their aims constitutionally, turned to sporadic violence which was easily put down. The effect was to solidify white opinion still further. White liberals were easily discredited as exponents of social mixing and equal rights. Although the English-speaking press of South Africa continued to be highly critical of the government's performance—and paradoxically to be, as time went on, the freest opposition press in the continent —its opposition was essentially about means, not ends.

Quiescence amongst the blacks, Coloureds, and Indians is often explained in terms of repression, implying that the granting of normal civil rights would have led to peaceful change; but this is only part of the explanation. Probably more important was the effect of the combination of 'economic cement' and 'linked utilities'.[1] Not only did the South African boom ensure that 'anticipated incomes were outstripped by real incomes'; it also demonstrated to blacks that their higher incomes were linked with the improvement of white men's incomes. Instead of increasing poverty amongst the three non-white groups, there was increasing prosperity. The combination of prosperity and

[1] These terms are used by Edward Feit, *African opposition in South Africa* (1967). See pp. 10–22 for his highly convincing argument.

repression is always likely to stimulate the ordinary man's conviction that economics is more important than politics; and so it proved amongst those groups in South Africa whose political rights were being eroded or removed. It was a source of disappointment, even annoyance, to anti-apartheid campaigners abroad that the victims of apartheid showed so little inclination to combine against it. As in Rhodesia after 1965, the combination of repression with prosperity proved to be sufficient explanation.

Such influences did not operate to discourage opposition abroad. In the 1950s and 1960s international opposition to South Africa built up to a point perhaps never reached in respect of any other state, or not reached without war breaking out. It combined hostility from states with hostility from groups of people within states. The opposition from states that had begun with pre-independence India, extended in the 1950s to all the Asian, African, Middle East, and Latin American states represented in the UN, with the possible exception of Israel. In the 1960s some European states without colonies and with a liberal view of racial questions, notably the Scandinavians, increased the number. To all these groups were added, from the start, the communist countries of Eastern Europe and the Soviet Union, as well as North Korea, North Vietnam, Cuba, and China. Most West European and North American states were at first ambivalent, but by the mid-1960s the only state habitually voting with South Africa on questions involving South African racial policy at the UN was Portugal. Britain and Australia, which throughout the 1950s had supported it at the UN, not because they agreed with apartheid but because they regarded it as a matter of domestic jurisdiction, abandoned this position in 1961, rather later than Canada, New Zealand, and the US. The determination with which these states opposed South Africa varied greatly: some appeared to do so from deep conviction, others from prudence, others from habit, and others again from cynical calculation of their individual interests. To all, however, it had become a normal practice to denounce apartheid.

Left-wing, liberal, and other minority groups opposed apartheid in much the same way as in the 1930s they had opposed Nazi Germany. The communist parties of the world, whether inclined towards Moscow or Peking, could unite in condemnation of South Africa and in attempts to attract others to communist causes under an anti-apartheid banner. Trade unions and Labour parties passed resolutions supporting UN General Assembly propositions that South Africa be brought to book. Proponents of civil rights and of minority groups' struggles for equality attacked apartheid even if they had nothing to do with Africa, because the South African regime was the only one which elevated racial discrimination into a principle.

Public opinion in the older Commonwealth countries, especially Britain, was greatly affected. Political refugees from South Africa, whether white or non-white, mostly fled to Britain, where they found ready acceptance in left-wing, church, and civil rights groups and in the press. A variety of anti-apartheid organizations sprang up.[1] Strong feelings against South Africa were apparent in the churches, in student organizations, in most organs of mass communication, in academic circles, and in many popular books. British opinion, reflected in journals like the *Observer*, the (*Manchester*) *Guardian*, and *The Economist*, made an impact on Australia, Canada, and New Zealand. Few countries can ever have had so bad a press as South Africa. Much of the turbulence came from intellectuals, but in the end the man in the street was affected in the main sphere in which South Africa had been widely known in Britain, Australia, and New Zealand—sport. In the 1960s Rugby Union tours between South Africa and New Zealand were endangered by the South African government's insistence that Maoris should not be included in New Zealand touring teams; in 1968 an MCC side to tour South Africa was banned by that country because it included a former Cape Coloured player, Basil d'Oliveira; in 1970 agitation in Britain brought about the cancellation of a South African cricket tour; in 1971 the same occurred with a South African tour of Australia.[2] All this was new.

The interaction between state and private opposition to South Africa's policies was considerable. The communist states encouraged left-wing movements in non-communist countries; the South African refugees fed these and the liberal movements; vocal minorities pressurized their governments. Above all, the African states, from 1960 onwards, tried to make up for their own incapacity to influence South Africa by putting pressure on the major powers to act. For a decade after 1957 the western and communist powers were competing, at the diplomatic level, for the good opinion of the new African states; it is not surprising that they should have paid attention to the criticisms of South Africa. The African states exerted pressure indirectly as well through sympathizers in the western states, such as the anti-colonialists in Britain. South Africa was thus not only an international issue but also a domestic issue in all Commonwealth countries, where few were prepared to stand up for its indefensible approach to racial questions.

The UN provided the main arena for the attack on apartheid.[3] Following India's criticism of South Africa at the first session of the General Assembly,

[1] A number are described in Harold Soref & Ian Greig, *The puppeteers* (1965), a book to be read with caution, since the authors' anti-communist fervour sometimes obscures their judgement. For a strong statement of the contemporary case against South Africa, see Colin & Margaret Legum, *South Africa: crisis for the west* (1964).

[2] For some of these incidents, see Terry McLean, *The Bok busters* (1965) and Irving Rosenwater, 'The South African tour dispute', *Wisden Cricketers' Almanac 1971*, pp. 128–41.

[3] See Millar, *Commonwealth & UN*, ch. 4, for a long and detailed account of the issues of South African treatment of Indians, South-West Africa, and apartheid, as dealt with by the UN. See also Dennis Austin, *Britain and South Africa* (1966), pp. 95 ff. for a condensed account. Millar's treatment of domestic jurisdiction (a matter of some importance in the Commonwealth context) may be compared with that of M. S. Rajan, *The UN and domestic jurisdiction* (1961).

the offensive was progressively enlarged. It was already well established before the advent of the new African states, but their presence gave it impetus. Three issues were brought forward. The first in point of time, the treatment of Indians in South Africa, was gradually merged into a full-scale attack on the second, the whole practice of apartheid. The third, which had been before the UN since 1946, was South African control of South-West Africa through the League of Nations mandate. Smuts had refused to agree to the transformation of the mandate into a UN trusteeship agreement; his successors took the same line. The matter had been continuously before the General Assembly without any effect on South African control of the territory.

Indeed, it can be argued that there was no change in South African policy on any of the three issues, and that the attacks at the UN had amounted to no more than beating the air. In spite of resolutions of the Assembly, and attempts to get the Security Council to impose economic sanctions, neither the South African government's control of its country nor its electoral support were affected. Britain and the US, while willing to join in condemning apartheid as a policy, were not prepared to regard South Africa's actions as a breach of the peace, thus justifying intervention. South Africa was certainly isolated; and, to the extent that there is such a thing as 'world opinion', it was decisively against South Africa. But the South African economy continued to grow, the world (including some communist states) to trade with it, and the western powers to support South Africa's continued existence as a member of the international community. This was the position in 1969, after more than twenty years of Afro-Asian opposition at the UN.

The constant international opposition to the Nationalist government and to apartheid had some obvious effects in South Africa itself. For a time it encouraged resisters to think that they would get international support for their attack on the government, and that reprisals against them would not be so savage as if only white South African opinion had to be considered. The relative freedom of English-speaking white liberals probably owed something to the government's desire not to alienate opinion in other English-speaking countries, especially Britain. But international support was counter-productive. Although sympathizers abroad might subscribe money to defend resisters at the treason trials which the government held, they could not directly affect the operations of the government, and their very generosity and support could be represented to the electorate as evidence of an international conspiracy against South Africa, which was reinforced by the money and training given by the OAU and by communist states to South African 'freedom fighters': white electors naturally felt apprehension and hostility towards such efforts to overthrow the state structure from which they derived their privileges. There seems little doubt that one of the main effects of international opposition was to draw the Afrikaans and English-speaking groups closer together in support of the government, thus reducing what had been traditionally the major cleavage in South African politics. The myth of an international conspiracy engineered by communists was a potent one.[1]

III

In discussing international opposition to the South African regime we have moved ahead in time to the end of the 1960s, well after South Africa left the Commonwealth. It is now necessary to go back to 1960, the year of the 'wind of change' speech, of the Sharpeville incident, of Verwoerd's declaration of a referendum to decide whether South Africa would become a republic, and of the first overt condemnation of South Africa within the official Commonwealth context.

To the world at large the main message of Macmillan's 'wind of change' speech was the importance of African nationalism and British support for the independence of former colonies. To the South Africans, however, its importance lay rather in those passages in which, while paying tribute to South African achievements and recognizing the peculiar nature of the problems of the country, Macmillan stressed that Britain fostered fellowship between the different communities in the colonies which it led towards self-government and rejected the idea of any inherent superiority of one race over another. He had also pointed out that, while Commonwealth countries respected each other's sovereignty in matters of internal policy, in 'this shrinking world in which we live today, the internal policies of one nation may have effects outside it. . . . I would myself expand the old saying so that it runs "Mind your own business, of course, but mind how it affects my business too".' In effect, he disengaged Britain from public support for South Africa:

As a fellow member of the Commonwealth we always try and, I think, we have succeeded, in giving to South Africa our full support and encouragement, but I hope you won't mind my saying frankly that there are some aspects of your policies which make it impossible for us to do this without being false to our own deep convictions about the political destinies of free men to which in our own territories we are trying to give effect.[2]

[1] See J. E. Spence, *Republic under pressure* (1965), ch. 2, and Edwin S. Munger, *Afrikaner and African nationalism* (1967), ch. 6, for the closer relations between the two white groups. In the myth-making field, many Afrikaner pronouncements would provide examples, but a single one from an academic source may suffice. The editor of the collected volume of Prime Minister Verwoerd's speeches, who was Professor of History at Pretoria University, wrote of the UN: 'This organization . . . soon deteriorated into a battle scene between the Western democracies and Communist Russia. In order to assert itself in this world body, the latter *engineered the membership* of a large number of young and altogether immature states from Africa and Asia' (A. N. Pelzer, ed., *Verwoerd speaks*, 1966, p. liv; emphasis added). A man who could believe the italicized words could believe anything.

[2] The quotations are from Mansergh, *Documents 1952–62*, pp. 347–51. See Pelzer, pp. 336–9 for Verwoerd's reply, in which he defended S. Africa as a link between black and white states. See also p. 562 for Verwoerd's explanation in April 1961 that, while Macmillan had 'lightheartedly dropped a hint' in the speech about future British behaviour at the UN, he had 'said so candidly' in conversation with Verwoerd.

The essence of the speech was that South Africa could no longer count on British support at the UN, and it raised doubt whether Britain might withdraw support in other spheres too. It induced something of a note of uncertainty in South Africa and gave Macmillan some room for manoeuvre in his future negotiations with other Commonwealth countries in Africa.[1]

Macmillan's statements about South Africa have to be seen in the context of Verwoerd's announcement, a fortnight before, that the South African electorate would be asked in the near future to decide whether South Africa should become a republic. Verwoerd had also raised the matter of continuing membership of the Commonwealth, and had said he would announce what the government's policy was on this before the referendum. Amongst the considerations he would have in mind would be the position in Britain; in particular, if the Labour Party came to power and displayed the same hostility as it was showing in opposition, he would seriously consider 'taking the lead in no longer allowing South Africa to remain a member'. Similarly, if the policies of other members of the Commonwealth meant 'quarrelling around one table', he might take the same view. He was making it clear that South Africa's future membership of the Commonwealth would depend on how the members treated South Africa.[2] Macmillan, for his part, responded by refusing to bind himself to acquiesce in all that South Africa might do.

On 21 March the Sharpeville incident occurred. It was to be, in many ways, a watershed in South African affairs, increasing the severity of the government's handling of internal opposition, and intensifying opposition abroad. It arose from PAC demonstrations against the pass laws which were intended to be non-violent. At Sharpeville, near Vereeniging in the Transvaal, a large crowd of Africans was fired on by a handful of young white policemen, who were scared of suffering the fate of white and black police at the hands of an angry mob in Natal a few days before. The officer in charge had given no order to fire. The police fired for only a few seconds, most of the mob immediately turned to flee and were shot from behind. Sixty-seven Africans were killed and 186 wounded. Similar events at Langa near Cape Town produced fewer casualties. Press photographs of the unintended massacre at Sharpeville were seen throughout the world and increased the sense of outrage which had been building up in many countries. International reactions were widespread and highly condemnatory; nor was world opinion improved by the measures taken by the South African government to restore order. They included the

[1] There is something of a dismissed Lord Chancellor's pique in Lord Kilmuir's statement (p. 316) that 'the principal effect of the "wind of change" speech was, of course, the secession of South Africa from the Commonwealth' and that it 'enormously encouraged some of the new members of the Commonwealth to strike a dramatic pose as the guardians of the rights of man', though note should be taken of these views. One cannot, however, agree that S. Africa's departure was 'a direct consequence of one unguarded phrase in a single speech' (p. 317). There was nothing unguarded about it, and more than one phrase was involved.

[2] Pelzer, pp. 332–5 (speech of 20 Jan 1960). Also in Mansergh, *Documents 1952–62*, pp. 358–62.

banning of public meetings and of the ANC and PAC, the declaration of a state of emergency with 1,200 pre-dawn arrests of people of all races, and in the next two months some 17,000 further arrests.[1] From one point of view such firmness had the desired effect—there were no other massive demonstrations of African discontent in the 1960s. But adverse effects abroad resulted in renewed and extended diplomatic pressure. It is against this background that the Commonwealth treatment of South Africa's proposed republican status, at the Prime Ministers' Meetings of 1960 and 1961, must be viewed.

IV

Much has been written about these meetings, especially the second.[2] It is desirable here to show how discussion ebbed and flowed, and who took what position. Beforehand, it is worth making some general points about the way in which the two meetings led to South Africa's withdrawal.

It is clear from the record that there was little or nothing of a concerted attack on South Africa, despite what some South Africans said afterwards. The other Commonwealth leaders made plain their dislike of apartheid, but did so from a variety of standpoints and seemed more often to be competing with one another than co-operating. Towards the end of the 1961 meeting there was something of a competition to exceed one another in criticism; but this followed on a long period of hesitancy for most of them, during which the possible consequences of discussing a member's domestic circumstances against its will were being inwardly debated. 'Use every man after his desert, and who should scape whipping?' had long been an unspoken Commonwealth precept.

Perhaps because of this widespread initial hesitancy, the personal element seemed to be of greater importance at these meetings than in some others. Tunku Abdul Rahman, Eric Louw, Nehru, Nkrumah, and Diefenbaker figured in significant episodes which might have turned out quite differently if other men had been in their places. In particular, Louw's conduct in 1960 provoked adverse reactions from the Tunku. Nkrumah's manoeuvring, in turn, had important effects in 1961.

The combination of the 'domestic issue' aspect and the special character

---

[1] The account of Sharpeville is based on Munger, p. 108, and on Robertson, p. 205. Details of world reactions are in Peter Calvocoressi, *South Africa and world opinion* (1961), pp. 3–11. See pp. 26–7 for the fall in S. African share prices and the drain of capital out of the Union. The success of the government's repressive measures restored the economic situation, and the S. African boom was resumed.

[2] The material includes S. A. de Smith, 'The Commonwealth and South Africa', *Univ. Malaya Law R.*, Dec 1961; J. D. B. Miller, 'South Africa's departure', *JCPS*, Nov 1961; Peter Harnetty, 'Canada, South Africa, and the Commonwealth', ibid., Nov 1963; Menzies, *Afternoon light*, ch. 9; and Macmillan, *Pointing the way* (1972), chs. 6 & 10. There is a section in Mansergh, *Documents 1952–62*, pp. 356–400. I have also had the benefit of a narrative prepared by Mrs M. Cooksey.

of the discussion made some of the prime ministers search for 'international' aspects of apartheid, especially those with particular application to the Commonwealth, in order to dignify the protests which they wished to make about the policy. Contrary to some beliefs, the whole discussion did not turn on whether South Africa, as a republic, could remain in the Commonwealth, although this was the formal occasion for it. After Sharpeville some prime ministers felt impelled to bring up apartheid as an issue in its own right, if this could be squared with existing Commonwealth conventions. The republican issue, which was of great importance to the South Africans, did not matter to anyone else. In the upshot, in spite of the divergent approaches and the hesitations, the decisive aspect seems to have been the sense of responsibility which a number of prime ministers felt towards their own electorates and towards those Africans who were as yet unrepresented but whose cause was eloquently pleaded in private messages and public statements by Julius Nyerere, and who were thus present, as it were, unseen.

Some of these circumstances were foreshadowed in Commonwealth parliaments after Macmillan announced in December 1959 that a Prime Ministers' Meeting would take place in May 1960. British discussions did not mention South Africa but were about whether the Federation of Rhodesia and Nyasaland should attend the meeting although it was not independent, while Nigeria, which would become independent shortly after the meeting, would not attend. There was also some demur because the Federation of the West Indies was not being invited.[1] But South Africa was mentioned in the Canadian parliament in January 1960, after a meeting between Diefenbaker and the Canadian Labour Congress, which had asked for South Africa's 'exclusion from the councils of Commonwealth nations'.[2] Diefenbaker said he would not support any action to exclude the Union 'regardless of my strong feelings in respect of discrimination'. Pressed by the opposition, however, he said there were 'no vetoes on discussion'.[3] Verwoerd's announcement of 20 January that there would be a referendum on the question of a republic excited little interest in Britain, Canada, or elsewhere in the Commonwealth.

Sharpeville changed the situation. It was debated in a number of Commonwealth parliaments and in a great many newspapers. In the Indian parliament on 23 March, when the matter was raised, Nehru displayed the hesitancy which was to characterize a number of other Commonwealth leaders:

> Normally . . . this is not a matter which this House should discuss, I mean some internal matter within the internal jurisdiction of some other country . . .
>
> Nevertheless, something has happened at the Langa township near Cape Town

[1] HC Deb., 15 Dec 1959, cols. 1249–51. Macmillan also had to face opposition from Nkrumah to the attendance of the Federation of Rhodesia and Nyasaland, when he visited Accra in January 1960. Nkrumah was not, however, in favour of Nigeria's being invited (*The Times*, 8 Jan 1960).

[2] Richard A. Preston, *Canada in world affairs 1959–61* (1965), p. 201.

[3] Canada, HC Deb., 29 Jan 1960, pp. 491–2.

which has shocked the conscience of the world . . . so that a situation arises when our normal approaches and even normal rules and procedures are not always adequate to deal with it.

I do admit that it would be wrong, at the present moment, to discuss this matter. . . . But I am not clear in my mind how far it should not be permissible some time or other later to find some way for this House to express its opinion . . .[1]

He did not want a formal resolution at this stage, but three days later changed his mind and sponsored one deploring the events at Sharpeville and Langa, and expressing sympathy to the Africans who had suffered in these cases and from the policy of racial discrimination. He extended the idea of abnormality which he had previously expressed:

. . . It is not the custom of this House normally to consider such matters which are supposed to be in the internal jurisdiction of another country, nor indeed would we like the other countries to consider matters in the internal jurisdiction of this country . . . Nevertheless, sometimes, things happen . . . which are not normal at all . . . and then it becomes difficult or undesirable for some normal convention to come in the way of the expression of the feeling which is deep-seated and powerful. . . .[2]

In the parliament of Malaya, whose prime minister, Tunku Abdul Rahman, would be attending his first Prime Ministers' Meeting, there was a shrill debate on a mild resolution, the note of shrillness being voiced by the Tunku himself. The resolution recognized the South African government's responsibility 'for its own internal policies and administration' but expressed 'abhorrence' at the violence used in pursuance of apartheid. Speaking of the coming meeting, the Tunku said:

. . . Are we going there just to talk platitudes with a country whose hands are stained with red blood of innocent human beings?. . . . Are we to stand by and say nothing, do nothing? I think not—and I intend to speak out, be it at formal meetings or informal meetings of Commonwealth Prime Ministers . . .

Those who rule South Africa today . . . do not conform to our Commonwealth ideas and ideals of human rights and justice, and I am beginning to think whether a country like South Africa has any right to be within this family of nations. . . .[3]

Nevertheless, he made a distinction between the shootings and the policy, saying that if there had been no shooting, this motion would not have been brought up and adding that apartheid policy was 'purely a domestic and internal affair of South Africa'; it was only 'because it was followed by these atrocities that we have taken this stand'.[4] Thus the Tunku was clearly seized with the traditional Commonwealth convention of non-interference in domestic affairs. That convention was the main theme of Menzies on 29 March and again when the Australian parliament debated Sharpeville two days later. As he put it:

[1] India, Lok Sabha Deb., 23 Mar 1960, p. 7547.   [2] Ibid., 28 Mar 1960, pp. 8373-4.
[3] Malaya, HR Deb., 26 Apr 1960, pp. 602-8.   [4] Ibid., p. 629.

... I should offer a word of warning against the danger of abandoning certain principles which are of very great importance not only in the British Commonwealth of Nations but also in the world at large. . . . The greatest of these principles is that one government . . . does not interfere in matters which are within the domestic jurisdiction of another. . . . We do have our own native population and we do have . . . our own responsibilities in respect of Papua and New Guinea. If we are too free in asserting that what happens in South Africa is a matter for international jurisdiction, we may well step out of the light into the darkness on this matter. . . . We may well find that . . . somebody will be willing to assert at some time or other . . . that we, in relation either to our own internal population or to the population of our Territories, are also subject to international condemnation and international jurisdiction . . .[1]

Australian caution about interference in domestic jurisdiction was of long standing. Article 2(7) of the UN Charter had been strengthened at San Francisco in 1945 by Dr H. V. Evatt, then the Labor minister of external affairs when Menzies was leader of the Opposition, and Evatt had applied the clause to Indian attacks on South Africa in the General Assembly. Menzies, on taking office in 1949, had reinforced the Evatt position to a considerable degree.[2] His strong belief in the principle, and his great reverence for Commonwealth conventions, explain the attitude he continued to take about South Africa in the Commonwealth. So far as Sharpeville was concerned, he allowed a resolution of sympathy to be passed by his parliament, but no more, in spite of the Opposition's wish to go further in condemnation of South Africa and instruct him to bring up the matter at the coming meeting of Commonwealth prime ministers.[3]

In Canada there was a 'poorly attended and somewhat perfunctory' debate on South Africa on 27 April 1960,[4] during which the Opposition wanted Canada to dissociate itself from South Africa. 'We cannot refuse to face the situation', said Pearson, 'that South Africa may drive herself out of the Commonwealth by forcing a choice between her policies and the views of other members';[5] and in saying this he was not only unconsciously prescient but also echoing the line taken by Macmillan at Cape Town. Diefenbaker contented himself by warning against public disapproval and again pointing out that there would be informal discussions.[6]

These overseas Commonwealth debates were all expressions of concern, though they varied in aim and intensity. The most striking debate, however, occurred on 8 April 1960 in the House of Commons in London. John Stonehouse, an Opposition member, moved the following motion which was adopted without a division:

[1] Aus. HR Deb., 29 Mar 1960, p. 369.
[2] For an extended treatment of this point, see Norman Harper & David Sissons, *Australia and the UN* (1959), pp. 61–4 & ch. 6.
[3] Aus. HR Deb., 31 Mar 1960, pp. 779 ff.   [4] Preston, p. 202.
[5] Canada, HC Deb., 27 Apr 1960, p. 3323.   [6] Ibid., p. 3340.

That this House, deploring the present racialist policies now being pursued by the South African Government, under which non-Europeans are consistently denied normal human and political rights, including the right of campaigning for a peaceful change in the laws under which they live, and the recent declaration of a state of emergency and the many arbitrary arrests, fearing that a continuation of this repression is threatening the security and welfare of all races living in the Union of South Africa and good relations between members of the Commonwealth, urges Her Majesty's Government to take the opportunity at the forthcoming Commonwealth Prime Ministers' Conference to bring home to the South African Government the strong feelings of British people on this question; and restates its firm belief that peace and tranquillity in South Africa can only be secured in the long run on the basis of freedom and equality and a full respect for the inherent dignity and humanity of all men.[1]

It was remarkable that a Conservative government should have permitted such a resolution to be adopted about the government of a country with which Britain had close ties.[2] The fact that it did so suggests that Macmillan and his cabinet endorsed two of the beliefs expressed in the motion, which were certainly widely held in Britain at the time. They were that repression following from apartheid in South Africa was threatening the welfare and security of all races there (i.e. that a 'blood bath', as it was often called, was inevitable unless the South African government changed its ways), and that the situation threatened good relations between members of the Commonwealth. The first belief could lead even the most hardened Conservative to believe that the South African economy (heavily laced with British capital) might disintegrate if there was no change in the government's policy. The second could be shared by all those Conservatives who considered, as Sir Ivor Jennings said in 1960, 'that the process whereby six dependent peoples of the British Empire have been converted, within the space of 13 years, into independent nations of the Commonwealth will be regarded by history as a tribute to British statesmanship', and for whom 'the mysticism which formerly surrounded the Empire now surrounds the Commonwealth'. Jennings concluded that its members would not regard it as worthwhile to break up the Commonwealth merely because a minority government in South Africa insisted upon a racial policy which hardly anybody outside the Union was prepared to defend.[3] Macmillan's mind was almost certainly running along these lines.

[1] HC Deb., 8 Apr 1960, col. 774. The debate generally was on predictable lines and could serve as an example of conventional wisdom of the time. Mention should be made of the speech by Bernard Braine (cols. 834–8), which tried to break new ground in suggesting assumptions on which the Commonwealth could be said to operate.

[2] This may, in fact, have been the high-water mark of 'Commonwealth' feeling in the Conservative Party (i.e., of the conviction that independence for colonies and the enlargement of Commonwealth membership were goods in themselves). See Goldsworthy, pp. 366–72, for the reaction which soon set in.

[3] Sir Ivor Jennings, 'South Africa and the Commonwealth: constitutional problems in admitting republics', *Optima*, Sept 1960, p. 120.

V

The Prime Ministers' Meeting began on 3 May 1960. It was the first since 1957. Before it started several heads of government, including Diefenbaker, Nash,[1] Ayub, Menzies, and Nehru, were either quoted or reported as not wishing to put South Africa in the dock; the attitude of Nkrumah was not known.[2] Only the Tunku was said to be anxious to raise the matter of South African racial policy. This he did, when, as the junior prime minister present, he was asked to respond to Macmillan's opening speech of welcome. Louw, who was representing South Africa because of the attempted assassination of Verwoerd at Johannesburg on 9 April, agreed to meet other heads of delegations for informal discussion, provided it was recognized that Commonwealth conferences did not discuss the internal affairs of member countries; and an interim communiqué was issued accordingly.[3] The initiative in suggesting this procedure was taken by Menzies, who had discussed it beforehand with Macmillan. In the private discussions, for which the prime ministers were split into two groups, he was impressed by what he considered to be moderation on the part of the Tunku, Ayub, and Nkrumah. They showed a willingness to appreciate the position of the white population in South Africa but had sharp comments to make about the treatment of Africans and Asians.[4] They raised the questions of Cape Coloured representation, of the Bantu franchise (for which the Tunku suggested a token representation), and of the kind of personal discrimination to which they would be subjected if they went to South Africa. According to Menzies, Sharpeville was not mentioned, but South Africa's reluctance to receive diplomatic missions from some Commonwealth countries was.[5]

Menzies may have been satisfied with these informal discussions, but the Tunku was not. He was incensed by reports of a press conference which Louw gave after lunch on the day the private discussions began, although he did not know what Louw had said until he read the newspapers next morning. He then issued a statement accusing Louw of forestalling the results of the talks, and said he would have nothing more to do with them. 'It is obvious that his character is uncompromising and his attitude unyielding', said the Tunku. Louw had taken the line that the talks enabled him to provide information to the others, whereas the Tunku thought they were designed to reach a firm understanding. There was something of a scene between the two before the

---

[1] Walter Nash was prime minister of New Zealand during the Labour government of 1957-60; otherwise Labour was in opposition for the period covered by this book.

[2] The Times, 30 Apr; Observer, 1 May 1960.

[3] The Times, 4 May 1960.   [4] Menzies, pp. 194-5.

[5] Ibid., pp. 199-201. This is part of a subsequent correspondence between Menzies and Verwoerd, which Menzies prints in full; it is a fascinating glimpse of the two men's divergent approaches.

meeting adjourned for the weekend.[1] Over the weekend Nkrumah withdrew an invitation to visit Ghana that had been extended to Louw some time before. On the Monday the prime ministers decided almost at once to send their advisers out of the room while they discussed apartheid. Next day, after such an unpropitious start, Louw had to bring forward the question of South Africa's status in the Commonwealth if it decided to become a republic. Nkrumah had already obtained approval for Ghana's continued membership as a republic.[2]

In one way the matter should have been just a formality. The prime ministers had some years earlier given approval to Ceylon's continued membership if it should become a republic (which it had not done). According to Menzies, they had already agreed, at the end of the apartheid discussion, that, in spite of their feeling about racial policy, South Africa was still welcome in the Commonwealth as a monarchy.[3] But Louw's abrasiveness (what one London newspaper called his 'sheer pigheadedness')[4] had irritated a number of them, and they were coming, in any case, to feel that they must speak out more strongly against apartheid. Nehru and Nkrumah brought up the question of South-West Africa. Menzies objected that this was a UN question and that, in any case, if they were prepared to have South Africa as a monarchy, its transformation into a republic would make no difference to its behaviour in respect of South-West Africa. Macmillan smoothed things over by suggesting that a decision to approve membership of South Africa as a republic, in advance of the proposed referendum, would perhaps influence the South African vote and thus constitute a form of intervention in South Africa's affairs.[5] There was something in this, since the question of Commonwealth membership was a live issue in South Africa. In the end it was agreed that if South Africa decided to become a republic, and subsequently wished to remain a member of the Commonwealth, it should ask for the consent of the other Commonwealth governments either at a meeting of prime ministers or, if this were not practicable, by correspondence.

The communiqué issued at the end of the meeting contained a reference to the informal discussions with Louw about South African racial policy, and added that the other ministers 'conveyed to him their views on the South African problem. The ministers emphasized that the Commonwealth itself is a multi-racial association and expressed the need to ensure good relations between all member states and peoples of the Commonwealth'. This was an unusual statement, and the Tunku and Ayub were quick to say it should have been stronger.[6] As it was, Louw objected to it and refused at first to have it in

---

[1] *The Times*, 6 May 1960. See also the Tunku's speech, Malaya, HR Deb., 20 June 1960, p. 1064ff.

[2] *The Times*, 10 May 1960.   [3] Menzies, p. 196.

[4] *FT*, 11 May 1960.   [5] Menzies, pp. 196–7.

[6] *The Times*, 14 May 1960; extract from the communiqué in Mansergh, *Documents 1952–62*, p. 362.

the communiqué. He was spoken to in 'pretty stringent terms' by Menzies during a short adjournment, and then consented.[1] The meeting was followed by a statement in Dublin by Nkrumah to the effect that if the UN secretary-general was

unable to agree with the Government of South Africa on such arrangements as would adequately help in upholding the purposes and principles of the Charter, then the Government of Ghana for one would find it embarrassing to remain in the Commonwealth with a Republic whose policy was not based upon the purpose and principles of the United Nations.[2]

This was a somewhat muffled threat; but there was no equivocation about a resolution adopted by the conference of independent African states (including Ghana) at Addis Ababa in the following month, which invited 'the Independent African States which are members of the British Commonwealth to take all possible steps to secure the exclusion of the Union of South Africa from the British Commonwealth'.[3]

The same conference adopted a number of other propositions relevant to South Africa's position in the community of nations. These amounted to economic war against South Africa, by way of boycotts of goods from that country (which some states had already begun), and the interruption of rail, sea, air, postal, telegraphic, and radio communications. African states were called on to close their ports to South African ships, and their airports and air-space to South African aircraft. In July Ghana 'exacted from any South African citizen seeking to enter Ghana a formal renunciation of policies of racial discrimination'.[4] It was becoming clear that countries which supported South Africa would encounter increased hostility from the growing number of independent African states.

Less than a year elapsed between the 1960 and 1961 meetings of prime ministers. During this time there must have been a certain amount of correspondence between them about South Africa. The Tunku told his parliament in June 1960 that all he proposed to do at that stage was to ask the premiers of 'all countries in the democratic world' what he should do in the matter and how they proposed to subscribe to whatever action Malaya might take, 'because if we go any further than that I do not think we should have their support'.[5] Nehru said in August that he too had written to the other Commonwealth prime ministers.[6] We know from Menzies's memoirs that in July and August he was in correspondence with Verwoerd, urging him to take some account of the criticisms expressed at the 1960 meeting but discovering that Verwoerd would not move an inch in racial policy, because to do so would

---

[1] Menzies, p. 196.   [2] *I Speak of freedom*, p. 229.
[3] Calvocoressi, pp. 64–6. Nkrumah was also under other African pressures to leave the Commonwealth (see W. Scott Thompson, pp. 171–2).
[4] Calvocoressi, pp. 31–3.   [5] Malaya, HR Deb., 20 June 1960, p. 1071.
[6] India, Lok Sabha Deb., 25 Aug 1960, p. 4839.

mean 'a possible thin end of the wedge'. Menzies wrote of the possibility that South Africa might be expelled. He counselled Verwoerd not to seek Commonwealth approval of republican status by correspondence—one of the means canvassed by the 1960 meeting—but to make application in person at a Commonwealth conference 'at a time when the Republic had been substantially established but perhaps not actually proclaimed'. On such an occasion it would be possible to discuss 'in the frankest possible fashion the principles upon which and the procedure by which a membership of the Commonwealth, either new or continuing, should be determined'. He believed that people like himself, Macmillan, Nash, and Diefenbaker would think it a misfortune if South Africa were not in the Commonwealth.[1]

The reference to Diefenbaker suggests that his attitude showed no sign of a change from the caution that the Canadian prime minister had expressed before and during the 1960 meeting. However, at some stage in the next few months (according to Macmillan, by November 1960) Diefenbaker became convinced that he should take a strong line on South African racial policy when the prime ministers met again. As in other matters, his motivation is hard to discover. Whether it was because of the set of his mind towards Declarations of Rights, or his sense of public opinion, or his appreciation of Canada's position in the Commonwealth, or his conviction that the Asian and African members should not stand alone within the Commonwealth circle in their opposition to apartheid, is not known at the time of writing.[2] In the event, his change of attitude was to be of considerable importance in 1961.

Meanwhile, however, Verwoerd announced on 3 August 1960 that the referendum would be held on 5 October. His statements showed that he was principally concerned with the cleavage between Afrikaans and English-speaking South Africans. It was to be a republic 'which will seek to retain its membership of the Commonwealth'. If continued membership were refused, the republic would be established without it; and Verwoerd explained that, in such an event,

since the fault will, without any doubt, not lie with the United Kingdom and other friendly disposed Commonwealth countries, the present policy of maintaining cordial relations and co-operation by agreement in many matters, such as economics and defence, will be continued.

His argument was that, if membership were refused, it would mean that 'younger non-white member countries would be exercising a predominant influence in this matter'; in these circumstances, if it were outside the Commonwealth, South Africa would have a better chance of retaining friendship with the older Commonwealth states.[3]

[1] Menzies, pp. 198–210.
[2] See Harnetty, *JCPS*, Nov 1961, pp. 37–8 for some discussion of the point. Macmillan, *Pointing the way*, pp. 293–6, is an illuminating later source.
[3] Pelzer, p. 408.

There is no reason to believe that Verwoerd was insincere in his wish to retain membership of the Commonwealth. From the start he had envisaged the possibility that South Africa might be forced out by the Afro-Asians; he was not prepared to accept continued membership under humiliating circumstances such as some form of probation, but gave English-speaking South Africans a promise that if the Commonwealth continued to operate as it had in the past, the South African government would happily retain membership. It was the Afrikaner nationalists who wanted the republic, while it was the English who wanted continued membership of the Commonwealth. If he could, he would give both what they wanted; but if the Commonwealth proved to be different from what the English-speakers had grown up to expect, they would agree with him that South Africa should not seek to retain membership on sufferance.[1] His approach was quite consistent, before and after the referendum. In many ways, while based upon the Afrikaner sense of the past, it was more forward-looking than that of his opponents in the United Party. They clung to a symbolism of the Commonwealth which was appropriate to its past but hardly to its present; he saw both the hostility of the Afro-Asian members and the likelihood that, if South Africa had to withdraw, its relations with Britain and the white members would not be gravely impaired.

The referendum attracted 90·73 per cent of the electorate; 850,458 (52·05 per cent) voted for a republic, and 775,878 (47·49 per cent) against. The voting by provinces was significant:

	Yes	No
Transvaal	406,632	325,041
Cape Colony	271,418	269,784
Orange Free State	110,171	33,438
South West Africa	19,938	12,017
Natal	42,299	135,598

Source: Pelzer, p. 410.

To a great extent, the Afrikaans and English-speaking groups had divided along language lines. The English-speakers in the big cities and in Natal had followed their traditional dislike of Nationalist symbols. The Afrikaners had shown themselves faithful to the traditions of the Boer republics. This does not seem to have disturbed Verwoerd. He had a majority, and his post-referendum speeches contained no fuel to kindle English fires of resentment: he was for reconciliation, for a just appreciation by each side of the cherished traditions of the other, for a closer link between the two in common loyalty to South Africa, and for defiance of those (misguided, in his view, rather than wicked, except for communists) who opposed apartheid. The colour question had been of little consequence during the campaign. It was a dialogue between the two white groups.

[1] Ibid., pp. 407–8, 431 ff.

When Verwoerd left for London on 3 March 1961, to present South Africa's request for continued membership to the Prime Ministers' Meeting arranged for the coming week, he mentioned in his parting message the hostile demonstrations which the press said he would face there:

Such demonstrations take place regularly there, also in respect of local affairs. Neither you, nor I, need take much notice thereof. In London, the city of millions, it is easy to gather large groups consisting of ignorant persons and inexpert fanatics, professional and politically motivated demonstrators, and frequently leftist exiles from other countries. These persons represent neither the heart nor the mind of the British people. We would be doing an injustice to a friendly country were we to judge it by this or to allow our feelings towards it to be influenced thereby.[1]

Was this the case?

VI

An honest answer must be yes and no. Verwoerd was right to the extent that London had all sorts of demonstrations, that these often contained the same people whatever the subject, and that often these people had little to do with the subject of the day. But this was not the whole story. Along with the professional demonstrators of the left and the South African exiles went a considerable movement in British opinion, disturbed by what it considered to be the brutal racialism of South Africa, and anxious that Britain should not be tainted by further formal assocation with it—to the extent that Commonwealth membership represented formal association. No one who followed British opinion at the time could argue that the opposition to South Africa was confined to the groups mentioned by Verwoerd, prominent as those might appear in the newspapers and on television. There was also a broad band of feeling, obvious in the young but by no means confined to them, which rejected the idea of continued connection with South Africa, for what were considered to be good and sufficient British reasons—those associated with a liberal political system, a rejection of colour bars, and a conviction that the Commonwealth would work better without South Africa. When *The Times* could say that the Commonwealth could not afford to 'drift rudderless through the world, a hulk without principles', and that to keep the Verwoerd government as a partner with the other governments would be to register a gross anomaly,[2] and *The Economist*, on the same day, could write of 'the implacable contradiction between the Commonwealth doctrine of racial equality and the Verwoerd doctrine', something more than the views of professional demonstrators was being expressed.

The situation of the Commonwealth in 1961 had much to do with the sense of uneasy urgency with which many British people approached the problem

[1] Ibid., p. 497.   [2] Editorial, 'The One Apart', 4 Mar 1961.

of South Africa.[1] Asian and African membership was in everyone's mind. The Prime Ministers' Meeting was to begin on 8 March; on 2 March the Queen left New Delhi after a highly successful visit which seemed to epitomize the smoothness of post-independence relations with India, to which Commonwealth membership was believed to have contributed so much. Nigeria, the biggest of Britain's African colonies, had gained its independence some months before and would be represented at a Prime Ministers' Meeting for the first time. The conditions of independence for Sierra Leone had already been published; those for Tanganyika were in the last stages of discussion. The Federation of Rhodesia and Nyasaland was in a critical condition following the report of the Monckton Commission; it was becoming increasingly clear that there would be constitutional advance for Northern Rhodesia and Nyasaland, in spite of the objections of the federal government. To many people, British policy in Africa, and the future of the Commonwealth, seemed poised between success and failure. Of the younger generations, only those whose interest was concentrated on South Africa for business or family reasons could think of that country in the same way as white South Africans thought of it. To the rest, South Africa was more likely to seem an obstacle to the kind of future which Macmillan had envisaged in his 'wind of change' speech. If the Commonwealth was to be disrupted because South Africa clung to its racial policy and insisted that this was domestic jurisdiction when so many others said it was not, the outcome would be unacceptable to a great many—a majority, it seemed—of those who were articulate and politically minded.

A long correspondence in *The Times* from 1 to 13 March exposed these ideas, and also those of people who wanted South Africa to stay in the Commonwealth. The conflict of generations was reflected to some extent, though people under 30 do not normally write to *The Times*. The writers under 50 were more in favour of dropping South Africa than the older ones, to whom usually the salient facts about South Africa were not those of the present but of the past: of South Africa's British connections and its help in two world wars. Few were prepared to state the economic implications—a point worth recollecting in the light of later British emphasis upon the importance of South Africa as a trading partner.[2] The discussion was essentially political. The main reason advanced by those who wished to keep South

[1] References for what follows about the 1961 conference are to be found in my article in *JCPS*, Nov 1961. Where later material has been available, direct reference is made to it.

[2] There were, however, advertisements attributed to 'A Group of British Friends'. They said: 'Do you know that: 1) South Africa even now is the largest buyer of motor cars and commercial vehicles made in England, except for North America. 2) Nearly one out of every five Pounds of the nett overseas investments of the British Public is profitably and safely invested in South Africa. This is already nearly £1,000,000,000. 3) Nearly half the total tonnage of cargo (49·4%) handled by the great port of Southampton is between Britain and South Africa. LET US WORK TO KEEP THE COMMONWEALTH TOGETHER' (*The Times*, 6 Mar 1961). It is worth noting that very few of the British critics of S. Africa suggested cutting economic ties at this stage.

Africa in was that the Commonwealth association might influence its government to adopt more liberal policies. Only South African correspondents defended apartheid as such.

Against such a background, one can see something of the problem facing Macmillan and his Commonwealth secretary, Sandys, as the meeting approached. Both wished the Commonwealth to be preserved and South Africa to remain a member. Both were committed to rapid advance in Africa and to the enlargement of the Commonwealth by the addition of African members as these became independent. Both were aware of the strong current of anti-apartheid opinion in Britain. They rejected apartheid, but knew of the close connections between the British and South African economies. What line were they to take?

According to Verwoerd,[1] he was told that the British proposed, as a matter of tactics, to side with the Africans and Asians in condemning apartheid: 'they would state it very strongly, even more strongly than they would have preferred to say it to us'. The aim was to 'convince the other Prime Ministers that they could follow her lead since Britain shared their views but nevertheless wished to retain the Union as a member of the Commonwealth'. If this is correct, then Macmillan hoped to use the very condemnation of apartheid as a means of retaining South Africa. It was a neat scheme, but perhaps too neat. Verwoerd's account of Macmillan's intended tactics (in which he acquiesced) is supplemented by Menzies, who says[2] that he discussed matters beforehand with Macmillan, and that they agreed to try to handle the South African question in two parts. First there would be a constitutional discussion in order to establish the convention that a change to republican status should be regarded as a domestic affair, needing only to be notified to other members. 'On this principle, South Africa would automatically continue its membership as a Republic.' Once this was disposed of, 'there should be a debate, in full conference, on South African affairs, with South Africa as a participant and not a petitioner'.[3] To succeed, these tactics would depend on an awareness by the other members that a direct refusal to retain South Africa on the ground of its racial policy would be to expose each of them subsequently to possible attack, or even expulsion, for offences peculiar to itself but judged to be incompatible with Commonwealth membership.[4] The principle of domestic jurisdiction could be sustained if members were convinced of the dangers to themselves of its being breached in South Africa's case. Macmillan's scheme would enable him and others to attack apartheid, but to divorce this from the technical question of membership.

[1] Pelzer, pp. 558–9.

[2] Menzies, pp. 212–13; see also Macmillan, p. 297.

[3] Verwoerd's testimony agrees with that of Menzies: the constitutional issue was 'to be discussed . . . as a technical matter and then disposed of' (Pelzer, p. 531).

[4] According to the *Spectator* (3 Mar 1961) the CRO had quietly made this point in each of the Commonwealth capitals.

Before the meeting began it seemed that the plan might succeed. No head of government said beforehand that he wanted South Africa to be expelled. The Tunku reiterated his opposition to apartheid but said his approach would be different from last time; the other Asians would not be drawn. The prime minister of Nigeria was also uncommunicative. Nkrumah, the last to arrive, said he would bring up the question of South Africa if no one else did, but added that personally he wished for no show-down on South Africa.

The story of the meeting itself may be told briefly. In essence, Macmillan's scheme for separating the constitutional and apartheid issues miscarried. Other heads of government wished to combine the two, and Verwoerd agreed. Nehru, Nkrumah, and Diefenbaker have each been identified by different observers as the decisive figure in shifting the whole discussion towards apartheid and its incompatibility with the principles which the Commonwealth was assumed to embody. Nehru showed considerable activity in forcing an analysis of the problem upon the other delegations. Nkrumah, at first inclined towards quietism, was galvanized into action when told that an article by Nyerere, expressing the determination not to make Tanganyika a member of the Commonwealth if South Africa remained one,[1] would appear in London the day before South Africa was discussed. He decided to take the initiative in the debate. Diefenbaker insisted that there was no 'automaticity' about a new republic's remaining in the Commonwealth, and wanted it laid down that non-discrimination in respect of race and colour was an essential principle of the Commonwealth. The debate extended over three days (13, 14, and 15 March).

It is clear that no one demanded the expulsion of South Africa from the Commonwealth, though the possibility was certainly raised of such a demand in the future. What did happen was that suggestions were made for conditions of Commonwealth membership which would be unacceptable to South Africa, and that some members threatened to leave the Commonwealth if South Africa remained. South Africa could have stayed in the Commonwealth for the time being on sufferance. At one stage of the meeting the prime ministers came very near to agreeing on a joint communiqué which would have continued South Africa's membership but stated the contradictory views on 'the racial question' of Verwoerd on the one side and the remaining prime ministers on the other.[2] It soon became evident, however, that some would interpret the situation as allowing them to raise South African racial policy at any time; some would later suggest South Africa's expulsion; and some would leave if South Africa stayed. In these circumstances Verwoerd chose to withdraw South Africa from the Commonwealth, to resign before being forced out.

---

[1] Private information. Nyerere's article appeared in the *Observer*, 12 Mar 1961. It is reprinted in *JCPS*, Nov 1961, pp. 72–4, and in a slightly longer form in Nyerere, *Freedom and unity* (1967), pp. 108–13.

[2] *JCPS*, Nov 1961, pp. 71–2.

South Africa was not expelled. It left because its prime minister felt this was the best way to handle a situation which would otherwise, in his view, have become intolerable, not only for South Africa but also for Britain.[1] The leave-taking was relatively dignified; while commentators and participants after-wards stressed Verwoerd's inflexibility, they also remarked on his good manners. The fact that South Africa's resignation was not effective from the moment when it was expressed, but from 31 May, the day of proclamation of the republic, enabled the loose ends of South Africa's Commonwealth con-nections to be tidied up.

There were numerous post-mortems on the decision.[2] They emphasized the fact that there had initially been widespread reluctance to see South Africa go, and that, if Verwoerd had been prepared to make concessions, a number of the prime ministers (though not all) might have been prepared to urge him to stay. The decisive, because highly symbolic, point seems to have been Verwoerd's refusal to accept diplomatic representatives from African fellow members of the Commonwealth. This, about which Menzies had previously warned him, and which Sandys said 'bit very deep', was something of a point of no return. The final assault upon South Africa's racial policies, in which Nehru, Sir Abubakar Tafawa Balewa, Nkrumah, and Mrs Bandara-naike took part, must have been fierce.[3] I have been told, by a private source, that much of the vigour of the final debate arose from Verwoerd's 'brutal if honest answer' to the question of how a non-white prime minister would be treated if he visited South Africa.

Most of the prime ministers were pleased at the outcome, although Macmillan was suitably funerary. Diefenbaker, Nehru, Sir Abubakar,[4] and Holyoake (who had replaced Nash for New Zealand)[5] all thought the Common-wealth would be strengthened by what had happened, a view very widely expressed in the British press after the meeting.[6] The same view was taken by

[1] Verwoerd's explanation of why he acted as he did (given in his speech to the S. African parliament on 23 March 1961) is very detailed and extremely convincing. He enumerated four alternatives which he could have chosen, and then gave five reasons for taking the fourth (Pelzer, pp. 538–9; also in Mansergh, *Documents 1952–62*, pp. 386–7).

[2] Mansergh, *Documents 1952–62*, pp. 365–400, contains extracts from the speeches in their parliaments of Diefenbaker, Macmillan, Verwoerd, Nehru, Menzies, and Nkrumah. Unless otherwise stated, quotations are from these. It should be noted that Nkrumah showed some of his customary equivocation; see *The Times*, 23 Mar 1961.

[3] It is described to some extent by Menzies and in Verwoerd's speech in parliament. The only participant who seems to have made public a full account of her statement is Mrs Bandaranaike (see *Ceylon Daily News*, 17 Mar 1961).

[4] 'What happened last month . . . literally purged the Commonwealth. It is my belief that the Commonwealth can now wield tremendously powerful influence for good in world politics . . .' (Nigeria, HR Deb., 17 Apr 1961, p. 1747–8).

[5] 'I believe that by its determination to stand for the principle of racial equality the Commonwealth, far from beginning to disintegrate, has demonstrated its strength and its capacity to serve great and worthwhile ideals' (NZ Deb., 4 July 1961, p. 220).

[6] *The Times* editorials of 16 & 17 Mar 1961, 'The Commonwealth Preserved' and 'Salutary Crisis', were typical.

the official opposition parties in all their parliaments. Apart from Sir Roy Welensky, who was in any case a minor figure, the one prime minister to continue to deplore South Africa's departure was Menzies. Throughout the meeting he had objected to the introduction of what he regarded as irrelevancies and improprieties, and he continued to do so when encountering hostile criticism from the opposition on his return to Australia. As before, his main contention was that the rule of non-interference in members' domestic affairs, which he regarded as basic to the Commonwealth and as particularly vital for Australia, had been broken and might be broken again in the future. Unlike the others, he did not think the Commonwealth would be better for South Africa's having left.

An interim judgement on the significance for the Commonwealth of the South Africa issue was given in the following year by the experienced Canadian observer, John Holmes. Two ways of looking at the Commonwealth had been at issue, he wrote:

first there was the traditional conception of the institution as a kind of family, a family of mixed blood but nevertheless a family in that it had no reason for existence except that it shared a common origin. It had been regarded as observing British principles of government and law and as recognizing the tradition that the members did not judge one another's domestic policies.

He went on to say that against this was the

increasing insistence of new members that adherence to the more recent principle of racial equality took precedence over the preservation of the family. . . . The offence of South Africa posed an issue which could not be ignored as the tendency grew to justify the very existence of the Commonwealth by its nonracialism. Most of the Prime Ministers were aware of the implications of driving South Africa out, but they did so because they realised that there was no alternative if the Commonwealth was to be preserved at all.

He believed that what had been gained was a pride in the Commonwealth in the new African states which could not otherwise have existed. 'What is lost is the more flexible relationship of the past.'[1]

This fair judgement accorded with what most political leaders and students felt throughout the Commonwealth. For the time being the Commonwealth had rid itself of the embarrassment of a non-conforming member. But Holmes was prophetic in including in this comment a reminder that, in spite of the Africans' pride in the institutions they had helped to create, more difficult problems were still to be faced. 'The Commonwealth itself might well be shattered by differences over the processes of liquidating colonialism in East and Central Africa—not to mention Angola and the Republic of South Africa.'[2]

[1] 'The impact on the Commonwealth of the emergence of Africa', *Int. Org.*, 16 (1962), pp. 298–9.
[2] Ibid., p. 296.

For the time being these disturbing possibilities could be put aside. In Britain there was little disposition to penalize South Africa after its withdrawal: the bilateral relations between the two countries continued very much as before, with legislation to regularize the situation in those cases in which the existing statutes required alteration.[1] Verwoerd had evidently received assurances about continued co-operation in trade and defence before he announced the decision to withdraw;[2] the charge made by some of his South African opponents that he might endanger preferential trade arrangements proved to be wrong, and there was no difficulty about continuing the Simonstown agreement. South Africa remained in the sterling area. South African citizens in Britain who held positions closed to aliens were given until the end of 1965 to decide whether to apply for British citizenship or to give up these jobs. Although now aliens, South Africans continued to come to Britain in much the same numbers, and British people to emigrate to South Africa. The two countries exchanged ambassadors instead of high commissioners, but otherwise went on much as before.

In South Africa itself, the change seems to have had a politically dampening effect on the English-speaking population, impelling it further towards agreement with the Afrikaners and away from a sense of kinship with Britain. The combination of a republic and withdrawal from the Commonwealth, put into effect on 31 May 1961, cut these people off from the symbols which their political leaders had supported with fervour and even fury during the 1920s, 1930s, and 1940s, and to which they had continued to give diminished loyalty in the 1950s. There seems to have been little reaction, except from radicals and from those visionaries who could say: 'I no longer feel myself to be fully in touch with my own past or with that of South Africa as a whole'.[3] A sense of the past was all very well, but when it led the leader of the United Party, Sir de Villiers Graaff, to the limp statement that Verwoerd was at fault because, in London, 'all the hon. gentleman was asked to do was to sit still and then he could not be put out of the Commonwealth', and that 'it is nothing to have to sit still and suffer indignities for one's country',[4] it had clearly exhausted itself. The salient facts, as a correspondent of *The Times* put it (28 March 1961), were that most white South Africans thought that Verwoerd did the right thing, and nearly all white South Africans believed in racial segregation.

---

[1] The problems of legal change are discussed in de Smith, pp. 183–90. A transitional bill was introduced in parliament in May 1961, and the position was consolidated by the South Africa Act of 1962.

[2] His minister of finance, introducing his Budget in Cape Town while the Prime Ministers' Meeting was still in progress, was able to say that if South Africa ceased to be a member of the Commonwealth, this would have no effect on trade relations (S. Africa, HA Deb., 15 Mar 1961, p. 2998).

[3] These words are from an eloquent article by the S. African novelist Dan Jacobson, 'Alienation of a South African', *Guardian*, 18 Mar 1961. Undoubtedly it expressed a point of view to be found in S. Africa, but the writer was living in London when he wrote it.

[4] S. Africa, HA Deb., 23 Mar 1961, p. 3515.

Verwoerd got a hero's welcome when he returned, and his explanation of what he had done was accepted. After 31 May the English-speakers may or may not have lost some of what they previously regarded as their self-respect and their special identity. At all events their monarchism dropped from them like an old cloak. As Verwoerd had foreseen, withdrawal from the embarrassments of a Commonwealth in which Africans and Asians were beginning to predominate gave white South Africans a sense of relief. It would now be possible to get on with fruitful bilateral relations with Britain, Australia, and other Commonwealth members which seemed to have interests in common with South Africa.

VII

The 'business as usual' relationship between Britain and South Africa gave something of a formalistic look to the departure of South Africa from the Commonwealth. Politicians and publicists might say that the Commonwealth was now free to display even more convincingly its commitment to multiracialism; but the fact that Britain behaved no differently towards South Africa, apart from a change in its voting at the UN and the adjustment of certain institutions to which the word 'Commonwealth' had been applied, emphasized the stylized aspect.[1] Something of the same impression was given at the meeting of Commonwealth prime ministers in 1964. For the first time the prime ministers committed themselves to multiracialism, though in rather ambiguous terms. They said 'it should be an objective of policy' to build in each country a structure of society offering equal opportunity and non-discrimination irrespective of race, colour, and creed. 'The Commonwealth should be able to exercise constructive leadership', they said, in applying democratic principles so that different racial groups could exist and develop as free and equal citizens.[2] These were cautious words which could be interpreted by each as he wished. In respect of South Africa, the African members (to whom Tanzania, Sierra Leone, Uganda, Kenya, and Malawi had been added since 1961) pressed for further measures, but were rebuffed. The communiqué stated:

The Prime Ministers reaffirmed their condemnation of the policy of apartheid practised by the Government of the Republic of South Africa. Some Commonwealth Prime Ministers felt very strongly that the only effective means of dealing with the problem of apartheid was the application of economic sanctions and an arms embargo. It was recognized however that there was a difference of opinion among Commonwealth countries as to the effectiveness of economic sanctions and as to the extent to which they regarded it as right or practicable to seek to secure the

[1] S. Africa ceased to be a member of the Commonwealth Sugar Agreement, for example, and of the Imperial Cricket Conference, which was something of an exception amongst Commonwealth bodies in respect of its name; it never changed to 'Commonwealth', but became the International Cricket Conference in 1965. S. Africa did not return.
[2] Cmnd 2441, p. 2 (CS, 21 July 1964, p. 718).

abandonment of apartheid by coercive action, of whatever kind. But the Prime Ministers were unanimous in calling upon South Africa to bring to an end the practice of apartheid, which had been repeatedly condemned by the United Nations and was deplored by public opinion throughout the world.[1]

The rejection of economic sanctions and an arms embargo was overwhelmingly a matter of British government policy, since the trade of other members of the Commonwealth with South Africa was insignificant alongside Britain's. At no point was the government prepared to consider economic sanctions.[2] The African states had brought the question of an arms embargo before the Security Council at the end of 1963, securing resolutions which called on member states not to provide arms to South Africa. The Conservative government in Britain agreed to stop the sale of arms for internal use which could be employed to enforce the policy of apartheid, but reserved the right to supply arms for external use, which might be involved in joint arrangements for the protection of the sea routes. These reservations, stemming from the Simonstown Agreement and the arrangements which it envisaged, did not meet the wishes of the Africans. Their efforts at the 1964 Prime Ministers' Meeting brought no more satisfactory result, but soon after the British general election of that year the new Labour government decided to issue no more licences for arms, except in respect of current contracts.[3] The issue was to remain one of disagreement between the Labour and Conservative Parties.

As we have seen, the attacks on South Africa at the UN and elsewhere became more intense in the 1960s, but to little avail. The attempt to have the International Court of Justice declare that South Africa was acting illegally in South-West Africa came to grief with a close but nullifying judgment in 1966.[4] Attempts at comprehensive boycotts were a total failure. Once again, South Africa's economic strength, together with its government's capacity to hold down dissident movements, helped to explain the African states' failure to get more than paper support for their demands. There was no question of the determination of the majority in the General Assembly to do something about South-West Africa. It even changed the name to Namibia to dramatize the alleged illegitimacy of South African rule. But whenever the Assembly tried to go further, it was faced by the South African government's refusal to yield and the major powers' refusal to strike. The South African economy continued to boom, to provide opportunities for investment by multinational

---

[1] Ibid., p. 6 (CS, p. 721). There was a similar but briefer statement in the communiqué of the 1965 Prime Ministers' Meeting, and others in 1966 and 1969.

[2] The question of sanctions is discussed exhaustively in Austin, esp. ch. 6. See Ronald Segal, ed., *Economic sanctions against South Africa* (1964) for several contemporary assessments of the practicability and effect of sanctions.

[3] CS, 21 Jan 1964, 79 ff.; 22 Dec 1964, pp. 1239–41.

[4] The Court was evenly divided. Its judgment, on the casting vote of the president, Sir Percy Spender from Australia, was to the effect that the petitioners (Liberia and Ethiopia, the only black African states which had been members of the League of Nations) had failed to establish their legal right or interest.

companies based in Britain, Europe, and the US, and to absorb large quantities of imports, especially from Britain. The Labour government itself showed how significant the South African market had become, when it suffered a brief convulsion over arms sales in December 1967.[1]

The dispute occurred against the background of a South African request for a lifting of the arms embargo imposed three years before, and a worsening economic situation in Britain which compelled the cabinet to look for cuts in expenditure and ways of increasing exports. The foreign secretary had been engaged in negotiations for some time with the South African government: he thought it wise to resume the sale of weapons for external defence, especially since, 'if we didn't supply, France or someone else was waiting on the doorstep pressing the South Africans to let them do it at our expense'. Both he and the defence minister wanted to resume the sales, 'within the context of the difficult economic situation'. A further factor was that the South African government might bring pressure to bear on the Smith regime in Rhodesia. There was an upheaval in the Parliamentary Labour Party when it became known that ministers were thinking of modifying the embargo, and the prime minister, who had been involved in some of the earlier discussions, drew back from the idea. In the end the cabinet decided to allow the embargo to stand. What is striking about the dispute is that, while it was about arms to South Africa, it began as a matter of retaining or increasing trade, and went on to become a quarrel about leadership and cabinet solidarity. Labour back-benchers and junior ministers were exercised over the issue of seeming to acquiesce in South Africa's racial policies, but cabinet ministers, preoccupied with economic and defence considerations, and aware of the limited nature of the equipment in question, did not regard agreement with a UN embargo as imperative. Nor, it seems, did they regard Commonwealth pressures as being of primary importance.

South Africa had become too big and important an international quantity for the British government to wish, or to be able, to discriminate effectively against it. Furthermore, by 1967 the African states had become less influential, within the Commonwealth and the international community, than in 1961. Many of the hopes of peaceful African development under independence had been disappointed; instability seemed to have become endemic. Although the larger number of African states had increased their capacity to mount campaigns in the UN, in practice their power had proved negligible. In Britain's case expectations about African membership of the Commonwealth had already been soured by African demands over Rhodesia. After the Commonwealth meeting of September 1966 (see ch. 10) no British government was

---

[1] There are three accounts of this, two by cabinet ministers and one which may well have a cabinet minister's approval. They are Harold Wilson, *Labour government*, pp. 470–6; George Brown, *In my way* (1971), pp. 170–4; and Williams & Reed, pp. 230–4. These have been used as sources.

likely to show much deference to African opinion. The other non-African members of the Commonwealth, while mostly acquiescing in declaratory African demands, were not prepared to take further steps against South Africa if these might adversely affect their own interests.

The difficulties of the African states in mounting an effective campaign against South Africa, especially within the Commonwealth, were accentuated by the so-called 'outward policy' of South Africa from 1966 onwards.[1] This represented a determination to break out of the formal isolation into which that country had been thrust, while capitalizing upon the presence upon (or within) South Africa's borders of newly independent but weak states. It was a revival of the already mentioned ambitions of Smuts, Strijdom, and Louw. South Africa, as the strongest state on the African continent, could be of great help to others, and might be able to draw around it a cordon sanitaire against incursions from further north. Lesotho, Botswana, and Swaziland (the sovereign states created from the former High Commission Territories), obviously could not offend South Africa without damaging their economies. Malawi, while separated from South Africa by Rhodesia and Mozambique, was a sound prospect for influence because of the estrangement between President Hastings Banda and the radicals in other parts of Africa, and because it too was heavily dependent on South Africa for employment.

Rhodesia and the Portuguese territories of Angola and Mozambique presented more difficulty, because of their problematic future and the differences between Portuguese and South African racial policy; but the efforts of the OAU to assist 'freedom fighters' in these territories, as well as in South Africa, provided a common source of interest. South Africa might, of course, overreach itself if it tried to shore up collapsing regimes, but for the time being the risk was worth taking. South Africa was cautious, in the late 1960s, in assisting Rhodesia and the Portuguese. If these regimes should eventually topple, it would be troublesome but not necessarily fatal for South Africa; meanwhile, their continued existence, in the face of guerrilla action helped by other countries (including the Soviet Union and China), was a source of assurance for South Africa itself as well as a means of emphasizing South Africa's strategic value to the western powers.[2]

---

[1] Some helpful sources on this topic include J. E. Spence, 'South Africa's "new look" foreign policy', World Today, Apr 1968; Dennis Austin, 'White power?', JCPS, July 1968; G. M. E. Leistner, South Africa's development aid to African states (1970); and James Mayall, 'Malawi's foreign policy', World Today, Oct 1970. I have also read with profit James Barratt, 'The outward movement in South Africa's foreign relations', Newsletter no. 3, S.A. Inst. Int. Aff., Aug 1969.

[2] During the Kennedy administration in the US there were frequent suggestions that the US government was either giving or encouraging help to resistance movements in the Portuguese territories, on the ground that these were genuine non-communist nationalist movements fighting an anomalous European regime. By the end of the decade American policy was very different. Something of the same change was apparent in policy towards S. Africa.

THE SOUTH AFRICAN PROBLEM

In the Commonwealth context, the success of South Africa's 'outward policy' with the former High Commission Territories and Malawi was a blow to the hopes of the governments of members such as Tanzania, Kenya, and Uganda, pledged to outlaw South Africa and to work for African unity. On the one hand they could not deny either the economic needs of the new states which were establishing diplomatic relations with South Africa, or the fact that these had gained their independence and Commonwealth membership by the same means as themselves: while weak, they were not 'phoney'. Seretse Khama and Hastings Banda, the leaders of two of them, had as good an anti-colonial record as Kenyatta or Nyerere. There was accordingly no attempt to expel these states from the OAU. Nevertheless, the more 'normal' appeared to be their relations with South Africa, the less credible appeared the OAU contention that the South African regime was an offence against humanity. By the end of 1969 other African states, including the Ivory Coast and the Malagasy Republic, had begun to talk of 'dialogue' with South Africa. With the failure of the campaign for economic boycott, and with a falling-away of African support for all-out hostility, the members of the Commonwealth opposed to South Africa made what looked like a last effort to use its machinery to isolate South Africa. The issue was that of arms supply by Britain. It arose in the long term from the Simonstown Agreement, and, in the short term from the change in government in Britain after the general election of 18 June 1970.

VIII

Consideration of the debate over arms for South Africa at the Commonwealth Heads of Government Meeting at Singapore in January 1971 goes beyond the time-scale generally observed in this book. It is included here because it exemplified the change in the South African problem that had occurred during the decade 1961–71. Although no longer a member, South Africa still occupied members' attention.

Before the 1970 election, influential members of the Conservative Party were known to believe that arms sales to South Africa should be resumed, for much the same reasons as the Labour foreign secretary in 1967.[1] The South African government had protested strongly against the continuance of the Wilson government's embargo, arguing that it was contrary to the spirit of the Simonstown Agreement;[2] in any case, the Conservatives had never endorsed the extension of the restrictions in December 1964. At the Lord

[1] See Geoffrey Rippon, 'South Africa and naval strategy', *Round Table*, July 1970, for a representative view of this kind. The views of Sir Alec Douglas-Home, who became foreign and Commonwealth secretary in the new government, are expressed at length in Young, *Douglas-Home*, pp. 243–4.

[2] See, e.g., *The Times*, 12 Jan & 22 May 1970. Merle Lipton, 'British arms for South Africa', *World Today*, Oct 1970, gives the background to the S. African statements.

Mayor's Banquet on 16 November 1970 the new prime minister, Edward Heath, said of the agreement: 'Under these arrangements we have an obligation to supply to South Africa the maritime equipment she requires to fulfil her side of the agreement'. While the government did not wish to encourage apartheid, 'the defence of the great sea routes around the Cape of Good Hope is of vital importance to us'. The matter was being discussed with colleagues in the Commonwealth. They were not being asked to abandon their principles on apartheid, which indeed the government shared. 'But we do ask our Commonwealth colleagues to accept that our right to take decisions in pursuance of British interests is no less than theirs to pursue the policies which serve what they consider to be their own interests.'[1] There was considerable criticism of the government's position in Britain itself. Expressions of concern came from African sources. As the Singapore meeting drew near, it became clear that this would be the main issue discussed.

At Singapore,[2] in a meeting plagued by declamation at unconscionable length, the two sides of the argument were deployed. The British line was that the use of Simonstown was essential to Britain's keeping watch on the sea-lanes in the South Atlantic and Indian Ocean. This need had increased since the Soviet Union had put a naval presence into the Indian Ocean. Any 'marine equipment' Britain might sell to South Africa was the price to be paid for the continued use of Simonstown. No African state had said Britain should give up Simonstown, and there was no practicable alternative to it. Britain had an obligation to provide a limited range of marine equipment, but South Africa had agreed in writing not to use any of this against its neighbours, and, if South Africa did so, Britain would cut off the supply. It was not a matter of assisting or condoning apartheid, but of continuing a naval policy which benefited all Commonwealth states around the Indian Ocean.

Heath's argument, in its full sense, received little support except from Australia and New Zealand. It was clear that the African states were against it, though in varying degrees, and some of those who spoke did not appear to have read the agreement or to know where Simonstown was. The gist of the argument was that Britain could not be obliged to supply arms, since the Wilson government had not held this view. Any form of support for South Africa was support for its regime. If Britain went ahead with the supply of marine equipment, this would be a signal for other arms suppliers, some of whom were still holding back because of the UN resolution. Some said that Britain had made no real effort to find a substitute for Simonstown. There were suggestions that, if Britain went ahead, some African states might restrict

---

[1] *Survey B & CA*, 4 Dec 1970, p. 1050.

[2] I was in Singapore throughout the meeting, and permitted to attend British and other press conferences. The treatment of the issue here is drawn from information gained then from a number of sources. Special mention should be made, however, of Nyerere's pamphlet, *South Africa and the Commonwealth*, distributed at Singapore.

British trade and investment and consider leaving the Commonwealth. Above all, it was asserted that in the Commonwealth one basic principle was implicitly accepted by each member. 'If we are not opposed to racialism', wrote Nyerere, 'we have no business sitting down together in an association which consists of representatives of all the racial groups in the world.' Britain was asked to 'combine its interests with those of free Africa, and of those members of the Commonwealth who share our bitter hostility to racialism and colonialism'.

In the upshot, Heath refused to accept any sort of direction from the meeting. While agreeing to the setting up of a 'study group' to consider the position of the sea-lanes, he made it clear that his government retained its right to take such action as it considered necessary to give effect to its global defence policy, in which the facilities at Simonstown constituted an important element.

This was virtually the end of the matter. The study group was never set up. In the following month the British government issued a White Paper containing an opinion from the Law Officers about the extent of Britain's obligations to South Africa, together with correspondence between the two governments for some years past.[1] It then announced that certain helicopters for anti-submarine frigates would be provided.[2] No member left the Commonwealth. There were no punitive restrictions on British trade and investment anywhere in the Commonwealth. The storm had blown itself out. The minimal character of the 'arms' supplied was presumably the reason. The storm might revive if major arms were involved.

This illustration of how the South African problem had changed within the Commonwealth shows that for the militant Africans it was still the same problem, but plainly harder to solve, since South Africa's departure from the Commonwealth had not materially changed relations between it and Britain, the strongest and richest member, which continued to trade with it and refused to mount a full arms embargo. In spite of increased African membership, African influence had begun to decrease: after a failure to persuade Britain to use force in Rhodesia (for reasons explained at length below), there was a failure to prevent the sale to South Africa of arms which, while intended for external use, were a symbol of co-operation with what should be an outcast regime.

For other Commonwealth members, the South African problem, from being a simple matter of declaring oneself for multiracialism and against apartheid, had become transformed into one of calculating the importance of naval equipment in terms of a strategy which few could define and none could be sure of. It was also a matter of how to choose between the alternatives of trade and intercourse with an increasingly powerful market and supplier, and

[1] Cmnd 4589, 1971.
[2] See *Survey of Current Affairs*, Mar 1971, pp. 123–7, for a summary of the White Paper, the government's announcement, and the subsequent parliamentary debate.

the idealistic position espoused by Nyerere, in which states should deliberately accept being poorer if that would help to get rid of an abhorrent regime.

For Britain there was still a South African problem, not necessarily more acute than in 1961 but certainly more complex. Apartheid still flourished and still troubled the consciences of many British people. Moreover, it continued to disturb relations between Britain and most of the African Commonwealth members, since Britain's trade and investment were among the reasons for South Africa's prosperity, which in turn enabled it to keep its non-whites under control and to embark on its 'outward policy'. In spite of the failure of the black African states to bring down the South African regime, they remained a force in the world, and their voice was important to Britain.

In addition, the whole issue had been further complicated by the question of Rhodesia, to which we now turn.

CHAPTER 9

RHODESIA (i): THE LOST DOMINION

T HE subtitle harks back to a passage in an earlier volume in this
series:

New Zealand was . . . an example of the process by which a white colonial people,
determined to possess and rule, substitutes its will for that of the imperial trustee.
The white men claim self-government as their British birthright; and how can the
claim be denied? But how can the Empire's promises to its Native subjects be
denied? A compromise is sought. The claim to self-government is granted; but with
reservations of oversight and veto which safeguard the imperial trust. The reservations prove to be inconsistent with the principle of colonial autonomy. In substance
they are from the beginning ineffective; in form they become irreconcilable with the
dignity of a growing nationality. At last a Dominion is born.
Southern Rhodesia started on this path in 1923, when her white population was
only 33,000. Her progress during the ensuing years was rapid . . .[1]

In the chapter in which this passage appears, W. K. (now Sir Keith) Hancock
dealt with the beginnings of the Rhodesia problem. In a later book he questioned, in direct terms, whether Southern Rhodesia's advanced constitutional
status was something to be pleased about.[2] But Southern Rhodesia never
become the dominion of which he had written; it lost the chance of that status
through the passage of time and a change in British policy. The New Zealand
example no longer applied.

That example, like those of Australia, Canada, and South Africa, represented
a kind of structural fault in British colonial policy—the ultimate preference for
white settlers' 'British birthright' over 'the Empire's promises to its Native
subjects', in cases where the pressure from the white settlers was difficult to
withstand. This situation had not obtained in such diverse other dependencies
as India, the Sudan, Nigeria, or Uganda, where there had been few or no
white settlers, or where it had been policy to discourage a permanent white
element; it did obtain in Canada, Australia, New Zealand, and South Africa.

In Africa north of the Zambesi the argument had been loudest in Kenya,
where the doctrine of 'paramountcy' of 'Native' interests had been asserted by
the British government in 1923. In that same year the white settlers of Southern
Rhodesia achieved internal self-government. The Kenya settlers had been
caught in the paramountcy snare before they could attain that status; they
never acquired it thereafter. Those of Southern Rhodesia, while not much

---

[1] Hancock, *Survey*, ii, pt 2, p. 122.   [2] Hancock, *Argument of empire* (1943), p. 52.

more numerous, escaped the snare; as self-governing citizens they did not come under the administrative supervision of the Colonial Office.[1]

Southern Rhodesia was a throw-back to the days before the issue of paramountcy had been thought of: it was a nineteenth-century-type colony in which a nineteenth-century solution was sought by the white inhabitants who, when their right to full control over their native peoples was questioned, could point to the example of the old dominions. Indeed, they could go further and point to constant encouragement by British governments, to tacit recognition through the presence of their prime minister at Imperial and Commonwealth conferences, and to the fact that their formal link with Britain had consistently been through the Dominions and Commonwealth Relations Offices, not the Colonial Office. To them 'dominion status' was a legitimate right; any delay in granting it did not mean that they did not deserve it.

To successive British governments of the 1940s and 1950s, on the other hand, the grant of such status to Southern Rhodesia became more and more difficult because, in the meantime, self-government was being planned for other African colonies in which the rights of the Africans were recognized as paramount. In Southern Rhodesia the whites were outnumbered between ten and twenty to one by the blacks. If independence were granted to the whites alone, this would make nonsense, or at the very least hypocrisy, of what Britain was doing in other parts of Africa, since no logic could justify the simultaneous granting of political rights to Africans in Nigeria or Uganda and the withholding of the same rights from Africans in Southern Rhodesia. If the Rhodesian whites would agree to a gradual transfer of control to Africans, as it seemed they might do in 1961, then the British dilemma would be eased, even if the rapid pace of pan-African opinion and organization might not permit it to disappear. But if the white Rhodesians refused to allow such a transfer—as in 1963 they did—then the British dilemma would become more acute with each new manifestation of African independence elsewhere in the continent.

It was the fate of both Britain and Rhodesia that the structural fault which Rhodesia embodied should become starkly evident at the very worst time for both. For Britain it happened when newly independent African states were still being introduced into Commonwealth membership, when the conventions and understandings of the Commonwealth system were under strain, and when international opinion, focused through the UN, was directed towards the rights of subject peoples. For the white people of Southern Rhodesia it came after a series of shocks caused by the breakdown of authority in the newly independent Congo and widespread disturbances throughout the Federation

[1] The Office had been aware of the problem for many years, e.g. in 1906, when self-government was being considered for the defeated Boer colonies. Its head wrote: 'I am afraid that it is impossible to devise effectual means of controlling the native policy of a self-governing Colony', and his Assistant added: 'We may by provisions in the new Constitutions prevent things from getting worse, but once Responsible Government is granted we cannot do anything towards making things better' (quoted in Mansergh, *South Africa 1906–61* (1962), pp. 68–9).

of Rhodesia and Nyasaland, of which Southern Rhodesia had been a part since 1953. It also came when they were alarmed about the sudden expansion of the Commonwealth and the withdrawal, under Afro-Asian pressure, of South Africa. Above all, they feared that their own security and prosperity would disappear beneath a black flood. The result was a prolonged and bitter convulsion of Commonwealth relations. Even before the Rhodesian UDI of 11 November 1965, the Commonwealth had been disturbed by pressure upon Britain from African members to delay Rhodesian independence until Africans were in control. After UDI the issue of Rhodesia dominated two further meetings of Commonwealth prime ministers but remained unresolved. UDI was an affront to British pride and to the pride of the independent African states.

The departure of South Africa from the Commonwealth had seemed to herald a period of increasing co-operation and understanding between the African and the remaining original members. The effect of the Rhodesian issue was first to reduce this expectation, and then, after UDI, to substitute for the South African question another to which the Africans had an answer (the use of force against the white regime in Rhodesia), which Britain and the older members would not accept.

I

To understand the dilemma which the Rhodesian UDI presented one must recall the country's origins and its ten years as part of the Federation of Rhodesia and Nyasaland. This is not the place to relate a history of Southern Rhodesia,[1] but it is important to stress the fact that it was no ordinary colony. It had begun as an enterprise of Cecil Rhodes's chartered British South Africa Company, which from 1890 onwards occupied what became known as Northern and Southern Rhodesia and administered them for nearly thirty-five years before they were separated, the first to become a Crown Colony and the second a self-governing colony with responsible government. From 1923 onwards the Rhodesian settlers had, in practice though not in theory, full control of their country's affairs. The Imperial government retained certain rights of disallowance. A tradition of local control had been continuous from 1890 onwards, so that a Rhodesian minister could claim in 1966, after UDI:

Britain has never governed Rhodesia. . . . Unlike other territories in Africa to which Britain has granted independence in recent years, Rhodesia, in view of her fully self-governing status, has never been administered by the British Colonial Service, or, to use a common term, by 'expatriates'.[2]

[1] Some books which illuminate the question include Philip Mason, *The birth of a dilemma* (1958); Richard Gray, *The two nations* (1960); L. H. Gann, *A history of Southern Rhodesia* (1965); Colin Leys, *European politics in Southern Rhodesia* (1959); and Patrick Keatley, *The politics of partnership* (1963).

[2] Desmond Lardner-Burke, *Rhodesia* (1966), p. 10.

Two points are of importance when we are considering the later situation. The first is that the number of settlers was always small in comparison with the number of Africans over whom they exercised control. The 1922 referendum which decided Southern Rhodesia's future constitutional course showed 8,744 voters in favour of responsible government, and 5,989 for joining the Union of South Africa.[1] The number of white voters had trebled by the time of another referendum thirty years later, to decide whether they would enter the Federation, but was still barely 46,000.[2] Figures for total European population rose from 33,620 in 1921 to 68,954 in 1941 and 135,596 in 1951. Of this latter figure less than a third (i.e. 32·7 per cent) had been born in Southern Rhodesia. Another 30·5 per cent had come from South Africa and 28·8 per cent from the British Isles.[3] There were some 224,000 white Rhodesians when UDI was declared[4]—the population of a middle-range English city such as Leicester. There were just over 4 m. black Africans. The discrepancies of scale, which could be ignored in the mental climate of the 1920 and 1930s, could not be brushed aside by any British government in the 1960s.

The second point is that, during the first thirty years of responsible government, most Rhodesian politicians had been anxious that Northern and Southern Rhodesia should be amalgamated. The separation of the two territories in 1923 had been followed by Colonial Office policies of paramountcy in the North, while in the South responsible government had enabled white men to decide 'native' policy largely on their own terms. The discovery of rich copper deposits in the North made amalgamation more attractive from a Southern standpoint. The resulting growth of a significant white population on the Northern copperbelt (reaching about the same size in 1953 as Southern Rhodesia's in 1923) provided a link which settler leaders on either side of the Zambesi were keen to consolidate. The British government refused to agree to amalgamation because of the obvious dislike of the Northern Rhodesian Africans for what they regarded as discriminatory practices in the South.

Both of these aspects of Southern Rhodesia's development—the small size of the white population in comparison with the number of Africans, and the continual attempt to amalgamate with Northern Rhodesia—have to be viewed in the context of the economic situation in Central and Southern Africa between the two world wars and afterwards. The trend of economic development led Northern and Southern Rhodesia towards closer association with one another, and with South Africa. They were also linked to some extent with

[1] We are sometimes entitled to muse over the 'ifs' of history. If as few as 1,378 people had voted the other way in this referendum, there would have been no future Federation of Rhodesia and Nyasaland, and, more important, Southern Rhodesia (and according to Sir Roy Welensky (p. 56), Northern Rhodesia as well) would in 1961 have been as much a part of S. Africa as Natal, and would have left the Commonwealth with the rest of S. Africa. Britain would then have had no remaining 'settler' colony to complicate its African policies and its Commonwealth relations.

[2] Keatley, p. 425.   [3] Leys, pp. 73–6.

[4] Kenneth Young, *Rhodesia and independence* (1967), p. 8.

Nyasaland, a contiguous British colony. Northern and Southern Rhodesia were landlocked: if their copper and chrome and tobacco were to get to world markets, it had to be through South Africa or Mozambique. Railways were built to both adjoining countries, but South Africa was the main outlet. The original settlement had come from the South, and day-to-day economic contacts continued to be primarily with South Africa rather than with Europe. A steady number of white farmers and artisans continued to migrate from South Africa.[1] Both Northern and Southern Rhodesia absorbed African workers from neighbouring territories, of which Nyasaland was one of the main contributors to the workforce on the copper-belt. Southern Rhodesia's industrial future depended, to a considerable extent, on being able to sell manufactured goods to neighbouring territories, especially Northern Rhodesia, and to provide them with certain raw materials such as coal. Anyone viewing the scene with detachment would have said that these neighbours could not help influencing one another through the ordinary transactions of economic life, whatever the political boundaries between them.

Southern Rhodesia's form of settlement and its economic development combined to make it a sort of younger brother to South Africa and elder brother to Northern Rhodesia. With South Africa, its relationship was that of a brother with a difference: the Afrikaner traditions had not been transplanted to Rhodesia, and the relationship was very much with the English-speaking tradition in South Africa. It was customary to emphasize the British background of Southern Rhodesia's institutions and for its 'native' policies to be in line with those espoused by English-speaking South Africans rather than with apartheid. Ostensibly, the Southern Rhodesian franchise was a 'colour-blind' one, based upon money, not the colour of a man's skin; in practice, like the traditional 'colour-blind' franchise in the Cape, it prevented Africans from gaining seats in parliament.

With Northern Rhodesia, on the other hand, Southern Rhodesia's link was that of a permanent white population possessing a variety of skills and other resources with a smaller but much less permanent white population engaged largely in mining and without the same direct responsibility for native policy. It was an economic relationship somewhat akin to that which South Africa had with Southern Rhodesia.

Britain's link with this complicated interlocking system was largely external. So long as South Africa was in the Commonwealth, and African self-government had not advanced far in Britain's other dependencies, the British role as South Africa's partner and as the ultimate sovereign over Southern and Northern Rhodesia could be sustained without much difficulty. Direct policy was required only in Northern Rhodesia, which, because of the spectacular

---

[1] There were also a great many unofficial contacts corresponding to the movement of white people. Many Rhodesians were educated in S. Africa; Southern Rhodesia played as the equivalent of a S. African province in the Currie Cup cricket competition.

growth of the copper industry, did not present the same problems of economic underdevelopment as some other British colonies. No doubt there were people within the British governmental system who perceived the widening gap between Southern Rhodesia's type of self-government and the type that Britain was providing elsewhere in Africa; but, while there was some concern about the consequences of the situation, there was little disposition to deal with them in advance.

Partly, this was due to the fragmentation of responsibility in Africa between different British government departments. Southern Rhodesia's relations with Britain (and with the Federation while it existed) were conducted by the CRO, which, because it was also responsible for relations with South Africa and for the administration of the High Commission Territories, represented the British government south of the Zambesi. To the north, west, and east, the Colonial Office was in charge, except during the Sudan's period as a dependency under the Foreign Office. The CRO dealt on diplomatic terms with South Africa and quasi-diplomatic terms with Southern Rhodesia; it is hardly surprising that much the same tone and many of the same methods were used in communications with both. Britain had never governed Southern Rhodesia; it was the prisoner of the past, once the need arose to exercise the sort of pressure which could be exerted, with little difficulty, by a colonial secretary upon a colony such as Nyasaland or the Gambia. In colonies the governor was in complete charge of the local executive and was subject to orders from Whitehall. In Southern Rhodesia the governor had as little executive power as had the governor of an Australian State. The Southern Rhodesian government could not be compared, in power and authority, with the British government; but in practical terms it was better equipped to negotiate with British ministers than any governor or legislature in a Crown Colony.[1]

Whatever else had happened, Southern Rhodesia would have constituted a problem for Britain by the 1960s. The combination of white pressure for closer association with Northern Rhodesia, and black pressure from countries which had either gained independence or would soon do so, would have forced Britain into something other than its accustomed quietism about the self-governing colony. The task of readjustment was delayed (though it was made, if anything, more complicated) by the existence of the Federation of Rhodesia and Nyasaland between 1953 and 1963.

II

The Federation was an imaginative, if peculiar, attempt at solving the

---

[1] The problem of fragmentation of responsibility is well illustrated in Lord Alport's account of 'two Secretaries of State conducting separate constitutional conferences more or less simultaneously at a distance of 4,000 miles from each other' in January 1961, in respect of different parts of the Federation (Alport, pp. 26–7).

British problem in Central Africa.[1] Its origins have been briefly described by one who was Commonwealth secretary in 1951:

The idea ... originated with the [Attlee] Labour Cabinet. Although some, like Mr James Griffiths, had serious doubts, it was decided to explore the possibility of a federation. ... Arguments for a federation were powerful. Only a large unit could provide a reasonable base for economic advance, for a real university and the like. Above all, the incorporation of Southern Rhodesia with its northern neighbours seemed the only way of countering its gravitation towards South Africa.[2]

These motives were common to the moribund Attlee government in its last months and to the Churchill government which succeeded it. The colonial secretary, Oliver Lyttelton, said in parliament, on the Federation Bill, that federation might 'be the solution to the great problems, most of them inter-racial, with which the Continent of Africa is unquestionably faced in 1953'.[3] It was recognized that racial problems were growing, especially in Northern Rhodesia; it was hoped that accelerated economic growth in what was, in many ways, an economic unit would promote interracial harmony, and that the influence of an interracial parliament (to which each of the three territories had to send two African representatives) and an interracial university would encourage partnership between the races.

But the Federation was not comparable to other federations in the Common-wealth which had prospered, notably the Canadian and Australian. Those had been made by self-governing units freely deciding to come together for certain purposes, and the British government had had little or no responsibility for them. In this case only one of the three units was self-governing (Southern Rhodesia), and that only to the extent that its white minority was regarded as the 'self'. The other two were proceeding towards more representative institu-tions, but were both still controlled by local governors and the Colonial Office. Their dependent status was not altered by the constitution of the Federation, which provided for a federal government with federal powers but for the preservation of the existing governments in the units: this meant that Northern Rhodesia and Nyasaland remained under the Colonial Office. The federal

[1] There is an extensive documentation for the Federation. See the books by Alport, Welensky, and Keatley; Young, chs. 2–5; Richard Hall, *Zambia* (1965), ch. 6; Mason, *Year of decision* (1960); Edward Clegg, *Race and politics* (1960); John G. Pike, *Malawi* (1968), chs. 4–5; also Cmds 8753 & 8754 of Jan 1953 and Cmnd 1948 of Feb 1963. Mansergh, *Documents 1952–62*, has a section on the Federation (pp. 115–62), including a 'description of the Federal Scheme', pp. 119–26.
[2] Gordon Walker, 'The British Labour party and the Commonwealth', *Round Table*, Nov 1970, p. 508. By 1953, when the Federation was set up, the Labour Party had changed its view; see Mansergh, *Documents 1952–62*, pp. 129–32 for Attlee's second reading speech, which stressed African opposition. This remained the Labour Party attitude throughout the life of the Federation. For the 1953 division of opinion within the Labour Party, see Goldsworthy, p. 228.
[3] Mansergh, *Documents 1952–62*, p. 127.

government was a responsible one, accorded the same relationship with Britain through the CRO as Southern Rhodesia had previously had; but Southern Rhodesia retained that same status, whereas Northern Rhodesia and Nyasaland had not attained it.

The Federation was thus an association of the unequal, so far as its units were concerned. It was also an association of the unequal in respect of its citizens since, although the federal franchise was more generous towards Africans than the existing Southern Rhodesian franchise, the great mass of the population in all three territories was unrepresented in the federal legislature. It was a white man's parliament, mitigated by the presence of a few Africans. The government, first under Sir Godfrey Huggins (later Lord Malvern) and then under Sir Roy Welensky, was a white man's government.

This inequality might not have impeded effective government had it not been coupled with an inequality between the units which involved control of two of the territories by governors and a Colonial Office who wished to make Africans less unequal as citizens than either the federal or the Southern Rhodesian government was prepared to accept.[1] Broadly speaking, while Northern Rhodesia and Nyasaland were fully exposed to that growing consciousness of the 'wind of change' which caused the British government to defer increasingly to the claims of African nationalism, and while the federal government temporized in the matter, the underlying political forces in Southern Rhodesia were determined to enforce white man's control, not to give it up. An explosion could hardly be avoided. In the end it blew up the Federation.

The explosion—a long-drawn-out affair, spread over some five years and involving African disturbances in the three parts of the Federation—did not occur during the Federation's first five years. This was a period of very considerable economic growth, with a great deal of British and American investment, not only in the highly profitable copper industry of Northern Rhodesia but also in expanding industry and commerce in Southern Rhodesia, the capital of which, Salisbury, had been selected as also the capital of the Federation. In the opinion of *The Times*, writing in 1958, 'the phenomenal economic development in the early federal period [had] been due largely to widespread belief in the investing countries that the Federation was a safer proposition than the Union [of South Africa] because its racial policies were sounder'.[2] These racial policies had proved rather more liberal than the traditional policies of Southern Rhodesia, and had, at that stage, not been strongly challenged by the white Rhodesians, whose numbers were increasing through

[1] See e.g. Sir Roy Welensky's account of the secret dispatch of the governor of Northern Rhodesia, Sir Arthur Benson, in June 1956, and its effect on relations between the federal and Northern Rhodesian governments (Welensky, p. 70). See also Hall, *Zambia*, p. 164. For examples of the CO and CRO 'at daggers drawn' over Federation matters, see Macmillan, *Pointing the way*, pp. 134 & 165.

[2] Editorial, 'A Panic Measure', 3 Feb 1958.

immigration spurred by economic growth, and to whom the Federation must have seemed attractive because it was prosperous.

There had been no break in political leadership, since the prime minister of Southern Rhodesia had become the prime minister of the Federation, and his party remained in control of both, having changed its name and absorbed white political parties in the other two territories. To a motion calling for equal treatment of all races in public places in the Federation in 1954, Sir Godfrey Huggins had replied to the African mover, 'Be a little patient. Your time is coming.' It was better to avoid incidents: 'why spoil it and rush things in this deplorable fashion?', he said.

There is going to be inequality and differentiation. To pretend there is not, is to deceive everybody. Let us get on on the basis that we hope over a period of time to wipe out all these things as the African advances and the European becomes more enlightened. Let us do this for the sake of developing the country economically, which is what we have got federation for, not for the preamble—that was forced upon us.[1]

This speech contained in a nutshell the case presented by optimists, both in Salisbury and in London: the African would advance, but he must be patient, and the European would become more enlightened. Economic development would facilitate both processes. It was not usually suggested in Salisbury that the Europeans should learn 'the art of being submerged without actually drowning',[2] though it was often hoped in London that they would. Rather, white Rhodesians wanted European leadership to continue, so that 'partnership' between the two races would be between senior and junior partners, not between equals.[3] In the first few years of the Federation there was little indication that it would be otherwise; and the contrast between the Federation, apparently so 'British' in character, and South Africa, moving since 1948 so plainly towards Afrikaner republicanism, certainly made the Federation an attractive prospect to many in Britain.

The question of the Federation's international status, especially in relation to the changing membership of the Commonwealth of Nations, was brought up officially in 1956–7, when the movement of the Gold Coast and Malaya towards full membership was well under way. Up to this time the position of both Southern Rhodesia and the Federation had been embodied in Huggins,

[1] *The Times*, 31 July 1954. The reference to the Preamble is presumably to the entrenchment of the rights of Northern Rhodesia and Nyasaland to separate governments which would continue to control their land and to promote the political advancement of their peoples.

[2] 'Compromise in Capricorn', *The Economist*, 22 Oct 1955. The art, it was said, 'can be seen practised in the West Indies, where the black majority rules at the polls but the whites reign in society and enjoy the full influence conferred by education and business leadership'. Numbers, culture, and pan-Africanism prevented the art from flourishing in Central Africa, though it has been successfully practised, to some extent, in Kenya.

[3] See Leys, *European politics*, ch. 8, and his 'Power and principle in Central Africa', *The Listener*, 12 Sept 1957 for a cool but convincing assessment of dominant political ideas amongst white Rhodesians.

who became Lord Malvern in 1955. He had attended meetings of Commonwealth prime ministers since the Imperial Conference of 1937. This attendance had been based upon an invitation to Southern Rhodesia to attend the
Ottawa Conference of 1932, because this was an economic conference, and had
been confirmed thereafter on application from the Southern Rhodesian to the
British government. Huggins did not participate in constitutional discussions
and those affecting Commonwealth membership; he was not, for example,
invited to the 1949 meeting. Nevertheless, he had become something of a
fixture. In 1956 the prime ministers stated in their communiqué that,

taking into account the twenty years' attendance first by the Prime Minister of
Southern Rhodesia and now by the Prime Minister of the Federation of Rhodesia
and Nyasaland, [they] agreed that they would welcome the continued participation
of the Prime Minister of the Federation of Rhodesia and Nyasaland in meetings of
Commonwealth Prime Ministers.[1]

It was the opinion of Sir Robert Menzies that neither Huggins nor his successor, Welensky, was present 'as of right', since 'his country was not fully independent and therefore not a Member of the Commonwealth. But he was
present in continuation of a long-standing courtesy extended for many years.'[2]

Courtesy, however, was not enough. Huggins made it clear in 1956 that he
had always wanted the Federation 'in its own sphere [to] advance in constitutional status to complete independence irrespective of the position of the three
constituent territories, which would have their own separate, direct relationship with the United Kingdom government'. He thought the time had come
for complete independence to be granted to the Federation in its own sphere,
with the object 'merely to improve our international status vis-a-vis other
countries outside the Federation. This would enable us to talk to other countries as a separate State and not as someone else's child'. On his return to
Salisbury he explained that the British government had thought his proposal
legally impossible—since Northern Rhodesia and Nyasaland would still
remain the responsibility of Britain—but this he could not accept because it
was in total contradiction of the advice he had received when Federation was
being discussed. His solution of the 'native' problem was that the Federation
and Britain should conclude a treaty embodying all those safeguards for native

---

[1] Mansergh, *Documents 1952–62*, p. 132. There had been some earlier public discussion of
Huggins's attendance in 1954, when Sir Winston Churchill was asked in parliament why the
Federation was being asked to the 1955 Prime Ministers' Meeting, and Malta, the Gold
Coast, and Nigeria were not: they too were not quite sovereign states. Churchill answered in
terms of Huggins's personal qualities (*The Times*, 15 Dec 1954).

[2] Menzies, *Afternoon light*, pp. 216–17, from which some of the detail above is also taken.
There is a discrepancy between Sir Robert's recollection of these matters and the 1956
communiqué: he dates the consideration of the matter by the prime ministers from some time
after 1956, and applies it to Welensky, whereas clearly it came up in 1956 over Huggins.
Perhaps it came up more than once. A private source informs me that in 1956 the objection to
any idea of Huggins's attendance 'as of right' came from S. Africa.

interests which at the time were embodied in the federal constitution. He did not succeed in 1956, largely, he thought, because there had been a campaign in the Colonial Office to suggest that he wanted 'amalgamation by the back door'.[1]

In 1957 the new federal prime minister, Welensky, did obtain some concessions from a sympathetic Commonwealth secretary, Lord Home, and colonial secretary, Lennox-Boyd.[2] In a comprehensive attempt to upgrade the status of the Federation, Britain agreed to recognize a convention that it would not amend or repeal federal Acts without the consent of the federal government. It also agreed that in principle all civil services in the Federation should be locally based, and that, in the words of the joint communiqué,

> responsibility for External Affairs will be transferred to the Federal Government to the fullest extent consistent with the fact that, until the Federation becomes a separate international entity, there is a certain responsibility which in international law the United Kingdom Government must continue to have; the transfer to include, *inter alia*, the passage of a United Kingdom Act to enable the Federal legislature to make laws with extra-territorial effect.

This was an advance, so far as the federal government was concerned; but it was not an advance to agreed independence or full Commonwealth status, neither of which was attained by the Federation before its demise. It was enabled to appoint some diplomatic envoys, but in international terms it remained 'someone else's child'.[3]

Meanwhile the status of Southern Rhodesia was unaffected. Its ultimate status did not become an issue either in British politics or in Commonwealth circles; for the time being the hopes of most of its active politicians were centred on the Federation rather than upon 'dominion status' (a term still used in Rhodesia well after it had ceased to be current in other parts of the Commonwealth) for Southern Rhodesia itself. By those acquainted with the situation, it

---

[1] *The Times*, 3 Aug 1956.

[2] Ibid., 27 Apr 1957; Welensky, pp. 76–7. A private source intimates that in 1957 the federal government suggested an exchange of high commissioners with Canada, with some British support. The Canadian government demurred on account of the Federation's status, and said commissioners (not high) might be exchanged. The offer was not accepted. Ironically, the British government had previously opposed a Canadian suggestion of an exchange of high commissioners with the Federation of the West Indies, which had much the same international status as the Federation of Rhodesia and Nyasaland.

[3] There is some historical interest in the proposals advanced in G. H. Baxter & P. W. Hodgens, 'The constitutional status of the Federation of Rhodesia and Nyasaland', *Int. Aff.*, Oct 1957, since the first of the authors was a former assistant under-secretary in the CRO who had chaired the conference of officials which laid the groundwork for the Federation in 1951, and the second was a former private secretary to the first governor-general of the Federation, Lord Llewellin. The article suggested ways of overcoming the obstacles to 'the Federation's being recognized as an international person and accepted as a full Member of the Commonwealth'. In part they followed Huggins's proposals of the year before, especially in respect of a treaty, and in part depended upon interpretations of Commonwealth status which, while appropriate to the 1930s and 1940s, had little or no chance of general acceptance after 1957.

was sometimes said that 'Southern Rhodesia could have had dominion status any time after 1938, but chose to forgo this immediate possibility in the hope of achieving a wider federal arrangement'.[1]

That arrangement lasted for ten years, the first five of which, as has been said, were years of prosperity and economic advance, while the second five were punctuated by violence and by the growth of African nationalism in two of the three federal units. In that period the problem of Rhodesia as a Commonwealth issue began to arise, partly because of increased African influence in the Commonwealth at large and partly because of a steady growth of determination amongst Southern Rhodesian whites that they must be left to decide their country's future for themselves.

The prime cause of the break-up of the Federation was the pressure of African nationalism in Northern Rhodesia and Nyasaland, which took the British and federal governments by surprise. If they had agreed to put down the national movements with the heavy hand that characterized South Africa and later Southern Rhodesia, the course of events might have been entirely different. But there was no such agreement, no matter how much the British government might represent itself in public as supporting Welensky. Britain had too many other irons in the African fire to give full support to the white settlers of the Federation. In spite of the existence of a Conservative 'Rhodesia lobby' in the House of Commons,[2] the Conservative government of 1959–63 did not regard itself as bound to support the Federation through thick and thin. The point may be illustrated by reference to the 'secession' issue.

It was a matter of constant concern to supporters of the Federation that the constituent units might be allowed to break away from it.

Just so long [wrote G. H. Baxter and P. W. Hodgens] as there remains even in theory United Kingdom legislative power to undo what has been done in creating the Federation, there will be a strong human temptation for many African leaders to agitate against it rather than join in making it work, in the hope that a change of government in the United Kingdom might result in the Federal settlement being undone.[3]

Welensky had already told the colonial secretary that it was necessary

to make it plainly and unmistakably clear to the Africans that there is no possibility of secession from, or a break-up of, the Federation; that they must get used to the idea that their future lies within the Federation, and that at the review of the Constitution the question of secession will not even be considered.[4]

He got what he regarded as a 'quite unconditional undertaking'[5] from the colonial secretary that there would be no question of secession.

[1] Ibid., p. 452. Baxter's espousal of this statement gives it some credibility.
[2] See Goldsworthy, p. 366–7.   [3] Baxter & Hodgens, p. 451.
[4] Welensky, pp. 73–4; part of a letter to the colonial secretary, New Year 1957.
[5] Ibid., p. 74.

Within three years, after there had been disturbances in Nyasaland,[1] the Macmillan government appointed a special commission under Lord Monckton to consider the constitutional position of the Federation. Welensky fought hard to have the question of secession excluded from the commission's consideration, and thought that he had secured promises from the British government (specifically from Macmillan) that secession would not be considered by the commission when making its recommendations;[2] but in fact British members of the commission were told that they could interpret the terms of reference to include secession,[3] and when its report was published, it was clear that secession had in fact been considered. The commission did not recommend secession for any unit of the Federation, but did recommend that the possibility of secession should be included in constitutional arrangements for the future.[4] In the eyes of the federal government, this was a betrayal; but to the British government (as to the chairman and members of the commission) it was a recognition of the facts: in view of the widespread opposition to Federation in Northern Rhodesia and Nyasaland, it could survive only if the possibility of secession was included in any future constitution.[5]

The Monckton report's reference to secession was an earnest of the future; its qualified optimism about Federation was not. Its publication in October 1960 was followed in December by the Federal Review Conference, which the constitution required to be held not less than seven nor more than nine years after the Federation was set up. This proved to be no more than an occasion for competing oratory between the African nationalists of Nyasaland and Northern Rhodesia, and the federal delegates led by Welensky.[6]

Political advancement in the two northern territories had brought to positions of influence Hastings Banda and Kenneth Kaunda, the two men who were to dominate their later politics. The Federation could not survive if the

[1] These were the subject of the Devlin report (Cmnd 814), which rebuked the Nyasaland government for heavy-handedness, and claimed that there was considerable African opposition to Federation.

[2] Welensky, ch. 6, esp. pp. 160–1. See Macmillan, *Pointing the way*, pp. 140–2, for his side of the story.

[3] Birkenhead, pp. 342–3. According to Lord Butler, a member of the cabinet which decided to appoint the Commission, 'the arguments which persuaded the government were largely couched in terms of our own domestic politics: that is to say, it was held to be for the good of the Federation if Church and middle-of-the-road opinion at home could be reassured by a dispassionate and widely-based inquiry, and if the Labour Party could be dissuaded meanwhile from any firm commitment to break it up' (*Art of the possible* (1971), p. 209).

[4] For background, see Birkenhead, ch. 35. The official title of the report is *Report of the Advisory Commission on the review of the constitution of Rhodesia and Nyasaland*, Cmnd 1148 (1960).

[5] 'We thought that the only way to avert or postpone secession was to persuade Africans to give Federation in an amended form a fresh trial. We were convinced that the only way to persuade them to do so was to say: "You have nothing to lose by giving Federation a fresh trial because, if you do so, and still dislike it in its modified form, you may secede"' (Lord Molson, one of the Commissioners, in Birkenhead, pp. 356–7).

[6] The account in Welensky, pp. 285–90, is tendentious but has the ring of truth in describing the atmosphere. See also Alport, pp. 23–5, and James Barber, *Rhodesia* (1967), pp. 41–2.

forces represented by these two men were to get what they wanted. The Macmillan government cast the die in favour of African control of the two territories, and pressed ahead with new constitutional arrangements for them.

It is not surprising that Welensky and his ministers complained; what was more important for the future was the strengthening of the conviction of many white Rhodesians that Southern Rhodesia must get independence at the same time as, or no later than, the other two component parts of the Federation. Nyasaland, a small, backward territory with few white settlers, could become independent without troubling white Rhodesians too much; but Northern Rhodesia was another matter. In September 1961 the British government announced that it was proposing to examine the Northern Rhodesian constitution afresh, although it had already published proposals in June. In the meantime there had been riots and disturbance in that territory. It was brought home to white Rhodesians that they must safeguard their own future.[1] As will appear, Southern Rhodesian whites had voted for a more liberal constitution in their own territory only a few months before; but their subsequent voting behaviour showed them moving rapidly in a retrograde direction.

There is no evidence of the exact point in time at which the British government decided collectively that the Federation would have to be wound up. In March 1962 a Central African Office was set up under R. A. Butler, to sort out responsibilities and provide a unified policy in place of the divergent approaches of the CO and CRO. In just over two years, however, dissolution was complete, in spite of Butler's desire 'not to leave any territory out on a limb'. The obsequies of the Federation were observed at a conference at Victoria Falls in July 1963, when arrangements were made for the disposal of its assets and liabilities, together with the staff and activities of its government.[2] Nyasaland was represented only by observers, but the predominantly African Northern Rhodesian government was fully represented. The conference agreed that certain common services maintained by the Federation, such as the Rhodesian railways, the Kariba Dam, and Central African Airways, should be continued as co-operative ventures, and made important decisions about the future of the Federation's armed forces. It was agreed that

the position in regard to the operational control of the armed forces should revert to that which obtained before 1953 when Southern Rhodesia was responsible for her own forces and the United Kingdom Government had operational control of the Forces in the Northern Territories. . . . The physical assets of the forces would in general remain with their present units.[3]

[1] See Alport, pp. 88–91 for comment on this British decision, which in his view was 'made in isolation to ease a local situation without any regard for the wider, long-term consequences'.

[2] Cmnd 2093 (1963) gives details. See Butler, ch. 10, for the responsible minister's account of the operations of the Central African Office and the hopes he held for a time that some sort of association might still be retained between the three territories.

[3] Cmnd 2093, p. 12.

These inoffensive words disguised the fact that Southern Rhodesia would in future have a much bigger and better equipped air force and army than ever before, while the newly independent states would have little to show. The self-governing status of Southern Rhodesia ensured that it would get the lion's share of what was available. The Northern Rhodesian government agreed.[1]

In September, however, the UN Security Council was asked to consider the control of the armed forces, and an attempt was made to call on Britain not to make the transfer; the British government was forced to use its veto for the first time since Suez in order to defeat this resolution.[2] Relations between the former constitutent parts of the Federation were not, in fact, very difficult when the Federation was dissolved (apparently amicable trade arrangements were made between them),[3] but the pressure of African opinion was closing in upon Southern Rhodesia now that the possibility of its becoming independent as a white-dominated state was more obvious. The matter of the arms transfer had been raised in the Security Council by one Commonwealth member, Ghana, and supported by another, Uganda.[4]

III

From 1960 onwards the Southern Rhodesian issue became intensified through doubts about the future of the Federation, especially in the light of Iain Macleod's policies in Northern Rhodesia and Nyasaland. Directly, Southern Rhodesia had nothing to do with what was done in these territories, since its own relations were with the federal and British governments, but in other respects its political affairs were bound up with theirs. The same political parties were represented in the federal and Southern Rhodesian parliaments; Salisbury was both the federal and the Southern Rhodesian capital; and Southern Rhodesia had been the strongest influence within the Federation. The basic political aim in Southern Rhodesia remained what it had always been, to ensure that no British government interfered with the control of local affairs by white Rhodesians. The argument for this was that otherwise the prosperity and progress of the territory would be destroyed. The question of how to achieve the aim decided the course of Southern Rhodesian politics until UDI on 11 November 1965, and afterwards.[5]

[1] According to Harold Wilson (*Labour government*, p. 21) the Labour Party in Britain considered opposing the transfer of armed forces to Southern Rhodesia, but decided not to, after consultation with Kenneth Kaunda.

[2] Barber, p. 185. Southern Rhodesia had been discussed at the UN for over a year, in spite of protests from the British government, which lost its principal spokesman, Sir Hugh Foot, who resigned because of its negative attitude towards reform of the franchise in Southern Rhodesia (see Foot, *A start in freedom* (1964), ch. 10).

[3] *CS*, 4 Feb 1964, p. 124.

[4] W. Scott Thompson, p. 391.

[5] Two good books on the events leading up to UDI are Barber, and Young, *Rhodesia and independence*. The first is basically hostile towards the Southern Rhodesian government and the

When the Federation began to fall apart, Southern Rhodesia was still being governed by the party which, under Huggins, had been in office throughout the 1930s and 1940s. Its current name was the United Federal Party (UFP), and its leader was Sir Edgar Whitehead, who had taken office in 1958 after the deposition of Garfield Todd, Huggins's successor. It became the Rhodesia National Party (RNP) in 1963. Up to 1962 its main opposition came from the Dominion Party, a body rather further towards the right and less inclined to pay attention to African interests, which was merged into the Rhodesian Front (RF) in 1962. African nationalists were organized in the National Democratic Party (NDP), led by Joshua Nkomo. This was transformed, at the end of 1961, into the Zimbabwe African People's Union (Zapu), after having been banned for incitement to violence, like its predecessor, the African National Congress (ANC), which existed from 1957 to 1960 before being banned—as Zapu was in due course. Nkomo had been leader of all these bodies, but his headship was challenged in 1963, when Zanu (the Zimbabwe African National Union) split with Zapu, under Ndabaningi Sithole.[1] Both white and black political parties in Southern Rhodesia were thus liable to splits and changes, but the basic situation remained: one or two white parties with varying views of white supremacy faced one or two parties committed to African control and linked with African nationalist parties in other territories. Each side claimed the passive support of the rural Africans and of some of the urbanized Africans, and hoped to influence the British government to side with it. The African parties had connections with the anti-colonial movement in Britain, with the OAU, once it was formed, and with African states at the UN;[2] the white parties also had their connections in Britain, especially in the Conservative Party, and with politics in South Africa. The basic constitutional position, which had been slightly liberalized in 1957 and was to be again in 1961, was that the electorate, supposed to be based on capacity rather than race, was very largely white, and would remain so for a very long time in spite of provisions for increased African participation.

The more liberal 1961 Southern Rhodesian constitution, for which Whitehead campaigned energetically,[3] had been put together at a conference in Salisbury earlier in the year, attended by all the organized political groups (including the NDP) and chaired by Duncan Sandys, the secretary of state for Commonwealth relations, whose forceful management ensured that only the Dominion Party representatives dissented from the changes which the new constitution embodied. Nevertheless, Nkomo and Sithole soon reversed their

---

second basically sympathetic, but both are well documented and represent substantial efforts to arrive at the truth.

[1] The author of *African nationalism* (1959), a useful source of background to nationalist thinking.

[2] Day, *International nationalism*, is especially helpful on the external relations of the African nationalists.

[3] See Cmnds 1291, 1399, & 1400, 1961, for details.

previous approval, on the ground that although the constitution provided
more opportunities for Africans, it did not provide for 'one man one vote'.
Whitehead's strenuous campaigning at a referendum on the new constitution
in July 1961 resulted in its approval by 41,949 votes to 21,846.[1] Two aspects of
the campaign proved important in the long run. The UFP campaigned for a
multiracial future, presumably with the aim of enlisting higher-income
Africans to support it instead of the NDP; and Whitehead gave many people
the impression that, because the constitution restricted formal British powers,
it either involved independence in itself or was the prelude to an independence
already promised by the British government. The first aspect alienated many
waverers who had previously not been prepared to vote for the Dominion
Party, and helped to precipitate the formation of the Rhodesian Front. The
second had the same effect in that, once it was seen that the constitution did
not provide for independence and that the British government did not intend
to grant independence, many white Rhodesians turned towards the more uncompromising policies of the new Rhodesian Front.

The fruits of the 1961 referendum and its surrounding circumstances were
seen in December 1962, when the Rhodesian Front unexpectedly won a general
election on the new voting roll—an election boycotted by the African nationalist
leaders in the belief that they would get what they wanted more quickly by
denouncing the new constitution than by trying to work it. Whitehead had
continued to forecast a multiracial future. His tactics gave him support
amongst the few Africans who voted, but lost him the election amongst the
white voters.[2] Winston Field, the RF leader, found himself in office at a time
when relations with Britain were becoming the most urgent issue in Rhodesian
politics, on account of the rapidly approaching independence of Nyasaland and
Northern Rhodesia. The Federation was dying. It was symbolic that Field had
previously been the Dominion Party leader in the federal parliament, while
his lieutenant, Ian Smith, had sat there as a member of the UFP; now both
had returned to Southern Rhodesian politics to defend what they regarded as
vital interests.

Field began an exchange of correspondence with Butler,[3] which was to lead
in due course to Field's attendance at the Victoria Falls conference of mid-
1963 which wound up the affairs of the Federation. Field began by making a
formal statement that his government would not attend the conference unless
it received in writing an acceptable undertaking that Southern Rhodesia
would receive its independence concurrently with Northern Rhodesia or
Nyasaland, whichever gained independence first. In reply, Butler said independence would have to wait on the results of the conference, but made it

[1] Barber, p. 110; see chs 4–6 for the general political situation.
[2] Ibid., ch. 7 & App. II.
[3] A series of white papers gives more detail of communications between the British and
Southern Rhodesian governments than we possess of most aspects of Commonwealth relations.
They are Cmnds 2073 (1963), 2807 (1965), and 3171 (1966).

clear that thereafter a further conference would be necessary with Southern Rhodesia, in order to settle finance, defence, and other matters, including constitutional questions. Field found this latter condition unacceptable, since the constitution had been settled so soon before, with British participation. However, Butler stated that Southern Rhodesia's attendance at the conference was a prerequisite to discussion of independence. In the end, after Field had come to London for talks, he agreed to come to Victoria Falls. Butler concluded the correspondence by reminding Field that in London they had talked about the possibility that Field's government would amend the constitution to broaden the basis of representation in the Southern Rhodesian legislature, and about 'the future development of policy of non-discrimination'. These were not stated to be requirements before the British government would grant independence, and Butler affirmed that Britain would continue to refrain from legislating for the internal affairs of Southern Rhodesia; but the implication was clear: there must be a move towards multiracialism, or there would be no independence.[1]

Field revealed in his own parliament on 18 June that he had been told in London that there was opposition to independence for Southern Rhodesia from members of the Commonwealth, particularly the newer ones. He had replied 'that nothing would satisfy these people but the departure of all Europeans, and that we are not prepared to appease in this way'. He had also heard from the Canadian, Australian, and New Zealand governments that they hoped Southern Rhodesia would move towards a franchise whereby the African had the same rights as the European.[2] Thus, the Commonwealth had been brought into the forefront of the argument about Southern Rhodesia's future.

Field had less than a year to go before he was replaced as prime minister by Ian Smith in April 1964. In the meantime the British government made clearer the demands that had been foreshadowed in Butler's letters. The immediate issue of Field's deposition was his failure to secure independence, and his lack of persistence in threatening UDI.[3] His views do not seem to have differed significantly from his successor's, but he was less stubborn and less impressive. His replacement by Smith seems to have sharpened the whole approach of the Southern Rhodesian government. Smith epitomized in himself the dominant aspects of Southern Rhodesian society; it will help to make the issues of the Rhodesian affair clearer if he and what he stood for are described.

Smith was the first local-born prime minister of Southern Rhodesia. He came of 'small man' stock rather than from the moneyed professional and business groups who had normally provided Southern Rhodesia's leaders. His father, an emigrant from Scotland, had been attracted to the little mining

---

[1] This paragraph is digested from Cmnd 2073. See also Young, ch. 4, for the background as related to him by Field. See Butler, p. 226, for a correction of Young.
[2] CS, 30 July 1963, p. 656.   [3] Barber, pp. 190-3; Young, pp. 99-107.

village of Selukwe, and had worked as a farmer, a butcher, a baker, and a garage man. 'Cattle, race horses, and sport' comprised the atmosphere in which Ian Smith was brought up.[1] He went to Rhodes University in South Africa, breaking off his course to enlist in the RAF in World War II. He was shot down over Italy, fought behind the German lines with Italian partisans, then got across the Alps to join the allied forces in France. After the war he finished his degree at Rhodes and returned to Selukwe to farm. He was elected to the Southern Rhodesian parliament in 1948 as a Liberal Party member, and then, after five years, to the federal parliament for the UFP, becoming its Chief Whip. He broke with the UFP over its support of the 1961 constitution. He helped to form the Rhodesian Front—which, indeed, had many UFP men amongst its foundation members—and was made treasurer in Field's ministry. It is not likely that his opinions changed much with these changes in party.

Smith stood for the control of Southern Rhodesia by 'civilized' people, by which he understood those like himself, together with a slowly growing number of Africans who had accepted white men's standards. He seems to have been quite unmoved by the wish of successive British governments that Rhodesia should rearrange its racial policies to bring them into line with those in colonies under British control, especially in respect of the franchise. He was a Rhodesian nationalist in the sense that he wanted what he regarded as Rhodesian standards to prevail in Rhodesia, and not to have standards set by people from elsewhere, whether they were British or African. His attitude to the British demand for 'safeguards' in the constitution was: 'They know it will never affect *their* lives, so *we* should accept this; it will assist them in getting out of the predicament in which they find themselves'.[2] His politics were those of Rhodesia, described by Lord Alport as 'the politics of Lilliput' and essentially parochial in character.[3] To Smith and his ministers, the basic complaint against the British government was that it was interfering in things which it did not understand and which, in effect, it had promised to leave alone; moreover, it was doing so at the behest of countries which did not deserve to be listened to. 'The British attitude is one of appeasement, without any thought of the future of this part of the world', wrote Lardner-Burke; and he went on to express the basic indignation of white Rhodesians:

If our skins were black, we would have our Independence—the British could not have cared less. . . . When, oh when, will they see sense? When will they realise that their policy is so completely wrong? When will they realise that for the benefit of human beings, irrespective of colour, they should stop interfering with things they know nothing about?[4]

Lilliput or not, the British government was faced with a tenacious form of

[1] This, and most of the detail in the paragraph, are from Young, ch. 6.
[2] Ibid., p. 228.
[3] Alport, pp. 217 & 57–8; see also ch. 7 for a penetrating survey of political attitudes.
[4] Lardner-Burke, pp. 76 & 86.

nationalism when it attempted to tell the white Rhodesians what to do about the franchise. The fact that other British colonies, and former colonies, were involved by reason of the contrast between the progress of their Africans and those of Southern Rhodesia was not an argument which Smith and those like him would accept. Besides the danger of 'one man one vote' to their own interests, they pointed to the instability and lack of democratic freedoms of various newly independent African states; the example of the Congo was eagerly put forward, and reinforced by others as time went by.[1] Rhodesians with an international outlook, and those connected with the international business community, might take a different view, and stress the importance of Commonwealth and world opinion if Rhodesia was to prosper; but the dominant note amongst the smaller men, even (perhaps especially) those recently arrived from Britain, was of determination to retain Rhodesia's privileges and autonomy.[2] Young asserts that 'to most British politicians', Smith seemed 'a foreigner in all but language—a man of convictions so outdated, of tastes so naive, as to make mutual understanding almost impossible'.[3] Yet he was not so different from his predecessors. No white Rhodesian leader faced with the prospect of black majority rule would have acquiesced to suit the convenience of British ministers.

IV

The Commonwealth became a matter of immediate concern for the government of Southern Rhodesia only when the Federation was breaking up and Southern Rhodesia was actively seeking independence. However, the British government had recognized at an early stage that the Rhodesia question would need to be settled in Commonwealth terms, and not simply as a bilateral matter between London and Salisbury. Since Ghana's independence in 1957 the views of Commonwealth African states had been of direct concern to the CRO; the impending independence of Nigeria, Britain's biggest colony in Africa, made African opinion all the more important. Some of the considerations which led Macleod to quicken the pace of decolonization from the end of 1959 were applicable also to questions affecting Rhodesia. If it was necessary that colonies should become independent sooner than expected, it was also desirable that they should be members of the Commonwealth thereafter; certainly their future was considered very much in these terms.[4] But if they

---

[1] See, e.g. *Rhodesia in the context of Africa* (1966), the theme of which is the question, 'What have our detractors to offer us but the re-enactment of tragedy that has overtaken one African country after another?' (p. 70).

[2] See Perham, pp. 294–308, for a perceptive article of 1966, in which the white Rhodesians are described as 'a micro-nation'.

[3] Young, p. 128. A civil servant who had much contact with Smith disagrees strongly with this assertion, maintaining that Smith was 'honest and not un-British', but came to office with that great mistrust of British ministers which had become endemic in Rhodesia.

[4] I do not know of any case in which British ministers talked in advance of a colony

were members of the Commonwealth they would be informed of British colonial policy, and it would be advisable if they concurred. Certainly it would be undesirable if they objected.

The custom was for British ministers to report constitutional progress to each meeting of Commonwealth prime ministers, not as something for the meeting to decide but as something in which its members were closely interested. In strict legal terms, the advancement of colonies was Britain's business and no one else's; in political terms it was desirable that other Commonwealth members should concur in, and if possible applaud, the progress which Britain was making. If they could be associated in some way in that progress— as India and Pakistan had been in preparing for the independence of the Sudan, and Australia, India, and Pakistan in that of Malaya—this was all to the good.

It was presumably in pursuance of such an opinion that, in drawing up a list of those who might serve on the Monckton Commission, Macmillan in June and July 1959 suggested the inclusion of Malayans, West Indians, and Indians.[1] According to Welensky, he even suggested a Malayan as chairman at one point. The suggestions were strongly opposed by Welensky and Whitehead (who thought them 'intolerable'), and were dropped, although Macmillan returned to them some months later, to be told by Welensky that he could not agree to reopen the question. It was agreed, however, that the commission should include a Canadian (Professor Donald Creighton) and an Australian (F. G. Menzies, the brother of the prime minister). There were no white Rhodesian objections.

Perhaps this was why Australia, Canada, and New Zealand were brought in to 'try to force [Field's] hand', as he put it, when Butler was persuading him to attend the 1963 Victoria Falls conference.[2] Field cannot have been too distressed, because in October he said in a broadcast that his government would continue to put its case to the world, 'and particularly the older Commonwealth'.[3] However, Field and his government were disturbed by a speech in the House of Commons on 15 November by Sandys, in which he said:

We are asked by the Government of Southern Rhodesia, what are your terms for independence? What are the changes which would satisfy you? Our answer is that

achieving independence *outside* the Commonwealth, although this course had in fact been taken by Palestine, Jordan, and the Sudan, and was to be taken in 1960 by British Somaliland. The Middle East has been very much a special case in British colonial policy. What was done there does not seem to have had any effect on policy in black Africa, any more than in Southeast Asia or the Caribbean or Pacific.

[1] The authority for this statement and those which follow is Welensky, pp. 145–54.
[2] Young, p. 81. There is a reference to Sir Robert Menzies's correspondence with Field in Menzies, *Afternoon light*, with the information that Field considered Southern Rhodesia to be already a member of the Commonwealth, until he was corrected (p. 216).
[3] *CS*, 7 Jan 1964, p. 32.

this is not just a matter of satisfying us. The question of Southern Rhodesia's independence is one in which the whole Commonwealth is acutely interested. If we were to give independence to Southern Rhodesia on terms which were unacceptable to our fellow members we would be likely to cause grievous injury to the unity of the Commonwealth, and to the image it presents to the world. It is clear, therefore, that the whole Commonwealth will have to be consulted. I am wondering whether we might not go further than that. Might it not perhaps be possible for other members of the Commonwealth to help in a more positive way in the task of finding a generally acceptable solution?[1]

It appears that Sandys had in mind a conference at which Sir Robert Menzies, Lester Pearson, and President Nyerere would discuss Southern Rhodesia's independence with himself and Field. Field said he was not prepared to discuss Southern Rhodesia's problems and affairs with any other country than Britain.[2] Sandys replied with a message dated 7 December 1963 which laid down, more clearly than anything else on record, the position of the British government. 'The present difficulty', he wrote, 'arises from your desire to secure independence on the basis of a franchise which is incomparably more restricted than that of any other British territory to which independence has hitherto been granted.' (This, it is clear, remained the nub of the problem throughout the discussions between the two governments, up to and after UDI.) Sandys also brought in the Commonwealth question. 'This is how I see things', he said:

If Southern Rhodesia were to be offered independence on a basis which was unacceptable to Commonwealth opinion, not only would Southern Rhodesia's application for membership certainly be rejected, but the unity of the Commonwealth itself might be seriously threatened. The first is a prospect which I know you would be most reluctant to contemplate. The second is a risk which we would be most unwilling to take.

Having explained that he never had any thought of asking the Commonwealth to 'sit in judgment' on Southern Rhodesia, as had been suggested in the parliament in Salisbury, Sandys wrote that his government was 'most anxious to carry Commonwealth opinion with us' and believed they would be more likely to secure a realistic understanding of Southern Rhodesia's problems 'if we were to invite a few representatives of Commonwealth Governments to try to help us to find a generally acceptable solution' rather than present them with a cut-and-dried settlement. Since this was a European and African issue, he thought it right to confine initial consultation to the governments of two

---

[1] HC Deb., 15 Nov 1963, cols 584–7, for the whole speech. It is of considerable importance since it was the first official pronouncement on Rhodesia following the replacement on 18 October of Macmillan by Sir Alec Douglas-Home as prime minister. In the new cabinet Sandys retained his secretaryship of state for Commonwealth relations and the colonies and was also given responsibility for Central African Affairs, in place of Butler (*CS*, 22 Oct 1963, p. 882).

[2] Cmnd 2807, p. 6.

European and two African countries, and he suggested that the ministers of external affairs of these countries should be invited to have frank discussions with Field and himself, without any fixed agenda. He said the talks would be entirely exploratory and consultative in character:

They would not in any way affect the respective responsibilities of our two governments for the ultimate solution; and there would of course be no question of asking you to bind yourself in advance in any way to accept any advice which might be given.

He said that Canada, Australia, and New Zealand had expressed favourable interest in his statement in the House of Commons and he had no doubt they would 'go along with this plan, if it was agreeable to you'.[1]

On 13 December Field rejected this proposal saying it was without precedent in British colonial history, that it would be construed as a breach of the principle of exclusive responsibility which Britain claimed at the UN, and that:

The attitude of Commonwealth Governments towards this question is in our opinion likely to be conditioned either by doctrinaire considerations or by considerations of national interest which will have little or no bearing on the best interests of the people of Southern Rhodesia of all races now and in the future.

He said too that he could detect little evidence of objectivity in the approach of Commonwealth governments.[2]

A further exchange of messages took place after Field had made a hurried visit to England with some franchise proposals. Sandys wrote on 22 February 1964, mainly about a possible UDI, since there had been numerous press statements to the effect that this was being contemplated by Field's government. Sandys accurately foretold much of what eventually occurred, in terms of British, Commonwealth, and foreign reactions to UDI. On the Commonwealth he indicated that he did not think Field's proposals would be acceptable to any member government, and he had evidently obtained Canadian, Australian, and New Zealand approval for this statement. The crux of the matter was that 'we are not prepared to take action which might precipitate resignations from the Commonwealth'. He indicated that the question of Southern Rhodesia's membership of the Commonwealth was not the issue.

What we are concerned with is the likely reactions of other Commonwealth Governments to a decision by the British Government to grant independence to Southern Rhodesia, at a point of time when the franchise is incomparably more restricted than that of any territory which has acquired independence in the last 50 years.[3]

The final reference would have special significance for Southern Rhodesians, since the country which had gained independence with a restricted franchise could only be the Union of South Africa.

---

[1] Ibid., p. 7.   [2] Ibid., pp. 8–9.   [3] Ibid., pp. 10–11.

Field did not reply till 3 March. In the meantime Pearson, Menzies, and Holyoake had written to him to no avail,[1] and he had made clear, in his parliament, what he thought of the Commonwealth African states. They were 'mainly republics with their varying degrees of one-party dictatorship; some just flirting with communism, some obviously in love with communism if not already married to it'. They wished to interfere in Southern Rhodesia to divert attention from the appalling inefficiency, nepotism, and corruption in their own states.[2] In his reply to Sandys he said that for Southern Rhodesia the issue was not the impact of independence on the Commonwealth

but the preservation of our Constitution, which is essential to our freedom, against the efforts of international and Commonwealth forces to circumvent, and even suppress it. No one should know better than yourself that this Constitution is the very basis for the orderly advancement of the Africans here; and for this reason it is regarded as an obstacle by the enemies of the country. There is no doubt that African Nationalism in this country is directed and financed by Communist countries.[3]

From this point onwards, especially after Field's replacement by Ian Smith next month, the Rhodesia issue proceeded on two fronts: one on which the British government tried to persuade the Rhodesians to liberalize the franchise so as to ensure an African majority in due course; and another on which Britain withstood increasing pressure from Commonwealth countries to impose majority rule in spite of the Rhodesian government's disagreement. The two were closely connected.

The 1962 Commonwealth Prime Ministers' Meeting had been preoccupied with British entry into the EEC, and the question of Rhodesia was brought up only indirectly. The London representatives of Zapu handed in a petition about the franchise. However, between this meeting and the following one, in July 1964, the number of independent African members increased and the efforts of the Southern Rhodesian nationalists to influence them were redoubled. In 1963 Nkomo and his supporters appealed to Commonwealth heads of government to prevent independence for Southern Rhodesia under its existing consitution. Sithole, the rival leader, called for an emergency Commonwealth meeting to deal with the matter. Both groups made their presence felt at the 1964 meeting of prime ministers.[4]

The representations of Zapu and Zanu were not, of course, the only influences brought to bear on the Commonwealth leaders. The independent African countries, such as Tanzania, Sierra Leone, and Nigeria, were imbued in varying degrees with pan-African sentiment. The OAU had recently been formed and was an important focus of African attention, especially since an OAU summit meeting was to be held in Cairo immediately after the Common-

---

[1] Young, p. 103.   [2] S. Rhod. LA Deb., 26 Feb 1964 (Barber, p. 180).
[3] Cmnd 2807, p. 13.   [4] Day, p. 45.

wealth meeting in London. This was the first Prime Ministers' Meeting for
Kenya, Uganda, and Malawi (the former Nyasaland). Northern Rhodesia, it
was known, would soon be independent as Zambia, and the whole process of
dissolution of the Federation had been widely discussed throughout Commonwealth Africa. Southern Rhodesia remained an anomaly. The structural fault
in British colonial policy lay exposed for all to see at a time when relatively few
people in Britain were prepared to advance the former arguments justifying it,
and when African opinion was bitterly opposed.

v

In preparing for the Prime Ministers' Meeting of 1964, the British government was in a difficult position. At home, its tenure was insecure: not only had
Sir Alec Douglas-Home become premier the previous October in an atmosphere of dispute, in which some of the most prominent members of the
Conservative Party (including Iain Macleod) refused to serve in his cabinet,
but the sense of urgency about African affairs was ebbing in the party.[1] As
everyone knew, there was to be a general election before long; and there was a
widespread feeling that the Labour Party would win it, as in fact it did.[2] It
was highly desirable, from the government's standpoint, that the meeting
should be a success, since it would be one of the most publicized events of
Douglas-Home's administration. And it was important that the new African
states should not clash too bitterly with Britain over Rhodesia, since the break-
up of the Commonwealth would damage Britain's position in the world and
would strengthen the position of the Southern Rhodesian government.
Rhodesia would obviously be one of the main points of discussion. For the
British government, two questions stood out: whether the prime minister of
Southern Rhodesia should be invited to the meeting, as he had been before the
formation of the Federation; and what sort of case Britain could put forward in
respect of the Southern Rhodesian franchise and the prospects of independence.

Douglas-Home was questioned in the House about an invitation to
Southern Rhodesia a week after he had announced the Commonwealth meeting. He replied that the only persons entitled to attend as of right were prime
ministers of fully independent countries, and that 'therefore, before issuing
invitations to the Prime Minister of any country which is not independent, the
British government have always thought it right to satisfy themselves that this
would be generally acceptable to the other members.' He had accordingly

[1] The *Spectator's* political commentator believed that in February 1964 at least 100
Conservative MPs favoured granting independence to Rhodesia under white control without
delay, and that no more than thirty progressives were 'clinging with many a longing backward
glance' to Macmillan's 'wind of change' policy (quoted Goldsworthy, pp. 371–2).
[2] During the Commonwealth meeting, it was reported that fourteen of the visiting heads of
government had initiated talks with Harold Wilson as leader of the Opposition (*Guardian*,
15 July 1964).

asked Smith if he wished the other members to be consulted about an invitation. Smith had replied in the negative, since he claimed that he was entitled to be invited as of right. He was being asked to reconsider his position.[1] It was already known that Ghana opposed Smith's attendance: its High Commission in London had stated that its government was 'astounded' by the possibility that Southern Rhodesia might attend, and that the proposal had no basis in law or precedent. If any part of the former Federation was invited, it should be Northern Rhodesia, because of its universal suffrage and lack of racial discrimination.[2] Nehru had said in New Delhi that he would be opposed to Southern Rhodesia's inclusion if he were asked.[3] Whether the British government wanted Smith to attend or not,[4] it was not going to invite him in the face of such opposition. He did in due course consent to the other Commonwealth members' being asked; but this was no help, since Pakistan and Kenya joined in the opposition.[5] Douglas-Home explained to him that he had consulted the other prime ministers, and that the consensus of opinion was that, in view of the size of the modern Commonwealth, meetings should in future be confined to the representatives of fully sovereign states.[6]

This meant that Smith was being let down lightly, but he did not choose to interpret it in this way; rather, he said:

We are excluded now not because we are no longer loyal to the Crown or to the ideals on which the Commonwealth was founded. Nor was our case judged on its merits. We are excluded because the Commonwealth has outgrown itself and there is no longer room for us among the motley of small countries which have recently acceded to independence and been admitted to the Commonwealth without regard to their adherence to the ideals and concepts on which it was founded.[7]

Such a reply was likely to increase the dislike of Conservative backbenchers for the discussion of Rhodesian affairs at the Commonwealth meeting; but the government had at least been protected from a direct clash between Smith and African heads of government, such as had occurred in the case of Verwoerd in

[1] HC Deb., 30 Apr 1964, cols 583–4.   [2] *The Times*, 25 Apr 1964.
[3] *Guardian*, 28 Apr 1964. This was one of Nehru's last statements on Commonwealth affairs.
[4] According to *The Times*, in April many Conservative backbenchers considered it 'inconceivable' that Southern Rhodesia should not be represented 'at talks that might be crucial for it' (3 Apr 1964). An editorial on 1 May ('Inviting Mr Smith') said 'a discussion without Mr Smith would be *Hamlet* without the Prince. . . . Ghana and India should reconsider their objections.'
[5] *DT*, 26 May 1964. Canada is also believed to have been strongly opposed.
[6] Douglas-Home's public announcement is in HC Deb., 9 June 1964, cols 239–40. He said the consensus represented 'nearly all' the leaders consulted.
[7] *The Times*, 8 June 1964. Smith was quoted as being even more expansive at a banquet of the Sons of England Society in Salisbury, to the effect that 'the Queen today is the mouthpiece of party politicians and can't speak her own mind and heart' and that 'if anyone thinks they can interfere in our affairs and tell us how to run our country and how to lower our standards to appease outside opinion and the Afro-Asian bloc, then I will say—that will be the bloody day'.

1961, and it still maintained (as it had at the UN) that the granting of independence to Rhodesia was its own affair; other Commonwealth members could express their views but could not usurp the British right of decision. On what basis, though, was the decision to be made? What kind of franchise in Southern Rhodesia would be practicable in the circumstances of that country, in line with the conditions for independence in other British dependencies, and acceptable to other members of the Commonwealth?

The question was not fully answered; perhaps it never could be. Yet it took up an inordinate amount of time in the consultations between the British and Rhodesian governments in the next two years, always with the Commonwealth aspect apparent. Sandys had already indicated to Field that the franchise was the main problem in any British decision to grant independence; Smith's accession as prime minister had provided an opportunity to take the matter further. Writing to him on 20 May 1964, Douglas-Home reiterated Sandys's point of 7 December 1963, that the Southern Rhodesian franchise was 'incomparably more restrictive than that of any other British territory to which independence has hitherto been granted', and emphasized again that Britain would not legislate in respect of the franchise. He added, however, that while he fully understood the desire of the people of Southern Rhodesia to achieve early independence, he suggested that Smith might consider initiating some new compromise proposal, which, while not meeting the demands of extreme African opinion, might offer sufficient advance to secure acquiescence. The British government, either alone or in conjunction with other Commonwealth governments, would be glad to help in any way possible to bring about 'a generally acceptable solution'.[1] But Smith proved as awkward as Field, and as little prepared to help the government. He dismissed the point about the restricted franchise by saying 'it seems unbelievable that the criterion by which the right to sovereign independence is judged by the British Government can so ignore the history of experience already abundantly clear in the newly independent African States'. And he counter-attacked with what, to those who read it in London, must have seemed some justice:

> The situation is being made impossible. You ask us to alter the franchise but you will not tell us how it must be altered to meet your approval. You then withhold your grant of independence until such time as we amend the franchise to meet your requirements. With all respect to you personally, can anything be more unreasonable and more calculated to prolong the present state of uncertainty with all its attendant difficulties for Southern Rhodesia?

With this, with a request that the British government 'give me in writing, and for publication, either their terms for independence or their considered reasons for refusing independence on the basis of the 1961 Constitution', and with a

[1] Cmnd 2807, p. 16. Home and Sandys also asked Smith to come to London for talks either just before or just after the Commonwealth meeting in July, but he preferred to wait until September (ibid., p. 17).

reminder that the issue of independence was one for Britain and Southern Rhodesia, not for any other government in the Commonwealth or elsewhere, Douglas-Home had to be content until he met Smith after the Commonwealth meeting.[1] Meanwhile the Africans had to be faced.

It was made clear before the prime ministers actually met that the African members expected Britain to do more than simply negotiate with Smith's government. Obote, of Uganda, set the tone on his arrival by saying that, while he recognized Southern Rhodesia as an issue facing the British government rather than members of the Commonwealth, 'in Uganda our view is that power is in London. It is not an internal affair of Southern Rhodesia. It is an internal affair of the British government.' During the period of internal self-government in Uganda and British Guiana the British government had interfered in these countries' affairs. 'Why do they not interfere in Salisbury?'[2] Much the same point was made by others,[3] and the Ghana High Commission issued a booklet entitled *Britain's Responsibility in Southern Rhodesia*.[4] The foreign ministers of the African members took what the *Observer* described as 'the unusual step of arranging a meeting among themselves to discuss their attitude towards Southern Rhodesia', on the eve of the conference itself.[5]

There does not appear to have been a full consensus—Ghana, as in later situations, was inclined to stand apart from the others—but on the opening day it was reported that most of the African members had agreed on the following general line. The British government would be asked to recognize that the present constitution had failed; to institute a transitional period in which Southern Rhodesia would proceed to majority rule before independence was achieved; and to hold a conference of all political groups in that country to work out a new constitution. In return, the African members would help by trying to persuade the Southern Rhodesian nationalists to compromise on their demand for immediate universal adult suffrage.[6] The issue was debated mainly on this basis.

The formal basis of discussion was an item entitled 'Progress of dependent territories toward independence', placed on the agenda by Britain. The British government outlined its policy on independence for various colonies, and stated that 'Southern Rhodesia would attain full sovereignty as soon as her governmental institutions were sufficiently representative'.[7] Consideration of Southern Rhodesia took place in the wake of an emotional discussion of the

[1] Ibid., p. 19.   [2] *The Times*, 4 July 1964.
[3] e.g., Sierra Leone and Kenya: *Guardian*, 7 July 1964.   [4] Ibid., 4 July 1964.
[5] *Observer*, 5 July 1964.   [6] *The Times*, 8 July 1964.
[7] The British statement was included in the conference communiqué, issued on 15 July (Cmnd 2441, p. 4; *CS*, 21 July 1964, pp. 717–24). An interim statement on Southern Rhodesia and British Guiana was issued on the 10th (*The Times*, 11 July 1964). The description of conference proceedings which follows derives from the communiqué, from Pearson's report to the Canadian parliament on 17 July (*External Affairs*, Aug 1964, p. 359), and a broadcast by Menzies on 19 July (*CN*, July 1964, p. 32). Where newspaper references have been used, these are given.

South Africa problem, during which some of the prime ministers had called for economic sanctions and an arms embargo; they had also, at the instigation of Pearson of Canada, subscribed to a declaration on racial equality which was later included in their communiqué. The British Guiana issue, which was discussed at the same time as that of Southern Rhodesia, was itself emotional and explosive, involving disorder, racial strife, and the presence of British troops.

Essentially the African members called on Britain to treat Southern Rhodesia as the same sort of colony as their own countries had been—i.e. as one in which such matters as the franchise, the judicial system, and the defence arrangements were all British responsibilities. Obote and Kenyatta asked Britain to stop being vague about the responsibility for Southern Rhodesia, not to depart from 'one man one vote' as an aim, and to call a constitutional conference which those persons in detention in Rhodesia, such as Nkomo and Sithole, would be able to attend.[1] Pearson supported these requests, but evidently Menzies did not, since he believed, with Douglas-Home, that 'the Government of Southern Rhodesia was constitutionally responsible for the affairs of that territory'.[2] Much was made of the possibility of violence in Southern Rhodesia if moderate African opinion were not taken into account, Pearson believed that the greater danger was not speed but delay, and that 'unless some early progress is made . . . the African majority might be driven increasingly to despair and to the acts of desperation that despair can engender'. Kenyatta and Nyerere were reported as offering troops to help Britain if necessary.[3] According to the London correspondent of an Indian paper usually well informed on these occasions:

Delegate after delegate put the onus on Britain for doing something more [than simply negotiate with Smith] . . . a common factor was the convening of a constitutional conference of all the Southern Rhodesian parties.

In principle the British Government may not be opposed to the idea, but it has so far rejected a formal commitment in this sense, on the grounds, first, that Mr Ian Smith will refuse to attend such a conference, and secondly that the African leaders are under detention and it is not within Britain's power to order their release.[4]

The final communiqué reflected the gap between Britain and the Africans (though Menzies was said by one reporter's informant to be 'more British than the British', and more concerned about the white settlers than Douglas-Home).[5] It contained no promises by the British government other than its

[1] *DT*, 11 July 1964.
[2] On the political prisoners' issue, according to Menzies's own account, he got into some trouble because 'some people present thought . . . that I was advocating the imprisonment of political opponents. I regret to tell you I took the opportunity of saying that I was one of the few at the table who didn't imprison his political opponents.'
[3] *NYHT* (Eur. edn), 11 July 1964.
[4] *Hindu*, 12 July 1964 (dispatch from K. S. Shelvankar).
[5] *Guardian*, 16 July 1964 (report by Patrick Keatley).

original statement that sufficiently representative institutions would be necessary before independence.[1] Britain's responsibility was fully acknowledged. Any attempt at UDI was condemned, and it was made clear that no member would recognize it if it were made. Although Douglas-Home had been under continuous and often hostile pressure, Britain could be said to have come well out of the ordeal. The collapse of the Commonwealth, which had been widely forecast before the meeting, had not occurred.[2] Clearly, however, the Africans expected some further action by Britain.

In Salisbury, Smith appears to have been relieved, although he complained that the prime ministers had broken with precedent by their detailed discussion of domestic affairs. He had before him a report from his high commissioner in London, to the effect that Douglas-Home had 'done a splendid job', supported only by Australia. New Zealand, it said, had sat on the fence, the Asians had been indifferent, and the Africans (and Canadians) were looking for trouble. Pearson's 'reasonable' drafting of certain passages in the communiqué had, however, been adopted in place of a 'vitriolic' alternative from Nyerere. It was thought that Menzies and Holyoake were both 'personally sympathetic' towards Rhodesia, but they would not commit their governments.[3] Smith must have been confirmed in his conviction that little or no advantage was to be gained from the Commonwealth.

A meeting between Douglas-Home, Sandys, and Smith took place in London in September 1964. It followed numerous references in Rhodesia to the possibility of UDI, and visits by Smith to South Africa and Portugal, countries which might be expected to give at least tacit support to any action which preserved white control in Rhodesia. The record of the exchanges between the British and Rhodesian ministers[4] suggests that Douglas-Home and Sandys were anxious to avoid UDI but had no practical franchise proposals to advance. Instead, they appear to have felt that if Smith could get a satisfactory expression of African opinion in favour of the existing constitution, this would be enough to enable them to say that sufficiently representative institutions existed and independence could be granted. Neither seems to have regarded the opinions expressed by other leaders at the Commonwealth Prime Ministers' Meeting as binding upon Britain, although they wished to see some deference paid to the demands for a constitutional conference and the release of political prisoners.

Douglas-Home felt that a test of African opinion about independence on the basis of the 1961 constitution, 'if based on some form of referendum or the

---

[1] Although it was reported that Nyerere and Kenyatta thought an undertaking had been given that a constitutional conference would be held (*The Times*, 16 July 1964).

[2] Pearson had shown prescience when, on arrival, he had been asked to comment on the suggestion that the Commonwealth was on the verge of breakdown. He replied: 'I have been in government service in one form or another since 1927, and the Commonwealth has been breaking down since then' (ibid., 8 July 1964).

[3] Young, pp. 142–3.   [4] Cmnd 2807, pp. 21–39.

equivalent, could be argued to be a sufficient alternative to a conference as a means of ascertaining the wishes of the population', but if it did prove possible for Southern Rhodesia to proceed to independence, it would subsequently be necessary to arrange a conference if only for the purposes of general "tidying up". On the political prisoners, the British ministers seemed satisfied with Smith's assurance that no one was in prison for 'purely political reasons'. Douglas-Home certainly envisaged the possibility that Southern Rhodesia might have to accept independence outside the Commonwealth because of some African members' continued opposition.

The real problem was how to be sure that Rhodesian African opinion supported independence under the 1961 constitution. Smith offered an indaba of the chiefs and headmen, a method which gave little or no opportunity for detribalized, urban Africans to be heard. Home and Sandys wanted a referendum. The point was not fully settled, but the British representatives made it clear that an indaba would not be enough, and in the subsequent communiqué the British government 'reserved their position'. So matters stood until the day before the British general election, when Smith informed Douglas-Home that he needed to hold an indaba in a week's time so as to protect chiefs and and headmen from further intimidation. Douglas-Home replied that the British government could not regard this as representing the opinion of the people as a whole.[1] Next day the situation had changed: Harold Wilson had won a bare majority.[2]

VI

Wilson had met Smith once, and impressed him as businesslike and reasonable.[3] Their exchanges, as recorded in White Papers, suggest some empathy between them, in spite of the differences in the positions they took up, in the backgrounds of experience from which they operated, and in the slogans which they employed. Each was a politician aware of the other's difficulties; neither was a patrician; each could see why the other was acting as he did. There is a hint of more understanding between them than there had been between Smith and Douglas-Home and Sandys. This may explain in part why they met so often, even after UDI; it certainly helps one to understand why Wilson persisted in his efforts to find a solution which Smith could commend

[1] Smith expected the message to be dealt with by the new prime minister, whoever he was, but it got to Douglas-Home quicker than Smith had calculated. Douglas-Home's immediate response surprised Smith, who was thereafter confronted with more of a bi-partisan British policy than he had anticipated (Young, pp. 159–61). The exchange of messages is in Cmnd 2807, pp. 39–41. The speed of reply is said to have been due to Sandys, not to Douglas-Home.

[2] It is ironic, but worth recording, that Nyerere, Kaunda, and Obote sat around a radio in Dar es Salaam listening to the election results: 'At the news of every Labour victory we cheered, and when the Tories won we groaned', said Kaunda afterwards (Richard Hall, *The high price of principles* (1969), p. 43).

[3] Young, p. 156.

to the Rhodesian Front. Their early exchanges, however, were cool, after Smith's indaba proposal and his refusal to agree to the British government's condition that Arthur Bottomley, Wilson's Commonwealth secretary, should see Nkomo and Sithole in detention. It was some time before they came to grips.

Meanwhile, Wilson issued a public statement on 27 October in which he spelled out much of what Sandys had previously told Smith about the unpalatable consequences for Southern Rhodesia of an attempt at UDI.[1] Smith's main riposte was to tax Wilson with a letter he had written during the British election campaign to Dr Mutasa, a Rhodesian African, saying that the British Labour Party was totally opposed to granting independence to Southern Rhodesia so long as its government remained under the control of the white minority, and had repeatedly urged the British government to negotiate a new constitution with all the African and European parties, in order to achieve a peaceful transition to African majority rule.[2] Wilson did not publicly take up Smith's challenge about the letter. Instead, he adhered to the previous government's position: 'We have an open mind on the timing of independence in relation to progress towards majority rule . . . but the granting of independence must be on a basis acceptable to the people of the country as a whole'.[3] From this point onwards, over several years they moved slowly through an intermittent series of detailed discussion of the franchise, of A rolls and B rolls, blocking thirds and quarters, cross-voting, Senates, a House of Chiefs, a treaty, a royal commission, and special entrenchment procedures. We will not follow them into this thicket of detail, although the documentation is ample,[4] but will consider how the Commonwealth aspect affected the discussions, before and after UDI.

Wilson announced in February 1965 that a Commonwealth Prime Ministers' Meeting would be held in London in the second half of June.[5] Between this announcement and the meeting, Smith's main step was to issue a White Paper of his own in April, the purpose of which was to show that Southern Rhodesia would not suffer greatly from a UDI, even if Britain and other countries took the steps that Wilson had threatened. Rhodesian business interests appear not to have shared the Smith government's view, but it was firmly held, and helped Smith to overwhelming success in a general election on 7 May, when the Rhodesian Front won 50 out of the 65 seats in the Legislative Assembly.

[1] The text of this statement was left out of Cmnd 2807. It is in *CS*, 10 Nov 1964, together with statements in support from Commonwealth countries and the US—and a forecast of S. African policy from Verwoerd.

[2] The text of Wilson's letter is in Young, p. 171. Smith's repeated inquiries about it are in Cmnd 2807, pp. 47 ff.

[3] Ibid., p. 48.

[4] See the remainder of Cmnd 2807, which goes up to the UDI; Cmnd 3171, which carries the story on till the *Tiger* talks of December 1966; and two other White Papers: Cmnds 3793 (1968) and 4065 (1969).

[5] HC Deb., 4 Feb 1965, cols 1280–3.

Meanwhile Britain received gentler treatment at the hands of the UN than might have been expected. A move by the Soviet Union to demand that Britain revoke the Rhodesian elections got support from no one else, and the Council adopted an innocuous resolution which largely followed British policy. The signs, it seemed, were set fair for the 1965 Prime Ministers' Meeting.[1]

After the 1964 refusal to admit Smith, any attempt to invite him to this meeting would seem to have been useless, but Smith issued a statement deploring the absence of an invitation, and it was reported that Wilson was at first willing to ask the other prime ministers to allow Smith to be present when Rhodesia was discussed.[2] As we have seen, the meeting occurred just before a proposed Afro-Asian conference at Algiers. Also, it was the first to be attended by Kaunda. One might have anticipated, therefore, that African pressure would be stronger and more effective than in 1964. It was very strong, but not so personal. There was still something of a honeymoon between the African leaders and the British Labour government. The communiqué differed little in substance from the 1964 one except that the British government went some- what further in regard to a constitutional conference, which had again been urged by the African members. It 'would be ready to consider promoting such a conference in order to ensure Rhodesia's progress to independence on a basis acceptable to the people of Rhodesia as a whole' if the discussions being held with Southern Rhodesia did not develop satisfactorily. This was vague, but a little more definite than what the Africans had achieved in 1964. Their views were expressed in a statement that 'other Prime Ministers' (i.e. some other than the British prime minister) 'welcome the statement of the British Govern- ment that the principle of "one-man-one-vote" was regarded as the very basis of democracy and this should be applied to Rhodesia', and in references to political prisoners and to an appeal by the Africans for the British government to suspend the 1961 constitution and appoint an interim government if the Rhodesian government refused to attend a constitutional conference and release the detainees.[3]

Nyerere dissociated Tanzania from the communiqué. He said that, while the British government's basis for negotiations rested upon agreement on the principle of majority rule, upon an improvement in the franchise to give Africans a 'blocking third' in the Assembly, and upon a Rhodesian under- taking that there would be no reversal in progress to ultimate majority rule, this was not enough. Explaining his refusal to join the other African leaders, he said:

I am not concerned about timetables. I know that this is a tough, difficult business and that it cannot be done in a hurry. But this does not matter so much as long as the

[1] The information in this paragraph is from *CS*, 25 May 1965, pp. 486–95.

[2] *The Times*, 5 Feb 1965. There is no mention of this in Wilson's *Labour government*. His account of the discussions on Rhodesia at the Prime Ministers' Meeting is on pp. 114–19.

[3] See *CS*, 6 July 1965, pp. 623–4. Wilson describes the communiqué as 'an essentially compromise draft' (p. 118).

objectives of achieving independence *on the basis of majority rule* were established in advance. But it was the adamant refusal of Mr Wilson to commit the British Government to these six words that caused all the trouble.

In Nyerere's view, the British government remained free, in terms of the communiqué, to negotiate with Smith on the basis of majority rule being deferred indefinitely after independence was granted. So long as this remained the position, the rest of the British concessions were simply 'blah-blah'.[1]

There had clearly been differences of view amongst the African leaders. Nyerere, the most logical and outspoken, was not fully typical. He had made his position clear before the meeting began. If there was a Rhodesian attempt at UDI, this would be rebellion; if there was no UDI, Britain should call a constitutional conference; and if Smith did not attend, this would be rebellion too. It would not be physically impossible to put Smith in prison. 'I know what would have happened to us if we had rebelled', Nyerere had said.[2] But when Banda of Malawi had arrived in London, he had accused Nyerere's Tanzania of harbouring Malawian rebels;[3] and during the meeting Sir Abubakar Tafawa Balewa, of Nigeria, was reported as having said that the Africans in Rhodesia should have some experience of government before they took over full control.[4] At the meeting the foremost radicals were Nkrumah, Nyerere, Obote, and Kaunda, but Nkrumah and Nyerere had already clashed in 1963 over the proposed East African Federation and in 1964 at the OAU meeting, in respect of freedom fighters and Ghanaian proposals for African union. Nkrumah, after presenting the African members' main demands at the opening of the Rhodesia discussion,[5] evidently decided to play a moderate part rather than support Nyerere.[6] Obote appears to have been appeased by the British concession of considering a constitutional conference.[7] This left Kaunda as the leader most vitally concerned, and the one most likely to support Nyerere.

Kaunda was probably troubled in his conscience before deciding to support the communiqué rather than Nyerere. On the one hand in his burning idealism he was more akin to Nyerere than to anyone else at the conference; on the other he was aware that if Britain and Rhodesia could find a peaceful solution, this would make his task of government easier in Zambia, which remained heavily dependent on Southern Rhodesia for much of its trade and services, and which still had a substantial white minority without whom the copper industry could not be carried on.[8] Smith had threatened in his White Paper that if, following a UDI, Britain took economic reprisals, Rhodesia would

---

[1] *Observer*, 27 June 1965.   [2] *The Times*, 17 June 1965.   [3] Ibid., 15 June 1965.
[4] *Guardian*, 23 June 1965.   [5] Wilson, p. 114.
[6] W. Scott Thompson, pp. 330–3, 352–3, 390–1.   [7] *FT*, 25 June and *DT*, 26 June 1965.
[8] Kaunda is one of the most interesting figures of the period in Commonwealth affairs. See his appealing autobiography, *Zambia shall be free* (1962), written before he took office; *Zambia: independence and beyond* (1966, ed. Colin Legum), his speeches; and Hall, *High price of principles*, about his experiences after independence.

consider the repatriation of foreign workers and their families. There were 500,000 of these from Zambia and Malawi in Rhodesia. Repatriation would create acute problems for Kaunda. The railways and power from the Kariba Dam were essential to Zambia; yet these could be disrupted if the Rhodesian government chose. Rhodesia had formidable armed forces; Zambia did not.[1]

Kaunda was convinced that Britain should take responsibility for whatever happened in Southern Rhodesia. He told the Royal Commonwealth Society in London:

Make no mistake. Former British colonies and the rest of the world will turn their backs on Britain if, through her weakness or refusal to face her responsibilities, she allows another South Africa to emerge in Southern Rhodesia.[2]

He offered Britain Zambian facilities if military action should be needed against Rhodesia, and cited British Guiana, Malta, and Cyprus as cases in which constitutions had been suspended and troops used to keep order;[3] after the meeting he emphasized that Zambia would never agree to independence for Rhodesia on the basis of transferring power to a minority—'never, never'.[4] Yet he agreed to the communiqué which left the British government such a free hand. Perhaps the reason was that, according to Richard Hall, the Zambians had been told in private by Wilson that he would send troops to Rhodesia if there was a breakdown of law and order. In Hall's view, by a breakdown of law and order, Wilson meant communal rioting and civil disturbance of a kind which, in British colonies, normally called for the dispatch of British troops to safeguard lives and property; but Kaunda and the other Zambians interpreted it as either the use of draconian methods by the whites against black nationalists, or simply an illegal declaration of independence which to Wilson was a constitutional matter, not one of law and order.[5] If Hall is right, Wilson's promise could have tipped the scale with Kaunda.

Whatever the reason, Wilson had weathered the Prime Ministers' Meeting with nothing to tie his hands except the promise to consider a constitutional conference in loosely defined circumstances. Menzies and Pearson, in their respective statements,[6] supported Wilson. 'I must say I thought Mr Wilson and his Government went as far as any government could go on this matter', said Menzies. Pearson said it was 'a very difficult conference'. He had been reported as going along with the Africans, though deprecating the use of force.[7] Wilson wrote to Smith on the day the meeting ended:

[1] Kaunda's reply to Smith's White Paper is in *Zambia: independence and beyond*, pp. 217–21.
[2] Ibid., p. 224.
[3] *Guardian*, 22 June 1965. Kenya and Tanzania also offered facilities.
[4] Ibid., 30 June 1965.
[5] Hall, *High price of principles*, p. 112. There is no mention of this in Wilson's book.
[6] Menzies's statement is in *CN*, June 1965, pp. 349–50, and Pearson's in *External Affairs*, Aug 1965, pp. 326–7.
[7] *FT*, 22 June 1965.

Our purpose during the meeting has been to try to keep the temperature down and the ground clear for negotiations on which we are engaged with you. I am grateful for your own forebearance at this time and your understanding of the difficulties which I have been facing here.

He stressed the wide support at the meeting for a constitutional conference; but he also emphasized Britain's sole responsibility for Rhodesia's independence, and how the British government had 'refused to be deflected from negotiations between the two Governments as the next step'.[1]

There were in fact further negotiations, but they do not seem to have got very far. Cledwyn Hughes, the British minister of state for Commonwealth relations, visited Rhodesia in July, but little came of the visit; in the middle of September Smith told Bottomley that he was still expecting 'definite and concrete opinions' but had not received them. He also asked for British views on independence outside the Commonwealth. In reply Bottomley brought up the 'Five Principles', which had been put forward by Bottomley and Lord Gardiner during a visit to Rhodesia in February and which represented the British government's requirements for independence.[2] As stated by Bottomley, they were:

(i) The principle and intention of unimpeded progress to majority rule, already enshrined in the 1961 Constitution, would have to be maintained and guaranteed.
(ii) There would also have to be guarantees against retrogressive amendment of the Constitution.
(iii) There would have to be immediate improvement in the political status of the African population.
(iv) There would have to be progress towards ending racial discrimination.
(v) The British Government would need to be satisfied that any basis proposed for independence was acceptable to the people of Rhodesia as a whole.[3]

These principles, not quite so ambiguous as the Four Freedoms but having something in common with the highly flexible Panch Sheela, were the basis of future discussion with Smith. They involved neither one-man-one-vote nor majority rule before independence. In effect, they were Sandys's and Douglas-Homes's requirements codified. As such, they met the same difficulties: Smith was prepared to give up neither the reality of white control nor the possibility of perpetuating that control by future constitutional change. Wilson had little capacity to apply pressure. Possibly he thought that the widely-expressed opposition to UDI of business interests in Salisbury would suffice to prevent

---

[1] Cmnd 2807, pp. 61–2. Smith replied that a conference would be interference in Rhodesia's internal affairs, and that he was not interested in what other members of the Commonwealth said.

[2] In fact the five principles had been originally enunciated by Sandys and Douglas-Home, and had been put before Smith as a basis for discussion during his September 1964 visit to London. Smith, according to Douglas-Home, then expressed 'no sort of objection to them' (Young, *Douglas-Home*, p. 201).

[3] Cmnd 2807, pp. 65–7.

it; in any case, he had many other matters to attend to, at home and abroad. Smith, in contrast, had a relatively simple polity to govern. Its overriding concern was independence, in the light of which all other questions paled. The 'micro-nation' of white Rhodesia became, throughout 1965, convinced of the inevitability and desirability of UDI.[1] A decision is said to have been made by Smith and his cabinet well before September 1965.[2]

Rumours of what might happen in Rhodesia were widely current, though there was no certainty about what form UDI might take. Smith visited London early in October, to no avail.[3] The British government, following this visit, took the precaution of obtaining royal approval of Lord Mountbatten's appointment as governor of Southern Rhodesia, if the Smith regime should attempt to seize the local fount of lawful authority in the person of the existing governor, Sir Humphrey Gibbs.[4] At the end of the month Wilson himself visited Salisbury, in a last attempt to come to terms.[5] This too was of no avail. On 11 November Smith made his illegal declaration of independence. Southern Rhodesia was not to be a dominion after all.

[1] The mood is well described in Barber, pp. 299–300.
[2] Young, *Rhodesia and independence*, pp. 211–12.
[3] Wilson, pp. 146–9.　　[4] Ibid., pp. 150–1.
[5] See ibid., ch. 11, for a vivid account of this journey.

CHAPTER 10

RHODESIA (ii):
THE COMMONWEALTH AFTER UDI

I N the many pages of published communications between Wilson and Smith
in the months before UDI, there is relatively little mention of the Commonwealth. The minutiae of constitutional change occupy most of the space.
Nevertheless Wilson did make at least one effort to resurrect the suggestion
about Commonwealth mediation made earlier by the Conservatives. On 12
October 1965 he suggested to Smith that 'a collective Commonwealth voice'
might be able to produce proposals worthy of consideration. He had spoken to
Menzies, who had said that if Smith would receive it, he would take part in
a small Commonwealth mission of 'respected senior statesmen', who would go
to Rhodesia and examine the whole situation. Wilson suggested that the prime
ministers of Nigeria and Ceylon 'and perhaps one other Commonwealth
country' might also take part. Smith's reply was lengthy and strong. He
reiterated the view that the Commonwealth had no jurisdiction in the matter.
In any case, 'a mission in keeping with your suggestion must have within its
ranks people who have openly expressed themselves as enemies of the present
Rhodesian Government and Constitution'. He quoted Tanzanian, Zambian,
and Indian statements which suggested that a Commonwealth mission would
be no use.[1] Again it was clear that whereas the British government viewed the
Commonwealth as a valuable bridge between peoples and races, the Rhodesian
government saw it as a source of African and possibly communist influence.[2]
Smith said publicly in the Legislative Assembly on 1 July that the question of
whether Rhodesia should seek independence within or without the Commonwealth was very much in the balance:

[It] depends on which faction in the Commonwealth gains the controlling influence.
If it is those nations . . . who believe in maintaining standards and principles, then
I believe Rhodesia will wish to retain its links. On the other hand, if it is those
nations who have rejected all those things that we believe in, then I feel that we will
have nothing in common with the Commonwealth and it would be hypocritical for
us to retain our association with them. . . .
   We have conclusive proof that three countries to the north of us, fellow members
of the British Commonwealth, are aiding and abetting the training by Chinese
communists of saboteurs against Rhodesia.[3]

[1] Cmnd 2807, pp. 95–8, for the exchanges on this point.
[2] Ibid., pp. 81 & 114–15.   [3] *CS*, 20 July 1965, p. 663.

Whichever these countries were, they were not, of course, 'fellow members of the British Commonwealth'. By this time, presumably only Rhodesians were likely to think of their country as a 'member' of the Commonwealth, British or not, and not many can have believed that, if Britain granted Rhodesia independence under the Smith government and the 1961 constitution, it would be acceptable to the others as a fellow member. Smith could afford to deride and ignore the Commonwealth. Indeed, his statements suggest he was more concerned about the effects of UDI upon Rhodesians' attachment to the monarchy.[1] Wilson, in contrast, could not ignore the Commonwealth. He had come to office with the reputation of a strong 'Commonwealth man'; he subscribed to the sort of viewpoint that had impelled Sandys to write, 'We are not prepared to take action which might precipitate resignations from the Commonwealth'. There had already been, on 12 October, a public threat by Nyerere to withdraw Tanzania from the Commonwealth if Britain granted independence before making full arrangements for majority rule.[2] Others might follow, creating a sense of disturbance in Britain, where 'Commonwealth' was still a word of power with parliamentary and public opinion.[3]

I

A word of power, no doubt; but what was the Commonwealth as a political factor? As we have seen, the 1964 and 1965 Prime Ministers' Meetings had not produced either unanimous or practical policies on Rhodesia, although most of the overseas members had agreed on what they wanted Britain to do. The Commonwealth factor included a number of discordant elements.

First and most obvious were the African militants, represented in their most strident form by the public utterances of Nkrumah's government in Ghana, at their most logical and attractive in the arguments of Nyerere, and at their most urgent in those of Kaunda. Obote of Uganda and Margai of Sierra Leone were others in this group. With variations, their position was that, having either experienced the use of force by British administrations in their own countries or seen it deployed in such other colonies as Aden, British Guiana, and Cyprus, they saw no reason why Britain should not use it against the Smith regime in Rhodesia. The arguments used by the British government—that Rhodesia was unique, because of its long tradition of responsible government,

---

[1] Two days before UDI, the Rhodesian government sent a letter to the Queen, signed by all its members, stressing how dear the person of the sovereign was to all the peoples of Rhodesia, and ending, 'whatever happens there will still be found among all Rhodesians that same loyalty and devotion to the Crown which have guided and sustained us since our country was founded' (ibid., 23 Nov 1965, p. 1164).

[2] Ibid., 26 Oct 1965, p. 1015. It is of some importance that in this same speech Nyerere rebuked the refugee Rhodesian nationalists for their divisions and lack of practicality.

[3] Wilson regarded Commonwealth opinion as one of the four 'dimensions' or 'constituencies' which the British government had to take into account, the others being Rhodesian opinion, British public opinion, and the UN (Wilson, p. 181).

its substantial armed forces, etc.—seemed to them largely irrelevant, if not hypocritical. They believed that the reason why Britain had not used force was the reluctance of the British to fire on white men, a reluctance which, in their view, had not existed in the case of coloured people, or even those (like the Cypriots) who, while white, were not 'kith and kin' to the British themselves. The African militants could deploy additional arguments which were less emotional. They could, for example, cite the opposition of all the white Commonwealth members to apartheid, and assert that if the Smith government were allowed the independence it claimed, another South Africa would be created in Southern Rhodesia. They could also argue that both the stated basis of British colonial policy in other parts of Africa and the declarations about racial equality of the 1964 and 1965 meetings would be undermined by a mere appearance of acquiescence in the Smith position. They could argue too that in other African countries, notably Kenya, white people had been able to live as before under a system of majority rule; why then should the white Rhodesians be given special privileges?

Next along a spectrum which led from militancy to passivity were probably the Caribbean states, especially Trinidad in the person of Eric Williams, and the Indians, anxious to retain good standing in Afro-Asian circles, where the Indian position was under pressure from Pakistan, Indonesia, and China. They, together with the Pakistanis and Ceylonese, were liable to counsel moderation in private and support extremism in public. Some African states—especially Kenya and Nigeria—were animated by a general sense of African nationalism, but were cautious about the use of force in the Rhodesian situation. These, like most others, still had ties with Britain which they did not wish to prejudice. Such a heterogeneous group of states would probably vote for an extremist resolution at the UN, and not oppose it publicly at a Commonwealth meeting, but would not go so far in condemnation of Britain as the militants.

Next, in the direction of passivity, was Malawi, an awkward quantity for the other Africans, because of its close connection with the Rhodesian imbroglio since the days of Federation, and because of Hastings Banda's view that Malawi would suffer if outside pressure were exerted on Rhodesia. The thousands of Malawian workers in Rhodesia would be among the first to be affected; Malawi was economically dependent on Rhodesia and South Africa in a great many ways; and Banda himself was being opposed by younger men whom he had banished and who had taken up the cause of the 'freedom fighters' against whom Rhodesian police and military effort was directed. The Malaysian position was somewhere near Malawi's, but less vocal.

Beyond Malawi in the spectrum lay the white members of the Commonwealth, uneasy in this situation which they had not created but which had uncomfortable resemblances to aspects of their own development. The Canadian government generally supported the Africans, except on the use of force, but emphasized the need to keep the Commonwealth together, and suggested using the resources of the UN. The New Zealand position oscillated between the Canadian and Australian, but came to rest somewhat closer to the Australian, which was given special force by the strong personality of Menzies. Menzies wanted no Commonwealth or UN interference: he wanted Rhodesia to be viewed as a problem for Britain alone, to be solved in whatever way suited Britain. There were strong Australian reasons for stressing the principle of domestic jurisdiction in situations of this kind.

There was, indeed, a good deal of difference in the background to the Canadian and Australian positions. Pearson, untroubled by participation in the Vietnam war or Malaysian-Indonesian confrontation, could operate from the normal Canadian assumption that the Commonwealth was a valuable bridge between peoples and continents, and that multi-racialism was its essence. He could, and did, refer appreciatively to Diefenbaker's siding with the Africans and Asians in 1961, when South Africa had withdrawn. With no Canadian problems at the UN, but with the experience of successful Canadian participation in UN peace-keeping activities, he could view with equanimity the possibility of UN action on Rhodesia. Menzies, on the other hand, concentrated upon the issue of Britain's sole responsibility for Rhodesia, largely because of conviction that this was right, but also, presumably, through wariness of possible UN and Commonwealth interference in Australian affairs. Australia's experience at the UN had been different from Canada's: no troops for the peace-keeping operations (but some policemen in Cyprus); continual defensiveness in the face of questioning about Australian policy in New Guinea; and a tradition of stressing the sanctity of domestic jurisdiction because of the danger of UN interference in Australian immigration policy. Menzies had supported South Africa's continued membership in 1961; since then he and his government had viewed with distress the appearance of one-party regimes in Commonwealth Africa, and had been disturbed by the possible growth of communist influence. There was thus no basic solidarity amongst the members of the 'old Commonwealth', although none was in favour of the use of armed force. Canada showed the greatest sympathy with African wishes, Australia the least.

What was the British position, in the face of a Commonwealth which, in spite of its lack of harmony, could not be ignored? Undoubtedly the British government wished to preserve, in Africa, the good reputation it had gained by its policy of granting independence. What had been a matter of mingled expediency and belief with the Conservatives was one of even greater belief (though necessarily also of expediency) for the Labour Party, traditionally opposed to imperialism and thinking of itself as the creator of the 'new Commonwealth' through Attlee's decision to grant independence to India. In more recent years opposition to racialism had sharpened within the party and amongst articulate opinion in Britain. 'The argument is about racial equality. Implicit acceptance of racial equality has been an obligation of Commonwealth membership ever since India became independent', said Bottomley in the first Commons debate after UDI. 'Britain's attitude to racial equality is well known.' He also pointed out that British 'kith and kin' in Rhodesia were not the only ones in Africa. There were large British communities in Zambia, Kenya, Tanzania, and most other Commonwealth countries in Africa. If the British government took a one-sided racial view of the situation in Rhodesia, racialism might be the reaction of other governments in Africa.[1]

Thus there were arguments of both principle and prudence for heeding Commonwealth opinion about Rhodesia. The point was endorsed in another debate in December by Douglas-Home, who was by now Conservative spokesman on foreign and Commonwealth affairs (he had been replaced as Conservative leader by Heath). Wilson, in his view, had been right, 'in weighing up the balance, always to consider the reactions of the Africans in the Commonwealth countries'; but he added that, while the right way to satisfy them was to ensure that there would be majority rule in Rhodesia, the wrong way was 'to tag along behind those extremists who want force'.[2]

Force and majority rule were the two issues dividing Britain from the African governments, though the British position was not simply negative. It may be summed up in five points, the first three negative, the last two positive. Britain's policy was:

a. not to accept UDI;
b. not to give it any semblance of legality;
c. not to use force unless the governor of Rhodesia said that law and order had broken down;
d. to employ economic sanctions against the Smith regime;
e. to work for a viable constitutional government in Rhodesia, majority rule not being regarded as a feasible proposition for the time being.

Basically, these points of policy were common to Wilson, to his predecessors, and (after his electoral defeat in 1970) to his successors. They all regarded (a), (b), (d), and (e) as the most important. It was in respect of these that Britain invited Commonwealth help. To the militant Africans, however, (c) was what mattered, since they doubted both the desire and the capacity of the British government to make a success of (d) and (e). So they continued to demand the use of force in the service of majority rule in Rhodesia, to be instituted as soon as possible.

Wilson had ruled out the use of force before UDI. In talks with African leaders (including Nkomo and Sithole) in Salisbury in October, he said he regarded it as his duty

to remove from their minds any idea or any hope they might have had that Rhodesia's constitutional problems were going to be solved by an assertion of military power on

---

[1] HC Deb., 12 Nov 1965, cols 523 ff.   [2] Ibid., 20 Dec 1965, cols 1988 ff.

our part, whether for the purpose of suspending or amending the 1961 constitution, of imposing majority rule tomorrow or any other time—or for that matter of dealing with the situation that would follow an illegal assertion of independence. To quote the words I used to them: 'If there are those who are thinking in terms of a thunderbolt hurtling from the sky and destroying their enemies, a thunderbolt in the shape of the Royal Air Force, let me say that thunderbolt will not be coming, and to continue in this delusion wastes valuable time, and misdirects valuable energies.'

He had also explained his position on majority rule to Rhodesian Africans:

Secondly, I said: "Although successive British Governments are deeply and irrevocably committed to guaranteed and unimpeded progress to majority rule, the British Government, who alone through the British Parliament have the legal power to grant independence, do not believe that in the present tragic and divided condition of Rhodesia, that majority can or should come today, or tomorrow. A period of time is needed, time to remove the fears and suspicions between race and race, time to show that the Constitution of Rhodesia with whatever amendments may later be made, can be worked, and is going to be worked, and that the rule of law, equally with the maintenance of essential human rights, will be paramount. And the time required cannot be measured by clock or calendar, but only by achievement.[1]

Wilson stuck tenaciously to his position on the use of force, although he was later to modify, under pressure, his insistence that majority rule need not be introduced before independence (see below). His argument on force was to be that economic pressure, in the form of sanctions administered first by Britain, then through Commonwealth and UN means, would bring the Smith government down. It is possible that military force was considered but rejected before this emphasis on economic pressure became the official policy.

In *The Times* of 4 August 1965 (an ambiguous anniversary) its Defence Correspondent wrote that serious thought was being given by the government to the problem of planning for a possible military intervention in Rhodesia. Such intervention might follow from an internal political dispute involving the Rhodesian armed forces, from a straight UDI, or from a request by Zambia for military aid. It was clear, according to this article, that Rhodesia would be difficult to invade: the problems were different from those faced by Britain in other colonial situations, for reasons involving numbers of troops (the Rhodesian armed forces were substantial), supply (Rhodesia was landlocked), and morale (the Rhodesians were 'British' in all but their determination to disobey the British government). Although this article was described by the minister of defence, Denis Healey, as 'irresponsible speculation',[2] it is quite likely that military opinion was consulted and proved hostile to any suggestion that an invasion of Rhodesia would be easy or bloodless, or, indeed,

[1] Ibid., 1 Nov 1965, cols 629–49.
[2] *The Times*, 5 Aug 1965. For a version of Healey's views on the great difficulties of using force, see Williams & Reed, pp. 189–91.

should be undertaken at all.[1] In any case, the prospect of governing a Rhodesia which had been subdued by force must have daunted a British government which had no more recent experience of governing a defeated white people in an African setting than its efforts in the Transvaal and Orange Free State after the Boer War.

Wilson did agree to a Zambian request, soon after UDI, to provide air cover, since Zambia had received so little from the division of the Federation forces. However, the British forces kept to the Zambian side of the border and did not venture into Rhodesia. In the event of a Rhodesian attack, Wilson stated, Britain would not 'stand idly by'; but the operation did not go nearly so far as the militant Africans wanted. Wilson said he had not agreed to Kaunda's request for ground forces to 'take out' the Kariba generating station, one of the legacies of Federation which was on the Rhodesian side of the Zambesi. He also made it clear that the RAF contingent was going to Zambia to 'prevent the stationing of other air forces in Zambia, wherever they may come from, as a means of providing air cover for President Kaunda'.[2] The requests from Kaunda had followed a meeting between his vice-president and Kenyatta, Nyerere, and Obote, in Nairobi.[3] It is possible, as Hall suggests, that it was the prospect of an OAU 'liberation army' operating from Zambia that goaded Wilson into this particular action. More likely, perhaps, was the desire that Zambia should not call on some other major power for protection against Rhodesian military pressure. The RAF detachment may also have been regarded as a form of psychological warfare against Rhodesia, along with radio broadcasts.[4]

The British government appears to have feared the wider consequences which might flow from any attempt at military action against Rhodesia, but especially from military intervention which was prolonged and not immediately a success. Wilson's speeches after UDI, like his sombre final statements to Smith, contain numerous references to the possibility of wider conflict in Africa. In the Commons on 12 November he said that the danger of great powers getting a foothold in Africa could not be dismissed. Chinese attempts at penetration had become a by-word; other nations might wish to emulate the

[1] Young asserts (p. 329) that the commander of the British Land Forces in the Middle East, who had accompanied Bottomley to Zambia, believed enormous forces would be necessary, even to cross the Zambesi. There is a military appreciation of the problem in W. F. Gutteridge, World Today, Dec 1965. Readers who do not despise imaginative approaches to serious matters will find special interest in Douglas Hurd & Andrew Osmond, Send him victorious (1969), in which pp. 104–7 contain operational orders for the subjugation of Rhodesia, prudently set in the year 1975; they are, however, severely practical.

[2] HC Deb., 1 Dec 1965, cols 1429–41. Young says (p. 332) that the RAF planes had to use Air Traffic Control at Salisbury to get safely into Ndola and Lusaka, their airports in Zambia.

[3] Young, p. 325.

[4] Hall, High price of principles, pp. 125–6. Private information suggests that some African governments (notably Ghana) had alerted parts of their forces to serve in a 'liberation army'. See CS, 10 June 1966, p. 618 & 30 Sept 1966, p. 990, for the British government's setting up of a broadcasting relay station at Francistown in Bechuanaland.

success they thought China was having. Certain states might be glad of the opportunity of establishing a foothold with the substantial backing and the aura of legitimacy provided by a resolution of the UN. There was, indeed, the prospect of a 'red army in blue berets'[1]—of a Russian contingent in a UN peacekeeping force. To a Britain that had been disturbed by the prospect of Russian intervention in the Congo imbroglio four and five years before, this was not an idle speculation. In any case, even if the Russians did not participate, there still might be an OAU army or substantial African contingents in a UN force; in addition, Rhodesian nationalists might set up a 'government-in-exile' and be recognized by some African states, in and out of the Commonwealth, although not by Britain. It did not take much imagination to think that Rhodesia, if mishandled, could 'set Africa ablaze', as the point was sometimes emotionally put.

More immediate, however, was the possibility that action against Rhodesia might trigger some conflict involving South Africa. In Britain a section of opinion had been seeking sanctions against South Africa because of apartheid, and there had been persistent Afro-Asian pressure to the same end at the UN.[2] Britain, as South Africa's main trading partner and a source of investment capital, had been under special pressure, to which it had not acceded except in terms of arms supply. South Africa and Rhodesia were identified in the minds of many African leaders, and probably in the minds of many people in both those countries. From a British standpoint the two problems were formally quite separate but were plainly linked. The same political forces, at home and abroad, were calling for strong action in both cases; unforeseen consequences might flow from Britain's taking that action. Nevertheless, in the Rhodesian case Britain had full formal authority to do what it thought fit against a rebellion within one of its own dependencies, while in the South African case it would be acting against a sovereign state. What was discipline in the one instance would be akin to war in the other. The British government certainly did not want war with South Africa, either in direct terms or as a result of disturbance in Rhodesia; nor did it wish to impose economic sanctions on South Africa. Its own trade would suffer badly if it did. South Africa might well become involved in assistance to the white regime in Rhodesia if that regime were menaced by other African states through the efforts of either a 'liberation army' or groups of 'freedom fighters'. South Africa would hardly stand idly by if its northern frontier were set alight. True, it would hardly welcome sanctions or boycotts against Rhodesia, because of its opposition to boycotts against itself; Verwoerd said so publicly on the day Smith declared UDI.[3] But it would not be so troubled by these as by the use of military force, and

---

[1] HC Deb., 12 Nov 1965, cols 619 ff.   [2] See Austin, pp. 12–20.

[3] CS, 21 Dec 1965, pp. 1291–2. Verwoerd said: 'It is self-evident that ... it is of exceptional importance for the Republic of South Africa that its normal intercourse with its Rhodesian neighbour should continue as in the past.' This policy was pursued to a degree which nullified most of the economic discrimination exercised against Rhodesia by others.

they would not be likely to cause so much unforeseen disturbance in the general position in southern Africa. The same reasoning applied to Portugal, which would also be affected by any action against Rhodesia.

Lastly, in any assessment of the policy to be pursued towards Rhodesia's UDI, the Wilson government must have been influenced by the political situation at home. The Labour Party had a bare working majority in the House of Commons. A public opinion poll taken in October 1965, a month before UDI, showed that, of those interviewed, only 2 per cent were in favour of the use of armed force if Rhodesia declared itself independent without British consent; 15 per cent were in favour of trade restrictions; 63 per cent thought Britain should refer the matter to the UN; while 18 per cent thought no action at all should be taken. There was little or no difference between people with the three different forms of party attachment, Labour, Conservative, and Liberal. Moreover, when asked where their sympathies lay when thinking of Rhodesia, only 29 per cent of the sample had said they lay with the Africans, and 28 per cent with the Europeans. The remainder had said 'neither', 'both', or 'don't know'. In this case there was a slight increase in the proportion of Labour supporters whose sympathies lay with the Africans, but they represented only 35 per cent.[1] Clearly, there was no pressing demand for force in the interests of the Africans, which was what the African members of the Commonwealth had been urging on Wilson. Other considerations apart, the use of force might be political suicide, especially if it was not an instant success.

The British position, then, rejected force and stressed the need for economic action involving as many as possible of the countries which normally traded with Rhodesia. From the beginning, it was expected that there would be difficulty in persuading South Africa and Portugal to participate in any way, but diplomatic pressure might induce them not to be obstructive. Once economic sanctions had 'bitten' it was optimistically hoped that a change of government might take place in Rhodesia.[2] In the meantime, Britain's Commonwealth partners must be patient.

The divergences within Commonwealth opinion were dramatized at the Commonwealth Parliamentary Association's conference at Wellington a few weeks after UDI. In a long and often acrimonious debate on Rhodesia, the use

[1] NOP *Bulletin*, Spec. Suppl. I, Rhodesia, Oct 1965. 81% of those questioned did not know that Europeans comprised only 5% of Rhodesia's population. A further poll nearly a year later, in September 1966, showed that 16% thought force should be used, and 72% that it should not. Those against force were very divided in their alternative, though leaving things to the UN got more support than other possibilities. Again there were no significant differences between party supporters (ibid., Sept 1966, p. 11). In December 1966, when asked if force should be used *if sanctions failed*, 20% said it should, and 74% that it should not (ibid., Spec. Suppl., Rhodesia, Dec 1966).

[2] The emphasis was upon trying to stop Rhodesia getting essential supplies, especially oil, and preventing the sale of Rhodesian exports, especially tobacco, sugar, and metals. No doubt the Rhodesian government suffered considerable difficulties, but S. Africa and Portugal soon knocked enormous holes in the sanctions net, and these were never mended. For admirable summaries of sanctions provisions, see *CS*, 1965, 1966, and succeeding years. (See also p. 240 n. 7.)

of military force was urged on Britain by the leaders of delegations from Nigeria, Zambia, India, Jamaica, Uganda, Pakistan, Sierra Leone, Kenya, Ghana, Tanzania, and Trinidad, and by those speaking from Ceylon and Barbados. Economic sanctions were derided: they would be 'unworkable, weak and silly', said the leader of the Zambian delegation; Uganda believed that, if effective, they would merely make the Africans suffer. Persistently it was pointed out that Britain had used force (and was still doing so) in other dependencies. Britain, Australia, and New Zealand were isolated in deploring any use of force. Canada and Malaysia, while not calling upon Britain to use it, appeared to agree to its use by the UN. Speakers from some small, still dependent, territories such as Gibraltar and British Honduras were against force, but there was no doubt of the division between the major countries. The leader of the Trinidad delegation expressed it: 'What form does the line-up take? With disgust and horror I say that it is purely and entirely a question of colour.' The completeness of the division was emphasized by the fact that both government and opposition members of the British, Australian, and New Zealand delegations took the same line.

There was special fervour in the demands for force from those African countries styled the militants in this chapter, but the emotional attachment of the other coloured delegations to this point of view was plain, whatever qualifications prudence might cause them to make. The structural fault was again laid bare. Yet it would probably be wrong to conclude from such an emotional occasion that Britain had lost all influence with the countries urging strong action, or that they would not continue to accept British initiatives in certain situations. Rather, it was a matter of loss of respect: the sense that Britain had been found wanting and inconsistent in a sphere in which its other actions had been praiseworthy and right.[1]

II

The African member-states did not confine themselves to the Commonwealth in trying to stiffen the British government's sense of resolution. At both the UN and the OAU, where they were accustomed to concert their policies whenever possible, they tried to force the same points home. The OAU heads of state conference at Cairo in July 1964 had opposed the notion of a possible UDI and had said it would support a government in exile if necessary; it had also called on Britain to arrange a constitutional conference.[2] At Accra in October 1965 the heads of state had been even more trenchant in their criticism of British policy. As well as supporting the line taken by African leaders in Commonwealth meetings, they called upon the UN to regard UDI, if it

[1] CPA, General Council, *Report of Proceedings of 11th ... Conference held in Wellington December 1965*, pp. 1–47.
[2] *CS*, 18 Aug 1964, p. 815.

occurred, as a threat to international peace. A committee consisting of the UAR and four Commonwealth states (Kenya, Nigeria, Tanzania, and Zambia) was appointed to consider further action.[1]

At the UN, immediately before UDI, there was a flurry of African activity. On 12 October 1965 the General Assembly passed, by 107 to 2 (Portugal and South Africa), with one abstention (France), a resolution condemning any illegal declaration of independence, and calling on Britain to transfer power to a representative government if there were such a declaration. Britain did not vote because of its demurrer on the UN's competence in respect of Rhodesia.[2] On 5 November there was a much stronger resolution, indicting South Africa and Portugal as well as Rhodesia, and calling for stern measures; this was passed by 82 to 9, those opposed including Canada, Australia, and New Zealand as well as the US. There were 18 abstentions. The separate vote for including a demand for the use of military force was passed by 68 to 34, with 4 abstentions.[3] The African states thus had asserted the voting majority which they had been able to command at the UN for some years; but this sort of supremacy did not avail because of the disinclination of the major powers to take enforcement action.

On 12 November, on Britain's initiative, the Security Council condemned the UDI and called on all states not to recognize it and to refrain from helping Rhodesia. On 20 November the Council went further. A compromise between a British motion and one from the Ivory Coast called on Britain to quell the rebellion, and other states to do their utmost to break economic relations with Rhodesia. Both resolutions were adopted by 10 votes to nil, with France abstaining, on the ground that Rhodesia was an internal matter involving no conflict between states.[4]

By the time of the second Security Council resolution, the Smith regime was still in power and the African states had brought no effective pressure to bear on Britain, from either the OAU or the UN. If there was such a thing as a world public opinion, it was certainly against Smith and partly against Britain's lack of decisive action; but neither Britain nor anyone else was being compelled to take such action. The African states' next attempt was through the OAU, this time at an extraordinary meeting of the OAU Council of Ministers special foreign ministers' meeting at Addis Ababa on 3 December. What has been described as a 'gust of emotion'[5] swept this meeting (held in camera) at a suggestion from the Zambian foreign minister, Simon Kapwepwe, that members should sever relations with Britain if by 15 December it had not crushed the rebellion and restored law and order, preparing the way for a

[1] Ibid., 7 Dec 1965, p. 1230.
[2] Res. 2012 (xx): GAOR, 20th sess., suppl. 14, pp. 53–4.
[3] Res. 2022 (xx), ibid., pp. 54–5.
[4] Res. 217 (1965) (SCOR, 20th yr, Resolutions, p. 8). Britain took the line, after UDI, that Rhodesia was now a fit subject for UN discussion and support of British policy.
[5] W. Scott Thompson, p. 393.

majority government.[1] Kapwepwe was identified with the more militant group in the Zambian government urging Kaunda not to accept the conditions Wilson was imposing on the use of British forces (see pp. 208–9).[2] At the OAU meeting he acted on his own initiative, without orders from Kaunda.[3] Some of the Africans present were worried by the resolution, but they were not heads of governments, and they thought it best to follow a radical line. What were the heads of governments themselves to do?

Most of the Commonwealth leaders, it is clear, found the OAU resolution an embarrassment. Kenyatta announced that Kenya would not break relations with Britain, since this 'would not be effective and could in fact be abortive'.[4] Sir Abubakar said Nigeria would not break relations: 'other ways of putting a quick end to the minority regime must be devised and devised very quickly'.[5] But it was Kaunda's position which proved decisive for most. He said:

It is not within my province to tell other nations whether they should break their ties or not. But as President of Zambia I feel it my duty to express to my fellow leaders the difficult position in which Zambia would find herself in the circumstances which would follow such an action. . . .

This is what I am explaining when I write to other OAU nations. I have always maintained that Rhodesia is a British responsibility and as such it is Britain's duty to get us out of the difficulties caused by the illegal declaration of independence.[6]

In the event, only Tanzania and Ghana, amongst Commonwealth members, broke off diplomatic relations with Britain; and neither left the Commonwealth.[7] But the strains in the situation were becoming more serious.[8] A temporary means of bringing African and British leaders together was suggested by Sir Abubakar: a special Commonwealth Prime Ministers' Meeting, to be held in Lagos and devoted entirely to Rhodesia. It would be the first on non-economic questions to be held outside London, and the first organized by the newly-formed Commonwealth secretariat.

[1] CS, 21 Dec 1965, p. 1296.
[2] Guardian, 2 Dec 1965; see also Hall, High price of principles, p. 161.
[3] Private information.
[4] Guardian, 11 Dec 1965.
[5] Ibid., 10 Dec 1965.
[6] FT, 9 Dec 1965.
[7] Canada represented British interests in Tanzania, and Tanzanian interests in Britain. In Accra the commercial section of the High Commission stayed behind, and exercised its political functions. The British military training mission stayed (W. Scott Thompson, p. 394). Nyerere gave his reasons for breaking relations with Britain in the Observer, 12 Dec 1965, saying: 'We shall not leave the Commonwealth. . . . That is a multinational organization not a British one, and is therefore for the moment, at any rate, unaffected by our decision.'
[8] Their seriousness was shown by the British prime minister's reception at the General Assembly on 16 December. Some twenty African delegates walked out as he spoke. 'There is no denying that it hurt; I was a passionate believer in the independent Commonwealth. I had gone to great lengths and risked not only political unpopularity but even parliamentary defeat in our total opposition to the policies of the Rhodesian Front. But all one could do was to be good-tempered about it' (Wilson, pp. 185–6).

III

At their meeting in June 1965 the prime ministers had appointed Arnold Smith, from Canada, to be the first secretary-general. He had begun to assemble his staff before UDI. A key appointment had been that of A. L. Adu, a former head of the Ghanaian civil service and secretary-general of the East African Common Services Organization, as one of the two deputy secretaries-general. It was clear, at the time of the secretariat's formation, that African affairs would bulk large in its work. Adu was known and respected by all the African member governments. Arnold Smith was known to share the sense of the importance of Africa in the Commonwealth that had characterized Canadian policy in the preceding decade.

The growing tension over Rhodesia, following Smith's appointment, led him to make a tour of East and Central African Commonwealth countries in October.[1] He found much speculation about the possibility of African countries' resigning from the Commonwealth if Britain did not take what they regarded as proper steps to discipline Rhodesia. It seems likely that each of the heads of government whom he saw was himself in favour of staying in the Commonwealth but was apprehensive of the effects of a decision by others to walk out. UDI was declared when Arnold Smith was in Kenya. His advice probably helped to keep each country in the Commonwealth at this stage; but when he returned to London he warned that the Rhodesian crisis could lead to the disintegration of the Commonwealth if it were handled inadequately. If there was one African withdrawal, this could lead to four or five others, which would have an effect on Asian countries. He emphasized too that most African countries were sceptical about sanctions as so far proposed, and thought Britain morally committed to move Rhodesia towards majority rule.[2] When the OAU resolution was passed, Smith was able to tell member governments in Africa that, if they did decide to break relations with Britain, this did not mean leaving the Commonwealth. The recent break of relations between Pakistan and Malaysia (see p. 91) was a case in point; neither had left the Commonwealth.

The secretariat's capacity to influence African states may well have been increased by the suspicions of it voiced in some Conservative quarters in Britain, and, even more, by the curious notion of some of the Rhodesian leaders that Britain was going to 'hand over' Rhodesia to the secretariat, thus

[1] See CSG, *Ann. Rep.*, 26 Aug 1966, p. 6.

[2] *The Times*, 27 Nov 1965. The British government appointed a special envoy of its own to East and Central Africa on 27 October, when the CRO announced that Malcolm MacDonald, high commissioner in Kenya, would become special representative in Kenya, Malawi, Tanzania, and Zambia. This post was somewhat analogous to his role as commissioner-general in Southeast Asia between 1948 and 1955, since when he had been high commissioner in India, and governor-general and high commissioner in Kenya. His task appears to have been that of both mediator and advocate. He accompanied Wilson to Lagos in January 1966.

washing its hands of the whole problem.¹ There was, of course, a risk, to the extent that, if the secretariat was widely thought to be specially concerned with the militant Africans, its influence might be diminished with other members of the Commonwealth who disliked the militant approach. The secretariat could hardly be blamed, however, for making the preservation of the Commonwealth one of its main tasks in a time of tension.²

Sir Abubakar's proposal for a conference at Lagos did not meet with full approval. Menzies announced that Australia would not accept the invitation; he thought the meeting

unlikely to do more than record and emphasize diferences. No unanimity of view could be achieved, and considerable bitterness would be disclosed . . . To have [Britain] attacked and threatened at a special conference would be a grave departure from proper practice in a Commonwealth gathering.

In a later statement Menzies said the Australian high commissioner in Nigeria would attend as an observer only, adding as an extra reason for the decision that

if Britain can be instructed and coerced by the Commonwealth—or most of its members—in a matter which is, by concession, hers and hers alone to deal with, then Australia can some day be instructed or coerced on some matter in which the sole jurisdiction resides with Australia.³

This line was not taken by any other prime minister, but Wilson himself was said to hesitate for some time before deciding to go,⁴ and Ghana and Tanzania boycotted the meeting.⁵ A combination of short notice (only three weeks) and the caution felt by some heads of governments about committing themselves meant that this meeting had a smaller proportion of heads of government than most. Britain, Nigeria, Cyprus, Canada, the Gambia, Malawi, Malta, Sierra Leone, Singapore, Uganda, and Jamaica were represented by those at the head of affairs; Zambia, Malaysia, Trinidad, Ceylon, India, Kenya, New Zealand, and Pakistan by lesser ministers or officials. The Australian observer sat at a separate table for the opening and closing plenary sessions. He did not attend the business sessions.

¹ This opinion was voiced by Lord Graham, one of Smith's ministers (Young, p. 339), and is to be found in Lardner-Burke, pp. 70–1.
² *The Times* wrote of the Lagos conference that, in spite of 'the explosive issues of southern Africa and of race . . . the African leaders should reflect that to wreck the Commonwealth will not solve these problems' (editorial, 'Mr Wilson's Message', 7 Jan 1966).
³ *CN*, Dec 1965, pp. 849–50 & Jan 1966, pp. 37–8. These were Menzies's last statements as prime minister on a Commonwealth topic. He resigned on 20 January.
⁴ *The Times*, 4, 5, & 7 Jan 1966. Wilson did not announce his decision until five days before the meeting began. Bottomley would have led the delegation if Wilson had not gone; there was no suggestion that the Australian lead should be followed. It is said that Wilson was persuaded by Pearson on a visit to Ottawa (private information). See Wilson, p. 189, for an informative statement.
⁵ Ghanaian diplomats were active in Lagos during the meeting, however.

The Lagos meeting convened in January 1966 in an atmosphere of tension in Nigeria, a prelude to the disasters that were to occur soon after the Commonwealth leaders left. Two days before the meeting opened, there were reports of continued violence in the disturbed Western Region, and seven people were killed in riots in Lagos itself.[1] The atmosphere was unlike that of the normal Prime Ministers' Meeting in London. All the visiting delegations were quartered in the one hotel, in which the meeting itself was held; this was heavily guarded. There was an almost complete absence of the national journalistic entourages which had become (and continue to be) ever-present elements in the diplomacy of such meetings. The formal work was done in two days (11 and 12 January), although there had been discussions between senior officials beforehand. The secretary-general announced on the eve of the meeting that three topics had been agreed on: the ending of the Rhodesian rebellion as soon as possible; the consequential future of Rhodesia; and Commonwealth co-operation with Zambia, in the event of future sanctions.[2] The actual discussions were largely secret, apart from some reports of what Wilson and Sir Albert Margai, of Sierra Leone, had said on the first day.[3] A working party of officials discussed details.

Perhaps because of these inducements to practicality rather than oratory, the communiqué was more businesslike than usual.[4] The prime ministers[5] reaffirmed Britain's responsibility for Rhodesia 'but acknowledged that the problem was of wider concern to Africa, the Commonwealth and the world'. They stated their opposition to racial discrimination, and noted the British government's view that a period of direct rule would be needed in Rhodesia,[6] preparatory to a constitutional conference which 'would be for the purpose of recommending a constitution leading to a majority rule on a basis acceptable to the people of Rhodesia as a whole'. On military force, 'it was accepted that its use could not be precluded if this proved necessary to restore law and order'. So far, the communiqué was not markedly at variance with Wilson's previous position, and showed a considerable acceptance of the British position. A paragraph followed, however, which was to be the subject of much later controversy:

In this connection the Prime Ministers noted the statement by the British Prime Minister that on the expert advice available to him the cumulative effects of the

---

[1] *The Times*, 10 Jan 1966.   [2] Ibid., 11 Jan 1966.

[3] Ibid., 12 Jan 1966. There is a brief account in Wilson, pp. 195–6, in which most attention is given to a speech by Lee Kuan Yew which Wilson greatly admired. Wilson says the conference 'ended in an atmosphere of unity, even euphoria', but gives the impression that it would have been a failure if he had not used the phrase 'weeks not months', 'based on the advice we were receiving that the oil sanctions and the closure of the Beira pipeline would bring the Rhodesian economy to a halt'.

[4] Cmnd 2890 (*CS*, 21 Jan 1966, pp. 84–7).

[5] The difficulties of the continued use of this term at such meetings were illustrated by the fact that only ten out of the nineteen representatives were prime ministers.

[6] The prime minister of Malta dissociated himself from the reference to direct rule.

economic and financial sanctions might well bring the rebellion to an end within a matter of weeks rather than months. While some Prime Ministers had misgivings in this regard, all expressed the hope that these measures would result in the overthrow of the illegal regime in Southern Rhodesia within the period mentioned by the British Prime Minister.

The communiqué then proceeded to the setting up of two continuing committees to work with the secretary-general in London. These had been proposed by Pearson.[1] One would review regularly the effect of sanctions and Zambia's special needs. The other would co-ordinate a special Commonwealth programme of assistance in training Rhodesian Africans for administration and other tasks. The first of these—known as the Sanctions Committee—would, it was said, recommend the reconvening of the Prime Ministers' Meeting when it judged this necessary. In any case, there would be another meeting in July if the rebellion had not ended by then. The Sanctions Committee would also advise whether it thought UN action was necessary. Some governments reserved the right to propose mandatory sanctions through the UN.

In spite of the forebodings of Menzies and others, Britain had not done badly out of the Lagos meeting. Wilson had clearly been adroit, except for his 'weeks, not months' statement; Pearson had helped him to secure a compromise; the Asian members had not been troublesome;[2] the most radical leaders—Nkrumah and Nyerere—had not attended; most important of all, it seemed that Kaunda was satisfied, in spite of his not having been at Lagos. Wilson met him in Lusaka for four hours afterwards, and Kaunda made clear that he had softened his demand that there should be a time limit on sanctions before force was resorted to. The general atmosphere between the two men seems to have been cordial.[3] Hall says that Kaunda was told by Wilson that he would soon win a general election in Britain, and with an increased majority could take a harder line towards the Smith regime. 'Even military intervention need not be ruled out', according to Hall, 'for if the experts were to be believed, the sanctions—on oil in particular—would have reduced Rhodesia to confusion and lawlessness'. Kaunda was convinced, and told his cabinet so.[4] At the end of January, Wilson announced a further turn of the sanctions screw, designed to cut off all British trade with Rhodesia—while assisting Zambia—and to deny

---

[1] According to a statement by his minister for external affairs, Paul Martin, on 4 April 1966, to a parliamentary committee (*External Affairs*, May 1966, pp. 224–9).

[2] The highly approving tone of editorials in *Dawn* and *The Hindu* (17 Jan 1966), and *Straits Times* (14 Jan 1966) probably reflected the relief of the Pakistan, Indian, and Malaysian governments that they had not been called upon to assume unwelcome responsibilities.

[3] *The Times*, 14 Jan 1966.

[4] Hall, *High price of principles*, pp. 133–5. Wilson's brief report of the conversation (p. 196) mentions none of this. Whether military intervention was being considered or not, military administration of Rhodesia after sanctions had had their effect apparently was. See the article by *The Times* Defence Correspondent on 14 Jan 1966.

credit to the Smith regime.[1] Before that (on 25 January) he had made a long report to the Commons about how an interim government might be expected to work.[2] It had said little or nothing about the Commonwealth, being confined to Britain's direct responsibility, but seemed highly confident of Britain's capacity to bring the Smith government to satisfactory terms. It had added a Sixth Principle to the previous Five: no oppression of the majority by the minority or of the minority by the majority.

Two developments characterized the remainder of 1966, setting the stage for a disturbing, bad-tempered Prime Ministers' Meeting in September—forecast after Lagos by Lee Kuan Yew when he said 'I hate to think what the next conference will be like if the Smith regime has not been brought down. Feelings and tempers will be very different.'[3] The two developments which led to such acrimony in September were the deterioration of African stability on the one hand, and the failure of sanctions on the other.

From the Lagos meeting onwards, Commonwealth Africa in 1966 presented an unimpressive face. A few days after that meeting had ended, Nigeria was shaken by violence and a coup in which Sir Abubakar was assassinated in especially revolting circumstances, and what had been a vigorous though corrupt parliamentary system was replaced by military rule which proved unable to keep the divided regions together in peace. In February newspapers of the same day carried accounts of the overthrow of Nkrumah in Ghana and the suspension of the constitution by Obote in Uganda.[4] Former ministers continued to be arrested by the new military regime in Nigeria; General Ironsi, who had succeeded Abubakar, was himself murdered in July. Obote's seizure of power was followed, before the year was out, by a bloody affray in which the Kabaka of Buganda was forced to flee the country. Nkrumah's removal from power eliminated, for the time being, the most actively militant of the African states. Obote's action against the Kabaka discredited another of the more prominent militants. The upheaval in Nigeria not only deflected that country's attention to domestic matters, but, in company with these other events, provided further arguments for those—in Britain, South Africa, and elsewhere—who maintained that the 'one man one vote' formula led to instability and ultimately to black dictatorship. In contrast, Rhodesia itself remained peaceful, partly because of efficient policing and the inefficiency of the 'freedom fighters' trained in Ghana, Tanzania, and Zambia, but also because sanctions had failed to bite.

There can be little doubt that Wilson miscalculated the effect of the sanctions he had imposed directly, and of those which might be imposed by other countries. He had been misled by assurances from persons in Rhodesia that the Smith regime would collapse if hit hard by sanctions, and would be replaced by more loyal elements, including the army.[5] In fact, sanctions had

---

[1] Young, p. 334.   [2] 723 HC Deb., cols 39–42.   [3] *Straits Times*, 15 Jan 1966.
[4] *The Times*, 25 Feb 1966.   [5] Private information.

the reverse effect: they consolidated support behind Smith. Above all, Wilson was misled about the extent to which South Africa would co-operate. South Africa had said that 'normal trade' would continue between itself and Rhodesia; but there were two possible interpretations of such a term. That which Wilson evidently believed South Africa meant at first was that normal trade would be the level which had existed before UDI. The other, which, it became increasingly clearer, was actually held by the South African government, was that it meant trade in the goods which had previously crossed the border, and even of others, such as oil, which had not, irrespective of levels. After the first few months South Africa made no attempt to keep the levels down. Whatever diplomatic pressure the British government tried to exert was ineffective.[1]

In any case, as indicated in the previous chapter, South Africa, Rhodesia, and Zambia formed something of a single economy, symbolized by the line of rail. Whatever hurt Rhodesia would be likely to hurt Zambia too. Kaunda's lack of enthusiasm for sanctions, and his desire for quick action by force, were explicable in terms of Zambia's economic position, which required that copper should go out through Rhodesia and coal come in from it. Smith held Kaunda in a noose which could be tightened at any time.[2] Moreover, Zambia's prosperity rested not only upon the copper mines' continuing to produce and market the copper but also upon the presence of a substantial number of white technicians and miners, with close links with Rhodesia and South Africa. Whichever countries might decide to cut off their trade with Rhodesia, Zambia could not do so, since even a large part of its food supply came from the south. From the Zambian point of view, any delay in imposing British rule on Rhodesia meant further difficulty in imposing sanctions. Zambia might be freed to some extent from dependence upon the Rhodesian and Portuguese transport systems; but this would mean either airlifting supplies or transforming the existing bush track which led to Tanzania. In fact, both were done, a costly airlift of oil being maintained for some time at British expense, and a 'hell run' with road tankers from Tanzania being operated before the road could be improved, again with British assistance. By 1968 Zambia had reduced Rhodesia to third, instead of first, amongst its suppliers of imports; but this had meant more than a doubling of imports from South Africa, and Rhodesia still accounted for £13·1 m. worth of imports.[3]

To look so far ahead is to see what difficulties UDI created for Zambia in material terms, and how much better it would have been for President Kaunda if the Smith government had been quickly brought to heel. There was the emotional dimension of the problem as well. Kaunda and his colleagues were African nationalists: they believed that it was morally wrong for white men to

---

[1] Young describes the effect of sanctions in various places, esp. pp. 356–7, 513–14, 590. See also p. 404 for Verwoerd's statement of 25 January 1966 (after Lagos) to the effect that S. Africa would have nothing to do with boycotts and sanctions.

[2] See Hall, *High price of principles*, esp. pp. 162–8, for Zambia's difficulties.

[3] *The Times* Special Report on Zambia, 24 Oct 1969, p. V.

continue to govern a black majority. Kaunda summed up his position in Lusaka in March 1966, when he said that Britain had no political or moral right to 'keep the majority of people in Aden down by force' and at the same time to 'allow a band of unprincipled and racially minded men to get away with it' in Rhodesia. Economic sanctions were not enough:

> Force in Rhodesia may even, to the British government's mind, become inevitable, but alas, it may be so late as to involve a considerable loss of life, which we in Zambia have stood against.
>
> This may sound paradoxical in that we have been advocating force in Rhodesia by the British government, but the whole basis of our advice for the use of force in the situation has been that the longer the British government waited and was later forced by the circumstances of the situation to use force, the more human life would be lost.[1]

This speech was made three weeks before the general election in Britain on 31 March. Rhodesia was not a major issue, but still represented some difference between the parties. Wilson had campaigned on the need for Ian Smith's regime to return to constitutionality: there should be no talks with an illegal government, no recognition of an act of rebellion against the Crown. The Conservatives denied that their proposals would recognize rebellion, but they did call for talks; they did not insist that Smith should repudiate independence before the talks began.[2] Kaunda may well have hoped that Wilson would adopt more drastic measures once his majority was increased from a handful to 96 over all other parties; but in fact it was the Conservative line that Wilson took when his majority was assured. Following a much-publicized decision of the UN Security Council early in April, which—despite African opposition on the ground that it was at the best a half-measure—gave Britain the right to intercept by force tankers carrying oil destined for Rhodesia,[3] and following renewed efforts by the African states to bring pressure to bear on Britain,[4] Wilson announced on 27 April that there would be what became known as 'talks about talks', i.e. discussion with the Smith regime of whether a basis existed for a return to constitutional government in Rhodesia.[5]

The statement shattered whatever trust Kaunda still had in Wilson, and after it, the tone of Kaunda's statements changed: the element of rancour and resentment increased; the element of confidence in British good faith declined. The situation was made worse by Kaunda's hearing of Wilson's intention on the BBC news, not through official channels, as the official message reached him too late.[6] This unfortunate echo of an earlier crisis in Commonwealth

---

[1] Ibid., 9 Mar 1966.   [2] Ibid., 22 Mar 1966; see the editorial, 'Rhodesia's race'.

[3] SC Res 231 (1966). For this and other Security Council debates and decisions on Rhodesia, see ch. 7 of Andrew Boyd, *Fifteen men on a powder keg* (1971).

[4] These efforts, planned by an 11-nation African summit meeting in Nairobi (*The Times*, 4 Apr 1966), included a special committee of African states at the UN to exert further pressure there (*NYT*, 20 Apr 1966).

[5] HC Deb., 27 Apr 1966, cols 708–14.   [6] Hall, *High price of principles*, p. 149.

relations, the Chanak affair of 1922, indicated the current state of 'consulta-tion'. Zambian reactions were more direct and characteristic of the 1960s than those of Canadians in 1922. Windows were smashed at the British High Com-mission in Lusaka, and the Union Jack was torn down in protest against the shooting of seven Zanu 'freedom fighters' in Rhodesia; a week later the charges against those who had attacked the High Commission were withdrawn.[1]

But what could Kaunda do? He had little or no means of exerting effective pressure on Britain. The talks about talks went on between British and Rhodesian officials in Salisbury, producing no significant result. The Common-wealth Sanctions Committee met in London, issuing uninformative state-ments;[2] the African states tied themselves in knots at the UN, especially with a Security Council resolution in May, which secured only African, com-munist, and Jordanian votes, and was defeated.[3] Zambia continued to demand the use of force (as the unsuccessful UN resolution had done), but to no avail.[4] Kaunda could not do without British financial help and there was no one else to turn to for military protection, dissatisfied as he might be with the restric-tions placed on the use of the few British forces sent to Zambia. Eventually he began to talk about leaving the Commonwealth. On 12 July, on being installed as chancellor of the new University of Zambia, he said that 'if leaving the Commonwealth is the only way Zambia can show that soulless cleverness wins rounds but not victories, then we must take this step'.[5] But he did not take it. Instead, he announced on 23 July that Zambia was carrying out a deliberate plan of disengagement from the Commonwealth in protest at Wilson's hand-ling of the Rhodesia question. Zambia would attend some Commonwealth occasions but not others; the decision whether to make a complete break would be made in September, when the prime ministers met again in London.[6]

It had been decided at Lagos that they would meet in July, but Wilson announced in the Commons on 5 July that the secretary-general had consulted with other governments and it had been agreed 'that it would serve the general convenience if a meeting were held from 6 to 15 September in London'.[7]

---

[1] *CS*, 13 May 1966, pp. 509–10.

[2] See e.g. ibid., 10 June 1966, p. 618. In fact the Committee met eleven times in London between the Lagos conference and the end of August 1966. It was chaired by the Canadian high commissioner and attended by high commissioners and often by Bottomley. Kapwepwe attended twice. Aid to Zambia was also discussed, and senior officers of the secretariat made several visits to Zambia (CSG, *Ann. Rep.*, 26 Aug 1966, p. 7).

[3] See Boyd, pp. 242–4, and *NYT*, 25 May 1966 (article by Drew Middleton).

[4] See, e.g., the letter from the Zambian minister of home affairs, *The Times*, 17 May 1966.

[5] *CS*, 22 July 1966, p. 754.   [6] Ibid., 19 Aug 1966, p. 873.

[7] HC Deb., 5 July 1971, cols 51–2. According to the Australian Dept of External Affairs, there was discussion about meeting in some other capital, following the Lagos precedent. Zambia made a firm proposal that this meeting be held in New Delhi; India agreed subject to its being acceptable to the other members. 'Nonetheless, the practical advantages of London won its acceptance as a venue for the September meeting' (*CN*, Sept 1966, p. 562). The secretary-general announced the postponed date on the same day as Wilson.

Kaunda, in his chancellor's speech, had said Britain had 'organized' other Commonwealth members into accepting the postponement, 'but they have no ability to organize me to remain within that organization'. There were few other developments of consequence before the prime ministers assembled, except that Kaunda met Obote, Nyerere, and the Kenyan vice-president, Joseph Murumbi, at the end of July in Dar es Salaam. It was reported that he had urged them to leave the Commonwealth with him if Wilson refused to take harsher measures against Rhodesia. However, the absence of Kenyatta was thought to represent discouragement on the part of Kenya, and Obote was said not to be enthusiastic. No statement was issued after the meeting.[1]

IV

The situation before the Prime Ministers' Meeting of September 1966 was fairly clear. The British government persisted in a refusal to use force unless there were a breakdown of law and order in Rhodesia, and was reluctant also to advocate mandatory sanctions through the UN or to declare that it would not allow independence without majority rule. Its refusal to use force can be attributed, as we have seen, to the possible consequences of such an action in southern Africa and doubts about its effectiveness, and to domestic reactions in Britain. Hence common sense and its wish to retain some bargaining counters in negotiation with Smith's government no doubt accounted for its reluctance to demand mandatory sanctions and to insist on majority rule. There was little evidence that its position had caused it trouble at home, except in some quarters on the left, but it faced strong opposition from the radical African Commonwealth members, despite Nkrumah's fall, Ghana's subsequent preoccupation with domestic affairs, and Obote's subdued tones since the flight of the Kabaka. Some African states—notably Kenya and Nigeria—were not likely to press for extreme policies. Malawi was actively opposed to them. But most African leaders were liable to support extreme positions, partly in order to sustain the line of argument that had brought independence to their own countries and partly because of reactions within the OAU against a contrary view. The OAU was in fact powerless against those who fell out of line—by the end of 1966 it had fallen into greater disarray than usual; to the extent that Nyerere believed 'there must be a devil somewhere in Africa'[2]— but the complex interrelations of African states, and the interdependence of their diplomacy, made them hesitate to disagree with one another unless it seemed absolutely necessary.

[1] *Dawn*, 28 July 1966.

[2] After an OAU summit meeting in Addis Ababa, Nyerere said it had demonstrated that Britain and France had more power in the OAU than the whole of Africa put together. He said wryly: 'Africa is in a mess. There is a devil somewhere in Africa. I am a good superstitious African, and I believe in devils. There must be a devil somewhere in Africa' (*Guardian*, 11 Nov 1966).

The Asian and Caribbean members, while not directly involved, were emotionally committed to curbing the Smith regime, and would have found it difficult to oppose suggestions for the use of force and for mandatory sanctions. They were not, however, a solid front. Malaysia had been released from the thrall of confrontation which had made it so anxious for African support at the 1964 and 1965 meetings, while Singapore was still concerned for such support, in the light of its own expulsion from Malaysia in the previous year and Pakistan's hesitancy about Commonwealth membership. India and Pakistan were, as usual, divided over Kashmir and were still suffering the after-effects of their 1965 war; neither could wish to quarrel with the Africans if the other was not doing so.

The Mediterranean members, Malta and Cyprus, took different lines. Malta was opposed to the use of force and to direct rule; Cyprus, much closer to the Afro-Asian group at the UN, supported the radical position of the most vocal African states. Even the 'old dominions' were divided, though not sharply. Whereas the Canadian government's main concern was to build bridges and bind up wounds, so keeping the Commonwealth in being, the Australian and New Zealand governments had little to offer beyond support for Britain, and both deplored the pressure which Kaunda and others were trying to sustain.[1]

There was by now a sameness about the debates on Rhodesia, whether they occurred in the British House of Commons or the annual meeting of the Commonwealth Parliamentary Association.[2] The British government adhered to its basic position, though it amended the details from time to time; sanctions were disturbing but not ousting the Smith regime; the militant African states were still trying to overthrow the Rhodesian regime, but could not themselves muster the necessary force and could not make Britain do so. Other states had other things to attend to, and not only Rhodesia divided the OAU. It is not surprising that Kaunda and Nyerere expressed their displeasure by not attending the 1966 London Prime Ministers' Meeting, or that, in spite of their absence, the division of view between those who attended should have been wider than before. The more remote seemed decisive action, the more intensive became the war of words. Yet this process could not continue indefinitely. The war of words reached a peak in September 1966 and thereafter declined— so much so that at the next meeting, in 1969, Rhodesia received much less attention, although Ian Smith's government still maintained its illegal independence.

---

[1] Although he was no longer in office, Sir Robert Menzies's article in *Sunday Telegraph*, 24 Apr 1966 ('Let's have reason on Rhodesia') is probably representative of Australian and New Zealand official opinion in 1966.

[2] See e.g. CPA, General Council, *12th Commonwealth Parliamentary Conference, Ottawa, report of proceedings* (1966), pp. 6–94, where the argument on Rhodesia took much the same lines as in the preceding year, though with rather less vehemence.

The September 1966 meeting, which Wilson, in retrospect, was despondently to describe as 'a nightmare conference',[1] was again attended by relatively few heads of government. Of the 22 member nations present, 14 sent their heads of government, of whom 10 were prime ministers and one an acting premier. The remainder—including such important members as Kenya, India, Pakistan, Ghana, Zambia, and Nigeria—were represented by men of lesser stature. *The Times* found that there might be 'some collective wisdom displayed in this absenteeism':

Sir Albert Margai touched on it when he remarked that many leaders preferred to send representatives when the dominant issue was one that might inconveniently put a strain on their good relations with Britain. By playing down the significance of a meeting that is a consequence of decisions taken at Lagos in January—by, as it were, making this Prime Ministers' meeting a "non-event"—heads of government may be taking their own precautions to ensure that the Commonwealth survives at the level at which it operates most effectively—which is not necessarily a prime ministerial level. The fewer Prime Ministers present when tempers run high, the fewer there are to make irreversible decisions or gestures later regretted.[2]

In this context the key figure was Kapwepwe, the Zambian foreign minister. From what some participants in the meeting have said,[3] there seems to be little doubt that he came to London determined to take Zambia out of the Commonwealth if its demands were not met, and that in this he had the acquiescence—though probably not the wholehearted conviction—of his president. If he had walked out, it would have been on the explosive issue of majority rule which would have compelled some of the other African representatives to follow him. Whether this would have meant a large number of withdrawals of members is another matter; Kapwepwe might have been no more successful in London than in Addis Ababa the previous December. But there was certainly the possibility that the heated atmosphere would engender resignations on the heels of the walk-outs. For this reason, a number of the moderates at the meeting attempted to use the Afro-Asian caucus as a means of toning down Zambia's demands, of 'surrounding Kapwepwe'. While this greater emphasis on the caucus and on collective action was to some extent successful in its purpose, it had the drawback of alienating the Australians and New Zealanders, who were incensed by the indignity of twiddling their thumbs while the caucus argued in private during periods when the meeting should have been in session. Wilson, likewise excluded from the caucus, was also annoyed. Pearson was not pleased.[4]

[1] *Labour government*, p. 277. His general description, including notes of one of his speeches, occupies pp. 277–87.

[2] *The Times*, 3 Sept 1966, editorial 'Changing Commonwealth'.

[3] In private discussions.

[4] Wilson, p. 284, quotes Pearson as saying it was 'intolerable' that the caucus should make them wait so long for its decisions. On the other hand, note must be taken of the secretary-general's view: 'These "group" consultations while unusual, and by general agreement not to

By the standards of earlier Commonwealth meetings, Britain and the old dominions had a right to be incensed. Given the changed nature of the Commonwealth and the desirability of keeping its membership intact, one could argue that they ought to accept some indignity and exasperation as the price of permitting African declamation to exhaust itself and of enabling compromise proposals to be accepted. But it could also be argued that heads of any governments, Commonwealth or not, do not come ten or twelve thousand miles to wait around while the sort of negotiation normally carried on by officials and junior ministers is conducted in a near-by room, especially if they do not know what is happening there. In any case, the element of bad manners involved in leaking information to the newspapers, while contributing little to actual discussion, was conspicuous at this meeting. It had an adverse effect on Holyoake and on Harold Holt, who had succeeded Menzies as prime minister of Australia. It angered Wilson considerably.[1]

The actual course of events can be summarized fairly briefly, since much of the argument was the same as at the 1964 and 1965 meetings, and at the special meeting at Lagos. Beforehand, Kaunda said publicly that he would not be coming because of his 'disgust' at the British government's behaviour: he was reported as saying that 'when the history of the period came to be written it would reveal many undertakings and promises which had been broken by the Prime Minister'. Kaunda was said to be bitter about promises contained in letters written to him by Wilson, which he alleged had been broken. He was also concerned about the announcement, before he had been informed, that RAF planes would be withdrawn from Zambia.[2] Kapwepwe was said to be briefed with three demands; if these were not met, Zambia would leave the Commonwealth. They were that Britain should use force if Smith was still in power after a certain time; that if Britain could or would not use force, there should be a concerted Commonwealth initiative to the same end; if these proposals were turned down, there should be a unanimous Commonwealth approach to the UN for mandatory sanctions and the use of force.[3] The proceedings of the meeting are explicable in terms of these demands and the related demand for no independence before majority rule (Nibmar).[4]

The meeting opened on 6 September, in the shadow of Verwoerd's assassination in the South African parliament in Cape Town. It was news of

---

be accepted as a precedent, served on this occasion to assist in the eventual reconciliation of views and the emergence of the elements of a consensus' (CSG, *Second Report*, 1968, p. 16).

[1] Wilson says that the delegates agreed to his suggestion that they should 'brief only on their own contributions and not seek to paraphrase the speeches of others', but that this was 'observed almost exclusively in the breach' (p. 278).

[2] *The Times*, 31 Aug 1966. There is a long article by Kaunda in *Sunday Times*, 4 Sept 1966, in which he repeats previous charge and demands; it may fairly be taken as a summary of his position.

[3] *Keesing's Contemporary Archives*, 1966, p. 21637.

[4] Both Nibmar and NIBMR were widely used as contractions. The CSG's *Second Report* used Nibmar, and his *Third Report* NIBMR.

uncertain significance—Verwoerd was not killed by an African—but it emphasized the central part which southern Africa was to play. Wilson offered to vacate the chair because of his direct involvement with Rhodesia, but this offer was declined. He spoke of the loopholes in sanctions, of Zambia's need to import from other places than Rhodesia, of British aid to Zambia, and of the possible need for mandatory sanctions on oil. He showed no inclination to yield on Nibmar or on demands for the use of force and for general mandatory sanctions. Tunku Abdul Rahman appealed to other premiers, notably those of Zambia and Sierra Leone, not to break up the Commonwealth. 'If we have to vent our wrath let us take it out of Britain and not out of the Commonwealth', he said, pointing out that Britain was not the head of the Commonwealth but only a member nation.[1] On the next day, however, Lee Kuan Yew's speech made it plain that there was the possibility of a mass walk-out of African and Asian delegates if British policy was not more forthcoming. His own wish was for more effective sanctions, supported, if necessary, by force, but the Zambian delegates who spoke demanded both direct rule and Nibmar. They also charged that British offers of aid to Zambia were based on the proviso that they would be reconsidered if Zambia decided to leave the Commonwealth or break with Britain.[2] In the next couple of days a succession of speakers called for sterner measure and for Nibmar; Wilson's refusal was supported by no one but Australia and New Zealand. Kapwepwe's original demand was widely endorsed, among others by Malaysia and Canada which, however, left themselves some latitude for possible mediation.[3] Pearson was prepared to consider the use of force, but only under a mandatory Security Council resolution.[4]

Divisions of this kind persisted, until it seemed likely that two widely differing communiqués would have to be written, one by 'the Five' (Britain, Australia, New Zealand, Malta, and Malawi) and the other by 'the Seventeen' (the others represented); the meeting would thus agree to differ. Kapwepwe left for Zambia to report to Kaunda, on his departure accusing Wilson of being a racialist.[5] By this stage the emphasis in Afro-Asian-Caribbean demands seems to have shifted from the use of armed force to Nibmar and mandatory sanctions, which, the British government believed, would not only make negotiation more difficult with the Smith regime but might also reduce the support still given to the British government by the governor of Rhodesia and a few other prominent Rhodesians. Wilson's position was perilous: he was being asked to throw away what he regarded as a possible winning hand in Rhodesia in order to preserve the Commonwealth in its existing form.

[1] *The Times* & *Straits Times*, 7 Sept 1966.
[2] *The Times*, 8 Sept & *Straits Times*, 9 Sept 1966. 'The actual combat of British troops— eyeball to eyeball—with white Rhodesians is, of course, unthinkable for a popularly elected British government', said Lee.
[3] *The Times*, 10 Sept 1966.   [4] Wilson, *Labour government*, p. 281.
[5] *The Times*, 14 Sept 1966.

He was extricated by a combination of his own efforts and those of his British colleagues (in conceding something on both Nibmar and mandatory sanctions), of Pearson and Arnold Smith, of the Asians, and of Kenya and Uganda.[1] When the final compromise caucus proposals were put forward, the task of spokesman was allotted to Lee Kuan Yew. He had joined the African discussions, as had Swaran Singh, the Indian foreign minister (the Tunku had not attended).[2] Eventually it proved possible, under the chairmanship of Pearson, for a drafting committee to find an agreed formula. But there was no doubt of either the continued distrust of Wilson by many of the Africans, or of Holt's and Holyoake's annoyance with the African caucusing and delay, and what they regarded as the disproportionate amount of time spent on Rhodesia.[3]

The communiqué[4] repeated some of what had been said by previous meetings—that Rhodesia was Britain's responsibility but also of wider concern, that any political system based on racial discrimination was intolerable, that political prisoners should be released and the principle of one man one vote applied. 'Most' of the heads of government affirmed the need for a strong attitude by Britain and the desirability of Nibmar; they also wanted Britain to refuse to resume discussions or negotiate with Smith. Wilson countered by saying there would be no settlement that did not conform to the Six Principles, and made much of the fifth (about acceptability to the people of Rhodesia as a whole). The British government's intentions were given rather more clarity by a point-by-point statement of what would be done. After the illegal regime had ended, a legal government would be appointed by the governor and would 'constitute a broadly based representative administration'. There would be normal political activities and a release of political prisoners. A constitutional settlement, with the objective of majority rule, would be negotiated with the interim administration, on the basis of the Six Principles. This settlement would be 'submitted for acceptance to the people of Rhodesia as a whole by appropriate democratic means'. The British government must be satisfied that this test of opinion was fair and free and 'would be acceptable to the general world community' and, again, the government would not consent to independence before majority rule unless the people of Rhodesia as a whole were shown to be in favour of it.

A quite new element appeared in the British promise to inform the Smith regime that if it did not return to legality two things would happen: the

---

[1] A credible account, probably astray in some of its details, is in *Observer*, 18 Sept 1966, entitled 'The night they saved the Commonwealth'. See Wilson, pp. 279–86, for the British prime minister's version.

[2] Josey, *Lee Kuan Yew*, pp. 504–6. The Tunku, when refusing, is said to have stated, 'I am not a caucusian'. (From a private source.)

[3] Holt's views are expressed in *The Age* (Melbourne), 14, 17, & 20 Sept 1966. See *The Times*, 19 Sept 1966, for Holyoake.

[4] Cmnd 3115 (1966); *CS*, 30 Sept 1966, pp. 978 ff.

government would no longer be prepared to submit to parliament any settlement involving independence before majority rule; and if it had full support from other Commonwealth countries at the UN, it would, before the end of the year, sponsor a Security Council resolution for selective mandatory sanctions. Ian Smith was thus being told that unless he formally submitted to the governor as the symbol of British sovereignty, he would forfeit the possibility of independence under something like the existing Rhodesian constitution; if he remained recalcitrant, the British government would adopt Nibmar. He was also being told that sanctions would tighten in three months' time. That period did not, by the provisions of the communiqué, apply to the submission to the Governor; but the two proposals were linked in such a way as to make it easy to assume—as did *The Times* in its headline on 15 September —that Smith was being given a three months' ultimatum on all grounds. The sanctions point was clearer. The Sanctions Committee set up at Lagos reported that, 'though sanctions had undoubtedly depressed the Rhodesian economy, they were unlikely at their present level to achieve the desired political objectives within an acceptable period of time'. The heads of government were broadly agreed on the need for stronger sanctions, but they disagreed on whether these should be selective or general. In agreeing to sponsor a Security Council resolution, Britain was taking the same course as it had immediately after UDI—that of leading the pack instead of being pursued by it. Whether South Africa and Portugal would take any notice of UN sanctions once these were mandatory rather than voluntary was another matter.

Wilson said after the meeting that the Commonwealth had been 'tested in the heat of the flames this week. It will never be quite the same again. It may well be stronger.'[1] There were what had become the normal sighs of relief from the newspapers that the Commonwealth was still intact, and the Kenyan and Ugandan representatives pronounced themselves satisfied;[2] Kaunda decided not to withdraw for the time being.

v

Wilson sent his Commonwealth secretary, Herbert Bowden, to Salisbury for talks soon after the Prime Ministers' Meeting ended, and again in November. In between, a set of proposals went to Smith from the British government, by way of the governor.[3] These included three propositions which, in due course, were turned down by the Rhodesians. One, which had been suggested by Whitehead, was for an Act of Union between Britain and Rhodesia, which would enable white and black Rhodesians to sit in the British parliament. (It does not seem to have been taken very seriously.) The other two brought in the Commonwealth. One was for 'a mission, fact-finding and mediatory, of

---

[1] *The Times*, 16 Sept 1966.   [2] Ibid., 15 Sept 1966.
[3] Wilson, pp. 304 & 319; see also his speech, HC Deb., 8 Dec 1966, cols 1609–10.

Commonwealth leaders headed by the prime minister of Canada and consisting of other Commonwealth leaders, all of whom ought to have been acceptable to Mr Smith'. The other was for a 'high-level commission of constitutional experts' to be drawn from Commonwealth sources and headed by Sir Douglas Menzies, a judge of the High Court of Australia and a cousin of Sir Robert. Again the old Commonwealth was being used to tempt the Rhodesian government into accepting advice from outside; but again the offer was refused. Bowden did, however, make enough progress on his second visit to persuade Wilson that face-to-face contact with Smith should be tried again.

Meanwhile, the African states had been busy at the UN and in the OAU. Resolutions were passed by the General Assembly on 22 October and 17 November, the first calling for 'one man, one vote' in Zimbabwe (the African name for Rhodesia), the second demanding oil sanctions and the use of force and condemning Portugal and South Africa for their support of the illegal regime. The strength of the African position in the General Assembly was shown by the voting: in the first case 86 were in favour and 2 against, with 18 abstentions; in the second 89 in favour and 2 against, with 17 abstentions. South Africa and Portugal were the countries opposed, in both cases. The abstentions included Britain, Canada, Australia and New Zealand, as well as a number of West European countries.[1] Such voting strength was not, of course, a compelling reason why Wilson should stiffen his attitude towards Smith: it was a hollow majority which Britain could afford to ignore, since there was no direct means through which the majority could enforce its will. But the British government did not wish to alienate Commonwealth African states any further, and did not want its future relations with Afro-Asian states to be hindered by perpetual reference to Rhodesia.

The OAU passed a strong motion on Rhodesia at its meeting in Addis Ababa from 5 to 9 November, although a quarrel between Ghana and Guinea and the absence of a majority of heads of state indicated the strains behind the façade of unity. Nyerere was especially prominent in pressing the case against Britain's failure to act decisively. He issued a memorandum entitled 'Rhodesia: The Case for Action' which called for a meaningful collective statement addressed to Britain, but he was forced to admit that only a minority of African states had broken off relations with Britain, as requested by the OAU resolution of a year before. As in earlier situations, he and those who felt like him could muster an overwhelming vote on paper but could not get action.[2]

Wilson met Smith aboard HMS *Tiger*, off Gibraltar, for talks from 3 to 5 December. The aim was to provide for a 'return to legality' and for agreement on a future Rhodesian constitution. This time the two sides came nearer to agreement than at any earlier or later discussions. Wilson and Smith agreed on a 'working document' for a revised constitution after the return to legality,

[1] GA Res. 2138 (XXI) & 2151 (XXI): GAOR, 21st sess., suppl. 16, pp. 68–9.
[2] *The Times*, 7 Nov 1966; *Africa Research Bulletin*, 1–30 Nov 1966, p. 653.

and even discussed the personnel of the interim government to be set up after legality had been resumed.[1] While the document was regarded by the British government as satisfying all Six Principles, except in the very long term it preserved something very like the existing structure of government in Rhodesia, did not provide for a rapid approach to majority rule, and left the question of whether the proposed arrangements would be acceptable to 'the people of Rhodesia as a whole' to a royal commission, not to a referendum. Independence would be given 'at the earliest possible date' after the commission had given an affirmative verdict in its 'test of acceptability'.

Smith could hardly hope for a better settlement, especially in the light of Wilson's promise to the Commonwealth prime ministers that if the Smith regime did not return to legality the British would insist on Nibmar. Here were terms which Smith could accept with every likelihood that he would emerge as the prime minister of a legally independent Rhodesia. His eventual rejection of them is explained by Wilson as due to the fact that when Smith returned to Salisbury, 'the extremist party bosses exerted their pressure and invoked all the grass-roots threats of which they were capable'.[2] Yet Smith had insisted throughout the discussions that he must consult his cabinet. Some account must be taken too of the almost incurable suspicion with which by this time Smith and other Rhodesian politicians regarded any British proposal, especially one by Wilson.

On Smith's rejection, Wilson lost no time in redeeming his promise to the Commonwealth prime ministers, which he did in parliament on 20 December.[3] The policy of the government was now, he said, 'as set out in paragraph 10 of the communiqué which was issued at the end of the meeting of Commonwealth prime ministers in September and endorsed by a clear majority vote in this House on 8 December'. The proposals made to the illegal regime were 'no longer on offer'. The government had been prepared to make a unique exception in the case of Rhodesia and had gone to 'extreme lengths to work out a constitution which would have meant independence before majority rule'. This had been rejected and 'we have carried out what the House has endorsed: our obligation to the Commonwealth'. The government was thus fully committed to Nibmar, a point which was spelled out some months later by George Thomson, the minister of state for Commonwealth affairs, in an address to the Royal Commonwealth Society, although he stressed that it was not committed to immediate majority rule. Instead, 'from the date of a return to legal government in Rhodesia, there would have to be a very considerable period of careful preparation for majority rule'.[4] The policy was Nibmar, but it was interpreted

[1] See Wilson's account, *Labour government*, pp. 307 ff., and *CS*, 23 Dec 1966, pp. 1297–309, which includes a copy of the 'working document', Wilson's parliamentary explanation, Smith's reasons for refusing to accept the document, and a Commonwealth Office statement in reply. See also Cmnds 3159 & 3171 (1966).
[2] Wilson, p. 321.   [3] HC Deb., 20 Dec 1966, cols 1175–83.
[4] *Survey B & CA*, 23 June 1967, p. 626.

as a return to the 1961 constitution (which had promised eventual majority rule) and a continuance of Rhodesia's dependent status for some time.

Wilson's statement of 20 December also redeemed the promise about mandatory sanctions. The Commonwealth Sanctions Committee became active, and as soon as the result of the *Tiger* talks was known, it took up the question of which Rhodesian exports and imports should be the subject of sanctions. Following some disagreement, notably on whether oil should be included, there was a further meeting of Commonwealth representatives in New York.

When a draft resolution submitted by the British Government was discussed in the Security Council there were proposals to add to it a number of further items, including items which had been recommended in the Sanctions Committee. In particular Nigeria and Uganda, as members of the Security Council proposed the inclusion of oil and oil products.[1]

The British view was that the commodities selected for sanctions 'should be export commodities, since our experience has shown that it is in this way that we most effectively reduce Rhodesian economic activity and earning power'; asbestos, iron ore, chrome, pig-iron, sugar, tobacco, copper, meat and hides were those suggested. Britain was not, at first, prepared to include sanctions on the import of oil into Rhodesia, but the foreign secretary, George Brown, said that if a proposal to do so were made in acceptable terms, his delegation would not oppose it. 'I say this on the basis of the full understanding which it is clear also exists among delegations here, of the importance of not allowing sanctions to escalate into economic confrontation with third countries.' This and another statement to the effect that selective sanctions 'must not be allowed to develop into a confrontation—economic or military—involving the whole of Southern Africa'[2] presumably referred to South Africa and Portugal, which were no more likely to observe mandatory than voluntary sanctions, and which supplied all Rhodesia's oil.

The final form of the resolution, adopted on 16 December, included oil as well as the exports originally proposed by Britain. According to the Commonwealth secretary-general:

The terms were substantially as had been discussed and recommended in the [Commonwealth] Sanctions Committee. All four Commonwealth members of the Security Council (Britain, New Zealand, Nigeria and Uganda) joined in supporting it, although both Nigeria and Uganda continued to hold—and express—strong doubts about the likelihood of selective sanctions achieving the political objective

[1] CSG, *Second Report*, p. 19.
[2] *Survey B & CA*, pp. 53–8, which is the source for other statements in the text about what happened at the UN. See also Boyd, pp. 246–52, according to whom (p. 248), Brown 'told the Commonwealth representatives at the UN the day before the debate opened [that] Britain would not accept a wording that implied the taking of any action to prevent South Africa or Portugal passing on oil to Rhodesia'.

and were under strong pressure from the Afro-Asian Group to seek comprehensive mandatory sanctions.

Thus both the initiation and the provisions of the Resolution were substantially the result of Commonwealth consultation. It marked the first time in the history of the United Nations that the articles in Chapter VII of the UN Charter on mandatory economic sanctions had been invoked.[1]

This was indeed the case, and the Commonwealth could be regarded as having achieved some measure of meaningful discussion. But the prospect was not hopeful. Kapwepwe had appeared before the Security Council for Zambia to denounce the sanctions proposal and to call for the use of force; France had abstained from the vote; and South Africa said again that it would have nothing to do with sanctions and boycotts, a statement which was borne out by events. 'Normal trade', interpreted so as to provide both an outlet for Rhodesian exports and the supply of essential imports, including oil, continued to prevail between South Africa and Rhodesia.

No doubt the Smith government was disturbed by the changed attitude of the British government and by the proclamation of selective mandatory sanctions; but its plans must have been well laid, especially its understandings with South Africa and Portugal. It continued on its way, uttering its usual denunciations of the UN and the Afro-Asian bloc, and on this occasion trying to gain some extra support by abortively soliciting the prime ministers of Australia and New Zealand.[2] A Rhodesian office continued to be maintained in London; a 'Rhodesian Information Service' was set up in Australia; Rhodesia continued to maintain that it was part of the Queen's dominions, and had its first gold coins minted in republican Pretoria, bearing the Queen's head. Sanctions still did not 'bite'. It became clear that other countries besides South Africa and Portugal were prepared to trade with Rhodesia inspite of mandatory sanctions. The African states, for their part, were distracted from the Rhodesian issue by a succession of other problems. The OAU heads of state meeting at Kinshasa in September 1967 was so much preoccupied with other African questions—including the civil war in Nigeria and a series of bilateral intra-African disputes—that Rhodesia was pushed into the background. The customary resolution was passed, and a 17-member committee of military experts set up to consider ways and means of assisting resistance movements in southern Africa; but the OAU was plainly unable to

---

[1] CSG, *Second Report*, p. 19.

[2] The Rhodesians evidently felt that these two governments were the most likely in the Commonwealth to see their point of view. On 20 December Holt, the Australian prime minister, announced that he had had communications from Salisbury asking him to send a fact-finding mission there which would report to himself, and also, with the New Zealand prime minister, to nominate 'members to a commission to test Rhodesian public opinion on constitutional proposals'. Apparently this commission was to be confined to the two Pacific countries. Holt called the proposal 'disturbingly unrealistic'. He stressed the continuing responsibility of Britain for any negotiation with Rhodesia (*CN*, Dec 1966, pp. 751–2).

exert any significant pressure on the Smith regime.[1] Another UN General Assembly majority in November 1967 (92 for, 2 against, 18 abstentions including the old dominions, Japan, and the US)[2] must have been little consolation, in the light of Rhodesia's capacity to survive the measures introduced nearly a year before.

In 1968, in the course of a chain of events begun in March by the Smith regime's decision to hang certain Africans and continuing with a declaration by the Judicial Committee of the Privy Council that the regime was not a lawful government, on 29 May the Security Council moved from its previous position of selective to comprehensive mandatory sanctions, following considerable discussion in the Commonwealth Sanctions Committee, which recommended very much what the Council eventually decided.[3] It forbade all trade with Rhodesia, except for certain items justified on medical, humanitarian, and educational grounds. Again South Africa refused to comply.

The British Order in Council giving effect to the new sanctions was at first rejected by the House of Lords (which decided not to press its rejection), but came into operation in June.[4] It had also been opposed by the Opposition in the House of Commons. Somewhat similar disapproval was expressed in Australia, where the attorney-general, Nigel Bowen, told a convention of the Liberal Party (the senior partner in the government coalition) that many Australians had a 'profound distaste' for sanctions, and that this distaste was 'shared by very many Government members in the parliamentary party and, I might say, by very many ministers'; he felt, however, that Australia's international standing would be damaged if it did not observe the Security Council resolution.[5] Whereas three years before there had been fairly widespread agreement amongst conservative-minded politicians in Britain, Australia, and New Zealand about the need to apply pressure to the Smith regime, the failure of the pressure to get results and the apprehensions which had been aroused by an apparent extension of UN jurisdiction had now come to the surface.[6] Not only was the Rhodesian situation causing political difficulties; it was disturbing social life: according to Bowen, the Australian government had recently had to refuse two golf teams entry into Australia.

Wilson still hoped for a settlement. After three months of 'secret diplomacy', centring on two emissaries, Sir Max Aitken and Lord Goodman, he again met Smith on a warship, HMS *Fearless*, at Gibraltar.[7] The talks, from

---

[1] *Survey B & CA*, 13 Oct 1967, pp. 1034–7.

[2] Ibid., 22 Dec 1967, p. 1280.   [3] CSG, *Second Report*, pp. 20–1.

[4] *Survey B & CA*, 2 Aug 1968, pp. 715–22, for the UN and British debates.

[5] *Canberra Times*, 16 Sept 1968.

[6] There were legitimate grounds for thinking that the Security Council, in treating UDI as a threat to peace, had gone farther than its founders had ever envisaged. For a lively polemic expounding this view, see C. B. Marshall, *Crisis over Rhodesia* (1967), esp. ch. 4. But see also Boyd, pp. 222–34.

[7] Wilson's account is in pp. 565–70 of his memoirs. See also *Survey B & CA*, 25 Oct 1968, pp. 979–87 & Cmnd 3793 (1968).

9 to 13 October, were conducted in a reasonable atmosphere. This time no 'working document' was initialled by the two leaders, as at the *Tiger* talks, but the British government produced a modified version of the *Tiger* proposals which Smith took back to Salisbury. The Commonwealth secretary, George Thomson, went there for further talks in November, to find the proposals unacceptable to Smith and his colleagues. They raised a number of objections, but laid most stress on their opposition to the safeguards which the British government wished to introduce against Rhodesian amendments to entrenched clauses in the proposed constitution. Thomson had to report to parliament on his return that there remained 'fundamental disagreement on several major matters of principle'. Nevertheless, the British government's *Fearless* proposals remained on the table.[1]

The outstanding feature of these, to the naked eye, was that they appeared not to have been affected by Wilson's Nibmar pledge. They were closely akin to the *Tiger* proposals, differing only in some of the ingenious detail with which successive schemes abounded. Wilson, in explaining the proposals in parliament, maintained that his position had always been that if there were some 'substantial change of circumstances', the British government could go back to its Commonwealth partners and ask for reconsideration of Nibmar.[2] The *Fearless* proposals had repeated the former notion of a royal commission 'for the purpose of testing the acceptability to the people of Rhodesia as a whole of a new Independence Constitution based on any agreement to be reached'. An affirmative statement by this commission would presumably constitute the substantial change of circumstances, especially since the new constitution was to have the title of 'Independence' constitution. Wilson would then be able to argue that he had been released from his Nibmar pledge, and that Rhodesian independence could proceed on the basis of the new constitution. Such an interpretation was hardly likely to appeal to men like Nyerere and Kaunda.

The *Fearless* talks and their aftermath were met by two General Assembly resolutions. One of 25 October specifically called upon Britain not to grant independence unless it was preceded by the establishment of a government based on free elections by universal adult suffrage and on majority rule, and called upon all states not to recognize independence if it were not preceded by the prior establishment of such a government. This was passed by 92 to 2, with 17 abstentions. On 7 November a stronger resolution, aimed especially at South Africa and Portugal but reiterating the demands of 25 October, was passed by 86 to 9, with 19 abstentions and 11 absences. On this occasion Britain, Australia, and New Zealand voted against.[3] The UN resolutions in which, as usual, African Commonwealth states were the prime movers, had been accompanied by discussions in the Commonwealth Sanctions Committee

---

[1] Thomson's speech is in HC Deb., 18 Nov 1968, cols 896–912.
[2] For Wilson's speech see ibid., 15 Oct 1968, cols 207–23.
[3] GA res. 2379 (XXIII) & 2383 (XXIII): GAOR, 23rd sess., suppl. 18, pp. 57 & 58.

in London, at which, according to the secretary-general, 'some members . . . expressed deep anxieties and stated that the *Fearless* proposals did not represent an adequate guarantee for ensuring African majority rule in Rhodesia; and they affirmed that the Nibmar pledge must therefore form part of any honourable settlement'.[1] It was clear that Wilson would face further remonstrations at the meeting of Commonwealth prime ministers scheduled for January 1969.

VI

Wilson prepared for this meeting with a somewhat defiant though vague speech at the Lord Mayor's banquet in London on 11 November. While indicating that there was a fierce desire on the part of other Commonwealth countries to assert their independence, he felt it necessary to emphasize 'that Britain has also achieved her independence'. Human rights, he said, were at stake not only in Rhodesia, but also in Gibraltar—'and the issue is not one whit reduced by the fact that we are talking about 23,000 and not four millions'. Pointing out that the 23,000 had expressed their unanimity about their future in a free ballot, he went on to say: 'We have a right to ask for—what we have so far not been given—the support of the whole Commonwealth in this issue'. He followed up this reference to some African countries' votes at the UN against self-determination for the Gibraltarians by referring to the suffering that was taking place in Nigeria. He made no apology for *Fearless*.[2]

Careful preparation had been made for the meeting, which was held on 7–15 January 1969. The secretariat tried to see that as many heads of governments as possible attended, in particular, Kaunda and Nyerere. In the event, 24 of the 28 heads of government were present, with only Pakistan, Kenya, Ghana, and Nigeria represented by lesser figures. The composition of the meeting probably worked against the African militants' interests, apart altogether from the recollections of the distressing scenes in 1966 and the sense of frustration and even boredom with which, by now, many people approached the Rhodesian question. Five new members were present, of which Lesotho, Botswana, and Swaziland were too much beholden to South Africa for their economic existence to be expected to take a strong line about Rhodesia.[3] The other two, Barbados and Mauritius, were linked only tenuously with the Afro-Asian bloc. There had also been changes in the representatives of existing members. Ceylon had returned to relatively conservative rule under Dudley Senanayake; Harold Holt had died, and Australia was represented by John Gorton, somewhat less of a 'Commonwealth man'; above all, Pearson of Canada, who had been consistently sympathetic to the African point of view and prepared to assist in finding formulas, was replaced by Pierre Trudeau,

---

[1] CSG, *Second Report*, p. 22.

[2] British Information Service Backgrounder G507/b, 12 Nov 1968.

[3] Sir Seretse Khama of Botswana did, however, call for direct rule in Rhodesia and the withdrawal of the *Fearless* proposals (*The Times*, 10 Jan 1969).

whose government was subjecting all Canada's normal assumptions about external policy to a sceptical re-examination. Moreover, Rhodesia was not the only topic of consequence: two others, the Nigerian civil war and the immigration policies pursued by Britain on the one hand and the East African members on the other, were very much in the minds of many of those attending, especially the Africans. These two topics, which in fact were not discussed in the formal meetings of the conference itself, none the less diverted attention from Rhodesia.

Recollection, boredom, frustration, vital interest, scepticism, and the pressure of other issues thus conspired to put Rhodesia into a different perspective from that in which it had appeared to the meetings in 1964, 1965, and 1966. When the communiqué of the meeting stated that 'some Heads of Government reiterated their call on the British Government to use force to quell the rebellion in Rhodesia', these 'Heads' comprised Kaunda alone.[1]

The two main speakers on Rhodesia were Wilson and Nyerere[2] (Thomson was deputed to put the British case at the start of the debate, which Wilson wished to wind up). Thomson said that the *Fearless* proposals remained on the table, but Nibmar was still British policy. He refused to renew the Nibmar pledge in terms that might put *Fearless* out of court.[3] In reply, Nyerere did not call for the use of force but spoke mainly on Nibmar, 'on which he had stood out alone in 1965', his case being, according to Wilson, 'all the more effective in that it was utterly restrained and reliant on withering understatement'. Under the 'test of acceptability' envisaged in the *Fearless* talks, the Rhodesian Africans would remain under the Smith regime: if the test was positive, in the eyes of the Royal Commission, Britain would give full recognition to that regime; if it was negative the regime would still remain in force, the only difference being that Britain did not provide recognition. Either way, the condition of the Africans would be the same. In his words:

> Let us not make any mistake about the unreality of this choice. Real and justified fear of an oppressive government does not only exist in communist states. It exists in Rhodesia now. Organized opposition—by Africans especially—to the minority government has been smashed by the ruthless use of police power, of intimidation, and of economic pressures. . . . To ask a people to express their opposition to this coercion in the full knowledge that having done so they will be at the mercy of it, is exactly the same as asking people to vote contrary to the instructions of the man with the gun. . . .

He did not see that conducting a test of opinion through a Royal Commission would make the result any better because, though there was to be complete

---

[1] Private information.

[2] Wilson's account of the meeting is in *Labour government*, pp. 592–603. From what he says of Neyerere's speech, it is likely that the substance of this is to be found in Julius Nyerere, 'The African view on Rhodesia: objections to the *Fearless* proposals', *Round Table*, Apr 1969, pp. 135–40. Material in the text is from these two sources unless otherwise stated.

[3] Wilson, *Labour government*, p. 594.

immunity for those giving evidence to the Commission, and its members would be free to move anywhere and talk to everyone, it would be operating in an area controlled by the minority regime with the police and army working for it. 'Is this immunity really very meaningful under these circumstances?'

Nyerere went on to suggest conditions for a 'real test of opinion' which, in their extent of British control, went far beyond anything the British government had been prepared to put forward in either the *Tiger* or *Fearless* proposals. He concluded:

If every other country in the world gave up sanctions and recognized the Rhodesian regime, no Commonwealth country could do so and retain the Commonwealth boast that it is united in anti-racialism. The Commonwealth stands for something basic to the future of mankind; but only while it stands firmly against racialism and minority racial domination. The fact that we are not strong enough to achieve the result we need quickly must not cause us to give up our principles.

In the subsequent discussion, according to Wilson, 'twenty-three countries, give or take a number of qualifications, were against Britain, and five for us'. The five were Australia, New Zealand, Malaysia, Malawi, and Canada, the last of these in 'basic' agreement, but with a willingness to understand the African point of view. Wilson's reply, while dwelling on the anti-racial stance of the Commonwealth, reiterated Britain's incapacity and unwillingness to use force in Rhodesia. He then tackled the main point of African opposition, the possibility that the royal commission would report that the people of Rhodesia as a whole were willing to accept the *Fearless* terms as a basis for independence. This, he said, would constitute a 'substantial change of circumstances' and would justify Britain in reconsidering Nibmar and saying so to the other members of the Commonwealth. Wilson's key question was:

If the people of Rhodesia—having had the constitutional proposals put to them, having regard to the consequences of accepting them, and having regard also to the consequences of present conditions continuing, and from their point of view deteriorating—decided for acceptance, should any of my colleagues outside Rhodesia say that the Rhodesians were wrong; that they knew better than the Rhodesians what was good for them?

It was clear that the British government was firmly attached to some scheme such as *Fearless*; and subsequent discussion turned largely upon how acceptable was the 'test of acceptability' through a Royal Commission. Nyerere pointed out that the implication of Wilson's references to the Gibraltar case was that a referendum was what was needed in Rhodesia. This was not accepted, although it was agreed that the Royal Commission could recommend a referendum if it thought this necessary. *The Times*'s editorial on 11 January was headed 'The End of NIBMAR'. It was a fair summing-up.[1] Rhodesia

---

[1] The official communiqué gave rather fuller details of the discussion than before, broadly following but in some details amplifying the account here. See Cmnd 3919 (1969), paras 24–5; *Survey B & CA*, 31 Jan 1969, pp. 89–100.

was not to disrupt the next meeting of heads of government in 1971, whatever it might still do to the atmosphere of Commonwealth relations.[1]

During the remainder of 1969 the Rhodesian position deteriorated so far as any settlement was concerned. Smith, having poured scorn, in his usual fashion, on the efforts of the Commonwealth prime ministers,[2] continued desultory exchanges with the British government.[3] He also brought forward proposals for a new Rhodesian constitution which would never lead to majority rule: the most that could be hoped for would be eventual parity between European and African representation in the lower house.[4] A referendum in June asked the Rhodesian voters whether they wanted a republican form of government, and whether they approved the constitutional proposals already made known. 61,130 were in favour of a republic and 14,327 against; 57,724 agreed to the proposals and 20,776 did not. The governor thereupon resigned and his resignation was accepted. The residual missions were withdrawn from London and Salisbury.[5] The Commonwealth Sanctions Committee continued to meet and to be largely responsible for UN initiatives on sanctions,[6] but a UN report published in June revealed that Rhodesian exports worth £106 m. had nevertheless reached other countries (i.e. UN members and others) in 1968.[7]

Rhodesia was declared a republic on 2 March 1970.

VII

Only an enemy of the Commonwealth could maintain that the effects of Rhodesia upon it were anything but bad. None of the parties was pleased. Even for the white Rhodesians there was no great gain, although their sense of self-importance was satisfied and the predictions of their government were vindicated: sanctions caused strains and restrictions upon economic growth, and the isolation of Rhodesia by other countries emphasized its dependence upon South Africa. For Britain, Rhodesia represented a form of prolonged and irritating humiliation, since neither the symbols of imperial power nor the efforts of 'world opinion' had sufficed to prevent a rebellious colony from going its own way, and Britain had been widely pilloried as a 'racist' country which would willingly fire on coloured men but not on its kith and kin. For the

[1] Nyerere told a meeting of students on his return to Dar es Salaam that Tanzania would leave the Commonwealth if Britain settled the Rhodesian situation on the *Fearless* terms (*The Times*, 15 Jan 1969).
[2] Ibid., 8 Jan 1969.   [3] See Cmnd 4065 (1969).
[4] *Survey B & CA*, 20 June 1969, pp. 542–5.
[5] Ibid., 18 July 1969, pp. 615–16.   [6] CSG, *Third Report*, p. 3.
[7] S/19252 & Add. 1 (SCOR, 24th yr, suppl. Jan–June 1969, p. 195). Boyd argues (pp. 262–9) that the effect of sanctions was greater than the statement in the text might suggest. See also two articles in *JCPS*, July 1969 (R. B. Sutcliffe, 'The political economy of Rhodesian sanctions', and T. R. C. Curtin, 'Total sanctions and economic development in Rhodesia') and the references quoted there.

African states, whatever the satisfaction they might have gained from UN and OAU resolutions and from majority sentiment in Commonwealth meetings, Rhodesia was a source of frustration. Not only had the African mobilization of 'world opinion' failed to shift Britain from its course on the use of force and on pressure upon South Africa and Portugal; the African states themselves had been unable to provide either armies of their own or sufficient incitement to Rhodesian guerrillas to threaten the stability of the Rhodesian regime.[1] For other Commonwealth members Rhodesia came to represent embarrassment or annoyance, or both. Those states with their own dominant problems, such as India, Pakistan, and Cyprus, had to turn aside from these to listen to protracted statements of the African case; unless a vote in favour of African resolutions could be turned to the advantage of their own diplomacy, it represented an interruption to that diplomacy in aspects directly concerned with the Commonwealth. For Australia and New Zealand, Rhodesia presented an unwelcome choice between their customary support for Britain and a hesitant recognition of the growing diplomatic importance of the African states, which, while uncertain in its application, still required attention. No one really benefited from this long-drawn-out and distressingly indeterminate issue.

Similarly, the effect on the Commonwealth as an institution was bad. The Rhodesian issue set members against one another, especially, but not solely, the Africans against Britain.[2] The explosive racial basis on which the discussion was conducted was bound to exacerbate suspicions about British policy and to generate bad feeling: when Kapwepwe called Wilson a racialist, and Wilson replied so hotly, both were expressing the underlying emotions innate in such a question. It was widely accepted in Britain that white Rhodesians were kith and kin and this was accepted by some Afro-Asian leaders (such as Lee Kuan Yew) as sufficient explanation of why Britain did not use force against them; yet Wilson relates that Hastings Banda was 'the only African I have ever heard use the phrase "kith and kin" except as a term of abuse'.[3] The other 'white' Commonwealth countries were rendered correspondingly sensitive (though they reacted in rather different ways) by this underlying feeling.

Not only were relations between individual members damaged by Rhodesia; so too was the machinery of the Commonwealth itself. A series of conferences obsessed by the problem led to a lopsided development of priorities. Rhodesia

[1] For an account of guerrilla activities, of the help given to them, and of the mixed feelings engendered in Zambia and Tanzania, see John Day, 'The Rhodesian African nationalists and the Commonwealth African states', *JCPS*, July 1969. For a critical account of the OAU's incapacity to affect events, see Anirudha Gupta, 'The Rhodesian crisis and the Organization of African Unity', *Int. Stud.*, July 1967.

[2] A high commissioner from one of the less militant African states told me in October 1969: 'We felt we were being conned ... In a way we knew we would be but there was a vague feeling that perhaps this government [i.e., Wilson's] would be different from the others.'

[3] *Labour government*, p. 114. Cf. the sensitive treatment of this issue in Mazrui, *Anglo-African Commonwealth*, ch. 3, and James Barber, 'The impact of the Rhodesian crisis on the Commonwealth,' *JCPS*, July 1969.

was important, but it was not all-important; yet in 1964, 1965, and 1966 it virtually excluded discussion of any other question. Here, on ground to some extent of their own choosing, the Commonwealth was tested by the Africans, and found wanting. It did not, in the view of most of them, guarantee multi-racial justice; and it was powerless to force the British government into a course which it was not prepared to take. The manner of conducting confer-ences, the conventions of behaviour which had hardly needed to be codified because they were so widely understood, and the assumption that what a member regarded as a domestic concern was to be treated as such, were all thrust aside in the fruitless pursuit of a dominant African goal. In the wearing struggle for it, not only tempers but also the fabric of the association were frayed.

Yet for one Commonwealth institution, the secretariat, the Rhodesian issue provided opportunities which might not otherwise have occurred. It was a difficult matter to start the secretariat's operations just when the Common-wealth was being convulsed by Ian Smith's UDI, but the disruptive quality of the issue meant that without this organization it might not have been possible to contain it. After the turmoil of 1966, only a slow process of mending enabled the 1969 Prime Ministers' Meeting to be the success it was widely acclaimed to be. The existence of the secretariat meant that a special, detached figure of standing with a Commonwealth focus, the secretary-general, could act as an envoy between the parties in a way which would have been impossible for the CRO in a dispute in which Britain was the main object of other mem-bers' complaints. The secretariat also provided a base for the Commonwealth Sanctions Committee, which, while largely ineffective in a situation which was beyond its control, could not, in the prevailing situation, have been successfully incorporated into the machinery of British government as, for example, the Commonwealth Economic Committee had previously been.

In spite of these opportunities given to the secretariat, the dominating character of the Rhodesian issue, coming so soon after the South African one, caused a kind of equation of the Commonwealth with Africa in the 1960s. To large sections of the British public, the identification must have seemed com-plete, and may have led to disapproval of the Commonwealth because it was the means through which African demands were made on Britain. To the non-African members, the close identification of Africa and the Common-wealth was mostly unwelcome and often troublesome. To the Africans them-selves, while this identification may sometimes have been a source of pride and of opportunity, the Rhodesian result was such as to create frustration and annoyance rather than any feeling that the Commonwealth was a potent political instrument.

Perhaps the worst thing that Rhodesia did to the Commonwealth was to damage, and possibly to destroy, what in terms of these Commonwealth *Surveys* might be called the Hancock vision: the notion that, following the

Empire, the Commonwealth stood for 'the government of men by themselves', which Hancock identified as the central point of 'the liberty, the ideal, the aspiration—the *mythus* of the Commonwealth of Nations'.[1] In one way and another, such a notion had not only survived but flourished down to the 1960s. Innumerable orators, giving the *mythus* their own interpretation, had located it in parliamentary government, national unity, multiracialism, majority rule, and the like. No one, of course, located it in permanent domination of a black majority by a small white minority. Rhodesia showed that Britain was unable, or unwilling, or both, to enforce the *mythus* upon a colony over which its sovereignty was undoubted but its control tenuous, and which was ruled by a white minority. As we have seen, all British governments recognized a commitment to multiracialism and to eventual majority rule; but domestic considerations stood in the way of enforcing these in Rhodesia.

It could be argued that the British were being consistent even though they were unable to put their consistency into practice. Time and again British representatives pointed out how different Rhodesia was from other colonies, in that Britain had no control over its armed forces and police. Time and again they stressed the degree of self-government which the Rhodesians enjoyed and which it would be unreasonable to withdraw from them—apart from the great and unresolved problems of direct rule which such a withdrawal would involve.

Such arguments, while understandable to the old dominions and acceptable to those sections of their public opinion which still saw imperial responsibilities in terms of their own countries' experience, were unacceptable to many newer Commonwealth members on two grounds. One was scepticism, since the reluctance to use force which the British displayed in Rhodesia had not applied in Kenya, Aden, British Guiana, India, or Cyprus—indeed, in almost any of the newly independent members. The other was doctrinal: if the British were serious in what they had said about majority rule in the other African colonies,[2] then they were under a moral commitment to apply the same principles in Rhodesia. Why should what was right in Zambia or Kenya be wrong in Rhodesia? Britain did not, indeed, deny this latter reasoning, and the Five (or Six) Principles were designed to incorporate these principles. But there was still a structural fault in British colonial policy: it was difficult for Africans to accept the sincerity of the British claim that practicality was all that prevented Britain from enforcing such principles in Rhodesia. Instead, their tendency was to believe that Britain made a virtue of necessity in proclaiming

[1] Hancock, *Survey*, i, 61–2.

[2] The one exception had been Zanzibar, in which, in Nyerere's words, 'sovereignty was transferred to a minority government; the result was a bloody revolution, with all the consequences which follow from such an event—and which are still following' (*Round Table*, Apr 1969, p. 135). I have been told that the British action in granting independence to Zanzibar at the end of 1963 intensified the suspicions of some African leaders, including Nyerere, about what the British government might do in Rhodesia.

majority rule for colonies which it no longer wished to govern, while preserving an underlying preference for white men's control in such cases as Rhodesia and South Africa. The Commonwealth *mythus* necessarily shrivelled in the face of such a belief.

One further effect of Rhodesia deserves attention. Rhodesia brought the Commonwealth more directly into the sphere of UN politics than any previous issue. At one level, it enhanced the Commonwealth's importance, since the tendency of both the OAU and the Afro-Asian group at the UN was to accept the leadership of the Commonwealth African countries, especially on sanctions, and the sanctions strategy, from 1966 onwards, was influenced by the Commonwealth Sanctions Committee in London. But this was not the only level. At another and more important one, the Commonwealth became directly subordinate to the UN and the OAU, since the strategy to be pursued at the UN by the Africans was determined by themselves in consultation with other African states, not with the other members of the Commonwealth. Some of those other members willingly followed the African line, since it suited their general posture in foreign policy. Others again, however, notably the old dominions and Britain itself, were left out of the discussions and found themselves either opposed to what the Africans wanted (especially on the use of force) or forced to abstain. The UN thus became a divisive force within the Commonwealth, mirroring and enlarging existing differences, and serving as a means whereby the militant African states could co-ordinate and concentrate their pressure upon Britain. To see the matter in this way is to omit altogether consideration of whether it was sensible or proper for Britain to take the Rhodesia question to the UN after UDI, following the period in which it had maintained that the UN had no jurisdiction in the matter. The UN would have had much the same relation to the Commonwealth as an association whether Britain had done this or not, since the Africans would still have continued to force Rhodesia on to the attention of the General Assembly.

In sum, then, the Rhodesia question was bad for the Commonwealth's continuance as an informal association based upon some degree of mutual trust and understanding. Trust ebbed; understanding was obscured; the Commonwealth's prestige declined because some of its members thought it was being used as a means to achieve ends to which they did not subscribe, while others thought it a whited sepulchre of principles which expediency had laid aside. The central issue was British policy. Could it have been different? If it had been different, would the Commonwealth have been in better shape?

As we have seen, British ministers were, to a great extent, prisoners of the past. In the 1950s great hopes had been pinned on a multiracial solution in the Federation, but there was not much of a concerted attempt to assess how Rhodesian practice was diverging from British policy elsewhere in Africa, and what effect this divergence might have upon Commonwealth relations. Fragmentation of advice to the cabinet, concentration upon particular cases, changes of minister and of government, attention to major issues elsewhere were all factors in the situation. Yet, to an extent not clearly seen by British ministers, a Commonwealth problem was building up. The Commonwealth was not conceived in advance as a means of channelling and making consistent British policy towards Africa; instead, it had been a slow growth stimulated by particular circumstances, such as Indian independence, acquiring its assumptions and institutions by pragmatic means, and essentially concerned with post-independence questions. The onset of the African campaign for majority rule in Rhodesia took other Commonwealth members and the British government almost unawares: neither had been prepared to deal with such a determined and single-minded approach.

In two respects the British government might have taken a different course from the one it adopted. First, it might have washed its hands of Rhodesia quite early, or simply disowned it as an intractable issue once Smith had made his illegal declaration of independence. Britain would thus have foregone responsibility for future developments, and left the Africans to do what they could in the UN and elsewhere. The attraction of such a policy, in hindsight, is that Wilson would not have been led into undertakings which he could not keep, and Britain would not have had to go through the exhausting and abortive negotiations on *Tiger* and *Fearless*. It would have been a concession to realism, an act of abrogation on the part of an imperial power which was no longer willing (because largely unable) to enforce its wishes. But it would have had some adverse consequences. The Commonwealth would almost certainly have been affected, since the African states would still have maintained that Britain should have put its principles into practice, and it is probable that some would have withdrawn. If opinions differ about whether this would have been a disaster, there is no doubt that both Douglas-Home and Wilson thought it would be highly undesirable, since their wish to preserve the Commonwealth was a factor in shaping their policy. Hence abrogation, while an act of realism in one sense, might have been unrealistic because unworkable in another, since it would have gone against the conception of the Commonwealth and of Britain's place in it that was still current amongst British ministers. Nor would it have preserved Britain from attacks at the UN. And, above all, it would have meant washing Britain's hands of responsibility for the black Rhodesians, who were, in a sense, Britain's wards. No cabinet would have been likely to do this.

The second alternative course would have been to use force. Opinions differ on the practicality of this. The British government consistently maintained that logistics and the state of its forces prevented it; no doubt memories of Suez had an influence. As against this, various people have told me that a parachute drop from bases in Zambia might have met with no resistance, some of the senior officers of the Rhodesian army having made it known privately that they would not resist the Queen's forces lawfully deployed. Even if this were true, however, there would still have been considerations to make the British government pause.

Supposing there had in fact been bloody fighting: how would British public opinion have taken this? In July 1968, according to an opinion poll, only 16 per cent of the British public thought force should have been used in 1965, and these included only 19 per cent of habitual Labour voters. The 16 per cent had grown from 2 per cent who had said, in October 1965, that force should be used if UDI was declared; but they were still only a small minority.[1] Racialism in Britain itself might well have been stimulated by clashes between British and white Rhodesian troops at the request of black members of the Commonwealth. There must also have been doubts about how to govern Rhodesia after a military victory. None of these considerations would have mattered if the British government had been seized by a firm conviction that nothing— including the risk of bloodshed in Rhodesia and the estrangement of South Africa—mattered in comparison with the overriding need to impose the Six Principles on Rhodesia. But there was no such conviction in Britain. Colonial policy had been the province of a few, not a matter of mass determination. Now, for the first time since the 1930s,[2] it was becoming a mass issue on the most awkward of questions, involving the deliberate use of armed force against a white community thought of as strongly 'British' in loyalty and sentiment. There was no evidence of strong support for such a policy anywhere except on the extreme Left. The Six Principles were not an affirmation of a deep British belief which had to be enforced, whatever the consequences. It is not surprising that Wilson rejected this second alternative.

Whichever way British policy went, it would have meant trouble for the Commonwealth and for the British government. As the atmosphere at the 1969 meeting showed, only time, and the realization that no generally satisfactory solution was likely to emerge, could reconcile the two sides within the Commonwealth to the point at which they saw how little was to be gained from further disputation. But the *mythus* would never be the same again.[3]

[1] NOP *Bulletin*, Nov 1968.

[2] This is a reference to the debate over the Government of India Bill, which so convulsed the Conservative Party. India was never a 'colony' in the strict sense, but it was a dependency, and I include it amongst colonial issues in the broad sense.

[3] On 24 November 1971, after long and delicate negotiations, Sir Alec Douglas-Home signed an agreement with Ian Smith on behalf of the Heath government. This agreement involved proposals for a settlement, not dissimilar to, but going further in the British direction than, the *Fearless* proposals (see Cmnd 4835, 1971). Douglas-Home, in commending the proposals in the House of Commons, said he was conscious that Britain's influence on the Rhodesian situation was running out, but 'we must exercise it while anything of it remained, to try to obtain the best deal we possibly could for the Rhodesian African' (see HC Deb., 1 Dec 1971, cols 464–600, for the debate). A British commission of inquiry reported in May 1972 (Cmnd 4964) that, while the proposals were acceptable to the great majority of Europeans, the majority of Africans rejected them.

CHAPTER 11

THE AFRICAN DIMENSION

IN the 1950s the Commonwealth's most obvious dimension was an Asian one. The constitutional triumphs of 1947 and 1949, which had kept India, Pakistan, and Ceylon in the association in spite of their anti-colonial and republican inclinations, were still fresh in the minds of publicists and politicians. At the Fifth Unofficial Commonwealth Relations Conference at Lahore in 1954, 'much emphasis was placed rightly and inevitably on the Asian viewpoint on Commonwealth and world affairs'.[1] Yet by 1969 it is doubtful whether anyone would have talked about 'the Asian viewpoint'. A series of upheavals and conflicts, described in Part II, had made it clear that Asian Commonwealth members displayed no unity of outlook. Asian questions had become interruptions to Commonwealth leaders' enforced concentration upon Africa. It was the African, not the Asian, dimension that mattered. The reasons are to be found on both sides.

There was no prospect of India's and Pakistan's agreeing except on such vague worldwide issues as colonialism and underdevelopment. They were primarily concerned with outwitting one another; they viewed all Asian issues in this light, just as they viewed the relations between the great powers. Where either could gain an advantage over the other by taking a particular stance, it would do so. In such a situation (paralleled to a certain extent by that which developed between Malaysia and Singapore) no distinctive Asian viewpoint was expressed at Commonwealth meetings, even though the ultimately divisive question of Kashmir was not allowed to be raised.

Africa, on the other hand, had after Ghana's independence in 1957 the advantage not only of novelty, which India and Pakistan had possessed ten years earlier, but also of apparent unity in pursuit of major objectives. While there were often acute disagreements between the African members, they had common purposes to pursue. Moreover, the pressures of international politics in the early 1960s combined to make the rest of the world pay particular attention to Africa. The change to an African dimension in Commonwealth affairs can be linked with a similar change on a larger scale.

I

By 1960, 'Africa's year', the super-powers were already concerned about Africa's future. Clearly, the increase in the number of African sovereign

[1] Nicholas Mansergh, *The Multi-Racial Commonwealth* (1955), p. 137.

states would cause a shift in the balance of forces in the General Assembly and other international bodies. Less obvious was the future political orientation of the various parts of the continent. How would the Muslim areas of the north view the politics of Europe, their neighbour across the Mediterranean, with which their contacts were of such long standing? Would the former French colonies continue to follow France's lead? Similarly, could the British expect to guide their former colonies on major issues? What roles, then, could the US and the Soviet Union play? Neither had been a colonial power in Africa. In this sense they were external to its affairs, but they were engaged in a worldwide confrontation, in which neither could afford to leave any area fully open to penetration by the other. Further, the Sino-Soviet rift had opened up the prospect of Chinese opposition to the influence of the two super-powers.

The super-powers, in spite of their wealth and technological accomplishments, were in addition handicapped by inexperience and lack of contacts in Africa. This was especially true of the Soviet Union, which had not only to gain basic knowledge of the continent's affairs but also to adjust its doctrines about ex-colonial areas before it could take advantage of such potential associates as the radical regimes in Ghana and Mali. From the standpoint of the US, Africa was important because the communist powers might entrench themselves there, because of its emotional significance for black Americans, because it involved such Nato allies as Britain, France, Belgium, and Portugal, and because it was a source of important raw materials, from gold to chrome.

Those European colonial powers connected with the US through Nato did not concert their colonial policies, except to the extent that the advances made by one were likely to affect the others. Britain's adoption of independence as a policy affected France; Belgium's unexpected decision to proceed with independence for the Congo, in its turn, affected Britain in neighbouring areas. Each colonial empire in Africa had been largely self-contained, separated by language and institutional barriers if not by natural frontiers. These barriers tended to persist after independence, since it was difficult to disentangle the African countries' economies from those of the metropoles, and often impossible to establish effective links between new states which spoke different languages and had no tradition of co-operation. The European countries, for their part, wished to continue their association with their former colonies, though each had its own way of doing so. The British way, of Commonwealth membership combined with economic aid related to the economic viability of the country in question, differed from the French, in which the provision of massive economic and sometimes military aid was conditioned by the former colony's acquiescence in French policies. Belgium attempted, with varying success, to re-establish influence in the disturbed Congo. For Portugal the question did not arise: Angola and Mozambique were not being groomed for independence, no matter how severe became the burden of military resistance to local insurgents.

Hence the formal ending of colonialism did not mean an end to connection with the former colonial powers. French preponderance was especially noticeable. It was no wonder that Nyerere said there was a devil in Africa, when he contemplated the amount of influence still wielded by Britain and France, which could not ignore the interest taken in their former colonies by the Soviet Union and China. Portugal was even more affected by the direct encouragement given to the insurgents by the communist powers.

Africa's situation as a focus of attention by the super-powers and the former colonial powers was demonstrated in the long-drawn-out crisis in the Congo, in which were manifest the wish of most African states that the US and USSR should not be drawn into an African confrontation with one another; the use of the UN as a means to this end, with the connivance of the US; the covert international support for Katanga; and the displeasure of the British and Belgian governments at UN actions which they considered contrary to their countries' interests. It was demonstrated again, as we shall see, in the Nigerian civil war, when the Soviet Union provided arms for the Nigerian federal government, the French and Portuguese aided its opponents, and the British government continued to supply arms to the federal government, partly to prevent the Soviet Union having a monopoly. In the Rhodesian situation, which seemed very much a Commonwealth affair apart from the part played by the UN, there was a further international dimension. The US support of sanctions owed much to its desire that the Soviet Union and China should not have a duopoly of influence with African nationalists; Wilson's argument for Britain's taking the matter to the UN was that otherwise Britain might find 'a red army in blue berets' in Central Africa at the behest of the Security Council; and the continuance of Smith's regime in Rhodesia strengthened the Zambians in their acceptance of the Chinese offer to help with the Tanzam railway, which would free Zambia from dependence on the Rhodesian and Portuguese rail systems.

Thus the developed countries' approaches to Africa in the 1960s were characterized by the super-powers' mingled apprehension and opportunity, and the former colonial powers' desire to retain connections in Africa. The Africans, on their side, developed a system of association and propaganda whereby, as far as possible, the gains from independence could be consolidated, new gains made, and the influence of the super-powers and former colonial powers could be tempered and sometimes nullified. The system was in no way perfect. It frequently broke down, most often through quarrels between the African states themselves; but it was notable in contrast with the lack of such a system amongst the former European dependencies in South and Southeast Asia.

The essentials of the system were, first, a vague but real sense of common interest on the part of the African leaders, and, second, an attempt to set up workable means of consultation and common policy, mainly through the OAU. The first of these was especially vulnerable because of the divergent cultural backgrounds of the elites of the new African states and because of the lack of contact and sympathy between their peoples, in spite of whatever sense of unity their leaders may have derived from student days in London, Paris, and New York. Nonetheless, it represented a genuine aspiration on the leaders' part, and was closer to reality than some other political aspirations: to say 'we are all Africans' was more self-evident than it would be to say 'we are all Asians'.[1]

The second essential was pursued through the OAU (set up after considerable difficulty and tenuously sustaining itself in the face of frequent animosity between the states and leaders represented), and through the African caucus at the UN. Commonwealth African states had little experience of diplomacy; their leaders' main experience, as we have seen, was of agitation for independence. They had not sat in metropolitan parliaments and exerted influence at the heart of colonial government, like some of the leaders of francophone Africa. Although this distinction was not complete—Sekou Touré of Guinea, for example, was as much an agitator by nature and experience as Nkrumah— it was sufficiently marked to render the two sets of leaders often antipathetic to each other's style and objectives. Nevertheless, except where their sense of vital national interests was affected, they managed to work together on the main propaganda issues. Especially in the earlier 1960s the Commonwealth was a principal means used by the Commonwealth African states to exert pressure in respect of these issues.

On paper, as we have seen, the Africans achieved considerable success with their campaigns. This was partly because of their habit of caucusing and achieving a consensus for General Assembly votes. It was also because these votes were swollen by those of the communist bloc, of other former colonies, and normally of the Latin American states. In the 1960s there was a natural coalition for condemnation of South Africa and Portugal, as in the 1950s there had been for attacks on France's policies in Algeria. But, except for the adherence of the Soviet Union, this was a coalition of those lacking in military and economic power. On such issues as Rhodesia and South-West Africa, the strength of the denunciation often increased in inverse ratio to the effectiveness of the campaign.

---

[1] Mazrui, *Towards a pax africana*, esp. ch. 3, is of great interest on this point. Cf. W. E. Abraham, *The mind of Africa* (1962), and Nyerere: 'There is one sense in which African unity already exists. There is a sentiment of "African-ness", a feeling of mutual involvement, which pervades all the political and cultural life of the continent. Nationalist leaders all over Africa feel themselves to be part of a greater movement; they recognize a special responsibility to the political unit in which they happen to belong, but feel personally involved in the triumphs and setbacks of all other African countries. . . . But with all this, African unity is at present merely an emotion born of a history of colonialism and oppression . . .' ('A United States of Africa', *J. Mod. Afr Stud.*, 1/1 (1963), p. 1).

Africans, lacking the power to go beyond declamation, naturally looked for all available diplomatic opportunities to declaim. Not only the General Assembly, but the meetings of such UN specialized agencies as Unesco and the ILO, echoed to the denunciation of South Africa and Portugal; so did the International Olympic Committee and other bodies connected with sport, and a variety of scientific and similar bodies in which western liberal opinion could be enlisted. For as Britain, France, and Belgium gave up their empires, South Africa stood out as a bastion of the kinds of regime which African nationalists and western liberals found most repugnant—in the Portuguese territories one which refused to recognize a specific African personality and right of self-determination, asserting instead the virtues of a Catholic civilization based in Lisbon; in South Africa an established white settler regime, so long and so firmly in place that it recognized no European base but asserted its own right to govern in spite of its minority status; and in Rhodesia a similar though often different regime, less assured but almost as determined not to permit erosion of its power. Into this situation the Commonwealth was thrust willy-nilly. Indeed, it was hardly thrust, but found itself there already. Its new members were determined to use it for their own ends, while the older ones, unfamiliar with Africa, did not know what to do at first, though their positions became firmer as their experience grew.

In seeking explanations of the new militancy which the African states brought to Commonwealth discussions, one must also attach some weight to the prevailing international climate. The massive paper majorities which the Africans obtained in the General Assembly on South African and Rhodesian issues were reflections of the view taken of Africa in the 1960s by the super-powers, the European powers, the Latin Americans, and the Asians alike—that the newly independent African states must not be alienated but must be given their heads on African issues. Amongst the developed countries, there was a basic division between those of the communist bloc, which were pre-pared to advocate harsh measures against the South African and Rhodesian regimes, and those of the west, which were not; but on the symbolic and declamatory issue of opposition to racialism all were prepared to join. In this respect the Commonwealth's discussions and declarations mirrored what was going on at UN headquarters.[1]

South Africa and Rhodesia, issues on which Britain was subjected to heavy pressure by the African members of the Commonwealth, represent the most important element in Africa's impact on the Commonwealth. There was to be another African issue which resembled that of Southern Africa, involving great-power interests, African nationalism, anxious concern in the OAU, pressure upon the former colonial power to alter its policy, the Commonwealth

[1] 'Mirror' is not an exact term. In Commonwealth discussions there was often more of a 'family' atmosphere than at the UN; and disappointment and distrust may often be more acute in a family atmosphere than in that of a theatre or a forum.

as an instrument in the pursuit of some members' aims—but the element of racialism was lacking and the other elements were mixed in different proportions to produce a quite different result. This was the civil war in Nigeria between 1967 and 1970. A brief examination of it will show the African dimension of the Commonwealth in another light.

II

Nigeria was a country with acute regional and tribal differences; its northern, eastern, and western regions had been constantly at loggerheads over the disposition of power and political advantage. The biggest tribal group in the east, the Ibos, had spread into other regions and achieved success in many walks of life, largely because of their adaptability and their aptitude for the education provided by the Christian missions, especially the Roman Catholic. They had thus created resentment amongst the peoples of regions to which they had migrated. The small group of officers who planned the assassinations, including that of the prime minister, Sir Abubakar Tafawa Balewa, in January 1966 were mostly Ibo; so was General Ironsi, who took over as head of a federal military government pledged to eliminate corruption and the abuses perpetrated by the political parties.

Ironsi declared Nigeria a unitary state in May 1966, with the aim of eliminating the former regions. He was himself the victim of another coup in July, this time led by officers from the north, who installed a military government under Lt-Colonel Yakubu Gowon. Within the next few months the massacre of Ibos in the north caused a mass exodus of them to their homeland. Lt-Colonel Ojukwu, the military governor in the east, emerged as the Ibo champion, and there was talk of secession. A conference at Aburi, in Ghana, in January 1967, seemed to provide some common ground between Ojukwu's position and that of Gowon and the other military governors, but this proved illusory. In May Gowon divided the country into twelve states, three of which would be in Ojukwu's eastern region; Ojukwu responded by announcing secession from the federal republic and the constitution of the eastern region as the sovereign Republic of Biafra. Hostilities began six weeks later.[1]

The war was to last until January 1970.[2] Although at first the federal government looked like winning quickly, its shortage of trained troops soon became evident, and the Biafrans managed to strike back. In due course the federal forces captured the ports which provided Biafra with an outlet to the

[1] This description of the events leading up to the war is a summary one and may not do justice to the complexities of the situation. See S. K. Panter-Brick, *Nigerian politics and military rule* (1970), for careful essays on the circumstances leading up to the war and for useful documents. For Ojukwu's version, see C. Odumegwu Ojukwu, *Biafra* (1969). For earlier background, Okoi Arikpo, *The development of modern Nigeria* (1967) is concise and informative.

[2] See Roy Lewis, 'Britain and Biafra: a Commonwealth civil war', *Round Table*, July 1970, for a shrewd assessment of the situation at large. The title is somewhat misleading.

sea. They then settled down to a slow campaign of attrition which depended largely on blockade for its success. The effective borders of Biafra contracted until, by the end of the war, there were probably more Ibos outside them than within. Ojukwu's campaign, aided by a tendentious and effective propaganda organization centred in Geneva, attracted much sympathy in other countries, and he must have received a good deal of financial support, but in the end the superior force of the federal government told. Ojukwu retreated to political asylum in the Ivory Coast. The fears of genocide expressed by Biafran supporters proved to be groundless when the federal government took over; its treatment of former opponents was highly magnanimous.[1]

During the war there was a peculiar line-up of sympathizers and opponents. The federal government had the support of Britain—hesitant at first—and of the Soviet Union, and retained its position as an established government, embodying full sovereignty, in the eyes of the UN and of the OAU. Support for Biafra was less official but emotionally stronger. It came from South Africa, Portugal, Rhodesia, and France, and from a few African states (see below). Biafra also got sympathy from Israel and China. All these powers acted for their own reasons, and mostly under cover. The fact that the Soviet Union was providing the federal government with military aircraft, while the UAR supplied airmen to fly them, was sufficient reason for some. Others, of which France was the most notable,[2] presumably wished to reduce British influence in Africa and simultaneously the pretensions of the anglophone members of the OAU. Nigeria's oil resources, which would have been largely under Biafran control within the original Biafran boundaries, undoubtedly had some influence.

One can argue (as Harold Wilson does)[3] that French arms kept Biafra in the field for the last fifteen months of the campaign, during which conditions within the Biafran perimeter became steadily worse. Starvation amongst the Ibos aroused world-wide concern amongst church groups, both Protestant and

[1] Biafran claims about genocide persisted in spite of the reports of the international observer team, a body of military experts appointed by Britain, Canada, Sweden, Poland, the UN, and the OAU, at the invitation of the federal government in September 1968. The existence of such a body was largely unprecedented in such a conflict. Its reports were highly circumstantial and prescient, even though Biafran propaganda attempted systematically to discredit them throughout the world. See e.g. the report of January 1969, Cmnd 3878 (1969).

[2] A French government statement of 31 July 1968 said that 'the blood spilt and the hardships endured for more than a year by the population of Biafra demonstrate their will to affirm themselves as a people'. It went on: 'In consequence, the present conflict should be resolved on the basis of the right of people to dispose of themselves and should permit the appropriate international procedures to be applied.' At a press conference on 9 September de Gaulle said the Federation was 'employing war, blockade, extermination and famine to subdue Biafra' and questioned whether it was conceivable 'that the people of the Federation, including the Ibo, might resume a life in common'. He said France was helping Biafra within the bounds of possibility, but had not taken the decisive step of diplomatic recognition because Africa's political development was the concern of Africans. He did not rule out recognition for the future (*Survey B & CA*, 31 Jan 1969, p. 106). Formal recognition never came.

[3] *Labour government*, p. 560.

Catholic, and in many liberal-minded people. Britain was criticized for continuing to provide arms to the federal government, thus prolonging the war. An unusual coalition of people from left and right, concerned to alleviate suffering and impatient with the limitations which recognition of the Nigerian federal government's sovereignty imposed on their governments, developed in Britain, Ireland, the Scandinavian countries, and Canada. There was endless argument about the conditions under which relief supplies could be got into the diminishing Biafran area; relief agencies of the Catholic and Protestant churches and the International Committee of the Red Cross (ICRC) were drawn into controversies about whether Ojukwu or the Federal government was to blame for hindering the deliveries.

The civil war proved difficult for the OAU, since, like the Katanga case, it exposed basic problems arising from the collapse of the European empires and their legacy of artificial boundaries which had nevertheless acquired legal sanction. Indeed, founders of the OAU had recognized the need to affirm the principle of territorial integrity, no boundary changes to be made without the consent of the established regimes. Ojukwu's regime in Biafra rested its case on the general principle of self-determination, but Gowon had the trump card of the established regime. In due course four African states—Tanzania, Zambia, the Ivory Coast, and Gabon—recognized Biafra.[1] But all the other African states continued to recognize federal sovereignty, and the OAU's collective action was based on this. Stresses within the organization were considerable, especially because of the French support for Biafra. As time went by, African support for Gowon's regime increased, partly because of Biafra's association with Portugal and with rightists generally, because the occasional Biafran use of European mercenaries appeared to give a Katanga cast to Ojukwu's whole operation, and because Ojukwu was losing. The OAU appointed a consultative mission at its Kinshasa meeting in September 1967,[2] and thereafter retained the main responsibility for attempts at mediation, while formally agreeing with Gowon's government that the matter was an internal Nigerian affair. The first of the original Biafran hopes—that Biafra would be accepted as a member of the OAU, as of the Commonwealth and the UN[3]— was thus dashed; and neither of the other two bodies showed any inclination to affirm Biafra's independence. The Commonwealth was, however, involved in two ways: through the positions taken by individual members, and through the activities of the secretariat.

III

Britain was the Commonwealth member most concerned, because of the

[1] See Nyerere's article, 'Why we recognized Biafra', *Observer*, 28 Apr 1968, for his reasons, which may not have been those of all the others.
[2] *Survey B & CA*, 13 Oct 1967, p. 1036.
[3] See Ojukwu, pp. 193–6, for the declared objectives of Biafra.

international implications of the civil war and because of considerable domestic agitation over the British policy of continuing to supply arms to the federal forces. 'Long before the major parliamentary debates in June and August 1968', writes Harold Wilson, 'Nigeria had replaced Vietnam as our major overseas preoccupation. It took up far more of my time, and that of ministerial colleagues, and far more moral wear and tear than any other issue.'[1] In discussing those debates, which cut across party lines, he explains part of his government's attitude towards the problem. Commenting on the replies to criticisms by Michael Stewart, the foreign and Commonwealth secretary, Wilson says:

> What he could not say was how far Nigeria would have been put in pawn to the Russians had we refused [to continue to supply arms]. Whatever military supplies we felt it right to withhold, they did in fact provide; they were tightening their grip on Nigeria's life. The hawks in the Nigerian Military Government gave short shrift to our—as they saw it—pedantic arguments, especially those which linked our arms supplies with pressure to negotiate for a cease fire. They were concerned with the "quick kill". It would not have taken more than one false step, perhaps one incautious word in Parliament, to have produced a purge in the Nigerian administration which would have put the pro-Russian hawks in control.[2]

These anxieties were reinforced by anxieties about France, which at this stage was still pursuing de Gaulle's policy of opposition to 'les Anglo-Saxons'. British support for the federal government, backed at one remove by the US (though the US refused to sell arms to either side in the civil war),[3] evidently convinced the French president that support for Biafra would strengthen France's position in Africa. Wilson said, of August 1968, that Colonel Ojukwu's worldwide search for arms was not succeeding, not for lack of finance but because he was finding it harder to obtain supplies and, once he had lost the ports, to fly them in. 'At this point General de Gaulle took a hand and supplies were made available to the fullest extent that they could be got through to the Colonel's beleaguered troops. The world knew what was going on, yet it could never be proved.' In reply to press inquiries the Quai d'Orsay maintained that they knew nothing and that this was a matter for the Elysée, but the Elysée, 'where the energetic M. Foccart was masterminding the operation', blandly referred all inquiries to the Foreign Ministry. 'Not that France was supplying arms to Biafra. All the arms went into the arsenals of the Governments of the Ivory Coast and Gabon', but national stocks of these governments were rapidly replenished when they were diminished by shipments to Biafra.[4]

The involvement of the Soviet Union and France in the civil war, which was

---

[1] *Labour government*, p. 558.

[2] Ibid., pp. 559–60. It should be noted that generally Wilson is highly complimentary to Gowon.

[3] See Waldemar A. Nielsen, *The great powers and Africa* (1969), pp. 323–5 for a useful but uncritical account of US policy.

[4] *Labour government*, p. 560.

regarded by some in Britain as a 'Commonwealth' matter because Nigeria was a Commonwealth member, typified the complicated nature of African affairs in the late 1960s. The civil war was a domestic affair, yet major powers were involved. Britain had long since given up any control over Nigeria, yet had responsibilities as its principal arms supplier and many connections resulting from its former colonial status. The British government was inclined to defend its arms policy by saying that it wished to retain some influence in Nigeria, yet that influence was not sufficient to end the war. Wilson himself visited Nigeria at the end of March 1969, and then went on to Addis Ababa for talks with Emperor Haile Selassie, who was the main figure in the OAU's attempts at mediation.[1] He was unable to make any headway with mediation, since Ojukwu would not meet him, but he did manage to clarify some of the intentions of the federal government and to prevail upon it to stop indiscriminate bombing. Britain thus exercised some influence, but it was marginal. It did not satisfy those people who were unimpressed by talk of sovereignty, who disregarded the international politics of the affair, and who concentrated upon the relief of suffering.

This same situation prevailed in Canada. Trudeau was under parliamentary pressure to bring up the matter at the UN, either in the General Assembly or in a committee; to seek Commonwealth action to deal with the problem;[2] and to attempt unilaterally to arrange a ceasefire. He rejected all these proposals because the civil war was a domestic affair, and because there was no doubt of the 'hostility and opposition from almost all African states' that would result. But Canada did press hard for humanitarian action, made representations to the Nigerian government, provided large sums of money to the ICRC, and supplied Canadian Hercules aircraft for Red Cross food airlifts—although only one of these was able to operate before the airlifts were stopped by wrangles over access to the stricken areas. Canada contributed to the observer team which rejected charges of genocide against the federal authorities. Trudeau's position, summed up, was:

. . . it would be wrong for the Canadian Government to assist the Nigerian government militarily, but it would be equally wrong for the Canadian government to assist the rebel regime politically. Each is an act of intervention. Each would be a presumptuous step, an arrogant step, I would say, for a country so distant as Canada. What Canada can do, and what it must do . . . is to attempt to feed the children who will starve to death without help.[3]

Similar sentiments prevailed in most other non-African Commonwealth

---

[1] See ibid, pp. 623–39, for an account of his journey.

[2] The Commonwealth secretary-general took the unusual step of testifying before the Parliamentary Standing Committee on External Affairs and Defence, to explain the various attempts at mediation (*External Affairs*, Dec 1968, p. 487).

[3] The description of the Canadian position is based on Trudeau's speech in parliament on 26 November 1968 (ibid., pp. 486–95). The quotation is from his speech of 27 November 1969 (Canada, HC Deb., 1969, p. 1319).

governments, which wished to see the civil war end but not to become involved. The Australian government, for example, sent one of its diplomats to Addis Ababa while the two sides engaged in negotiations under the auspices of the OAU in September 1968, 'to impress on both delegations Australia's concern over the destructiveness of the fighting and its hopes for the early achievement of a cease-fire'. It also made gifts of relief supplies through Unicef and the ICRC.[1] The general policy adopted by Commonwealth members was that the war was a Nigerian affair, and an African affair, but not an international responsibility.

The two members which recognized Biafra, Zambia and Tanzania, cannot have been pleased at the outcome. Humanitarian impulses were aroused in Kaunda and Nyerere by what they regarded as an attempt by the Nigerian federal government to bomb Biafra into submission; but the only other African states that accorded recognition were the Ivory Coast and Gabon, with neither of which they were in sympathy on other issues.

The difficulties of Commonwealth members over Nigeria were strikingly illustrated in a BBC broadcast on 6 January 1969, on the eve of the Commonwealth meeting of that year. Those taking part included Lee Kuan Yew from Singapore, Holyoake of New Zealand, Obote of Uganda, and J. S. Gichuru, the minister of finance of Kenya.[2] The interviewer, James Mossman, persistently tried to get them to discuss Biafra in such terms as: 'Do you think it's constructive for Britain to supply arms to Nigeria?' 'Do you think the Commonwealth has a responsibility to try to stop [hundreds of thousands of people being killed]?' 'As members of the Commonwealth is it reasonable that you should have a view on that—was Britain right to arm one side?' Holyoake would not discuss the issue; Lee said Mossman was becoming sententious and pompous; Gichuru said the Commonwealth had a moral responsibility, but it was impossible for the Commonwealth to go into a country which was independent; Obote did not like military government but would go no further.[3] Clearly, sovereignty was paramount. It was the fundamental ground on which the Commonwealth rested, and these leaders, like the rest, were not prepared to disturb it unless Nigeria invited them. To those onlookers who wanted action to prevent suffering, this seemed like equivocation. To many in Britain, also, it seemed odd that Commonwealth members should refuse to discuss the spilling of blood in Nigeria because it was a domestic matter, but should be ready enough to make demands about Rhodesia, although no blood had been shed and Rhodesia was formally a British responsibility.

When the heads of government communiqué was released there was no mention of the civil war. There had in fact been some discussion outside the

[1] *CN*, May 1969, pp. 195–7.
[2] Extracts are taken from Josey, *Lee Kuan Yew and the Commonwealth* (1969), pp. 18–22.
[3] There may have been something of a presentiment about this. Obote was deposed by his military commander, General Amin, while absent from Uganda attending the next Commonwealth Heads of Government Meeting, at Singapore in January 1971.

conference, and even a suggestion from one or two delegations that it should be discussed within it, but apart from an informal gathering at which Chief Awolowo of Nigeria explained his government's position, nothing was done. The Biafran delegation in London, which had been supposed to meet the Nigerians, did not turn up.[1]

As a group, the Commonwealth heads of government could not and would not intervene. But, paradoxically, the Commonwealth secretary-general had been able to do so.[2]

IV

The events before the civil war, including the failure of the Aburi conference, led the Nigerian government to agree to the secretariat's taking an interest in the situation. A. L. Adu visited all the regions of Nigeria in March 1967. The secretary-general visited Lagos not long before the fighting began, and was given approval in writing by Gowon to use his good offices; this approval gave the secretariat standing. Without it further action would have been impossible, since Nigeria insisted, and most other Commonwealth governments agreed, that the war was a domestic matter. The outbreak of hostilities in July intensified the secretariat's efforts. For a time, representatives of both sides consulted separately with the secretary-general in London. In October he arranged secret discussions between them, but these broke down before any substantial progress had been made.

In January 1968 there seemed to be a possibility that the Biafran representatives would agree to certain compromise proposals, which included a return to the twelve-state federal structure, access by the Easterners to the sea through Port Harcourt, and the establishment of a Commonwealth peace-keeping force. The secretary-general flew again to Lagos in the early part of February to consult with Gowon. The federal authorities were unable to accept the general principles which the secretary-general put forward as a basis for discussion, but agreed that there was scope for a further meeting of the two sides. For a time thereafter Ojukwu proved difficult, but talks in London eventually produced a meeting at Kampala in Uganda from 23 to 31 May 1968. These talks, organized and serviced by the secretariat, showed that the positions of the two sides could not be reconciled, even when compromise proposals were put forward by the secretary-general. In the end the Biafrans walked out on instructions from Ojukwu. Much the same applied to talks arranged by the OAU in July and August. French pressure was clearly stiffening the Biafran resolve. At the Commonwealth Prime Ministers' Meeting in January 1969, as we have seen, further opportunities for discussion were avoided by the Biafrans. This did not prevent the secretariat from trying

---

[1] *The Times*, 9 Jan 1969; Wilson, *Labour government*, pp. 600–2.
[2] The following section is based mainly on CSG, *Second Report*, pp. 7–8 & 22–26.

again later in 1969, but the federal government understandably wanted some assurance of Biafran participation before it would agree to talks; Ojukwu would not provide this. There remained, for some time, the possibility that a Commonwealth peace-keeping force might be called upon to help in the event of a ceasefire. The actual circumstances of the war's end—a surrender by Biafran forces, after the Biafran enclave had been greatly reduced in size—meant that no such force was needed; thus its possible composition did not become a matter of official consideration by Commonwealth governments.

The secretariat's efforts at a negotiated settlement, and those of the OAU, were, in the secretary-general's words, 'throughout complementary and in no way competitive'. If there had been sizeable opposition within the OAU to Commonwealth efforts, the Nigerian government would presumably have withdrawn its approval, and there would then have been no basis on which the secretariat could proceed. On the Commonwealth side, the secretariat received many expressions of approval from Commonwealth governments, although one or two informally expressed doubts. The Commonwealth as a whole was not asked to give approval to the secretariat's operations, which were based upon written permission from the Nigerian government.

v

In 1953 Africa, in Commonwealth terms, meant a number of British colonies which were advancing slowly towards self-government, and a founder member, South Africa, which had a policy towards coloured people at variance with Britain's but was firmly enshrined in the Commonwealth. By 1969 South Africa had gone, driven out by African, Asian, and Canadian pressure; Britain had been harried for five years by African members to enforce its principles in Rhodesia; and the Commonwealth secretary-general, by permission of an African member, was attempting to help in settling an African civil war. So much had changed that the two pictures had little in common.

As we have seen in assessing the impact of Rhodesia on the Commonwealth, African issues brought a new tone to Commonwealth discussions and imposed on Britain pressures much more intense than those previously employed by overseas Commonwealth members. Further, any lingering notions of colonial issues being domestic to Britain, or of issues arising within the Commonwealth being confined within it, were put out of court. South Africa, Rhodesia, and the Nigerian civil war all showed that Commonwealth questions could be tossed backwards and forwards between the UN and the Commonwealth, with the OAU as intervener.

One must connect this change in Commonwealth tone and procedure with a decline in British belief in the Commonwealth, and connect that in turn with the apparent failure of African states to live up to either their domestic protestations or their advice to others. Rhodesia precipitated an illustrative exchange of letters in October 1966, between Margery Perham and Duncan Sandys.[1] Dame Margery was provoked by Sandys's reference at a Conservative Party conference to 'a sea of chaos and carnage' which Rhodesians saw to the north of them, and his statement that Conservatives did not want Rhodesia 'to go the way of Ghana, Nigeria and Zanzibar'. These, she wrote, seemed strange sentiments from ex-ministers who had played their part in the decolonization of Africa and who should have been able to assess the strength of the forces of African assertion, and of other forces at work which made it expedient to yield to that assertion. The causes of these events 'lay deep in the strange situation which had kept so much of tropical Africa out of the main currents of world development and then exposed it to them so suddenly and so lately', with the result that African leaders had had 'to convert arbitrary regions of tribal Africa into states and nations'. Britain must watch mistakes and atrocities with distress, but not forgetting that 'as in Zanzibar and the Sudan, we are not without some responsibility for them', though were they much worse than those committed by mature and western nations?

Sandys in reply said that in so far as Britain was responsible, it was largely because it had introduced universal suffrage without sufficient preparation; it would be 'irresponsible for us to press the Rhodesians to commit the same mistake'. He had met 'nobody here or in Rhodesia' who did not accept that majority rule must come in due course, but many (like himself) wished to ensure that the 'one man, one vote' principle would not (as in Nkrumah's Ghana) be carried to the point 'where all is decided by the one vote of one man'. Britain wished to see Rhodesia evolve into a broadly-based democracy in which all races would play their part and not 'as in the sad case of Nigeria, to be torn asunder by rival ethnic groups seeking to impose their domination on one another'.

These two opposed points of view typified those of the British people in the 1960s, proud of Britain's legacy in Africa and anxious that it should be preserved. The movement in Sandys's thinking since 1963 is especially striking and was representative of much wider opinion in Britain. Some were beginning to ask why France, which had begun its decolonization in less propitious circumstances than Britain, seemed to have left a more effective stamp on its ex-colonies and retained greater influence. Did this mean that the Commonwealth model for 'the government of men by themselves' had been a mistake after all?

It was natural, and indeed proper, that such questions should be asked—and natural too that the British should be inclined to blame their own policy for much of what happened in Africa after independence, especially since so many of them had been convinced that independence would be a success. The

---

[1] *The Times*, 18 & 20 Oct 1966. For an experienced, detached, and wise assessment of the aftermath of independence in African states, see James O'Connell, 'The inevitability of instability', *J. Mod. Afr. Stud.*, 5/2 (1967), pp. 181–91.

sense of omnipotence which imperial power fosters is not completely dispelled on the morrow of independence: it shows itself sometimes in a desire to continue to guide the destinies of former colonies from afar, sometimes in a conviction that imperial policy was in all matters the deciding factor and that local and external factors need not be considered. One must avoid this latter state of mind in considering the behaviour of the Commonwealth African states in the 1960s.

It is true that the African leaders were greatly influenced by what they had learnt from Britain, and that much of what they said was expressed in terms of British liberal thinking, however it might diverge from their practice. The Lusaka Manifesto of 1969, for example, is an impressive statement of liberal principles. But the main reasons for their actions after achieving independence arose from local and international circumstances. They acted as they did because the African continent was largely released from European control, but the south was still under the thumb of local white men. This lay behind their pressure for the liberation of Southern Africa from European rule. In this the Commonwealth African states were supported by Algeria, the Congo, Somalia, and Ethiopia. In some cases the campaign to liberate the rest of Africa may have served to divert attention from domestic corruption and confusion. But whatever the reason, the result was the same: in Africa itself and in world forums, helped and hindered by the diverse policies of the developed countries of the northern hemisphere, African states strove to break the white grip on the South. They did not succeed. In the process the Commonwealth was both damaged and changed.

In the light of hindsight, it is understandable why the leaders of African states should have pressed Britain so hard on Rhodesia. They had achieved apparent success in driving South Africa out of the Commonwealth, only to find that it remained as powerful as ever in southern Africa, perhaps more so. Their own declaratory aims in Africa were being undermined by dissension in their own countries and a lack of African response in Angola, Mozambique, Rhodesia, and South Africa. To a great extent, they were barred by under-standings with the francophone states from criticizing French policy in the supply of arms to South Africa and trade with Rhodesia. Britain was their allotted target; it was also, in comparison with others such as France and Portugal, a comparatively easy and congenial target.

The machinery of the Commonwealth gave the African states an unusual opportunity for bringing pressure to bear upon Britain, especially the institu-tion of the Prime Ministers' Meeting, which attracted so much attention in the British press and customarily enabled the Africans not only to present their own case but also to marshal opinion amongst their sympathizers in Britain. The gatherings of prime ministers focused attention on African matters as nothing else could in Britain. The temptation was found irresistible by most of the African leaders. The occasion was ready-made: the stage set, the target vulnerable, the audience—including the Commonwealth correspondents of most of the quality London newspapers—sympathetic. Some of the Africans, such as Albert Margai and Hastings Banda, took themselves so seriously that their pompous interventions told against them. But others—especially Nyerere —were able to combine personal attractiveness with an appeal to the British liberal conscience, in a way somewhat comparable to Nehru's in the 1950s but more effective because directed with more force at clear-cut objectives.

If the British government found these occasions embarrassing, it was, to some extent, being repaid in its own coin. In the 1950s there had been widespread British self-congratulation at the smoothness with which problems were surmounted at Prime Ministers' Meetings, and the ease with which contact had been established with the Asian members of the Commonwealth. Now, in the 1960s, the British government was faced with its own instrument turned against itself. As we have seen, India and Pakistan, for their own reasons, had not used these meetings to exert pressure on Britain, although Pakistan had tried to do so in respect of Kashmir. It suited them to observe the conventions. The African states did not; they had a joint cause to foster, although they might differ among themselves about how much pressure to apply. In the event, the stridency and emotion with which the African case was presented over Rhodesia in 1966 proved counter-productive: the attack did not move the British government to any great extent, and it turned much British opinion against the Africans. Even though the attack was renewed in 1969,[1] it did not have the same force as before. In adapting a Commonwealth institution to their own ends, the Africans had not only greatly changed it but also overreached themselves.

They were, on the other hand, largely responsible for the growth of another Commonwealth institution, the secretariat. Originally suggested by Nkrumah,[2] and adopted with some initial hesitancy by some of the older members, the secretariat gained much of its stature from the urgency of African issues: it provided a bridge between Britain and some of the Africans during the split over Rhodesia, it was the agency through which the Commonwealth Sanctions Committee operated, it tried hard to shorten the Nigerian civil war, and its economic activities owed much to African needs. While never a passive instrument of African demands, as some of its critics claimed, it was clearly consonant with the new African dimension which the Commonwealth had acquired.

VI

To sum up the African impact on the Commonwealth with any precision is extremely difficult, since the impact was so widespread, and the Commonwealth was so clearly changed after it had been experienced. Africa was such

---

[1] And again at Singapore in January 1971, over arms for S. Africa.
[2] See below, ch. 17.

an explosive force in Commonwealth terms that one is tempted to attribute to it all the changes that took place in the 1960s. This would be wrong, as previous chapters have shown and subsequent ones will also show. But Africa represented dynamism, spectacle, conflict, and the expression of radical principle. The force of its impact came not simply from diplomatic pressure but from the fact that the African case rested upon ground which previously the Commonwealth had accepted as its own. Self-determination, multiracialism, one man one vote: not all the older Commonwealth members might practise these wholeheartedly, but all, with the exception of South Africa, had espoused them as principles, and they were often stated to be the foundations of the Commonwealth itself. In the process of changing the nature of the association, altering its procedures and lengthening its communiqués, the African members not only damaged that fragile sense of unity which members had previously felt but also challenged the sincerity of previous protestations about what the Commonwealth stood for. The African insistence upon making majority rule a reality in southern Africa was expressed at a time when opposition to racial discrimination had already become a passionately emotional issue in the US, in Britain, and elsewhere, and was becoming a kind of crusade with younger people of radical opinions.

The combination of such a climate of opinion with the interest in Africa displayed by the super-powers and other developed states meant that the Africans had not only a ready-made stage for their efforts in the Commonwealth, as in the UN, but also a ready-made audience in the older Commonwealth countries and elsewhere. Especially in Britain, but also in Canada, Australia, and New Zealand, many people on the left applauded the demands for sanctions against South Africa, action against the Smith regime in Rhodesia, and help for 'freedom fighters' in the Portuguese territories. It was no longer enough for supporters of the Commonwealth to wish that it could retain its character in spite of increased African membership; they felt they also had to find some way of understanding, and then pacifying or appeasing, the Africans if the Commonwealth was not to be pulled apart. Such an attitude explains why Douglas-Home, Sandys, and Wilson expressed themselves as they did in 1964 and 1965 about Rhodesia, and why, after the 1964 Prime Ministers' Meeting, Sir Robert Menzies said:

> The first thing that a Prime Minister of the old Commonwealth has to adjust himself to is that although this is not his vocabulary and these are not his ideas, they do exist and they must be received and understood. . . . The personal relations between all representatives were extraordinarily good.[1]

The basic difficulty of the African intervention, apart from its impact upon forms and procedures, was that it required the older members (and such members as India and Pakistan) to go further in action than they were

[1] *CN*, July 1964, p. 36.

prepared to. In the name of multiracialism, they were asked to support positions which, as sovereign states, they regarded as dangerous and undesirable. The British government and people were not prepared to use force in Rhodesia or to introduce sanctions against South Africa; the same was true of their counterparts in Canada, Australia, and New Zealand. Although fiery attitudes were sometimes expressed by the Asian, Caribbean, and Mediterranean members,[1] there was basically no inclination to turn the Commonwealth into the kind of instrument of policy that the militant Africans wanted. The association was not fitted for this purpose; Britain was not prepared to follow advice to make it so; and the other members, while desiring not to offend the Africans, showed no sustained inclination to follow the lines they proposed. Through their pressure, at the end of the 1960s the Commonwealth differed from what it had been at the beginning of the decade, but it had not become an instrument of further African liberation, except in declamatory terms.

The changes in the atmosphere and machinery of the Commonwealth brought about by the African members would probably have occurred in any case, though not so rapidly or so blatantly. They were very much in line with what was happening elsewhere in the international sphere. In the 1960s intergovernmental relations became more public and more personal, the meetings of heads of governments more frequent and more publicized. The Commonwealth Prime Ministers' Meeting, which had some claims to be regarded as one of the older regular forms of 'summit' discussion, could hardly be expected to remain unchanged. Its conventions of informality, privacy, and respect for domestic jurisdiction were not likely to withstand the increasingly declamatory style of international conduct. In particular, they could not have withstood the pressure of mass communications, the immediacy of confrontation which these (especially television) encouraged, and the heightened responses which they produced in the public at home and abroad. If the Africans had not taken advantage of the changed atmosphere, others would have done so for their different purposes.

---

[1] For example, in March 1970 the Indian deputy minister for external affairs promised, in the Indian parliament, that India would give Africans any assistance required, including military support, to liberate Rhodesia from white minority rule. He was under some pressure in the House at the time. The promise led to no action (*The Times*, 13 Mar 1970).

PART IV

COMMONWEALTH POLICY IN BRITAIN

CHAPTER 12

THE STERLING AREA, TRADE, AND AID

THE Commonwealth ties of trade, investment, and migration and the changes in their extent and direction are described in Chapter 20. This chapter is concerned with British economic policy, especially on trade, currency, and economic aid. Such policy is important because of its effect on Commonwealth relations and because it reflects the British swing away from the Commonwealth and towards Europe (discussed in Chapter 13). Other changes in British policy which to some extent paralleled it are discussed in Chapters 14 and 15. Together, the chapters in this Part help to explain why the British approach to the Commonwealth in 1969 differed so much from that in 1953.

I

The Empire and Commonwealth had never formed an economic 'bloc' in the sense of having integrated economic and financial policies towards the rest of the world, with a protectionist and inward-looking bias. In the nineteenth and early twentieth centuries, as the figures in Chapter 20 show, Britain was the main element in trade and investment for other parts of the Empire, but made no attempt to confine its economic interests to these, and indeed often found other parts of the world more attractive. In 1871, 1901, and 1931 Europe took more British exports than India, Australia, New Zealand, Canada, the West Indies, and the US combined. Trade with Europe was supplemented by trade with, and investment in, Britain's 'informal empire' in such parts of the world as Latin America, China, and the Middle East, where British influence was strong. The policy of free trade denied the virtue of any special arrangements with the Empire such as those which France made with its colonies. If British countries could find markets in Britain, well and good; if Britain found markets and profitable investments in their territories, well and good too. But it was not considered proper to give them special concessions, even though their representatives at Colonial and Imperial Conferences might ask for these and might take part in British political controversies such as tariff reform in order to put pressure on the British government to change its attitude.

However, while free trade was the official doctrine from 1846 to 1932, there were always people in Britain who wanted to make the Empire more of an economic unit. The Conservative Party was periodically disturbed by their efforts. It was not until the depression of the 1930s and the siege conditions of World War II that these efforts bore fruit, and then as a matter of temporary necessity. The preferences granted at Ottawa in 1932 did cause something of a shift in British trade, and this was intensified by the mobilization of resources among allies during the six years of World War II. It became a practical possibility that, as these wartime necessities persisted into the reconstruction period, a permanent policy might emerge whereby the Commonwealth would face world economic problems as a closely collaborating group. Could, and should, the Commonwealth and colonies become an economic bloc, parallel to the political bloc which many during the war had hoped they would become?

Just as such hopes were vitiated in the political sphere by the increasing complexity of world politics, by the disintegrating effects of colonial nationalism, and by Britain's incapacity to remain a great power, so it was in the economic sphere. In this sphere, however, hopes could be sustained longer, because of the close wartime association of Commonwealth countries in the sterling area, an association which continued, after the war, to furnish a binding element for the Commonwealth which had no replica on the political side. The sterling area's problems provide a natural point of entry into the period.

II

Sterling-area arrangements arose historically from convenience and were then systematized by necessity.[1] Before World War II a number of countries, mostly in the Empire but including others with close British connections, found it convenient to finance their trade in sterling, to relate or identify their currencies with sterling, and to make their principal borrowings in sterling. A banking network based on London facilitated this. The position was somewhat varied in the 1930s, when the depression caused some currencies previously identical with sterling to devalue (e.g. those of Australia and New Zealand), and when local central banks began to manage the currencies of Australia, New Zealand, South Africa, and India. But it persisted for all the countries of the Commonwealth except Canada (which was drawn naturally towards the US dollar rather than sterling) up to the outbreak of war.

The wartime sterling system gave coherence to the sterling area, a coherence which persisted for some time after 1945. The proceeds of the foreign-exchange earnings of all the members were pooled in London, under the custody of the Bank of England, and drawings on this pool were regulated by common principles of exchange control, put into practice by each country

[1] Two accounts which describe the sterling area from the standpoint of the early 1950s are Paul Bareau, *The sterling area* (1950) and Diana Spearman, *The sterling area* (1953). Official explanations can be conveniently studied in the documents in A. R. Conan, *The rationale of the sterling area* (1961). I have learnt a great deal from Susan Strange, *Sterling and British policy* (1970), the first book to put sterling into a continuing context of world politics and economics.

individually, but agreed upon in order to ensure that no country drew too heavily upon the gold and dollars which constituted the reserve. Britain was the centre of the allied effort, so far as the colonies and Commonwealth countries were concerned; and Britain was the natural centre of the sterling area. Each member country held its international balance in sterling, thus having an ultimate claim on Britain's resources but agreeing, in effect, not to press this claim if the war effort at large, and Britain's effort in particular, would thereby be damaged. In practice quite large balances were built up since, under wartime conditions, neither Britain nor the international economy could provide goods to offset them. They were, in effect, postwar credits, in the sense that the countries owning them could hope to get goods for them when the war was over. India and Egypt, in particular, accumulated large balances.[1]

At the end of the war Britain was in no position to provide goods to the full value of the accumulated sterling balances; nor could Britain or most of the sterling countries export to the US in sufficient quantities to obtain from dollar sources the goods which might offset the balances. Trade had to revive slowly as wartime arrangements merged into those of peace. For the time being, the need to conserve the sterling area's meagre reserves of gold and dollars by exchange control was self-evident. After the termination of Lend-Lease, Britain itself only managed to keep going by means of a large US loan in 1945. Some of the conditions of the loan related to the sterling balances, which American official opinion regarded with disfavour because they represented pent-up demand which could not be applied to American goods; because they could, in part, be regarded as wartime debts which ought to be written off as were Lend-Lease liabilities; and because the Americans did not want the dollars which they were lending Britain to be used to dispose of these debts. It was accordingly agreed in 1945 as conditions of the US loan that the balances would become convertible into other currencies by stages, that some of them would be 'adjusted as a contribution to the settlement of war and postwar indebtedness', and that the loan would not be used to repay British creditors.

The American hopes were not fulfilled, since Britain was unable to earn enough extra foreign exchange to make the pound both convertible and stable. In time, especially after the brief attempt at convertibility in 1947 and the British devaluation of 1949, it was reluctantly recognized by the US government that, although sterling-area arrangements had a protectionist effect in encouraging trade within the area, this was due less to intent than to the shortage of foreign currencies, notably dollars. A strong Britain, which the US desired on political grounds, could be secured only if the restrictions of the system continued—at least for the time being.

---

[1] The changes in sterling balances, grouped according to regions, are reflected in table 2 (p. 297), which shows UK liabilities in sterling from 1945 to 1969.

The intricate and often unrealistic negotiations about the American loan were typical of much of the economic diplomacy of the next decade. The future organization of world trade and finance remained extremely open and undecided. The US ideal of universal free trade and convertibility of currencies, which had been passionately embraced by F. D. Roosevelt's secretary of state, Cordell Hull, and had found expression in the loan agreement, was enshrined in a series of international agreements. These included the setting-up of the IMF and the World Bank, the abortive attempts to constitute an International Trade Organization and its replacement by the temporary (though long-lived) Gatt. Each represented a multilateral ideal which was unattainable in the immediate circumstances, but to which most countries gave lip-service. In the chaotic period of postwar reconstruction the practical task was to enable trade to flow through the jungle of tariffs, quantitative restrictions, non-transferable and inconvertible currencies, etc., which were the legacy of the war and continued to be policy weapons in a succession of balance-of-payments crises in most major countries.

The freedom of trade and investment in the sterling area, though maintained at the price of the retention of tight controls on trade and investment outside it, was exceptional in such a situation, and was recognized by the US and other countries as representing stability. Another area in which relatively unobstructed trade was achieved was Western Europe, where the OEEC, working with US aid and encouragement, managed to achieve a reasonable flow of trade and payments. Through a series of conferences Gatt negotiated several mutual reductions of tariffs and quantitative restrictions, while pursuing the traditional Hull hostility towards preferential systems and preventing their extension. Each of these processes was gradual; each affected British policy at large, though sometimes the effect was not seen until later.

Meanwhile Britain continued to operate the mechanism of the sterling area, which, to a degree which cannot be measured but seems to have been considerable, underlay and enhanced the British role in the Commonwealth in the late 1940s and early 1950s. The mechanism was largely that of co-operation between central banks, with the Bank of England as its centre. The Bank did not only supervise the exchange control (the central banks of member countries acting as its agents), but

was believed also to be responsible for much of the effective policy-making of the system; in addition, the United Kingdom Treasury controlled exchange reserves, fixing (in some cases) the amounts available for current use and in all cases discouraging expenditure whether in sterling or in dollars. Trade policy was conditioned by the necessity of limiting imports and saving hard currency; development plans were slowed up because imports of capital goods from the dollar area had to be deferred.[1]

---

[1] Conan, *The sterling area* (1952), pp. 153–4. Unless otherwise stated, facts in the following paragraphs about the operation of the system are from this work, ch. 5.

Since, however, co-operation between central banks was not sufficient to determine major lines of policy, this became the function of the meetings of Commonwealth prime ministers, especially after India, Pakistan, and Ceylon became independent. Although there was a clear formal distinction between the sterling area and the Commonwealth, there was no such distinction politically. In the public and the official mind the distinction became blurred, despite the fact that Canada was a member of the Commonwealth but not of the sterling area. Britain's leadership of the economic grouping helped to reinforce its traditional leadership of the political grouping.

To a surprising extent, the system gave general satisfaction. There were certain difficulties. India wanted the pooling of hard currencies to cease in 1946; South Africa held reserves of its own in gold and dollars after 1947; Australia proved unable to live within its dollar income in 1948; Ceylon was allowed in 1949 to keep its dollar earnings to itself; agreements had to be made with India and Pakistan to delay the release of large parts of their sterling balances. If sterling was in trouble, there was a strong tendency in British circles to blame the overseas members and to emphasize the lack of disciplinary elements in the situation. Hugh Gaitskell, after his experiences as chancellor of the exchequer in 1951, was very much of this opinion.[1] In some parts of the Commonwealth there were complaints about lack of information, though these were met to some extent by the setting up of a Sterling Area Statistical Committee in 1947 at the initiative of the UK Treasury. This consisted of officials from Britain and sterling-area countries. In 1949 the functions of another body, the Commonwealth Liaison Committee, which had been created by the Cabinet Office to keep Commonwealth members informed of what was happening in the OEEC, were enlarged to include dollar-saving policies and the discussion of sterling-area policies in general; it too was made up of officials. Canada was a full member, instead of only an observer, as in the Statistical Committee. The two committees were no doubt helpful, but the devaluation of sterling on 18 September 1949 without prior consultation of other sterling-area countries emphasized that sterling was Britain's currency after all, and that Britain made the crucial decisions about it.[2]

In the early 1950s it was still possible to talk of a choice between two lines of policy for Britain. One was to aim at consolidating the sterling area and the strength of sterling before going further in the direction of convertibility and dismantling controls on non-sterling imports. Policy since the war had in some respects reinforced the integrating tendencies of the war itself: the Labour government had continued many of the wartime bulk-purchase agreements, whereby commodities had been bought on contract from Commonwealth countries, which were able to plan production in the knowledge that British

[1] See his article, *New Statesman*, 20 Dec 1952.
[2] For this episode, see Mansergh, *Survey 1939–52*, pp. 342–5 and his *Documents 1931–52*, ii. 1021–45.

markets were available. Also, the stringent British restrictions on investments in non-sterling countries had not applied to those in the sterling area, with the consequence that previous British investment there was being buttressed with fresh supplies of capital, which increased the productive capacity of the sterling area as a whole. There was thus an argument for continuing the consolidation of sterling-area capacity, even though the type of economic development which this would mean fostering—both in Britain and in the overseas countries—might make the sterling bloc less able to face a multilateral world in the end, if it ever had to be faced. In spite of the efforts of Gatt and the OEEC, it was still possible to take the view that multilateral free trade was a chimera.

The other line was to press on to a more rapid achievement of convertibility and multilateral trade. This was perhaps a riskier proceeding, but it held out the prospect, if successful, of restoring Britain's place in the world at large as trader, financier, and middle-man. Such a view was characteristic of those who wished to see the City of London restored to its former place as a market for currency, commodities, and the like, and who saw state trading as a distorting and limiting factor in world trade.

On the whole, the Attlee government had been more favourable towards the first line. In doctrinal terms, its members were more willing to plan trade and investment, and less confident of ultimate US intentions, than their Conservative opponents. Moreover, in this as in so many other fields, the Labour government had largely carried on with wartime arrangements, irrespective of doctrinal considerations: both the sterling area and the bulk purchases were already in being, and it was easier to continue existing practice than to construct alternatives. The Conservative Party, on the other hand, had by 1951 become dissatisfied with the whole system of wartime and postwar controls, and was prepared to denounce them unless some good reason could be found for retaining them.

III

1952 was a year of considerable importance for Commonwealth economic policy. The Conservative government had come into office at the end of October 1951, committed to something like the second of the two lines just described. They encountered an acute balance-of-payments problem. When Butler, the new chancellor, met his senior Treasury officials for the first time, 'their story was of blood draining from the system and a collapse greater than had been foretold in 1931'.[1] The reserves, which stood at about £3,000 m., were being reduced by something like £300 m. a month, and seemed likely to reach the point at which it had been thought necessary to devalue in 1949. Butler at once took action to reduce imports and external spending, and in

[1] Butler, p. 157.

January 1952 a special meeting of Commonwealth finance ministers recommended drastic steps throughout the sterling area to curtail imports and reduce inflation,[1] but such measures could hardly take effect at once. Most sterling-area countries had suffered a sharp drop in export earnings with the collapse of the Korean war boom. Their commodities were now selling for much lower prices, but they were still importing at the levels of the incomes they had earned during the boom. It was hoped that, although the reserves would continue to fall, they would stabilize by the middle of 1952. For the next few months however, an atmosphere of crisis prevailed. Macmillan, now minister for housing, wrote in his diary on 29 February:

In spite of all our efforts to save imports, cut internal expenditure and generally do all the right things at home, we are going to be ruined by our customers in our capacity as bankers. The drain on sterling cannot be stopped unless something drastic is done about this.[2]

Allegations of prodigality in the overseas sterling area, which we have noted as likely to be made whenever sterling was under strain, were again in evidence.

A striking but unsuccessful effort to do 'something drastic' was the plan known as 'Operation Robot', put forward by the Treasury and the Bank of England at this time, supported by Butler, but rejected because of strong opposition from Lord Cherwell and senior members of the cabinet.[3] The essence of the scheme was that a large part of the sterling balances would be blocked, that sterling earned by non-residents of the sterling area would in future be freely convertible into dollars, but that the pound itself would be left free to find its own level of exchange with other currencies. There would thus be limited 'convertibility for foreigners', but not for anyone in the sterling area. The operation would probably reduce the value of the sterling balances quite markedly, in terms of what they would buy when they were unblocked and eventually made convertible; but it would, in a sense, 'solve' the British balance-of-payments problem. The reserves would be safe-guarded: the scheme, it was said, would 'take the strain off the reserves and put it on the rate of exchange'. In Butler's view, if adopted it would have given successive chancellors 'an external regulator for the balance of payments corresponding to the internal regulator provided principally by Bank Rate'.[4]

'Robot's' opponents, especially Cherwell, considered that it would be unfair to confront the Commonwealth governments with a totally new proposition, especially one closely affecting their interests, so soon after a Finance

[1] See Mansergh, *Documents 1931–52*, ii. 1045–8 for the communiqué.

[2] *Tides of fortune*, p. 381.

[3] I have assumed, on good authority, that the account of this episode in Earl of Birkenhead, *The Prof in two worlds* (1961), pp. 283–94, is substantially correct, and have used it freely, together with the references in Butler and Macmillan, and in Andrew Shonfield, *British economic policy since the war* (1958), pp. 216–18.

[4] Butler, p. 158.

Ministers' Meeting at which no mention had been made of it. There is no doubt that, if presented as a unilateral British decision, it would immediately have provoked great opposition in the rest of the sterling area, not least because, in its urge towards further convertibility, it would have meant that Britain had turned its back on further sterling-area planning. 'It was admitted that many countries might leave the sterling area.'[1] For these, as also for reasons more directly concerned with the British economy, the scheme was put aside, although 'the mood that conceived it remained'.[2]

What emerged instead was 'the collective approach', a term used consistently to describe the general policy adumbrated by a Commonwealth Economic Conference, held in London from 27 November to 11 December 1952[3] and attended by Commonwealth prime ministers and representatives of colonial governments. Butler announced its purpose in advance as an expansion of world trade, which Britain could not bring about alone. The help of the Commonwealth and the goodwill of the US would be needed in development and in the purchase of the sterling area's raw materials and exported goods. There must also be 'a strong and widely-respected sterling as a sought-after medium of exchange'. The conference was necessary because, unless the Commonwealth governments developed a common economic strategy, there was a danger that, in trying to save their own economies, they might inflict lasting damage on others. Butler added that the conference would consider the system of imperial preferences, and the part that international agencies might play in the solution of world economic problems.[4] In preliminary discussions between officials from Commonwealth countries, it appears that British proposals for early convertibility on something like 'Robot' lines were strongly opposed. The proposals eventually put to the conference in November had been considerably watered down.[5]

According to the conference communiqué the 'collective approach' would, by stages and within reasonable time, 'create an effective multilateral trade and payments system covering the widest possible area'. There was to be a 'progressive removal' of import restrictions, but the rate of progress would depend upon 'the advance towards equilibrium between the United States and the rest of the world'. Convertibility was the aim, but it could be achieved only if trading nations adopted policies conducive to the expansion of world trade, and if finance were available through the IMF 'or otherwise'. Acceptance of the scheme was to be sought from the US and European countries. In effect, the whole proposition was an appeal to the US, which was being asked to live up to the implications of its earlier belief in multilateralism by cutting its tariffs so as to let in more imports from the sterling-area and Europe, by modifying its shipping and 'Buy American' legislation, and by providing more

[1] Birkenhead, p. 287.   [2] Shonfield, p. 217.
[3] Its communiqué is in Mansergh, *Documents 1952–62*, pp. 401–6.
[4] *The Times*, 30 July 1952.   [5] Birkenhead, pp. 291–2.

international liquidity through investment abroad and through greater support for the IMF and the World Bank.

The difficulty was that the US was not yet prepared to do this. The Democratic administrations which had espoused the Hull policies had been replaced by a Republican administration with a Republican Congress, largely unprepared, for doctrinal and practical reasons, to take the steps that would make the 'collective approach' work. When Butler and Eden went to Washington in March 1953, to put the proposition, Butler records:

In a word, I asked the Americans to live up to the slogan which they had been dinning into me ever since I arrived at the Treasury, namely, 'non-discrimination'. But I certainly got no change out of them ... it was clear that the American team had been encouraged to pour cold water on the collective approach to convertibility, to tell us to put our own house in order, and to raise as few hopes as possible of Congressional support for better credit policies ...[1]

It must have seemed at the time as if the collective approach would not work, and that it might be necessary to try to integrate the sterling area more effectively, developing its resources as much as possible, and continuing to trade within it to the extent that those resources would permit. As we have seen, this was a choice constantly before the British government. Some ministers complained that such a choice would mean 'the danger of setting up an artificial system of exchanging high-priced goods in a new form of autarchy'; others maintained in reply, like Macmillan, 'that although American protectionism suffered from this effect in its early stages, the increasing size of the market and the corresponding opportunities for mass production completely altered the picture over a period of time. Might not the same be done in the sterling area?'[2]

The real questions were, to what extent could it be done in the sterling area, and for how long? There were obvious limitations. The US would not countenance an extension of the preference system; Canada and India were both against it.[3] In any case, all countries were committed under Gatt to set up no new preferences, and, even if they were not, the system could not be made to apply to all Commonwealth products. Commonwealth members depended on non-Commonwealth countries for certain major exports, such as wheat, wool, minerals, rubber, and tin, and also for key imports and certain forms of capital. Even though the British government was prepared to look again at the preference system, neither Britain nor Canada was likely in the long run to support any attempt at comparative autarchy, Britain because of its underlying inclination towards cheap food and raw materials, and Canada because any increase in preferences would not compensate for the continued discrimination likely to be exercised against it on currency grounds. Although there was certainly scope for some increase in Commonwealth trade, a closed bloc

[1] Butler, pp. 166–7.   [2] *Tides of fortune*, p. 386.   [3] *The Times*, 22 Sept 1952.

could not be formed. A well-placed Australian observer, Sir John Crawford, says of the critical character of the Economic Conference's decision to move away from discriminatory trade policies to systems of multilateral trading:

> What the communique principally fails to communicate is that the 1952 conference really turned its back on the hopes of some (including those held by the Australian Prime Minister) that the Ottawa road would be further explored, turning the Commonwealth into a more tightly integrated economic unit. The debate was not difficult nor was it prolonged, but it was decisive, simply because the case against was overwhelming.[1]

IV

This is not to say, of course, that the degree of economic integration which the sterling area had attained in 1952 vanished overnight, or that parts of it vanished at all. The immediate prospects for multilateralism and convertibility were poor, with the American response so cold. For the time being the system of exchange control remained in operation, and sterling-area policies were continued as before. At no time, in fact, did the US government avowedly take action to enable the collective approach to work in the way intended, but what it did was to change its policies in other respects and for other reasons, so that the effect was as if it had acceded to the collective approach when asked to. In the 1950s US policies of world-wide opposition to the Soviet Union and China necessitated an increasing flow of aid to countries in Asia, Africa, and Latin America; moreover, the US government put more drive into the IMF and the World Bank than could have been expected in 1952. The lull after the end of the Korean war boom was shown to be temporary. At the same time the economic recovery of Western Europe and Japan led to heavier demand for the primary products of the overseas sterling-area countries. There was also a consistent increase in the economic aid provided by developed countries. The total effect was to secure something like the result for which Butler and Eden had pleaded in 1953, thus enabling the British government to persist with its aims of 'the re-establishment of sterling as a general international currency and of London as an open financial market-place'.[2]

The increasing involvement of the US in the international trade-and-payments system, largely based upon political considerations, brought about something of a change of American attitudes towards the sterling area and a lessening of the pressures which, in the 1940s, had been brought to bear upon the British government to dismantle its organization. Throughout the 1950s, in fact, Britain and the Commonwealth countries were largely left alone to manage the system as they thought best. Although there was considerable change in the relative holdings in the sterling balances, the total did not vary much. In Britain attention tended to move away from the prodigality of

[1] J. G. Crawford, *Australian trade policy* (1968), p. 101.   [2] Strange, p. 64.

Britain's sterling partners to the problems of the British economy itself. British investment in the overseas sterling area expanded considerably. There were further sterling crises, but not of the magnitude of 1951–2. The advance towards convertibility proceeded slowly. There were still appeals for increased production of dollar-saving commodities by the periodic meetings of prime ministers and finance ministers. The December 1952 Economic Conference, while endorsing the collective approach, had also 'agreed that in sterling area countries development should be concentrated on projects which directly or indirectly contribute to the improvement of the area's balance of payments with the rest of the world'. Exchange controls were relaxed only gradually. In effect, the sterling area in the 1950s presented something of a schizophrenic face to the world: on the one hand the urge towards convertibility and an open economy was still being maintained by the British government, which wound up nearly all the remaining bulk-purchase agreements and returned commodity trade to private hands; on the other, British investment and economic aid were still concentrated very largely in the sterling area.

It was still difficult to distinguish effectively between the sterling area and the Commonwealth. Britain's leadership of the one continued to enhance its position at the head of the other. The gold and dollar reserve was a symbol, both of Britain's leadership (since sterling was British currency, and the management of the system was largely in British hands), and of the benefits which other countries might gain from close association with Britain. The point seemed especially applicable to countries like India and Pakistan, which were continually drawing down their sterling balances to finance their dollar expenditures. In the 1950s the contributions to the dollar pool of certain British colonies, especially Malaya and the Gold Coast, were very large indeed. It was possible, as late as 1958, to argue that distinct material benefits arose from Commonwealth membership because of the near-identity of the sterling area and the Commonwealth, and because the ultimate management of sterling-area policies was in the hands of the Commonwealth prime ministers.[1] There were arguments on the other side, the most telling being that one of the most prominent members of the sterling area was the Irish Republic which, not being in the Commonwealth, could not take part in conferences of prime ministers or finance ministers, but did not seem to suffer on this account. This argument could, however, be countered on the ground that the relationship between Britain and the Republic was so close as to make Ireland even more than a member of the Commonwealth, and on the other ground that the Commonwealth system gave the sterling area credence and cohesion, and vice versa; the Irish, it was said, were benefiting from a stability which others had created.

The stability was, however, relative not absolute. An important element in

---

[1] A contemporary example of such an argument will be found in the 1st edn of my *Commonwealth in the world* (1958), p. 271.

the change to a Conservative government had been the determination to restore the City of London to its position as a financial market-place. The process by which this took place is described by Susan Strange:

In December 1951 Britain re-opened London as an international market for dealing in foreign exchange. In May 1953 an arbitrage agreement between France, Belgium, and other West European countries allowed sterling held abroad to be freely transferred without official control. This was the foretaste of the major step taken in March 1954 towards freeing non-residents using sterling as an international transactions medium from the red tape of British exchange control. Hitherto, these controls had specified that only certain Transferable-Account countries and only sterling arising from certain current transactions could be freely transferred to other non-residents without official interference. From 1954 onwards, all the varying restrictions on non-resident sterling (outside the dollar countries) were unified. . . .

This liberalization of non-resident sterling in 1954 was followed by further steps in 1955. . . . The London gold market was also reopened and so were the pre-war commodity markets.

It was the reopening of these markets which made the latest step of full convertibility of sterling for non-residents sooner or later unavoidable. . . .[1]

It could be argued that these steps enabled Britain to keep up with, and benefit from, the growth in world trade and payments as Europe and Japan returned to the international economy, and that they allowed Britain to exercise traditional financial skills which had been in abeyance during the siege conditions of the war and immediate postwar years. As against this, they inevitably made sterling more vulnerable to speculators. Pressure upon sterling would arise in future, as before, from drains on reserves due to heavy spending on imports in Britain and throughout the sterling area, and from doubts about the future of the British economy; but it would be exacerbated by the ease with which funds could be taken in and out of sterling, and would force Britain to maintain high interest rates to encourage foreigners to keep their money in London. For the remainder of the 1950s and 1960s sterling remained a volatile currency.[2]

The British moves towards convertibility took place against a background of changing world trade, which affected the relative importance of the members of the sterling area. This change was reflected in the sterling balances.[3] The most notable feature in 1957 was the size of those built up by the colonies of Malaya, Ghana, and Nigeria. The first two became independent that year, while the third was approaching independence. India and Pakistan had drawn down their balances to a considerable extent, reflecting their development

[1] Strange, pp. 64–5.
[2] Macmillan can claim to have seen as early as 1955, when he was chancellor of the exchequer, the consequences of freeing commodity markets and supporting transferable sterling (see *Riding the storm*, pp. 5–6. See also ch. 4 for his account of how US pressure on the pound affected British policy in the Suez crisis of 1956.)
[3] See table 2, p. 297.

needs and their incapacity to match their imports with exports. In the colonies which had large balances, currency and marketing boards had been conservative in husbanding the proceeds of exports, and governments still under British influence had not embarked on major developmental schemes. It was an open question whether independent governments would take the same line or would follow the example of India. If they did, the pressure on sterling would be considerable. These countries (Malaya, Ghana, and Nigeria) had been amongst the principal dollar-earners for the sterling area in the 1950s, and their continued earning power was very much in the interests of the other members. If, however, they emulated India and Pakistan in running large balance-of-payments deficits and drawing on their sterling balances—especially if this happened at a time when their export prices were deteriorating—they would become a major problem for Britain and, by extension, to the other members.

Increasing uncertainty about the future behaviour of colonies nearing independence was one reason why there was so much debate in Britain about the value of the sterling area in 1957–8.[1] There were doubts about whether the sterling countries had the right machinery to ensure mutual discipline. 'There should surely be means', wrote *The Economist*, 'by which other members of the sterling club could bring some mild forms of pressure . . . to bear on those of their colleagues whose policies are plainly likely to plunge them into excessive deficits.'[2] The possibility of Britain's being embarrassed by such action was increased by India's policy of wholesale drawing down of its balances in 1956 and 1957. Sterling was under pressure in 1957, so much so that the British prime minister, perhaps making more of the situation than it called for, wrote to his chancellor:

For the moment [the future of the sterling area] hangs upon the slender thread of the high price of wool in Australia and a 7% Bank Rate in London. In the course of the next few months we must really search for an answer to some of these fundamental questions. It haunts us at every point and makes foreign policy, defence policy and home trade policy very difficult to carry on. . . .[3]

It cannot be said that the Macmillan or later governments found an answer to the problem of sterling, which was periodically under pressure from short-term holders and from the British trade balance, and would have been in deep trouble if long-term holders, such as the members of the sterling area, had joined in. The normal British reaction to a sterling crisis was to reduce government expenditure and delay investment programmes, which did not satisfy those critics who contended that Britain's major problem lay in not investing

---

[1] Some representative samples are in Shonfield, ch. 6, and 'What price the sterling area?', three talks by A. C. L. Day, John Wood, & J. R. Sargent on the BBC Third Programme (*The Listener*, 21 & 28 Nov 1957 and 2 Jan 1958).

[2] 'Prime ministers and the pound', 22 June 1957.

[3] Macmillan, *Riding the storm*, p. 361. The letter is dated 31 Oct 1957.

enough at home. These were especially likely to complain about the extent of British investment abroad, particularly the investment in sterling countries as part of the implicit bargain that they would have first call on British overseas capital in return for keeping their balances in London.

A. R. Conan[1] estimated Britain's total investment (i.e. public and private combined) in the sterling area in 1957–8, in comparison with the prewar position, as follows:

TABLE 1

British Investment in Sterling Countries (£ m.)

Country	Total		Business inv.		Public debt	
	1938	*1958*	*1938*	*1958*	*1938*	*1957*
Australia	650	900	200	600	455	253
New Zealand	150	200	25	100	122	68
South Africa	300	800	200	800	99	24
Rhodesia	75	300	50	200	12	83
India ⎫	600	400	300	300	240	1
Pakistan ⎭			30	50	—	—
Ceylon	100	100	75	75	—	—
Colonies	300	850	250	750	62	71
(inc. Ghana						
& Malaya)						

The British stake in the Commonwealth had changed considerably in character in twenty years. Government securities had become a much less important part of it, and business investment had greatly increased, but it had been concentrated in highly profitable areas, especially the old dominions and colonies which could show high returns, such as the Rhodesias, West Africa, and Malaya. There was some justice in Andrew Shonfield's contemporary comment that sterling-area investment could not

be fairly regarded as an effective instrument for furthering the progress of the under-developed countries. If the colonies are treated as a separate problem . . . then the system begins to look remarkably like an organisation for the promotion of British investment in Australia and South Africa, with Rhodesia thrown in. This does not seem quite so important in ethical or political terms as the people who constantly stress the vital need for more investment in the sterling Commonwealth generally make out.[2]

Clearly, there would be changes in the aid position as more and more colonies gained independence, to offset the lack of private investment. In the meantime there were problems in the economic relations between Britain and the old dominions. These were not serious in respect of South Africa, which

[1] 'Investment in the sterling Commonwealth', *The Times*, 19 Aug 1959. See also his *Capital imports into sterling countries* (1960).
[2] Shonfield, p. 132.

was continually gaining British investment and which had as its main export a commodity—gold—which was acceptable everywhere. Things were otherwise, however, for Australia and New Zealand on the one hand and Canada on the other. The investment question was not uppermost, since both Australia and New Zealand had benefited from a flow of British money, more on public account in New Zealand's case than Australia's but broadly sufficient in both. Canada could find the capital it wanted in the US, especially in mining and manufacturing, even though it built up a good deal of hostility towards foreign ownership. The problems in all three cases arose from an insufficient growth in trade. In 1957 the particular problems of Australia and Canada were highlighted by the renegotiation of the Ottawa Agreement between Britain and Australia, and a surprise proposal from John Diefenbaker, the newly elected Canadian premier, to divert 15 per cent of Canadian imports from the US to Britain.[1] Both revealed the increasingly complex nature of British trade relations with the old dominions, which could no longer be regarded simply as farms and granaries for the food which Britain could not or would not grow at home. New Zealand and Britain examined their joint relations in 1958, but to relatively little effect.[2]

Certain Australian farm industries, such as those producing wheat and meat, wanted a better position in the British market, in competition with both local and foreign producers. At the same time Australian manufacturers did not want their British competitors to be given more favourable conditions in the Australian market. While Australia wished to sell more foodstuffs in Britain, it recognized that its prospects were declining. It did not wish to retain high margins of preference for British manufactured goods in case it needed to bargain with other suppliers (such as Japan and the US) which, if given improved terms in Australia, might in turn look more favourably on the entry of Australian foodstuffs into their own markets. At the beginning of the negotiations the Australians seemed unyielding. Macmillan (then chancellor) wrote on 13 July 1956 that they wanted

to abolish (or whittle away to nothing) UK preferences in Australia, but keep—and improve—their favoured position in our market. We had two hours or more of tough negotiations—and got nowhere at all. I thought Bob Menzies seemed rather ashamed, but McEwen (Country Party) was ruthless and unsmiling.[3]

In the event, the Australians got some of what they wanted. Since they were able to show that Britain had been getting much the better of the exchange of preferences, it was agreed that British preferences in Australia could be reduced. They did not get all they wanted in respect of wheat, but were

---

[1] In the following paragraphs on these two events I have drawn heavily upon Crawford, ch. 9 ('Ottawa reviewed') and Trevor Lloyd, *Canada in world affairs 1957–9* (1968), ch. 3. Both are admirable guides.

[2] *External Affairs Review*, May 1958, pp. 22–3.   [3] *Riding the storm*, pp. 77–8.

assured of preferential treatment of a slightly wider range of goods in Britain. Problems of diversifying the types and direction of Australian exports remained. They were to be relieved in the following decade by a great surge of mineral exports to Japan and elsewhere, and massive exports of wheat to China, a new market.

The Canadian problem was perhaps less basic, since it arose less from an absence of markets than from disinclination to depend too much on the US. At the post-Suez general election in Canada in 1957, of which mention was made in Chapter 4, Diefenbaker made much of undue US economic influence in Canada, and promised to move closer to Britain in economic as in political matters. A few days after taking office, he left for the 1957 Commonwealth Prime Ministers' Meeting in London, where he was fêted by the Beaverbrook press and addressed meetings on the importance of the Commonwealth. To Macmillan, however, he seemed 'still the victim of his election oratory. He is a fine man—sincere and determined; but I fear that he has formed a picture of what can and cannot be done with the Commonwealth today which is rather misleading.'[1] It was difficult to know what Diefenbaker wanted,[2] but his actual proposal to the prime ministers was for a Commonwealth financial and economic conference to be held in Ottawa. After warnings from Menzies about raising false hopes, it was decided to hold the normal Finance Ministers' Meeting that year in Ottawa, where, in due course, preparations were made for the Montreal conference of 1958.[3] On his return to Canada, Diefenbaker announced his proposal to divert 15 per cent of Canadian purchases to Britain on 7 July.

The British response was to offer a British-Canadian Free Trade Area arrangement to come into operation over some twelve to fifteen years. This, it seemed, was the only way to achieve something like the Diefenbaker diversion, since new preferences were forbidden under Gatt, and a relaxation of certain Canadian tariffs which bore especially heavily on British goods would be unacceptable to Canadian manufacturers. The Canadian reaction was unfavourable. Canada was prepared to review government purchasing to see if more British goods could be bought on this account and to revise the practice of charging duty on goods bought abroad by Canadian tourists; but it would go no further.[4]

At the time, it was widely said that the British government meant little by its offer of a Free Trade Area, since it knew that Diefenbaker would not accept it. This may have been true; Diefenbaker had never said how he expected the 15 per cent diversion to be made. If he had gone into details, he would

---

[1] Ibid., p. 377.

[2] During Diefenbaker's visit to London I interviewed him for the BBC. It was the only time I have interviewed a politician but not been able to understand a word he said.

[3] Macmillan, p. 377.

[4] See The Times, 5 Oct 1957, for the joint communiqué on talks in Ottawa about the British proposal.

certainly have run into opposition from the traditional supporters of his own party, the manufacturers (especially in Ontario) who were wedded to tariffs and often saw the British as their most obvious competitors. Any substantial increase in British exports to Canada would have hurt them. If Diefenbaker was bluffing, the British called his bluff. His party's liking for increased tariffs was demonstrated early in 1958, when it introduced measures to improve prospects for local manufacturers, the effect of which was to restrict rather than facilitate the entry of British goods.

The large-scale conference which Diefenbaker had suggested in 1957 was held at Montreal from 15 to 26 September 1958 as the Commonwealth Trade and Economic Conference. It was attended by all the independent members of the Commonwealth, and by representatives from Nigeria, the West Indies, Kenya, Tanganyika, Uganda, Sierra Leone, and Hong Kong. Its report[1] was long and all-inclusive, in the sense that it provided something, but not much, for everyone. It announced the British intention of providing development loans from exchequer funds to independent Commonwealth countries, and of further relaxing restrictions on dollar imports. It said Commonwealth countries should work together 'in no exclusive spirit towards a multilateral trade and payments system over the widest possible area' but at the same time they should 'work towards an expansion of Commonwealth trade by all practicable means', and it was 'essential to the stability and progress of the countries of the sterling area and of the world trading community as a whole that [sterling] remains strong'. Convertibility was still the aim, but the decision about its timing must rest with Britain, 'who would, however, take into account the interests of the Commonwealth as a whole'. The incapacity of the Commonwealth to operate as a closed economic system was emphasized by references to the IMF in the context of world liquidity, to the World Bank in that of development, and to the need for 'the participation of the important producing and consuming countries throughout the world' in any plans to deal with instability in commodity prices. The most practical decisions of the conference were not about currency, trade, and investment, but about the extension of Commonwealth scholarships and the construction of a round-the-world coaxial-cable system. In economic terms its decisions echoed those taken in 1952. Perhaps, as *The Times* suggested, the 'sense of a Commonwealth purpose in economic affairs' had 'taken on new life';[2] but it was not self-evident. The 1960s were to see an extension of the lack of commitment of the Montreal communiqué.

V

After 1958 the Commonwealth entered a new period, the most important

---

[1] Cmnd 539 (1958) (Mansergh, *Documents 1952–62*, pp. 537–53).
[2] Editorial, 'A Real Success', 27 Sept 1958. For a more sober assessment, see 'Forward to freedom?', *The Economist*, same date.

feature of which was the decision of the British government to apply for entry into the EEC (see ch. 13). The background includes a number of related changes which helped to make that decision more likely in the first place, and easier to justify once it was made. These are discussed here in the context of British policy.

First, most of the restrictive aspects of the sterling-area system were dismantled, and sterling was made convertible soon after the Montreal conference, though Britain continued to give preference to investment in sterling countries. The British investor was never, in fact, given as much freedom to invest abroad as he might wish.

Second, there were significant changes in the composition and function of the sterling balances held in London. Their total quantity did not change appreciably, but their distribution did. The old dominions—Australia, New Zealand, and South Africa—continued to hold fairly stable balances. Their total external reserves rose with continuing prosperity, but this did not mean a substantial rise in their holdings in London. As South Africa had done for many years, Australia and New Zealand put much of the increase in their reserves into gold and dollars: in this way they were able to diversify their holdings while not 'rocking the sterling boat'. India, Pakistan, and Ceylon had drawn down their balances to the point at which any further reduction would have hindered their normal trading practices; their resources in foreign exchange were, in any case, now largely provided through international consortia (see below). The balances of the Caribbean countries rose, while those of the major African Commonwealth members declined slowly from the peak they had reached in the mid-1950s. Hong Kong, Malaysia, and Singapore continued to have substantial holdings.

The most striking development was the great growth in the balances of the Middle East oil countries. From an estimated nil figure in 1945 they rose to £562 m. in 1967. If this had not occurred, the whole sterling system would have been put under great strain at an early date because of the running down of colonial balances by newly independent countries, and the failure of the old dominions to increase their holdings in accordance with the growth in their overseas reserves.

By 1968 the Commonwealth side of the sterling area had become less important and the foreign side more so.[1] There were six major holders of sterling, between them accounting for three-quarters of the total balances, and each holding more than £200 m.: Australia, Malaysia, Hong Kong, Eire, Kuwait, and Libya. Since only two of these were full members of the Commonwealth, the earlier identification of sterling area and Commonwealth had become much less plausible. If there was a sterling club, it now had a more varied membership, and some of its members were less devoted than before. The original raison d'être of the sterling area—its members' practice of keep-

[1] See Strange, pp. 89 ff.

ing all or nearly all their overseas currency assets in sterling—had been gradually eroded. Their wider trading needs and their growing uneasiness about the strength of sterling caused them to keep an ever-increasing proportion of their reserves in gold and dollars. However, since the total reserves of the members operating in this fashion were rising, they were able to keep fairly stable amounts in sterling and thus cause little or no pressure on the pound. Contrary to widespread belief in Britain in the 1960s, at practically no time before the 1967 devaluation did the overseas official holders make any major moves out of sterling.

The period 1967–8 was one of major change in sterling-area arrangements, representing a culmination of some of the tendencies already described, including the move away from sterling and the uneasiness about sterling's stability. The pound was devalued on 18 November 1967, but not, according to the British premier of the time, because of any disturbance in the sterling area itself:

What forced us off parity was, basically, the economic consequences of the Middle East crisis, and in particular the closure of the Suez Canal; the proximate causes were the dock strikes in London and Liverpool, and, following their ending, financial manoeuvring within the Six [i.e. the members of the EEC].[1]

In contrast with the devaluation of 1949, most of the overseas sterling area members did not follow Britain and devalue their currencies in terms of the US dollar; instead they increased the diversification of their reserves, and there was a significant fall in the total of officially held sterling balances as considerable sums were thus switched. By the middle of 1968 this desertion of sterling threatened the further stability of the pound.

The upshot was a new stage in the history of the sterling area, though it was in many ways a logical development in the postwar history of sterling as a currency and of the growth of international monetary co-operation. Following close negotiations between Britain and each of the individual countries holding sterling, on 9 September 1968 twelve foreign countries (mostly European, but also including Japan and the US) agreed at Basle, in company with the Bank of International Settlements, to provide some $2,000 m. as a 'facility' to cushion blows to sterling. Britain promised to guarantee the value, in US dollars, of the greater part of the sterling reserves held by sterling-area countries. Each of these consented in return to hold not less than an agreed proportion of its reserves in sterling.[2] The overseas countries would thus be protected against any further British devaluation, while Britain would be spared the possible embarrassment of a precipitate run on sterling by discontented official holders. There were obvious gains on both sides. The overseas holders received a guarantee, while Britain was protected against runs of a

---

[1] Wilson, *Labour government*, p. 439. See the whole of ch. 23 for his account of the affair.
[2] Cmnd 3787 (1968), paras 7, 10–23.

kind which, coming from those countries which had previously been the most consistent holders of sterling, would have had a very bad effect on confidence generally. In many ways it was a recognition of reality. *The Times* said:

It marks the effective end of sterling as a reserve currency, a role the long-suffering pound has been finding increasingly difficult to play. The amount of the world's trade now conducted in sterling is much less than it used to be. . . . Britain simply no longer has the financial resources to carry on a reserve currency role.[1]

Although the Basle arrangements involved some awkward Commonwealth diplomacy,[2] they were a landmark in the development of the postwar monetary system. They created what was, in effect, a three-cornered agreement between the overseas sterling area, Britain, and the US and other major industrial countries. The sterling area now had legally binding rules for a diminishing relationship, in place of the much more flexible understandings of the earlier years. The situation was essentially contractual, an element in the general international monetary system rather than an extension of that wartime co-operation in which members had willingly taken part because of their political and economic ties with Britain. In press comment and politicians' statements about the arrangements, it was the stability of sterling, not the stability of the Commonwealth, that received attention: the earlier identification of the two had largely disappeared.

In the 1950s the overseas Commonwealth had consisted of a small number of sovereign states, most of them of significance in world trade, commanding a respectable and fairly stable balance in London, and important as major trading partners of Britain. In the 1960s it had changed in all three respects. By 1968 most Commonwealth members did not have the economic strength to hold a substantial reserve of the earlier kind, and were of decreasing importance in British and world trade. This is a further important change in the decade after 1958.[3] The new members mostly started independence with small sums to their credit, which were not replenished; in some cases, of which Ghana had been the most notable, they started with large sums and quickly exhausted them. The process did not occur as rapidly as might have been expected, since there was what Susan Strange has called a 'delay in monetary independence' in some cases, notably in Malaysia, Singapore, and East and Central Africa, where previous colonial arrangements for joint currency boards persisted for some time, with their heritage of caution in economic management. Neverthe-

---

[1] Editorial, 'A Stronger Pound', 9 Sept 1968.

[2] Wilson says the Basle propositions were 'not easy to accept in the case of some of the newer countries, who had suffered a loss in the real value of their reserves through devaluation; Australia, too, presented special problems. But to each our negotiators had to make clear that we could not make special concessions or derogations to any one country which were not available to all' (*Labour government*, p. 551).

[3] For a wise account of some of the economic problems of colonies' transition to independence, see Sir Hilton Poynton in London Univ., Inst. of Commonwealth Studies, *The changing role of Commonwealth economic connections* [1971].

less, the general tendency was clear enough. The African dimension of the Commonwealth meant new ways in economics as in politics. Most new members needed economic aid from the start.

Only one English-speaking African state in the years after its independence looked as though it might be able to build up its reserves instead of drawing them down. This was Nigeria, which was fortunate both in its size, making for a more viable economy than most, and in its possession of profitable oil reserves. Unfortunately, however, internal political disintegration and strife, and the civil war over Biafra, postponed the prospect at least for a number of years.[1]

In addition to the new members with constant need for aid (largely, though not entirely, from Britain, since international bodies and the US were also available to help them), several older members had exhausted their resources and acquired debts so large that consortia of creditors (including Britain) were formed to 'ensure that sufficient new foreign investment and economic aid [was] forthcoming to enable the client state to meet their revised requirements for debt-servicing'.[2] These included India, Pakistan, Ceylon, and Ghana. The problems which they represented could not be solved within a Commonwealth framework. Unlimited entry for their products into Britain would not do it, since they needed much wider markets; and their development needs far outran anything that Britain alone could provide. The consortia could do little more than keep them going at the level of income, welfare, and trade which they had achieved before their reserves ran out. In general, the underdeveloped states of the Commonwealth could not look forward to effective economic growth, unless they had the special resources (and the comparatively low populations) of a Singapore, a Malaysia, or a Zambia.

The decade was also marked by a further diminution of the system of Commonwealth preference. This arose partly from the system's incapacity to satisfy the needs of particular export industries in the old dominions, partly from the out-dated ad valorem basis of some of the preferences, and partly from the fact that the system hardly applied in Africa, and so was insignificant for most of the newer Commonwealth members. The Australian claims of 1956–7, described above, were similar to those which Canada had made on Britain in negotiations in 1947 and 1958–9, and which had resulted in the preferences between them becoming a matter of choice rather than agreement. In November 1958 New Zealand made an agreement with Britain on similar lines to Australia's, allowing it to reduce the margins of preference on British goods. In addition, the long process of Gatt and similar negotiations had reduced the most-favoured-nation duties in the British tariff, so narrowing the margin of preference available to that large quantity of Commonwealth goods which came in duty-free. Britain did achieve some exceptions, especially for colonial

[1] Strange, pp. 103 & 122.
[2] Ibid., p. 120. See also John White, *Pledged to development* (1967).

products, but the general effect was to lessen the overseas countries' advantage.[1]

The general effect of preferences was a matter of argument. Professor Harry Johnson, using figures available in 1966, calculated the gains and losses in rough terms. His conclusions were:

... On a net basis, one could say that for the countries shown the system redistributes annually about £36½m. among the members. Of this total, about £15¼m. comes from New Zealand, £9m. from Australia, £7½m. from the United Kingdom, and the remaining £4¾m. from various of the less-developed members of the Commonwealth, the largest contributors being Trinidad and Tobago, Malta, and Malaya and Singapore. Of the same total, two-ninths goes to advanced Commonwealth countries, no less than one-sixth going to the Irish Republic. Of the remainder going to the less-developed countries, India and Hong Kong receive the lion's share, £11m. and £9½m. respectively; Mauritius receives £1⅞m., and the remaining £6½m. is divided in smaller portions among a number of countries. ... Incomplete calculations ... suggest that the total implicit transfer from the United Kingdom is probably of the order of magnitude of £18m., making it a somewhat larger contribution than New Zealand.

He emphasized that the most striking aspect of these figures was the small size of these implicit transfers relative to the national incomes of the major Commonwealth countries—'tens of millions of pounds in contrast to thousands of millions of pounds'. The contrast implied that the ending of Commonwealth preference would have little effect on the national incomes of the members and that any resulting losses to less-developed members could easily be made good by an increase in development assistance provided by the developed to the less-developed members of the Commonwealth.[2]

However, the difficulty for overseas Commonwealth members arose less from a fall in the net value of preferences than from the dislocation which would be caused to their polities and economies by losing the British market for industries which had arisen to serve it. Most of these would be unable to compete with similar European industries if those were given a preferred position in the British market. Australia was especially noted for such industries: for example, exports of dried and canned fruits and dairy products contributed comparatively little to the national income, but they earned foreign exchange, alternative markets were hard to find, and the resources which went into the industries could not readily be switched to other uses. New Zealand's position was much more extreme, as was that of the sugar producers of the Caribbean, Mauritius, and Fiji.[3]

---

[1] COI, *Commonwealth preference* (Aug 1961), pp. 5–7. See also *CS*, 18 Feb 1966, for more recent inquiries into the effects of preferences.

[2] Harry Johnson, 'The Commonwealth preferences: a system in need of analysis', *Round Table*, Oct 1966, p. 376.

[3] Commonwealth sugar producers were sustained throughout the period of this book by the Commonwealth Sugar Agreement, the one survivor of the bulk-purchase arrangements of

The African Commonwealth members and certain others were largely untouched by the Commonwealth preference system, which had been worked out hurriedly in 1932 to satisfy the old dominions and a limited number of colonies, and was, in any case, inspired by the economic difficulties of the 1930s, not those of the 1960s. Gatt prevented extensions of it. In the 1960s a new possibility arose to meet the needs of the newer states: generalized preferences. These, which were amongst the proposals made by the less-developed countries (l.d.c.s) at Unctad in 1964, would differ from Commonwealth preferences, which had been essentially quid pro quo arrangements on a bilateral basis, one country giving concessions in its own market in exchange for concessions in another's. The Unctad scheme was for a tariff preference for l.d.c.s' industrial products in the markets of the developed countries without any quid pro quo. The proposal met with indignant resistance at first from the US, Japan, and the developed countries of Western Europe. It was accepted by Britain, which agreed to extend preferences to l.d.c.s outside the Commonwealth, so long as any loss which this might represent to Commonwealth countries was made up by compensating advantages for those countries in other developed countries' markets. Australia accepted the idea at once; Canada did not. Australia introduced a limited scheme for generalized preference in 1966, Canada and New Zealand in 1970. While generalized preferences did not solve the problems of the l.d.c.s in the sale of traditional export commodities, they did offer some hope for the growth of manufacturing industries which might otherwise find themselves completely shut out of foreign markets by established local protectionism.

Another development of the period, already mentioned, was the increased importance in world trade of countries which had recovered from wartime difficulties and postwar prostration: these included such formidable exporters and importers as Japan and Germany. Together with the increased US involvement in the economies of Afro-Asian countries, this meant a wider range of both markets and suppliers for Commonwealth countries. It also meant, in some cases, access to new sources of investment, for example considerable Italian business activity in Zambia. Earlier Israeli activity in Ghana was one of the many instances in which external powers showed an interest in Commonwealth countries on broad strategic grounds, in order to offset possible activity by their rivals. The general effect was to weaken the British

---

World War II. It was concluded in 1951 between Britain and the sugar industries of Australia, S. Africa, the West Indies, British Guiana, Mauritius, and Fiji. S. Africa left in 1961. Swaziland, India, and Rhodesia entered in 1965. Each country was paid a negotiated price for a quota of sugar for the British market, the price being based on weighted average costs in all producing areas, with some addition for the l.d.c.s. It was normally above the 'world price' (a somewhat artificial concept because of the widespread protection of sugar and the fact that only residual quantities reached the free market). See *Survey B & CA*, 24 Apr 1970, and D. B. Jones in London Univ., *Changing role of Commonwealth economic connections*.

position in economies which, in colonial days, had often unthinkingly preferred British goods, even when no formal preferential arrangement existed.

The change was not confined to the overseas countries. Britain was itself
the prime example of a turning away from Commonwealth markets and
suppliers towards its traditional areas of interest in Europe; and the British
application to join the EEC, while capable of interpretation as a desertion of
the Commonwealth, could also be regarded as a return to those channels of
trade which were most natural before the exigencies of depression and war
caused Britain to turn to the colonies and Commonwealth for temporary
relief. As figures in Chapter 20 show, by 1956 Europe was only just failing to
exceed India, Australia, New Zealand, Canada, the West Indies, and the US
combined as a market for British goods. In 1961 it exceeded their combined
total with ease. The significance of the changes could be interpreted in different
ways: to some in Britain they were a call for action to restore Commonwealth
trade; but increasingly they spelt out to others the lesson that Europe, especially Western Europe, was the market which Britain must safeguard at all
costs. Macmillan said that at the end of 1955 he was haunted by the fear that
Britain might fall between two stools and was convinced that from the purely
economic point of view, the importance of the Commonwealth preference
system must decline. 'What would be our position if we found ourselves
excluded from the benefits of the large European market which seemed likely
to develop?'[1] As we shall see (ch. 13), the British government tried other
expedients before finally deciding to apply for entry into the EEC. In the
latter half of the 1950s British ministers were prepared to consider various
possibilities for increasing British trade. What is significant, however, is that,
although British overseas investment was largely confined within the sterling
area (and to some extent Canada), substantial increases in trade did not
follow this investment. Britain's invisibles benefited, but not to the same
extent its proceeds from exports. The investment in Commonwealth countries
did not breed substantial demand for British goods, whereas increasing
incomes in Europe evidently did. It is not surprising that, when the EEC
seemed likely to close the doors of the West European market on Britain
unless Britain could get in beforehand, the British government chose to seek
entry.

VI

The record between 1953 and 1969 suggests that there were frequent moves
towards a stronger Commonwealth element in Britain's external economic
relations but no policy of concentration on the Commonwealth to the exclusion
of other possibilities. The Commonwealth moves arose in the first place from
the postwar difficulties of sterling, and from the pressures of the early 1950s,
before the flow of US aid and military expenditure loosened the channels of

[1] *Riding the storm*, p. 72.

trade. They can also be associated with a desire to retain a British presence in particular areas, such as Southeast Asia, where British military activity continued until the end of the period.[1] But from 1952 onwards, with the adoption of the collective approach (in which the Commonwealth states concurred), the main thrust of British policy was towards an open, multilateral world economy in which Britain would buy in the cheapest market and sell in the dearest, and which would employ to the full the traditional skills of the City of London. The argument was that only if Britain was strong could it assist Commonwealth countries by buying their goods and lending or giving them money. It is ironic that the ultimate outcome was a British application to enter the EEC, which was anything but multilateral in trading terms; but the important point is that the philosophy embraced by the Conservative government led to the dismantling of bulk-purchase agreements and the advance towards convertibility, and that it was adhered to after Britain's application to enter the EEC was rejected in 1963. It was, in any case, a philosophy aided by Gatt, which allowed little opportunity to help the trade of the overseas countries, and by Britain's close association with the US.

The irksome problem of commodity prices and markets was probably insoluble within the Commonwealth framework where even in the wartime and postwar years it had caused considerable strain.[2] The move towards international commodity agreements, in which Britain joined from 1959 onwards by its adherence to those for sugar, wheat, coffee, and tin, was necessary, given the increasingly complex character of world production and demand, but it did not solve the problems of the producing countries. Only with the Commonwealth Sugar Agreement, an arrangement perpetuated because of the monocultural economies of so many colonial territories, did Britain persist with sustained 'Commonwealth' action—which was, in fact, a system of subsidies from the British consumer to the sugar-producing West Indies, Mauritius, and Fiji, and to a lesser extent to Australia. There had been some modest encouragement to commodity producers in the colonies from the 'buy sterling' adjurations of the Prime Ministers' Meetings in the 1950s, but this proved disappointing:

Retribution was apt to follow as soon as it became possible, and internationally necessary, to relax import restrictions which had been imposed to protect the balance of payments, and which are only justified under GATT for that purpose and not for trade protection. At that point it becomes evident that the stimulated extra production, hitherto fortuitously protected by such restrictions, cannot face the cold

---

[1] See Strange, pp. 96–103.

[2] See Poynton, in *Changing role of Commonwealth economic connections*, pp. 8–11, for an unusually frank account of the difficulties involved in bulk-purchase agreements—that they led to charges of exploitation against the buying country, and to 'straining the doctrine of collective responsibility within the British government almost to breaking-point'. Poynton was Deputy Under-Secretary of State (Economic), CO, 1948–59, and Permanent Under-Secretary, 1959–66.

wind of free competition from non-sterling sources, and the producers will press for continued protection which cannot be given under the international Queensberry rules. Britain has been in breach of Gatt for many years by retaining quantitative restrictions on citrus, cigars and bananas for the protection of the West Indian producers. In 1955 we were able to secure from the Gatt, with the support and advocacy of some of the West Indian representatives, a small relaxation of the general "no new preference" rule. We were henceforth allowed to increase preferential margins in this country in order to help colonial producers to market their commodities here against foreign competition. We were *not* free, however, to extend the new margins in independent Commonwealth countries.[1]

There were thus penalties as well as opportunities for colonies which gained independence; even if they could receive special consideration in the British market in spite of Gatt, this had to be withdrawn after independence, since Britain's freedom of action did not extend to sovereign states. So any attempt to concentrate long-term attention on Commonwealth production would have been vain.

By 1961–2 the multilateral view had triumphed in Britain, only to be merged in a 'European' view, which accepted that the Commonwealth's commodity problems would have to be accommodated within the framework of the EEC. Thereafter no Conservative government was likely to put forward general (apart from occasional and piecemeal) schemes for intensifying the Commonwealth trade network. After de Gaulle's rejection in 1963 of the British application for entry into the EEC, however, there was a period when Commonwealth solutions could still be regarded as feasible, if Britain had the political will to apply them.

In February 1964 Harold Wilson, as leader of the Opposition, put forward a 'plan for Commonwealth trade' which, in his view, would put right the situation which had deteriorated since he ceased to be president of the Board of Trade in 1951.[2] He mainly criticized the dismantling of bulk-purchase contracts, and said his party's policy for Commonwealth countries included the negotiation of specific preferences for the award of public contracts to British firms in return for guaranteed markets for their primary produce; the expansion of those British industries which served capital development in these countries; joint activity in working for world-wide commodity agreements to stabilize prices of primary commodities; an expansion of international liquidity; more exchange of scientific information; the adoption by bodies in advanced countries of similar bodies in the l.d.c.s, with British help; the creation of a pensionable career service for work in the Commonwealth and of a Ministry of Overseas Development. He also pledged that a Labour government would not consider entry into the EEC on any terms which would reduce Britain's existing freedom to trade with the Commonwealth.

[1] Ibid., p. 10.
[2] HC Deb., 6 Feb 1964 (in Harold Wilson, *The new Britain* (1964), pp. 101–24).

Wilson took office eight months later, and at the Commonwealth Prime Ministers' Meeting in June 1965 he put forward three propositions which followed from his 1964 plan. The first was a conference of trade ministers; the second a meeting which he hoped would create permanent machinery for co-ordinating development programmes, so that Britain could enlarge its industrial capacity to serve them; and the third, closer Commonwealth consultation on aircraft requirements. 'All these', he says, 'were agreed in principle, but I was acutely disappointed at the outcome.' Despite the initiatives proposed by Douglas Jay at the Commonwealth trade ministers' conference, which was held in London in 1966, 'there was virtually no willingness to improve intra-Commonwealth trading arrangements'. The developing countries were more interested in aid, and the developed countries—particularly Australia, and to a lesser extent Canada—'were not disposed to adopt arrangements which put their own domestic manufacturers at risk', though they wished to continue long-established agricultural exports to Britain. There was also the development of strong non-Commonwealth trade ties, for instance between Australia and Japan, Canada and the US, to which long years of neglect of Commonwealth trade had contributed. There was, in fact, 'nothing under the sun more *laissez-faire* than Commonwealth trade'.[1]

At the 1966 trade conference the British representatives did suggest reciprocal agreements with other Commonwealth governments to give 'national treatment' in public procurement; no doubt Wilson's ideas about aircraft requirements would have been accommodated within this policy, together with the supply of power, transport, and other equipment in overseas development programmes. The response, according to the communiqué, was poor: 'Ministers agreed to consider the extent to which their governments in their public purchases might place orders in other Commonwealth countries where commercial and other considerations made this practicable.'[2] Wilson's other suggestions seem to have been overwhelmed by the general desire of the trade ministers to ensure that any further approach by Britain to the EEC should not damage their preferences, and by their wish to see international, rather than Commonwealth, action to curb trade practices contrary to their interests.

Wilson was, in fact (in a quite sincere and purposeful manner) bringing a 1951 approach to bear on a situation which fourteen years had radically changed. During that time the overseas Commonwealth countries had become much further embroiled in attachments outside Britain. Perhaps, as Wilson believed, this was due to 'long years of neglect of Commonwealth trade' by the Conservatives; but it was also due to long years of increased activity by Britain's competitors. If Britain had been consistently able to offer up-to-date passenger aircraft to all the Commonwealth countries setting up national airlines, the VC-10s of the 1960s would presumably have prevailed over the Boeings and Douglases; but by the time Britain had large aircraft to offer,

[1] Wilson, *Labour government*, p. 117.   [2] *CS*, 24 June 1966, p. 686.

those airlines were already accustomed to getting what they wanted from the US. In regard to Canada's orientation towards the US and Australia's towards Japan, the period since 1951 had seen massive US investment in Canada combined with a continually irritating British refusal to buy Canadian goods on currency grounds (a refusal which the Labour government had endorsed before 1951); it had also seen the opening in Japan of large markets for Australian minerals and wool, which Britain, whatever its policies, could not have matched. Wilson was, in any case, arguing from a position of British economic weakness. It was hardly likely that Canada and Australia could be persuaded in the mid-1960s to throw over these associates in return for promises which Britain might not be able to keep.

So far as the underdeveloped members of the Commonwealth were concerned, Wilson seems to have been surprised that they wished to talk about aid rather than trade; but their post-independence economies had, in a number of cases, been largely built on the foundation of aid, in particular US aid which was tied to American purchases. Unless Britain could replace this aid, while simultaneously maintaining the British aid which these countries had got since independence, it might have been contrary to their interests to provide special trading concessions to Britain. In fact, total British aid was reduced rather than increased in the next few years, as will be seen.

The general swing, then, was away from intensifying the Commonwealth economic network in the latter part of the 1960s. Many of the overseas members had no strong incentive to intensify it. Wilson and his party, for reasons of sentiment and tradition, did have an incentive; but the thrust of opinion amongst British businessmen and officials was towards Europe, in line with the movement of actual British trade. When Wilson's government in its turn decided to enter the EEC, the swing was very much confirmed; and there was a kind of final confirmation in 1970, with the election which brought Edward Heath, the British negotiator in Brussels in 1962, to office. There were still those prepared to argue that Britain ought to give special attention to the Commonwealth, but they were few.[1] Often their position was based on the special advantages of the Commonwealth as a framework for economic aid, since it contained both rich and poor countries which had certain things such as language in common. This, while capable of being developed as a political argument, was not sufficient to convince many businessmen, politicians, and officials that Britain could become more prosperous by concentrating on the Commonwealth and not on Europe.

There was something of a symbiotic relationship between the decline of the sterling system's restrictions and the growth of British conviction that

---

[1] See, e.g., several of the contributors to Paul Streeten & Hugh Corbet, eds., *Commonwealth policy in a global context* (1971), esp. Michael Lipton, pp. 198–220. See also Lipton's argument in Lipton & Clive Bell, 'The fall in Commonwealth trade', *Round Table*, Jan 1970, pp. 39–50. See also Guy Arnold, *Economic co-operation in the Commonwealth* (1967).

'Europe' was Britain's destiny. When de Gaulle exercised his second veto against British entry on 16 May 1967, he made the reserve role of sterling one of his main grounds. He, like many other Europeans, had been impressed by Britain's apparent wish for exclusive markets in Commonwealth countries but also by what he felt to be collusion between Britain and the US in upholding a privileged system. If Britain was to be a major partner in the EEC, it could not retain a private economic empire of its own. The reasoning was largely out of date, but there was truth in it to the extent that the operation of the sterling area in the 1950s, especially the restriction of external British investment to sterling countries, had symbolized a connection between Britain and Common-wealth countries which, if continued in its most stringent form, could not have been accommodated within the framework of the EEC. In fact, as we have seen, Britain had been quietly dismantling this connection since 1952, retain-ing only those aspects which, at the time, seemed most likely to safeguard sterling. The French objections were in most respects belated; they would have made more sense in 1961–2, when they were not brought up at all. By 1967 only the remnants of the earlier sterling system were still in operation. It was not simply that Britain, for its own purposes, had dismantled most of the equipment; it was also that other sterling countries, for various reasons but partly because they no longer had confidence in sterling, had been shifting their reserves.

In 1968 and 1969, when the pound was under heavy strain, the British chancellor, Roy Jenkins, asked the Australian government to co-operate in stemming a flow of sterling into Australian equities. He was met, he said later, by a blank refusal and a threat to switch even more Australian sterling into gold and dollars. In the event, Australia settled for a minimum of 40 per cent of its reserves in sterling, a striking contrast to its earlier full confidence in British currency. The exchanges between the two governments were evidently harsh; 'not much kith and kin about that', said Jenkins.[1] This was an extreme but significant example of the attitude which major members of the sterling area were taking by the end of the 1960s: lacking confidence in sterling as a reserve, because of the fear of devaluation; still hungry for British investment, but on their own terms; and inclined to believe that Britain, on entering the EEC, would turn its back on Commonwealth development and concentrate on Europe, partly from choice, and partly because the EEC rules required that the first call on members' investible funds should be the EEC area itself. The fact that Britain had refrained from operating exchange control against sterling-area countries, while retaining controls of varying degrees of severity

---

[1] *Canberra Times*, 21, 22, 23, 28 July 1971. It should be noted that the Australian govern-ment had been perturbed by the action of Jenkins's predecessor, James Callaghan, in institut-ing in May 1966 a 'voluntary programme' of restriction of the flow of investment to Australia, New Zealand, South Africa, and Eire. The programme, operated through the Bank of England, continued until it was abolished in the Budget of 1972.

against the rest of the world, was insufficient to reassure them about the future.

The sterling area, as described in these pages, officially died on 27 June 1972, when the 'scheduled territories'—the only legal definition it had ever been given—were re-defined by the Bank of England as Britain (including the Channel Islands and the Isle of Man) and Ireland. Payments to the former members of the area were now to be subject to exchange control, especially in respect of portfolio investment. There were still sterling balances, and the Basle agreements remained in force, to be honoured if the 'floating' pound moved below an agreed figure in terms of the US dollar; but the sterling area was a thing of the past.

VII

From 1953 to 1969, in contrast with trade and currency, British policy continued to maintain a Commonwealth bias in respect of economic aid and investment. Three periods can be distinguished. The first, from 1953 to 1958, was one in which the Colombo Plan was the main element in official aid to Commonwealth members, with private investment as the main contributor to their development; the colonies were looked after by means of Colonial Development and Welfare funds and the Colonial Development Corporation (CDC). The second, from 1958 to about 1964, was marked by an extension of British policy to enable Commonwealth members to obtain government-to-government loans, and by special efforts for newly independent African states. The third, 1964 to 1969, was a period in which British aid policy was centralized in the Ministry of Overseas Development, there was a levelling-off of British aid because of balance-of-payments problems, and the CDC was transformed into a body dealing with Commonwealth members as well as colonies, underlining the changed character of the Commonwealth and of smaller members' aid requirements. Over the whole period aid for developing countries was greatly expanded and new international institutions were created to handle it. The entire operation became more sophisticated and hard-headed as the intractable nature of development problems became clear.[1] For Commonwealth countries, Britain was not the only, or even, in some cases, the main source of aid. But British aid was especially important to the smaller ones, which no one else would help with their problems of debt service and the payment of pensions, apart from their need for development.

Between 1953 and 1958 the British government's emphasis was on private investment in the member states. The Colombo Plan[2] was the main vehicle of direct assistance, largely confined to technical co-operation rather than capital aid. The Plan soon became a widely international affair, so far as both donors

---

[1] For a general conspectus of the aid position, see Lester B. Pearson, *Partners in development* (1969).

[2] See Mansergh, *Survey 1939–52*, for the origins of the Colombo Plan.

TABLE 2

UK Liabilities in Sterling, 1945–69 (£ m.)

End of year	Aust., NZ, & S. Africa	India, Pak., & Ceylon	Caribbean	East, Central, & W. Africa	Middle East	Far East	Other sterling area	Non-sterling countries
1945	305	1,358	54	205	—	142	284	1,254
1946	266	1,314	58	217	1	193	286	1,329
1947	255	1,218	54	253	1	198	260	1,343
1948	379	957	57	314	8	195	255	1,087
1949	491	790	58	346	8	201	282	1,083
1950	685	820	69	436	19	284	285	1,067
1951	615	837	70	551	19	399	254	1,085
1952	462	668	77	612	36	430	284	838
1953	573	660	92	675	61	438	301	885
1954	530	672	107	773	101	426	311	994
1955	359	728	104	765	170	465	283	943
1956	404	570	118	748	212	498	292	834
1957	493	371	134	701	248	479	301	811
1958	428	248	136	683	312	517	318	970
1959	521	281	132	660	340	607	311	946
1960	339	236	140	595	370	695	310	1,577
1961	492	208	154	516	388	722	332	1,120
1962	493	178	175	481	416	765	358	1,064
1963	669	212	190	407	415	664	385	1,290
1964	697	179	196	442	452	661	421	1,370
1965	538	191	213	425	541	731	422	1,474
1966	482	141	227	404	556	770	504	1,662
1967	460	115	236	341	562	707	561	2,167
1968	447	198	278	364	411	714	469	2,708
1969	381	274	243	441	462	854	518	2,063

Source: Bank of England, Statistical Abstract, No. 1, 1970, pp. 125–43. The Bank does not publish the holdings of individual countries, but groups them. It should be noted that there was a change in the method of computation after 1962 (ibid., p. 159). UK claims have not been included, so the figures are not net.

and recipients were concerned, and lost the Commonwealth focus derived from its formulation at a Commonwealth conference.[1] There had been some evidence of slightly changed British intentions at the Prime Ministers' Meeting of December 1952, which formulated the 'collective approach'. Britain would 'facilitate' the financing of schemes in other Commonwealth countries which would contribute to the sterling area's balance of payments, but it would need to be sure that the country in question was also contributing. On the same occasion it was announced that a group of British firms, with government encouragement, was forming a company to further development in the colonies and Commonwealth countries. This became the Commonwealth Development Finance Corporation (CDFC), but it had little effect since its activities were overshadowed by those of the CDC, set up in 1948 to assist the development of British dependencies. At the Finance Ministers' Meeting of 1954 the British government announced that overseas governments could borrow in London for general development programmes as well as particular projects. Continued devotion to the private sector was emphasized by a White Paper in July 1957.[2] 'It is through the investment of privately owned funds that the United Kingdom has made its most valuable contribution to development in other Commonwealth countries', it said, 'and Her Majesty's Government considers that this should continue'. A clear distinction was drawn between colonies and independent Commonwealth states:

> The Government has always recognized a special responsibility for the Colonies, and this is the justification for its policy of applying Exchequer funds to developments in Colonial territories through such means as the Colonial Development and Welfare Acts and the Colonial Development Corporation.
> Her Majesty's Government has also considered the special problems arising from the achievement of independence by Colonial territories. Because of the political and economic ties which bind the Commonwealth countries together, Her Majesty's Government retains the closest interest in their well-being and economic development. But the special responsibility which Her Majesty's Government has for Colonial dependencies ceases when they achieve independence. The Government therefore does not envisage Government to Government loans as a normal means of assisting such countries. Their interests can better be served if they build up their own credit and thus make use of the facilities for raising money on the London market or elsewhere. . . .

A similar distinction was drawn in respect of the CDC. It should not invest money in new schemes in any territory after independence; this would be 'inappropriate for a United Kingdom statutory corporation, particularly one whose essential purpose is the fulfilment of the United Kingdom's special responsibility towards its own dependent territories'. It would, however, be

[1] The memoirs of Sir Percy Spender, who was Australian delegate at Colombo in 1950 and largely responsible for putting forward the final form of the Plan, show that it was always intended to embrace other powers, especially the US (*Exercises in diplomacy*, 1969, Pt II).
[2] Cmnd 237 (1957). The main sections are in Mansergh, *Documents 1952–62*, pp. 668–83.

able to help with advice and management, so long as this involved its own funds.

The White Paper did not have quite the same reservations about technical assistance. In spite of its own needs, the government was 'determined to make special efforts to meet the needs of the less developed Commonwealth countries', though Colombo Plan arrangements would suffice for the Asian members. It was noteworthy, however, that in regard to Ghana, which had become independent a few months before, the provision of experts would depend upon mutual cost-sharing.

In general, the tone of this White Paper was highly protective of the colonies and cool towards the independent members; if government money was available, the colonies would get it. One can glimpse behind the phrases a clash of interests between Treasury, CO, and CRO, with the CO winning. There had been a clear change from the earlier tradition of making colonial governments pay for themselves, apart from small amounts from Development and Welfare funds. Now those funds had been greatly expanded, and colonial territories could hope for help in other ways. The traditional attitude had, however, been transferred to newly independent countries. These, it appeared to be assumed, would hardly be seeking independence if they could not look after themselves. Yet in a very short time there was to be a reversal of policy.

At the Montreal conference of 1958 Britain announced its intention to make Commonwealth assistance loans from exchequer funds to both independent Commonwealth countries and colonies, those to independent countries to be tied to British exports. This was a major step forward, the results of which were visible in the rising figures for loans in the next few years (see p. 301). Perhaps more important was the growth of the consortium arrangements mentioned earlier, especially for India and Pakistan. In each case Britain became part of a team instead of an individual donor: its contributions to these major operations were, of course, individual in the sense that they came from British funds, but they formed part of a system of periodic pledges of financial support, agreed between major industrial powers and supervised by the World Bank. These pledges were worked out in accordance with agreed assessments of the planning requirements of India and Pakistan. Most of the money was in the form of loans. As well as the consortium arrangements, in September 1960 a special Indo-Pakistani agreement related to the division of the Indus waters. Under the aegis of the World Bank, a number of countries, including Britain, Australia, Canada, and New Zealand, agreed to help finance the project. A further development of a Commonwealth kind was the decision of the prime ministers, in May 1960, to set up a Special Commonwealth Aid to Africa Plan (SCAAP), under which assistance would be given to African members by more developed Commonwealth states.

Between 1958 and 1964 a pattern was set for economic aid from Britain to new African members. It was quite different from what had occurred with the

Asian members, and was repeated in respect of Mediterranean, Caribbean, and Pacific colonies as these became independent. Essentially it consisted of a grant broadly reflecting the aid which the country would have received towards its current development programme if it had not become independent, together with assistance loans on the lines set out in 1958, and in some cases aid to help with the compensation of retired expatriate officials and the commutation of their pensions.

Technical assistance, a growing field in all the categories of countries receiving British aid, was given a minor Department of Technical Co-operation to itself in 1961, to co-ordinate and direct activities in the Commonwealth and elsewhere. The CDC was freed from the restrictions affirmed in the 1957 White Paper. By the Commonwealth Development Act of 1963 it became the Commonwealth Development Corporation, permitted to 'carry on the full range of its activities in any part of the Commonwealth except in those countries which became independent before 11 February 1948'.[1] This was the date on which it had been originally set up to serve the dependencies. Its role now became that of continuing to foster the enterprises in which it had been engaged before independence, and of finding new ones, in co-operation with newly independent governments.

By the time the Wilson government took office in 1964, the quantity and character of British aid to Commonwealth countries were very different from ten or even seven years before. Table 3 illustrates the position.

It will be seen that, in spite of the advance to independence of some of the biggest and most important dependencies, the aid to the colonies was still considerable, while that to independent Commonwealth members had increased greatly, as had aid as a whole. There was little increase in bilateral aid to countries outside the Commonwealth, or to agencies through which multilateral aid was provided. British aid was essentially directed towards Commonwealth countries. Its other main characteristic was that more than half of it was in the form of loans. The normal rate of interest was that at which the British government could borrow on the domestic market, together with a small management charge. In effect, the government was borrowing on behalf of overseas governments at the current rate of interest. In September 1963 important changes in this respect were announced in a White Paper, following discussions in the Development Assistance Committee (DAC) of the OECD, a body of increasing importance in the aid field. Whereas loans had previously been for a maximum of 25 years, with a grace period of 7 years for the repayment of principal, these were now to be extended to 30 and 10 years respectively, and in needy cases there would be a waiver of interest for 7 years, thus substantially reducing the effective rate of interest for the loan as a whole.[2]

[1] Cmnd 2147 (1963), p. 19. Much of the information in the preceding paragraphs is from this White Paper.
[2] Ibid., p. 14.

TABLE 3

British Economic Aid, 1954–5 to 1962–3 (£ m.)

	1954–5	1955–6	1956–7	1957–8	1958–9	1959–60	1960–1	1961–2	1962–3 (provisional)
Bilateral aid									
Colonial Territories* (total)	55·3	45·3	46·0	47·3	49·0	57·6	71·8	95·5	60·6
Grants	35·6	33·0	37·6	41·1	37·3	40·3	38·9	56·6	40·4
Loans	19·7	12·3	8·4	6·2	11·7	17·3	32·9	38·9	20·2
Independent Commonwealth (total)	3·4	2·3	1·9	4·7	25·8	39·7	45·6	44·5	62·3
Grants	0·6	0·6	0·6	2·7	5·0	5·0	10·2	12·5	20·6
Loans	2·8	1·7	1·3	2·0	20·8	34·7	35·4	32·0	41·7
Other Countries (total)	7·5	28·8	11·8	10·3	10·7	12·4	12·5	13·8	15·0
Grants	5·7	7·8	6·8	6·1	5·7	7·4	8·7	10·4	8·7
Loans	1·8	21·0	5·0	4·2	5·0	5·0	3·8	3·4	6·3
Total bilateral aid	66·2	76·4	59·7	62·3	85·5	109·7	129·9	153·8	137·9
Multilateral aid	10·4	5·9	15·6	18·8	24·0	19·9	21·2	6·3	9·9
Total aid	76·6	82·3	75·3	81·1	109·5	129·6	151·1	160·1	147·8

* Includes aid given before independence to territories now independent, and to the Federation of Rhodesia and Nyasaland.

Source: Cmnd 2147 (1963), p. 15. The 1962–3 figures were, in fact, slightly underestimated: total bilateral aid for that period was £141·6m. instead of the provisional £137·9m. Technical assistance is included in Grants.

The debt burden on developing countries was becoming a matter of wide international concern. The contrast in tone with the 1957 White Paper was substantial.

Wilson took office with a determination to improve the aid position. He writes:

First a new ministry, that of Overseas Development, was set up under Barbara Castle, with a seat in the Cabinet. Its duty was to administer Britain's aid programme abroad, previously the responsibility of a minor department . . ., and to do it with a new instruction that aid was to be granted not so much as a charity but as a real means to development, particularly within the Commonwealth. I intended also that it should have wide responsibilities. In my very early ministerial career I had seen a good deal of the work of the Food and Agriculture Organisation (FAO) of the United Nations, and other specialised agencies. I was very anxious that all Britain's responsibilities in relation to these organisations should be centred in the Ministry of Overseas Development. With one exception (the World Health Organisation) responsibility was so transferred and a new zest was put into the job of overseas development, despite the fact that Barbara was never able, against the background of financial stringency, to get the funds that she really wanted to have at her disposal.[1]

The new zest was clearly apparent under the leadership of Sir Andrew Cohen, who headed the ministry; there was more effective co-ordination than before; but it is doubtful whether the element of 'charity' was any less—indeed, it became, in one sense, even greater, since the terms of new development loans continued to be eased to such an extent that, in 1969, 91 per cent of new bilateral British loan commitments were interest-free. However, some 43 per cent of bilateral aid was contractually tied to the purchase of British goods and services.[2]

What Wilson said last was still more important: his government did increase the total of British aid, but not at the same rate as in the comparable period before the 1964 election. Financial stringency was, as he says, the reason. When one takes into account the effects of inflation, British aid in real terms may well have declined during the government's term of office. Details of bilateral aid between 1958/9 and 1968/9 are given in Table 4.

The figures are notable for the substantial increases in grants to small, poor, newly independent countries such as Malawi and the former High Commission Territories. This represented a new aspect of aid programmes: the provision of money, not for development, but to make up budgetary deficiencies. There were political reasons why Malawi should not have to turn to the regime of Ian Smith or Lesotho, Botswana, and Swaziland to South Africa.

By 1969 little initiative was being exercised by Britain in respect of aid to major Commonwealth countries, which were under the aegis of the World Bank. Smaller countries were very much dependent on British aid on gaining

[1] *Labour government*, pp. 10–11.
[2] COI, *Britain's international investment position* (1971), p. 59.

TABLE 4

UK Government Bilateral Economic Aid (£ m.)

(Years ended 31 March)

	1958-9	1959-60	1960-1	1961-2	1962-3	1963-4	1964-5	1965-6	1966-7	1967-8	1968-9[1]
Total bilateral aid	85·5	109·7	130·2	155·4	141·6	158·3	174·9	185·3	196·0	188·8	177·1
Grants[2]	48·0	53·9	59·8	81·4	73·7	71·7	91·5	91·8	91·8	88·6	90·7
Africa	16·3	18·2	25·2	45·3	40·1	38·6	51·9	46·3	42·1	38·7	38·6
East African Community[3]	0·4	0·5	0·5	4·2	2·7	2·6	3·6	3·9	3·3	2·4	2·5
Federation of Rhodesia & Nyasaland	0·1	0·3	0·6	0·2	0·4	0·2	1·1	0·2	0·4	0·2	—
Gambia	0·1	0·2	0·3	0·5	0·4	1·4	1·1	1·4	1·0	0·4	0·1
Kenya[4]	2·1	1·7	1·2	11·3	7·8	8·1	7·7	7·1	3·5	4·2	4·0
Libya	3·2	3·2	3·2	3·2	3·2	3·3	3·3	—	—	—	—
Malawi (formerly Nyasaland)[4]	0·3	0·3	1·8	2·5	2·0	6·2	8·7	8·6	5·7	5·4	4·7
Mauritius	0·1	0·1	1·1	1·3	1·3	0·6	0·4	0·4	0·3	0·3	1·8
Nigeria[5]	3·4	4·0	5·3	1·6	1·7	0·9	1·4	2·1	2·4	2·4	3·1
Zambia (formerly N. Rhodesia)	0·3	0·4	0·2	0·9	0·6	0·9	5·5	3·3	6·5	3·9	4·4
Sierra Leone	0·2	0·9	1·2	2·7	1·1	0·6	0·2	0·2	0·4	0·3	0·3
Somali Republic[6]	1·4	1·1	2·5	1·5	1·0	—	7·9	10·5	11·3	11·8	11·5
Botswana,[7] Lesotho,[8] & Swaziland	1·3	1·7	2·0	4·6	4·8	5·2	4·4	2·9	2·3	1·3	1·2
Tanzania	1·5	1·5	1·9	6·0	7·5	4·5	2·4	2·1	2·4	2·0	2·1
Uganda	0·6	0·9	1·3	3·1	4·6	3·1	4·0	1·8	1·8	1·9	2·8
Other	1·3	1·5	2·0	1·8	0·6	1·0	0·2	1·8	0·8	2·2	0·1
America	6·6	8·6	6·9	8·9	7·2	6·2	5·8	6·6	9·5	9·9	7·9
Guyana (formerly British Guiana)	0·7	1·0	1·3	1·3	0·7	0·8	0·4	0·5	2·1	1·1	0·6
British Honduras	1·2	1·0	0·6	1·7	1·5	1·0	0·8	0·6	1·1	2·4	1·5
Other West Indian Territories	3·4	4·0	3·4	4·3	3·7	2·9	3·3	4·2	5·3	5·4	4·6
Jamaica	1·0	1·8	1·3	1·5	1·1	0·4	0·5	0·4	0·3	0·2	0·3
Trinidad and Tobago	0·2	0·7	0·2	0·1	0·1	1·0	0·2	0·1	0·2	0·2	0·2
Other	0·1	—	0·1	—	—	0·1	0·5	0·7	0·7	0·7	0·8
Asia	10·5	12·6	12·9	14·9	15·3	17·7	21·6	26·1	25·9	22·0	18·5
India	0·3	0·3	0·4	0·4	0·5	0·6	0·8	0·7	0·7	0·7	3·2
Jordan	1·5	2·6	2·5	2·8	2·0	2·0	2·0	1·9	1·8	1·9	0·6
Malaysia[4]	5·2	5·1	4·8	4·7	5·5	2·8	3·9	4·4	4·2	4·9	3·8
Pakistan	0·3	0·4	0·4	0·4	0·8	0·9	1·0	0·9	0·7	0·9	0·7
South Yemen (formerly South Arabian Federation)	2·0	2·7	2·6	3·3	3·9	5·3	7·1	10·1	10·4	6·1	0·8
Indus Basin Development Fund	—	—	0·3	0·5	0·3	2·9	3·3	4·2	5·3	5·4	4·6
Other	1·1	1·5	1·9	2·8	2·3	3·2	3·5	3·9	2·8	2·1	4·8
Europe	12·4	11·8	11·5	6·6	5·5	4·8	7·2	6·4	5·9	6·5	6·5
Cyprus[4]	7·6	7·6	6·5	3·5	4·8	4·0	6·1	5·9	5·5	4·6	5·8
Malta	4·6	4·0	4·7	2·7	0·5	0·5	1·0	0·3	0·2	1·9	0·5
Other	0·2	0·2	0·3	0·4	0·2	0·3	0·1	0·2	0·2	—	0·2
Other grants	2·4	2·7	3·4	5·6	5·6	4·5	5·0	6·4	8·4	11·5	19·2

Loans (gross)	1958-9	1959-60	1960-1	1961-2	1962-3	1963-4	1964-5	1965-6	1966-7	1967-8	1968-9[1]
Africa	37.5	55.8	70.4	74.0	67.9	86.6	83.4	93.7	104.2	100.2	86.4
East African Community[3]	4.0	12.3	31.5	40.0	23.2	34.3	30.0	34.7	29.3	20.2	22.2
Federation of Rhodesia & Nyasaland	—	—	4.3	4.6	2.1	1.5	2.8	1.4	2.1	1.8	0.2
Kenya	0.9	2.4	8.4	12.1	4.5	7.1	10.2	8.1	6.6	5.0	5.5
Malawi (formerly Nyasaland)[4]	1.2	—	0.3	1.9	0.4	3.0	1.3	1.7	3.2	2.9	3.0
Mauritius	0.7	0.2	0.6	0.1	0.8	1.0	0.1	1.2	0.5	1.0	0.7
Nigeria	—	—	6.2	6.2	3.0	1.1	4.3	10.2	5.4	2.2	3.4
Zambia (formerly N. Rhodesia)	—	—	—	—	1.0	3.0	0.8	0.7	0.8	0.7	0.3
Sierra Leone	—	1.5	1.7	0.1	1.1	2.1	0.8	1.9	0.5	0.7	0.4
Southern Rhodesia	—	—	—	—	3.9	—	—	—	—	—	—
Botswana,[7] Lesotho,[8] & Swaziland	0.5	2.2	3.0	2.8	2.3	0.4	0.9	1.8	3.8	0.6	0.8
Sudan	0.4	2.4	1.7	—	—	0.3	1.3	1.4	1.4	0.4	0.2
Tanzania	0.3	0.6	2.0	3.9	2.6	3.0	3.2	3.0	1.6	0.2	1.1
Uganda	—	3.0	3.0	3.6	3.7	2.5	1.9	2.4	3.1	1.3	6.6
Other	6.9	2.0	4.5	0.7	1.0	3.3	2.3	0.9	0.3	3.4	1.9
America	—	—	—	—	—	—	—	—	—	—	—
Argentina	—	—	—	1.2	1.3	1.9	1.9	1.5	3.2	0.3	0.2
Brazil	5.2	1.1	1.6	2.6	1.7	1.5	1.5	1.2	0.7	0.6	0.2
Guyana (formerly British Guiana)	0.4	0.6	0.6	0.3	0.1	0.8	0.8	0.1	0.7	0.4	0.6
Other West Indian Territories	—	—	—	1.4	0.4	0.6	0.6	0.1	1.3	—	0.3
Chile	—	—	2.3	1.0	1.7	0.2	0.5	2.0	0.8	0.1	0.7
Jamaica	0.1	0.4	—	—	—	0.5	1.2	2.2	—	—	—
Trinidad and Tobago	1.1	—	—	—	0.1	0.9	—	0.1	0.7	0.3	0.2
Other	—	—	—	—	0.1	0.1	—	—	0.7	0.6	0.2
Asia	23.9	36.5	32.2	26.1	32.2	36.5	41.6	43.3	59.3	62.1	46.8
India	18.8	33.0	28.1	17.2	22.3	26.0	30.1	32.1	43.2	40.9	30.9
Iran	1.7	0.1	0.1	1.7	0.1	0.7	0.7	0.7	1.3	1.7	0.6
Jordan	0.6	0.5	0.5	1.8	0.7	0.7	0.7	0.7	0.8	0.9	0.7
Malaysia	1.0	0.4	0.7	6.2	0.8	0.5	0.3	0.4	0.4	—	0.8
Pakistan	1.2	1.7	2.7	0.3	7.4	8.2	9.3	9.4	9.0	13.1	8.0
Other	0.6	0.8	0.3	0.8	1.0	1.0	1.3	0.6	4.5	5.4	5.7
Europe	2.7	5.1	2.2	0.5	5.5	7.0	5.1	8.4	8.1	8.3	5.5
Malta	—	1.8	0.5	0.8	2.0	3.2	2.0	1.2	1.0	1.8	1.2
Turkey	2.7	0.9	—	—	3.5	3.1	3.1	7.0	6.9	5.8	3.9
Yugoslavia	—	1.1	1.6	0.3	0.1	3.5	—	—	—	0.5	0.3
Other	—	1.3	—	0.5	0.2	0.1	0.1	0.2	—	0.2	0.1
Other loans[9]	—	—	—	0.5	1.6	—	—	0.2	0.2	8.3	10.0

[1] Provisional. [2] Including technical assistance. [3] Formerly the East Africa High Commission and then the East African Common Services Organization. [4] Including emergency assistance. [5] Including loans for Nigeria Special List 'B' officers. [6] Disbursements up to July 1960 were made to British Somaliland. [7] Formerly Bechuanaland. [8] Formerly Basutoland. [9] From 1967-8 the figures include exchequer advances to the Commonwealth Development Corporation which are not available by country after 1966-7. These amounted to £8.2m. in 1967-8 and £10.0m. in 1968-9.

Source: UK, Ann. abstract of statistics 1969, pp. 266-7.

independence, and in some cases afterwards; such countries do not lend themselves readily to the large-scale investigations of multilateral agencies, and rudimentary administrations probably fare better with donors whom they know and who speak the same language. There had been a significant change of approach when it became clear that new members of the Commonwealth would require different forms of aid from those which had sufficed for the Asian members. The Asian dimension of the Commonwealth had meant, broadly speaking, that members were treated much as the old dominions had been: they were assumed to be solvent, credit-worthy, administratively stable, and capable of either providing their own experts or paying for those they might need. The Colombo Plan had been an innovation, but not a large one. The African dimension called for a different approach, because it soon became apparent that African states and other small new states did not share the characteristics listed but needed loans on special terms and grants for new purposes.

Commonwealth recipients of aid did not, in the mass, depend on Britain alone, or even mainly, for development aid: it was estimated that in 1960–5 developing countries in the Commonwealth received some £980 m. from Commonwealth donors but £2,523 m. from other donors.[1] This picture is, however, distorted in terms of individual countries' experiences. India and Pakistan, the biggest Commonwealth countries, got most attention from international bodies and non-Commonwealth donors (especially the US). Peter Williams calculated that whereas Britain was responsible for only 7·5 per cent of the total bilateral aid going to India and Pakistan, it was responsible for 80 per cent of what went to other Commonwealth countries.[2] This distinction emphasizes the role played by Britain in helping the less populous and newer members.

For most of the period of this book, the term 'Commonwealth aid' was a misnomer if it meant any system of centrally-administered Commonwealth aid. In this the Commonwealth differed from the EEC, which had a Development Fund administered by the members as a whole. Four Commonwealth members—Britain, Canada, Australia, and New Zealand—had aid programmes, but these were not co-ordinated.[3] Each served the particular interests of the country in question. Thus Australian aid was concentrated in Papua-New Guinea and Southeast Asia; New Zealand's in Southeast Asia and the Pacific; and Canada's in Asia, Africa, and the Caribbean. Both the Colombo Plan and SCAAP were purely bilateral in operation; 'it might be unkind', wrote Williams, 'but certainly not unjust, to observe of SCAAP that

---

[1] Commonwealth Secretariat, *Flow of intra-Commonwealth aid 1966* (1968), p. 14.

[2] Peter Williams, *Aid in the Commonwealth* (1965), p. 23.

[3] See G. J. Thompson, *New Zealand's international aid* (1967); OECD Secretariat, *Australia's international development assistance* (1969) (also for the aid programmes of those three countries).

it is not very Special, and is certainly not a Plan'.[1] Nevertheless, each of the four donor countries put by far the greater part of its total aid into the Commonwealth. In 1968 countries within the Commonwealth received nearly 90 per cent of British bilateral aid, almost 85 per cent of Canada's, and much the same proportion of Australia's and New Zealand's.[2] In June 1967 a modest start was made with a centrally-administered Commonwealth Programme for Technical Co-operation. A meeting of officials at Nairobi laid down a plan, the working of which was reviewed at a further meeting in Barbados in September 1969, and commended in due course by the Commonwealth prime ministers. Essentially a small operation, the scheme was staffed by the Commonwealth secretariat and aimed at giving Commonwealth members the benefits of one another's expertise, in particular at helping the smaller states to draw on advisers from those more developed.[3] It was not a replacement for the technical-assistance programmes of the four donor countries but a means of supplementing them. Nevertheless, Australia refused to take part in the scheme, revealing the suspiciousness which had been the norm in its government's attitude towards the secretariat.

VIII

The importance of Britain in the economies of Commonwealth members, especially the newer and less developed, will be apparent from what has been said above. Yet in each of the spheres considered—currency, trade, investment, economic aid—it is clear that the wider world became more important to most Commonwealth countries, and Britain less so, as the international economy expanded in the 1960s. For currency and economic aid, there was a growing institutionalization and sharing of responsibility, through the activities of the Bank of International Settlements in the Basle agreements, and those of the World Bank and the OECD in rationalizing and sharing responsibility for aid. For trade, and to a lesser degree for investment, there was a wider range of buyers and sellers for Commonwealth countries to choose from, and also some degree of institutionalization, shown in the international commodity agreements and the expanding activities of the World Bank.

Britain was affected by such developments in its own right and as the traditional centre of most other Commonwealth countries' external economic operations. In its own right it found the Commonwealth less of a growth area for trade, and progressively less attractive as a form of support for sterling. Western Europe became much more attractive as a trading area. British investment continued to flow towards the Commonwealth, as did British aid; but the fact that other Commonwealth countries increasingly bought and sold

[1] Williams, p. 10.
[2] Commonwealth Secretariat, *Flow of intra-Commonwealth aid 1968* (1969), pp. 22-30.
[3] See CSG, *Third Report*, pp. 19-23.

in non-British markets meant that any programme for increasing Common-wealth trade, such as Wilson suggested in 1965, languished because it did not carry prospects of obvious gain for Britain's or the overseas countries. It is a chicken-and-egg question to ask whether Britain's or the major Commonwealth countries' indifference came first: the two are inseparable, since both arose from the changed conditions of the international economy. Yet there will always be the lurking question whether Britain might have made more of its Commonwealth economic connections. Whatever the answer might have been, the reason why it did not try very hard, in terms of policy, can be summed up in a word: Europe.

CHAPTER 13

BRITAIN AND THE EEC

BRITAIN's attempts to enter the EEC in the 1960s brought to a head the question whether Britain's European interests were more important than its Commonwealth interests. In spite of Britain's substantial economic links with Europe and its participation in European wars, relations with the Commonwealth had traditionally been regarded as superior. The Commonwealth, especially in its earlier form as the Empire, was Britain's creation, in which British institutions, the English language and an inscrutable providence had combined to create something unique:

> Time and the ocean, and some fostering star,
> In high cabal have made us what we are.

Europe, on the other hand, was where the lamps periodically went out, causing a waste of British blood and treasure before they could be lit again.

This is an extravagant but basically accurate description of British sentiment on those occasions when the country's destiny and associations were being discussed. Churchill had said that if Britain had to choose between the narrow seas and the open sea, she would choose the open sea.

Such views were still dominant in 1952, when Eden gave an address in New York. It was designed, in part, to warn the US, which favoured closer British integration with Europe, that 'if you drive a nation to adopt procedures which run counter to its instincts, you weaken and may destroy the motive force of its action'. Eden went on:

This is not something you would wish to do, or any of us would wish to do, to an ally on whose effective cooperation we depend. You will realize that I am speaking of the frequent suggestions that the United Kingdom should join a Federation on the Continent of Europe. This is something which we know, in our bones, we cannot do. We know that if we were to attempt it, we should relax the springs of our action in the Western Democratic cause and in the Atlantic Association which is the expression of that cause. For Britain's story and her interests lie far beyond the Continent of Europe. Our thoughts move across the seas to the many communities in which our people play their part, in every corner of the world. That is our life: without it we should be no more than some millions of people living on an island off the coast of Europe.[1]

Not all Eden's ministerial colleagues agreed with this doctrine,[2] but it was

---

[1] Speech at Columbia University, 11 Jan 1952 (RIIA, *Documents 1952*, pp. 43–4).
[2] Sir David Maxwell Fyfe (as he was in 1952) wrote later that the breakdown in 1963 of

sustained throughout the 1950s. The main British response to the growth of European institutions intended to bring about further integration was a sceptical one, British participation in Europe being largely confined to security arrangements, schemes for freer trade in manufactures, and functional co-operation of various kinds. There was little difficulty for Commonwealth countries in this sort of 'Europeanism', especially since it was customary for British ministers to insist that food, drink, and tobacco, which comprised the main Commonwealth products with free access to, and preference in, the British market, would not be included in any closer economic arrangements with Europe. As Macmillan told an audience at Christchurch, New Zealand, in January 1958, when speaking of the EEC in its initial stages, 'it was obvious that in view of all our long history, all our obligations to our Commonwealth partners, especially in respect of food and other agricultural products, we clearly could not join this European Customs Union. We decided without the slightest hesitation that we could not join it.'[1]

Yet not much later Macmillan's government took the steps which culminated in an application in 1961 to join the EEC. To see why there should have been such a momentous change of attitude, we must glance at the history of Britain's relations with Europe since World War II.[2]

I

After World War II there arose in Western Europe a movement for integration with Jean Monnet as its chief theorist and protagonist and such leaders as Reynaud, Spaak, Van Zeeland, Adenauer, and Schuman as its practical men.[3] Apart from the economic sense of bringing more closely together areas which had traditionally shared transport systems, rivers, ports, and the like, the 'Europeans' saw, in varying measure, three other great advantages to be got from a united Europe. One was an end to the kind of conflict which had seen France and Germany at each other's throats three times in three-quarters of a century. A second was the perpetuation of the alliance against the Soviet Union. The third was the opportunity of creating, through integration of Western Europe, an economic power which could stand alongside the Soviet Union and the US.[4]

Britain's application to enter the EEC 'had its roots in 1951–52. . . . No doubt, we few pro-Europeans in the Cabinet, Macmillan and myself, should have done more at the time. But against us there were senior Ministers of the stature and authority of Eden and Salisbury, supported hesitantly but inevitably by Churchill' (Kilmuir, pp. 188–9).

[1] 'The Commonwealth and the European Free Trade Area' in COI, *Commonwealth tour: quotations from the speeches . . . of the Prime Minister . . .* (1958), p. 27.

[2] For further detail, see Miriam Camps, *Britain and the European community 1955–63* (1964), which has an opening chapter on 'The background: 1946–54'.

[3] For the arguments of 'Europeanism', see ibid., ch. 1, and Uwe Kitzinger, *The challenge of the common market* (1962), ch. 1, together with documents in Pt I of Kitzinger's *ECM & C*.

[4] This feeling, so often present amongst advocates of an integrated Europe, was elegantly

Although British governments of the late 1940s and 1950s shared these aims, especially in regard to security, they were not attracted by the idea of total integration. This was partly because Britain's unique relationship with the members of the Commonwealth was felt to require British independence, and partly because memories of the 'special relationship' in which Britain had stood with the US in World War II (during which it had been cut off from Western Europe) were still strong and were assumed to represent the normal state of relations between the two countries. From about 1949 Britain's relations with Europe were considered to be effectively handled by OEEC and its derivatives in economic matters, and by Nato in security matters. Both had the added advantage that the US was a member, so that the focus became 'Atlantic' rather than 'European'. This smack of the open sea suited the British, especially the Foreign Office. It suited some of the 'Europeans', especially when Western Europe required American aid; and it suited the US government in the earlier stages, though, as the 1950's advanced, US pressure for Britain to come closer to the states of Western Europe grew.

The first effectively 'European' institution (i.e. one which assumed European integration, as distinct from those which were concerned only with co-operation between states) was the European Coal and Steel Community (ECSC), evolved from the Schuman Plan of 1950 and put into operation as a supranational body in 1953. The Attlee government in Britain refused to commit itself to supranationalism in this form, but decided to maintain a tenuous 'association'; the Churchill government concurred. The members of the ECSC (France, West Germany, Italy, Belgium, the Netherlands, and Luxembourg) went on to form the European Atomic Community (Euratom) and the EEC, the three Communities eventually being merged in one. They also tried to form a European Defence Community (EDC) in response to the need to integrate German forces in those of Nato: this failed in 1954 because the French Assembly rejected it. It was the failure of the EDC that led the 'Europeans' to create the EEC. This body, it was hoped, would achieve by economic means the eventual integration which existing bodies and schemes such as EDC had failed to achieve.

The main features of the EEC can be briefly stated.[1] It was to form a customs union with a common external tariff against the rest of the world. Agricultural trading within the Community would operate within a system of managed marketing, whereby agricultural products would be admitted from

---

and memorably expressed by Maurice Faure, the principal French negotiator over the EEC, in presenting the treaty to the French National Assembly on 5 July 1957: 'Voyez-vous, mes chers amis, nous vivons aujourd'hui sur une fiction qui consiste à dire: il y a quatre "Grands" dans le monde. Eh bien, il n'y a pas quatre Grands, il y en a deux: l'Amérique et la Russie. Il y en aura un troisième à la fin du siècle: la Chine. Il dépend de vous qu'il y en ait un quatrième: l'Europe' (Camps, p. 88 n). It was too early to include Japan as a fifth.

[1] For further detail see Pt II of Kitzinger, *ECM & C.*

outside only to the extent that they did not compete adversely with Community products. There was to be 'harmonization' of several aspects of economic and social policy, including social services, transport, cartels and monopolies, migration of labour, and conditions of work, and members' policies in the location of industry and the use of transport were not to create unfair advantages for one set of industrial producers over another. There was to be free movement of capital and labour throughout the Community. At the insistence of France, certain past and present colonies of members (especially in Africa and the Caribbean) would be granted 'association': a special fund would be built up to assist their economic development, their products would be permitted free entry into the EEC area, and they would be able to protect their domestic industry against the EEC. European states outside the EEC could also apply for associate status on different but unspecified terms. There were to be appropriate institutions—including an Assembly, Council, and Court of Justice—to represent the interests of member states and adjust grievances. In addition, there was to be an executive and initiating body, the Commission, to embody the Community's supranational character. The ministers of the Six met first at Messina in June 1955 to agree on aims and on the methods of preparing a scheme; the task was completed with the signing of the Treaty of Rome in March 1957. The treaty was quickly ratified, and (together with that of Euratom) came into force at the beginning of 1958.

The British reaction was erratic but generally sceptical. After the Messina meeting British 'experts' sat in on the meetings of the drafting committee for the treaty, but were withdrawn when the British government was asked to declare its intentions. In July 1956 Britain took a step of its own, proposing in the OEEC (to which the Six as well as the other states of Western Europe belonged) that the idea of an industrial free-trade area for the whole of Western Europe should be examined. In this scheme the proposed EEC would be treated as a unit, and would, it was hoped, practise free trade in manufactures with the other countries of the area. Consideration dragged on until November 1958, by which time it had become clear that France, in particular, and the other EEC members in varying degrees, wished to get on with the rapid construction of the EEC, in which their own special interests were specifically embodied, and not to launch into the wider but shallower waters of the British proposal. Politically speaking, 'Europeans' saw no advantage in the proposal: it did not involve any sort of integration, and seemed to be designed to give Britain all it wanted, while not giving the continental countries any advantage in Commonwealth markets, and preserving Commonwealth advantages in the British market. During the following twelve months, Britain looked for, and found, a second best: this was the European Free Trade Area (Efta), resulting from the Stockholm Convention of November 1959, with Austria, Denmark, Norway, Portugal, Sweden, and Switzerland as members with Britain. (Finland became an associate soon after.) Commonwealth countries, which had given their approval in general to the free trade area idea at the Montreal Conference of 1958, were not perturbed.[1]

But Efta did not satisfy the British government, which soon turned to the idea of joining the EEC, in spite of the difficulties this was likely to create with the Commonwealth countries, and in spite of the strong reservations which, throughout the 1940s and 1950s, most British politicians and officials had held against anything which went beyond functional co-operation with Western Europe. The process was gradual. Macmillan as prime minister needed little or no persuasion. He has said that, early in 1952, 'I was much distressed by a memorandum compiled in the Foreign Office on European integration, which was given a wide circulation. It seemed to me to be based upon a complete misapprehension of the reality and strength of the movement for European unity'. He prepared a fighting reply. The argument which most concerned him was the claim that because of its position as a world power, Britain could not join a movement for integration but could only associate with it in a friendly fashion. He thought this 'seemed to duck the whole question'. Britain could not, 'of course' join a federation which would limit its membership of the Commonwealth or association with the US, but there could be a confederation based on consultation between governments, with a Consultative Assembly 'to create a European public opinion'. European currencies could be linked to sterling and a European preferential area could be created 'interlocking with our own system of Imperial Preference'. Specialized but not supranational authorities could be set up, e.g. for defence and heavy industry, and Britain could participate in a European army.

If we did nothing, the French, German and Italian federal system—"Little Europe" —might, in spite of all hesitations, come into being,—but without Britain. It would be encouraged by the United States, and in the long run it would represent both an economic and political danger to Britain and even to the Commonwealth.[2]

These sentiments, so different from Eden's of the same year, needed little alteration to meet the challenge of the successful creation of the EEC in succeeding years.[3]

---

[1] Mention should be made of the proposal of the Sixth Unofficial Commonwealth Relations Conference (held at Palmerston North, New Zealand, in January 1959) that 'The governments of the United Kingdom and the other Commonwealth countries should urgently consider the advisability of conducting joint negotiations with the European group [i.e. the EEC]. In such negotiations it was felt that the Commonwealth should, with a view to obtaining a satisfactory solution, be prepared to consider variations in the system of imperial preference which at present obtains within it' (see C. E. Carrington, *The Commonwealth relations conference 1959,* (1959), p. 30). This proposal, expanded by one of the delegates, Peter Thorneycroft, in two articles (*Manchester Guardian,* 4 & 5 May 1959) was unkindly dismissed by Macmillan on 13 June 1961, on the ground that 'the concept then put forward was totally unrealistic, having regard to the economic interests of the various Commonwealth countries and of Europe' (462 HC Deb., cols 203–10; Mansergh, *Documents 1952–62,* p. 633).

[2] *Tides of fortune,* pp. 468–9. See also chs 3 & 14 of *Riding the storm.*

[3] Macmillan was well aware of the differences between himself and Eden during the long

By early 1960 there had arisen a changed attitude to Europe in Whitehall, especially in the Treasury and the Foreign Office.[1] This was paralleled by shifts in business and press opinion. The EEC looked like a success; Britain's attempts to outflank it, while not entirely a failure, seemed unlikely to provide the major market which growth-minded economists and businessmen wanted. In addition, there were strong political reasons for concentrating on Europe. Macmillan wrote on 9 July: 'Shall we be caught between a hostile (or at least less and less friendly) America and a boastful, powerful "Empire of Charlemagne"—now under French but later bound to come under German control?'[2]

The change of heart in the key government departments was signified early in 1960 by a report from the Economic Steering Committee, an interdepartmental body under Sir Frank Lee, who had previously been at the Board of Trade but was now joint permanent secretary to the Treasury. This committee, asked to consider the range of options available to Britain, pronounced in favour of an application to join the EEC.[3] The discussions were highly confidential: fewer people were involved than in a normal Whitehall examination of a major change in policy; empirical studies of economic effects were not undertaken on any large scale, and the conclusions of the committee carried the sense of an act of faith rather than a disinterested weighing of possibilities.[4]

Throughout 1960 the move towards EEC membership became more pronounced, though it was still confined to departmental circles and to confidential discussions between ministers. At the Commonwealth Prime Ministers' Meeting in May there was only perfunctory and general discussion, British ministers apparently indicating that they thought negotiations with the Six were unlikely to be resumed for some time and that Britain might decide to give up its right to preferential treatment in the Commonwealth, 'doubtless pointing out that this would give the Commonwealth countries a useful counter for bargaining for better access for their own goods in the markets of the Community'.[5] As Reginald Maudling later made plain, the British again promised that in any future negotiations they would safeguard the arrangements for entry of Commonwealth food, drink, and tobacco in the UK

period of negotiation about EDC: 'I felt that I could not make him understand the depth and scope of my anxieties. He was always looking for a solution of the short-term problem—the rearmament of Germany and her admission to NATO. My eyes, rightly or wrongly, were fixed upon a more distant future—the organisation of Europe in the second half of the century, and the place which Britain and the Commonwealth should hold in a great design' (*Tides of fortune*, pp. 480–1).

[1] Well described in Nora Beloff, *The General says no* (1963), pp. 88–91.

[2] *Pointing the way*, p. 316. [3] Camps, pp. 280–1. [4] Private information.

[5] Camps, pp. 286–7. The 1960 Prime Ministers' Meeting was largely concerned with S. Africa (see ch. 8). The section of the communiqué on 'European trade problems' was brief. It 'expressed concern at the prospect of any economic division in Europe and its possible political implications', drew attention to Commonwealth countries' markets in Europe, called for adherence to GATT in European policies, and called on Europe to make its contribution to 'the economic development of the less advanced countries' (Mansergh, *Documents 1952–62*, p. 554).

market. Serious discussion with the Commonwealth countries on the implications of Britain's decision to join the Six did not begin until the autumn.

In the meantime, while Macmillan may well have decided to pursue membership of the EEC,[1] he continued to be concerned about how to go about it, and what damage it might do to the Commonwealth. On 1 August, when Duncan Sandys became Commonwealth secretary, Macmillan wrote to him pointing out the obvious problems and adding:

> Finally, there is the question that we would really be discriminating *against* the Commonwealth. I know how keen you are on the European Movement, as I have always been. I am not satisfied that there is not a way to be found [of] getting over the Commonwealth difficulty. If you could put your acute and active mind to the study of this you would be doing a great service. It is perhaps the most urgent problem in the Free World today.[2]

It was a week later, after a visit to Bonn in which he had canvassed ideas of modifying the EEC by enlarging Efta that he asked Sir Frank Lee's committee to consider in detail the various suggestions open to Britain, including entry into the EEC under conditions which retained the Commonwealth's share of the British market for non-industrial products. He told President Eisenhower that Britain had 'no clear plan', but that while there was 'some Commonwealth anxiety', this was confined for the moment to the technical matters which the Commonwealth finance ministers were to discuss in September.[3]

In their communiqué the finance ministers 'accepted that in any negotiations that take place the essential interests of Commonwealth countries should be safeguarded and full account taken of the continuing importance of intra-Commonwealth trade'. As Miriam Camps points out,[4] the change from the definite 'food, drink and tobacco' promise previously made, to the vaguer 'safeguard the essential interests of the Commonwealth'—a phrase which the British were henceforward to use time and again—was a considerable step. It released Britain from something very close to a contract and gave it much more room for manoeuvre: any judgement on these 'essential interests' would, in the last analysis, be made by the British government.

Whenever the actual decision to try for membership of the EEC was made, it was clearly a fact on 20 March 1961, when George Ball—in London on behalf of the recently inaugurated President Kennedy to discuss policy

---

[1] Camps, p. 282, says he had already agreed with the conclusion reached by Sir Frank Lee's committee. Lee read her book in draft, as well as a draft of my chapter in which her point on Macmillan was quoted. He raised no objection. Nora Beloff maintains that Macmillan made up his mind 'by Christmas 1960 when he took a few days off at Chequers. . . . It was then that he cast himself in the historic role of the man destined to carry Britain into Europe' (Beloff, p. 104). However, this appears to have been when he composed his 'Grand Design', some of which, reproduced in *Pointing the way*, pp. 323–6, implies that he may have hoped France and Germany might be persuaded to agree to arrangements which would not necessitate Britain's adhering to the Treaty of Rome as it stood.

[2] *Pointing the way*, p. 317.   [3] Ibid., pp. 321–2.

[4] Camps, pp. 317–18 for the extract from the communiqué also.

matters with the British government—was asked to meet Edward Heath, the Lord Privy Seal,[1] and some senior civil servants including Lee. He writes:

I detected in the atmosphere of the Heath meeting the glimmerings of something quite new. It was clear to me that Edward Heath, Sir Frank Lee and their colleagues had quite sincerely decided that Britain's interest was no longer in merely gaining a European beach-head from which she could frustrate efforts to build economic and political unity. They were now willing—and had said so at the meeting—to do a number of things they had up till then rejected: to embrace the idea of a common external tariff, to agree that joining the Common Market would include accepting its political institutions 'as a full member', to agree to all treaty provisions including those having nothing to do with tariffs, and to harmonize British agriculture with the general agricultural policy of the Community. . . . They identified [Britain's] future with that of Europe.[2]

Why had these men come to these conclusions—in particular, why had Conservative politicians and senior civil servants, usually the last men to change a long-held assumption, decided that Britain should seek entry into the EEC? The reasons were complex.[3]

Someone like Macmillan, whose main interest lay in political security for Britain and Europe alike, would put foremost the need to ensure that Europe was not economically divided in ways which would encourage political divisions and perhaps war. Britain needed to be closely involved in any permanent European structure, partly because the structure might otherwise work against British interests, and partly because, as the structure grew, the US would inevitably pay more attention to the 'European' than to the British point of view because of the EEC's concentration of economic and military strength. Britain's value to the Commonwealth countries, as a market and a source of development capital, would dwindle if Britain were not politically influential and could not maintain economic growth. If Britain did not get into the EEC, significant economic growth would be impossible. The speed of economic growth in the EEC countries, compared with the rest of Europe, and the greater rise in British exports to Western Europe than to other parts of the world, suggested that the key to British expansion lay in access to the markets of the Six. Conversely, Britain's growth would be sluggish or might stop if British goods were excluded from these markets by a high external tariff. If Britain were in the EEC, it would eventually have free access to a

---

[1] Heath had recently been given responsibility for European affairs. He was in charge of technical talks with the French, Germans, and Italians, which had recently begun.

[2] Ball, pp. 78–81.

[3] What follows in the text is a mélange of various sources, including the speeches of Macmillan and Heath, of which Macmillan's pamphlet, *Britain, the Commonwealth and Europe* (published by the Conservative Central Office in 1962 and containing the substance of his opening speech to the Commonwealth prime ministers in 1962) is one of the most significant. Use has also been made of *Britain and the European communities: background to the negotiations* (HMSO, 1962), the popular guide prepared for the government by the Information Division of the Treasury.

market of as many as 250 m. people (allowing for other countries joining too) which would enable it to concentrate on highly sophisticated, complex capital-intensive industries such as electronics and computers. There would be no reason to think that, with the rapid growth in living standards on the Continent, European industries could undercut British industries by means of cheap labour.

There were two other influences at work. The first was that US policy favoured British integration with Europe.[1] What George Ball said to Heath's meeting in March 1961, on being asked how the Kennedy administration would react if Britain applied for accession to the Rome Treaty, had to be taken seriously. He felt that British participation was an indispensable element of European stability, and that participation in Efta, which lacked 'political content' but involved economic discrimination against the US, was less acceptable to the US government than participation in the EEC, in spite of the economic discrimination which that too involved.[2] Such opinions were bound to impress a government led by a man like Macmillan, with considerable experience of the Americans, who saw no future in British attempts to ignore or belittle them. Macmillan's understanding of the new administration's views was further clarified when he visited Washington in April and Kennedy said he wanted Britain in the EEC for two reasons: economically the US thought it would be better to deal with one large group rather than with two groups; bargaining on tariffs and trade would be easier. Politically they hoped that Britain as a member would be able to steer and influence the Six.[3]

The second influence, harder to define, was that of 'Europeanism' in Britain itself. Here it is necessary to make a distinguish between 'Europeans' of the Monnet persuasion (of whom there were a number, often highly dedicated, but not a great many), and others moving in the same direction, who were vaguely dissatisfied with a purely British stage for national effort, who found the Commonwealth either boring or distasteful as a field of enterprise (often because of its imperialist past), and who thought that 'going into Europe' would be at least a change, and might prove to be exciting.[4] Elements of intellectual fashion and of reaction against established notions of national patriotism and the Commonwealth combined with a sense of malaise, of constriction and impatience, for many members of the articulate elite. One

[1] Sir John Crawford, permanent head of the Australian Dept of Trade up to 1960, makes the point that since 1956 Australia had, in Gatt, resisted those elements in the EEC's common agricultural policy which threatened American as well as Australian agricultural interests, but that, while 'the Americans also saw the threat to American exports . . . not until 1960 did they actively express concern. Up to that point the political importance to them of Franco-German unity in Europe overrode difficulties of this kind . . . Not until the Kennedy Round did Washington begin to take a really strong line on agricultural protectionism in Europe' (Crawford, p. 270).

[2] Ball, p. 79.   [3] *Pointing the way*, pp. 350–1.

[4] This point is developed further in my essay (pp. 27–45) in Coral Bell, ed., *Europe without Britain* (1963), leaning heavily on the symposia in *Encounter*, Dec 1962 & Jan 1963.

should not give too much weight to this; but one should not ignore it altogether. It provided a sympathetic intellectual climate for the British government's gradual conversion to the idea of entry into the EEC.

But as well as uncertainties about how the idea might be received by the farmers, the trade unions, and the Conservative Party, there was a major difficulty: 'the Commonwealth aspects of the question overshadowed all others, politically, economically, emotionally'.[1] Why should this have been so?

II

In the first place, British politicians' statements had themselves made the Commonwealth seem important to Britain. In March 1960, for example, Macmillan had spoken to the Central Council of the National Union of Conservative and Unionist Associations about the forthcoming Commonwealth Prime Ministers' Meeting, saying that after this meeting he would be going to summit talks. He went on: 'Americans and Russians have far greater wealth and strength but Britain will be able to speak—and I hope lead—not merely from her own position as a single island but as the centre of this great community'.[2] Allowing for some pardonable exaggeration suitable to the audience, this was the kind of statement which British politicians of both sides were accustomed to make in the 1950s and, with decreasing fervour, in the 1960s. The Commonwealth was, as well as something to be proud of, something useful. It added stature to Britain's international posture; it was also still in use as a decolonizing mechanism, whereby colonies approaching independence could be assured of membership of an international association of some prestige, and newly independent countries in Asia and Africa were kept informed about the decolonizing process.[3] Although it was not an economic unit, and did not provide the massive 'home market' which British industrialists were increasingly seeking in Europe, it did provide a number of important export markets for British goods. The combination of past habits, preferential arrangements, investment by British firms, wartime experience, and dollar-saving within the sterling area, had created for a time something close to a protected market abroad, even though British firms had not always been able to take advantage of it. Simply as a matter of British interest, in the sense of an area in which Britain had something of a privileged position, the Commonwealth could not be ignored.

The difficulty arose not in recognizing that the Commonwealth had been and might continue to be an area of importance to Britain but in satisfying the great variety of interests which the Commonwealth countries had acquired in

---

[1] Camps, p. 338.   [2] *The Times*, 19 Mar 1960.

[3] This is a reference to the fact that the British government was accustomed to report progress in colonial independence at each Commonwealth Prime Ministers' Meeting, and to ask the existing members to accept new ones when they were about to gain independence.

Britain. It was compounded by the fact that, diverse as were the interests in the British market of the Commonwealth members in, say, 1960, the colonial territories approaching independence added to the complexity of the situation. There was even one (Hong Kong) which no one expected to become independent, but which had done well out of free entry into the British market. And the difficulty was increased because the rights and interests of Commonwealth countries in Britain, which they could be expected tenaciously to uphold, were almost exclusively economic, bearing no relation to the political aims uppermost in the minds of those who directed British policy. Neither the textile manufacturers of India nor the wheat farmers of Australia could be expected to be concerned about whether Europe was divided or whether it could stand alongside the US and the Soviet Union; but they were intensely concerned about access to the British market. The Indian and Australian and other overseas Commonwealth governments would be bound to voice their anxieties and to take little account of the large but cloudy political possibilities envisaged by the British government. In the past Britain had acquired certain responsibilities towards the products of Commonwealth countries, for reasons which seemed good at the time. Now those responsibilities stood in the way of a smooth transition into the EEC.

It is worth considering briefly what the responsibilities were. First there was the preference system, a confusing and much misunderstood affair.[1] Some aspects of it dated from before the Ottawa Conference of 1932, but it was largely the outcome of the arrangements made then, and subsequently amended by agreement and by change of circumstance. There was no single system of preference (each formal preference was embodied in a bilateral agreement between Britain and the country in question), but, once established for any country, the same treatment was given to all other Commonwealth countries even if they had no trade agreement with Britain and did not give British goods preferential treatment over foreign goods or free entry.[2] Most Commonwealth products entered Britain duty-free, though some Commonwealth countries doubted the advantage which this practice gave them in competition with other suppliers; New Zealand, for example, after having been able to sell all its butter to Britain on bulk purchase from 1939 to 1954, found the going difficult afterwards on a basis of free entry and wanted protection against Denmark, Holland, and other European suppliers. In the main, however, it was only in such overcrowded fields as wheat, butter, wine, and fruits that Britain was called upon to provide either a clear preference margin or a system of quotas which would guarantee Commonwealth producers a part of the market.

[1] In what follows I am such indebted to COI, *Commonwealth preference*, which incorporates the results of studies of the 1961–2 situation which were not available at the time, and compares these with earlier studies.

[2] CRO *List 1964*, p. 153.

The most outstanding case was sugar. Under the Commonwealth Sugar Agreement (which ran until 1969 and so provided a breathing-space for Commonwealth sugar producers, whatever might happen about the EEC), Britain agreed to pay a price higher than the world price and guaranteed certain quotas to the Caribbean and East African Commonwealth countries, Australia, Fiji, and Mauritius. The quota arrangements for wheat and butter (and for meat) favoured Commonwealth producers. But in the main, Commonwealth producers relied upon the principle of free entry, although some of them had protested at times about the special advantages given to the British farmer.

Britain received no uniform treatment from overseas Commonwealth countries in return. There were certain preferential advantages for the British seller in the markets of Canada, Australia, and New Zealand, the Caribbean countries, Rhodesia, Ceylon, Cyprus, Malta, and Mauritius, but in Africa only Sierra Leone gave Britain any preference. India and Pakistan offered only very slight advantage. Between 1948 and 1961–2 margins of preference for British goods had not noticeably fallen in Canada, New Zealand, Ceylon, Cyprus, and Malta, but they had done so in Australia, India, Malaya, Rhodesia, and Hong Kong. It was the cautious conclusion of the Board of Trade in 1965 that 'a few years ago' (which would be roughly when the issue became important in relation to the EEC), 'the United Kingdom and the overseas Commonwealth Preference area as a whole, on roughly comparable values of trade, enjoyed preferential benefits of a similar order of magnitude'.[1] This kind of averaging, while necessary for any overall assessment, was not of much use in distinguishing between the position in different markets. In fact, Britain probably enjoyed much more preference in the New Zealand than in the Australian market, and more in that than in Indian or Pakistani markets.

Besides the advantages certain Commonwealth countries obtained through preference, bulk quotas, and free entry, there were at least two other advantages which might be threatened by the provisions of the Treaty of Rome. These were free access to the London money market, and Commonwealth citizens' rights to enter Britain freely to take jobs.[2] Taken altogether, the advantages which the Commonwealth countries enjoyed constituted an unwieldy package which, while it might be seen as a whole in Britain, took on a different shape in each overseas country, whether independent or still a colony.

In practice it was possible to sort these varying economic claims into five sections, each of which would have to be dealt with somehow if Britain was to redeem its promise to 'safeguard the essential interests of the Commonwealth'; for every country concerned was sure that its interests were essential.

First came the sugar interests. Until 1969 some acceptable arrangement

[1] Ibid., p. 10.
[2] This right was reduced but not destroyed by British legislation in 1962. See below, ch. 14.

could possibly have been worked out with the EEC countries, although the Commonwealth sugar suppliers were likely to be uneasy because some Caribbean and African sugar producers were EEC associates, who might increase their supplies to Europe on a preferential basis, and since Europe itself was a sugar producer with beet farmers who would be only too glad to increase production if they had a sheltered market and guaranteed prices.

Next were the Asian manufactures, including the textile and other labour-intensive manufactures of India and Pakistan and the industries of Hong Kong. The British market had been open to these on a basis which often annoyed British manufacturers but which, it was felt in London, enabled the Asian countries to establish their manufacturing industries more firmly by giving them the British market as a growth area, but since there were areas in Europe in which labour-intensive manufacture was still carried on, especially in textiles, it was unlikely that France and Italy would consent to free entry of products so clearly in competition with their own.

Third were the manufactures of the developed Commonwealth countries, Canada, Australia, and New Zealand, of which Canada's had gained a discernible footing in the British market. Each had heavily protected manufacturing industries, mainly concerned with supplying their home markets but sometimes able, because of local specialization, to compete successfully in Britain.[1] It was most unlikely that the Six would allow more than a temporary advantage for these products.

Fourth, and most difficult of all, were the temperate foodstuffs of Canada, Australia, and New Zealand, which were in direct competition with those grown in Western Europe, especially in France, which clearly hoped to increase production so as to supply any enlarged EEC. Canada was protected to some extent by the fact that hard wheat was not grown in Europe in any quantity, but Australia grew soft wheat, and there would be no difficulty in expanding European production at the right price. New Zealand lamb and Australian mutton were reasonably secure, because European producers and consumers were not interested in them, but beef was vulnerable. The greatest problem was dairy products. Western Europe was capable of producing a mountain of butter and cheese at any time, and seemed likely to do so. Even if the EEC were not enlarged further when Britain came in, French, Dutch, and German producers could provide enough to absorb the British market; and if Denmark and Ireland joined, as seemed likely, the prospects for butter and cheese from New Zealand, Australia, and Canada would be remote indeed.

Finally, there were tropical products other than sugar. Some of these, such as jute (vital to Pakistan) and rubber (vital to Malaya), were admitted duty-free into both Britain and the EEC and would retain their markets in any event. Tea, India's and Ceylon's main export to Britain, entered Britain free

[1] For example, the universal acceptability of Australian lawn bowls is something of which their manufacturers are justifiably proud.

but was subject to a duty in the EEC. None of these seemed likely to provide much difficulty, but it looked otherwise with copra, cocoa, and palm-oil, the main exports of the West African Commonwealth countries. These were in direct competition with the products of the former French and Belgian colonies in Africa. If preference had to be given to these former colonies, which already had associate status with the EEC, then Nigeria, Sierra Leone, and Ghana would suffer. The obvious solution was for them too to be granted associate status, but African politics had prejudiced Ghana and Nigeria against this solution. In their case an economic interest had been transformed into a political interest, which no amount of British negotiation with the Six could settle.[1]

The various positions taken by Commonwealth members will be made clearer when we come to the 1962 Prime Ministers' Meeting. In the meantime, we can see how essentially intractable the problem of 'the Commonwealth' was for the British government, if only because it was not one problem but many. Customary political rhetoric demanded that Britain continue to refer to 'the Commonwealth' as if it were a single entity. In some respects it was: all parts of it needed capital, all wanted markets, all had been accustomed to look to Britain for special favours. Yet each had gone about its business with Britain in a different way, corresponding to the circumstances of its own growth. None could be blamed if it saw 'Commonwealth interests' as overwhelmingly its own self-interests. There had been little complaint about this from Britain in the past. If the Commonwealth countries had been piecemeal in their demands, Britain had understandably been piecemeal in its responses.

III

We now turn to the history of the British application from the early part of 1961.[2] It should be remembered that, while a major part of the task of Macmillan, Heath, and their officials was to convince the Commonwealth countries that their interests would be safeguarded and the Six that these interests were worth considering, they also had to satisfy British opinion about the desirability of entering the EEC, and to reconcile the proposed new responsibilities with those in Efta. As well as the economic considerations which inevitably took first place in any detailed discussion, the government had to keep in mind the problems of closer political association, which were bound to be brought up by the Six at some stage. They would also be raised by the other parties involved, especially when these did not appear to be getting what they wanted on the economic front. Any negotiation would therefore be detailed, complex, and rife with misunderstanding.

[1] For a thoughtful and illuminating background to African opinion at this stage, see Mazrui, 'African attitudes to the European economic community', *Int. Aff.*, Jan 1963, pp. 24–36.
[2] See Camps, chs 10–14, and Beloff, pp. 104 ff.

Before asking parliament to approve an approach to the EEC, the government decided to send ministers to a number of Commonwealth countries in June and July 1961, in order to achieve whatever understanding was possible about their interests.[1] The ministers had a mixed reception.[2] Thorneycroft, in his visits to India, Pakistan, and Ceylon, seems to have had a fairly smooth passage, although the governments of the first two made it clear that they were concerned about the possible effects on their exports of manufactures. He encountered no difficulty in Malaya and Singapore. The communiqués of John Hare's visits to African capitals were short and gave little indication of opinion. In the West Indies (where the short-lived Federation was still in being) Lord Perth found a predictable response: there were specific West Indian interests which Britain would be expected to safeguard. The obvious (and in this case outstanding) difficulties were experienced by Duncan Sandys in New Zealand, Australia, and Canada, where he, as a convinced 'European' with a strong, thrusting personality, found himself fencing with ministers who were often just as thrusting and who were prepared to speak bluntly. This was especially true of Australia and Canada, where ministers faced early elections.

New Zealand ministers made it clear 'that they could not at present see any effective way of protecting New Zealand's vital interests other than by maintenance of unrestricted duty-free entry'. Sandys replied that it was difficult to reconcile this with the principles of the Rome Treaty, and that 'it might therefore be necessary in any negotiations to explore other methods of securing comparable outlets for New Zealand exports'. He also pointed out that the British market could not, in any case, absorb an increase in New Zealand agricultural production. The New Zealand ministers said they would have to reserve their position but, in response to assurances that they would be consulted before any negotiations and that Britain 'would not feel able to join the EEC' unless 'special arrangements to protect the vital interests of New Zealand' were secured, they said they would understand it if, after considering the views of Commonwealth countries, the British government should open negotiations. This was as much as—perhaps more than—could have been expected from them.

Moving to Canberra, however, Sandys confronted a government in which

[1] For further study of Commonwealth interests, the following books will be helpful: Crawford, *Australian trade policy*, and H. G. Gelber, *Australia, Britain and the EEC 1961 to 1963* (1966) for Australia; Lyon, *Canada in world affairs 1961–3* (1968); Dharma Kumar, *India and the European economic community* (1966); P. N. C. Okigbo, *Africa and the common market* (1967), esp. for Nigeria. Tom Soper, *Commonwealth and common market* (1962), is a useful contemporary Fabian pamphlet. Asghar H. Bilgrami, *Britain, the Commonwealth and the European union issue* (1961), attempts to cover the whole range. Pierre Uri, ed., *From Commonwealth to common market* (1968) is better.

[2] The various communiqués issued after these visits are collected in Cmnd 1449 (July 1961), from which any quotations here are made. See also Mansergh, *Documents 1952–62*, pp. 634–45.

the prime minister, Menzies, had the gravest doubts about the political consequences of joining the EEC, and his deputy, John McEwen, who was both
minister for trade and leader of the Country Party, had the clearest and most
pessimistic view of how entry would affect Australian farmers. The Australian
ministers, in stating that they did not object to Britain's applying (Sandys
made it plain that he had not asked them to express an opinion on whether
Britain should apply), flatly 'made it clear that the absence of objection should
in the circumstances not be interpreted as implying approval'. They also
stressed that 'Australia should be in a position to negotiate direct on Australia's
behalf when details and arrangements affecting items of Australian trade were
being discussed'. No other country made this point.

In Ottawa Sandys found the Diefenbaker government in a state of gloom,
occasioned partly by the disturbance to Canadian exports which British entry
into the EEC would create and partly by the recognition that the end of free
entry into the British market would prevent further expansion of those Canadian manufacturing industries which had been built up under protection and
which, it was thought, could not effectively compete in US markets. Diefenbaker's government had inherited a tradition which was both protectionist and
imperialist. The British proposal struck at both elements simultaneously. The
communiqué on this occasion was bleaker and gave less detail than either of
the other two.

The Canadian Ministers indicated that their Government's assessment of the
situation was different from that put forward by Mr Sandys. They expressed the
grave concern of the Canadian government about the implications of possible
negotiations between Britain and the EEC, and about the political and economic
effects which British membership . . . would have on Canada and on the Commonwealth as a whole.

Sandys could reply only that Commonwealth governments' views would
be carefully considered before a decision was taken. In this case, as in the
others, the point was made that the British government had not yet made a
decision.

Whether it had or not seems to be a fine distinction since, in spite of the
resistance which Sandys had encountered, the last of his communiqués with
Commonwealth governments on 14 July was followed, on 31 July, by Macmillan's announcement to the House of Commons that the government had
decided to make a formal application. The motion carried by the House on
3 August said this was 'to see if satisfactory arrangements can be made to meet
the special interests of the United Kingdom, of the Commonwealth and of the
European Free Trade Association'; and the House accepted the undertaking
of HMG that 'no agreement affecting these special interests or involving
British sovereignty will be entered into until it has been approved by this
House after full consultation with other Commonwealth countries, by

whatever procedure they may generally agree'.[1] The prime minister's speeches contained the customary obeisances to Commonwealth consultation.[2]

The British application was soon under way. In October Heath would make his opening statement in the negotiations at the EEC headquarters in Brussels. There was, however, still another shot in the locker of those Commonwealth countries which wished to register their dislike of what Britain proposed to do. It was fired at the Commonwealth Economic Consultative Council meeting at Accra in September. These meetings had always previously produced communiqués in which the virtues of correct economic behaviour were hymned in terms sufficiently general to satisfy all concerned. This time, apparently at the instigation of the Canadian delegation, but certainly with the support of India, Australia, and the host country, Ghana, the British government was faced with the embarrassment of widespread disapproval.[3] The communiqué recorded that, after British representatives explained why the application was being made, 'all other Commonwealth representatives expressed grave apprehension and concern regarding the possible results'. There was reference to imperilling the Commonwealth relationship and weakening its cohesion; there was doubt whether 'the United Kingdom with its other international and domestic obligations could possibly secure in the proposed negotiations an agreement which would protect Commonwealth interests adequately and effectively'.[4]

In general, the Commonwealth sky was clouded for the British government; and it was not improved when Canadian representatives, consulted when the government was assembling its brief for the Brussels negotiations, 'were instructed not to give any indication of priorities but rather to insist that all . . . existing interests be fully protected'.[5] A further storm in a Canadian teacup, when Heath's opening statement at Brussels on 10 October was not officially released to Commonwealth governments, made things no better.[6]

One must not, however, overemphasize the difficulty which Commonwealth opposition created. It had more awkwardness than force. From a British standpoint, the cries of anguish from Ottawa and Canberra in particular seemed very much responses to the demands of minority interests, and to have a strong electoral aspect. Similarly the African objections to association arose from political circumstances, and might not carry much substance if those circumstances changed. It was unhelpful for Diefenbaker and McEwen to seem to want every conceivable interest satisfied before giving any benediction to British entry, but it was not a complete impediment. In practice, the parties to the argument recognized that all Commonwealth interests could not be satisfied, that most Commonwealth countries did not have alternative patrons

[1] *Britain & the European communities*, p. 3.
[2] See Mansergh, *Documents 1952–62*, pp. 645–50.   [3] See Peyton V. Lyon, pp. 448–52.
[4] Mansergh, *Documents 1952–62*, pp. 650–1.   [5] Peyton V. Lyon, p. 452.
[6] Ibid., pp. 454–5. See Mansergh, *Documents 1952–62*, pp. 651–6 for a debate in the House of Commons on this matter.

from whom they could get the same kind of treatment as from Britain, and that, in consequence, Britain would have the critical voice in deciding what was the best package of concessions to be obtained for Commonwealth producers. The dangers, from the government's standpoint, were of two kinds. In the first place, the multiplicity of Commonwealth interests demanded that all should be considered at some stage, even if it was clear that not all could be satisfied. This meant that the negotiations would be protracted, and that Britain, forced to operate on such an extended front, might not be able to deploy effectively its most potent arguments against the resistance of the Six— arguments about the attractions of the British market for the EEC producers. Secondly, there was the danger that Commonwealth demands, while being received sceptically in British governmental circles, might carry more influence with the British people, particularly with the rank and file of the Conservative Party.

Heath's speech at Brussels[1] devoted considerable space to the Common-wealth. He began this section by stressing the great importance of Common-wealth trade in maintaining the Commonwealth association, and the likelihood that the EEC would not wish either to disrupt Commonwealth members' trade or incur their hostility if their interests suffered. There were analogies with the situation when the Rome Treaty was being negotiated: 'your prob-lems concerned a considerable number of countries which were in varying constitutional relationships with members of the Community'. These problems had been settled without damaging the interests of those countries, through two alternative solutions: by giving them continued access to the market of the country with which they had previously been connected (as for Morocco and Tunisia in the case of France), or by giving them full association and thereby gaining 'a preferential position for their products in the Common Market as a whole'. Commonwealth trade was more extensive perhaps, but not too much so: '36 per cent of our imports come from the Commonwealth; but I think I am correct in saying that over 20 per cent of metropolitan France's imports come from territories having a special relationship with her'. Heath went on to suggest that either association as it was being newly worked out[2] or arrange-ments—as in the case of Morocco, Tunisia, and Surinam—whereby access to the UK market would continue, would meet the needs of most tropical countries involved. He suggested that it might also be desirable to proceed commodity by commodity, and brought up some of the hard cases already

[1] Although made on 10 October, and widely summarized immediately afterwards, the full text of the speech did not appear in the press until 28 November (see *The Times* of that date), and was then published as a White Paper (Cmnd 1565, from which quotations here come). This was a classic case of the unwisdom of not releasing publicly a statement which was bound to be the subject of gossip and to arouse unnecessary fears. In fact, when released it was seen to be both skilful and aware of Commonwealth interests.

[2] Arrangements for association under Part IV of the Treaty of Rome were at this stage being revised in company with associated territories.

mentioned. He suggested zero levels for the EEC tariffs on commodities such as tea (vital to India and Ceylon) and cocoa (vital to Ghana), and for certain materials—aluminium, wood pulp, newsprint, lead, and zinc—which were important to Canada, and, in the last two cases, to Australia. On manufactures from the old dominions Heath was cautious, but indicated the need to avoid the creation of reverse preferences (as he pointed out, the Community had not created a tariff in respect of any commodity from any country connected with one of its members where none existed before). He gave special attention to the problem of manufactures from l.d.c.s, especially in Asia, saying, 'you will probably agree that it would not be in the general interest that the United Kingdom should erect fresh tariff barriers to cut back such trade'.

On temperate foodstuffs, after indicating the magnitude of the problem, particularly for New Zealand and Australia, he called for a principle of 'comparable outlets' in the operation of the EEC's common agricultural policy which was still in the making. Duty-free, levy-free, or preferential quotas, market-sharing agreements, and long-term contracts were possibilities mentioned; but he did not apply these to particular items, clearly hoping that the field for negotiation would be left open so that his team could produce arguments relating to each one. The Commonwealth Sugar Agreement was buttressed by mention of its being recognized in the International Sugar Agreement, but no further proposals were made on sugar.

Negotiations now began.[1] They were long and involved; since Britain had other things to worry about besides Commonwealth interests, and since the negotiations were necessarily private and depended so much on considerations additional to the matters actually being discussed—e.g. the relations between the Six themselves, the developments in their own politics, the influence of their overseas associates, the interest taken by the US, the problem of political union, the internal politics of Britain and changes in its own economic position—not much reliable information became public. Straightforward negotiation was in any case made difficult by the fact that the Six were still discussing details of the common agricultural policy and their conditions of association with former African colonies which had become independent since the Rome Treaty was signed.

Some strain arose from the position of Britain as negotiator on its own behalf and on behalf of Commonwealth countries. Some of these maintained their own special delegations in Brussels during the discussions, but the only one to demand a special position at the negotiating table was Australia, to which this right was given on certain matters. The Canadian government was reluctant to say what it regarded as most important, presumably lest this cause its other interests to be disregarded. New Zealand made its position clear to all and

---

[1] See, for more information, Camps, ch. 11, Gelber, chs 6 & 7, and, for agricultural problems, Michael Butterwick & Edmund Neville Rolfe, Food, farming and the common market (1968), pp. 73–9.

seems to have elicited most sympathy from the Six. Its diplomacy was especially persuasive, but since its problems were those of direct competition with European farmers in fields in which New Zealand farmers were generally more efficient, it had a hard case to present. Australia was the busiest of the Commonwealth countries, seeking solutions not only in Brussels but also in Washington. In regard to wheat, in particular, it tried simultaneously to secure concessions from Britain and the Six and some sort of international arrangement which would bring together world producers and consumers. But as with other temperate products, it confronted a series of interdependent relationships which meant that solutions had to benefit the farmers of the Six if they were to be received favourably there, had to stabilize the Commonwealth producers' existing position if they were to be popular there, and had to take account of the position of producers who were neither of the Six nor of the Commonwealth. Pierre Uri put the dilemma succinctly:

To preserve free entry into Great Britain is to deny the Common Market producers the outlets upon which they count, and is diametrically opposed to the Common Agricultural Policy. . . . To eliminate protection is to effect a sudden reversal, to the benefit of Europe, of the preferences enjoyed by the Commonwealth. To give sales guarantees to Commonwealth products is to establish a preference system unacceptable to the United States. . . . In the context of the present agricultural policies the problem seems insoluble.[1]

As stories of disappointment at Brussels became current, and pressure grew from Commonwealth members, a Prime Ministers' Meetings was announced for September 1962. At this it was hoped that the terms of Britain's possible entry into the EEC might be discussed. Although the British government, anxious for speed and for an acceptable package to produce at this meeting, increased its efforts in Brussels, the best it could manage was an interim set of conclusions, many of them indefinite, arrived at with ministers of the Six in August.[2] Some matters were fairly clear. It was agreed that existing dependencies, 'with certain possible exceptions', would be able to become associates under Part IV of the Treaty of Rome. It was also agreed that such association would be suitable for African and Caribbean Commonwealth members prepared to have it; if they did not agree, alternative arrangements would be discussed. With India, Pakistan, and Ceylon, the enlarged EEC would seek 'to negotiate comprehensive trade agreements . . . at the latest by the end of 1966'. Meanwhile tea would be given a nil tariff and, while cotton textiles would not continue indefinitely to enter Britain freely, the Common External Tariff would be applied to them in stages, and if this meant a decline in exports to the Community (measured on at least the 1959–60 basis), the situation would be restored. Other manufactures from these countries would also receive a

[1] *Le Monde*, 20 Jan 1962 (quoted in Gelber, pp. 155–6).
[2] To be found in Cmnd 1805, from which quotations here are taken.

staged application of the tariff until 1970. Earlier, arrangements had been worked out for manufactured goods from Australia, Canada, and New Zealand to have a similarly staged application up to 1970. Although received with distress by Australia and New Zealand—which seem to have regarded the arrangement less as one in its own right than as a precedent for staging operations for their other products—these terms looked reasonably generous.

As expected, temperate foodstuffs were the main trouble. The enlarged Community would be the biggest market in the world for food; the EEC ministers were prepared to agree that the policy it intended to pursue would offer reasonable opportunities in its markets for imports of temperate foodstuffs. They pinned their faith in world-wide agreements which it was hoped to negotiate; in the meantime there would be 'an intra-Community preference', which 'in the case of cereals . . . would not lead to sudden and considerable alterations in trade patterns'. They did give specific consideration to New Zealand and recognized its difficulties, expressing readiness to consider special provisions to deal with them, but went no further.

IV

Thus, when the prime ministers began to assemble in London for the meeting that was to begin on 10 September, none could be sure that he had got what he wanted, and some had got either nothing or something so vague as to constitute no promise at all. Moreover the meeting received more public attention in Britain than usual, because of the relevance of the issue to the arguments in and between the British political parties. The Labour Party, after some hesitation, was now pursuing a line of general scepticism, signalized by the fact that its leader, Hugh Gaitskell, had his own Commonwealth conference just before the official one began. It consisted of representatives of Labour and Socialist parties from several member states, including Australia and New Zealand, and leaders (sometimes chief ministers) from colonies such as Barbados, Uganda, Mauritius, and Singapore. The communiqué of the meeting published on the opening morning, said that, on the basis of the agreements quoted earlier, 'great damage would inevitably be done to many countries in the Commonwealth and therefore to the unity of the Commonwealth itself'. The essence of the complaint (one which Australian ministers had already made) was that 'while there appears to be a firm commitment to end Commonwealth preferences not later than 1970, and to give European exports a preference in Britain against the Commonwealth, no precise agreements which offer compensating advantages to Commonwealth countries have been reached'; and it called for 'precise agreements' before Britain entered the EEC. Particular attention was given to Commonwealth l.d.c.s, but temperate foodstuffs were not forgotten. According to George Brown, then deputy leader of the Labour Party, the influence upon Gaitskell of Walter Nash of New

Zealand was considerable and made things more difficult for those Labour men supporting entry.[1]

The Prime Ministers' Meeting was notable in several ways. One was that in its committee stages, dealing with particular aspects of the problem, representatives were present from several of the affected colonial territories, especially those, like Kenya, Uganda, Singapore, and British Guiana, which were near to independence. It was perhaps unfortunate that the leaders of these countries should experience, at their first such meeting (and the first for Sierra Leone, Tanganyika, Jamaica, and Trinidad as sovereign states), not only a measure of disagreement, but, more important, a degree of disclosure greater than usual at these meetings.[2] Clearly economic matters, especially trade, bring out divisions and the explicit expression of national interests (both the 1932 and 1952 Economic Conferences had been notable in this respect), but in 1962 the situation was more extreme than before. This time it hinged on whether Britain should transfer certain privileges in its market from the Commonwealth to 'foreigners'. *The Times*, nervous but benign on the opening day, made the point that 'in criticizing any Commonwealth Prime Minister's attitude in the next few days it will be necessary to remember that the price of his being a voice in London at all is that he shall remain in power at home'. It found something to sympathize with in most Commonwealth objections but found the African countries 'wholly irrational'. It was firmly opposed to the Diefenbaker and Gaitskell view that the prime ministers should meet again to give a final verdict when the EEC position was clearer. 'This week's meeting must be enough for the Commonwealth as a whole . . . a week hence the grand forum of the Commonwealth must pronounce a general blessing on Britain's going into Europe, or withhold it.'[3]

In fact, the grand forum did neither. The positions taken by the representatives varied considerably. A few were pleased with what had already been agreed with the EEC. Trinidad and Malaysia were in favour; Sierra Leone, while not wishing to express approval of the status of association opposed by its two West African neighbours, Ghana and Nigeria, seemed likely to accept. Cyprus, a European country, could apply for a different, less contentious, form of association. The Federation of Rhodesia and Nyasaland, which had not as yet been offered anything, was expansive about the benefits of association. These, however, were all comparative light-weights. The crucial

---

[1] *The Times*, 10 Sept 1962; George Brown, p. 217.

[2] The *Guardian* correspondent, Patrick Keatley, who was very experienced in these matters, wrote: 'Perhaps in the perspective of history, this London 1962 conference will be seen as the moment when the Commonwealth nations abandoned the fading fiction of partnership—in economic affairs—and recognised the brutal fact that they had become sovereign rivals. Certainly, this conference has seen the end of references to "mutual consultation", and a frank acceptance that all the weapons of standard international diplomacy had to be brought into play: the inspired report, the leaked text, the backstage *quid pro quo*' (*Guardian*, 19 Sept 1962).

[3] Editorial, 'Striking the Balance', *The Times*, 10 Sept 1962.

opposition came from what some journalists called the 'tough five'—Canada, Australia, New Zealand, India, and Pakistan. For once Nehru, in spite of his anti-colonialism and non-alignment, was yoked with Menzies.

To understand the positions taken by these five one must remember that all were fully aware of the negotiations which had been going on about their exports to Britain, and all knew, in fair detail, what the Six were likely to concede, as distinct from what they had publicly stated. Officials as well as ministers from the major Commonwealth countries had been in frequent consultation with their British counterparts, and in some cases with their counterparts on the continent. Each knew, moreover, that the British government wanted to enter the EEC, and that, whatever it might say in public, there was little likelihood that it would reject entry simply on Commonwealth grounds.[1] Britain's task was to get the best bargain it could for Commonwealth interests; but the application was a British application, and must be judged finally on how it would affect Britain. On the economic side, then, the prime ministers of the 'tough five' knew that they could gain little by the new proposals at the meeting. They may well have felt, however, that a show of resistance there would strengthen the hand of the British in the negotiations, especially if the French and others were being recalcitrant about Commonwealth issues. The problem was how far to go: if Commonwealth demands looked petty and unreasonable, they would be heavily discounted; if they were not pressed, they might be regarded as unimportant. There were also, of course, broad political considerations. Although Britain's entry into the EEC would not cancel its membership of the Commonwealth, the Commonwealth would not be the same if privileges in the British market were withdrawn. Often in the past, these had been cited as solid evidence of the advantages of the Commonwealth bond. If they were removed, the Commonwealth would not be the same.

Faced with these problems, which must have occurred to them in different guises but which obviously mattered to all of them, the leaders of the five responded in two broad ways.[2] Holyoake and President Ayub stuck closely to their economic briefs, which were clear-cut in each case: New Zealand's whole economy, said Holyoake, 'rests on the products of two animals—the sheep and the cow'; Ayub concentrated on the arrangements about manufactures which had been announced the month before, and suggested how they might be improved. The one was driving home the tragic plight which New Zealand

[1] The predominant feeling of most delegations was summed up by Sir Alexander Bustamente, the prime minister of Jamaica, as he stood on the steps of Marlborough House after one of the sessions: 'Whatever anyone says, Britain is going to join. There is no need for a multiplicity of words. They're bound to join, whatever we say' (*Guardian*, 12 Sept 1962).

[2] All five spoke on the second day of the conference. Their speeches were reported in considerable detail (see e.g. *FT*, 12 Sept 1962, where Ayub's and Holyoake's texts were said to have been issued officially, while Nehru's and Diefenbaker's came from 'unofficial sources'; the Ghana representative, who also spoke, issued an official text).

might suffer, the other attending to a matter of business. In both cases the economic approach was the more suitable.

The other three—Nehru, Diefenbaker, and Menzies—preferred to stress broad politics. Although India's material interests in the matter were very close to Pakistan's (as detailed discussions later in the week made clear), it was not in Nehru's nature to descend to economic detail alone. While mentioning what was proposed for exports of tea and cricket bats, he said he thought Britain's entry would build up new tensions by hampering the development of the poorer countries; the EEC was animated by the 'old colonial concepts', not entirely, but to a very great extent. He did not see how the Commonwealth could survive unless a very radical change were made in the proposals.

Diefenbaker also questioned whether the Commonwealth links would remain strong, since Britain might not be able to retain her world influence as a member of the EEC. Canada, in particular, would find it harder to withstand US magnetism if this were so. He was prepared to put forward alternatives to British entry, but only if the meeting wished him to do so; and he annoyed some of the British ministers through pointed references to what some of them, notably Maudling, had said earlier about the indispensability of the free entry of Commonwealth products into Britain. He envisaged a further Prime Ministers' Meeting.

Menzies was somewhere in between these two, but he also gave most emphasis to the political side. His reactions were significant for the British government, since he alone amongst the Commonwealth prime ministers was a figure of importance to British Conservatives. Holyoake, while approved of, was normally dismissed as provincial, and Diefenbaker, while extolled by the Beaverbrook press, was something of a figure of fun, when not an irritant. But Menzies typified for many Conservatives the sort of 'loyalty' which they expected of Commonwealth countries. As in his earlier speeches in Australia,[1] he said that the supranational character of the EEC implied some sort of federation of Europe in which Britain could hardly expect to exercise the same freedom of action—notably in regard to the Commonwealth—as existed now. Besides the political price to be paid for British entry, there was an economic price which, like the other, was still not fully known. Menzies did not object in principle to Britain's entry, but he could not be expected to approve the conditions of entry. 'You would not expect us,' he said, 'in a matter so full of implications for us—and many of them as yet unresolved—to pronounce a general benediction.' He also explained some of Australia's particular problems. His speech pointed to the need for further consultation, though he did not positively request another meeting.

Thus India, Pakistan, Canada, Australia, and New Zealand had all made it

[1] Menzies's speeches on the EEC question, which were amongst the most thoughtful and (in this writer's view) the most interesting he has made, will be found in *CN*, 32/7 & 8, 33/8 & 10.

plain that they disliked the terms for British entry. Speaking directly to the British ministers present, but indirectly to their own peoples and to the British electorate, they were saying that Britain was not only neglecting their interests but also endangering the existence of the Commonwealth. Yet they were not offering significant alternatives. Diefenbaker's, when it came, proved to be nothing more than that universal refuge, a world conference of Commonwealth countries, members of the EEC and Efta, the US and Japan and other countries 'to give consideration to how to deal with the trading problems before us in a way which will be to the mutual advantage of all'. This should pave the way for non-discriminatory tariff negotiations on a most-favoured-nation basis. Canada would be most willing and honoured to be host country.[1] This intervention was considered by many 'anti-climactic as well as inconsequential',[2] but no one else had anything better to offer, and the final communiqué was anodyne: it propounded good international trading practice in broad terms, explained the concessions the Six were prepared to make, but did not pronounce a benediction on the British application for entry. The other representatives 'took note' of why Britain had made it and recognized that Britain must make the final decision. The needs of the various members were rehearsed, and the cohesion of the Commonwealth was commended. No demand was made for a further meeting.[3] It was, in general, a victory for Macmillan, who soon afterwards secured another victory—more positive and even more important—at the Conservative Party conference.

It had been an unusual but revealing Prime Ministers' Meeting, clearly showing how the British government wished to lead and how the other governments wished neither to follow nor to lead but to influence. Twice during the week *The Times* reported that 'according to British observers, Commonwealth delegations have still not made any distinction between their "vital interests" and more marginal points of trade',[4] implying that Britain knew these vital interests better than the countries to which they were supposed to apply. Some of them, especially the smaller ones, had very clear ideas of their interests;[5] the bigger ones, as we have seen, had larger and often vaguer interests to consider, and easily slipped into the position of putting forward what seemed like fiddling and particularist arguments of a sort which, if taken seriously, were likely to hinder the swift exposition of the British case at Brussels. But it was clear that none of them had a viable alternative to offer Britain other than the status quo, which Britain was not prepared to accept. The Commonwealth was not an economic unit, and no one was

---

[1] Quoted in Peyton V. Lyon, p. 469.   [2] Ibid.

[3] The communiqué (Cmnd 1836) is in Mansergh, *Documents 1952–62*, pp. 656–60.

[4] 15 Sept 1962; see also 13 Sept.

[5] e.g. Dr Eric Williams, the prime minister of Trinidad, who welcomed association: 'The Commonwealth is a collection of independent sovereign states which can't take our goods and won't take our people. Australia only admits cricketers and Canada only admits domestic servants' (ibid., 13 Sept 1962).

prepared to take (or even to formulate) the drastic steps required to make it one.

The problem of association for the African members, which was a major political issue in itself, did not make the same impact on British public opinion as the obvious economic problems of temperate foodstuffs or the ominous statements about the destruction of the cohesion of the Commonwealth. The issue was an awkward one, but not insoluble. The two West African states concerned, Ghana and Nigeria, made their positions clear at the meeting. Though the arguments of both came to the same conclusion, the rejection of associated status, they were different in expression and in their likely outcome. Ghana rejected the idea outright on the ground that it would perpetuate Africa's 'colonial' economic status.[1] Sir Abubakar Tafawa Balewa of Nigeria concentrated on searching questions about what would happen to the sterling area and to Commonwealth privileges in the London money market after Britain joined the EEC. He showed no hostility to the Community as such, and indicated that Nigeria would be satisfied if it could obtain free entry into the enlarged common market for its produce.[2] In this he foreshadowed Nigeria's later conclusion of a special agreement with the EEC. The issue of association was, in fact, one which existed less between Britain and the African Commonwealth members than between some of those members and the new francophone states of Africa; it was an outcome of tensions and rivalries in the new pan-African organizations, and in due course was settled by new alignments there. Although it seemed to bulk large as a Commonwealth issue in 1962, it caused little trouble later.

V

Negotiations with the Six continued in Brussels up to the end of 1962. On 14 January next year de Gaulle held the famous press conference at which he pronounced that Britain was not yet a fit candidate for membership. He emphasized the dissimilarity of its economy to those of the Six; he also rejected the Anglo-American Nassau agreement providing for the supply of Polaris missiles to Britain within the framework of Nato.[3] On 29 January the French foreign minister moved the indefinite adjournment of the Brussels negotiations. A chapter was closed. Its summation, so far as Commonwealth questions were concerned, was made by the EEC Commission, in a frank and informative report to the European parliament, which showed that agreement had been near with Britain on some additional points of detail but that temperate foodstuffs were still a stumbling-block, and New Zealand butter

[1] Nkrumah did not attend the meeting, but sent his finance minister. An impressive document outlining Nkrumah's opposition is in RIIA, *Documents 1961*, pp. 179–82.

[2] *The Times*, 13 Sept 1962.

[3] See Kitzinger, *ECM & C*, pp. 182–91 for the text of the statement.

continued to be what an earlier Australian statesman had called, in another context, a lion in the path.[1] The British government, taking the view that the negotiations had broken down 'not because they were going to fail but because they were going to succeed',[2] reserved its policy for the future.

VI

Four years later Britain made a second effort to enter the EEC.[3] Between January 1963, when the French vetoed the first attempt, and May 1967, when the second was made, conditions had changed in several important respects. The EEC had continued to consolidate its organization and to dismantle its internal tariffs, but this had had no obviously detrimental effect on the economy of Britain, which continued to increase its trade with Western Europe, a result partly attributable to a general lowering of industrial tariffs through Gatt. Most Commonwealth countries too had increased their trade with Europe, although there had been a general decline in Commonwealth trade measured in percentage terms. In general terms, the Commonwealth countries occupied a decreasing proportion of Britain's exports and imports, and Britain's place in their trade was also declining. The reasons for these changes lay largely in the rapidly increasing capacity of the industrial countries of North America, Western and Eastern Europe, and Japan to absorb imports and to seek out markets for their sophisticated goods. Britain shared in this general rise in prosperity and found that, while other developed countries were often successful competitors against it, they were also suitable markets for many British products.

There had been important political changes. US pressure on Britain to join the EEC had relaxed with the death of Kennedy, the concentration of his successor's administration on Asia, especially Vietnam, and the continued rejection by France of the idea of integration. The EEC itself had suffered genuine crises, often as a result of French intransigence;[4] although its most ardent supporters still thought in terms of eventual political union, the idea was receding, partly because of the Gaullist insistence on national sovereignty, but largely because the Six, while gaining significant benefits from their mutual lowering of barriers, continued to be highly nationalistic in their social lives and in the ultimate protection of their national interests. The EEC had become more like an ordinary international organization; the notion of 'integration'

[1] See EEC Commission, *Report to the European parliament on the state of the negotiations with the UK* (1963), ch. 2.

[2] From Macmillan's broadcast, 30 January 1963 (*CS*, 12 Feb 1963, p. 169). See ibid., p. 167, for Heath's account of how the negotiations ended, and pp. 217–18 for a report of the subsequent parliamentary debate.

[3] Commentary and documents on this will be found in Kitzinger, *The second try* (1968). See also Uri.

[4] See Camps, *What kind of Europe?* (1965) for some of these.

became less significant as the postwar conditions which had created it receded.

There had also been political changes in Britain. Whereas the Labour Party in opposition under Gaitskell had become steadily more opposed to membership of the EEC—Gaitskell declaring that it would mean the end of 1,000 years of history, a repudiation of Britain's Commonwealth ties—Labour in power under Wilson sang a different tune. The kinds of economic considerations which had weighed with Macmillan's government, especially in respect of Britain's plight if it was unable to exploit an expanding market within the EEC, now weighed more heavily with Labour. Debates in the Parliamentary Labour Party in 1967 'were vigorous and well-informed, but much less passionate than those of 1962', according to Wilson.[1]

Thus Wilson's domestic position was easier in 1967 than Macmillan's in 1961. The Commonwealth too seemed less of an obstacle. This was partly because of decreasing British esteem for it—largely on account of the African events described in Part III—but also because the Commonwealth countries were less pressing in their demands. The difference in the African situation was especially striking. Nigeria had, in 1966, concluded a special treaty of association with the EEC, under which it would operate reverse preferences against Britain. Kenya, Uganda, and Tanzania had begun long-drawn-out negotiations to a similar end; Ghana had shaken off Nkrumah's leadership and was no longer either the opponent of the francophone African states or the apostle of African unity. In addition, the EEC had itself negotiated (in 1964) a new arrangement with its associated states (the Yaoundé Convention) which, in the changed circumstances of Africa, looked less liable to the charge of neo-colonialism than the original arrangements. For African and Caribbean Commonwealth members, in spite of the increase in their numbers, the way to association seemed much simpler.

Canada and Australia had moved from the positions which they had taken earlier. New Zealand, though still very much concerned about the future of its exports if Britain entered the EEC, had become more reconciled to the idea of entry. In Canada Diefenbaker had been succeeded by Pearson, who had strenuously opposed the Diefenbaker line during 1961 and 1962.[2] The traditions of the Canadian Liberals differed from those of the Conservatives; they were less opposed to economic dependence on the US and their leader gave much more emphasis than had Diefenbaker to the benefits to be obtained from British entry by Europe and the world as a whole.

In Australia there had been no change of government (except for the retirement of Menzies) and McEwen was still minister for trade; but in the meanwhile there had been a substantial shift in Australian exports, with minerals becoming much more important, and with new markets opening up in Japan and elsewhere for exports of food which previously had relied upon

---

[1] Wilson, *Labour government*, p. 338. The same was not to be true in 1971.
[2] See Peyton V. Lyon, pp. 444, 456, & 473.

the British market. With the departure of Menzies no one left in the government had the same devotion to a Crown Commonwealth ideal or such a desire to preserve the Commonwealth. Indeed, Sir Robert himself had been saddened by recent events in the Commonwealth, and wished to see the old dominions and Britain come to some economic arrangement with the US.[1] The continued expansion of the Australian population and economy, the discovery of new trading outlets, and the awareness that the EEC, while regarding New Zealand's plight as genuine, had little sympathy with any attempt to equate Australia with it, all served to make Australia less demanding than a few years earlier. The prime minister, Harold Holt, and McEwen, both warned that Australia's interests could be imperilled if Britain entered the EEC on conditions like those which had seemed likely in 1963;[2] but although McEwen made the homely point that 'a good sale of iron ore to Japan does not help the dairy industry if that industry loses the market that is so predominantly important', and Holt said that, while the proportion of Australian exports going to Britain had declined, the total value had actually increased in money terms, neither seemed unduly worried. Holt's main concern, in fact, seemed to be not trade but access to the London capital market.

New Zealand's position was still recognized as difficult by Britain and the EEC. When George Brown gave a full conspectus of the British case to the Council of Western European Union in July 1967,[3] New Zealand and sugar were the two Commonwealth issues which he treated as basic, in contrast to the multitude which Heath had put forward six years before. New Zealand had been safeguarded to some extent by a recent trade agreement, which guaranteed the free entry into Britain of meat and cheese till September 1972, together with a quota of at least 170,000 tons of butter a year.[4] Similarly, the Commonwealth Sugar Agreement was set to run until the end of 1974.[5] In both these cases, while Commonwealth interests were protected for the time being, the products in question represented those in which the EEC was or was likely to be in surplus, and for which its members would want to get as much of the British market as they could.

In spite of some diversification of exports since the previous attempt, New Zealand still depended to a great extent on the British market and would need special consideration; this the EEC was prepared to give, as before, but there was no agreement about what it should be. New Zealand public opinion had, however, been greatly affected by Britain's previous application. No longer was Britain regarded as a reliable partner. If one can say that a nation had lost its innocence, this had happened to New Zealand in 1961 and 1962. There-

---

[1] See Kitzinger, *Second try*, pp. 157–61 for extracts from Sir Robert's Ditchley Foundation Lecture, 28 July 1967, in which these points are made.

[2] See *CN*, 38/5, pp. 191–4 for their statements.

[3] See Kitzinger, *Second try*, pp. 189–200.   [4] *Survey B & CA*, 18 Aug 1967, p. 848.

[5] Kitzinger, *Second Try*, pp. 237–8, for the existing situation for both Britain and the Six in respect of both sugar and butter.

after all organs of opinion had steadfastly emphasized the need to diversify, to seek new outlets in Asia, to press for world schemes of food disposal, to come to terms with competing industries in the case of Australia, and to find whatever common ground could be worked out with Europe.[1] In rather the same way India and Pakistan had been trying to settle their less urgent problems by negotiating directly with the EEC after 1963, and had already been granted certain concessions.[2] Their governments were no longer in the same state of indignation as at the earlier stage.

Conditions thus seemed propitious for a second try. The British government made it; the EEC Commission approvingly appraised the consequences; but again de Gaulle exercised a veto.[3] This time he had nothing to say about the malign influence of the US but concentrated on the instability of the British economy—especially in respect of sterling—and the great difficulty of bringing it into line with the established practices of the Community. He glanced at 'the increasingly centrifugal trends that are appearing in the Commonwealth', and stressed the difficulty of reconciling Britain's imports of food from it with the agricultural policy of the Community. He was prepared to consider association but not membership. This the British government turned down; it wanted to be a full member or nothing, since only as a full member could Britain help to shape future Community policy.

New Zealand and the sugar producers could breathe again, but only for a short time; by the end of 1969 President de Gaulle had gone, and Britain was preparing yet again to try for membership. The election in 1970 of a Conservative government, led by Heath, Britain's chief negotiator at Brussels in 1961, was soon followed by a resumption of negotiations where the Labour government had left off. In spite of strenuous debate in the country and in parliament, and a near-split in the Labour Party, terms were agreed with the EEC in June 1971 and by parliament on 28 October; the Treaty of Accession was signed on 22 January 1972. The problem of New Zealand, which had been the one remaining Commonwealth difficulty of major proportions, appeared to have been solved through a relaxation of previous EEC attitudes.

In the White Paper setting out the government's reasons for joining, and explaining the terms, there was something of an obituary for previous anxieties about the Commonwealth.[4] It said that the Commonwealth did not by itself offer or wish to offer Britain alternative and comparable opportunities to membership of the EEC. Commonwealth countries were widely scattered and differed widely in political ideas and economic development, and with the

---

[1] Although, on the face of things, it might seem far fetched, since New Zealand was in direct competition with EEC farmers, some common ground could be found in the fact that the EEC Commission wished to reduce European production of food by eliminating the smaller and less efficient farmers over a period; this might then leave room for imports from the far more efficient New Zealand dairy farmers. See Sicco Mansholt, *Agriculture 1980—New Zealand and the EEC* (1969).

[2] Kitzinger, *Second try*, p. 289.   [3] Ibid., pp. 311–17.   [4] Cmnd 4715 (1971).

attainment of independence their political and economic relations with the UK had greatly changed and were still changing. They were developing trade and investment arrangements with other countries and the UK's share of Commonwealth trade had declined sharply: in absolute terms its exports to the Commonwealth had grown only slowly, whereas exports to the EEC had grown much more rapidly and in 1970 exceeded those of the whole of the Commonwealth. Moreover the EEC increasingly seemed a more attractive trading partner than the UK for many Commonwealth countries; it was significant that those in East Africa had given the Community trade preferences over the UK.

The White Paper went on to deny that membership of the EEC would mean that Britain would become increasingly 'inward-looking' and would trade and invest only with other members. It also denied that British aid would lessen; 'the aid given to the poorer nations by our European neighbours is proportionately greater than ours, and the Community has been the first of the major aid donors to introduce a generalised preference scheme . . .'. But much of it was devoted to aspects of British domestic change which membership would involve and which played a prominent part in the discussions of the following year, especially in the British Labour Party, which had now become officially opposed to entry on the terms obtained. Commonwealth questions became much less significant in the British debate.

VII

To some extent, the urge to 'enter Europe' represented a conscious turning away from the Commonwealth on the part of large sections of the British elite. One's broad impression is that this urge was not felt to the same degree by the man in the street: successive public opinion polls failed to produce a substantial majority of British people in favour of the change. For the elites in government, business, politics, and the press, however, the urge was strong. It sprang partly from disappointment in the Commonwealth, partly from the feeling that there was no effective alternative to membership of the EEC.

Wilson writes[1] of the 'well-documented choices before us' in 1967: 'entry, or those attractive sisters, NAFTA and GITA'. Nafta (North Atlantic Free Trade Area) was a scheme for joining the US and Canada with Efta, and perhaps later with Australia and New Zealand. Wilson's cabinet agreed that this was an unreal choice, because of US (and Australian) protectionism. Gita ('go it alone') was, they thought, 'not so much a constructive alternative as a fall-back if entry were denied to us'; but 'in or out of the Community we must be strong'. He does not mention any Commonwealth alternative. Perhaps his experiences of 1965–6 (see ch. 12) had convinced him that Commonwealth countries would not respond. It is more likely that, like so many other British

---

[1] *Labour government*, p. 388.

people, he had now given up the Commonwealth as a basis for constructive initiative. Britain appeared to need the Commonwealth less and less since the major Commonwealth countries showed less interest in Britain; at the same time the European economy seemed to become steadily more attractive for large-scale British activity, while Britain's sense of its political responsibilities was contracting to a European span.

Such a view was not accepted by many opponents of British entry,[1] but its constant reiteration meant its wider acceptance in Britain and in the Commonwealth countries: increasingly the weight of opinion there shifted in the 1960s to the belief that it was useless to try to stop the British from doing what they were determined to do. By 1967 most Commonwealth members were either preoccupied elsewhere or had lost much of their former intensity of feeling. Even Nkrumah before his deposition is said to have been making discreet soundings for some associate status with the EEC.[2] A number of countries which had formerly not been sure of their interests now knew them better.[3] It was only the hard cases—New Zealand in particular—that still thought the matter vital.

The applications to join the EEC did not mean that Britain was giving up the Commonwealth as an area of economic concern. British leaders said they believed that the Commonwealth would not suffer materially by Britain's entry, but would, if anything, benefit in the long run because of the increased prosperity which Britain was expected to enjoy and the increased influence which it would wield. Both of these, it was argued, would work to the advantage of Commonwealth countries. The annoyance which British ministers had evidently felt with Diefenbaker's and McEwen's approach was that it seemed to emphasize short-run and neglect the longer-run considerations. It was such feelings that led to the comments that the Commonwealth countries did not seem to know what their own vital interests were.

Even so, the importance of the EEC lay in Britain's turning away from the open sea towards the narrow seas. De Gaulle had said in his 1963 press conference that Britain was 'insular, maritime, linked through its trade, markets and food supply to very diverse and often very distant countries'.[4] The British applications were assertions that, while this had been true in the past, it would not be the dominant theme in the future. They represented a distinct choice, with decisive implications for the Commonwealth countries. The greatest shock was experienced by New Zealand, to which the British

[1] See e.g. William Pickles, *Britain and Europe—how much has changed?* (1967), and Leonard Beaton & others, *No tame or minor role* (1963).

[2] W. Scott Thompson, p. 363.

[3] See Okigbo, pp. 94–5, for an acute comment on the problem for newly independent countries of deciding their own interests (as distinct from the colonial powers', which previously had dominated discussion in such matters as trade and finance).

[4] Regrettably, the president said this was true of 'England', but the context shows that he meant 'Britain', which he used immediately afterwards.

market was still vital and in which British sentiment was still uppermost. For New Zealand in great degree, and for others in less, Britain's attempt to enter the EEC meant the end of an often implied economic determinism in Commonwealth affairs—the assumption that the Commonwealth automatically involved some kind of mutual economic benefit.[1]

[1] By June 1972 the New Zealand prime minister was openly talking about joint 'bargaining-off' of British preferences by New Zealand and Australia, in return for advantages for their own products: both would like to bargain for Japanese preferences for their primary products (*Canberra Times*, 22 June 1972).

CHAPTER 14

COMMONWEALTH IMMIGRATION

IN 1953 Britain was the only Commonwealth member which allowed un-hindered entry to citizens of all Commonwealth countries and colonies, permitted them to settle permanently without asking any questions, and gave them immediate citizen rights. Their status was sharply different from that of aliens, not only in the right to vote but also in respect of employment. The British Nationality Act of 1948 put in formal terms the existing equation between 'British subject' and 'Commonwealth citizen'. This equation was observed at the point of entry into Britain, as well as when entrants had settled. For a long time it had been a matter of pride to British people and to successive British governments that Commonwealth people could come and go freely. They did so, leaving behind some residue of seamen, scholars, and professional people, although they mainly stayed a while for study, experience, business, and pleasure, and then went home. It was widely felt that the practice encour-aged Commonwealth unity. Certainly, people in the old dominions and in such places as the West Indies valued free entry. The image of Britain as a 'mother country' depended upon it to a considerable extent: a mother who shuts the door is no mother.

The situation began to alter in the early 1950s, with the beginnings of sustained migration from the West Indies.[1] This, which was mainly due to shortage of labour in Britain, increased markedly after the McCarran-Walter Act of 1952 restricted West Indian immigration into the US. Except for special arrangements in Barbados, this new immigration was not directed towards particular jobs available in Britain: people came because it was known that there were opportunities in an expanding British economy, and the West Indian islands were stagnant. Roughly half came from Jamaica. Later in the 1950s the stream of West Indians was joined by streams from India and Pakistan. The immigration from the subcontinent was largely limited to people from clearly-defined areas, including the Punjab and Gujarat in India (four-fifths of the Indian immigrants being Sikhs), and Mirpur and Sylhet in

---

[1] A vast literature has grown up on Commonwealth immigrants in Britain. A short compre-hensive summary is Clifford Hill, *Immigration and integration* (1970). The publications of the Inst. of Race Relations include J. A. G. Griffith & others, *Coloured immigrants in Britain* (1960); Ceri Peach, *West Indian migration to Britain* (1968); R. B. Davison, *Commonwealth immigrants* (1964), Sheila Patterson, *Immigration and race relations in Britain 1960–7* (1969); E. J. B. Rose, ed., *Colour and citizenship* (1969); and an abridgement of this, Nicholas Deakin & others, *Colour, citizenship and British society* (1970). Two books by Paul Foot, *Immigration and race in British politics* (1965) and *The rise of Enoch Powell* (1969), while tendentious, are useful for knowledge of how political opposition to immigration developed.

Pakistan.[1] In these cases 'chain migration' was the norm: over a period of time, a single village or district might send scores or hundreds of people to settle in Britain, the earlier ones sometimes helping to provide finance, jobs, and accommodation for the later arrivals. Many of the Pakistanis, in particular, could not speak English. Immigration from India and Pakistan, in contrast with that from the West Indies, was at first overwhelmingly male.

These Commonwealth immigrants settled in London and the great industrial towns such as Birmingham, Bradford, Leeds, and the Black Country. They filled jobs for which labour was short in times of full employment, especially in transport and hospitals, and a variety of unskilled or less skilled jobs in factories. Their growing numbers put extra strain on housing: often the only houses available were those discarded by the British working classes when moving on to council estates. Like earlier groups of immigrants in other countries and in Britain itself, they were crowded into decaying areas near city centres. Their different social customs tended to excite comment and opposition. Their colour made them stand out from the grey, misty, raincoated mass which is the working class of an English industrial town. As time went on, their children began to cause problems for the educational and welfare services. Social contacts were troublesome when the migrants moved in to pubs and other places where they were unwelcome; in those Indian and Pakistani cases where no social contact at all was established, because of the language barrier and the immigrants' habit of associating only with one another, further local grievances built up.

The British governmental system was not equipped to deal with the problems of large-scale immigration. Indeed, from 1951, when a small welfare department in the Colonial Office was closed down, to 1965, no government department or agency was directly or solely responsible for immigrant welfare or integration, although some officials served on the committees of voluntary bodies.[2] To the extent that the problems of adjustment were not regarded as the task of the various High Commissions and their colonial equivalents, they were the responsibility of local government. Local authorities were given no special finance to deal with problems in the crucial areas of housing and education, and they were not encouraged to treat immigrants differently from British-born citizens. The Macmillan government was notable for its lack of action on any front during its first five years. It resisted the early suggestions from some MP's that immigration should be restricted; at the same time it failed to give any lead, or any money, to the local authorities which were experiencing the local tensions but could do little or nothing about them. A

---

[1] See Deakin, ch. 3.

[2] Patterson, p. 29. Jamaica organized help for its migrants to Britain as early as 1955, its organization later being taken over by the Federation of the West Indies during its short life, after which the individual governments continued the work. Indian and Pakistani High Commissions established similar activities.

major problem of social tension and public opinion was developing, but no official attempt was made to tackle it. Why?

Apart from the immense difficulties involved in making any change at all in the relations and responsibilities of central and local government, and the fading possibility that the problem might not last, there were Commonwealth considerations. It seems likely that discussion within the government centred on the control of entry of intending immigrants, even as early as 1957. According to Patricia Hornsby-Smith, then parliamentary under-secretary at the Home Office, writing in the context of a possible Bill to control immigration:

> The Home Office was at pains to point out the increasing numbers arriving and the inevitable social consequences arising from demands on housing and education, together with the overburdening concentration in limited areas. At that time, we were in the throes of several constitutional moves to grant independence and the most vehement opponents who, on then perfectly justifiable political grounds, were the then Commonwealth and Colonial Ministers, felt that any such Bill would sour our negotiations with various African powers. In the case of Kenya, it would have precipitated the anti-Asiatic moves now apparent . . .[1]

In 1958, when there was something of a recession in Britain, and immigrants from India and Pakistan were often the first to lose their jobs, arrangements were made with the Indian and Pakistani governments for voluntary restriction of emigration, whereby passports were issued only to those who could prove that a job was waiting for them, and high sureties were demanded.[2] These restrictions were readily evaded when employment rose again in Britain: agents were available to provide false passports and journeys through Europe. In any case, legal arrivals naturally increased when jobs were available.

In 1961 the government at last took action. Restriction of further immigration rather than expansion of immigrant welfare in Britain, was the action chosen. 'By 1961', writes R. A. Butler, then home secretary, 'I was persuaded that the rise of racial tension could be avoided only if it were anticipated. This in essence was the argument for the Commonwealth Immigrants Bill which controlled entry by a system of labour permits that in practice approximately halved the rate of net immigration.' He points out that a Gallup Poll in the summer of 1961 showed 67 per cent of British people in favour of some restriction, and only 21 per cent for the continuation of unrestricted entry.[3] In 1962, despite vehement Labour opposition and troubled sentiments expressed by editorialists and liberals of all parties, the Bill became law.[4] It did not alter citizenship rights once Commonwealth citizens had entered Britain, but restricted entry to those who were students or visitors, or had a work voucher

---

[1] From a letter dated 22 April 1969 to Paul Foot (*Rise of Enoch Powell*, p. 33).

[2] Griffith & others, p. 12.   [3] Butler, pp. 205–6.

[4] Extracts from the parliamentary debate, and the text of the Act itself, are in Mansergh, *Documents 1952–62*, pp. 727–37 & 741–7. For useful summaries of this and other legislation, see Hill, pp. 11–24.

from the Ministry of Labour, or were dependants of those entering or already in the country. It applied to people from all the colonies and Commonwealth countries, but since it had been occasioned by an influx of coloured immigrants, it was widely attacked as discriminatory.

The Labour government elected in 1964 (when opposition to coloured immigration was voiced in a number of constituencies) imposed further restrictions by administrative action announced in a White Paper of August 1965.[1] At the same time it tried to deal with problems of integration through a National Committee for Commonwealth Immigrants, and through a Race Relations Act, aimed at eliminating racial discrimination. Some months earlier a mission under Lord Mountbatten had gone to a number of Commonwealth countries—India, Pakistan, Jamaica, Trinidad, Malta, Nigeria, Cyprus, and Canada—to discuss means of reducing evasion and of regulating the flow of immigrants to Britain.[2] By this time both major parties were committed to continuing restrictions on Commonwealth immigration, although immigration from the Republic of Ireland—the biggest single source—remained unchecked because of the difficulties of border control.

Thus far, the British government's restrictions had been occasioned by the private acts of Commonwealth citizens, not by the actions of Commonwealth governments. In February 1968, however, a further step was taken because of the Kenya government's policy of replacing locally employed Asians (i.e. people of Indian descent) by Africans, where the Asians had not registered as Kenya citizens. The previous Conservative government had made provision in the Kenya independence settlement for these Asians to be able to opt for Kenya citizenship or retain their former UK and colonies (i.e. British) citizenship. As discriminatory measures increased in Kenya, those with British citizenship moved in greater numbers to Britain. In the three months ending January 1968, 7,000 arrived—more than in the whole of 1966. The Kenya Asians were a group limited in number and more readily assimilable in Britain than most immigrants from India and Pakistan since their level of education, skill, and wealth was generally higher. Nevertheless, in the atmosphere of the time they constituted a problem for public opinion in Britain, especially since there would probably be similar moves from Uganda, and the number of people theoretically capable of entering Britain freely under existing legislation, because they had a right to British passports, was said to approach 1 million.

Wilson says his cabinet was evenly divided on whether to apply special restrictions, and sent Malcolm MacDonald to try to find a solution through discussions with Kenyatta; but it soon decided on a Bill to limit work vouchers

---

[1] Cmnd 2739 (1965).

[2] Ibid., p. 5. Mountbatten's report was never published. This was widely taken to mean that most of the governments he saw were not prepared to take the responsibility of regulating the flow. His main task was probably to prepare the overseas governments for the changes to come.

for East African Asians to 1,500 a year and to withdraw the right of free entry of people with British passports whose parents or grandparents had not been born there.[1]

Although the Bill was passed, it posed, in a way, even more disturbing questions than the legislation of 1962. This time, the British parliament had been asked to restrict the entry of Commonwealth people who actually held British passports. It was true that they had gained these through tortuous processes involved in the independence of Commonwealth members with mixed and divergent populations; it was also true that the people in question had few links with Britain other than their education in English. None the less, their rights to British passports had been deliberately affirmed by the British government; now, only a few years later, the understood implications of those rights were being explicitly denied by the British government. In the minds of many, both Britain and the Commonwealth were brought into disrepute.

Over the period of these British measures, there were protests from the Commonwealth governments most concerned, although other members usually preferred to treat the matter as one of British domestic jurisdiction. Their own restrictive practices were the best reason why this should be so. The Jamaican prime minister and leader of the Opposition protested strongly to the British government in 1961, as did the prime minister of the Federation of the West Indies.[2] Since neither Jamaica nor the Federation was technically independent at the time, and did not attend meetings of Commonwealth prime ministers, these were perhaps not 'Commonwealth' protests, although in the context of the Bill to restrict immigration they certainly were. The Indian government, in a Lok Sabha debate of 4 December 1961,[3] stated that, while it was 'against illiterate or semi-literate Indians going to the United Kingdom or to any other country in search of employment', it considered there was a possibility of the proposed legislation 'rendering the position of a Commonwealth citizen even worse than that of citizens of non-Commonwealth countries'. It might also result in discrimination between the various member countries of the Commonwealth on the basis of colour. President Ayub of Pakistan said the Bill had damaged Britain's psychological advantage as the basis of the Commonwealth.[4]

At the 1965 Prime Ministers' Meeting the immigration issue was raised by Eric Williams of Trinidad and Donald Sangster of Jamaica, in spite of Wilson's efforts to keep the question outside the meeting by talking to prime ministers individually about the Mountbatten mission and the possibility of wider

[1] *Survey B & CA*, 15 Mar 1968, pp. 245–51, and Wilson, *Labour government*, pp. 504–5. In 1971 the Heath government put through an Act which brought Commonwealth citizens and aliens under a single system of control for the first time, particularly in respect of work permits. A 'right of abode' was established, giving free entry to Commonwealth citizens with a parent born in Britain. See *Survey of Current Affairs*, Mar 1971, pp. 146–50 & Dec 1971, pp. 613–14.
[2] *The Times*, 14 Oct & 18 Nov 1961.
[3] Mansergh, *Documents 1952–62*, pp. 738–40. [4] *Dawn*, 23 Nov 1961.

voluntary controls. It was reported that each of the countries in question (which included Cyprus and Malta in addition to Jamaica, Trinidad, India, and Pakistan) was likely to resist any such suggestion.[1] Williams explained afterwards to his parliament that the immigration issue involved, in addition to these countries, the smaller Caribbean countries and Nigeria, besides to a lesser extent Trinidad and Tobago. It also involved

two points of principle which Trinidad and Tobago and Jamaica insisted on including in the Conference record: the first, that in respect of job opportunities in the United Kingdom, Commonwealth citizens should have priority over aliens; the second, that in respect of any controls to be imposed, considerations of race and colour should be avoided. And yet, in the context of a conference in which the United Kingdom announced new procedures in respect of economic aid to developing countries, it was argued that migration was not a Commonwealth matter.[2]

In a conference attended by Sir Robert Menzies, it is not surprising that the latter point should have been made.[3] The context in which the results of Williams's and Sangster's intervention appeared in the communiqué was that of recognition by the meeting 'that the extent of immigration into Britain was entirely a matter for the British Government to determine'. The 'two points of principle' were put in terms of a hope, and of a welcome to an assurance from the British prime minister.[4]

The 1968 legislation led to even greater dispute. *The Times* considered that if it did not break the Commonwealth 'probably nothing will'. It was causing more offence than even the withdrawal from east of Suez. Britain was not only in hot and probably prolonged dispute with Kenya, Uganda, India, and Pakistan over it, 'but is widely accused of racial discrimination of the sort that forced South Africa out of the Commonwealth and which underlines the Rhodesian rebellion'.[5] So far as Kenya and Uganda were concerned, the offence arose because the British government asked for relaxation of the policies which were causing the accelerated emigration. It got no satisfaction, being told that these were the business of the local governments, and that it was Britain's business to look after those who were not local citizens. With India and Pakistan, it arose because their governments introduced visa requirements for Asians coming from Kenya. From a British standpoint, it was obviously desirable that people of Indian stock should go to India rather than Britain, whatever sort of passport they held, but India held out for a substantial increase in the numbers Britain was prepared to take. India could do little in negotiation with Kenya, and Indian wrath was publicly expended on Britain rather than on the government which had created the immediate difficulty for Asians.[6] In the end, after

---

[1] *DT*, 23 June 1965.   [2] Text provided by Trinidad High Commission, London.

[3] He had, it seems, strongly opposed any discussion of Australian immigration policy at the previous meeting in 1964. See *Sunday Telegraph*, 31 May 1964.

[4] *CS*, 6 July 1965, p. 623.   [5] Editorial 'Commonwealth Home Truths', 1 Mar 1968.

[6] *The Times*, 7 Mar; *Christian Science Monitor*, 18 Mar 1968.

much negotiation, the British and Indian governments agreed on a formula which would enable any Kenyan Asian with a British passport who was compelled to leave Kenya to choose whether to come to Britain or India. If he chose India, the British government would promise that he could come to Britain in future if he wished. In this way the Indian contention about ultimate British responsibility was satisfied, while the way was cleared for those who wished to go to India.[1]

By the next Prime Ministers' Meeting, in January 1969, Zambia and Uganda had joined Kenya in putting heavy pressure on Asians without local citizenship to vacate particular sorts of jobs—especially in trading—in favour of Africans. The British government appears to have favoured some general approach to the problem, which would involve others than itself in some responsibility for uprooted Asians, but it got nowhere. The African governments, after initial hesitation, refused to take part in general talks unless the British government unequivocally accepted responsibility for all their non-citizens. India was cautious about any general principles, although it continued to accept Asians who came from Kenya under the 1968 agreement with Britain. The Pakistani delegate suggested measures which would safeguard his people in both Britain and the African countries, but to little obvious effect. The Australian government abstained from the discussions, although the New Zealand and Canadian delegations took part. The upshot was that the communiqué recorded a request by 'some Commonwealth countries' to the secretary-general to examine in consultation with them 'general principles relating to short and long term movement of people between their countries and to consider the possibility of exploring ways and means of studying this subject on a continuing basis with a view to providing relevant information'. This looked like a bureaucratic way of saying 'do little or nothing'; and so it proved.[2]

To what extent the social tensions arising from Commonwealth immigration contributed to British disillusion with the Commonwealth is impossible to determine. One may perhaps be pardoned for thinking that it had much to do with the process. The constant use of the word 'Commonwealth' to describe people who were a source of dispute must presumably have had some effect. It can hardly have been a good one. Here was 'the Commonwealth', it was widely said, taking unfair advantage of privileges granted by Britain, and thereby causing social tension in Britain itself. Yet even if we admit that the effect on British public opinion was bad, we should still need, in order to

[1] *The Times*, 27 July 1968. For a helpful view of the actual situation in East Africa, see Anirudha Gupta, 'The Asians in East Africa', *Int. Stud.*, Jan 1969.

[2] *The Times*, 9, 10, 11, 13, 14, 15 Jan 1969; and Cmnd 3919 (1969), para. 38. This appears to have been the last prime ministers' communiqué printed as a British White Paper. The secretary-general's *Third Report*, presented to the Heads of Governments Meeting at Singapore in January 1971, showed that no more than a questionnaire had been issued, and not all members had replied to it (p. 6).

estimate the effect, to decide how much of the general lowering of Common-wealth prestige was due to the immigrant question and how much to such issues of policy as the EEC, Rhodesia, and 'east of Suez', each of which was prominent at the same time.

What is singular about the immigrant question, in contrast with the other issues, is that it affected the broad mass of the British people, whereas the other issues, while capable of capturing headlines in the newspapers, were essentially matters of high policy, the implications of which were not easily grasped by many men and women in the street. The presence of coloured people in a working-class neighbourhood was concrete, constant, and personal. It was essentially a domestic happening, whatever implications it might have of the kind described by Patricia Hornsby-Smith. It could kindle a different and more dangerous kind of political feeling from the other issues presented here. The very difference of this feeling, its alien quality so far as the normal give and take of British politics were concerned, troubled and even frightened the men who had to make high policy. Racial conflict was the last thing they wanted. At the same time they were reluctant to turn upside down many of the conventions of government in Britain in order to take the action necessary to render a multiracial society peaceable and productive. In the outcome, they chose restriction, whatever effect it might have on liberal opinion at home or Commonwealth opinion abroad.

If there were troublesome effects abroad, they were at least confined to a relatively small number of Commonwealth countries, although the number increased with time. West Indian migration, which caused difficulty in the first place, might have spent itself without British restrictions, since by the end of the 1960s opportunities had been re-established in the US and Canada, a more traditional and closer area for West Indian migration, and the flow was in that direction. Relations between Britain and the Caribbean countries might have been better if there had been no restrictions and the flow had, in time, turned elsewhere, but they would still have been adversely affected by West Indian fears of the consequences if Britain joined the EEC and by the lack of substantial British economic aid. India and Pakistan cannot have been greatly affected by the imposition of British restrictions, since the numbers involved were, in their terms, small, and they had already consented to voluntary restrictions. To their governments, the Sino-Indian and Indo-Pakistani wars must have had far more influence on their views of the Commonwealth. The East African countries and Zambia, while indignant about the British refusal to take all the local Asians they exported, had more serious things to think about in Rhodesia.

What damage, then, was done to the sense of Commonwealth by British restrictions on Commonwealth entry? Both in Britain and abroad, the main damage was to the conception of Britain as the one country which was colour-blind in its policies. Before the 1962 Act no one could say Britain was racialist;

afterwards it was widely said, even if it was only partly true. For people in Britain to whom the ideal of multiracialism was important what was most wounding was the discovery that many other British people were not prepared to regard coloured people, from the Commonwealth or anywhere else, as acceptable fellow citizens. For people from the overseas Commonwealth countries to whom Britain was the fount of culture and the deviser of institutions, there was sometimes distress that they could no longer enter Britain as of right. While this disappointment was most acute in the old dominions, it was also notable in such divergent places as Singapore and Nigeria, Ceylon and Tanzania. Some of those who could claim a common culture, through their knowledge of the English language and their admiration for British institutions, felt they were no longer so welcome at the source. It was not a large deprivation, especially in the light of the restrictions already practised by the overseas members, but it was a deprivation all the same.

Some violence was done to the susceptibilities of those people from the old dominions to whom the notion of 'British' as an all-embracing concept had not become alien. While there may not have been so many of these in Canada, there were still a great many in Australia and New Zealand. At first the immigration legislation seemed to threaten the institution of the 'working holiday', whereby people from these countries came to Britain in hundreds of thousands and stayed for a few years, earning their living and travelling in Europe the while. The British government attended to this problem.[1] But it could not eliminate the feeling of many from the old dominions that a right had been withdrawn for no good reason, and that, in any case, they were more deserving of free entry than the Irish. A sense of identification was certainly affected.[2]

The immigration question displayed, in miniature, a number of the themes of change in the Commonwealth from 1953 onwards. It showed how much less of a unity the Commonwealth had become, and how national interests had been sharpened in Britain's case as much as in that of any other member. It showed how British policy and opinion about the Commonwealth could change under the stress of circumstances. It showed how plastic were conceptions of the Commonwealth, especially in racial terms. What it did not show was any power of Commonwealth machinery to deal with such a problem. Migration, with its concrete social effects, proved to be less suited to multilateral discussion than larger issues of international policy.

There will continue to be argument about whether Britain was right to choose the policy it did. Given the state of public opinion in 1962, which demanded some restriction, any other policy would have been difficult to

---

[1] See Patterson, pp. 65–7.

[2] In February 1971 the new Agent-General for Tasmania arrived in Britain and was given the right to only a six-month stay, according to the stamp in his passport. The British government apologized publicly to him in October (*Canberra Times*, 29 Oct 1971). There are few more British places than Tasmania. It had had an Agent-General in London since 1886. He had not been treated like this before.

justify. At the same time dominant opinion amongst the articulate elite demanded that, if there was to be restriction, it must be non-discriminatory, i.e. it must apply to all Commonwealth countries and not only to some of them. If this latter condition had not obtained, other possibilities might have been open, such as a frankly racialist restriction of coloured people, or bilateral arrangements with particular Commonwealth countries, or financial and language tests, or some version of the 'patriality' which the British government inserted (and had to amend) in its 1971 Act. These latter possibilities, if adopted, would have prevented some of the distress and annoyance which arose in the old dominions, but at a price which the British government would not have been prepared to pay—the price of an indictment on grounds of racialism which would have had serious effects at home and abroad. In the upshot, the British restrictions proved to be less indictable on racial grounds than those of other white countries in the Commonwealth.

CHAPTER 15

CHANGES IN THE BRITISH APPROACH

I

A VERY experienced American, George Ball, writing in 1967, said of Britain since World War II:

... the contrast between her accepted position and the power she could command injected ambiguity into British policy. Every postwar government from Attlee's to Harold Wilson's has been unsure of England's real place in the world. What was Great Britain in the mid-twentieth century? Was she: (1) the industrial third "great power", (2) the leader of the Commonwealth, (3) a major European nation, (4) America's special partner, or (5) the West's "honest broker" with Moscow? Some of these roles were mutually contradictory, yet governments were tempted to try to play them all at the same time—and as a result they often stumbled over their own feet.[1]

This was to some extent an echo of Dean Acheson's much-quoted pronouncement in 1962 when, remarking that Britain had lost an empire but had not yet found a role, he noted that:

The attempt to play a separate power role—that is, a role apart from Europe, a role based on a "special relationship" with the United States, a role based on being the head of a "Commonwealth" which has no political structure, or unity, or strength and enjoys a fragile and precarious economic relationship by means of the sterling area and preferences in the British market—this role is about to be played out.

He believed that Britain, 'attempting to work alone and to be a broker between the United States and Russia', had seemed to conduct a policy as weak as its military power.[2] Both these comments excited some resentment in Britain when they were made, but they were broadly true.

It is difficult to be sure of constant factors in the foreign policy of a country under such different governments as those of Churchill, Eden, Macmillan, Douglas-Home, and Wilson, especially when one must also cast a forward look at the Heath government of 1970. But throughout the whole period certain aspects of the situation remained prominent. Britain was leading its colonies towards independence, now slowly, now quickly, but always in the same

---

[1] Ball, p. 72. See also ibid., ch. 7, 'The disadvantages of the special relationship', in which Ball indicates why he thinks US policy was wrong in prolonging special consideration for British interests.

[2] *The Times*, 6 Dec 1962.

direction, in spite of such difficulties as arose in Kenya, Cyprus, and Aden. The British economy was continually troubled by balance-of-payments problems: even when the balance was right, the memory of the past crises and the possibility of future ones worried prime ministers. All governments strove to maintain something of a 'special relationship' with the US, as shown by the concern over its fracture at Suez, by Macmillan's and Wilson's desire to be on special terms with Presidents Eisenhower, Kennedy, and Johnson, and by Britain's readiness to engage Indonesia during confrontation, thus marking out Britain's sphere of operations in Southeast Asia as parallel to the US involvement in Vietnam.

At the same time all tried to display some independence from the US, or at any rate some special separate role which the US could not play, as in the continuance of diplomatic relations with communist China, Macmillan's and Wilson's overtures to the Soviet Union, Wilson's Vietnam initiatives, and Eden's espousal of Indian views on Indo-China. It was not easy. All attempted, also, to exert some leadership in Western Europe, even though Churchill and Eden rejected organic union. There was not a total change, but rather a change of emphasis when Macmillan decided on entry into the EEC: it meant turning Britain's back on the open sea, but the back was already half-turned by Britain's heavy involvement in Nato and constant activity in OEEC and other European institutions.

Two statements from Macmillan's memoirs of his premiership from 1959 to 1961 will illustrate both the continuity of British official thinking and the dilemmas to which Acheson and Ball had drawn attention. Of the situation early in 1959, he wrote that despite the superior military strength of Russia and the US in terms of resources, population and armaments,

the position of Britain and her influence in world affairs was of real and sometimes decisive importance. Successive Governments, whether under Attlee and Bevin or Churchill and Eden, had not hesitated to assume a commanding role. I tried to follow their example. . . .[1]

Clearly there was every wish to assume a 'commanding role', yet later Macmillan quoted a long memorandum he wrote in December 1960, part of which summed up Britain's position:

3. Britain—with all her experience—has neither the economic nor the military power to take the leading role. We are harassed with countless problems—the narrow knife-edge on which our own economy is balanced; the difficult task of changing an Empire into a Commonwealth (with the special problems of colonies inhabited by European as well as native populations); the uncertainty about our relations [with] the new economic, and perhaps political, state which is being created by the Six countries of continental Western Europe; and the uncertainty of American policies towards us—treated now as just another country, now as an ally in a special and unique category.[2]

[1] *Pointing the way*, p. 61.   [2] Ibid., p. 324.

Just as clearly, a 'leading role' was impossible. But Britain must not be solely a US camp-follower: on this all postwar governments were agreed. Instead, a supporting but individual role was required, if it could be successfully assumed.

In playing such a role, for the earlier years of the period at least, the Commonwealth was a help. Its existence eased the task of decolonization. While the Commonwealth could not of itself remedy the British balance of payments, in the 1950s the existence of the sterling area, largely coterminous with the Commonwealth, eased the British position somewhat. The Commonwealth was useful in sustaining some special relationship with the US, even though the British government did not have the sort of leadership which the US might like, or which it might be encouraged to think Britain had. In World War II an important element in Churchill's special relationship with Roosevelt lay in the fact that he was the leader and spokesman of the British Commonwealth and Empire. Britain gained in stature because it spoke for others as well as itself.

This stature was diminished after independence was granted to India and Pakistan in 1947, but there was still a Commonwealth in which Britain acted as 'head' (note Acheson's statement above) and British leadership was accepted unless members had vital interests of their own to warrant divergence. Such a situation, actively furthered by Eden, largely obtained up to the Suez crisis in 1956, even though it had been damaged by Pakistan's acceptance of US arms aid in 1954 and the consequent sharpening of Indian non-alignment. After Suez Macmillan tried hard to restore the situation, while also attempting to assert a special role in Europe. In his memoirs there are numerous examples of his informing Commonwealth governments and those of France and West Germany of his visits to the Soviet Union and the US, and also the US government of his intentions in some especially intricate question of policy such as Cyprus. The impression is of an inner circle of associates and major allies.

II

The position which Macmillan allotted to the Commonwealth in the early years of his premiership did not differ greatly from that which British opinion generally, and Conservative opinion in particular, had traditionally given it. It was assumed that 'the unity of the Commonwealth' would reassert itself in times of trouble, and that in the meantime differences could be settled without damage to that unity. This conventional wisdom was still strong in 1953, when our period opens; something of it was seen in Chapter 1. It owed much to the experience of World War II. Eden relates how, in 1940, he tried to tell a Liverpool audience 'in one incident of the spirit of the British Commonwealth which the Nazis had so misjudged'. The incident was simply of meeting a Scot and a South African on a Middle East airfield, and of their both saying,

'It seems there is a job of work to be done'. Eden saw this as 'the vision of the men beyond the seas who see truly'. In commenting on it in the volume of his memoirs which appeared in 1965 he wrote: 'These thoughts and feelings are passing from our ken, sometimes through circumstances and sometimes through our own fault. We are the poorer for it.'[1]

Such an attitude was common until the Suez crisis, the effects of which Macmillan strove so strenuously to overcome, but as we have seen (ch. 4), some Conservative opinion in Britain turned against the Commonwealth because of Indian and Canadian opposition to British action at Suez. In Professor Mansergh's view, this was the first time that 'the traditional assumption that the Commonwealth was an asset came in for questioning that was often distressing but none the less persistent'; and he sees 'a link in psychological terms between the traumatic experiences of 1956 and the manner of the British application for membership of the Common Market six years later'.[2] Suez was indeed the beginning of Conservative disillusionment with the Commonwealth as an asset in external policy; but we should not assume that this disillusionment grew constantly until it reached its peak at the end of the 1960s. Rather there was a period of a few years—from about 1957 to 1961—when the Commonwealth got significant Conservative support, and during which Macmillan used it effectively for British policy.

Macmillan made two Commonwealth tours, both more extensive than any British prime minister had previously undertaken, as well as incidental visits to Canada. The first, in January and February 1958, took him to India, Pakistan, Australia, New Zealand, and Singapore. The second, in the same months of 1960, included Ghana, Nigeria, the Federation of Rhodesia and Nyasaland, and South Africa. He returned from the first with 'a new ardour and a new faith' and presented his cabinet colleagues with 'on the whole a cheerful picture'.[3] From his trip to Africa, where 'everything was in flux', he came back with qualified optimism:

Perplexing as were the problems as a whole, not merely racial but economic and social, there was a touching confidence in the ability of British statesmen to make an effective contribution to their solution. Moreover even where there were strong differences of opinion I felt there was a respect for the policy and point of view of the British Government.[4]

Such sentiments, communicated to his party, stilled many of the doubts remaining from Suez days; certainly, Macmillan was very well received by the press, especially after his 'wind of change' speech in Cape Town. It is not surprising that a Conservative pamphlet, published a month before the 1960 Prime Ministers' Meeting, should have begun:

No political party would now dare to suggest publicly that the Commonwealth

---

[1] *The reckoning* (1965), pp. 88–9.   [2] *Commonwealth experience*, p. 348.
[3] *Riding the storm*, pp. 411, 413.   [4] *Pointing the way*, p. 120.

has outlived its usefulness. Today every political party is anxious to establish a reputation for unwavering devotion to this great heritage.[1]

We have already noted the significance of the House of Commons vote on John Stonehouse's motion of 8 April 1960, which deplored South African racial policies, and which represents a kind of high-water-mark of Commonwealth feeling in the Conservative Party: no Conservative MP voted against it. One can see the influence not only of Macmillan's African tour but also of the widespread contemporary British belief that a Commonwealth which allowed South Africa to persist in its policies without demur was not to Britain's advantage.

It is from the Prime Ministers' Meeting of 1961, which led to South Africa's withdrawal, rather than that of 1960 that we can date the decline of many Conservatives' faith in the Commonwealth. Once more Macmillan explained this in part when he said that after South Africa ceased to be a member, arrangements with it in the sphere of defence and economic relations might remain unchanged, but the effect of its secession upon 'the extremist politicians in Salisbury must be considerable—and might prove fatal'. There were those 'even at home' who were beginning to wonder whether internal disputes in the Commonwealth 'could be tolerated indefinitely, and whether the Commonwealth concept could have any permanent value' in the present changing circumstances.[2] The reference to Salisbury is important. Macmillan says of Sir Roy Welensky that his 'close relations with the Right Wing of the Conservative Party, both in the Lords and the Commons, were notorious and dangerous'.[3] The combination of South Africa's departure and the contemporary negotiations with Welensky, which were unsatisfactory to white Rhodesians, lost the support for the Commonwealth of some influential Conservatives. The Commonwealth secretary, Duncan Sandys, stoutly maintained his support in a pamphlet published in January 1962, asserting that 'the bigger and the more world-wide the problem, the better is the Commonwealth suited to help in its solution', and that 'its influence cannot be other than pacific and constructive';[4] but real damage had been done to Conservative belief in the association.

The contemporary British move to enter the EEC caused further damage. The kind of Conservative opinion likely to approve this overlapped, but was not identical, with that which was alienated by South Africa's demotion from Commonwealth membership. Sandys bravely stated in his pamphlet that 'we have made it clear that if we are faced with the necessity of choosing between the Commonwealth and Europe, we should unquestionably choose the

[1] T. E. Utley & John Udal (rapporteurs), *Wind of change* (1960), p. 9.
[2] *Pointing the way*, p. 301.   [3] Ibid., p. 300.
[4] *The modern Commonwealth* (1962), pp. 22 & 25. Sandys could not complain that he had not been warned of impending troubles. An article in *The Economist* ('Mr Sandys's empire', 6 Aug 1960) accurately foretold four major difficulties which he would encounter as Commonwealth secretary.

Commonwealth'.[1] In the parliamentary party some did not think this assurance worth giving, since they valued Europe more than the Commonwealth, while others considered the choice unreal. As we have seen, all overseas Commonwealth governments had interests that might be jeopardized: the Accra pronouncements of the finance ministers in September 1961 showed how strongly the Commonwealth countries feared that Britain would not protect their interests. In addition many British 'Europeans' considered that the delay involved in laborious examination of Commonwealth claims in Brussels contributed to de Gaulle's veto. The Commonwealth seemed to be a liability, not an asset, in dealing with the EEC, though it was not necessarily so in dealing with Western Europe in the long term.

Two other main adverse influences on public and Conservative opinion were Commonwealth immigration, which became crucial in 1961, and the erosion of parliamentary government in the newly independent Commonwealth countries, which meant that the vision of the Commonwealth as a series of replicas of the Westminster system was discredited. It was all very well for Lord Kilmuir to write in 1963 that '*in spite of existing manifestations*, there are certain fundamental ideals which the people of the Commonwealth would like to see maintained: the rule of law, an independent judiciary, personal freedom, and, in the international sphere, tolerance and fair play'.[2] Whether the people of the Commonwealth would have liked these or not, a great many were not getting them. The point was to be further driven home to British opinion in the remaining years of the 1960s, as one after another of the Commonwealth states in Africa succumbed to one-party or military rule. The fact that parliamentary government survived in such diverse places as India, Ceylon, Malta, Jamaica, and Trinidad was insufficient to offset many people's disenchantment.

One can date the decline in Conservative support for the Commonwealth from 1961, but there is always a time-lag in such things. There had been little public questioning of the Commonwealth as a British asset before an article by an anonymous 'Conservative' appeared in *The Times* on 2 April 1964.[3] This was directed specifically at the Conservative Party, which still formed the British government. It called on the party to rid itself of humbug in external policy. The change in Britain's relative power in the world since 1939 had 'imposed a colossal revision of ideas on Britain and above all on the Conservative Party', in the course of which there had been much self-deception. 'Now the wounds have almost healed and the skin formed again beneath the plaster and the bandages, and they can come off. This means a revision of the Conservative Party's philosophy, policy and vocabulary on the Common-

---

[1] Sandys, p. 20.

[2] In Conference on the Future of the Commonwealth, *The future of the Commonwealth* (1963), p. 1 (emphasis added).

[3] The article, entitled 'Patriotism Based on Reality Not on Dreams', was the second in a series of three called 'A Party in Search of a Pattern'. They are usually regarded as having been written by J. Enoch Powell, MP, although he has neither confirmed nor denied this.

wealth, on defence, and on international relations.' It continued: 'The Commonwealth has really become a gigantic farce.' Most people, including most Conservatives, knew this and in their hearts despised the politicians who kept the farce going.

Not merely the non-European members, increasing at the rate of six or a dozen a year, but the so-called "old Dominions" have no present real ties with Britain other than such as history might have left between any two foreign nations. Indeed, resentment against the former ruling power or mother country makes some of them less well-disposed to Britain than to Germany, China, or Israel. And why should it be otherwise?

To participate in the fiction of the undefined and indefinable Commonwealth relationship might be harmless and sometimes profitable for Nehru, Nkrumah, or Makarios. 'They give nothing; they get any advantage that may be going.' But in citizenship, trade preference, and the use of the monarchy the absurdities it imposed on British laws and thought harmed Britain, and the Conservative party must 'break the spell'. Once the duty 'to maintain the fiction of a "worldwide commonwealth of nations" was disclaimed', it would no longer be necessary to create new Commonwealth countries or to call Commonwealth conferences which had no common purpose. British relations with Canada or British Guiana, Malta or India, Southern Rhodesia or South Africa, could then be put on a new basis corresponding to actual circumstances and interests.

This statement gave rise to a considerable correspondence, but its abiding interest lies in its comparatively accurate prevision of how British governments would behave for the remainder of the 1960s, whether they intended to or not.[1] 'The spell', by which the author presumably meant the long-standing conviction that Commonwealth relations were different from foreign relations, might not have been broken by his efforts; it was certainly weakened by events. The energetic efforts of Sir Alec Douglas-Home to institute new Commonwealth arrangements at the Prime Ministers' Meeting of 1964 were overtaken by the acrimony provoked by Rhodesia; similarly, as we saw earlier, Wilson's ideas on Commonwealth economic co-operation were nullified by the divergent interests of Commonwealth governments.

III

As the opinion polls quoted in Chapter 10 showed, it was by no means only opinion within the Conservative Party that was disillusioned with the Commonwealth; nor was this disillusion only a question of pique or wounded pride.

[1] Perhaps even greater prevision can be granted to a correspondent who wrote: 'The message of the three articles by A Conservative seems to be that after the last four or five years of radical, expansionist, reforming government the country needs a period of consolidation under a conservative-minded, inward-looking government such as the present-day Labour Party could give' (letter from R. N. Lines, *The Times*, 10 Apr 1964).

True, much propaganda favouring the Commonwealth in the 1950s had come from the Conservatives since they were the party of government which was operating the Commonwealth system, but the polls showed that opinion varied little between party supporters, and from personal observation, the same would seem to have been true of MPs. Replies to two questions asked by the National Opinion Poll (NOP) on 12 September 1966,[1] during the second disastrous Prime Ministers' Meeting of that year, seem to sum up widespread feeling about the Commonwealth in Britain at that time. First, respondents were asked 'How important is the Commonwealth to you?'. They replied (percentages):

	All	Conservative	Labour	Liberal
Very important	26	29	24	28
Quite important	28	31	27	34
Not very important	26	25	28	27
Not at all important	14	10	16	10
Don't know	6	5	5	1

Considering the strong-minded antithetical positions taken by many party spokesmen over the Commonwealth and Rhodesia, the replies to the second question are illuminating. It was: 'How would you personally care if some of the African countries left the Commonwealth because of the Government policy on Rhodesia?'. The answers were (percentages):

	All	Conservative	Labour	Liberal
Very much	13	16	11	14
Quite a lot	18	18	18	24
Not very much	30	29	32	30
Not at all	29	29	29	28
Don't know	10	8	10	4

The sense here is of apathy and bewilderment rather than of conscious disillusion; but it is certainly not of strong attachment, and there is little difference between the adherents of the various parties. The reality seems to be that a broad consensus of approval of the Commonwealth in the 1950s was developing in the 1960s into a broad consensus of apathy merging into disapproval, especially because of Rhodesia. The Conservatives may have been first to signal this feeling, because of their special connections; but it was not confined to them. As we shall see, the opinions expressed in 1966 were not to be lasting.

The question whether this consensus arose from wounded pride or had a stronger foundation requires more extensive discussion. Certainly, there was a basis for wounded pride in the erosion of parliamentary government, in the apparent ingratitude of some Commonwealth members for favours received from Britain, and in the accusations hurled at the British government from

[1] NOP *Bulletin*, Sept 1966, p. 10.

1964 onwards about Rhodesia and South Africa. As has been said, Harold Wilson felt genuinely hurt in December 1965 when some twenty African delegates walked out while he was stating the British case on Rhodesia at the UN, because he had passionately believed in the independent Common-wealth.[1] There was emotional force in such an experience. Yet much of the articulate anti-Commonwealth sentiment which developed in Britain in the 1960s was based less on emotion than on dissatisfaction with economic and military policies slanted towards the Commonwealth. Both of these, it was widely held, were self-defeating from Britain's standpoint.[2]

Arguments against the Commonwealth connection were summed up by a Conservative Party study group in 1967, which pointed to the decline in the value of Commonwealth trade since the early 1950s, to the fact that Common-wealth preferences currently operated to Britain's disadvantage and that many held that the sterling area aggravated rather than assisted Britain's balance of payments. What Britain needed was modernization, of industry, communica-tions, and the social service infrastructure. It could not afford to help developing countries, including those of the Commonwealth, unless it was economically strong, yet since the war it had disbursed nearly £2,000 m. in grants and loans to such countries, 90 per cent of it to the overseas Commonwealth—'aid which has on occasion been mis-applied'. Thus economically the Common-wealth was a diminishing asset for Britain, whose natural markets today were the sophisticated markets of the developed world. Heavy investment in the potential of Australasia, South Africa, and stable new Commonwealth states with natural wealth might be justifiable, but the key to successful investment was 'to invest in success, and trade success in the long run is seldom obtainable where political risks are high'.[3] Essentially, these arguments maintained that Britain was neglecting its own interests by following investment policies which had been pursued in order to preserve the sterling area. They also drew attention to the lack of growth in Britain's traditional Commonwealth markets. To say that Britain's natural markets were the sophisticated markets of the developed world provided a rationale for the direction in which Britain was moving. It was a denial of the view that a former imperial mission entailed further obligations.

A similar situation prevailed in questions of defence, as will become clear.[4]

---

[1] See above, p. 215, n. 8.

[2] For a contemporary viewpoint on these criticisms in 1966, see my article, 'British interests and the Commonwealth', *JCPS*, Nov 1966.

[3] *Policy for the Commonwealth*, report of a study group of the Conservative Commonwealth and Overseas Council (London, 1967, mimeo.), pp. 10–11. It should be emphasized that the words quoted represent the study group's interpretation of what critics had been saying, not the group's own conclusions.

[4] Three works which help to put defence policy in context are R. N. Rosecrance, *Defence of the realm* (1966); L. W. Martin, *British defence policy* (1969); and Neville Brown, *Arms without empire* (1967). Mayhew's *Britain's role tomorrow*, a highly partisan book when it appeared, has been very much vindicated by events.

IV

Traditionally, British defence policy had two aspects. These were the defence of the home islands, which necessitated occasional forays on to the continent of Europe, and defence of the Empire, which meant the maintenance of the fleet and of certain forces overseas. The fleet was common to both, since it had to protect colonial areas and British supply routes and also prevent invasion of Britain. The overseas forces were reduced in the nineteenth century, dependencies being mainly guarded by locally-raised forces under British command. The one major exception up to 1945 was the Indian Army, which still included a substantial British component. The dominions were responsible for their own forces. It was generally understood that these would be co-ordinated with the British effort in time of war, and added to British resources if not required for local operations. Broadly speaking, this pattern was adhered to during World War II, though the war against Japan entailed a different disposition of dominion forces from World War I.

From 1945 the two basic aspects of policy remained in being, but their content and interpretation changed. The home defence aspect was the more stable. It had two elements: membership of Nato, and the possession of an independent British nuclear force. Nato was the more fundamental, the nuclear force the more widely discussed. In 1957 British defence policy was altered to give more emphasis to the nuclear deterrent and less to conventional forces;[1] none the less Britain continued to provide forces for Nato and to take part fully in Nato planning. Indeed, the nuclear deterrent became something of an embarrassment. Reliance on it saved money in the short term, but involved heavy long-term expenditure on further refinement of the weapons. A prolonged and disputatious search for vehicles to carry them ended in the curtailment of the independence of the deterrent because of the need to obtain US Polaris missiles. However, since very few people expected that Britain would be called upon to use nuclear weapons, the disputes over nuclear policy were theoretical and, except for considerations of cost, had little effect upon the second aspect of defence policy, the maintenance of forces beyond Europe.

After Indian independence British overseas defence policy lacked an obvious centre of concentration. It could be argued that Britain still needed to defend its colonies, but this became less convincing as the colonies dwindled. Yet Britain had a long tradition of overseas operations, and possessed strategic bases such as Singapore, Aden, Malta, and Cyprus. In effect, a solution was found by transmuting the colonial role into one of reinforcing the US containment policy. Britain's membership of Seato and Cento provided a general justification; but the main concern was keeping the peace in Malaysia, the Gulf States, and South Arabia, with an ancillary task for a time in preserving

[1] See Cmnd 124 (Apr 1957).

the strategic bases. Essentially, this was the 'east of Suez' policy which came under heavy fire in the latter half of the 1960s.

Such a policy could readily be identified as 'Commonwealth', although it had not been undertaken on behalf of the Commonwealth as a whole. In general, Commonwealth members approved of it in the 1950s, even when they had reservations about the US posture. India, for example, mounted no opposition to the British role in Malaya, in spite of its dislike of Seato. The old dominions approved: Australia and New Zealand took part in the operations in Malaya, and South Africa would have liked to see a western alliance established in Africa. Moreover, the task was performed in areas which had been British possessions in colonial days, and in some cases still were.

Successive ministerial statements on defence in the 1950s emphasized the Commonwealth aspect. In 1953: 'The defence policy of the United Kingdom continues to be based on the closest possible co-operation with her partners in the Commonwealth and in NATO'.[1] In 1954: 'Close co-operation continues between the United Kingdom and the other Commonwealth countries in all aspects of defence.'[2] In 1955 it was recorded that the Commonwealth prime ministers had held a series of meetings on regional defence problems. 'Each was attended by representatives of those Commonwealth countries whose forces might in war be operating in the particular area under discussion.'[3] The 1956 White Paper described Australian and New Zealand participation in Malaya and the discussions with South Africa mentioned in Chapter 9.[4] In 1957, with the general re-thinking of defence policy, less emphasis was given to the Commonwealth except in respect of technical details such as the exchange of officers, the Commonwealth Advisory Committee for Defence Science, and co-operation with Australia in the rocket range at Woomera.[5] The 1958 White Paper was more reserved, referring only to Australia, New Zealand, the Federation of Rhodesia and Nyasaland, and South Africa.[6] There were no such references in the 1961 or even the 1962 White Paper, which was supposed to cover the ensuing five years. There was the customary reference to Malaya, but the general tone was cautious:

The need for garrisons of British troops to support the civil power in internal security emergencies has demonstrably diminished already and may be expected to diminish still further. At the same time, we may suffer restrictions on our freedom to use some territories for military purposes, and we must accordingly adjust our strategy.

Base areas would cease to be available in Kenya.[7] From then onwards, the 'Commonwealth' emphasis tended to be on Britain's provision of training for servicemen from other Commonwealth states.[8]

[1] Cmd 8768 (1953), para. 76.   [2] Cmd 9075 (1954), para. 71.
[3] Cmd 9391 (1955), para. 95.   [4] Cmd 9691 (1956), paras 91–2.
[5] Cmnd 124, paras. 65–6.   [6] Cmnd 363 (1958). para. 42.
[7] Cmnd 1639 (1962), paras 6, 17, 18.   [8] e.g. Cmnd 2270 (1964), para. 112.

One of the reasons for de-emphasizing the Commonwealth was that defence agreements with newly independent Commonwealth countries were not proving so successful as had been hoped, except in the case of Malaya. A change of government in Ceylon caused the termination of the Anglo-Ceylonese agreement in 1957. An agreement with Nigeria signed in January 1961 lasted only one year. When Sierra Leone became independent, it was announced that the agreement envisaged in earlier discussions would not be needed.[1] The explanation of the abrogation of the Nigerian agreement was that its scope and purposes had been 'widely misunderstood', and that, in particular, fears had arisen that 'Nigeria's freedom of action might be impaired and that she might even be drawn into hostilities against her wishes'.[2] This can be taken as typical of the situation with newly independent Commonwealth members after 1957, when Malaya, a somewhat special case, signed the agreement which was later to be applied to Malaysia. The other new members, especially in Africa, did not wish to be associated with the American alliance system. In addition, military agreements with a former colonial power were likely to be attacked in Third World circles as 'neo-colonialist'. Not only did formal defence agreements cease to be available to Britain. Some of the new states turned to other countries to train and equip their armed forces, although Britain continued to be the main centre. Canada and Israel entered the picture; Nigeria developed its air force with West German help; and the Soviet Union and China offered assistance which in some cases was accepted and in others refused.

There was something of a false dawn in Commonwealth defence co-operation in 1964 as a result of two events: the East African mutinies in January, and the beginnings of confrontation in Malaysia. The mutinies in Kenya, Uganda, and Tanganyika, largely over pay and status, were put down with the aid of British troops at the invitation of the three governments concerned. Since Kenya had obtained independence only the month before, there were still two British infantry battalions and a light regiment there, and a commando unit on an RN ship offshore. Other troops were brought from Britain and Aden. The mutinies were overcome without bloodshed, and British forces were soon withdrawn, except for some which gave logistic support in internal security operations in north-east Kenya. These were withdrawn by the end of 1964.[3] The whole operation reflected credit on the British government and troops and prompted suggestions that Britain might find an extension of its post-colonial defence role in helping new states to retain their internal stability. In fact, however, the reaction of new states' governments was largely one of shame and concern that British troops had had to be brought back, and none

---

[1] Relevant documents on these three decisions are in Mansergh, *Documents 1952–62*, pp. 573–5, 581–3, & 584.

[2] Joint statement of the two governments, ibid., p. 583. For further details, see Olasupo Ojedokun, 'The Anglo-Nigerian entente and its demise, 1960–2', *JCPS*, Nov 1971.

[3] Cmnd 2592 (1965), paras 74–7.

sought this kind of aid during the remainder of the decade.[1] For example, British troops took no part in the Nigerian civil war.

Confrontation in Malaysia (see ch. 6) was another example of British dexterity and moderation, but again it had no obvious outcome except the agitation against a sustained presence east of Suez and the reduction of British effort at the end of the 1960s. It also helped to foster objections to Commonwealth commitments in a broader sense, on grounds of cost. Sterling became convertible in 1958, soon after Britain abolished conscription, with the result that it became much more costly to maintain armed forces just when 'the foreign-exchange implications of keeping them overseas began to be of much greater consequence'.[2] It was estimated in 1967 that the British government was spending £257 m. annually to keep 160,000 men abroad; ten years earlier, double the number had been costing only £190 m. Some 40 per cent of British military spending occurred in Malaysia. It was further calculated that Britain was carrying a heavier burden of net defence payments than Germany, France, Italy, or Japan, and that the brunt fell on its balance of payments.[3] Such arguments reinforced the contention of many British publicists and financial authorities that Commonwealth defence, and especially the retention of bases overseas, was a luxury which Britain could not afford. The Germans and the Japanese, Britain's obvious competitors in world markets, had no comparable expenses. Nor were the forces satisfied with the provision being made for them. Christopher Mayhew put the case for them, after resigning in February 1966 as minister of defence for the navy:

The Government in fact treats our East of Suez role precisely as a Hindu treats his sacred cow—neither feeding it properly nor putting it out of its misery. The economic departments will not let the role be properly financed, and the overseas departments will not let it be wound up.[4]

Mayhew indicated that he would prefer it to be wound up, and this, to a great extent, was what happened. It was clear to him that there was little or no expectation of Commonwealth unity in defence, economics, and politics, and he wanted this to be recognized.[5] His views were shared by many outside his own party; increasingly they became the conventional wisdom of the next few years.

V

Nevertheless, by the end of the decade there were signs that, while the Commonwealth might still be regarded as a liability in certain situations, it had regained something of its former status in public opinion. A series of polls

[1] See the discussion of Nyerere's reactions in Mazrui, 'Anti-militarism and political militancy in Tanzania', *J. Conflict Resolution*, Sept 1968, and the general treatment in W. F. Gutteridge, *The military in African politics* (1969).
[2] Strange, p. 183. The whole of ch. 6 is of great interest in this connection.
[3] Ibid., pp. 184, 187. [4] Mayhew, p. 97. [5] Ibid., pp. 111 ff.

taken in 1969 showed that most British people still believed that it was a valuable institution. Two polls taken in January 1969, when the Prime Ministers' Meeting was held, gave roughly similar results. One conducted by Opinion Research Centre for the Gemini News Service showed remarkable consistency. To the statement, 'The Commonwealth is valuable and should not be allowed to break up', 67 per cent agreed, 20 per cent disagreed, and 13 per cent did not know. The figures were almost identical for people of all three parties and for men and women, although Liberals and women showed a higher proportion of 'don't knows'. To the contrary statement, 'The Commonwealth has outlived its usefulness and should be wound up', the figures were duly reversed—21 per cent of all respondents agreed, 66 per cent disagreed, and 13 per cent did not know. When asked whether it would be a good thing if the Commonwealth countries worked more closely together on trade and political matters, 76 per cent agreed, only 6 per cent disagreed, and 16 per cent did not know. Here there was some difference between Conservative and Labour voters, with more Labour 'don't knows'. On a final question, about whether Britain should resign from the Commonwealth, the original percentages were reproduced.[1]

NOP asked 'Do you think the Commonwealth is a worthwhile organization or do you think Britain would be better off if she withdrew from it?' The results were broadly the same, though marked by a slightly bigger proportion in favour of withdrawal and by a difference of the proportions of young and old who thought Britain should withdraw (percentages):

	All	Con.	Lab.	Lib.	21–34	35–44	45–54	55–64	65+
Worthwhile	59	60	59	60	58	53	59	58	59
Better to withdraw	28	29	26	28	35	33	29	24	18
Don't know	13	11	15	13	7	13	11	18	21

Source: NOP Bulletin, Jan 1969, p. 11.

Later in 1969 NOP asked: 'Do you think the future of Britain rests mainly with the Commonwealth, with the USA, with Europe or with none of them?' With the groups listed above, the results were (percentages):

	All	Con.	Lab.	Lib.	21–34	35–44	45–54	55–64	65+
Commonwealth	30	33	29	32	18	26	35	37	38
USA	11	14	9	10	14	12	10	12	9
Europe	24	23	25	31	33	30	23	16	13
None	15	13	16	13	17	16	14	14	11
Don't know	20	17	21	14	18	16	18	21	29

Source: NOP Bulletin, Nov 1969, Spec. Suppl. 1.

Analysing the results further, NOP found that those most pro-Europe were the professional, senior managerial, and administrative workers and the post World War II generation. Those born before the Great Depression and the

[1] Round Table, Apr 1969, pp. 170–1.

general strike—i.e. those more conscious of British imperial history—supported future links with the Commonwealth rather than Europe. The large proportion of 'don't knows' suggests that the question was too much for many. The answers did, however, emphasize a point often made—that enthusiasm for 'Europe' was a matter very largely of the elites and of those young people who had first-hand experience of Europe in other circumstances than war. The Commonwealth's appearance at the head of the list was perhaps a recognition of the basic interests, by no means all of them political, which Britain shared with Commonwealth countries.

This point was expressed with some emphasis by Michael Stewart, the foreign and Commonwealth secretary, before the Royal Commonwealth Society on 19 February 1970, in a speech in which he attempted to reconcile Britain's entry into the EEC with its continued Commonwealth membership. Quoting Pierre Trudeau to the effect that, after the 1969 Prime Ministers' Meeting the association had reached 'a new plateau of maturity, a new sense of entity and practical interdependence based on mutual self-interest', he said that the Commonwealth relationship, being expressed so extensively in terms of people from many varied countries meeting together for purposes of common use and common interest, had a vitality of its own and was 'of a different nature' from the relationship the UK would have with fellow members of the EEC. He believed Britain would continue to show that its devotion to the Commonwealth was 'no mere matter of words' and was in no way qualified by the belief that a united Europe, including Britain, 'would be to the general advantage of us all'.[1]

In spite of the opposition at the 1971 Heads of Government Meeting at Singapore (described in ch. 8), this kind of statement continued to be made by senior ministers. So long as the Commonwealth was not an active brake on the pursuit of British interests—and it had become much less so, with the decline of the Rhodesia issue, the virtual certainty of entry into the EEC, and the subsidence of the immigration issue—the steady gains to be made from a continued association with Commonwealth countries could be counted. The new type of Commonwealth 'system', described in Chapter 18, was more acceptable to the Britain of the 1970s than the way the previous system had operated in the 1960s.

---

[1] *Survey B & CA*, 13 Mar 1970, pp. 259–60.

PART V

DIPLOMATIC CHANGES

CHAPTER 16

COMMONWEALTH FOREIGN POLICIES

NICHOLAS MANSERGH assessed the position of the Commonwealth at the accession of Queen Elizabeth II in a previous volume in this series, observing that questions of status had by then been decided, and that new questions needed to be asked:

> What was of interest, therefore, was no longer the status of the dominions but the ways in which the independent member nations of the Commonwealth regarded their membership, and the part it played in the shaping of their outlook and the determination of their policies. Had the weighing down of the scales on the side of autonomy impaired unity? Did the nations now mean more than the Commonwealth which collectively they comprised?[1]

We have just seen that, in the case of Britain, the answer had become clear by 1969: by then the Commonwealth ranked much lower in the British scale of values. The nation mattered more than the Commonwealth. But this outcome was not confined to Britain. We shall see that the same might be said of every other Commonwealth member.

I

To start with Canada, the senior member, which after World War II had experienced a transformation of the near-isolationism characteristic of the long reign of Mackenzie King:[2] as indicated in Mansergh's previous volume, Nato had created a new orthodoxy for Canadian foreign policy. It seemed to provide an especially suitable means of engaging Canada permanently in European affairs, especially for a Liberal government. King had made the unity of Canada an overriding consideration. In bringing Canada alongside Britain and France, Nato appeared to settle a conflict of opinion between English- and French-speaking Canadians about intervention abroad. (There was no similar move to enter Seato.) By consolidating Canada's alliance with the US in a context of consultation and joint action with European countries, Nato acknowledged the facts of Canada's geographical position while bringing

---

[1] Mansergh, *Survey 1939–52*, p. 369.

[2] See ibid., pp. 340–2, for Canada's part in setting up Nato. A Canadian diplomat summed up the change: 'Mackenzie King, in the 1920s and 30s, sought for a foreign policy that divided us the least. During the last years of his regime and under his successor, Louis St Laurent, we began the search for a foreign policy that united us the most' (Escott Reid, 'Canadian foreign policy, 1967–77: a second golden decade?', *Int. J.*, 22/2 (1967), p. 172).

in other states to mitigate the relationship between the US giant and what Canadians liked to call their own country, a 'middle power'.

The second preoccupation of Canadian external policy in the early 1950s was the Commonwealth, especially India.[1] Emphasis upon the Commonwealth's multiracial aspect and on India's independent line provided a useful counterweight to association with the US. The Indian connection gave Canada access to non-aligned thinking, injected some of the substance into Canadian policy (in regard to Indo-China in 1954 and Suez in 1956), and provided the biggest outlet and the easiest justification for Canadian economic aid.

The Commonwealth was readily identified with a specifically Canadian strand of altruism. It was no accident that St Laurent, Diefenbaker, and Pearson devoted special attention to it and stressed its idealistic aspects. When Diefenbaker spoke against South Africa in 1961 and Pearson tried to achieve some compromise between Britain and the Africans in 1966, they were acting in similar ways. Although Diefenbaker disagreed strongly with the action taken by St Laurent and Pearson over Suez, they defended it in Commonwealth terms not dissimilar from those which Diefenbaker later used to justify his stand over South Africa.

Nato did not prove so satisfactory in the awkward world of the 1960s. The nub of the complaints, as these developed,[2] was that it offered no solution to Canada's problems of defence connection with the US (since, contrary to what might have been expected, Nato's writ did not run in North America, and the defence arrangements between the two countries there were exclusively bilateral), while it associated Canada with US policy in matters which called for an independent approach, such as Vietnam. Further, it was argued that the Canadian government's self-satisfaction with Nato led it to neglect urgent problems at home, especially the increasing demand of Quebec for more autonomy and consideration.[3] Thus, at a time when Nato was experiencing considerable strain in relations between the US and its partners in Western Europe, it had also become a symbol of dislike for those Canadians who were at odds with their government's general approach to foreign policy, and to those (not always the same) who wanted it to concentrate more on questions of national unity. Norad (North American Defence Agreement), the separate Canadian-American agreement for North American integrated air defence, was a target for those who objected to US interference in Canadian affairs.

---

[1] See M. S. Rajan, 'The Indo-Canadian entente', ibid., 17 (1962), pp. 358–84.

[2] Three critical books are James M. Minifie, *Peacemaker or powder-monkey* (1960), Stephen Clarkson, ed., *An independent foreign policy for Canada?* (1968), and Lewis Hertzman & others, *Alliances and illusions* (1969). See also James Eayrs, 'The military policies of contemporary Canada', in Richard H. Leach, ed., *Contemporary Canada* (1967), pp. 225–69.

[3] Ramsay Cook, *Canada and the French-Canadian question* (1966) is a helpful work for non-Canadians. I have found Donald V. Smiley, *The Canadian political nationality* (1967), ch. 3, useful for the formal issues between Quebec and the federal government.

That interference had become public in January 1963, following the Diefenbaker government's reluctance to agree to Canada's accepting nuclear weapons on its own soil.[1]

The Trudeau government's announcement in April 1969 of its intention to reduce Canadian forces in Europe (though not to leave Nato) offered the prospect of greater concentration on the domestic front.[2] While this decision was a response to difficulties at home, it was also a recognition of the fact that Europe did not need as much protection, because of its own increased economic strength and because of US-Soviet détente.

Canadian concern for the Commonwealth, manifest throughout most of the events discussed so far in this book, waned appreciably when Trudeau replaced Pearson in April 1968. Inevitably, French-speaking Canadians regarded the Commonwealth as part of the English-speaking heritage. Now a government concerned to emphasize Canada's bilingualism wished to redress the balance. In his policy statement for the election which returned him with a massive majority on 25 June 1968 Trudeau had said: 'Parallel to our close ties with the Commonwealth we should strive to develop a close relation with the francophone countries.'[3] Canada proceeded to open up new diplomatic posts in French-speaking countries (mostly in Africa) and to give more emphasis to this aspect of its foreign policy, while still supporting the Commonwealth as a worthwhile association. Trudeau's interventions in the 1969 and 1971 meetings of Commonwealth heads of government were more subdued and less significant than Pearson's or Diefenbaker's had been. When the Canadian government published the results of a wide-ranging foreign-policy review in October 1970, the only mention of the Commonwealth was in the context of economic development—and then in a passing phrase, along with 'la Francophonie'. In a document which specifically condemned 'an over-emphasis on role and influence obscuring policy objectives and actual interests',[4] this was not surprising. The days of Canada's role as a 'middle power' and a 'bridge' were past, though there was no saying whether they might be resumed if a Canadian government with a different style emerged.

The distinction between 'role and influence' and 'policy objectives and actual interests' can be disputed: there is, in fact, no clear-cut difference between them, since interests are not immutable but derive in part from the perceptions of the statesmen who formulate them, and policy can very readily encompass a role and strive to acquire influence. None the less, there had been something synthetic about Canada's Commonwealth role in the 1950s and 1960s. Grounded in history when it involved an attempt to help the West Indies, in its Asian and African aspects it had been more a matter of

[1] The story will be found in Peyton V. Lyon, ch. 3.

[2] John W. Holmes, 'The new perspectives of Canadian foreign policy', *World Today*, Oct 1969, provides good background.

[3] Ibid., 16 Aug 1968, p. 760.

[4] Canada, *Foreign policy for Canadians* (1970), pp. 26 & 8.

diplomatic finesse. Canadian policy-makers could argue that Canada would assist the western cause by showing sympathy with ex-colonial countries, and by capitalizing upon its own absence of colonial guilt; but this was to a large extent an operation at the edges of national concern. It did not affect the massive problems of relations with the US and of national unity at home, in spite of a widespread conviction that national unity would be assisted by a prominent role as an honest broker in international politics. The change from Pearson to Trudeau was of great interest to foreign observers. Although the two men's emphases were quite different, especially in Commonwealth relations, they belonged to the same party and had much the same electoral support. It appeared that Canadian domestic considerations were still paramount, as in the days of Mackenzie King.

II

Australia and New Zealand were situated differently from Canada in the 1950s and 1960s; after the Korean war both were actively involved in three other wars: the Malayan Emergency, confrontation between Indonesia and Malaysia, and Vietnam. Participation in these conflicts was both the product of, and a stimulus to, the particular view these countries took of world politics. Both clung to Anzus as a guarantee and strongly supported Seato. Throughout the period both had conservative governments, except for the three years 1957 to 1960 in New Zealand, when there was a Labour government differing little in assumptions from its predecessors and successors.

Exemplified by Menzies and Holyoake, these governments protested their close identification with Britain, although they often found current British policy unpalatable, especially the attempt to enter the EEC; other instances were the British refusal to send troops to Vietnam and the readiness of the British government to defer to black African opinion over South Africa and Rhodesia. It was not that Australia and New Zealand were opposed outright to what Britain was doing, or even that the two were always of one mind. It was rather that politicians who had been brought up to believe in British leadership, and whose parties had gained electoral support for their past assertions of 'loyalty', were now faced with difficulties in following or even supporting British policies. An extension of diplomacy and military connections in Southeast Asia meant constant attention to the behaviour of countries such as Thailand and Indonesia; membership of Anzus meant an overriding concern for what the US government might be thinking. For most of the period, on most issues with the notable exception of Suez and the 'off-shore islands' crises of 1954 and 1958,[1] the two governments pursued a line summed up by Holyoake when arguing against those of his critics who wanted 'a qualified alignment':

[1] Reese, ch. 14, is enlightening on this and other episodes.

... What that means, I'm not sure. I suspect it means they welcome a United States obligation to us, but don't want to have any obligation in return. They really want a one-sided ANZUS Treaty, a free ride, with the right to criticise the driver. If you want to criticise the driver, you need to pay your share of the costs of the journey.[1]

Australia and New Zealand remembered their crucial need for American help in World War II, and because they feared communist expansion in Asia, they stuck to this line throughout the Vietnam war. The upshot of the war called for radical reappraisals. The reduction of US ground forces and Nixon's Guam doctrine that Asian countries would in future be primarily responsible for their defence were blows to the assumption that, if US allies were sufficiently loyal, the US would continue to bear the brunt of defence against communism in Asia. The advent of multipolarity—probably less welcome to these two countries than to any others in the Commonwealth—brought complications in the international situation for which they were little prepared.[2]

To both Australia and New Zealand, the Commonwealth had traditionally meant Britain. As we have seen, after their initial pleasure at finding that Asian countries could fit snugly into the Commonwealth system, both governments were disturbed by India's non-alignment and by the changes that took place in the Commonwealth's structure and concerns. Britain's attempt to enter Europe, its east of Suez policy and recurrent balance-of-payments crises were no comfort. Neither country had been especially solicitous of British economic interests. We have seen that Australia's international economic interests rapidly became more diversified in the late 1950s and the 1960s, while New Zealand remained more dependent upon the British market. Constant balance-of-payments problems prevented New Zealand from turning to other suppliers but also prevented it from buying all it might want. Australia, in contrast, was able to widen its range of suppliers because of a constant inflow of capital (much of it from Britain) and high prices for its growing exports of minerals.

At the end of the 1960s both countries were manifestly less dependent on Britain than ever before and less concerned about Commonwealth ties. Their external policies had been concentrated on Southeast Asia and the US. If the 'era of negotiation' enunciated in President Nixon's inaugural address of 20 January 1969 led to a US-Chinese détente, they might be expected to remain preoccupied with Southeast Asia but to show more initiative in the Pacific; in the latter event, their interest in the Commonwealth might revive somewhat, because of the Commonwealth status of Fiji, Tonga, Western Samoa, and Nauru, and its possible (though problematical) extension to an independent Papua–New Guinea. Such a development would be easier for New Zealand

[1] Keith Holyoake, *A defence policy for New Zealand* (1969), p. 12.
[2] Some of the two countries' problems are discussed in Bruce Brown & others, *New Zealand and Australia: foreign policy in the 1970s* (1970).

than for Australia. Menzies's disenchantment with the Commonwealth had been clearly evident in his two successors, Holt and Gorton.

In general, the old dominions had discovered that Britain was no longer an effective mediator for them in world politics; that it was now more natural for them to deal directly with the US; that their own powers of political initiative were strictly limited, except in situations peripheral to the main arena of conflict; and that the Commonwealth was not essential to their main concerns. Canada had used the Commonwealth as a means of fashioning a role and exerting influence, and as part of the search for a foreign policy that 'united us most'. By the end of the 1960s this emphasis was diminishing. Australia and New Zealand had been glad to assume the Commonwealth mantle in their joint military operations with Britain during the Malayan emergency, but this, as we have seen, was something of a convenient cloak for designs which were Southeast Asian rather than Commonwealth. Otherwise, apart from continuing their military interest in Malaysia and Singapore, they had found the association a source of embarrassment and disappointment in those critical aspects which involved Africa, although its social and traditional elements continued to influence them.

III

The external policies of each partner of the quarrelling pairs of South and Southeast Asian states, India and Pakistan, Malaysia and Singapore, can be understood only in relation to the other partner, i.e. Indian foreign policy is predominantly about Pakistan and vice versa, Malaysian about Singapore and vice versa. The other member of the Asian Commonwealth, Ceylon, throughout the 1950s and 1960s was largely enmeshed in domestic preoccupations and did not figure prominently in international politics. When it did, as in Mrs Bandaranaike's leadership of the 'non-aligned' group in connection with the Sino-Indian conflict of 1962, this activity was essentially within the Afro-Asian context. Ceylon was not prominent in Commonwealth relations, except for the perennial problem of its Indian Tamils.

During this period India and Pakistan were both members of the anti-colonialist group at the UN, and took part in the campaigns against racialism in Africa and in the quest for assistance in economic development. In 1953 both were still formally non-aligned, but the signing of the arms agreement between the US and Pakistan early in 1954—a fateful step—gave a much sharper edge to Indian suspicions of the West. This particular American decision displayed an inability to appreciate the situation in the Indian sub-continent and to recognize that the conflict between India and Pakistan took precedence, in the minds of the two governments, over all other questions, including those involving the great powers. The same inability was apparent in US policy during the Sino-Indian war of 1962 and the Indo-Pakistani war of 1965.[1] As we have seen, Pakistani adherence to Seato and Cento depended very much on what these pacts might contribute towards Pakistan's capacity to fight India, and on how they might resolve such questions as Kashmir in Pakistan's favour. When they failed to satisfy in these respects, Pakistan retained membership of them but turned towards China for further support. Inevitably, India turned towards the Soviet Union, which achieved a special status in 1966 by acting as honest broker to bring India and Pakistan together at Tashkent, but thereafter inclined more towards the Indian side. It signed a friendship treaty with India in August 1971.

Such a coincidence of Soviet-Indian interests, which had been maturing for a long time,[2] had to be seen in the context of the subcontinent, just as much as Pakistan's earlier connections with the US and China. India did not wish to assume responsibility for all the policies of the Soviet Union, any more than did Pakistan for those of the US. For each, any international connection had to be viewed primarily in terms of its impact on the other. This is not to say that they neglected all other issues, or that they never had wider aims. But their propinquity and frequent friction affected all their external policies.

In operating within Third World and Afro-Asian institutions and within the Commonwealth, India and Pakistan again directed their attention mainly at one another. It has already been suggested that, largely because of the influx of new African states, their influence in the Commonwealth waned in the 1960s compared with its significance in the 1950s. In the earlier decade Indian membership of the Commonwealth had all the advantages of novelty; as a triumph of British statesmanship, it was highly acceptable to liberal and mildly leftist-thinking people in the English-speaking countries; it seemed to carry with it an air of authority, as if Nehru spoke not only for India but for Asia at large. Certainly this was the impression which Eden as British foreign secretary and Casey as Australian minister for external affairs (perhaps Pearson too) conveyed to foreigners until India's refusal to accept the British line on Suez—and even afterwards, to a certain extent. Pakistan was less influential because obviously so much less united and so racked by faction.

In the 1960s this whole picture changed. India was no longer the exemplar of radicalism in the Third World. Once it fell out with China, the air of authority passed. The new situation was emphasized by Nehru's personal decline. After the 1962 war India was a suppliant rather than an arbiter, a state which had to defend itself against two adjacent enemies instead of one, a one-time leader of the Third World which now had to be carefully handled by other Third World states in case they should incur China's enmity by seeming to be too closely engaged with it. Although this situation suited

[1] The same was true in the Indo-Pakistani war of 1971. Wherever American diplomacy may be at home, it is not in the subcontinent.
[2] See Mansergh, *Survey 1939–52*, pp. 358–9.

Pakistan, that country was unable to capitalize upon it, since its own inherent weakness and its equivocation towards its formal allies made a firm policy difficult to sustain.

The African states, once their conceptions of their local interests became firm, did not look for leadership from the subcontinent, in the Commonwealth, or anywhere else. As we have seen, their attention was concentrated upon Africa's own problems. The main use of the UN, the Commonwealth, the non-aligned meetings, and other international gatherings was to further African aims in Africa. Although they were often divided, they were not so acutely or permanently divided as India and Pakistan. In consequence, they could work together more often and more effectively. It was only on international economic questions that India and Pakistan managed to work together at all.

In such circumstances, the Commonwealth was mainly, for India and Pakistan, an arena in which they could eye each other to see that neither obtained advantages unavailable to the other. Pakistan did manage, once or twice, to use Commonwealth institutions to further its aims in Kashmir; on the whole, however, India was vigilant to prevent this, and very largely successful. In the absence of any special political privileges for one or the other, it helped both economically to belong to the Commonwealth. The way in which their earlier diffidence about South Africa's membership was reluctantly but rapidly overcome, once it became clear that African opinion was both determined and important, was a sign that, while the Commonwealth had been congenial to them in the 1950s, they could not afford to retain its comfortable conventions when playing for bigger stakes in the 1960s. Alignment and non-alignment, the slogans to which Pakistan and India respectively had adhered in the 1950s, had become much less relevant to their problems by 1969 because the rapprochement of the two sides transformed the former Cold War situation. New associates were now needed; in addition, the structure of pressure and propaganda which the African states had created was a significant aspect of the 'world opinion' which both courted. The Commonwealth, accepted in the first instance since it provided continuity because of Britain's former control of undivided India, became less important in the affairs of the subcontinent after Nehru's death. The sense of continuity was vestigial. So were the advantages to be gained in the economic sphere, once Britain's determination to enter the EEC had been resuscitated in the new circumstances of 1967. By the end of the 1960s neither India or Pakistan had much to lose or gain from the Commonwealth, materially speaking.[1]

---

[1] Pakistan left the Commonwealth on 30 January 1972, following the action of certain Commonwealth countries (Australia, New Zealand, Fiji) in recognizing Bangladesh, the former East Pakistan which had become independent with the help of Indian arms. The Pakistani move was apparently a substitute for breaking off diplomatic relations with these Commonwealth countries and with Britain, which was expected shortly to announce recognition of Bangladesh.

IV

The problems of the other quarrelling pair, Malaysia and Singapore, were cast in a different mould. They did not go to war with each other. Instead, their verbal disputes were carried on within a system of common defence against communist insurgents and, for a time, against confrontation by Indonesia. Their need for such defence forced them to co-operate and also to press for continuance of a British military presence within their own borders, and for the retention of token contingents there by Australia and New Zealand. This foreign-policy environment was quite different from those of other Commonwealth states.

In Singapore, where the Chinese community was a clear majority, a governing party based largely but not entirely on the Chinese (the People's Action Party, led by Lee Kuan Yew), attempted to gain a foothold in Malaya after the incorporation of Singapore, Malaya, Sabah, and Sarawak in the Federation of Malaysia in 1963. The ruling Alliance in Malaya, in which the Malays were dominant, responded by ejecting Singapore from Malaysia. It was in essence the communal balance within the total area which decided that Singapore would become a sovereign state. The rift between the two governments was deep. None the less, they recognized that each would endanger itself if they carried their disagreement to the point of either ceasing to maintain co-operation against their joint adversaries or gaining temporary political advantage by seeking a removal of the 'Commonwealth' military presence represented by Britain, Australia, and New Zealand. Co-operation and antipathy thus continued to go hand in hand. It was a curious situation in which the three external Commonwealth countries were expected to make co-operation easier for Malaysia and Singapore by not only deterring Indonesia (and, to a lesser extent, the Philippines) but also deterring extreme elements in Malaysia and Singapore from arousing antipathy to the point of violent conflict.

Such conflict could not be tolerated by either government, largely for economic reasons. In Malaysia an open season for Malay hotheads would have meant attacks on the Chinese business class, with consequent economic chaos. In Singapore a direct communal conflict, extending from Malaya, would have pitted a Chinese majority against a small Malay minority, and probably led to demands by the Malays in Malaya for stern action against Singapore by the Malaysian government. Even if the situation did not deteriorate to this point, much of Singapore's value as a reliable marketing and investment centre would have been lost if it had suffered constant communal violence. For each, violence would jeopardize what was, in Asian terms, a high standard of living.

For Britain, Australia, and New Zealand, the position was acceptable so long as all three wished to retain forces in Malaya and Singapore as part of their contribution to a general western defence of Southeast Asia, alongside the US effort in Thailand, the Philippines, and Vietnam. By the end of the 1960s, however, the British government was ceasing to play an active role east of Suez, and the Vietnam war had effectively destroyed the likelihood that the US would continue to keep large numbers of troops in the area. Australia and New Zealand, while reluctant to see either Britain or the US go, were not prepared to keep more than token forces outside their own borders. This left a position in which both Malaysia and Singapore could still benefit marginally from 'Commonwealth' military assistance, although the margin was smaller than at any time since either had achieved independence.

Yet the Commonwealth was still important to them, especially to Singapore. Social and economic links with Britain and Australia were strong. Once Singapore split off, it needed quick recognition. Commonwealth acceptance helped. Active intervention in Commonwealth relations, typified by Lee's acting as spokesman for the African states over Rhodesia in 1966, showed that an articulate, adroit state could play a notable part in the Commonwealth, even if it was small. Moreover, the circumstances of Southeast Asia gave the Commonwealth status of Malaysia and Singapore a special significance in the 1960s, within the context of the Vietnam war and of US-sponsored military activities in general. The Malayan area was regarded by both the British and American governments as 'a Commonwealth affair', and Malaya did not join Seato when it became independent in 1957, although it became a member of the Commonwealth. Thereafter the Malayan prime minister, Tunku Abdul Rahman, was able to dissociate himself (sometimes quite strongly) from Seato and its activities, while getting from the Commonwealth members of Seato (Britain, Australia, and New Zealand) the internal and external defence which his country needed. The same was true of Singapore after its departure from Malaysia.

Absence from direct dependence on the US meant that Malaysia and Singapore did not have to respond to the American call for 'more flags in Vietnam', as did Korea, Thailand, the Philippines, Australia, and New Zealand. This meant escaping some of the international opprobrium which participation in this war brought upon these other states. One can argue, of course, that it was association with Britain rather than membership of the Commonwealth which gave Malaysia and Singapore this sort of immunity, an immunity that might have disappeared if the Wilson government had responded to the American call. Nevertheless, the arrangements were described as 'Commonwealth', and the Wilson government refused to respond; so some degree of credit may go to the Commonwealth.

v

Much has already been said about the pan-African policies of the African Commonwealth members, which were co-ordinated in the OAU, with the

UN as the focus. But, as Professor Mazrui has pointed out, this unanimity at the UN did not necessarily mean that there was a high degree of consensus among African countries, if only because the African issues brought to the UN were often those which least divided African states. There was a reluctance to take issues like the Nigerian civil war, the Ethiopian-Somalia dispute, the Malawi-Tanzanian disagreements, or the Algerian-Moroccan border question to the UN, for there was an ethos in inter-African relations which put a premium on trying to solve this kind of African problem within the African continent itself.

I have had occasion to call this ethos the principle of continental jurisdiction. . . . And African policy-makers, sometimes led by Emperor Haile Selassie of Ethiopia, have often emphasised the desirability of keeping major domestic contentions between Africans away from the chambers of the world body in New York.[1]

In the 1960s it was the experience of the Commonwealth too that African members brought before it the questions on which they were largely united, especially South Africa and Rhodesia, rather than those on which they were divided. For example, the divisions between Tanzania, Kenya, and Uganda over East African federation were not raised at Commonwealth meetings; neither were those between Ghana and Nigeria when Nkrumah was trying to extend the influence of his pan-African ideas over the whole of the continent. Thus the joint pressure exerted by African states at Commonwealth meetings was only part of the picture. If taken as the whole, it would give a mistaken impression of both unanimity and idealism. More often the policies of African states were characterized by idealism in global or African terms, but also by cautious and conservative nationalism in those matters affecting their specific local interests.[2] In one case, that of Tanzania, a well-placed observer perceived these two aspects as part of a whole, as a 'continued attempt to evolve a locally derived overall strategy for development, and to see foreign relations primarily from the perspective of what helps or hinders the further-ance of this policy'.[3] But Tanzania was fortunate in having a leader of remark-able calibre, a regime of considerable stability, and an economy and a society not subject to shocks as violent as those which affected many other African states.

The individual foreign policies of the Commonwealth African states have usually been influenced first by internal problems and then by relations with

[1] Mazrui, 'Geographical propinquity versus Commonwealth cohesion', in Streeten & Corbet, p. 21.

[2] Two articles in the *J. Mod. Afr. Stud.* show these characteristics in respect of Kenya and Nigeria: John Howell, 'An analysis of Kenyan foreign policy' (6/1, 1968) and Douglas Anglin, 'Nigeria: political non-alignment and economic alignment' (2/2, 1964).

[3] Catherine Hoskyns, 'Africa's foreign relations: the case of Tanzania', *Int. Aff.*, July 1968, p. 462. For other material on Tanzanian foreign and domestic policies, see Nyerere's two books of speeches, *Freedom and unity* and *Freedom and socialism* (1968), and three articles on him by William Edgett Smith (*New Yorker*, 16, 23, & 30 Oct 1971).

neighbours. Nkrumah gave Ghana an entirely individual policy which, arising from his own efflorescence of personality, collapsed with his own removal. Ghana's attention then shifted dramatically to the foreign problems arising directly from its balance-of-payments crisis and the domestic adjustments required to resolve that crisis. Relations with neighbours, which had been intense and often adverse because of Nkrumah's attempts at subversion of other African regimes, became simpler and easier, except in 1969 when Ghana, again acting on account of its internal economic problems, began to send home migrant workers to near-by states. Nigeria had operated a cautious, westward-leaning foreign policy before the internal tempest overtook it in 1966; thereafter most foreign issues were judged in terms of that struggle. Tanzania, Kenya, and Uganda, deeply affected by the military mutinies of 1964, spent the decade of the 1960s in constant argument about whether they could construct a satisfactory federation to succeed the arrangements for common services which they had inherited from colonial days. Tanzania, relatively homogeneous in comparison with the other two, did not suffer the combined problems of inter-tribal rivalry and friction across borders (Kenya with Somalia, and Uganda with the Sudan) which troubled them. Two West African states, Sierra Leone and the Gambia, found foreign policy very much a matter of relations with the states alongside them.

The problems of two others, Zambia and Malawi, embraced the double clash between African states and between them and regimes in Africa run by white men. Malawi and Zambia disagreed violently in their approaches to the white regimes of the south. Malawi was prepared to co-operate with them. Zambia was not. It received help from Tanzania, and moral support from many other African states, but it was unable to persuade the British government to use force against Rhodesia and was also unable to sever its economic links with Rhodesia and South Africa. For it, as for other African states pursuing the objective of an Africa ruled by Africans, the capacity of the Portuguese in Angola and Mozambique to withstand guerrilla attack was a constant source of frustration.

In sum, African members of the Commonwealth could and did pursue continent-wide aims, but their principal preoccupations arose from internal disturbances (leading to coups in Ghana, Nigeria, Sierra Leone, and Uganda, and to attempted coups and tribal conflicts elsewhere), and from the problem of amicable arrangements with the states on their borders. As a talking-point, pan-Africanism was a relief from these local distractions, and a means of asserting an African personality in the world at large, but it was not enough. Nor were states outside Africa much help. The Commonwealth African states, with a few small exceptions (Malawi, the Gambia, and the former High Commission Territories in southern Africa) did not receive aid from Britain on the same scale as did the former French colonies from France. The US and the Soviet Union, obsessed not with Africa itself but with nullifying one

COMMONWEALTH FOREIGN POLICIES 381

another's influence in Africa, were disappointing as aid-givers and awkward as associates. Tanzania and Zambia found China prepared to construct the Tanzam railway on fair terms and without obvious strings, but Chinese funds were limited. In any case, other states were inclined to fear Chinese subversion, as they feared US or Soviet-inspired subversion. France, with its own former colonies to look after, was not disposed to extend its activities except to Biafra. Possibly British adherence to the EEC, with associate status for most of the Commonwealth African countries, would bring a more consistent form of development aid.

One developed country was anxious to help African states on its own terms. This was South Africa. By the end of the 1960s its outward policy had borne fruit in Malawi and Lesotho, Swaziland and Botswana. Even the OAU had been sympathetic to the Lesotho delegate's plea, 'what would you do if you were in our position?', when Lesotho applied for membership and the question of association with South Africa came up.[1] But the idea of close connection with the South African regime was still abhorrent to most African states, especially Zambia, which stood to gain most from it. The South African problem, in no way solved by UN scoldings, remained a running sore.

In international terms, there is a contrast between the circumstances of the Asian and African members of the Commonwealth, in that the Asian states were established during the Cold War and had to contend with its problems, whereas the African states, with the exception of Ghana, did not appear on the scene until it had ended. Africa escaped the problems of choice of the Cold War: non-alignment had become a catch-word, not a real option, by the time they adopted it. Only during the Congo crisis did the US and the Soviet Union face each other in Africa south of the Sahara, and then there were so many intermediaries (notably the UN secretariat and the African members of the UN) that the situation did not resemble that in Asia a decade earlier. The African states were not conscious, as the Asian states had been, of two great powers looking over their shoulders. Some of the insouciance and some of the 'unity' of their approach to world problems can be attributed to this fact. In contrast, the Asian Commonwealth states remained highly conscious of the rivalry between the two super-powers, even after other major powers had begun to exert influence in world politics.[2]

VI

The 'old dominions', the Asian members, and the African members comprise the 'heavyweights' of the overseas Commonwealth. They have most of

---

[1] From a private source.

[2] For another assessment of the character of multipolarity at the end of the 1960s, and its significance for Afro-Asian states, see Robert L. Rothstein, *Alliances and small powers* (1968), ch. 8.

the wealth and population and most experience in diplomacy. The 1960s witnessed the advent of certain smaller states in the Caribbean and Mediterranean, to be followed at the turn of the decade by four in the Pacific[1] and one (Mauritius) in the Indian Ocean. All islands except Guyana, all small and poor, almost all took the orthodox Afro-Asian line on major issues at the UN, while having special problems of their own, including continued economic dependence on Britain.

After the collapse of the Federation of the West Indies in 1962, Jamaica and Trinidad became individual members of the Commonwealth, there to be joined by Guyana and Barbados in 1966. In spite of the differences between them, so often stressed by their nationals, these countries' problems were very similar: over-population (except in Guyana), reliance on single crops (mostly sugar), and underlying ethnic antagonisms. More thoroughly influenced by British example than most other Commonwealth members, they were profoundly affected by the restrictions imposed on immigration into Britain, and by the problems of association with Canada and the US, especially in respect of migration and aid. Commonwealth membership was a natural and obvious choice for them; but the uncertainties of the sugar market in the event of Britain's entry into the EEC, and the realization that the important decisions concerning their future would be made in the American hemisphere, inclined them more towards their own side of the Atlantic. Trinidad's action in joining the Organization of American States in 1967 was an earnest of how they might be expected to behave.

Malta and Cyprus had been British possessions because of the traditional importance of the Mediterranean in British strategy. As that strategy altered—mainly through the reduction of British naval power and its replacement in the Mediterranean by that of the US and other Nato members—the significance of the two islands to Britain waned. Both had become members of the Commonwealth for the sake of the advantages of continued association with Britain, Malta because of its naval base and Cyprus because of Commonwealth preference for its exports. But neither was essentially British in background. Malta was drawn towards Italy and Libya, Cyprus towards Greece and Turkey. Malta, having failed to achieve organic union with Britain, became independent in 1964 with an agreement involving heavy British subsidies and the preservation of the naval base—a precarious foundation in view of the ebbing of British interest in the area. Cyprus, after constant internal turmoil, had had its independence guaranteed in 1961 by Britain, Greece, and Turkey —again a precarious situation because the co-operation of the last two, reluctantly given under pressure from the United States, was constantly undermined by communal tension in Cyprus itself.

For Mauritius, Nauru, Tonga, Fiji, and Western Samoa a questionable

---

[1] Amongst the 'four in the Pacific' I have included Nauru along with Fiji, Tonga, and Western Samoa, although Nauru did not become a full member of the Commonwealth.

future stretched ahead in the 1970s. Mauritius could be regarded as ultimately falling into a South African sphere of influence, but this would be disconcerting and potentially disrupting for its people and also unpopular with other Third World states. The Pacific countries had close economic ties with Australia and New Zealand, emigration to which might prove a suitable outlet for over-populated islands, provided Australia and New Zealand would agree. The traditional Pacific powers, Japan and the US, both loomed large for them; but how first to attract, and then to domesticate, the flow of foreign capital was a problem which none could easily solve in advance. It is not surprising that these islands, like those of the Caribbean, were strong supporters of the Commonwealth association at a time when others had cooled towards it. They came to it late, without the rancorous experience of Commonwealth meetings in the mid-1960s and after a long and harmonious association with Britain. In 1971 Fiji was the only Commonwealth state other than Australia and New Zealand still to incorporate the Union Jack in its flag. A British connection, if continued, might help to offset pressure from Japan, the US, and Australia. The Commonwealth was something special to belong to; otherwise such small new states might well feel lost in the crowded corridors of the UN.

VII

It is significant that, by the end of the 1960s, the most enthusiastic members of the Commonwealth should be the newest and smallest. The pressures and attractions of a wider world had absorbed the others, including Britain. Both politically and economically, a variety of associations was available to all but the least important of the members. Some, like Canada, Australia, and India, were conducting their diplomacy in a directly individual fashion, in pursuit of what they saw as national interests; others, while taking refuge in such bodies as Unctad and the OAU, pursued national interests in whatever forum would listen to them. The Commonwealth was an instrument which all could use, but its usefulness varied from one member to another.

CHAPTER 17

CHANGES IN COMMONWEALTH MACHINERY

I N the 1950s, when this writer talked to people in the CRO in London, some of them spoke of themselves as involved in 'the Commonwealth system'. This was not an exact term but it was frequently used and clearly meant something important. They believed that they were engaged in an activity different from ordinary diplomacy, and that Britain's relations with other members of the Commonwealth were not the same as those which it had with other countries, even the US. What happened to this 'system', even recognizing that it was loose, incomplete, and in no sense rigid?

I

First, what was the Commonwealth system, and how did it operate in the 1950s? It was essentially a system of parallel diplomacy, based on the assumption that relations between Commonwealth members had a family quality which other sorts of international relations did not, and that this family quality justified a different structure of consultation and negotiation from that which normally obtained. These assumptions had been taken over from the CRO's predecessor, the Dominions Office. The Commonwealth system was part of the diplomatic system at large, but it was assumed to be diplomacy with a difference: not self-contained, but separate. It required, for Britain but not for any other member of the Commonwealth, a separate diplomatic service. The system comprised a number of interlocking elements: criteria of membership, meetings of prime ministers and of other ministers and officials, certain co-operative institutions, the CRO in London operating its own Commonwealth service, special relations between prime ministers, and high commissioners representing Commonwealth members in one another's capitals. Let us look at these elements separately.

In the 1950s there was no significant change in the criteria for membership, as these had been finally established through the decision in 1949 that republican India should remain a member. There was a gap of eight years before Ghana and Malaya became members in 1957; in the meantime the older members came to terms with an Asian presence in the form of India, Pakistan, and Ceylon, and vaguely looked forward to the eventual entry of Africans. All members except Britain were former British dependencies, but it was not assumed that all dependencies would automatically become members on attaining independence, any more than that independence was a certain future for all or even most of them. The example of the Sudan in 1956 confirmed those of Burma in 1947 and Israel in 1948: none had sought Commonwealth membership on becoming independent. South Africa was a 'difficult' member, but had been so ever since it became a dominion. It, along with the others, recognized the Queen as symbolic Head of the Commonwealth, and agreed to seek further confirmation of its membership if it decided to become a republic; these were the only formal requirements for a member, except that it should, in the first instance, be acceptable to all the other members.

The occasional meetings of prime ministers (irregular, but occurring at roughly two-yearly intervals) were the most visible aspect of the system, and of Commonwealth relations at large, even though they were held in camera. Emphasis was laid in public upon their informality and the fact that they did not pass resolutions. Lord Normanbrook, who had acted as secretary for many of them, declared in 1964 that there were no precise rules of procedure but that over the years certain conventions had grown up. First, on international questions no formal decisions would be taken and no attempt made to formulate 'Commonwealth' policy, though there was nothing to stop each government 'separately and independently [pursuing] a policy . . . consistent with that of the other Commonwealth governments' on a particular matter; in practice, he said, this had often happened, and had strengthened the influence of Commonwealth countries in world affairs. Secondly, the prime ministers did not discuss the internal affairs of a member country, except at its own request. Thirdly, disputes between one member and another would not be discussed 'save with the consent of the parties to the dispute'. These, however, were not immutable rules: procedure could be adapted to meet new situations, and issues not debated in plenary session could be debated outside the conference room.[1]

There was ample room for discussion, not only in terms of the rules, but also physically. In the 1950s the members were few enough for the meetings to be held in the Cabinet Room at 10 Downing Street—an appropriate arrangement, since it had been traditional for dominion prime ministers to be members of the Privy Council, and to attend an occasional cabinet meeting when in London. Until a fairly late date, Prime Ministers' Meetings were largely discussions between Privy Councillors who met not to reach agreement but to exchange views. The position of the British secretary of the cabinet as also secretary to the meetings of Commonwealth prime ministers grew naturally out of this situation.

The responsibility for Prime Ministers' Meetings lay partly with the CRO and partly with the Cabinet Office. The CRO conducted the negotiations preceding the announcement that a conference would be held; the Cabinet

---

[1] Lord Normanbrook, 'Meetings of Commonwealth prime ministers', *J. Parliaments of Commonwealth*, 45 (1964), pp. 250–1.

Office took over from that point onwards. The staff of the secretary to the cabinet was temporarily augmented from the CRO to provide a conference secretariat. The initiative in holding a meeting was taken by the British government, which sounded out others, issued invitations, and fixed dates in accordance with the convenience of the various heads of government. Macmillan records that in 1959 Walter Nash of New Zealand wanted a Commonwealth Prime Ministers' Meeting before the international 'Summit meeting' which Macmillan was trying to arrange; after discussion with Menzies Macmillan was able to dissuade him from insisting on a Commonwealth meeting, and seems to have retained the initiative.[1]

The meetings were, in fact, very British affairs, and were held only in London, although the possibility of their being held elsewhere was often mooted. The British prime minister took the chair. It was the British government's practice to pay the expenses, while in Britain, of each overseas prime minister, his wife, his private secretary, and one senior official. Other costs, including fares and the payment of other members of the prime ministers' entourages, were met by the countries concerned. The agenda for the meetings were a matter of consultation, items being included when there was something of a general consensus and no opposition. Prime ministers took advantage of their being in London to see a variety of people with financial, trading, and other connections with their countries, thereby emphasizing the non-governmental links between Britain and the overseas members of the Commonwealth.

In addition to the plenary sessions at which the prime ministers discussed world affairs, in economic as well as political terms, and questions of membership, the meetings provided opportunities for overseas prime ministers to have personal discussions with the British prime minister, and for those with similar interests to have what were, in effect, sectional meetings. In Normanbrook's words, 'there have usually been some sessions attended by less than the full number'.[2] On most occasions in the 1950s, however, the general appearance of the meeting was one of agreement with Britain: the picture drawn of them in Chapter 1 is a fair depiction. The ceremonial dinner at Buckingham Palace and the photograph of the Queen with her prime ministers continued to be features of each occasion, as did the weekend at Chequers.

These meetings of prime ministers were paralleled and buttressed by meetings of other ministers and officials, sometimes in the form of full ministerial meetings (most often by finance ministers), and sometimes on specific problems or in officials' seminars. At the UN, where there was, by convention, a 'Commonwealth seat' amongst the non-permanent members of the Security Council, it was customary for Commonwealth representatives to

[1] Macmillan, *Pointing the way*, p. 94. There is an interesting account of organizing Prime Ministers' Meetings in the early 1950s in George Mallaby, *From my level* (1965), pp. 136–49.
[2] Normanbrook, p. 253.

meet once a week under British chairmanship, while the General Assembly was sitting.[1] It was also customary for Commonwealth ambassadors in Washington to meet once a fortnight in the British Embassy, 'to exchange views and consult informally together'.[2]

The prime ministers had, at various stages in the past—mainly in the days of the Imperial Conference—agreed to the creation of a number of co-operative institutions, most of which were located in Britain. The most notable of these were the Commonwealth Agricultural Bureaux, but there were also the Commonwealth Economic Committee, the Commonwealth Shipping Committee, the Commonwealth Scientific Committee, and the Commonwealth Telecommunications Board. Each had a governing body on which all members of the Commonwealth were represented. K. C. Wheare, examining these in 1960, considered that in all cases their functions were 'those of providing information and advice and acting as a medium of consultation'. He found 'only one example of co-operative administration through a permanent institution in the Commonwealth where the institution [was] not engaged almost exclusively in the exchange of information or consultation': this was the Imperial War Graves Commission. To him, it proved a rule: 'it is only in a matter where policy can be agreed upon and politics can be ruled out that an institution with administrative functions can be set up by Commonwealth Members'.[3] Indeed, the whole emphasis of the system—an unstructured and unintended system, not one which had been consciously thought out—was on consultation; for most matters, experience had shown that politics could not be suppressed.

The CRO was, to a great extent, the centre-piece of the system, although it was formally a department of the British government and not a joint Commonwealth undertaking. With a secretary of state in the cabinet, it had a specific task to perform within the British government (as well as its task of putting British policy before Commonwealth governments). A former holder of the post put it thus:

The over-riding responsibility of the Secretary of State was to maintain the distinction of Commonwealth relations. He had, in fact, to educate Whitehall. His officials had to see that every other Department, the activities of which might impinge upon the interests of any other Commonwealth country, took these interests into account and provided the necessary flow of information for transmission to Commonwealth countries. Officials of the Commonwealth Relations Office also served on all interdepartmental committees whose business might have a Commonwealth bearing.[4]

[1] For a somewhat lyrical picture of the Commonwealth at the UN in this period, see Pendennis in *Observer*, 28 Sept 1958.

[2] Franks, ch. 2, p. 17.

[3] Wheare, pp. 133–5. S. Africa continued to be represented on, and to pay for the work of, the Imperial (later Commonwealth) War Graves Commission throughout the 1960s, in spite of its having left the Commonwealth.

[4] Gordon Walker, 'Commonwealth secretary', *JCPS*, Nov 1961, pp. 24–5.

It was in order to 'educate Whitehall' that the CRO maintained an establishment in London and was represented on a great many interdepartmental committees.[1] Through it went all communications from Commonwealth governments, and it was the channel through which they were informed of the British government's intentions. Although the other members' high commissioners in London had the right of access to other British departments, the CRO was the effective means of communication on major matters. Its methods were praised by C. J. M. Alport, its minister of state in 1960, who said that, with the consent of other members, it had in effect over the past thirty-five years been acting as a Commonwealth secretariat.

It has been a collecting house for ideas and information of common interest to the independent members. It has helped to evolve for the Commonwealth a set of diplomatic procedures which avoided the formalities and stiffness of normal protocol. We do not despatch formal notes of protest to each other, shrouded in the blinding light of the latest publicity technique, nor do we spend our time assuring each other to our highest consideration at the end of communications designed to prove that the exact opposite is the truth.

Goodwill was taken for granted even in cases of violent disagreements, which were much easier to resolve because of the informality of the approach. 'I have no doubt that in the Commonwealth context such methods of diplomacy are the most effective, and I sometimes think that in this field the Commonwealth can teach a number of lessons to the older diplomatic world.'[2]

The CRO was proud of its distinctive task. It came to assume, in addition to the responsibility for putting the British point of view before other Commonwealth members and theirs before the British government, that of public relations for the Commonwealth as a whole. The pamphlets about the Commonwealth produced by the Reference Division of the Central Office of Information under its directions had no counterpart elsewhere in the Commonwealth. Since no other member had a separate department and minister to deal with Commonwealth relations, it is not surprising that the CRO should have been virtually alone in this field. It is certain that its fervour was unmatched elsewhere. Although ministers of overseas members often made statements about the value of the Commonwealth, they normally echoed these British publications and the speeches of Commonwealth Secretaries—with the exception of Canada, the one other member whose government took the Commonwealth idea so seriously as to extend and develop it.

The departmental situation in other Commonwealth members varied in

[1] The working of the CRO in the 1950s can be studied in GB, Select Committee on Estimates, *Third Report*, sess. 1958–9, from which part of the evidence presented by the CRO is in Mansergh, *Documents 1952–62*, pp. 748–52. See also W. J. M. Mackenzie & J. W. Grove, *Central administration in Britain* (1957), pp. 224–8, and my article, 'The CRO and Commonwealth relations', *Int. Stud.*, July 1960.

[2] C. J. M. Alport, 'The philosophy of independence: the work of the Commonwealth Relations Office', address to Royal Commonwealth Soc., 26 May 1960 (text from CRO), p. 11.

accordance with their past circumstances. In each there were special provisions in their Departments of External Affairs; in India and Pakistan these were styled after independence, Ministries of External Affairs and Commonwealth Relations.[1] The fact that the British cabinet secretary acted as secretary to Prime Ministers' Meetings led to a close connection between the Cabinet Office in London and its counterparts in other Commonwealth countries. In several of these 'for a long period Prime Ministers in most dominions retained the External Affairs portfolios in their own hands'.[2] This was true of Canada up to 1947, of South Africa to 1948, and of New Zealand and India until later. In Australia the two portfolios were separated quite early, but relations with Britain remained in the hands of the prime minister's department. Patrick Gordon Walker has drawn attention to the importance of the links between cabinet secretariats,[3] and it is clear from personal testimony that these, and other direct links between CRO officials and those of other countries, enhanced the harmony of Prime Ministers' Meetings in the 1950s. Officials met beforehand to discuss possible items for the agenda; they accompanied the prime ministers in the meetings themselves; and they drafted the communiqués which reconciled national viewpoints, though often at the price of blandness and platitude. They got to know each other well. Since prime ministers often corresponded with one another between meetings, the contacts between their closest advisers acquired an importance in their own right.

The distinctive link between countries in the Commonwealth system was provided by high commissioners. These were a visible sign of the difference between Commonwealth and other forms of diplomacy, since no other group of states used a special term to describe their diplomatic envoys to one another. It had been chosen originally to stress the fact that these were not envoys in the accepted sense of an ambassador from one head of state to another: how could the King send an ambassador to himself? In spite of the recognition of the divisibility of the Crown, this same title was preserved for the representatives of one of the monarch's realms in another, the high commissioner being appointed by one government to the other government, not to the monarch or the governor-general. When republics appeared in the Commonwealth, and later other monarchies such as Malaya, the title was retained, though in these cases high commissioners were accredited between heads of state. The question of status had been settled before our period began. High commissioners everywhere took precedence with ambassadors. The name was almost the last vestige of the *inter se* doctrine—although one could argue that the whole notion of a Commonwealth system was itself a projection of that

---

[1] See Heather J. Harvey, *Consultation and co-operation in the Commonwealth* (1952), pp. 198–202, from which one may infer that the first use of 'Commonwealth Relations' was to describe the former Indian Department of Indians Overseas after 1944.
[2] Mansergh, *Survey 1939–52*, p. 406.   [3] *The Commonwealth* (1962), p. 244.

doctrine ('the ghost of the British Empire sitting on the grave thereof'), in spite of its practicality and its widespread acceptance in the 1950s.

High commissioners not only signified the special quality of Commonwealth relations by their titles but also in their operations. The CRO described the situation in its submission to the Estimates Committee in 1959:

> The principal difference in [the conduct of official business] between a High Commissioner and a foreign Ambassador in a Commonwealth capital is that whereas the Ambassador must do all his business through the Department of External Affairs, the High Commissioner is entitled to deal direct with other departments of Government. The result is that the High Commissioner and his staff at appropriate levels have contacts of an informal sort throughout the machinery of Government. A point of particular note is that the UK High Commissioner has closer and more frequent contact with the Prime Minister of the Commonwealth country in which he is serving than is the case with foreign heads of mission. Practice on this point naturally varies, but in Australia, for instance, on all important matters and whenever a formal approach is called for, the High Commissioner deals direct with the Prime Minister.[1]

Such access by a British high commissioner to an overseas prime minister was not paralleled, to the same extent, for the overseas countries' high commissioners in London;[2] these had to be content with the Commonwealth secretary, but could claim that they saw him regularly and thus had access to the British cabinet.

Taken together, these various elements did constitute something of a system. The main danger to it lay in the likelihood that, as the members' interests and activities diversified and as their numbers grew, the family quality would be insufficient to sustain the system in the spirit which had been appropriate to it in earlier decades. Not self-contained, but separate; but separate for how long and in what terms?

II

So far as membership was concerned, there were no changes in principle in the 1960s, merely great changes in numbers and in relations between members. The prospect for the Commonwealth of a significant increase in the number of British colonies gaining independence stimulated some discussion in Britain in the 1950s. At first, especially in 1954, when there seemed a possibility that South Africa might attempt to blackball newly independent African states, it seems that interdepartmental discussions, which came to nought, were held on the idea of a two-tier Commonwealth of 'senior' and

---

[1] Mansergh, *Documents 1952–62*, p. 751.
[2] For one case of British high commissioners' relations with overseas prime ministers, see Mallaby, pp. 61–84. This is a unique instance of a high commissioner writing about his job.

'junior' members.[1] As has been seen (in ch. 8), South Africa accepted the presence of Ghana when the actual moment came. Another scheme which came to nothing was advanced sometimes by Sir Eric Harrison, the Australian high commissioner in London, presumably on behalf of his prime minister, who is believed to have put something of a like proposition before the prime ministers in 1957. The scheme comprised a 'British Commonwealth' or 'Crown Commonwealth' within the general circle of Commonwealth countries, consisting of the old dominions (perhaps only Australia and New Zealand; he was not very specific). Within the inner circle there would be close co-operation and consultation; beyond, the others could do as they wished.[2]

The recognition that the large number of colonies seeking independence might overcrowd the Commonwealth caused the Commonwealth prime ministers in 1960 to agree that 'a detailed study' should be made of 'the constitutional development of the Commonwealth, with particular reference to the future of the smaller dependent territories'.[3] It seems that the problem was studied at the official level, but no further mention of it was made in communiqués from Prime Ministers' Meetings. Instead, colonies continued to seek and gain membership as they became independent, until at the beginning of the 1970s Tonga, with a population of less than 90,000, was accepted. Nauru, with 6,000, had become a 'special member' in 1969. The older and bigger countries had evidently decided that they must admit such small fellow members, although at an earlier stage it is said they were unwilling to accept the New Zealand dependency of Western Samoa when it was approaching independence.[4] In due course Western Samoa successfully applied for full membership. A stage short of Commonwealth status was reached by six of Britain's island dependencies in the West Indies when in 1967 and 1969 they were made autonomous but not fully independent and were designated 'Associated States', with access to Commonwealth functional meetings. Like Nauru, they did not attend meetings of heads of government. The main effect of this increase in numbers was on the conduct of Commonwealth meetings and on the Commonwealth secretariat, a body rather more favoured by the smaller than some of the larger members. In Commonwealth

[1] See e.g. Colin Legum in *Observer*, 4 Apr 1954, and 'Status in the Commonwealth', *The Times*, 16 Dec 1954.

[2] Sir Eric Harrison was a man about whose utterances it is very easy to be unfair. These references are to *Australian Newsletter* (London), 13 Dec 1956 & 7 Feb 1957, and *The Times*, 6 Dec 1956.

[3] See Mansergh, *Documents 1952–62*, pp. 285–90, for a Commons debate in April 1959, and p. 362 for the 1960 communiqué. See also Kenneth Robinson, 'The intergovernmental machinery of Commonwealth consultation and co-operation', in W. B. Hamilton & others, eds, *A decade of the Commonwealth* (1966), pp. 93–5. For contemporary views see Sir Hilary Blood, *The smaller territories* (1958) and Gordon Walker, 'Policy for the Commonwealth', in T. E. M. McKittrick & Kenneth Younger, eds, *Fabian international essays* (1957), pp. 191–3.

[4] See J. W. Davidson in *Pacific Islands Monthly*, Jan 1969, p. 27.

meetings, the members, no matter how small they were, were 'equal in status', both by tradition and in their role as universally recognized sovereign states.

One other question was whether a member of the Commonwealth would remain so if it entered some form of federation, confederation or union with one or more other states which were not members of the Commonwealth. The point arose first over the reported Ghana-Guinea union of 1958, and then over British entry into the EEC. Neither was a serious issue. The Ghana–Guinea union quickly proved abortive; British entry into the EEC, so long delayed, would be into an economic community in which members retained their formal sovereignty and autonomous foreign policies. A European federation would be another matter; but that had not become a practical possibility.[1]

One clear rule emerging after 1965 was that a country seeking membership should apply to the Commonwealth secretariat, which would then approach the existing members to test their views. The process became more complicated as the number of members grew. Some uncertainty exists about whether intending members can be blackballed, as it was envisaged they might be in the much smaller Commonwealth of the early 1950s, when bringing forward new members was the responsibility of the British government. S. A. de Smith has put the later position:

> There is no settled rule that the consent of the existing full members must be unanimous—it is believed that Pakistan declined to express any view when Singapore applied for membership—but the fact of strong minority opposition might lead to withdrawal of the application, and foreknowledge of such opposition would probably result in a decision not to proceed with a projected application. . . . But as far as is known, no territory whose application has been sponsored by the former metropolitan power has been rejected.[2]

Recognition of the Queen as Head of the Commonwealth and as a symbol of the free association of its members remained a necessity for members, though for a majority she was not head of state.

There had been, at one stage, a suggestion in Britain that the Commonwealth might be 'expanded' to take in other states, since, in the words of the Expanding Commonwealth Group, 'the free association of communities of Commonwealth citizens, which is the Commonwealth of Nations today, contains the seeds of a world system for which the "middle Powers" are craving'.[3] Not surprisingly, no state that had not been a British dependency tried to join it. Even the news from the chairman of the Group that a former prime minister of Japan had told the Queen in October 1954 that his country

---

[1] See Wheare, pp. 118–19.

[2] S. A. de Smith, 'Fundamental rules—forty years on', *Int. J.*, Spring 1971, p. 354. It has been suggested to me that Pakistan attempted initially to reject Singapore's application but, was prevailed upon to withdraw this rejection.

[3] Expanding Commonwealth Group, *The expanding Commonwealth* (1956), p. 12.

wished to join the Commonwealth[1] had no concrete result, although it has been suggested that Norway and Nepal were interested. The Commonwealth remained essentially the body which the great majority of ex-dependencies joined. That was the thing to do. It was not automatic, either in terms of application, or (more to the point in the 1960s, as Rhodesia demonstrated) in terms of acceptance. Nevertheless, the massive growth in numbers brought acute problems to the Prime Ministers' Meetings, the centre-piece of the Commonwealth system.

III

Symbolically, by January 1971 these meetings had acquired a new name, Commonwealth Heads of Government Meetings, since ten of the thirty-one members represented at Singapore in that month did not have prime ministers as their heads. Botswana, Cyprus, the Gambia, Kenya, Malawi, Pakistan, Tanzania, Uganda, and Zambia had executive presidents, and Nigeria a military government. Besides the increase in numbers there were also changes in tone, procedure, control, issues, and assumptions.

Already in 1964 Lord Normanbrook felt that 'such difficulties as have arisen have been mainly due to the increase in numbers, not to the changes in the composition of the association'.[2] 10 Downing Street could no longer contain the swollen meetings, even with strict observance of the rule that each country could have only two seats at the table, and two behind for advisers. The Queen's provision of Marlborough House for Commonwealth meetings, effective from 1962, was generous and suitable, given the increased numbers; but ironically, it brought the meetings back to the venue of the Imperial Conference (the last of which had been held next door at St James's palace in 1937) and to something more like the atmosphere of those conferences, with their large staffs and solemn tone. The intimacy of meetings in the 1950s was no longer possible. Each country had to be heard, especially after the South African and Rhodesian questions obliged each one to declare itself on matters which were furiously debated at the UN, in the OAU, and in Third World circles generally. There was still room for personal feeling and even friendship amongst the Commonwealth leaders, whose meetings together gave them more opportunity to assess one another than they could get from their ministers' and officials' reports; but the former atmosphere, it seems, was gone.

Changes in size and tone were necessarily linked with changes in procedure. A gathering of thirty countries cannot conduct itself like a body of six or eight. New procedures arose from a combination of increased numbers and determined efforts to change British policy, first over the EEC and then, to a much greater extent, over Rhodesia and South Africa.

It became a matter of course for some members that prepared speeches should be issued publicly, in place of the previous more discreet system

---

[1] Patrick Maitland, *Task for giants* (1957), p. 9.   [2] Normanbrook, p. 252.

whereby some indication was given to the press of each member country of the main trend of discussion, with its own position highlighted. The change to the distribution of prepared speeches in advance was less important than the fact that speeches were being made for public consumption, not for discussion within the meetings. The likelihood of 'leaks' meant that, while the meetings were still nominally held in camera, more emphasis was laid on distinctions between different kinds of session. Macmillan, in describing the 1960 meeting which first considered South African apartheid, distinguishes between 'plenary', 'informal', and 'restricted' sessions, the first being the normal assembly of prime ministers and their advisers, the second a group of prime ministers with the South African representative 'upstairs', and the third a meeting of all the prime ministers in full session but without any advisers.[1] It was necessary to hold the 'informal' sessions because it was only at these, at first, that South Africa was willing to have discussions of its racial policy.

At Singapore in 1971, in contrast, there were three types of session, known this time as 'plenary', 'executive', and 'secret'. The 'plenary' sessions were as before. The 'secret' sessions corresponded to the 'restricted' sessions of 1960, being confined to heads of government and the secretary-general. The 'executive' sessions consisted of heads of government with one adviser each and a small group from the secretariat. Both of the latter two types were meant to push business on and allow heads of government to have the same freedom of discussion, without set speeches, as they had had in the 1950s; but there were two results which betokened the new conditions. One was that some heads of government were frank and spontaneous in the 'secret' sessions but read out their original prepared speeches in later 'plenary' sessions, so as to be able to release them for use by the press. The other was that some of them expressed annoyance at having to keep silent about what happened in the 'secret' sessions, since this did not happen at the UN, where each leader could speak from the rostrum to the world. In contrast, the British and some of the older members' representatives made comparisons with the deliberations of a cabinet, the model on which the meetings had originally been based; by convention these were secret.

A further development in procedure, which arose over the Rhodesia issue, and has already been discussed (ch. 10), was caucusing. This too seemed alien to the British and older members; but it had become standard at the UN and other international gatherings by 1965, especially for the African states. From their point of view it was unreasonable to condemn in one international forum what had become standard in others. However, its effectiveness depended upon basic agreement between those who practised it; if this was strained, as at the 1969 and 1971 meetings, the practice could become embarrassing to those involved in it. It could also cause lengthy delays in meetings. From a

[1] *Pointing the way*, pp. 171–4.

traditional standpoint, it was a violation of established practice, an offence against the spirit which was supposed to characterize the meetings. Some of the older members might ruefully have exclaimed like the Cardinal in *'Tis Pity She's a Whore*:

> Why, how now, friends! what saucy mates are you
> That know nor duty nor civility?
> Are we a person fit to be your host,
> Or is our house become your common inn
> To beat our doors at pleasure? What such haste
> Is yours, as that it cannot wait fit times?
> Are you the masters of this Commonwealth
> And know no more discretion?

but the old situation could never be restored.

Changes in size, tone, and procedure were accompanied by changes in control, appropriate to the new circumstances and relieving Britain of responsibilities which could be troublesome when most of those attending the meetings were trying to put pressure on the British government. By the end of the 1960s the British prime minister was still chairman when the meetings were in London, but this was as host, not because of traditional primacy. Sir Abubakar took the chair at Lagos in 1966, and Lee Kuan Yew at Singapore in 1971. A more important change was the handing over to the Commonwealth secretariat of responsibility for organizing the meetings from 1966 onwards. The doubling of the secretary to the British cabinet and secretary to the Commonwealth meetings had worked well in its time, but it had become desirable to have a neutral instrument in which no single country would have a predominant voice, and it was increasingly difficult for a British official to be recognized as performing this neutral function. When the cabinet secretary had to take the chair at a stormy meeting of officials, held to draft a communiqué for what had been a stormy meeting of heads of government, there was a temptation for others to charge him with collusion with the other British officials present, despite his attempt to be detached.

The changeover to the secretariat was smooth. A draft agenda was arranged by the secretariat with the high commissioners' offices in London, any member being entitled to object to a draft. Although the agenda remained provisional until the meeting actually began, the form approved by senior officials on the preceding day was usually adopted. The secretariat staffed the meeting and the host country continued to provide hospitality to the heads of government and their wives, and other local expenses such as security. It is doubtful if officials from countries other than Britain felt that there was a change of atmosphere; to some British officials and politicians who, when meetings were held in London, had ceased to be hosts in more than a geographical sense, a change may have been apparent.

Changes in control were symbolic rather than substantial: the same aims were pursued by the secretariat as previously by the Cabinet Office and the CRO. But as earlier chapters have made clear, there were substantial changes in issues and assumptions. Lord Normanbrook's three conventions remained the general assumptions of the meetings, but they had been bent and strained— some would say broken—in regard to colonialism and in the related matter of racialism. There were strenuous efforts to formulate 'Commonwealth' policy on Rhodesia and South Africa on the ground that these had become 'international questions'. Apart from these vital matters, the conventions were observed. The Nigerian civil war was regarded as an internal matter and was not discussed; the Indo-Pakistani conflict continued to be kept off the Commonwealth agenda; the African members reserved their African disputes for the OAU, although in general, from 1964 onwards the Commonwealth meetings were used to exert pressure on Britain to pursue particular policies in Africa rather than as occasions for an exchange of views. This was not all that happened at Commonwealth meetings, but it was what took much of the time and filled the headlines.

At Singapore in 1971 the heads of government at last issued the first Commonwealth Declaration, codifying the principles which members were said to hold in common.[1] These included belief in the UN as an influence for peace; in the liberty of the individual, representative institutions, and guarantees for personal freedom under the law; in opposition to racial prejudice; in a free flow of international trade, and of adequate resources for the developing countries; in international co-operation as essential to remove the causes of war and to foster tolerance and development; and in the Commonwealth as one of the most fruitful associations for these purposes. There were no penalties for violation of the principles, nor was specific reference made to the conventions about members' internal affairs and disputes between them, although the declaration did say that each was 'responsible for its own policies'. It might be regarded as a requirement for future members, or even as a standard for existing members to live up to, if the political forces within the Commonwealth chose to make it so; but the section on personal freedom and representative institutions could so readily be used in retaliation against those who wished to indict others on racial and colonial grounds that it could hardly be regarded as more than a debating platform. The Declaration offered no solution to the problem of how to conduct Commonwealth meetings. Indeed, the British prime minister said in parliament afterwards that, in the discussions on the Commonwealth in the 1970s, 'many Heads of Government said that they feared there was a danger that the Commonwealth was developing into a mini-United Nations, and there was no point in having an organization like that when there was already a complete United Nations'. They therefore wanted the Commonwealth to change the way it conducted its meetings,

[1] *Survey of Current Affairs*, Feb 1971, p. 65.

and the secretary-general was asked to seek the views of governments as to how that could best be done.[1]

While in the political sphere Commonwealth meetings became noisier and more contentious, in the economic sphere they were more frequent but quieter. As was shown in Chapter 12, there was considerable economic diplomacy between Britain and the other members. The Montreal conference of 1958 attempted to provide a more formal focus for this diplomacy by setting up the Commonwealth Economic Consultative Council to cover the kinds of discussions which had been going on. It would consist of finance and economic ministers, meeting as occasion demanded, and would also involve meetings of officials where necessary. In practice, the finance ministers usually met each year before the meetings of the World Bank and the IMF, to which they would be going in any case. Their discussions were normally preceded by talks at official level. Except for the outburst at Accra in 1961, described in Chapter 13, these meetings were staid and did not attract headlines. They provided opportunities for discussion of currency and trade questions. The trade ministers held a separate meeting in 1966.

The diplomacy of the sterling area, largely conducted by central banks and treasuries, rarely achieved publicity except in specialized financial papers. It was regarded as technical rather than political; presumably some governments did not wish to see contrasts made between the flamboyancy of their political positions and the anxious conservatism of their attempts at economic management. This diplomacy was a matter for 'insiders', both as participants and as observers. It reached its peak in 1968, when Britain sent Bank of England and FCO or Treasury officials to each member of the sterling area to discuss dollar guarantees. Some day we may learn the full intricacies of the movement of reserves, especially in the late 1960s, and of the discussions that surrounded them; but the time is not yet.

IV

The Commonwealth secretariat arose from an unexpected decision by the Prime Ministers' Meeting of July 1964—unexpected in the sense that previous experience had suggested inflexible opposition to the creation of such a 'centralized' body, but not entirely unheralded.[2] Before that meeting the British prime minister, Sir Alec Douglas-Home, had made it clear that he wanted the Commonwealth to show more cohesion and undertake more joint projects, especially in economic development. There had been an important parliamentary debate in February, in which Harold Wilson, as leader of the

---

[1] Ibid., p. 66.
[2] Note should be taken of an article by Charles Carrington, 'How to improve the CRO', *The Times*, 18 Dec 1959, in which a secretariat on something like the lines which emerged is suggested.

Opposition, had put forward a ten-point plan of Commonwealth policy for Britain, and the prime minister outlined some new schemes for increasing Commonwealth co-operation.[1] Before the July meeting Douglas-Home continued to emphasize the idea of 'giving the Commonwealth association new meaning and new life';[2] at the meeting itself, he put forward seven proposals to this effect—some of which, such as the Commonwealth Foundation and third-party financing of aid projects, later became effective, either as independent bodies or as activities of the secretariat.[3] He had not included a secretariat. The CRO, well aware of the tradition of opposition to this, would hardly have advised it, but others did. Evidently the publicity given in advance to Douglas-Home's proposals had stimulated other Commonwealth leaders to make their own suggestions.

It was reported that Dr Eric Williams had suggested five new Commonwealth bodies—a secretariat, a development fund, a technical assistance pool, a conciliation commission, and a Press Council; Milton Obote a secretariat 'to co-operate and conciliate the member states'; Nkrumah a 'central clearing house to prepare plans for trade, aid and development, and serve all Commonwealth members equally'; and Mrs Bandaranaike 'some sort of conciliation machinery for disputes between members, provided they agreed'.[4] Later discussion has given the main credit to Nkrumah, whose proposal may well have been most clearly expressed and closest to what eventually emerged. Certainly the African members supported the idea sufficiently strongly for the prime ministers to instruct their officials to meet on 11 July to discuss the creation of a permanent Commonwealth secretariat. According to Nora Beloff, 'the idea had taken the "white" members of the Commonwealth, particularly Britain, completely by surprise: similar proposals had been put forward at previous conferences but always by the white members and had been suspected by the new members as "neo-colonial" '.[5]

Taken by surprise or not, the old dominions and Britain responded readily to the idea of a Commonwealth secretariat. Sir Robert Menzies recalled ruefully that he had suggested something similar before World War II and afterwards, but with no success; he was glad, however, that

for the first time in the history of the Commonwealth there is to be established a Secretariat which is based on the proposition that the Commonwealth is a continuing thing, an enduring thing, and that the machinery ought to be made available to enable it to continue more effectively. That, I think, is quite a remarkable achievement and a very powerful answer to the pessimists.[6]

Lester Pearson reported to his parliament in slightly more cautious terms; the ghost of Mackenzie King was hovering at his elbow, it seems. He said that it

---

[1] HC Deb., 6 Feb 1964, cols 1356–476. The whole debate is of interest.
[2] Royal Academy dinner, 29 Apr 1964.   [3] *The Times*, 14 July 1964.
[4] *FT*, 10 July 1964.   [5] *Observer*, 12 July 1964.
[6] Broadcast of 19 July 1964 (*CN*, July 1964, p. 37).

was significant to realize that the pressure towards 'this kind of consultative centralization' came from the newer countries, 'which in many ways are or should be most suspicious of the older members in this regard', but who were very much aware of its practical value to them 'in providing a broad range of information which it is difficult to obtain with the inadequate diplomatic and government services they now have or perhaps can afford'. He believed the situation had greatly changed since the early days, 'and it is something we should try to work out on a genuine Commonwealth basis', though this should be done without interfering with existing channels of communications or confusing 'what is in many respects a very satisfactory method of co-ordination and exchange of information'. They must be sure that the basis of the new secretariat was sound 'and that we are adding an institution of value and not simply an additional agency for the free play of Parkinson's Law'. Canada would be glad to participate in the study of a possible basis for a secretariat.[1]

The prime ministers had decided to have a secretariat, but they had not decided just what it would do. Their communiqué said that they were anxious that some permanent expression should be given to the desire for closer and more informed understanding between their governments on the many issues which engaged their attention and for some continuing machinery for this purpose. They had therefore instructed officials to consider the best basis for establishing a Commonwealth secretariat. This would, among other things, disseminate information to member countries on matters of common concern, assist existing official and unofficial agencies to promote Commonwealth links, and help to co-ordinate the preparations for future Heads of Government Meetings and, where appropriate, meetings of other ministers. This secretariat, recruited from member countries and financed by their contributions, would be at the service of all Commonwealth governments and would be 'a visible symbol of the spirit of co-operation which animates the Commonwealth'.[2]

This left much to be decided on what the secretariat would do, on determining the respective financial contributions of members, and in deciding on staff. A meeting of senior officials chaired by Sir Burke Trend, the cabinet secretary, was held in London in January 1965 to decide on these details.[3] It was greeted by *The Times* with an editorial[4] which said that now that there was discontent with British administration, 'a body is needed which the Commonwealth as a whole will staff, control, and own'. It was needed because 'the political unlikeness, or incompatibility, of Commonwealth members is now its most obvious feature'. The Commonwealth, to succeed, 'must be more than a

[1] Statement in Canadian House of Commons, 17 July 1964.
[2] Cmnd 2441, p. 9 (*CS*, 21 July 1964, p. 724).
[3] The list of those attending is in B. Vivekanandan, 'The Commonwealth secretariat', *Int. Stud.*, Jan 1968, p. 320.
[4] 'Tools for a New Age', 4 Jan 1965.

British-based, British-inspired institution', and the Secretariat would help in this, by building up new relations and concerting new priorities.

There were some inevitable disagreements about how the new body ought to operate, reflecting the approaches of different members. The African states and Canada were for a maximalist approach to the secretariat's functions, i.e. for giving it a fairly open opportunity to decide what matters were of Commonwealth concern and how they ought to be pursued. The main proponent of a minimalist view was India, probably because the Pakistani delegate is said to have taken up some of the suggestions at the 1964 Prime Ministers' Meeting and proposed that the secretariat should have the function of arbitration in political disputes among the member countries[1]—something no Indian representative could accept. There were also arguments about the distribution of financial responsibility, and the extent to which the secretariat staff would enjoy diplomatic immunities and privileges. In the end the officials produced an Agreed Memorandum,[2] although they needed a further meeting in June 1965 to give it formal shape. They had settled the maximalist-minimalist question in January by adopting a highly antiphonal position. Some thought of the secretariat as simply a 'post office'; others wished it to possess some power of initiative.[3] The actual memorandum is too long to quote here, but can be summed up as an invitation to the proposed secretary-general to extend the secretariat's activities if he could gain agreement from enough Commonwealth governments to make the enterprise worthwhile. The basic activities proposed for it—those of organizing meetings, providing information, and fostering Commonwealth institutions—were not a matter of much argument. Britain was to pay 30 per cent of the cost, Canada 20·8, India 11·4, Australia 10·4, and the other members 1·5 per cent, except for New Zealand and Pakistan, which would pay 2·5 and 2·4 per cent respectively. The staff was to be recruited on as wide a geographical basis as possible within the Commonwealth, consistent with efficiency, competence, and integrity.

The 1965 Prime Ministers' Meeting had the task of choosing the first secretary-general. The field was a wide one, enlivened by the piquant point that two international civil servants born in Australia (Sir Robert Jackson and George Ivan Smith) were proposed by African states but were not supported by Australia. Sir Robert Menzies is said to have been dissatisfied with all the nominations and to have suggested, late in the day, the name of C. S. Peiris, the director-general of the Ministry of External Affairs of Ceylon, but he had already been appointed Ceylonese ambassador to West Germany.[4] The eventual choice, approved unanimously, was Arnold Smith, assistant under-secretary of external affairs in Canada, who had been a prominent Canadian

---

[1] Vivekanandan, p. 321.   [2] Cmnd 2713, July 1965.
[3] See editorial, 'What Powers?', *The Times*, 15 June 1965.
[4] Sir Robert's comments (including his statement that he had not heard of George Ivan Smith until his name appeared in the list of nominees) are in *CN*, June 1965, p. 351.

adviser at recent Prime Ministers' Meetings after serving as ambassador in Cairo and Moscow. It fell to Arnold Smith to set up the secretariat and make it work. Some of his actions in the first few years have already been discussed in Chapters 10 and 11. It was a tribute to his constructive efforts that, when the question of reappointment came up five years later, 25 heads of government were in favour, two were undecided, and only one was against.[1]

The secretariat developed a number of new Commonwealth functions while attending also to the old ones.[2] It extended its operations to the smallest Commonwealth countries, and pioneered a scheme of technical assistance which enabled third countries to finance the operations of others in assisting those least developed, in spite of some grumpy opposition at first from the Australian government, which refused to participate in what seemed to it to endanger its own system of economic aid. In accordance with the recommendations of a committee set up by order of the Prime Ministers' Meeting of 1965,[3] the secretariat also absorbed the staff and activities of the Commonwealth Economic Committee and the Commonwealth Education Liaison Unit. It was also recommended that the executive secretary of the Commonwealth Scientific Committee should become Scientific Adviser to the secretary-general, and that, if the moribund Commonwealth Air Transport Council became active again, the secretariat should provide it with administrative services. The secretary-general, it was suggested, should be closely associated with, but not in charge of, such bodies as the Commonwealth Institute, the Commonwealth Agricultural Bureaux, and the Commonwealth Telecommunications Board.

By the end of 1970 the secretariat had Divisions of Establishment and Finance; Development, Aid, and Planning; Finance, Trade, and Commodities; International Affairs; Education; and a Legal Division and Medical and Scientific Advisers, as well as an Information Officer. Its staff was drawn from a wide range of member countries.

V

The creation of the secretariat was one, but only one, of the influences shaping the fortunes of the CRO in the 1960s. It was far more affected by the status of the Commonwealth in British policy. As colonies became independent, their relations with Britain were transferred from the Colonial Office to the CRO, symbolizing the change from surveillance to diplomacy. This meant

---

[1] Richard H. Leach, 'The secretariat', *Int. J.*, Spring 1971, p. 390.

[2] The best source is the three reports of the secretary-general, covering the first year of the secretariat's operations, Sept 1966–Oct 1968 and Nov 1968–Nov 1970. See also Leach & Vivekanandan, *New Commonwealth*, no. 9, 1970, and Derek Ingram, *The Commonwealth at work* (1969).

[3] Commonwealth Secretariat, *Report of the Review Committee on Intra-Commonwealth Organisations*, Aug 1966.

new problems in handling countries which had neither the same ties with Britain nor the sophistication in foreign policy of countries such as Canada and India. In the end the CRO absorbed what was left of the Colonial Office. However, as more states gained independence, and as Commonwealth relations became increasingly entangled with general international relations over such issues as South Africa, Rhodesia, Cyprus, and Malaysia, there was a growth in criticism of the CRO as the emblem of a Commonwealth system which was connected with but separate from the diplomatic system at large; at last it was merged with the Foreign Office. The changes in the CRO's circumstances may be summarized as follows.[1]

First, the question of the comparative functions of the Commonwealth Relations and Colonial Offices, and of British staffs serving overseas, excited discussion in Britain throughout our period until the two offices were merged to form the Commonwealth Office on 1 August 1966. During the 1950s the Colonial Office continued to recruit for posts at home and abroad, but there was constant concern amongst overseas officials about what would happen to them when major colonies became independent states and pushed ahead with 'localization' of jobs. It was recognized that this would mean redundancy for many British officers. At the same time it was clear that the new states would need to employ expatriates, especially in technical and professional posts. To many people it seemed obvious that a 'Commonwealth civil service' was required, in order to provide stable employment for those who would be turned out of permanent jobs when the colonies became independent, but whose skills would still be required by independent and dependent territories alike.[2] The difficulty, as others saw it, was that this might mean a large pool of officers who were the continued responsibility of the British government but who might not be wanted by independent Commonwealth governments, whether their objective needs seemed to dictate the employment of such officers or not. For technical and professional men, contract work could be arranged; for administrative people, the difficulties were greater, since it was here that newly independent governments would want to 'localize' quickly, and the Home civil service would not be likely to welcome an influx of middle-aged men whose experience had lain elsewhere.

The whole argument began to come to a head as African advance quickened, and particularly as Nigeria moved towards independence. The Select Committee on Estimates, examining the CRO in the first half of 1959, reported that it was anxious that the office should not miss the opportunity of strengthening itself 'by filling its vacancies in the new Commonwealth countries as far

---

[1] A useful source is J. A. Cross, *Whitehall and the Commonwealth* (1967), ch. 6.

[2] See, e.g., two articles, 'A Commonwealth Civil Service?', *The Times*, 7 & 8 Sept 1953, and the subsequent correspondence, especially Gordon Walker's letter of 9 Sept, one of the few to emphasize the diplomatic problems involved. See also the interview with Sir Angus Gillan, *New Commonwealth*, 1 Apr 1954; the House of Commons debate, 2 Apr 1954; and Sir Charles Jeffries's article, 'Staffing Oversea Public Services', *The Times*, 23 June 1958.

as possible from the Colonial Service officers in those countries'. It noted, however, that the CRO did not share this view, since it was 'anxious that there should be no risk of the new High Commissions' being confused with the old colonial administrations'. The two anxieties cancelled out one another in terms of action. Although the Committee urged 'that the CRO should throw over its inhibitions',[1] there was no development of the kind it envisaged, apart from some extension of the open competition for places. It is said that some Commonwealth governments, on being consulted, said they did not want ex-colonial officers in the Commonwealth service.

In the following year the Estimates Committee examined the Colonial Office with more verve. Its report[2] envisaged the creation of a Commonwealth Advisory and Technical Service to take up the slack of the Overseas Civil Service after independence, and a full merger of the CRO and the Colonial Offices. There was a persistent belief amongst the members of the Committee that a 'dichotomy' between the Colonial and Commonwealth Relations Offices was preventing a 'dynamic' Commonwealth policy from emerging.[3] The CRO, in evidence, was clearly anxious that its diplomatic function should be recognized as its prime one, and that this should not be damaged by the committee's enthusiasm for placing Colonial Office and Overseas Civil Service officers in jobs after they had become redundant. At the same time the CRO was somewhat on the defensive about its organization and some of its other functions, such as its formal responsibility for the High Commission Territories. (These were, in fact, transferred to the Colonial Office at the end of 1961, following South Africa's withdrawal from the Commonwealth.) The Colonial Office, in evidence, showed a better recognition of the CRO's role than members of the Committee, and suggested a merger on approximately the same lines as those which were eventually accepted.

The subsequent parliamentary debate showed that, while the committee may have been premature in its enthusiasm, and defective in sympathy for what the CRO had to do, it was in tune with the times. The prime minister announced on publication of its report that he was considering the possibilities of a future merger between the two offices,[4] and the colonial secretary stated that, while merger was not yet feasible, there would be study of the possibility of creating a joint department to deal with technical aid. This would be responsible jointly to himself, to the foreign secretary, and to the Commonwealth secretary.[5]

[1] Select Committee on Estimates, *Third Report*, para. 16.

[2] Select Committee on Estimates, *Fourth Report*, Sess. 1959–60, Colonial Office. Readers of my highly critical article on the report ('The Colonial Office and the Estimates Committee', *Public Administration*, Summer 1961) should be sure to read the sturdy reply by Sir Godfrey Nicholson under the same title in the Summer 1962 issue.

[3] This view was widespread amongst Conservative back-benchers at the time. For an expression of it, see Utley & Udal, ch. 6.

[4] *The Times*, 14 Dec 1960.   [5] 632 HC Deb., 19 Dec 1960, cols 1017–24.

This latter move soon took place. In July 1961 the Department of Technical Co-operation was created to take over technical assistance work, and also to help administer the Colonial Development and Welfare Act. It provided posts for Colonial Office officials and contract work for many former members of the Overseas Civil Service, as well as others. The Wilson government made it an independent department in October 1964, under the name of the Ministry of Overseas Development (see ch. 12).

Meanwhile the CRO had suffered some temporary loss of functions by the creation of the Central African Office in March 1962, giving up its responsibilities for the Federation of Rhodesia and Nyasaland and for Southern Rhodesia. The new office also took over the Colonial Office's responsibility for Northern Rhodesia and Nyasaland (see ch. 9). In the same year the CRO and Colonial Office were brought closer together by being given a single secretary of state, although they remained separate departments. The Central African Office was wound up in 1964; then its functions and staff were returned to the CRO. On 1 August 1966 the CRO and Colonial Office were merged in the Commonwealth Office, under a secretary of state for Commonwealth affairs. Its principal task was now plainly diplomatic; the remaining candidates for independence were small and insignificant.

There was still, however, the larger question of parallel diplomacy. Were Commonwealth relations so different that they required a separate system of diplomacy, or were they becoming so much like relations with other countries that they were better carried on within the ordinary diplomatic system? Even if British opinion regarded them as different, was there any evidence that other countries looked at them in the same way? Supposing they were different, did this justify separate treatment, since there were inevitably issues which involved both Commonwealth and foreign countries—at the UN, over Cyprus, over Malaysia, over Rhodesia? Even if the relations themselves were different, did this require a separate department and a separate service, confined to Commonwealth representation?

There had been more than one attempt to approximate Commonwealth to foreign relations. Eden records[1] that in 1942, after the fall of Singapore, Sir Stafford Cripps had suggested a single ministry combining the Foreign, Colonial, and Dominions Offices in the War Cabinet, less because of any need for combined operations than the need to have a small War Cabinet. More serious, from the standpoint of the CRO in its early years, had been the claim of the Foreign Office under Ernest Bevin in 1948-9

that it should handle all diplomatic contacts with the other members of the Commonwealth and all exchanges of view with them on foreign affairs. This argument was the stronger because the Foreign Office and its ambassadors were the source of the vast amount of diplomatic and international information sent to the rest of the Commonwealth.[2]

[1] *The reckoning*, p. 322.   [2] Gordon Walker, *JCPS*, Nov 1961; see also McDermott, p. 88.

The matter was settled by reaffirming the primacy of the CRO and by putting the relevant officers of the two departments alongside each other in the building they shared, so that communication was easy. But the right of the CRO actually to conduct relations with Commonwealth members had been confirmed, and was maintained throughout the 1950s. At the same time there were some further exchanges of staff.

The increase in the numbers of Commonwealth members meant that the overseas staffs of the two departments might be doing much the same work with much the same sorts of country, side by side, but with different headquarters in London. The growing sense of a need for change in organization has been described by Lord Garner:

> The most persuasive argument was that it did not make sense for diplomacy to divide the world into two, with the result that the Foreign Service knew little at first hand about the Commonwealth and the Commonwealth Service little about foreign countries.
> Policy considerations, however, were more complex. Clearly foreign affairs and Commonwealth relations were becoming more alike and there would be advantage in one Minister and one department taking a synoptic view of the whole world.
> Problems are indivisible and most world questions concerned both departments. On the other hand, there *is* a special relationship with Commonwealth countries and they are certainly not 'foreign'.[1]

In 1962 the government appointed the Plowden Committee to review the purpose, structure, and operation of the services representing Britain abroad. It reported in February 1964.[2] The CRO had asked that its own work be included in the Committee's review (which had originally been intended to deal only with the Foreign Office), and a former CRO permanent undersecretary, Sir Percivale Liesching, was appointed to the committee, which found that there should be a single Diplomatic Service, the core of its argument being:

> The makers of British policy must be in a position to see international problems broadly and to see them whole. At present they are not so placed. To take one example, the division of responsibility between the Foreign Office and the Commonwealth Relations Office for our relations with neighbouring countries in West Africa constitutes a weakness. This division makes it much more difficult to form a coherent picture of the political, economic and other interests of West Africa as a whole.

The fact that British missions were differently organized, that their personnel was drawn from different Services, and they lacked any direct means of communicating confidentially with each other made it harder to achieve effective consultation and identity of thought between them. The committee accepted

---

[1] Sir Saville Garner, 'Merger of Britain's Foreign and Commonwealth Offices', British Information Service G415/a, 9 Oct 1968.
[2] Cmnd 2276, Feb 1964.

that every effort was made to harmonize policies towards Commonwealth and non-Commonwealth countries, but where this succeeded, it did so 'in spite of the system' and involved much duplication and expenditure of time and effort.

With two Ministries, two overseas Services, two communications systems, the process of trying to hammer out a sensible world-wide policy is, with the best of goodwill, a wasteful and time-consuming process. At times of crisis these short-comings can prove disastrous. The division of responsibility is becoming an anachronism.[1]

Such powerful points would have been hard to refute. The Plowden Committee did not, however, go to the length of suggesting an immediate amalgamation of the Foreign Office and the CRO, but said that this must be the ultimate aim, for 'to take such a fundamental step now could be misinter-preted as implying a loss of interest in the Commonwealth partnership'. It pointed out that each other Commonwealth member had a single Department of External Affairs, and contented itself with a single Diplomatic Service as a first step.[2] This service was duly set up on 1 January 1965. Thereafter it was not long before the actual merger of the two offices, which was announced in March 1968 and took place in October, just over a year after the CRO had swallowed the Colonial Office. A final step was taken in November 1970, when the Heath government incorporated the Ministry of Overseas Development as a wing of the FCO.

No Commonwealth member objected publicly to the disappearance from the British cabinet of a separate secretary of state for Commonwealth relations. My information suggests that none objected privately, and that the only inquiries received by the Commonwealth Office in advance of the merger with the Foreign Office were from certain high commissioners in London, anxious that their privileges should be preserved. They were reassured. Presumably the lack of Commonwealth objection meant that, to Commonwealth govern-ments in the late 1960s, the 'Commonwealth system' could either be sustained without a special minister and department, or could be regarded as no longer significant. If so, this represented a different approach from that which the Irish government had displayed in 1959, when, on the Estimates Committee suggesting that the conduct of relations with Ireland should be transferred to the Foreign Office, the Irish minister for external affairs had publicly announced that 'no need to propose any change in the arrangement has arisen'.[3] In fact, the arrangement continued until the merger of the Commonwealth and Foreign Offices. Perhaps the link with Ireland was closer than with the majority of Commonwealth members. In any case, the pressure from within Britain itself for special treatment of Commonwealth countries had greatly relaxed by 1968. There was no sign of either the misinterpretation which the

[1] Ibid., para. 43.   [2] Ibid., para. 44.   [3] *Irish Times*, 31 Aug 1959.

Plowden Committee had feared, or of resistance from Commonwealth members.

Indeed, the FCO had hardly been established when a new basis was suggested for British overseas representation by the Duncan Committee.[1] Looking ahead to the 1970s, it divided overseas countries into two broad categories. One, the 'Area of Concentration of British diplomacy', would consist of a dozen or so advanced industrial countries in Western Europe plus North America, together with a few outside this zone, such as Australia and Japan. The other category, termed the 'Outer Area', would comprise the rest of the world.[2] It was in the Area of Concentration that Britain could expect to do most of its business and would need most of its representation. The report was not officially adopted by the British government, but it did serve to emphasize that the main lines of British interest would lie partly outside the Commonwealth and partly within it, though they would not be determined by the mere fact of its existence.

VI

Since the Commonwealth system had not been so plainly articulated outside Britain, there was less of it to change. By the end of the 1960s the Indian and Pakistani sub-departments had disappeared. There was no longer a 'Commonwealth seat' on the Security Council, and the regular meetings of Commonwealth representatives at the UN had ceased because of constant jarring disagreements over Rhodesia.[3] In Washington, New Delhi, Canberra, and elsewhere British envoys were about to begin meeting informally with their counterparts from the prospectively enlarged EEC, although they continued to meet occasionally with envoys from Commonwealth countries. The system of high commissioners still persisted, but with increasing approximation to ordinary ambassadorial arrangements. Although it had been a traditional feature of the Commonwealth system that members did not appoint consuls in one another's territory, since they could rely on the normal facilities of the other country, this convention had been undermined. The Plowden Committee had argued against it. By 1970 the Commonwealth secretariat reported:

Most Commonwealth countries continue to observe this convention; others have resorted to expedients such as giving consular officers other titles, such as that of commissioner or liaison officer; a few have ignored the convention. A case appears to exist for re-examining it, particularly as an increasing number of Commonwealth countries are becoming party to the Vienna Convention on Consular Relations, which should therefore regulate their consular relations.[4]

[1] Cmnd 4107 (July 1969).   [2] Ibid., paras 9–11.
[3] On these matters, see Millar, *Commonwealth & UN*, ch. 1. The regular meetings ended after the book was written.
[4] Commonwealth Secretariat, *Diplomatic service* (1971), p. 70. See also Robinson, pp. 104–5.

These were all significant changes in the 'system' which had been adopted either consciously or subconsciously by Commonwealth members on attaining independence. Taken by themselves, these changes suggest a weakening of the fabric, which indeed is what happened. General diplomacy had become as necessary for most Commonwealth countries as the Plowden Committee had found it for Britain, and each had its own Area of Concentration which cut across the bounds of the Commonwealth. Yet one should also mention that a number of regional arrangements which members took seriously, and which helped to define those Areas of Concentration, were based on Commonwealth foundations. They included the arrangements which the Caribbean countries were making between themselves; those between Canada and the Caribbean; those between Australia and New Zealand; those between them, Britain, Malaysia, and Singapore; those which the three East African Commonwealth members continued to make and re-make, and those which the Pacific Island members were constructing. These were partly complementary to, and partly a replacement for, the Commonwealth system as earlier defined.

CHAPTER 18

A COMMONWEALTH SYSTEM?

HERE we shall ask what sustained the Commonwealth system, and why it changed as it did. The previous chapter will have made clear that the use of the term 'system' was imprecise and figurative rather than exact, and that it could be used of two connected but separate things—of Britain's method of conducting its Commonwealth relations, and, beyond that, of the system of Commonwealth relations at large, symbolized by the use of the term 'high commissioner' to describe not only the envoys between Britain and other Commonwealth members, but also between those others.

I

In the beginning these two meanings were the same since, in the inter-war years, the dispatch of high commissioners had been essentially a to-and-fro traffic between Britain and individual dominions, not between one of these and another. The dominions had sent high commissioners to Britain for many years before it began to reciprocate after the decisions of the 1926 and 1930 Imperial Conferences that governors-general would be subject to, and appointed on, their local ministers' advice. In such a situation, they could not continue to act as local representatives of the British government. None the less, British high commissioners were not appointed to Australia and New Zealand until 1936 and 1939 respectively, and the notion of the governor-general as a special British emissary still lingered in those countries—perhaps in the minds of British prime ministers too.[1] The Commonwealth system, as passed on by the Dominions Office to the CRO, was part of a slowly burgeoning process of dominion autonomy of which the Statute of Westminster had been the symbol. It was already well established, in terms of pre-war and wartime experience, when India, Pakistan, and Ceylon began to take part in it in 1947.

It involved certain elements which were not necessarily in harmony but had become so through practice. It was highly informal, founded upon the easy exchanges between prime ministers, but also had formal elements, arising from the touchiness with which such men as Hertzog and Mackenzie King had approached anything which savoured of undue British influence. This attitude on the part of the South African, Canadian, and Irish governments had bred a reciprocal one on the part of the Dominions and Commonwealth Relations Offices, determined not to upset the overseas prime ministers and not to

[1] See e.g. Macmillan, *Riding the storm*, p. 412.

presume too far on their acquiescence in British policies. In contrast, the Australian and New Zealand governments had normally stressed the elements of unity and informality. They were eager, the others cautious, about affirming common policies; but all except Ireland had been involved in a common effort in World War II, and were predisposed to continue with the assumption of a common interest, provided the British did not presume too far. Canada's postwar internationalism made it more receptive than before, South Africa's election of a Nationalist government in 1948 less so. On the whole, however, the system which the Asian members joined showed considerable cohesion.

Part of this came from the monarchical element, always impossible to assess with any accuracy but plainly popular. Part came from the awareness of common institutions and like ways of thinking, and part from something to which little attention was paid at the time, but which has been highlighted by later contrast: the uniqueness of the dominions, and their lack of absorption in the general diplomatic system.

It was not simply that they had taken relatively few diplomatic initiatives in the 1930s and 1940s, in spite of their concern about international affairs at large. It was also that they could not be readily placed in a regional setting of like-minded or like-situated states. The kind of comment which the Plowden Committee made about West Africa in 1964 could not have been made about any of the dominions before 1947, with the possible exception of Canada. South Africa, Ireland, and the Pacific dominions did not have comparable foreign states alongside them; while Canada did, the very fact of this proximity to a similar but far more powerful state caused Canadian leaders to emphasize their country's separateness and to cultivate the Commonwealth as a counter-weight. Only Canada had a stronger trade partner than Britain, or got most of its foreign investment from another source. The economic, cultural, and defence ties with Britain put the other dominions in a unique position, in which relations with Britain seemed more natural, more obvious, and more permanent than any others—even when, as with the Irish and the Afrikaners, those relations were often feared and disliked rather than welcomed.

In such a situation, the special nature of the Commonwealth system was appropriate. The notion that the partners would consult before anything drastic was done by any of them was suitable to a family or club atmosphere. A particular 'style of conversation'[1] could be convincingly regarded as appropriate to the dominions' stage of development. The prime ministers could consult as persons; they could meet as Privy Councillors in the Cabinet Room at 10 Downing Street; they could even think of their own separate governments as being rather like departments in a single government, as indeed the Australians and New Zealanders often did. The question in 1947 and 1949 had been whether this sort of easy relationship could be continued if India (and

---

[1] A description used at the unofficial study conference at Lagos, 1962. See C. E. Carrington, *The Commonwealth in Africa* (1962), p. 39.

to a lesser degree Pakistan and Ceylon) were permanently part of it. According to Gordon Walker, the Foreign Office thought not:

Bevin argued the Foreign Office line—that it was not worth keeping India in the Commonwealth: it was not going to be morally committed to us, but we to it. To keep India in would lead to the breakdown of the old Commonwealth.[1]

In fact, republicanism such as India proposed was compatible with the Commonwealth system, so long as it did not involve active anti-monarchism, and so long as opposition to the beliefs of the other states was not pushed to the limit. A sense of common purpose could be suggested—and could indeed be present—even though common policies were no longer feasible. This is what happened in the first few years of the 1950s. India's republicanism and non-alignment were found to be compatible with the other members' positions. Even after Indian non-alignment had taken on a keener edge with the arming of Pakistan by the US, it was still possible for Commonwealth leaders in Britain and Australia to think of the Commonwealth system as both fitting and successful. The paean of Menzies in his Smuts Memorial Lecture of 1960 (quoted in ch. 1), can be paralleled from others of equally conservative and traditionalist mind, for instance in Sandys's 1962 pamphlet, *The Modern Commonwealth*. Lord Home (as he then was) wrote privately after three years as Commonwealth secretary: 'It is such a novel and exciting prospect that the written word can scarcely capture the spirit of the Commonwealth or its unity of purpose.'[2] C. J. M. Alport reaffirmed in 1960, while minister of state for Commonwealth relations:

Relationships within the independent Commonwealth, particularly between the United Kingdom and one or another of its members, are both stronger and at the same time more sensitive than they are between foreign countries anywhere. The independent Commonwealth expects special treatment from the United Kingdom and each country bitterly resents our failure to give it. If sometimes we feel that Commonwealth countries do not always give us the special treatment which they expect us to provide for them, I can assure you that each would enter into such an argument with an armoury of examples of Britain's failure to pay sufficient attention to their individual points of view.[3]

These were sincere statements about the Commonwealth system. They meant that, in spite of Asian and—for a time—Ghanaian membership, something like the former general situation could be said to prevail. But already significant factors were working against the continuation of the system, even before the other African states came into it.

[1] From Gordon Walker's diary, 9 Feb 1949 (*The cabinet*, p. 137).
[2] From a confidential Conservative Party paper, 2 May 1958 (quoted in Young, *Douglas-Home*, p. 118).
[3] Alport to Royal Commonwealth Society, 26 May 1960, pp. 5–6.

II

By 1960 the most obvious of these was the recognition that serious differ-ences of policy divided the members in international affairs, and that the system of consultation was now partial and selective rather than general. There was undoubtedly an increase in the number of telegrams which the CRO sent out to other members; according to Sandys in 1962, the number was then about 35,000 a year.[1] But, as Nicholas Mansergh pointed out:

> From the context in which these figures appeared it seemed that the public was expected to infer from them that the increase denoted a growing intimacy—to use a deplorable phrase firmly embedded in the Commonwealth vocabulary—in relations between Commonwealth governments. But it could also have meant—and this in retrospect appears the more likely—differences that were getting harder to resolve, coupled no doubt with a fashionable depreciation in Commonwealth cable currency.[2]

It was not just the Suez affair that demonstrated the substantial change in Commonwealth consultation by the latter part of the 1950s. India's non-alignment, while bearable by the other members which were allied with the US, had cut it off from the frank exchange of intelligence information, which was common between Britain, the US, Canada, Australia, and New Zealand. When Menzies and Harrison made their unacceptable suggestions of distin-guishing between the 'Crown Commonwealth' and the rest, this kind of consideration presumably affected their thinking. The idea was unacceptable to the British government, not because it wanted to share everything with the Indians (it did not), but because overt acceptance of a superior intimacy between Britain and the old dominions would devalue the Commonwealth for aspiring members, especially those coming from Africa. Yet the Menzies-Harrison line, while clumsy, did express an unpalatable truth: British officials and servicemen, and British politicians, were more likely to agree in policy and to feel a sense of intimacy with the older Commonwealth members than with the newer. This did not mean that they always agreed, or that there were no matters on which they would agree with the Asian members rather than with Australia or South Africa. But it meant that there was a basic dichotomy between those who were fully accepted within the US alliance system (making Pakistan an equivocal factor), and those who were outside it altogether.

Further, as we have seen (ch. 12), economic influences were working against a perpetuation of the Commonwealth system as understood in the 1950s. There was a widespread belief that economic ties, especially the preference system, held the Commonwealth together. When it became clear that Gatt would not permit that system to be extended, and that the British government

---

[1] Sandys, *Modern Commonwealth*, p. 10.

[2] *The Commonwealth experience*, p. 348. See also Wheare, p. 142, on the 'shoals of tele-grams': 'Is there much that is important in them? Does anyone of importance read them?', and Robinson, in Hamilton & others, eds, pp. 107–11.

was choosing multilateral trade and convertibility of sterling instead of continued bulk purchase and an intensification of trade within the sterling area, it appeared to many that the Commonwealth was losing its economic cement. Commonwealth governments could no longer count on a favoured place in the British market; and Britain's decision to join the EEC meant that natural tendencies to look elsewhere for economic ties were accentuated.

Thirdly, even before the African explosion, there was strong reason to doubt whether all Commonwealth members shared the same ideals, as was often suggested. South Africa under the Nationalists was hardly a congenial partner, however much it might be acceptable economically and in the context of world strategy. Pakistan had failed to develop a parliamentary system, in striking contrast to India. No sooner was Ghana independent than Nkrumah began to restrict his rivals' political activity. Bitter conflict in Kenya, British Guiana, and Cyprus, though these were colonies, cast doubt on the aims with which such countries might later seek in joining the Commonwealth.

Fourthly, and of more importance, was the steady growth of individual interests among Commonwealth members, including Britain. Partly political and partly economic, such interests did not necessarily lead to clashes; sometimes there was no clash at all, and sometimes individual members would find their most suitable companions inside, rather than outside, the Commonwealth. But the increased experience of the old dominions and the Asian members, the extension of their foreign policies and overseas representation, and their growing involvement in associations and alliances outside the Commonwealth meant a depreciation of the Commonwealth system, if only through inattention or neglect. Perhaps the same could be said of Britain. Certainly, in the late 1950s some Commonwealth leaders and officials felt that the British government was paying so much attention to decolonization that it had little time to spare for them. They may have been wrong; but in such matters it is often impressions that count.

III

In the 1960s, with so many sovereign states as members, the multiplicity of possibly conflicting interests was inevitably greater, and it was the more difficult to contain them within a single system. The economic interests which, when the new members were colonies, had been harmonized with Britain's through co-operative administration, currency boards, marketing boards, the CDC, and the like, were now no longer Britain's responsibility in anything like the same degree. They had a wider world (though a more dangerous one) in which to seek satisfaction.

Inevitably too, regional demands, which in colonial times had been only nascent or could be disregarded, now made themselves felt. Ex-colonies like the Gambia and Senegal and Malaysia and Indonesia perceived the benefit of co-operation with each other; Caribbean Commonwealth countries began to join the Organization of American States. Even without pan-Africanism, exemplified in the African members' demands about Rhodesia and South Africa, the growing complexity of members' interests would probably have made a Commonwealth system of the old type unworkable.

The fierceness of the African attack, and the specific nature of the pressure exerted, was something new in Commonwealth affairs. Dominion pressure in economic matters had been strong in the 1920s and 1930s, but it did not have the same edge and was not part of a concerted drive through a number of international organizations; it could plausibly have been regarded as part of the Commonwealth system. Apart altogether from its embarrassingly public nature, the African attack could not. An African interpretation of the position at the end of 1964 can be endorsed as broadly accurate:

... the Commonwealth had almost become an Anglo-African association. It was 'British' because the United Kingdom was still a kind of focal point of Commonwealth relations, and because the remaining old Dominions of Australia, New Zealand and Canada were still substantially 'Britannic'. The Commonwealth was now also crucially 'African' because the African states now constituted the largest single group of states and exerted substantial influence on Commonwealth decisions. There had, in fact, developed two centres of influence within the Commonwealth— Britain herself was one centre, the African group of nations was the other. The remaining members of the Commonwealth often found themselves in the orbit of one or other of these spheres.[1]

By the end of the decade, and especially with the addition of new non-African members, this situation of African superiority had begun to change, but for the crucial period 1964–6, when Rhodesia was so contentious a topic, the position was broadly as stated. One consequence was that British leadership, hitherto tacitly acknowledged, was, for the time being, effectively challenged.

The general trend of international politics at the time ensured that most other Commonwealth members would support the Africans, the Asian members being drawn into an uneasy caucus arrangement in 1966. Yet the fact that the caucus turned to Lee Kuan Yew, not to an African, to put its case, showed the basic weakness of the African position. African militants could go only so far with the pressure they regarded as essential. They could threaten to leave the Commonwealth—a threat first voiced as early as 1959, when Ghana and the not yet independent Nigerians used it in an effort to make the British government cast a UN vote against French nuclear tests in the Sahara[2] —but this was bound to lose force with repetition. They did not constitute a majority of members at any time. Unless they could gain support from other members, their position could not be sustained. At the same time their own unity was fragile, since the states in South Africa's orbit were unlikely to

[1] Mazrui, *Anglo-African Commonwealth*, pp. 27–8.
[2] Macmillan, *Pointing the way*, p. 94.

follow the more militant ones for long, and those were often divided on African questions. While the Asian and other members might go along with African militancy for a time, they could not be expected to do so indefinitely. Thus the African 'centre' of the Commonwealth was a transient phenomenon, at any rate in the form in which it existed in the mid-1960s, although it lasted long enough to help damage the influence of Britain, the other 'centre', and thus to damage further the Commonwealth system.

The adverse effects on the system originating in Britain itself have been discussed (chs 9, 11, 13, 15, and 16). In any case, British economic and military weakness was no foundation for strong belief in an institution which was essentially post-imperial: a slump in the imperial tradition had its effects on the special relationship which Britain was assumed to have with the legatees of that tradition, who in their turn had proved to be startlingly ungrateful. A sober but representative British view of the 'style of conversation' which had developed in the Commonwealth in the 1960s expressed a basic criticism in stating that when Commonwealth governments inveighed against Britain's application to join the EEC or its immigration laws and policies, they could reasonably argue that British policies of self-interest were having an adverse impact on their own economic interests or the interests of their citizens. But denunciations of British policy towards Rhodesia or arms sales to South Africa were 'basically assertions that British policy is inconsistent with the political and moral ideals for which the Commonwealth *ought* to stand'. No corresponding indulgence would be extended to British criticisms of such matters as flagrant violations of elementary civil liberties in a number of Commonwealth countries:

If there is to be one set of obligations binding and circumscribing Britain (or Western-aligned members), and another set of obligations, so nebulous as to be almost intangible, binding other members *qua* members, we may still have a Commonwealth, but not a Commonwealth which can meaningfully be described in any kind of constitutional terminology. If the Commonwealth cannot be so described, its future as a political association may be in jeopardy. For even in a loosely knit international organization there ought to be discernible rules of conduct deducible either from a broad community of purpose or from a convergence of self-interest.[1]

IV

Into such a situation in 1965 stepped the secretariat—to catch, as some might say, from failing hands the torch of Commonwealth. For a time the circumstances were both propitious and unpropitious for such a task—propitious in that the new secretary-general soon had opportunities for action in respect of Rhodesia, unpropitious in that these very opportunities caused some of the

[1] de Smith, *Int. J.*, Spring 1971, pp. 360–1. The adoption of the Commonwealth Declaration at Singapore in 1971 does not seem to me to invalidate this judgement, since it is the application of such a declaration that counts, not the words themselves.

members—notably Britain, Australia, and New Zealand—to fear 'that the Secretariat might intrude on policy decisions, which are, of course, the exclusive preserve of heads of government, both severally and individually', and 'that Marlborough House might become the instrument of Afro-Asian solidarity'.[1] The secretariat's special role in Rhodesian sanctions and its dependence on the goodwill of so many Afro-Asian members lent colour to these fears. They proved, however, to be of little substance: most of the secretariat's work lay in economic and related fields rather than political, and when it assumed further political activity, in the Nigerian civil war, its role was largely approved (or not actively opposed) by those who had previously demurred.

The advantages of the secretariat included the sense of a new start and a dynamic effort. Many thought on the same lines as a high commissioner in London in 1969, who told me that the other Commonwealth bodies were all 'too polite', and that it would do no harm if the secretariat stepped on a few toes in getting something done. Another advantage was that it could pay special attention to the needs and wishes of the smaller members. The older and bigger ones—Asian and African as well as 'white'—were well able to fend for themselves, attracting aid on their own account if they needed it, and informing themselves through their diplomatic networks of what was happening in world politics. The smaller ones were inexperienced and poor: they needed advice and help, which the secretariat gave, even to such minor non-members as Jersey, Guernsey, and the Cook Islands.[2] There was a further advantage in the multinational character of the secretariat's staff, which was representative of the Commonwealth in a way that had been impossible for the CRO to be.

Increasingly, the secretariat tried to provide a new Commonwealth system, or, perhaps more accurately, a new sort of centre for a modified version of the old one. Nothing could replace Britain as the source and origin of the elements which bound Commonwealth peoples together—the cultural, legal, political, and economic legacy which they shared, the English language, the sense of belonging to communities which had shared common experiences—but in Britain both the desire and the opportunity to operate a Commonwealth system had been greatly curtailed. The secretariat could utilize many of these elements to strengthen practical co-operation between the other members. The secretary-general rejected the metaphor of the Commonwealth as a wheel with Britain as the hub as anachronistic. Instead:

Any valid metaphor for this new Commonwealth with its 32 members . . . must express both its multilateral character, and the lattice-work nature of bilateral links between members, in which the relationships between for instance Canada and India, or Canada and East Africa, are close, important, and independent of the position of the former centre of an empire.

[1] Editorial, 'Less Caution Needed at Marlborough House', *The Times*, 21 Nov 1966.
[2] Leach, *Int. J.*, Spring 1971, p. 384n.

Its main role was to promote consultation and 'practical functional co-operation . . . across the lines of race, wealth and poverty, and region: differences
which . . . must not be allowed to fragment mankind.'[1]

To encourage a lattice-work of mutual relations within the Commonwealth,
the secretariat stressed the members' interests in such matters as economic
development, tourism, youth work, trade promotion, and training for diplomacy; it organized the Commonwealth Education Conferences and their
machinery, which grew in importance in the late 1960s; and its work was
supplemented by that of the Commonwealth Foundation, situated in the same
building.[2] The stimulation of functional co-operation, with the backing of
British traditions but not necessarily with any initiative from Britain itself,
implied a new sort of Commonwealth system, one in which the other Commonwealth members were interested in one another as well as in Britain, with
which connections had been so much greater in the past. It had previously
been the case that, when Britain suggested something and was bound to
support it, the others often stepped into line because of their overriding interest
in maintaining their connection with Britain. Multilateral action did not have
the same motive force. It would have to rely upon the awareness of the
members that they had needs in common, and the energy of the secretariat in
making sure these needs were first known and then, where possible, satisfied
within the bounds of the Commonwealth.

Such a system was, of course, not totally different from the old, and represented no abrupt break with the past—indeed, many of the activities had been
well under way before the secretariat was set up—but the new focus seemed
more appropriate to the more variegated Commonwealth.

The Commonwealth secretariat could not, however, replace that part of the
system which involved direct communication between Britain and the other
members, or between one of them and another. The specifically diplomatic
elements in the older system remained in being, but they were increasingly
harder to distinguish from ordinary diplomacy. The effect of the Plowden
report was to dilute greatly that section of British diplomats whose expertness
lay in knowledge of the Commonwealth: like the diplomats of other Commonwealth members, they now served wherever it was convenient to post them,
and acquired a much wider experience. The amalgamation of the Foreign and
Commonwealth Offices applied this same process to the diplomats' headquarters. The new Office included a Department for Commonwealth Co-
ordination, but otherwise its arrangements were functional and geographical,
not distinguishing between Commonwealth and foreign countries.[3] These
would, of necessity, stress bilateral and regional considerations in British
policy, at the expense of any notional common interest which Commonwealth

[1] Arnold Smith, 'The modern Commonwealth', *New Commonwealth*, No. 9, 1970.
[2] Education and Foundation activities are discussed in ch. 21.
[3] See chart in Commonwealth Secretariat, *Diplomatic service*, p. 22.

members might be assumed to have, or Britain to have in respect of them. This change led one observer to say that 'with the disappearance of a government department exclusively assigned to watch over Commonwealth relations, in Whitehall and throughout British Government the value and relevance of the Commonwealth have become not suddenly but nevertheless drastically diminished'.[1] If this were so, not everyone would be sorry. A former senior civil servant told me in 1970 that he had been equally opposed to the existence of the CRO and the Ministry of Agriculture, since it was 'bad in principle for a department to be the representative of a pressure group', and the CRO had represented Commonwealth countries in the same way as Agriculture had represented the British farmer. This point of view would have been strongly repudiated by CRO officials, who considered that they always remained aware of British interests, but, while it was not universal in Britain by the end of the 1960s, it was sufficiently pervasive in Whitehall to inhibit any attempt to resurrect the Commonwealth system.

V

One highly British insitution remained as a component of the Commonwealth—the monarchy. Queen Elizabeth II was Head of the Commonwealth throughout the period covered by this book. How did monarchy stand when the period was over? The question cannot be answered in simple terms.

When the Queen opened the new building of the Commonwealth Institute in London in 1962, she said: 'I suppose that, between us, my husband and I have seen more of the Commonwealth than almost any people alive. To us its diversity and unity and the friendliness of all its many peoples are alive and real.'[2] This was a statement of fact. From the beginning of her reign in 1952 the Queen had identified herself with the Commonwealth, and she and Prince Philip had reiterated, in speech after speech in many countries, their belief in the Commonwealth as a familial, multiracial body which could, through tolerance and understanding, ease the problems of countries which had to live together. But there were separable problems associated with the Queen's triple role as Head of the Commonwealth, monarch of her overseas realms, and monarch of Britain.

Much less has been written about the Queen's headship of the Commonwealth than about the other two roles.[3] This is partly because the role is solely symbolic—the Queen has nothing to do but be—and partly because, although it carries no distinct constitutional duties, there can still be uncertainty about the extent to which it makes the Queen, in some sense, the common property

---

[1] Peter Lyon, 'The Commonwealth in the 1970s', *World Today*, Apr 1971, p. 179.

[2] *The Times*, 7 Nov 1962.

[3] It is hardly mentioned in two of the adulatory books, Dermot Morrah, *The work of the Queen* (1958) and Dorothy Laird, *How the Queen reigns* (1961), or in a childish and catty one, Andrew Duncan, *The reality of monarchy* (1970).

of the members of the Commonwealth. For example, a fine tissue of speculation can be woven about whether the Queen's being Head of the Commonwealth entitles all members to have a say in any change in the succession, whether they acknowledge the Queen as head of state or not.[1] Such speculation has not been tested. Meanwhile, it is difficult for the inquirer to disentangle those tasks which the Queen performs specifically as Head of the Commonwealth and those which result from either or both of her other two roles. When she appears in the group photograph at a Prime Ministers' Meeting, that is clearly in her position as Head of the Commonwealth; the same applies when they and she exchange messages at each such meeting. Similarly, when Commonwealth heads of government come to see her individually, as they do during such meetings, and when they visit London for other reasons, it is clear that, if their countries do not acknowledge her as head of state, they are seeing her in her vaguer but more comprehensive part as Head of the Commonwealth. Again, when she visits a foreign country, she is met specially by the local Commonwealth ambassadors in a body, regardless of whether they represent her realms or not, and holds Commonwealth community receptions which are also comprehensive.

These ceremonial activities suggest that the symbolic headship of the Commonwealth carries with it the opportunity—though presumably not the obligation—to satisfy residual feelings of monarchism in those countries which have given up monarchy or, like Malaysia and Lesotho, have their own kings but find the British monarchy a striking example of monarchy as a principle. The British monarchy gets more space in such European and republican periodicals as *Paris Match* and *Der Spiegel* than any president's family; it is, in fact, the most interesting monarchy in the world. We need not wonder that royal attention should gratify Commonwealth leaders in the way that it evidently does. There may well be more residual monarchism than is often suggested.[2] There was little or no opposition to the idea of the Queen as Head of the Commonwealth amongst the new countries which became members in the 1960s. The only demurrer which this writer has found is Macmillan's record of Verwoerd's statement in 1960 that 'there was still a strong feeling in South Africa against recognizing the Queen as Head of the Commonwealth'. Macmillan was amazed by this statement: 'his attitude seemed to me not merely illiberal but definitely shabby'.[3]

A teasing question is whether the Queen ever requires advice (in the normal constitutional sense) in her role as Head of the Commonwealth, and, if so, to whom she should turn. Again it is possible to speculate on whether

[1] e.g. Wheare, ch. 7.

[2] See e.g. ch. 6 of Mazrui, *Anglo-African Commonwealth*, in which it is argued that republicanism in African Commonwealth countries was not necessarily because African nationalism was inherently opposed to monarchical values, and discusses the symbolism of Haile Selassie, the Kabaka of Buganda, and Seretse Khama in this context.

[3] *Pointing the way*, p. 154.

she is ever divested of her other roles (in each of which she is a constitutional monarch) and left simply with the functions of Head of the Commonwealth. Perhaps one such occasion was her tour of India and Pakistan in 1961, when both were republics, and when the British government did not arrange for her to be accompanied by a British minister but only by the Lord Chamberlain. Even in this instance, it is probable that the British government provided such 'fall-back' advice as she might need—and therefore was responsible for her remarks about 'basic democracies' in Pakistan, which were better received there than in India, where writers were quick to point out that Indian democracy was much more like British than anything which operated in Pakistan.[1]

In general, however, this situation would not arise. When visiting her realms the Queen depends on local ministers for advice, but normally when she visits Commonwealth countries, she does so primarily as Queen of the United Kingdom. No constitutional authority has suggested that the secretary-general could be a source of advice to the Queen as Head of the Commonwealth, although it is possible that in matters affecting the whole Commonwealth he might be available for conversations with her Private Secretary. Such occasions would more often be ceremonial than political, since it has not been the desire of any Commonwealth government that the Queen be embroiled in political argument. In the Rhodesian affair, for example, all her utterances were plainly the responsibility of the British government, in spite of Ian Smith's efforts to detach her from her constitutional position.

It is the Queen's situation as monarch of her realms outside Britain that potentially involves most debate. At the beginning of 1971 she was Queen of 11 Commonwealth countries. There were 21 others (including Nauru), of which 16 were republics and 5 had their own monarchs. Thus, while monarchy as a principle operated in exactly half the members, the Queen was the monarch of an actual minority. This gave rise to three interlocking potential or actual problems: the possibility that one realm might be seriously at odds with Britain or with another; the question whether each realm wants the monarchy to continue at the head of its constitution; and that of relations with the governments of the overseas realms.

The first of these, which could pose considerable difficulties, does not yet appear to have arisen. A possibility was the coup in Sierra Leone in 1967, which is dealt with below in the third category. A minor case arose over the fact that Australia took part in the Vietnam war and Britain did not. The Australian forces still recommend servicemen for British decorations. The award of one Australian VC required a year's correspondence between London and Canberra about the wording of the citation; there were complaints that Australian

---

[1] *The Times*, 8 Feb 1971; *Guardian* editorial, 11 Feb 1961. Still unanswered in formal terms is the intriguing question of why the British government, and not the governments of her other realms (in no way subordinate one to another) should have given this advice. In practical terms, of course, it is quite easy to answer.

recommendations should not have to 'run the gauntlet of the Commonwealth Relations Office'.[1] Inevitably, the fact that the British government had not seen fit to enter the war was suggested as a reason for the delay, although there had been similar complaints in the Korean war and World War II. This was a matter which could have been settled with a little more imagination and energy between the governments concerned; but the fact that it had not been, in spite of earlier instances, suggested that the Queen could be caught in a cross-fire of recrimination between two of her governments over a more serious dispute. On the whole, however, the fact that the Queen was removed from most contentious questions was an assurance that this sort of dispute would be rare.

There was considerable discussion during the period of the second question, whether each realm would wish to retain the British monarchy. This especially concerned Canada and Australia, since it was sometimes suggested that they might become republics. Though there had been adverse comment when Ghana became a republic, it was acceptable to British opinion that countries such as Cyprus, Nigeria, and Guyana should become republics. The Canadian case was the most serious. When the Queen visited Canada in October 1964 at the invitation of the prime minister, wild threats were made against her life by anonymous French Canadian separatists and she was booed in the streets of Quebec. Lester Pearson had 'relied on a tradition, perhaps now eroded, that the French are even warmer to the throne than the English Canadians'.[2] In this case the Quebec nationalists were not hostile to the Queen because she came from Britain but resented the action of the federal government in issuing the invitation as an assertion of the federal authority which they did not recognize.

English-speaking Canadians had traditionally used the Crown as a symbol of their own supremacy in Canadian politics. By the 1960s only a minority of Canadians could claim British ancestry. It was an open question whether Canada would want to continue attached to the British royal family, a point which was fully recognized by Prince Philip during his visit in 1969. He said:

The monarchy exists in Canada for historical reasons, and . . . in the sense that it is a benefit, or was considered to be a benefit, to the country or to the nation.

If at any stage any nation decides that the system is unacceptable, then it is up to them to change it. I think it is complete misconception to imagine that the monarchy exists in the interests of the monarch. It doesn't. It exists in the interests of the people. I think the important thing about it is that if at any stage people feel that it has no further part to play, then for goodness' sake let's end the thing on amicable terms without having a row about it.[3]

[1] Editorial, 'Awards for Bravery', *Sydney Morning Herald*, 28 Dec 1966.
[2] Editorial, 'The Queen and Quebec', *The Times*, 16 Sept 1964; for the events in Quebec, see *Sunday Times*, 11 Oct 1964.
[3] *The Times*, 20 Oct 1969.

This can be regarded as the doctrine on which the monarchy has operated. Efforts have been made to bring the Queen and her family into touch with people in her overseas realms, but it is recognized that monarchy does not suit everyone, and that changing circumstances in formerly 'loyal' countries might bring them to want an end to the system. Whether such a wish could survive the formidable barriers to constitutional change in Canada and Australia, as against newer members which can easily change their constitutions, is another matter.

In Australia the influx of European migrants since World War II is often said to have diluted monarchical sentiment, since many of these people, on being naturalized, do not see why they should swear allegiance to someone whom they have been brought up to regard as Queen of the United Kingdom. Australians of British stock too have complained about the retention of the monarchy in Australia, not because of its personal representatives but because it has been regarded as a symbol of the conservatism associated with honours[1] and in general with Sir Robert Menzies, a self-confessed 'Queen's man'. When Menzies's government proposed in June 1963 that the unit for the new Australian decimal currency should be called a 'royal', there was what the Treasurer, Holt, later described as wide and deeply felt opposition. When in October he announced that the unit would be called a dollar, this was widely welcomed. It was another minor incident, but indicative of the growing assertion of Australian nationalism—in small things, if not in matters of major policy.[2] In general, republicanism has made little headway in Australia.

Royal tours are one means of making royalty more meaningful for the overseas realms.[3] There have also been suggestions that the Queen might be shared between her eleven realms, spending a certain amount of time in each, or alternating between them year by year, but this is patently impracticable, and in any case would weaken the essentially British character of the monarchy, which is in practice its greatest strength. Its remoteness is in fact a strength, for the more remote it is, the less likely it is to be caught up in the local conflicts of a particular realm.

The third problem, that of the Queen's relations with her overseas governments, has seldom arisen, since most of these are fully parliamentary and peaceful and thus royal symbols are not involved in turmoil. There were, however, local disturbances about the use of power by governors-general in Pakistan

[1] Australia and New Zealand are amongst the few Commonwealth members still making recommendations for British honours, including, in particular, the OBE. The Australian States also exercise the right to recommend. Canada, which had made no recommendations for titles since 1935 but had continued to recommend for lesser honours, instituted a system of honours and awards of a Canadian kind to celebrate its centennial in 1967. They included no titles. There would be an Order of Canada, including medals for courage and service (*Survey B & CA*, 26 May 1967, p. 539).

[2] For a variety of views, see Geoffrey Dutton, ed., *Australia and the monarchy* (1966).

[3] There is a list of overseas tours by the Queen and Prince Philip from 1952 to 1967 in Christopher Hibbert, *The British monarchy today* (1968), pp. 49–55.

and Ceylon; and in March 1967 an army coup in Sierra Leone raised the question of how the Queen should behave when there was an overthrow of constitutional government. It is sound British doctrine that if such a thing occurred in Britain, she would have the power (which some would say she was bound to exercise) to act so as to preserve the constitution. There had been preliminary moves towards setting up a republic in Sierra Leone, but it was still one of the Queen's realms. No opinion was vouchsafed from the palace about the validity of the new government, despite the fact that it had put the governor-general under house arrest. The new regime was duly recognized by Britain, but a year later this regime was itself overthrown in another coup, which restored the parliamentary regime. Members of that regime, who had expected support from the Queen—or from the British government, the two being difficult for it to separate with complete assurance—took further steps to make Sierra Leone a republic, which it became in 1971. Many of those who worked to establish the republic believed that the Queen of Sierra Leone should have condemned the original coup, and that the British government should have advised her that this was a proper course to follow. They concluded that the British government had been more interested in economic interests than in parliamentary democracy.[1]

The reply is presumably that the Queen of Sierra Leone had no power with which to enforce whatever may have been her private views or those which she regarded as properly within her function as part of the Sierra Leone constitution, and that, in such a case, either inactivity or acceptance of advice from the British government was all that was open to her. This is the common sense approach. Its effectiveness depends on how often the monarch is called upon to make such choices. Since most of the realms are stable, the number of possibly awkward situations is not great. By 1971, however, they included Fiji, Jamaica, Malta, Mauritius, and Trinidad, none of which was entirely stable. If monarchy were involved in turmoil in these countries, as in Sierra Leone, to what extent could it be regarded as a unifying influence in the Commonwealth, described, on countless occasions, as its prime purpose?

On the whole, the policy of the British government and of the royal household has been to promote the Queen's Commonwealth ties in her capacity as Queen of the United Kingdom. When a high commissioner from one of the republics in the Commonwealth comes to present his credentials, the carriage sent for him has four horses and two postilions. The ambassador of a foreign country gets only two horses and one postilion. Gracious acts of this kind sweeten the atmosphere of Commonwealth relations. There have, however, been cases in which the interests of the United Kingdom in its monarch seemed to run counter to those of another Commonwealth member. An extreme example was the Queen's visit to Ghana in 1961, which is given a full chapter in Macmillan's memoirs.[2]

[1] From a private source.   [2] *Pointing the way*, ch. 17.

The essence of the problem was that, because of Nkrumah's repression and the fact that he was known to be in fear of his life, the Queen's visit might endanger her. At the same time, as Macmillan put the matter to the Queen, to cancel the visit 'would be a great act of policy on our side, and almost a declaration that we did not want Ghana in the Commonwealth. That would be a very grave step and not one to be lightly entertained'.[1] A previous visit had been cancelled because the Queen was expecting a baby. After much discussion, it was decided that the Queen would go, after the Commonwealth secretary had been sent to Ghana not only to talk to Nkrumah but to ride with him over the route that he and the Queen would take. In the event, the visit was a success; no violence occurred. The lesson was that at times a visit by the Queen to a Commonwealth country would have to be discussed in much the same terms as a visit to any other country, but with the added difficulty that if she did not go, the action might be construed as affecting the Commonwealth relationship.

Macmillan's view was that the acceptance by republican members of the Queen as Head of the Commonwealth could hardly be maintained 'on purely theoretical grounds': 'we owe it to the character and personality of the Queen herself and of the other members of her family, who by their constant visits and outstanding charm have carried the Commonwealth through this hazardous period'.[2] By the end of the decade, the British government's declining interest in the Commonwealth suggested that the Queen might have to undertake fewer such hazardous journeys in future.

It has already been mentioned that at various times people from other countries have referred to Britain rather than to the Queen, as the 'Head' of the Commonwealth. Historically, this is understandable; constitutionally, it is incorrect. The monarch is formally the symbol of the free association between the members of the Commonwealth. Her being Queen of the United Kingdom confers, in most Commonwealth respects, no greater status than her being Queen of Canada, Australia, or Jamaica. However, since her being Queen of those countries depends on her being Queen of the United Kingdom in the first place, there is a kind of union of constitutional doctrine and common sense in the notion that, since she is most obviously and basically Queen of the United Kingdom, it is the United Kingdom which, through her, is recognized as having some sort of leadership or headship in the Commonwealth. Even if the Commonwealth reached a *reductio ad absurdum* in which Britain was the only member of which Her Majesty was Queen (an unlikely but not impossible outcome during her reign or that of her successor), it would still be possible for the British monarch to be Head of the Commonwealth, provided the British government wished to retain this requirement and the other members were willing to accede to it. So long as the other members need Britain in one way or another, it is likely that they will perpetuate this way of showing that

[1] Ibid., p. 463.   [2] Ibid., p. 459.

the Commonwealth, while no longer British in name, is British in inception and cannot be totally divorced from its imperial origins.

To sum up the situation at the beginning of the 1970s, the Queen's position of Head of the Commonwealth remained largely inviolate, the other members readily agreeing to the British monarch's retaining this role.[1] The monarchy had remained useful to all who wanted to preserve the Commonwealth, since the Queen and her husband, increasingly experienced in Commonwealth affairs, had constantly stressed its value and tried to act as unifying elements within it, but its greatest value was for Britain. It was inevitable that the monarchy should be, in the broadest sense, an instrument of British policy in Commonwealth affairs as it was in foreign affairs. In any case, one would naturally expect Britain to derive more satisfaction from this highly British institution than other realms. Attachment to the throne was evidently a movable sentiment abroad: it had seemed to be strong in Durban, Cape Town, Johannesburg, and Salisbury, but had evaporated when the interests of the majority of people in those places were set against Britain's. The same might happen elsewhere, not necessarily to the disadvantage of British policy.

If Britain should become less interested in the Commonwealth, what future part would the monarchy play in a Commonwealth system such as the Commonwealth secretariat was striving to develop—one of a lattice-work of bilateral and multilateral co-operation, in which Britain did not necessarily take the initiative? It is worth remembering that it has been a tradition of the British monarchy, since the days of the Prince Consort, to encourage by patronage such activities as education, science, voluntary bodies, and the organization of the professions—those activities, in fact, which spread across the Commonwealth and had come to be regarded by many people, at the end of the 1960s, as providing whatever cement the Commonwealth possessed. The monarchy is thus well placed to continue patronage to these on a Commonwealth-wide scale. One would expect, therefore, that unless the British government were actively hostile to co-operation in such activities (which seems most unlikely), the Queen's position as Head of the Commonwealth would enable her and her family to continue giving support without any significant change of role.

VII

Such continued activity could not, however, sustain a Commonwealth system of the older kind, i.e. one which is an alternative or a rival to general diplomacy. Such a system still prevailed, to a certain extent, at the end of the 1960s between France and its former colonies, but had ceased to operate at

---

[1] A high commissioner did say to me in London, 'Some of my people wonder why the office does not rotate. After all, we have a King too!' See also the rather different proposals for rotation in James Eayrs, 'The overhaul of Commonwealth', *Round Table*, Jan 1967, p. 51. These swallows do not make a summer.

more than the formal level within the Commonwealth. Britain was less determined than France to retain influence over its ex-colonies, which were generally much more self-assertive than France's. Moreover, in the decline of the
Commonwealth system as formerly understood we can see exemplified four
of the five themes suggested in Chapter 2 of this book. It shows the influence
of a wider world and of a greater diversification of national interests within the
Commonwealth; the diminished unity and intimacy of contacts between
Commonwealth governments; the effect of significant changes in British
policy and opinion, leading towards closer attention to Europe and more
bilateralism in diplomacy with Commonwealth members; and a changing
conception of what the Commonwealth stood for.

It is important to recognize, in addition, that the third of the themes postu-
lated earlier—the steady growth in Commonwealth machinery, and in
co-operative use of that machinery—is also exemplified by the growth of the
Commonwealth secretariat (and the Commonwealth Foundation), with its
attempt to provide a lattice-work of contacts no longer dependent primarily on
Britain. At the beginning of the 1970s the aim of the secretariat was to develop
more of these contacts, by expanding the machinery of consultation, providing
further advisory services, and acting as a 'clearing house' whereby the experience of member governments, expressed in appropriate government papers,
could be made available to all.[1] These were modest proposals, likely to prove
more attractive to newer and smaller than to older and bigger members, but
they represented a contemporary means of continuing the advice and assistance to emerging states provided by the original Commonwealth system. And
the new system did also provide the prospect, for members of various sizes,
of a working alternative to universal and regional organizations, to both of
which they might be expected also to belong.

Note on Appeals to the Judicial Committee of the Privy Council
by J. E. S. FAWCETT

The role of the Judicial Committee of the Privy Council deserves brief
notice, which it should have in any survey of the Commonwealth. Appeal to
the Crown from the courts of its overseas dominions was long established, as
of right or by special leave, because the Crown was seen as the fountain of
justice, and as generally available, because the Crown was one and indivisible
throughout its empire. The function of the Judicial Committee was to hear
appeals and advise the sovereign as to whether they be allowed or dismissed.
This was the formal pattern, but it was early recognized that in fact the
Judicial Committee was not only a court rendering judicial decisions, implemented by order of the Sovereign in council, but was an appellate court, not
of the United Kingdom, but of the country from which the appeal came.

[1] See App. D of Commonwealth Secretariat, *Diplomatic service*, esp. pp. 182–4.

Whatever may have been the contribution of the Judicial Committee to the unity and harmony of Commonwealth law, self-government progressing to independence for Commonwealth countries made the Crown divisible, and the establishment of republics ended its authority, so that an important part of the historic base on which the Judicial Committee rested was removed. By whatever tests its Commonwealth influence is measured over the two decades after 1950, the result shows a continuing and perhaps inevitable decline.

In this period the Judicial Committee heard over 200 appeals from Commonwealth countries, the great majority turning on the administration of criminal justice and issues of commercial or matrimonial law. Sitting as it does as an appellate court of the country from which appeal is brought, such decisions of the Judicial Committee have for the most part only local application and interest; and it might well be asked whether the protraction and expense of proceedings in bringing such appeals to a tribunal sitting in London are really justified.

However, almost a quarter of the appeals heard in the period concerned issues that could be regarded as of common interest to other Commonwealth countries and the decisions upon them as having potential influence on future practice. Such issues are the role of the Crown in those countries still retaining it in their constitutional structure; the distribution of internal power between the various bodies and persons exercising public authority; and the constitutional protection of civil rights. It might then be asked how far the decisions of the Judicial Committee in these areas could be said to have a persuasive influence on law and practice in the Commonwealth, either because the particular issues were typical for several countries so that the decisions could have a useful and direct application in them, or because they reflected contemporary or progressive thinking. By the first test a persuasive influence could not be shown. Of forty-five appeals in the areas described, eleven came from Australia, ten from Ceylon, four from Canada, and four from Malaya or Malaysia, the remaining sixteen appeals being distributed over eleven countries. In substance, the decisions were concerned mainly with the interpretation of particular constitutional provisions, involving, for example, Federal-State conflicts in Australia, the jurisdiction of the Parliament of Ceylon, and analogous but isolated issues in Uganda and Trinidad. It is probable that the constitutional issues posed in Ceylon, and the handling of them by the Judicial Committee, were factors in the reform of the constitution and the establishment of the Republic of Sri Lanka. But it would be difficult to derive general conclusions, of wider application in the Commonwealth, from the decisions of this period or to deduce any principles of Commonwealth unity or constitutional synthesis from them. The handling by the Judicial Committee of UDI in Rhodesia was perhaps inevitably a legalistic exercise, which could have no general applicability, by reason both of the uniqueness of the situation and of the inherent political contradictions.

By the second test suggested, that decisions of the Judicial Committee may embody contemporary or progressive thinking on some of the issues raised on appeal, potential influence may and perhaps should be attributed to those decisions which deal with civil rights, though again such influence is likely to be limited to part of the Commonwealth only, namely the United Kingdom and its remaining dependencies. It is paradoxical that the Judicial Committee, though not acting as a tribunal of the United Kingdom, has handed down from London a number of decisions on the constitutional protection of civil rights, which is not so certainly extended to the inhabitants of that city. The United Kingdom could still learn from the rest of the Commonwealth that a single constitutional instrument, while not by itself a guarantee of civil rights, is nevertheless, as the commission on the constitution of Nigeria observed, a valuable first line of defence.

A further factor in the decline of the Judicial Committee is that Commonwealth countries have one by one been terminating appeals to it, and it is significant that the two countries from which more than half the appeals came in the period under review here have now terminated appeals in whole or in part. Ceylon, on becoming the Republic of Sri Lanka, abolished all appeals. Australia has, by legislation in and after 1968, abolished all appeals from State courts save those brought by special leave of the High Court, which is granted only if no exercise of Federal jurisdiction and no interpretation or application of the Constitution or any Federal law or instrument is involved. Only New Zealand of the 'old' Commonwealth, and fifteen of the countries that became independent from 1957 on now retain appeals to the Judicial Committee; while in Zambia the President may by order constitute it a court of appeal for that country.

Proposals have been repeatedly made for the establishment of a Commonwealth court of appeal, which would take the place of the Judicial Committee but differ from it, for example in having a more representative composition and in sitting perhaps in regional chambers. While the Judicial Committee as now composed has over thirty members, since it includes members of the Privy Council who have held high judicial office in Commonwealth countries, it consists in large part, when sitting to hear appeals, of Lords of Appeal in the United Kingdom. The notion of a regional Commonwealth court, analogous to the Judicial Committee, was put forward by the United Kingdom in the context of a settlement of the Rhodesian dispute but rejected in October 1969 by the Smith regime. This court would have been composed of the Chief Justices of Australia, Malawi, New Zealand, Rhodesia, South Africa, and the United Kingdom, and would have had jurisdiction to hear appeals against amendments of the entrenched provisions of a Rhodesian Constitution. An alternative proposal was that the existing Judicial Committee should have power to call for a referendum on a particular amendment.

The fact that the many and various proposals for a reformed Judicial Committee have made little headway serves only to confirm the conclusion from the experience of the last two decades that, neither as it is, nor as reformed, can it have any general Commonwealth function.

PART VI

NETWORKS OF CUSTOM AND CONVENIENCE

CHAPTER 19

NETWORKS OF ASSOCIATION

THE previous Part, with its account of changes in policy and machinery, can be interpreted to mean that by 1970 there was not one Commonwealth but at least seven. First were the old dominions; although Canada did not always find Australia and New Zealand easy bedfellows, there was sufficient in common between them (especially their connections with the US) to put them in a Commonwealth of their own. Next was the South Asian Commonwealth, consisting of India, Pakistan, and Ceylon. Third was the Southeast Asian Commonwealth, comprising Malaysia and Singapore; and fourth the African Commonwealth, though by 1969 this might have been divided into West, East, and Southern sections, each with three, four, or five members. The interests and experience of the former High Commission Territories, for example, were clearly distinct from those of the West or East African Commonwealth states, however much there might be an overlap in spirit. Fifth was the Mediterranean Commonwealth, composed of Malta and Cyprus, with primarily European populations and European links but hardly connected with one another except inasmuch as an upheaval in Nato or in the Mediterranean would affect them both. Sixth and seventh were the Caribbean and Pacific Commonwealths, the first consisting of Guyana, Jamaica, Trinidad, and Barbados, and the second of Tonga, Western Samoa, and Fiji (which became members in 1970) and Nauru (which became a special member in 1968).

These last two groups of small, poor island states with very similar problems were showing more awareness of their joint difficulties than the bigger states which had gained their independence earlier. The Caribbean members, for example, began a series of 'summit conferences' in 1963 and continued to co-operate on such matters as the disturbance in the British island of Anguilla in 1967; they also held combined conferences with Canada about extended Canadian aid. The Pacific island members, having had some joint experience at the South Pacific Conference and the Pacific Islands Producers' Association, formed in 1965, took part with Australia and New Zealand in establishing the South Pacific Forum in 1971.

These seven categories omit Mauritius, an island drawn towards Africa by location, India by origins, and the Caribbean islands and Fiji by a pressing interest in prices and markets for sugar. The seven regional categories correspond also to experience in time, since their members gained their independence at roughly the same stage. The differences between the categories are obvious, and the connections between them tenuous. While all have in common a relationship with Britain, it is not the same relationship. In fact, the further one pursues each member's actual relations with Britain, the more one is inclined to say that there is not one Commonwealth, or even seven, but as many Commonwealths as there are members, since each has had a distinctive network of connections with the former imperial power. One must also recognize the influence of the traditional Colonial Office doctrine that the colonies should not be governed as a whole but as separate entities. 'In the ultimate analysis', writes Professor Mazrui, 'what could a New Zealander have in common with a Jamaican or a Zambian if not the bonds of a shared British-ness?'[1] Yet this British-ness has not been the same all round: some of the networks have been distinctive to individual members, but most have been shared, to an unequal degree, by several and sometimes all. This was so before 1939, when Australia and New Zealand generally believed that their ties with Britain were different from, and closer than, Canada's and South Africa's. It was much more so by 1969.

In identifying these networks, we must put first the economic: Britain as a market, a source of investment and manpower, and a donor of aid; the other members as suppliers of raw materials, and markets for British goods.

Then there are the connections within the ambit of the English language, arising from educational, religious, administrative, and economic sources in the colonial period, and tending towards awareness of a distinctive culture. People of British stock were direct heirs of this, but it was readily assimilated by educated Indians, Africans, Chinese, and Ceylonese, though less readily by Afrikaners, Québecois, Maltese, and Cypriots. Such a culture embraced many things, from cricket on the one hand to English literature on the other. Nyerere translating Shakespeare into Swahili, and Menzies gazing at 'the long sweep of the Wye Valley above Tintern, with a Wordsworth in my pocket',[2] would probably agree more about literature than about politics, although the one would be looking for great ideas and the other for great traditions.

Thirdly, one can distinguish a network of similar institutions in most of the Commonwealth countries, arising in some cases from the creation of branches or imitations of British institutions (as with educational and professional bodies), and in others from the modification of transplanted British institutions in law and administration.

Fourthly, there is a network of ideas and assumptions. Often these are vague notions about standards of political behaviour, involving parliaments, civil services, judiciaries, and even armies, and including ideas about the nature of the Commonwealth. Again, the influence is clearer in the countries of British settlement, and in those which had of necessity to adopt British

---

[1] *The Anglo-African Commonwealth*, p. 41.

[2] See ibid., chs 7 and 8; and Menzies, *The British Commonwealth of Nations in international affairs* (1950), p. 25.

models for purposes of modernization, than in those communities which could draw upon different strains of European tradition, such as the Afrikaners and the people of Quebec, Malta, and Cyprus.

Some connections, such as the economic, military, and educational ones, have by their nature been more institutionalized than others. It is easy to concentrate attention upon the creation and dissolution of institutions, since these are definite things which appear to have beginnings and ends, and one can speculate more confidently about their influence than about the influence of language or ideas. Yet such a distinction may be artificial and even misleading. For instance, we know exactly when the Indian Army ceased to be under British control and became fully Indian in formal terms; but who can say that British standards ceased to operate at the same time, that the English language no longer constituted a bond between the officer corps of Britain and India, or that ways of thinking and forms of organization did not remain when formal control changed? It would be nearer the truth to say that in this, as in other examples, the networks of connection continued to exist, although their operation necessarily changed with the new circumstances of independence. In some cases, but not many, they were abruptly cut off. In others they declined gradually in importance, as new generations grew up unfamiliar with the former close connections.

Whether we regard these networks as responding to institutional treatment or not, it is hard to avoid the feeling that all of them were involved in the high politics described in Part II. From time to time, Prime Ministers' Meetings would take note of them, as when they commended attempts at greater educational co-operation within the Commonwealth or called for more trade within it. Where the networks involved obvious advantage or convenience, as in these cases, they were likely to become visible at the political level. Where it was more a matter of custom than convenience, the absence of specific attention by political leaders would not necessarily mean lack of effect and influence. It is best, perhaps, to visualize a continuous interaction between the official and unofficial aspects of Commonwealth relations, so that official policies and institutions both affected, and were affected by, the networks of connection in the cultural, educational, and economic fields.

There are several reasons why it is hard to go further than this in trying to assess the influence of the unofficial connections upon high policy. An obvious reason is that Commonwealth members were affected unequally by the various networks which we can identify. If we take the economic network (the most widespread and most talked about), this is clearly the case. The greater part of the outflow of British investment was concentrated in a few countries; the preference system was of vital importance to a few, and much the same few; the British market was much more important to some than to others; British aid was not distributed on a per capita basis, or on any other which might be said to have treated equally the various countries receiving it. Again, if one takes military connections, some Commonwealth countries continued to welcome British troops after independence, but the great majority did not. Even the spread of the English language was unequal, allowing for the fact that the mass of the people in African and Asian countries were in no position to learn it. The elites amongst Greek Cypriots and Maltese were less inclined to an English-speaking environment than those of India or Singapore. The point is that, while we can establish certain influences as having *some* effect everywhere (such as the English language and British administrative practices), we cannot say, without investigation, that they had the *same* effect.

Again, even when we establish the application of a particular network of connection to a particular country, we cannot be sure in advance that its effect continued to be the same as before. One cannot assume that a pre-independence tradition of parliamentarism (as in Nigeria and Ghana) or of transmitted social attitudes (as in Jamaica and Trinidad) would sustain itself against such pressures as personal ambition and tribalism in the first two instances, or the disappointments of emigration and the transmission of Black Power concepts in the other two.

Thirdly, any attempt to relate unofficial networks of connection to high policy must take account of the vastly more complex foreign-policy considerations of the principal Commonwealth countries; for example British foreign policy involves the great powers, the countries of Western Europe, the whole Commonwealth, and a complex of other influences (e.g. that of Spain in respect of Gibraltar, or that of South Africa), but the scope of Ceylonese foreign policy is infinitely narrower and more local. Whereas the question of sugar largely fills the foreign policy horizons of small states such as Fiji and Mauritius, India and Canada operate in a much more complicated environment. The more diverse the foreign policy environment of a Commonwealth country, the more difficult it will be to establish any sort of causal connection between its high policy and the networks described above.

None the less, the networks are there. Even Nkrumah, who seemed to discard so many British connections and to wish to replace so much of Ghana's British heritage with elements of his own (including his own head on the coins and stamps), is known, from wide testimony, to have been highly ambivalent about that heritage. The social groups which dethroned him were strongly British in their expression and motivation. One could construct (but only in impressionistic terms, since the evidence is patchy and often difficult to interpret) a different grid for each member, showing which networks mattered most and touched most heavily on which points of the national life.

The most complex of all would be the pattern or grid for Britain, especially since it has so often been oversimplified for political purposes, or merely in order to impose some coherence upon the situation. Whenever a British leader has said that 'the Commonwealth' wants this or that, or must be aware of such-and-such, or responds to treatment of a particular kind, or will not stand for something which is proposed, he has been using a kind of shorthand, because the complexities of association with each member, let alone the total of them, make any generalization about the Commonwealth's volition highly suspect, no matter how necessary it might seem in a domestic political context. We have seen how complex was the pattern of association, and of interests arising from the associations, in such matters as the EEC and Commonwealth immigration. Each issue of high policy discussed in Part II involved simultaneously a number of networks and their effects. But we cannot say exactly how.

The Commonwealth as a whole can thus be seen as an intricate total system, or system of subsystems, or network of networks, involving a variety of associations spread unequally over the whole, the inequality applying not only to the incidence of each network on the members at any point of time but also to the incidence on a particular member at different points of time. Jutting out of this, as it were, was what we have discussed as 'the Commonwealth system'. This formal system was assumed to possess qualities distinguishing it from normal diplomatic relations between countries foreign to one another. The basic reasons for such an assumption lay in the networks of informal, unofficial association. To the extent that these continued to be active, and not to be abridged by high policy, they provided a justification for the Commonwealth system. They and it changed together in effectiveness.

CHAPTER 20

ECONOMIC CONNECTIONS

ECONOMIC connections arose from the very nature of the British Empire
and were primarily connections between the overseas countries and
Britain rather than between those countries themselves. There were
exceptions: the fact of common British standards of law, language, and the like
encouraged some migratory links between these outer areas, as when Australian
miners went to South Africa and New Zealand, and Indian workers to Fiji,
Malaya, Mauritius, and East Africa. In other instances advanced dominions
like South Africa and Australia were strategically placed as trading and
transport centres for such places as Rhodesia and the Pacific Islands. There
was a long-standing economic link between Canada and the West Indies. But
in the main imperial and Commonwealth ties arose from Britain's economic
expansion abroad.

In Commonwealth terms, the three economic indicators most often used
have been 'men, money, and markets'—migration, investment, and trade.
Not only do these represent significant movements of resources; they were
also symbols of an interwar attempt to provide 'greater security and power for
"the Empire as a whole" ' by direct government policy, aimed at increasing the
flow of all three.[1] As we have seen (ch. 12), the period after 1953 was not
marked by such efforts, except to a minor extent in trade and rather more in
investment. None the less, the three indicators remain useful because of their
relevance to the past.

I

The nineteenth and early twentieth centuries, from 1850 to 1914, were
marked by Britain's supremacy as a provider of funds, markets, capitalist
enterprise, and manpower for the greater part of the Empire, and by the
existence of steady currencies in direct relation to the pound sterling. Canada,
because of its close connection with the US, was, in this period as in others,
something of an exception; elsewhere it was the British market which mostly
shaped the export trade of the overseas countries, just as it was British capital
that financed their transport industries and developed their local resources,
and British settlers who expanded the populations of Australia, New Zealand,
South Africa, and Canada.

In none of these fields, however, was Britain exclusively or even mainly
concerned with the Empire. British investors put their money where they

[1] Hancock, *Survey*, ii, pt 1, p. 149. See the whole of his ch. 3.

thought it would make the most profit. Rough figures for British investment show the following:

TABLE 5
British Investment Abroad: Totals (£ m.)

Area	1870	1885	1911
India	160	270	350
Australasia	74	240	380
Canada	20	113	375
South Africa	under 16	35	350
US	200	300	690
Europe and Near East	230	175	?
South America	85	150	585

Source: A. K. Cairncross, *Home and foreign investment 1870–1913* (1953), pp. 183, 185.

Some figures for trade, at thirty-year intervals up to the introduction of the second wave of imperial preference, make a similar point:

TABLE 6
British Trade with Selected Areas, 1871–1931 (£ m.)

A. Exports

Area	1871	1901	1931
India	19·1	35·8	33·1
Australia and NZ	11·1	29·7	26·8
Canada	9·2	9·6	22·7
West Indies	6·8	4·7	5·9
Africa (minus the North)	5·3	26·9	42·5
Europe and N. Africa	142·1	138·1	175·1
US	38·7	37·7	26·2
Latin America	20·6	22·5	30·3
Asia (minus India)	16·0	24·9	33·7
Middle East	13·6	14·6	13·0

B. Imports

Area	1871	1901	1931
India	30·7	27·4	36·7
Australia and NZ	14·5	34·8	83·5
Canada	9·3	20·4	34·9
West Indies	8·5	2·0	5·9
Africa (minus the North)	7·4	9·5	29·7
Europe and N. Africa	132·4	225·4	369·6
US	61·1	141·0	104·0
Latin America	22·5	26·7	82·7
Asia (minus India)	20·3	18·4	42·5
Middle East	20·5	18·0	20·5

Source: B. R. Mitchell & Phyllis Deane, *Abstract of British historical statistics* (1962), pp. 315–26. Exports include re-exports. Burma is included in India, Newfoundland in Canada, and Turkey and Egypt in the Middle East.

The investment figures show the great increase in British capital in the US and Latin America in the latter part of the period in comparison with a more gradual increase in India and the old dominions. The export figures show the continued and enormous importance of Europe, as do the import figures, though there is some counterbalance from the US and a growing dependence on developing areas in Australia, New Zealand, Canada, and Africa is evident. The older imperial areas—India and the West Indies—remained stable or slipped back as suppliers to Britain, and the 'informal empire' bulked large.

A similar emphasis upon areas outside the Empire is apparent when one considers British emigration, though here the comparison is narrowed: the US was until about 1900 the great magnet for British emigrants, taking more in most years than Canada, Australia, New Zealand, and South Africa together. After 1900 the US pull diminished. By the beginning of World War I the Canadian figure had outstripped the American, which in its turn was being equalled by Australia and New Zealand in combination. This trend continued with the lessened British migration between the wars.[1]

If, then, we wish to establish a true picture of British economic relations with the overseas Empire up to World War I, it has to be set against a background of British money, goods, and people going where it was thought they would do best rather than following the British flag. At the same time, we should recognize that the flag did ensure certain advantages: familiarity in language, law, and standards; an acceptable degree of political stability; a stable currency; and freedom from undue advantages to competitors. Other things being equal, the Empire was a good place in which to trade and invest. But they were not sufficiently equal to offset the effects of European propinquity, the attractions of Argentina, and the traditions of trade in the Levant and China. Similarly, a long-established British position in the West Indies and India did not guarantee an increase in British economic interest. The Empire was important but not all-important.

Between the wars the position remained much the same, subject to certain modifications.[2] One was sustained pressure from the old dominions for sheltered markets in Britain for their agricultural products, which they gained in part at the Ottawa conference of 1932. Another was local protectionism in the independent Commonwealth countries. These tended to raise their tariff barriers against British goods, but to encourage British firms to come in behind the tariff wall and establish subsidiaries which would rank as local industries while sustained by British capital and technical knowledge. A third was a slow revision of the conventional British attitude that development finance for colonies ought to come only from private sources: by 1939 the British government was becoming persuaded that it should take some direct

[1] B. R. Michell & Phyllis Deane, *Abstract of British historical statistics*, pp. 50–1.
[2] Hancock, *Survey*, ii, pts 1 & 2 is the standard work on this period.

action, and the Colonial Development and Welfare Act of 1940 was a foretaste of the substantial aid Britain was to give its colonies after World War II.

In spite of these changes, the Empire and Commonwealth, on the outbreak of war in 1939, constituted nothing like a comprehensive economic system, although it had more of the elements of a system than in the hey-day of free trade. British overseas investment was by now retreating from its 'informal empire', and finding greater attractions in the old dominions and in such rapidly developing areas as West Africa. It was imperial preference that gave the greatest appearance of system, though to some extent this appearance was deceptive. Britain fought hard at Ottawa to avoid paying through the nose for its vital foods and raw materials. Such important imperial commodities as wheat, wool, and rubber, and also many of the products of tropical Africa, remained outside the system. The products of the old dominions, especially those of which production had been expanded after World War I through soldier settlement, did get special consideration in Britain, and British manufactures were given an advantage over 'foreign' goods in return. There can be little doubt that the preferences benefited Canada, Australia, and New Zealand in selling to Britain, largely at the expense of Europe, the US, and Latin America, but there was no marked shift in British exports. In 1938 Europe still bought more from Britain than India, Australia, New Zealand, Canada, the West Indies, and the US combined, as in 1871, 1901, and 1931.[1]

During World War II Britain was largely cut off from European markets and sources of supply. Shortage of shipping and the need for guaranteed supplies of food and raw materials made it necessary to concentrate upon colonial and Commonwealth sources, and the US. Britain made bulk-purchase arrangements for a great range of the overseas products. While British export trade was necessarily restricted by the priority given to local needs, and by shortages of labour, raw materials, and shipping, British products did not have to meet Japanese and European competition in the colonies and Commonwealth countries. Mutual dependence within the Commonwealth was thus increased.

The situation may have been artificial from a long-term view, but it continued for some time after 1945 because Britain's other markets and suppliers were unavailable. Moreover, Britain was itself in need of sheltered markets and guaranteed supplies at known prices: British industry was in no position to switch its run-down machines immediately to general production for export, to rely solely upon its own earning power to meet its people's demands for imports, or to invest indiscriminately. Throughout the sterling area, exchange controls continued, and trade in sterling was preferred to any available alternative. In return, Britain restricted new overseas investment to sterling countries. Such a total arrangement came close to a siege economy for the colonies and Commonwealth as a whole, except for Canada, a dollar country.

[1] Mitchell & Deane, pp. 315–26.

In retrospect, it is easy to see that, once Britain and its European markets and suppliers had recovered from their wartime exhaustion, the siege economy would be neither practicable nor tolerable, and that the overseas countries, while wishing to retain their markets in Britain, would also be eager to try other sources of imports and investment. The US, which had suffered no diminution of its resources by the war but had experienced a substantial increase in productive power, had also gained new access to these overseas economies through the wartime alliance. It would be bound to figure more prominently in their plans for trade and investment. Japan would not remain a quiescent ex-enemy for ever. Above all, British governments and public opinion, schooled by a century of free trade, would be unlikely to want to continue Commonwealth bulk-purchase agreements for all the commodities which, after the recovery of competing sources of supply, could be bought more cheaply in the open market. In due course, investment opportunities outside the sterling area would again attract British investors.

II

Chapter 12 has described the rejection by Britain and other Commonwealth countries of a substantial development of economic links in favour of world-wide free trade in goods and capital. The combined effect of policy and opportunity can be seen in the drift away from intra-Commonwealth trade as the level of international transactions rose and their multilateral quality increased. Table 7 shows this for the main Commonwealth countries:

TABLE 7

Proportion of Intra-Commonwealth to Total Trade, 1956–68
(Percentages)

Country	Exports				Imports			
	1956	*1961*	*1964*	*1968*	*1956*	*1961*	*1964*	*1968*
Britain	39	35	28	22	42	35	30	23
Canada	21	20	20	13	12	16	13	9
Australia	49	38	37	34	60	48	39	36
New Zealand	72	60	57	51	78	72	69	63
India	50	44	35	25	40	31	20	16
Pakistan	35	34	36	24	35	32	21	33
Ceylon	50	50	46	44	46	45	37	35
Ghana	33	26	20	27	54	43	36	39
Nigeria	65	46	42	32	54	46	37	37

Sources: COI, *The pattern of Commonwealth trade* (1962), p. 7 and Commonwealth Secretariat, *Commonwealth trade 1968* (1969), pp. 137–8.

No single reason can adequately explain the increasingly multilateral character of these countries' trade, although one can find an explanation for Ghana's move in the opposite direction in the swing away from Nkrumah's economic policies after his deposition, and for the slowness of change for

Pakistan and Ceylon in the comparative stagnation of trade experienced by countries dependent upon a narrow range of primary products for export. For the remainder the reasons for increased trade outside the Commonwealth included the relaxation of import restrictions, especially upon dollar goods, in the later 1950s; the increase in non-Commonwealth aid for some of the overseas countries; constantly growing opportunities for trade with Western Europe, Eastern Europe, and Japan; and greater access to the US market. In spite of the adjurations of Commonwealth meetings in the 1950s to increase intra-Commonwealth trade, powerful influences were pulling in the opposite direction.

Nowhere is this clearer than in the case of Britain. Table 8 uses the categories previously employed to show the changing pattern of British trade between 1951 and 1969:

TABLE 8

British Trade with Selected Areas, 1951–69 (£ m.)

i. Exports

Area	1951	1956	1961	1965	1969
India	115·9	169·8	152·9	116·4	67·0
Aust. and NZ	437·0	369·0	327·7	410·5	445·1
Canada	140·1	182·3	228·2	208·1	310·9
West Indies	48·8	82·9	83·5	98·9	83+
Africa (minus the North)	372·5	452·7	448·5	558·2	—
Europe and North Africa	716·6	1,009·2	1,369·7	1,881·7	2,854
US	153·6	259·1	298·1	514·7	903·4
Latin America	160·9	137·3	175·3	160·7	248·3
Asia (minus India)	251·1	277·1	321·7	366·7	—
Middle East	146·5	169·7	211·6	247·7	502·4

ii. Imports

India	152·6	141·4	144·9	128·3	107·1
Aust. and NZ	419·1	433·1	333·7	427·7	453·7
Canada	260·5	347·5	349·4	458·2	506·4
West Indies	164·6	126·7	100·9	98·7	68+
Africa (minus the North)	393·9	417·3	400·9	604·7	—
Europe and North Africa	1,079·3	1,079·4	1,423·2	2,086·9	3,217·0
US	380·0	408·0	484·4	671·4	1,124·3
Latin America	269·8	254·4	278·0	289·7	355·7
Asia (minus India)	323·3	236·4	283·4	328·2	—
Middle East	245·0	245·5	331·2	325·4	695·7

Sources: B. R. Mitchell & H. G. Jones, Second abstract of British historical statistics (1971), pp. 136–40 and Ann. abstract of statistics 1970, pp. 247–8. The absence of some figures for 1969 is due to lack of compatability of the two sources.

Both exports and imports show mainly sluggish increase in the traditional areas of Commonwealth trade (and actual decline in the case of India), together with massive growth in the European market, and significant growth in trade with the US, the Middle East, and even Latin America. Using a yardstick we have used before, we can say that in 1956 Europe just failed to exceed India, Australia, New Zealand, Canada, the West Indies, and the US combined as a market for British exports; in 1961 it exceeded their combined total with ease; and in 1965 and 1969 it outranked them altogether, in spite of substantial rises in British exports to the US. On the import side, Britain's reduced dependence on imported food and basic materials, and its increased appetite for finished manufactures, militated against any growth in the market for traditional Commonwealth suppliers. It was not that Britain was substituting other suppliers for the same goods; rather, it was buying less of them and more of different goods.[1]

Markets for exports, rather than sources of imports, are what shape businessmen's views on where attractive trading areas are to be found. In the 1950s and 1960s the advantages derived in the Commonwealth from British traditions and preferences were less effective in providing markets for British goods than the rapidly rising incomes of West Europeans and Americans. The point is illustrated in percentage terms in table 9:

TABLE 9

British Exports by Areas and Selected Countries 1956–68
(per cent)

Area	1956	1959	1962	1966	1968
Non-sterling Area	57·1	60·9	65·6	68·6	71·6
North America	13·8	17·7	14·2	16·7	18·4
Canada	5·5	6·2	4·8	4·2	4·2
US	8·3	11·5	9·4	12·5	14·2
Western Europe	28·5	28·2	36·1	37·6	36·7
EFTA	11·7	11·3	13·3	14·7	13·9
EEC	14·5	14·9	19·6	19·0	19·4
USSR and East Europe	1·4	1·8	2·8	2·9	3·6
Latin America	4·2	4·5	4·1	3·1	3·6
Other non-sterling	9·3	8·9	8·4	8·1	9·2
Sterling Area	42·8	39·1	34·4	31·4	28·4
Australia	7·4	6·5	5·9	5·1	5·1
New Zealand	3·9	2·9	2·7	2·5	1·6
India	5·2	5·0	3·0	1·9	1·2
Pakistan	1·0	1·0	1·1	1·0	0·7
Malaysia and Singapore	2·5	1·8	2·2	1·8	1·5
Hong Kong	1·1	1·1	1·2	1·3	1·2
Nigeria	1·9	2·1	1·6	1·3	0·9
Irish Republic	3·2	3·2	3·5	3·6	4·2
South Africa	5·0	4·6	4·0	4·8	4·3
Commonwealth	39·8	41·5	30·8	26·0	22·7
Totals (£m.)	3,226	3,423	3,905	5,042	6,176

Source: COI, *The pattern of British exports* (1970), p. 8.

[1] COI, *Britain's external trade and payments* (1972), p. 2.

It is important to recognize that, in using percentages, we may gain a some-what misleading impression of the movement of Commonwealth trade in general and British trade in particular. As the last line of the table shows, British exports increased substantially in total value, so that a slight percentage decline in a particular country's share of British exports did not mean that it was spending less money on British goods; it might in fact be spending more. Nevertheless, just as Britain was getting smaller proportions of its imports and selling smaller proportions of its exports to Commonwealth countries, so they were trading less with Britain in comparison with their trade with other countries. Tables 10 and 11 show how, in the 1960s, most overseas Common-wealth members' trade with Britain declined in percentage terms.

TABLE 10

Commonwealth Countries' Exports to Britain, 1962–9
(Percentages of total exports)

Country	1962	1963	1964	1965	1966	1967	1968	1969
Canada	14	15	15	14	11	10	9	7
Australia	20	18	20	18	16	13	14	12
New Zealand	49	47	49	48	42	45	40	39
India	24	22	21	18	17	20	16	12
Pakistan	17	13	13	13	12	13	12	11
Ceylon	30	31	29	26	25	29	25	20
Malaysia	9	8	9	7	7	6	7	5
Singapore	5	5	5	5	4	6	5	5
Ghana	24	20	15	13	17	21	20	21
Nigeria	42	39	38	38	38	30	29	27
Rhodesia ⎫			23	20	—	—	—	—
Zambia ⎬	42	39 ⎨	32	38	32	27	29	26
Malawi ⎭			42	50	49	52	49	45
Hong Kong	17	18	18	14	14	13	13	12
Others	30	30	28	26	23	24	22	22
Total	20	20	19	18	17	15	14	12

Source: Commonwealth Secretariat, *Commonwealth trade 1966, 1968, & 1970.*

TABLE 11

Commonwealth Countries' Imports from Britain, 1962–9
(Percentages of total imports)

Country	1962	1963	1964	1965	1966	1967	1968	1969
Canada	9	8	8	7	7	6	6	6
Australia	30	29	26	26	25	22	22	22
New Zealand	42	40	38	37	37	32	31	31
India	17	15	12	11	9	8	7	7
Pakistan	18	14	13	15	15	13	12	13
Ceylon	21	19	16	18	17	16	15	17

Country	1962	1963	1964	1965	1966	1967	1968	1969
Ghana	34	33	27	25	26	30	28	27
Malaysia	20	20	19	20	19	15	14	13
Singapore	9	10	10	10	10	8	7	7
Nigeria	36	34	31	31	28	29	31	35
Rhodesia			30	30	—	—	—	—
Zambia	33	32	17	20	22	17	23	23
Malawi			23	25	31	28	31	30
Hong Kong	11	12	10	11	10	9	9	8
Others	26	25	23	22	23	21	20	20
Total	19	18	16	16	14	13	12	12

Source: As for table 10.

Some sense of long-term change can be gained by comparing the percentages in tables 10 and 11 for Britain's three major trading partners in the Commonwealth—Canada, Australia, and New Zealand—with those for 1950. In that year Britain had taken 15·1 per cent of Canadian exports and supplied 12·8 per cent of its imports. It had taken 33 per cent of Australian exports and supplied 48 per cent of imports, and 66 per cent of New Zealand exports, supplying 60 per cent of imports.[1] The change in twenty years had been massive. A phrase quoted earlier, 'not much kith and kin about that', applies also to trade.

The British propensity to invest abroad has been high for at least a hundred years. In spite of Britain's postwar economic difficulties, it remained the second biggest external investor, after the US; and its investments are much more widely distributed than those of the US, of which about half are concentrated in Canada and Latin America.[2] Moreover, it differs from other industrialized countries such as Germany, Japan, Canada, and Italy, which have a high degree of foreign capital invested in them. These pay out more than they get, whereas Britain gains. It also differs from Switzerland, the Netherlands, France, and Sweden, which also gain, in the greater magnitude of the British stake abroad.[3]

Explanations of this propensity are various, but have much to do with Britain's early status as an industrialized country with capital to spare, with the development of the London money markets, and with the growth of the Empire, which was a natural area for British investment, especially since the Colonial Stock Acts of the nineteenth century made the bonds of colonial (and later dominion) governments acceptable investments for British trustees. The US and the 'informal empire' in China and Latin America were also areas of substantial British investment before 1939, with the greater part of the total

[1] These figures have been taken from various editions of *Canada Year Book*, *New Zealand Official Yearbook*, and *Official Year Book of the Commonwealth of Australia*.

[2] The proportion used to be higher, but during the 1960s the US investments in Europe expanded more rapidly than those in the western hemisphere (see US, *Statistical abstract 1969*, p. 785).

[3] See Strange, table on p. 134.

going into basic utilities and resources such as railways, mines, plantations, and public utilities. Susan Strange's summing-up is apt:

British overseas investment in the past was distinguished from that of most other developed countries by both size and character. It was exceptionally large and very widely distributed in geographical location and type of enterprise. It was persistent and therefore resilient to setback, and productive of large new resources for re-investment. In character it was managerial and oriented to enterprise and economic growth.

British attitudes to overseas investment have consequently been unusually patient and unusually optimistic and confident. On the whole, British investors have been accustomed for a long time to suffer much less influence, intervention, or arbitrary appropriation at the hands of governments—especially of their own government. Continental European governments were much more inclined to interfere, and to try to manage their national capital markets in their own or their allies' interests.[1]

Some 55 per cent of the nominal capital value of British investments abroad in 1938 was in the Commonwealth. During World War II a process of dis-investment went on, with the result that in 1945 the total overseas stake was smaller by a third, but the Commonwealth element had dropped to 50 per cent, presumably because of the sale of assets in Canada, although the value of investment in Australia and South Africa increased on account of wartime industrial development.

In the postwar period, as we have seen, it was British policy to restrict overseas investment to the sterling area. There was no exchange control on the investment of capital to sterling countries. Investment in non-sterling areas was not prohibited, but was discouraged. It required special permission from the Bank of England, which prohibited portfolio but allowed some direct investment. In the 1950s the Commonwealth percentage of total overseas investment rose to 55 per cent in 1954 and 58 per cent in 1957. In the following decade the trend was to be checked.[2]

In the 1960s the same turning away from the earlier concentration on the sterling area began to occur in matters of investment. It was only in this decade that major efforts to compile official statistics for capital flows and stocks were instituted. This is an extremely complex and intricate area of statistics, in which the problems of definition, classification, and valuation are as intractable as those of collection. In spite of these problems, a broad picture, sufficient for present purposes, emerges from the following summary tables.[3]

Table 12 shows the consistent increase in total investment and the tendency

[1] Ibid., p. 141.
[2] The source for the preceding two paragraphs is UK, *Ann. abstract of statistics 1956*, p. 239 & *1959*, p. 236. Nominal capital values for total overseas investment (Commonwealth in brackets) were 1938, £3,454 m. (£1,962 m.); 1945, £2,417 m. (£1,211 m.); 1954, £2,128 m. (£1,178 m.); 1957, £2,102 m. (£1,234 m.).
[3] Apart from figures given by Strange, I have relied on two COI pamphlets, *Britain's international investment position* (1970) and *Britain's invisible exports* (1969).

for investment in non-sterling areas to overtake that in the sterling area in the late 1960s, in spite of premiums which made it more expensive. It also shows a move towards portfolio investment in the same period, to some extent accounted for by British buying of Australian mining shares.

TABLE 12

Flow of UK Private Overseas Net Investment, 1958–70 (£ m.)

A. *Overseas Sterling Area*

Year	Direct	Portfolio	Oil and Misc.	% of total inv.
1958	−79		−107	60
1959	−106		−59	54
1960	−160	+13	−54	62
1961	−124	−11	−51	60
1962	−122	+5	−33	62
1963	−135	+8	−36	51
1964	−161	+25	−51	47
1965	−186	+51	−63	54
1966	−119	+38	−61	47
1967	−142	−40	−44	49
1968	−177	−154	−21	48
1969	−311	−20	−46	55
1970	−209	−15	−39	38

B. *Non-sterling Areas*

1958	−65		−59	40
1959	−90		−48	46
1960	−90	+24	−55	38
1961	−102	+39	−64	40
1962	−87	+34	−39	38
1963	−101	−13	−43	49
1964	−102	−28	−82	53
1965	−122	+44	−91	44
1966	−157	+44	−49	53
1967	−139	−18	−80	51
1968	−233	−79	−68	47
1969	−236	−14	−40	45
1970	−277	−64	−110	62

Source: Strange, p. 145, corrected and amplified from *Ann. abstract of statistics 1971*, p. 272. Minus signs indicate an outward flow.

Table 12 is supplemented by table 13, which gives, for the years 1962, 1965, 1967, and 1968, the destination of the private direct investment shown in the first column of table 12—i.e. the amounts flowing to each area or country through direct investments by companies, excluding portfolio investment and oil, banking, or, prior to 1963, insurance.

TABLE 13

Net Outflow of British Direct Investment (£ m.) by Countries and Areas, 1962–8

	1962	1965	1967	1968
Non-Sterling Area	86·7	122·4	138·6	232·9
of which:				
US	10·2	22·5	51·5	84·2
Canada	8·2	18·8	33·5	29·6
EFTA	19·2	14·7	−8·4	18·8
EEC	29·2	32·1	29·9	72·8
Latin America	13·9	18·0	8·3	17·4
Others	6·1	14·2	23·4	6·2
Sterling Area	122·3	186·0	142·2	176·8
of which:				
Australia	48·4	55·6	54·3	79·7
New Zealand	8·0	10·7	−2·4	5·9
India	14·1	16·3	10·6	9·1
Pakistan	3·7	3·6	1·7	4·1
Ghana	2·9	8·2	3·0	3·0
Malay(si)a	6·3	5·4	12·6	0·7
Singapore	1·0	—	1·2	0·6
Nigeria	−4·6	7·4	−2·5	2·9
Zambia	—	−0·5	0·2	2·6
Hong Kong	2·9	1·0	0·1	5·5
Jamaica	−2·3	0·9	−1·3	1·1
Trinidad	3·5	0·2	2·7	−1·0
Kenya	0·9	−3·0	−1·9	1·6
Uganda	0·2	2·0	−0·3	1·0
Guyana	−1·6	−0·8	0·3	0·9
Irish Republic	3·2	12·0	6·8	2·4
South Africa	15·4	44·5	46·6	42·8
All Areas	209	308	281	410

Source: COI, *Britain's international investment position* (1970), p. 62. Minus signs here are the equivalent of plus signs in table 12 (as in the original).

Table 13 indicates the increasing importance of Western Europe and the US for investments by British companies in the latter part of the 1960s, a move parallel to that which occurred in trade. It also shows the very great attraction of Australia and South Africa for British investors in the sterling area, where they dwarf other countries. South Africa did not become less attractive as an area for investment after it left the Commonwealth but more so. Conversely, one is struck by the comparatively small investments in countries which bulked large in Commonwealth politics in the 1960s, such as Zambia, Uganda, Kenya, and Nigeria; by the relatively large figures for India; and by the lack of interest in New Zealand, a developed country comparable with Australia and Canada—largely explained by its small population.

For the same period, table 14 shows net earnings on British direct investment in critical areas. These largely confirm the conclusions drawn from the
flow of investment funds. The table shows that Malaysia and Singapore were
relatively profitable areas from old investment. There was a similar continuance of income from India, despite little new investment there.

TABLE 14

Net Earnings on British Outward Direct Investment, 1963–8 (£ m.)

	1963	1964	1965	1966	1967	1968
Sterling Area	213	250	251	237	236	286
of which:						
Australia	45	53	61	55	62	76
South Africa	47	62	57	60	65	76
India	21	21	25	18	18	20
Ghana	4	7	6	5	5	7
Nigeria	6	8	8	8	5	8
Malaysia and Singapore	21	22	23	26	20	24
Non-Sterling Area	116	121	149	192	201	282
of which:						
US	38	42	49	68	73	86
EEC	21	13	19	25	25	65
EFTA	7	9	8	8	11	13
Total (sterling plus non-sterling areas)	330	370	400	429	438	568

Source: Consolidated from table in COI, *Britain's international investment position*,
p. 21.

The picture of Britain's direct investments abroad needs to be kept in
perspective by reference to the sources of fresh capital. In established areas
(of which the Commonwealth countries provide a good many) the unremitted
profits of subsidiaries and associates of British companies form the main
source of capital, rather than new money raised in Britain itself. Unremitted
profits of subsidiaries accounted for one-third of net outward investment in
1960 and 1961, and rose to two-thirds in 1967 and 1968. The British stake
abroad is thus constantly reinforced by the success of the enterprises which
are established: it has been broadly characteristic of British companies abroad
that they repatriate only part of their profits and are sometimes content for
long periods with no profit at all.[1]

Table 15 gives book values of net assets, industry by industry, for direct
private overseas investment at the end of 1968. To the rough total of £5,600 m.
should be added some £1,650 m. for oil companies' net assets abroad, £500 m.
for insurance companies' direct investment in the US, and £6,150 m. for portfolio investment at estimated market value.[2] This table emphasizes the con-

[1] *Britain's invisible exports*, p. 71; and see Strange, pp. 140–1 for some bizarre past examples
of lack of interest in dividends.

[2] *Britain's international investment position*, p. 4.

tinued importance of British investment in Commonwealth agriculture, in spite of growing local control of plantations in some countries, a form of investment not paralleled to the same degree in non-Commonwealth areas. It also shows the great importance of British investment in mining in the Commonwealth and beyond it, and in manufacturing, which is largely concentrated in North America, Western Europe, Australia, and South Africa, with a smaller but significant stake in India. Transport is probably a declining field of investment, but distribution is substantial and will presumably grow in Commonwealth and non-Commonwealth areas alike. In general, the non-Commonwealth element continued to rise.

Given these facts about British investment abroad, we may turn briefly to some details of the situation at the receiving end—i.e. the degree of British investment in particular Commonwealth countries, especially in comparison with US investment, the other country mainly involved. Here again information is relatively meagre compared with information on trade.

Canada, one of the countries most experienced in charting foreign investment, estimated that at the end of 1967 British long-term investments totalled $Can. 3,576 m., accounting for 10 per cent of the total non-resident investment. This compared with 36 per cent at the end of 1939, before most of the wartime repatriations took place. After reaching a low point in 1948, the value of British investments increased each year until 1962, declined slightly in 1963, then increased again. US investment was 81 per cent of the total in 1967. European investment, while still less than British, was rising faster than either British or American.[1]

In India, by contrast, British investment appears still to be predominant, representing some 65 per cent of total accumulated foreign investment in 1962, with American only 15 per cent.[2]

For New Zealand, the evidence of annual capital movements suggests that in the 1950s and 1960s something like $N.Z. 20 m. of British capital was added each year, compared with somewhat smaller amounts of US capital (between $2 m. and $18 m.). British capital, the traditional source of investment in New Zealand, would seem to be predominant.[3]

This appears also to be the case in Australia, where figures on 'cumulative inflow' of overseas investment, both direct and portfolio, from 1947 to 1970 showed some 44 per cent from Britain, 39 per cent from the US and Canada, and 17 per cent from other countries. However, the British preponderance was to some extent a product of two factors—the longer standing of British investment and the greatly increased flow of portfolio investment in the late 1960s. The annual inflow of US investment had been greater than the British in four out of the six financial years, 1965–6 to 1970–1.[4]

[1] *Canada Year Book 1970–1*, p. 1203.   [2] Strange, p. 132.
[3] *NZ Official Yearbook 1971*, p. 737.
[4] The figures in this paragraph are from Australia, Commonwealth Treasury, *Overseas investment in Australia* (1972), pp. 16–17.

TABLE 15

British Direct Investments Overseas by Industry (book values of net assets at end 1968, £ m.)*

	Agriculture	Mining	Electrical & mech. eng.	Vehicles, shipbuilding & marine eng.	Other manufacturing	Construction	Distribution	Transport & communications	Shipping	Other activities	Total
Non-Sterling Area	45·2	194·1	166·3	44·7	1,258·8	31·5	565·5	96·7	7·7	207·6	2,618·3
Developed Countries	2·7	151·6	146·3	33·0	1,048·5	22·2	476·5	32·3	6·4	186·7	2,106·3
North America	..	149·0	72·0	18·8	684·7	14·3	210·3	14·8	..	122·5	1,286·9
Canada	..	137·9	62·5	..	253·1	..	131·9	7·2	..	68·9	686·9
United States	—	11·1	9·5	..	431·6	..	78·4	7·6	..	53·7	600·0
Western Europe	2·3	2·4	69·2	14·2	360·7	7·1	254·3	8·0	6·4	63·9	788·5
EFTA	..	..	8·5	6·0	56·0	..	57·8	..	..	17·7	152·7
EEC	..	..	60·7	8·2	299·2	4·5	196·4	4·9	6·1	45·6	628·9
Belgium and Luxembourg	—	..	6·6	..	19·6	..	71·7	..	..	11·3	112·3
France	..	..	19·3	3·8	74·8	..	58·6	..	..	16·9	180·5
Italy	..	..	8·2	..	28·3	..	17·0	..	..	5·3	60·3
Netherlands	..	..	10·7	..	56·1	..	13·9	..	5·2	7·3	96·5
Federal Republic of Germany	—	..	15·8	..	120·3	..	35·2	..	..	4·8	179·3
Developing Countries	42·5	42·5	20·0	11·7	210·3	9·3	88·9	64·4	1·3	20·8	512·0
Western Europe	16·9	13·4	..	5·2	21·2	..	12·4	..	..	6·1	67·8
South and Central America	3·8	—	9·8	..	148·8	..	36·3	14·2	..	5·0	233·4
Rhodesia	14·4	10·5	6·0	5·3	32·2	..	4·8	..	..	13·5	81·1
Other African Countries	..	9·7	—	..	..	..	23·8	41·0	..	10·9	105·6
Overseas Sterling Area	410·7	244·9	268·1	81·8	1,124·6	33·8	388·8	68·0	49·6	296·7	2,967·0
Developed Countries	80·8	165·6	225·4	70·0	839·2	15·2	195·6	19·8	30·3	168·7	1,810·7
Australia	71·3	110·2	143·9	43·9	402·2	7·7	78·7	14·3	2·8	91·4	966·4
Irish Republic	7·7	..	7·4	..	76·0	..	19·5	..	..	12·8	119·0
New Zealand	..	..	9·9	..	60·6	..	13·1	..	16·8	25·8	139·7
South Africa	..	55·0	64·1	11·8	300·4	6·5	84·3	..	..	38·8	585·6
Developing Countries	329·8	79·3	42·8	11·8	285·4	18·6	193·3	48·2	19·3	128·0	1,156·3
India	76·6	7·7	26·4	..	115·1	..	16·1	..	..	23·8	277·2
Malaysia	109·4	16·5	..	..	13·6	..	21·6	..	..	9·4	172·6
Commonwealth West Indies	62·7	..	..	..	37·6	7·0	32·4	9·6	16·8	50·8	217·9
Commonwealth Africa	31·5	52·8	4·3	1·7	70·0	6·4	83·8	7·2	0·4	30·8	288·9
West Africa	..	51·9	..	..	40·6	5·5	61·9	..	..	14·0	179·6
World	455·9	439·0	434·5	126·5	2,383·4	65·3	954·3	164·6	57·3	504·3	5,585·3
Developing Countries	372·4	121·8	62·8	23·5	495·7	27·9	282·2	112·6	20·6	148·8	1,668·3
Developed Countries	83·5	317·2	371·7	103·1	1,887·7	37·5	672·1	52·1	36·7	355·5	3,917·0
Commonwealth Countries	413·0	337·0	265·0	76·6	1,033·4	40·0	417·5	65·6	39·0	326·0	3,013·0

* Industrial and commercial investments other than oil, banking and insurance.   .. not available.   — nil or negligible.

It is fairly clear that in the developed Commonwealth countries, as in South Africa,[1] US direct investment has tended to catch up with British investment and may outdistance it. However, the investment policies of companies in both countries showed, in the late 1960s, a strong urge towards the EEC; it may be that only countries of proved high profitability, such as Australia and South Africa, will be able to withstand this competition. In the underdeveloped countries of the Commonwealth the main future interest of both Britain and the US is in extractive industries such as oil, mining, and forestry, together with growth industries like tourism in which such places as Fiji and the West Indies have natural advantages. The Asian Commonwealth countries have a possible future source of external investment in Japan, the policy of which has been to promote labour-intensive industries abroad (in fields such as textiles and assembly of the cheaper electronic devices) as its own labour shortages grow and its main effort concentrates more on capital-intensive fields. African Commonwealth countries cannot expect much private external investment, unless they have oil and minerals to be tapped. Again, the future of British investment abroad depends very much on Britain's policy in the EEC: it will have the opportunity (and formally the duty) of investing not only within the EEC itself but also in the former colonies of other members.

III

Migration between Britain and Commonwealth countries has long been a means of spreading knowledge and culture and of redistributing manpower. The traditional movement was of people from Britain seeking their fortunes abroad, always with the emphasis upon the greater opportunities available in the new countries of the Empire, especially Canada, Australia, New Zealand, and South Africa. There was also a parallel movement outwards of skilled people going for shorter periods to provide administration, specialized work, training, and the like to developing areas: the members of the ICS and the Colonial Service were not normally regarded as emigrants but did fulfil the economic role of temporary emigrants, in transmitting skills and practices to countries which would not have otherwise acquired them. Conversely, there was a movement into Britain from the Empire of returning settlers and specialists, and people born in the overseas countries who wished to strengthen their links with Britain through education and the like. The flow out of Britain was traditionally much the bigger. It was justified in terms of the need to strengthen imperial links and to provide a better life for Britain's surplus population. Whether assisted by governments or not, this pattern of migration persisted throughout the nineteenth and early twentieth centuries, until the depression of the 1930s and the restrictions on movement of World War II largely suspended its operations.

[1] See Austin, p. 155.

After World War II, and notably in the 1950s and 1960s, new elements appeared to complicate the pattern. Mass emigration from Britain to the traditional Commonwealth areas began again, and continued to grow, but British migrants now had to share Australia and New Zealand (as they had previously had to share Canada) with many immigrants of non-British stock, and there was a new emphasis on specific skills. But the main change occurred in the character of migration into Britain, as we saw in Chapter 14. More people came for training and temporary work, notably from Australia, New Zealand, and Canada; but the striking change, occasioned by full employment in Britain, was the arrival of more coloured people to settle. By the mid-1960s the word 'migration' probably meant, to the British man in the street, 'coloured immigration into Britain from the Commonwealth', whereas in previous periods it would have meant 'British emigration to the dominions'.

The statistics which follow are confined to migration into and out of Britain, with some details of the situation in the main countries receiving British migrants. As with investment, the actual figures need to be treated with reserve. Defining a migrant is a problem: in many of these figures, a migrant is defined as someone who has been in one country for more than twelve months and then goes to another in which he intends to spend at least twelve months, though not necessarily the rest of his life. He must be a Commonwealth citizen to be included in the British statistics, but need not be born in either the country he is leaving or the one he is going to. Until 1964 the British statistics show him travelling only by sea—although it was estimated that in 1952 one out of nine migrants to Canada went by air,[1] and the proportion going there and to the more distant areas by air must have constantly increased in the following years.

The inadequacy of the figures leads to discrepancies between sources. For example, in the tables below, the outflow from Britain to Canada, Australia, New Zealand, and Rhodesia combined, in 1963, is shown as 69,500; yet the Overseas Migration Board, using different measures, calculated it as 105,600.[2] Again, the British White Paper *Immigration from the Commonwealth* spoke of how, in the ten years after 1952, 'a substantial number of people from the Commonwealth began to think of settling in Britain', and went on immediately to say that the net intake from the Caribbean, Asia, East and West Africa, and the Mediterranean in 1961 had been 136,400; yet the official statistics of immigrants from the *whole* Commonwealth in that year gave a figure of 83,700.[3] The figures used can therefore be regarded as indicating little more than trends. They are probably understatements.

Table 16 shows the notable evenness of the flow of immigrants to Britain from Australia, New Zealand, and Canada, coming mainly for temporary periods of work (including study); it shows also the growth and decline in

---

[1] *Manchester Guardian*, 10 Sept 1954.   [2] *The Times*, 1 Jan 1965.
[3] Cmnd 2739 (Aug 1965), p. 2; *Annual abstract of statistics 1965*. p. 19.

TABLE 16

Immigration into Britain 1953–69 (000)[1]

Year	Australia	NZ	Canada	Rhod. & Nysald	India & Pak.	W. Indies	Other Comm.	S. Africa	US
1953	11·4	3·4	6·9	3·6	9·8	22·3		4·3	3·3
1954	13·5	4·4	9·4	2·2	10·6	9·9	19·1	4·9	3·9
1955	10·3	3·5	10·5	1·4	8·5	11·9	14·6	3·9	3·6
1956	10·1	3·2	7·9	1·3	7·3	10·5	14·1	3·7	3·4
1957	8·0	2·5	8·7	1·3	4·6	6·1	16·4	3·4	3·2
1958	8·5	2·8	11·9	1·7	4·8	7·4	14·9	3·2	3·9
1959	10·8	4·1	12·2	2·4	5·3	8·8	14·7	3·6	3·8
1960	12·6	4·7	11·2	2·9	5·4	15·6	15·6	6·0	4·1
1961	11·8	4·0	10·3	3·0	6·9	18·0	16·5	6·6	4·6
1962	12·3	3·9	7·4	2·2	5·3	11·3	16·4	3·4	4·6
1963	10·4	3·4	5·2	2·0	3·5	4·6	11·0	1·8	3·9
1964[2]	15·2	5·9	9·2	—	31·1	21·7	41·2	2·1	7·7
1965	19·1	6·5	9·1	—	28·5	21·1	40·3	2·7	8·3
1966	19·7	6·9	8·9	—	31·6	17·4	36·8	4·9	8·4
1967	27·8	7·7	9·9	—	45·9	15·2	34·0	3·3	7·4
1968	27·2	9·7	12·2	—	46·8	12·6	40·9	3·7	7·2
1969	25·5	6·9	12·7	—	38·3	12·0	34·5	3·8	7·7

[1] Before 1964, migrants *by sea only*; after, all migrants.
[2] From 1964, India and Pakistan include also Ceylon.

Source: Ann. abstract of statistics 1965, p. 19 and 1971, p. 21.

people from the West Indies (already discussed in ch. 14); and the low figures for migration from India and Pakistan in the 1950s and early 1960s, which shot up in the later 1960s. South Africa and the US, the other two main English-speaking countries involved in the British migration pattern, are added for comparison.

Table 17 deals with emigration from Britain for the same period to Commonwealth countries, to South Africa, and the US. It is generally accepted that emigration responds to both pushes and pulls—i.e. that the intending migrant is both pushed out of his own country by difficulties and disappointments there, and pulled by the attractions of the country to which he is going. The pushes and pulls vary for particular people and also with changing conditions in the countries concerned. The push outwards from Britain was strongest up to 1957 and after 1963, the intervening period being one of visible economic improvement. The pulls, as reflected by the figures, appear to be constant from New Zealand, increasing from Australia, and variable from Canada and South Africa. Economic difficulties in the late 1950s would explain the Canadian variation. The explanation for South Africa is partly political, partly economic: the low emigration there in 1960 and 1961 can be correlated with the highly uncertain political circumstances described in Chapter 8, while the steady rise afterwards is due to South Africa's increasing prosperity. Again, the figures do not suggest that South Africa became less attractive after it left the Commonwealth but rather the contrary. The table also shows for the late 1960s the return to the West Indies of an increasing number of migrants, and a smaller number to India and Pakistan.

In terms of traditional assumptions, it is perhaps surprising that so many British people should elect to emigrate in a period of sustained full employment in Britain itself. 'Shovelling out paupers' was an inaccurate but illuminating phrase to describe British emigration in the nineteenth century: though many people of means and education emigrated, most emigrants were of working-class origin, seeking greater opportunities than they could find at home. The explanation for massive emigration in the 1950s and 1960s lies partly in the practice of people joining relatives overseas, but much more in the fact that British full employment did not prove satisfactory for many. Moreover, newspapers and television kept telling them how much economic growth was taking place in other places, notably Western Europe, the US, and Australia. British people do not emigrate to Western Europe, and the US is too risky for those on low incomes and lacking high qualifications; but Australia, Canada, New Zealand, and South Africa, the traditional countries of opportunity, profited from the sense of frustration felt by many British people in the 1960s.

British policy towards emigration grew cooler in the 1950s and 1960s. In 1953 the Churchill government appointed an Overseas Migration Board to advise the Commonwealth secretary upon specific proposals for schemes of

TABLE 17

Emigration from Britain 1953–69 (000)[1]

Year	Australia	NZ	Canada	Rhod. & Nysald	India & Pak.	W. Indies	Other Comm.	S. Africa	US
1953	30·2	14·5	41·3	4·7	5·1		22·0	6·5	16·2
1954	34·5	10·4	38·6	3·6	4·3	1·8	19·4	5·9	14·4
1955	36·0	10·2	26·4	3·6	3·3	1·4	15·2	5·0	12·8
1956	32·2	11·5	41·5	5·2	3·1	2·3	13·7	4·8	13·9
1957	35·1	10·2	59·4	5·5	2·3	3·3	15·4	5·5	15·2
1958	37·4	10·8	16·0	4·2	2·9	4·1	13·2	5·3	9·7
1959	38·8	8·8	11·8	2·7	2·9	4·3	12·2	4·4	8·3
1960	39·2	6·5	10·9	2·0	2·8	3·5	11·8	2·8	7·8
1961	40·6	9·1	9·3	1·4	3·2	3·8	11·3	2·2	7·1
1962	35·5	10·8	10·7	1·6	2·9	6·4	10·5	3·6	7·9
1963	44·0	10·3	14·0	1·2	2·9	7·9	8·7	6·6	8·4
1964[2]	80·7	16·4	31·3	—	8·8	7·3	24·3	13·1	22·1
1965	92·0	15·7	42·2	—	9·5	7·7	24·1	11·8	20·7
1966	85·8	16·2	62·7	—	8·7	8·6	23·0	12·4	19·0
1967	87·1	17·5	65·8	—	7·6	8·4	23·0	13·2	26·3
1968	84·8	8·5	40·0	—	6·7	9·6	22·8	16·0	22·5
1969	98·5	10·4	34·2	—	10·0	9·1	24·4	19·4	14·9

[1] Before 1964, migrants by sea only; after, all migrants.
[2] From 1964, India and Pakistan include also Ceylon.

Source: As for table 16.

emigration to other Commonwealth countries. At first the Board appears to have considered that Britain should be more than a sleeping partner in formulating and carrying out migration policies. However, the only agreement on which it had to pronounce was that between Britain and Australia for assisted passages, together with some of the surviving schemes for emigration through voluntary societies. No Commonwealth government or any other body produced any new schemes for reference to it. After 1962, with the agreement of its members, the Board met only once a year; it was abolished in 1966. In 1967 the Wilson government approved the continuance of joint responsibility for the Australian scheme (its own contribution being limited to £150,000 a year, Australia paying about £8 m.), but in December 1971 the Heath government announced that the agreement would not be renewed when it expired in 1972. The minister making the announcement on 21 December stated that 'in the opinion of Her Majesty's Government the policy of financially subsidising emigration to Commonwealth countries which was conceived in the 1920s is no longer appropriate at the present time'.[1]

British argument about emigration seems to have concentrated on the 'brain drain', the emigration of highly qualified people at a time when immigration into Britain from such places as India and the West Indies involved so many unskilled people. A report of a working group in 1967[2] said that what was new was the highly selective nature of present British migration. The outflow of engineers and technologists had doubled in the previous six years; to North America it had quadrupled. The figures put forward were 3,200 engineers and scientists in 1961, compared with 6,200 in 1966. The comparable *net* losses, however, were nil and 2,700 respectively, reflecting the fact that the English-speaking countries constituted something of a common market in this field, and that Britain continually got back some of those it had previously exported, while also gaining skilled immigrants. In the years following the report, the situation was further affected by reduced research opportunities in the US.

British coolness towards organized migration schemes had something to do with the wish to conserve skilled manpower, but even more, presumably, with the plain fact that if Commonwealth countries wanted migrants they would pay for them, and a growing awareness that many migrants did not need assisted passages. On 4 January 1965 *The Times* reported that only Australia had an 'open door' policy in providing assisted passages to almost any British people who cared to come. New Zealand confined assistance to skilled workers under 35 if single and under 45 if married. Families must have a guarantee of employment and somewhere to live, and were limited to four children. Canada was even stricter: there was no subsidized fare, although loans were available, and unskilled workers were rarely admitted.

---

[1] *Manchester Guardian*, 10 Sept 1954; *Survey B & CA*, 12 May 1967, pp. 509–10; British Information Service press release 22 Dec 1971, G760/aa.
[2] Cmnd 3417, 1967.

A further point of importance was that, in contrast with the 1920s, Australia and New Zealand were admitting (and actively seeking) migrants from continental Europe. Australia had, by 1969, agreements for assisted passages with Malta, Austria, Belgium, Germany, Greece, Italy, the Netherlands, Spain, Turkey, and Yugoslavia;[1] in 1970 New Zealand, the last stronghold of distinctively British migration, extended its subsidy scheme to include Americans and West Europeans. In the previous three years it had been taking in a total of 25,000–30,000 immigrants a year, between 8,000 and 13,000 from Britain, 3,000–4,000 from Australia, and 2,500–3,000 from Europe and the US.[2] In the same period Canada had admitted 160,000–220,000 a year, of whom some 24 per cent had come from Britain and Ireland, 40 per cent from continental Europe, 11 per cent from the US, and 25 per cent from other countries, including significant numbers from Australia, Hong Kong, India, and the West Indies.[3] The Australian intake, between 150,000–180,000 a year in the same period, showed some 45 per cent from Britain and Ireland, 30 per cent from continental Europe, and 24 per cent of others, with significant numbers from New Zealand, the Indian subcontinent, and the US.[4]

In addition to the welcome which they gave to continental Europeans, Canada, Australia, and New Zealand widened the opportunities for coloured peoples to become permanent settlers, in contrast with their traditional harshness to them. The regulations for Canadian immigration introduced in 1967 had this effect; Australian entry procedures, operated under ministerial decision, were widened to include highly-skilled non-Europeans; and New Zealand gave entry to Polynesians and others who could show links with the country. English-speaking people from Asia were obviously those most likely to take advantage of the Canadian and Australian opportunities. This meant a wider range of intra-Commonwealth migration than before.

IV

Traditionally, Imperial Conferences had been interested in economic co-operation between Commonwealth governments in fields of transport and communication. The relevance of shipping, cables, and later airways to a widespread imperial structure was obvious. Some aspects of this interest remain.

Traditional co-operation has been most strongly maintained in telecommunications. From 1902, when the Pacific Cable Board was formed to manage a telegraph cable linking Canada, Fiji, New Zealand, and Australia, until 1949, when the Commonwealth Telecommunications Board was set up, there was a continuous history of partnership between Britain and Commonwealth governments. As we saw in Chapter 12, the Montreal conference of 1958

---

[1] *Official Year Book . . . Aus. 1970*, p. 149.   [2] *NZ Official Yearbook, 1971*, pp. 77–8.
[3] *Canada Yearbook 1970–1*, p. 267.   [4] *Official Year Book . . . Aus. 1970*, p. 146.

decided to extend the system further. Between 1958 and 1967 a comprehensive telephone cable network, linked by microwave systems across land areas, was laid to supplement or replace older forms of communications. Three main systems were involved: Cantat, from Britain to Canada; Compac, from Canada to Australia, by way of Fiji and New Zealand; and Seacom, connecting Australia, New Guinea, Hong Kong, Malaysia, and Singapore. In 1968 Commonwealth governments agreed on a new form of organization for the existing system,[1] which came into operation in 1969. In 1970 23 Commonwealth governments were partners in its operations.

In transport, the main area of Commonwealth co-operation has been in airlines, where BOAC has played an important part in helping to set up national airlines for other Commonwealth members and in co-operating with them when established.[2] Its predecessor, Imperial Airways, had done the same before World War II. With Qantas, the Australian national airline, and Air India, BOAC formed a tripartite partnership to cover not only the direct route from Britain to Australia and India, but also Tokyo, Hong Kong, and the North Atlantic. BOAC also established partnerships with Air Canada, East African Airways, Pakistan International Airways, Nigerian Airways, and Air New Zealand, in some of which it had originally held shares. In 1967 it wholly owned Bahamas Airways and Aden Airways, had a majority holding in Gulf Aviation and minority holdings in British West Indian Airways, Air Jamaica, Malaysia-Singapore Airlines, Cathay Pacific (based in Hong Kong) and Fiji Airways. Qantas and Air Canada also developed associations with Malaysia-Singapore Airlines on the one hand, and airlines in the West Indies on the other.

These various arrangements have enabled the companies to pool receipts in certain instances and to share technical services. From early situations in which the British company was dominant, the tendency has been for national airlines to develop with independence, but for a shared commercial interest to be maintained. The General Manager of Air India, B. R. Patel, is on record as saying of the tripartite partnership: 'It is entirely a business deal. But there is an affinity among us which makes negotiations easier than with certain other countries.' This is one sphere in which the characteristics of the Commonwealth have been readily adapted to commercial success, although one of the early aims of the system has not been achieved: major airlines have not flown British aircraft since the Boeing 707s appeared in the late 1950s, although smaller airlines have continued to do so. On the whole, however, 'a basically commercial situation has sensitively adapted itself to political evolution, neither sacrificing commercial integrity nor outraging political susceptibilities'.[3]

[1] See Cmnd 3547 (Mar 1968).
[2] For what follows, see 'Above the seven seas', *Round Table*, Sept 1965, pp. 348–57, and *BOAC News*, 28 Apr 1967.
[3] *Round Table*, p. 355 (and for the Patel quotation above).

Perhaps this is why the Commonwealth Air Transport Council, a body set up in 1945 to advise Commonwealth governments, did not feel obliged to meet from 1956 to 1966:[1] if commercial success can be achieved without them, governments are better out of the picture.

Telecommunications and airways stand out as economic activities in which Commonwealth members have been able to co-operate systematically over a long period. They have four common characteristics: a tradition extending back to colonial times; a widely shared common interest between the countries concerned; a highly technical quality; and the practice of governmental operation or regulation. Not many activities combine all four. Shipping, which might seem to come closest, breaks down on the second and fourth. Although there was a long history of Commonwealth discussion of shipping questions, arising from the desire of the distant dominions for cheap freight for their primary products, the preponderance of British private shipping prevented the growth of national shipping lines except in the case of New Zealand. A common interest did not emerge. Instead, Britain was very much a seller, while the other countries were buyers. Conferences and subsidies did not solve the problem. It is not surprising, then, that shipping did not follow the path of the airlines.

v

The search for a widely shared common interest between buyers and sellers lay behind the slogan of 'men, money, markets', propounded in the 1920s. It was hoped that the injection of British migrants and capital into the dominions would create markets for British goods; at the same time, sheltered markets in Britain for the goods produced by the migrants and capital would encourage further growth in the dominions. The process, once begun, would be strongly self-perpetuating. In practice, however, the slogan could not be equally or effectively applied in the restricted Commonwealth of the inter-war years: in agricultural production dominions competed with one another and with British farmers; migrants did not stay in the industries for which markets were supposed to be guaranteed; the dominions were not prepared to preserve their domestic markets for British manufactures, but wanted to protect their own infant industries. At best, the incomplete system which emerged provided special opportunities in Britain for a certain range of dominion producers, while giving the British manufacturer a somewhat easier market abroad than he might otherwise have had.

The much less homogeneous Commonwealth of the postwar years was even less suitable for such a slogan. While the prewar Commonwealth could, in some respects, be equated with that platonic model of British-dominion economic relations which the Australians and New Zealanders had so ardently

[1] Commonwealth Secretariat, *Report of Review Committee on Intra-Commonwealth Organisation*, p. 19.

publicized, the postwar Commonwealth could not. Its range of economic activities and of standards of living would not fit within the model—which, in any case, had never been wholeheartedly accepted by the British government or British opinion. In practice, as we have seen, a combination of circumstances and policy encouraged British investment and British emigration to overseas Commonwealth countries in the 1950s and 1960s, but these were distributed very unequally over the increasing number of independent Commonwealth members.

Men, money, and markets no longer constituted a trinity. The men and the money went where they were most at home and could make the most profit. Markets were not co-ordinated with the flow of men and money, once bulk purchase had been abandoned and multilateralism was in full stride. Britain returned to its predominantly European market; the overseas countries found new markets there, in the US, and in Japan. The paucity of British investment in the Commonwealth l.d.c.s was made up, to some extent, by economic aid from Britain and other donors. In no way, however, could the formal political equality of Commonwealth members be matched by economic equality. Established practices did maintain a certain minimum market for British goods elsewhere in the Commonwealth, and vice versa but, in a period in which economic growth was the watchword, Commonwealth markets proved less attractive as growth prospects than the European, American, and Japanese.

So, if we are looking for a pattern of Commonwealth economic connections between 1953 and 1969, we can say that these rested on an eroded traditional base, were unevenly distributed, favoured the developed countries rather than the less-developed, were still Britain-centred but were being replaced in various instances by connections with other developed countries, and exhibited in general the incapacity of the Commonwealth as a sufficient universe for the aims and activities of its members. We should also stress what emerged in part from the consideration of British policy in Chapter 12: that Britain and the other Commonwealth countries were involved, to a greater extent than ever before, in a web of world-wide discussions and agreements about trade, currency, and aid, symbolized by such bodies as Gatt, the EEC, the IMF, the World Bank, and Unctad. This aspect of multilateralism, largely unknown before World War II, would have been sufficient in itself to reduce the mutual dependence of Commonwealth members on one another, even if they had had the will to press for Commonwealth solutions wherever there seemed some possibility of success.

CHAPTER 21

A VARIED LEGACY

THE Caribbean narrator of V. S. Naipaul's novel, *The Mimic Men*, reflecting on his country's situation after he has had to leave because of a political failure, says: 'The empires of our time were short-lived, but they have altered the world for ever; their passing away is their least significant feature'.[1] A more precise attempt to show how Britain changed the world has been made by Sir Eric Ashby:

> The balance sheet for British colonialism includes four substantial assets: Christianity, representative government, educational institutions and the English language. Of course not all parts of the Commonwealth have drawn equally upon all these assets. Countries virtually empty of indigenous civilization, such as Australia and Canada, have made use of them all. Countries with ancient and venerable religions have made less use than others of Christianity; countries with a sophisticated indigenous language and literature have made less use than others of the English tongue. Representative government has been transplanted to them all, but in some Commonwealth countries it has had to be greatly changed to meet local needs. Of these four assets the most universally acceptable, and the least changed by the indigenous cultural environment, are the educational institutions exported by Britain to her Commonwealth.[2]

This chapter elaborates this statement, with some additions, such as sport, which is something which empires leave behind and which needs to be taken into account when the post-imperial network of connections is being considered. Representative government, and the military and administrative traditions which continue to matter in the life of Commonwealth countries, are omitted. The emphasis here is upon the aspects of culture which cluster around the English language, on religion, education, sport, and the professions. While the effect of these was not uniform throughout the empire, and has not been so since the colonies achieved independence, all have had significant influence.

We cannot measure that influence, although we can recognize how different the countries of the Commonwealth would have been without it. We can obtain figures for the number of books exported from Britain, the nominal adherents of the various churches which derive from British missionary activity, and the number of students from the overseas Commonwealth in Britain at any given

---

[1] Regrettably, he also says that 'on the subject of empire there is only the pamphleteering of churls', when he considers what has been written.

[2] *Community of universities* (1963), p. 92.

time, but none of these has the force and apparent authority of figures on trade or investment. We should use these sources where we can, but not believe that they tell us more than they do.

At the same time it is important to recognize that, although the spread of British cultural influences is an especially clear example of the 'rimless wheel' aspect of the Commonwealth, the reception of those influences has not been smooth and has often involved resistance. The local nationalistic reaction against ideas and practices from the metropole is one of the complex aspects of any study of the consequences of imperial control. It will be noted here as a constant, often creative, but frequently unpredictable element in the network of cultural links in the Commonwealth.

I

It is difficult to overstate the importance of the English language. We can think of its influence in various ways: as the language of administration in spite of objections, as earlier in Canada and South Africa and later in India; as a lingua franca in multiracial communities in which no other was acceptable or practicable, as in India, Singapore, Fiji, and Trinidad; as the means to higher education and the professions; and as the key to literature and ideas, both in its own right and as one of the major world languages. Writing of Nirad Chaudhuri's *Autobiography of an Unknown Indian*, William Walsh says that the development described there

is not just an evolutionary one in which a Western protestant astringency displaces the warm appeal of an Indian past—although it certainly *is* that. It is also a more personal and strenuous achievement which involves, on the one hand, hacking out an area of freedom and manoeuvre from a choked jungle of inheritance; and on the other, constructing a fresh identity which would join a questioning Western mind to a temperament laced with Bengali fury. The instruments of demolition and of building, and the elements out of which the new self was to be made, were concepts and principles, usages and styles, which Chaudhuri found, not in the imaginatively cramped local British population, or the restricted Anglo-Indian tradition, but in the immensely more inclusive source of the English language and its literature.[1]

This evolution must have occurred countless times, if not with such clarity and polish at least so as to make a wider world understandable and acceptable. The same is true, of course, of French. The two languages have been the means of introduction to the Western world for East, South, and Southeast Asia, for Africa (apart from the Portuguese territories), and for the Middle East. In the Commonwealth English has meant a massive flow of ideas to those who wanted to get on: it has been difficult, often impossible, to hold a position of any significance without proficiency in English. The exceptions, in places such as Canada, South Africa, Cyprus, and Malta, have been those of European

[1] *A manifold voice* (1970), p. 35.

communities with their own distinctive languages and with a sufficient weight of economic and social power to enforce the use of those languages in British possessions. While in non-European countries languages such as Hindi, Swahili, and Malay have advanced to national status after independence, English has continued to be indispensable as a language of commerce, higher education, and higher administration. It has provided a common culture or the assumption that one exists. When a Trinidadian High Commissioner quotes lines from Elizabeth Barrett Browning to an Australian who is distressed that he does not immediately recognize them, it says something about comparative education in Australia and Trinidad thirty years earlier, and something about the sense of a common heritage.[1]

It is generally regarded as one of the persistent strengths of the Commonwealth that meetings can be held without interpreters, documents circulated in English alone, and discussion related to basic concepts which the great majority of those present understand. The figure of Nehru at Prime Ministers' Meetings, speaking English with elegant fluency, became symbolic of the Commonwealth leader with intellectual roots nourished by an education in English; if a little romantic, the symbol still has a good deal of importance. Indeed, Ali Mazrui has pointed to the emergence of what he calls 'Afro-Saxons', especially in West Africa but increasingly in East Africa, who grow up bilingual in English and their own African language because their parents are highly educated and speak English to each other. In Africa, where most languages are tribal, there is not the same urge to extend and adapt them for national use as with Malay, Hindi, and Urdu. Instead, some African governments have been introducing English at an earlier stage in the education system than before independence.[2]

Education and administration do not exhaust the influence of English in the Commonwealth. Mass media for the elites have been developed in English, even when other competing languages were also used, as in India, Malaya, and Nigeria. Books, newspapers, radio, and television can all be viewed as networks of connection throughout the Commonwealth, with Britain as a focal point in most cases.

In 1971 Britain exported just under 55 m. books and pamphlets, of which Commonwealth countries imported just under half, i.e. some 25 m.[3] The US and South Africa were the two greatest importers outside the Commonwealth. Of the total value of £26,296,000 exported, some outstanding markets were (in £000):

US	15,600
Australia	9,374

---

[1] The lines were intended to describe the continuity of certain connections between Trinidad and Britain.

[2] Mazrui, 'Africa, the west and the world', *Australian Outlook*, Aug 1972, p. 127.

[3] These and subsequent figures for newspapers etc., are from *Overseas trade statistics of the UK*, Dec 1971.

Canada	4,563
South Africa	3,862
Nigeria	2,931
Ireland	2,395
New Zealand	2,036
India	1,348
Kenya	1,142
Jamaica	674

British publishers have managed to retain considerable markets in the Commonwealth by a long-standing agreement with US publishers, whereby neither side encroaches on the other's territory. At the same time they have been active in setting up subsidiary companies in the overseas countries, so as to qualify as local publishers under any form of protection that may be provided. They and indigenous publishing houses have benefited everywhere from the greatly increased expenditure on education that has characterized the period. They have of course had to take account of local agitation against traditional presentation in English textbooks, which put summer in the wrong months for people in the southern hemisphere and clothed the landscape with animals, plants, and flowers which those in the tropics were unlikely to come across. Probably all Commonwealth countries now have locally-written textbooks which emphasize local background and use local examples, but most of these are still written in English. There has been some cross-fertilization on a regional basis, with local publishing houses serving the primary and secondary levels of education in Malaysia and Singapore, Australia and New Zealand, the countries of East and West Africa, but in general literature and in higher education British publishers still have the leading role.

Something similar can be said of newspapers and magazines, although the immediacy of daily journalism means that local newspapers have a monopoly. Nevertheless there are numerous connections. The prevalence of 'Timeses' in what used to be the British Empire—*Cape Times, Times of India, Straits Times, Hindustan Times*, etc.—shows how pervasive were British journalistic practices, in areas where the papers catered largely for migrants and expatriates from Britain. Although most of these and other newspapers in English have been 'localized' in ownership, their links with Britain are still important. It is characteristic of them that news from Britain tends to overshadow other foreign news, which is often transmitted through British means. To a large extent, this has been due to the news agencies and the Commonwealth Press Rate. Reuters, the agency from which a great many Commonwealth newspapers get their overseas news, has been owned since 1947 by the newspapers of Britain, Australia, and New Zealand. London is the main centre for Commonwealth papers which have correspondents abroad, who tend to use British sources for much of the comment they get on events in other countries. The arrangement was encouraged by the British rate for press telegrams to Commonwealth countries. Before World War II it had been $2\frac{1}{4}d$ a word.

During the war this was reduced to a penny. The penny rate was retained until 1967, when the British government increased it to 3*d*, protesting, in the face of criticism, that the Commonwealth Telecommunications Board had consistently recommended an increase during 13 years of discussion, and that the real cost per word was nearer 7*d* than 3*d*. The British taxpayer was subsidizing the rate to a considerable extent.[1]

In 1971 British exports of newspapers and periodicals totalled £16,593,000 in value, with the Commonwealth accounting for £7,807,000 worth. This represented much the same proportion as for books, but the principal markets were differently placed (£000):

Australia	3,486
Ireland	2,329
Canada	1,998
South Africa	1,617
US	1,451
New Zealand	1,278

Other aspects of the newspaper industry helped to sustain Commonwealth connections. The long-established Commonwealth Press Union, which was set up in 1909 and includes most Commonwealth papers, continued to expand in the 1950s and 1960s, as did the Commonwealth Correspondents' Association in London. British journalists continued to migrate to jobs on papers in other parts of the Commonwealth, and Australians, New Zealanders, and Canadians to seek their fortunes in London. Indeed, the period witnessed something of a Commonwealth counterattack to earlier attempts to establish British control of newspapers in some parts of the Commonwealth, notably West Africa and Australia. The Thomson and Murdoch takeovers of such London papers as *The Times, Sunday Times, News of the World*, and *The Sun*, reminiscent in some ways of Beaverbrook's earlier efforts, meant that money originally made in Canada and Australia was being used to finance newspapers in England. It could hardly be said, however, that there was an expansion of Canadian and Australian propaganda. The papers were certainly not run with this in view.

One of the most obvious influences, yet one of the most difficult to assess, is that of British magazines. The *New Statesman* has been, since the days of the Indian independence movement, one of the main sources from which radical intellectuals in the overseas Commonwealth have drawn inspiration. No comparable Conservative influence is apparent except perhaps *The Economist*. In women's magazines and children's weekly papers, observation suggests that British influence is strong; George Orwell's comment in 1939 in his essay 'Boys Weeklies' that *Gem* 'was read in every corner of the British Empire, by

[1] From an address to the Commonwealth Press Union by Herbert Bowden, the Commonwealth secretary, on 12 June 1967 (British Information Service press release G187/a, 13 June 1967).

Australians, Canadians, Palestine Jews, Malays, Arabs, Straits Chinese, etc. etc.' still has some truth in it, in spite of the disappearance of *Gem* and *Magnet*, and the growth of the pop culture.

The influence of the BBC on broadcasting in the Commonwealth was rather like that of Imperial Airways and BOAC in airline development.[1] The Australian Broadcasting Commission, Canadian Broadcasting Corporation, New Zealand Broadcasting Corporation, South African Broadcasting Corporation, and All-India Radio all owed much to BBC example when they were founded in the 1930s. Relations between British and other broadcasting authorities grew closer during World War II, when BBC news broadcasts were used all over the Empire and Commonwealth; afterwards the extent to which local broadcasting authorities continued to re-broadcast the BBC Overseas Service was often an index of local national feeling, or at any rate of coolness towards Britain. Both the South African and Rhodesian authorities made it so. A Commonwealth Broadcasting Conference was established in 1945 as a standing association of public broadcasting bodies with a secretariat at Broadcasting House in London. It continued to meet at three-yearly intervals, taking into membership the broadcasting authorities of new Commonwealth members as these became independent, and with associate members from the remaining dependencies.

British influence was exerted in two main ways, through training courses for the engineering and programme staffs of overseas authorities (especially in television, in which Britain had a start over all), and in the sale of programmes. The former has become a substantial affair, subsidized by overseas development funds and recognized as part of the British aid programme. The latter was of lesser importance before television became general, but became more significant: both BBC and ITV sold television series all over the world, with special attention to Commonwealth countries. The trade in the opposite direction was only slight, although the BBC joined with Reuters, the ABC, the CBC, and the NZBC in Visnews, a service of news films, and with the CBC, ABC, and an American network to form Intertel, a programme of exchanged documentaries. The Australian, Canadian, and New Zealand authorities also took a hand in television training for the smaller countries of the Commonwealth.

Generally speaking, in respect of the written and spoken word British influence had to compete mainly with American, except for short-wave broadcasting, in which the communist countries, mainly the Soviet Union and China, aimed special programmes at Asian and African Commonwealth countries. Britain could claim, at the end of the 1960s, to be still the most

---

[1] A notable figure in both cases, as in the growth of Commonwealth telecommunications and of the Commonwealth Development Corporation after an inauspicious start, was Lord Reith. Although the matter is well outside our period, readers are assured that they will enjoy Lionel Fielden's account of what happened when Reith sent him to look after radio in India in the 1930s (*The natural bent* (1960), pp. 126–216).

significant influence in regard to books, radio, news services, and magazines; to be highly influential in television; and while outshone in films, to retain considerable influence even there. The 'influence' in question was only partially the kind of political influence which is associated with direct propaganda. It arose much more from the resources of a rich and long-lived way of life, and from emphasizing what were felt to be its most desirable aspects and institutions. Much of the influence, as in the past, must have come from the active demonstration that British democracy embraced acute differences of opinion on policy, especially on matters affecting relations between races and states. The BBC's Overseas Service continued to report the cleavage in British public opinion during the Suez crisis, for example. This was condemned in some quarters at the time as disloyal, but must have convinced many that the British were democratic in practice as well as in theory.

II

It is clear that the British Empire had a strong religious dimension, in the sense that British churches extended their operations to Britain's overseas possessions and that many of the connections arising from this activity have survived independence, though it is very difficult to gauge the numbers of adherents of various churches.[1]

British churches extended their influence through migration of church members to new countries such as Canada and New Zealand, and of missionaries to indigenous peoples. Both might apply to the same country, e.g. South Africa. They provided local institutions through churches, schools, hospitals, and the like, often where nothing of the kind had existed before. In due course, but especially after independence, these institutions were usually taken over by locally organized churches with local leaders. While these often identified themselves with national movements, they retained their links with the parent bodies from which they had sprung.[2] Thus, apart from the branches of the Roman Catholic Church established from Ireland, there are substantial numbers of Anglican churches, now largely staffed and directed by local people, and Presbyterian, Methodist and Baptist churches throughout the Commonwealth. Some of the local bodies have gone further with ecumenism than their parent churches, for instance, the United Church of Canada and the Church of South India. Especially in Africa there have been substantial moves away from the traditional missionary churches towards strictly local sects similar to those which have arisen amongst American blacks, and towards the more fundamentalist and pentecostal churches such as the Assemblies of God and the Seventh Day Adventists. In the old dominions the former dependence on

[1] See e.g. the heroic but incomplete attempts at enumeration in H. Wakelin Coxill & Sir Kenneth Grubb eds., *World Christian handbook* (1962).
[2] See e.g. K. Baago, *A history of the National Christian Council of India 1914–64* (1965).

clergy from the UK has been greatly reduced, although some migration continues.

Two of the activities of the churches connect, in a Commonwealth context, with other matters discussed in this book. One is education (see Section III); the other is a visibly increasing concern with social and political questions, especially racialism. In the 1950s and 1960s the concern of the World Council of Churches and the Roman Catholic Church with racial questions became evident; solicitous about the views of African and Asian Christians, both were ready to proclaim that racialism should be condemned in South Africa and Rhodesia. In Britain, Canada, New Zealand, and Australia churchmen put pressure on their governments not to condone apartheid or to give in to the Smith regime in Rhodesia. The break-up of the Federation of Rhodesia and Nyasaland was assisted by the Church of Scotland, which had substantial missionary interests in Nyasaland and gave support to Hastings Banda, who was one of its elders.

It seemed that, as support for the Christian churches ebbed in Britain and the old dominions, the clergy and laity still active in them were more responsive to appeals from the newer churches, especially in Africa. Such a response was itself evidence that a network of contacts continued to exist. It would be wrong, of course, to suggest that the network was confined to the Commonwealth. The resources available to the World Council of Churches came largely from the United States, and much of the opposition to apartheid and to colonialism was attributable to Scandinavian Christians. But views of the kind expressed in St Paul's Cathedral by Canon Collins at the time of the Coronation in 1953 (referred to in ch. 1) became increasingly more common in the 1950s and 1960s, in relation to decolonization, apartheid, and the Rhodesian issue. They were taken up by pressure groups, exchanged between the Christian communities of one Commonwealth country and another, and treated with respect by politicians. The shape of the Commonwealth at the end of the period owed something to the efforts of the churches, not least because the Church of England, allied with so many others in the Anglican communion, had ranged itself on the side of multiracialism.

III

The significance of educational institutions is obvious. Whatever local variations there may be in the primary schools, the secondary schools and universities throughout the Commonwealth owe much—some would say everything —to British models. The education of elites has been a powerful force in providing a common culture,

for Commonwealth leadership is largely in the hands of graduates, and, by virtue of the cohesion among Commonwealth universities, graduates from as far apart as

Singapore and Vancouver, Ghana and Aberdeen, find that they share common assumptions, common cultural traditions, common canons of criticism and facility in using a common language.[1]

The foundations of this cohesion have traditionally been laid in secondary schools (labelled high, grammar, or public) modelled on British originals, often under the control of the churches, often staffed by teachers from the British Isles and conforming to a pattern that has affected even the Roman Catholic Church. Kim's St Xavier's in Partibus, like Stephen Dedalus's Clongowes Wood, owed much to Dr Arnold's Rugby. The British influence was emphasized further in the later stages of colonial development in Africa and Asia by extending British public examinations to the colonies on a large scale, so as to provide an assured standard of matriculation.

The growth and expansion of colonial universities in the 1950s provided much of the backing for the network of Commonwealth educational connections which existed in 1969. Essentially, this was a matter of British colonial policy, and so will be treated only summarily here.[2] Before World War II the development of universities in the colonies had not been part of British policy; whatever took place was the result of local initiative, as it had been in the old dominions in their colonial days. The establishment of a university in Hong Kong in 1911 excited little help or interest in London; the establishment of a medical school in Singapore was not followed by university status. The wealthier and some of the brighter products of secondary schools in the colonies came to Britain for university education. They included such later Commonwealth leaders as Ramgoolam, Kenyatta, Lee, Eric Williams, Banda, Burnham, Busia, and Bandaranaike. India was in a different position, universities having been an object of the Government of India's policy since early in the present century. Even so, Nehru went to Cambridge. In 1945, however, following a report from the Asquith Commission on Higher Education in the Colonies, the decision was taken to make university education available throughout the colonies. This was a formidable task, not least because colonial administrators were not always favourable towards the idea. It was only in 1937 that the government of Nigeria had reversed its previous opposition to education abroad and granted scholarships for study in Britain.[3] Oxford and the London School of Economics were not regarded by many in the Colonial Service as good training-grounds for colonial leaders. Until the idea of deliberate progress towards self-government became official policy, the relevance of university institutions to colonial development did not become apparent. The Asquith Commission, however, viewed the need for them very much in this light; and

[1] Ashby, *Community of universities*, p. 95.
[2] For details, see A. M. Carr-Saunders, *New universities overseas* (1961); Ashby, *African universities and western tradition* (1964); and Sir John Lockwood, 'The transplantation of the university: the case of Africa', in Hamilton & others.
[3] Carr-Saunders, p. 33.

it was as a contribution to self-government that their development was pushed ahead in the 1950s.

In some cases, as in Hong Kong and Malta, this meant giving assistance to established but neglected universities; in others, such as Singapore, Uganda, and the Sudan, it meant the upgrading of existing institutions; but in West Africa and the West Indies it meant the creation of entirely new bodies, except in Sierra Leone. These, it was decided, would prepare their students for the external degrees of London University, thereby providing a guarantee that the degrees gained would be an adequate substitute for those which were so widely sought but so rarely obtained from Britain. The establishment of University Colleges in Nigeria, the Gold Coast, Rhodesia, and Jamaica (to serve the West Indies as a whole) followed in the 1950s.

In West Africa particularly, but to some extent in all these new and expanded institutions, the problems of standards and purpose arose, to remain when the colonies became independent Commonwealth members. The Asquith Commission had taken the view that the good of the colonies demanded nothing less than the standards operating in Britain itself, whether these applied to entrance and staff qualifications or examination passes. British practices were also adopted in the forms of government of the new university colleges which prepared students for the London external degrees; they were not government colleges but independent institutions, although their revenues came almost entirely from the British and colonial governments. In both respects there was controversy once the colleges got under way. The combination of London matriculation and the London degree structure meant that relatively few students were accepted at first. It was later found that students could be sent on scholarships to American universities which had lower entrance standards, while places were vacant in the colonies from which they had come. Again there was criticism that the range of studies in the new colleges was at first narrow, with surprising emphasis in some cases upon religion and the classics instead of on engineering and agricultural science. Later plans for university development in Zambia, Malawi, and Mauritius took careful account of these criticisms, and gave a different emphasis to the content and structure of these universities' proposed degrees.[1] So did the Australian Commission which reported in 1964 on the needs of higher education in Papua and New Guinea.[2]

The implementation of the Asquith and later reports meant that most of the colonies which attained independence in the late 1950s and early 1960s either had university institutions or had examples close at hand which could be followed or avoided in accordance with needs and experience. This did not solve all their difficulties; most were affected by the problems of localization

[1] See Lockwood, in Hamilton & others, pp. 270–3.
[2] *Report of the Commission on Higher Education in Papua and New Guinea* (Canberra, 1964), ch. 5.

of staff and relations with the government. In some cases, including Ceylon and Malaysia, there were also demands for the replacement of English by local languages.

Localization of staff was a problem in countries in which the supply of graduates of high calibre was small; relations with governments proved awkward, as in Ghana in the early 1960s and in Singapore later in the decade, when a strong local government, believing itself to be the embodiment of the national will, required staff and courses to be amenable to its demands. Both Nkrumah and Lee Kuan Yew wanted the local universities to conform to their programmes of national development; both were annoyed at times by the behaviour of expatriate staff, and Nkrumah went so far as to summarily dismiss members of the staff.[1] Lee, having expressed his disquiet as early as 1960,[2] later brought the Nanyang University under direct government control because of communist influence there and made one of his ministers vice-chancellor of the University of Singapore. These events had had their counterparts or near-counterparts in the history of universities in Australia and Canada; they were presumably part of that general process of reaction against British influence and practices which one recognizes as a likely nationalistic response when former colonies are becoming self-reliant.

The universities in the newly independent countries were helped by the Association of Commonwealth Universities (from 1948 to 1962 known as the Association of Universities of the British Commonwealth), which received a royal charter in 1963. By 1968, 182 Commonwealth university institutions were members.[3] The Association helped with staff appointments, with general advice on problems of administration, and provided opportunities to take part in its periodical congresses and conferences. This meant that the newer universities were able to discuss their difficulties not only with the British universities but also with those of Canada, Australia, New Zealand, and India, where the problems of localization and of relations with governments had a longer history and provided examples which were sometimes of more immediate use than those of Britain. Perhaps to a greater extent than in any other profession, the academic and administrative staffs of Commonwealth universities could think of themselves as part of a Commonwealth-wide community. This was not primarily a matter of having an Association but more because British academics continued to migrate to the old dominions, and expatriates continued to teach in most of the universities in Commonwealth Africa. In India, Pakistan, and Ceylon, and to an increasing extent in Malaysia and Singapore, where indigenous staff had become normal, contacts were maintained through postgraduate study in Britain and through the British Council's policy of subsidizing posts in particular universities where British academics could provide teaching that was not available locally.

[1] See Ashby, *African universities*, ch. 3.   [2] Carr-Saunders, pp. 207–8.

[3] CO *Year Book 1968*, p. 613. See also Ashby, *Community of universities, passim.*

We saw in Chapter 12 that the Commonwealth Economic Conference in Montreal in 1958 decided to establish the Commonwealth Scholarship and Fellowship Plan, on the initiative of Canada. There were to be 1,000 scholarships and fellowships, provided on a reciprocal basis by Commonwealth countries. The details were worked out at a Commonwealth Education Conference at Oxford in 1959. Britain had offered half and Canada a quarter of the thousand scholarships at Montreal; at Oxford, Australia, India, Pakistan, and New Zealand made further offers, so that the thousand was exceeded before the scheme began to operate. In the main, the scholarships were to be for postgraduate work, and the relatively few fellowships for senior scholars of established reputation.

Later Commonwealth Education Conferences, held every two years, continued to expand and refine the scheme, giving more attention to teacher training and other aspects which would materially assist the smaller and less developed Commonwealth members. Two administrative bodies supplemented the bilateral contacts through which the scheme would normally be implemented: the Commonwealth Education Liaison Committee and the Commonwealth Education Liaison Unit. After the establishment of the Commonwealth secretariat, these were incorporated into it, making co-operation in the provision of education one of its principal concerns. With the passage of time, the concept of education was altered to take account of special needs, such as those of the less developed Commonwealth members for medical awards and for scholarships to be for first degrees; but the scheme remained very much the kind of co-operative enterprise that had been envisaged at Montreal.[1] As the plan proceeded, Britain continued to play the major part in it, but the other more developed Commonwealth countries also took a larger share of the responsibility for scholars. Canada and Australia were already noted for the large number of overseas students at their universities and other tertiary institutions.

Nevertheless, the growth of universities in overseas Commonwealth countries hardly kept pace with the demand. Britain remained a magnet for their students, but there was a change in the proportions of undergraduate and postgraduate students coming there. At the start of the 1960s, 4,950 undergraduates and 2,531 postgraduates came; by 1968–9 the proportions had been almost reversed, with 4,668 postgraduates and 3,675 undergraduates.[2] In spite of the great attractions of postgraduate study in the US, Britain continued to be the main centre in which the Commonwealth graduate,

[1] See COI, *Britain and education in the Commonwealth* (1964), and Commonwealth Secretariat, *Commonwealth scholarship and fellowship plan, 9th Ann. Rep. 1968–9* (1969). For an example of secretariat thinking on educational issues, see Hugh Springer, 'Problems of aid in education in the Commonwealth', *Round Table*, July 1970.

[2] These and later figures are from W. H. Morris Jones & T. J. Johnson, 'A Commonwealth of learning', *Round Table*, Nov 1970, p. 389. Up-to-date figures are given in each issue of *A Year Book of the Commonwealth* (HMSO).

hoping for an academic career or its equivalent in research, got his higher degree.

Britain also remained a magnet for those wishing to study in other sorts of institutions besides universities. Of some 40,000 Commonwealth students and trainees in Britain in 1968-9, about a quarter were in universities, another quarter in technical colleges, and a half in professional or industrial training. Of the latter most were student nurses, who totalled nearly 15,000. As might have been expected from educational and constitutional development abroad, there were changes in the composition of students and trainees coming to Britain in the twenty years before 1969. Asians had made up more than half the numbers in the late 1940s, but in the peak year 1965-6 they accounted for less than a third. The numbers were Africa, 15,890; Asia, 13,644; western hemisphere (largely Caribbean), 12,156. Although government help had greatly increased, it was estimated in 1970 that more than three-quarters of the Commonwealth students and visitors were still privately financed.[1]

IV

In recognizing the widespread and often dominant character of British influence through language, education, and the mass media, we should not lose sight of the tensions this created, not only after Commonwealth members attained independence but well before. At least three kinds of related problem are involved. The first is that of predominantly British people overseas, especially in the old dominions, who wish to create a culture of their own but are conscious of the highly derivative character of what they have so far managed to achieve and the superiority of what is done elsewhere. A variety of responses has been noted. Edmund Wilson said of Canada in the 1950s: 'The critics seem very uncertain of themselves. They are inclined either to over-praise Canadian books or to be afraid to praise them.'[2] A. A. Phillips, an Australian, wrote:

> The dismaying circumstance is that . . . in any nation there should be an assump-tion that the domestic cultural product will be worse than the imported article.
>
> The devil of it is that the assumption will often be correct. The numbers are against us, and an inevitable quantitative inferiority easily looks like a qualitative weakness, under the most favourable circumstances—and our circumstances are not favourable. We cannot shelter from invidious comparisons behind the barrier of a separate language; we have no long-established or interestingly different cultural traditions to give security and distinction to its interpreters; and the centrifugal pull of the great cultural metropolises works against us. Above our writers—and other artists—looms the intimidating mass of Anglo-Saxon achievement. Such a situation almost inevitably produces the characteristic Australian Cultural Cringe—appearing either as the Cringe Direct, or as the Cringe Inverted, in the attitude of the Blatant

---

[1] Morris Jones & Johnson, p. 390.   [2] *O Canada* (1967), p. 105.

Blatherskite, the God's-own-country-and-I'm-a-better-man-than-you-are Australian Bore.[1]

Australians notoriously think they are unique; however, Phillips was writing about a more widespread problem, another facet of which has been stated by C. K. Stead: 'The New Zealand writer, then, is committed . . . to a country he is frequently prompted to describe in terms of its limitations—a society which cannot always satisfy his appetite for experience.' Stead goes on to speak of 'a tension . . . somewhere in the mind of every New Zealander between "here" and "there" '.[2] Such a tension is characteristic. It is especially difficult for those writers and thinkers from the old dominions and the Caribbean who may have been brought up to believe in the excellence of everything British, and who uneasily attempt to come to terms with this inheritance, with their own experience, and with the possibilities of distinctive forms of expression. Both extreme cultural nationalism and the uncertainty to which Wilson draws attention are compatible with this attempt at adjustment. But until 1962 (and to some extent afterwards) the Canadian or New Zealander or the West Indian had an alternative: if he was dissatisfied at home, he could come to Britain, if only for a stay of a few years, in which to absorb the atmosphere of the country from which his own culture had been derived.

The second problem is that it was more difficult for people belonging to a long-established non-European culture, such as the Hindu or the Chinese, to adjust to westernization. The task of blending such a culture with modern European industrial culture has been greatly facilitated by the English language in the Indian subcontinent and amongst the Straits Chinese, but it still produces tensions—as the career and writings of Nirad Chaudhury show. The troubled characters of Balachandra Rajan's novel *The Dark Dancer* and the young Malayan Chinese musician in Anthony Burgess's *Beds in the East* illustrate the difficulties involved in fashioning the blend and then of making it work. The decline of so many of the Indian universities from their former standards and of the English language in many parts of India shows how strong can be the influence of a dominant non-European culture and its politics when the prime incentives of the colonial period have disappeared.

The third problem concerns the Africans and others, such as Pacific Islanders, who do not have a sophisticated culture, whose movement towards the modern state and the modern money economy has been comparatively quick, and to whom the problems of adjustment, whether to British culture or any other, are different from those which arise in Asia. While the tension of such a situation can lead to extreme sophistication and artistic achievement, as in the novels of Chinua Achebe and Wole Soyinka, the sense of distance

---

[1] *The Australian tradition* (1958), pp. 89–90.

[2] 'For the hulk of the world's between', in Keith Sinclair, ed., *Distance looks our way* (1961), pp. 82–3. The whole of this book (subtitled 'The effects of remoteness on New Zealand') is worth attention.

between the old culture and the new remains very great, even in these remarkable works.

Among reactions in all three situations are extreme nationalism and the 'cultural cringe'. Often there is a need to break what Shils, in referring to the position in West Africa, called 'the vicious ring of dependence, lack of self-esteem, feeling of inferiority, and imitative provincial dependence'.[1] If the English language, with all that went with it, can be regarded as part of the reason why these problems exist, it is also part of the solution. It provides an escape from provincialism, as described by Davidson Nicol of Sierra Leone:

> If the intellectual community is not encouraged or has not got its roots in insti-tutes or universities which have links and connections with the outside world, it is likely to be crushed between politicians and a rising nationalistic middle class. It is also unlikely that without encouragement creative productivity will flourish in those writers, thinkers and artists who form the majority of the intellectual community. The contributions which West Africa could make to world culture would then be limited and would come largely from two extreme groups, the highly westernised and the completely primitive. Without an intellectual community of the type one envisages to feed and ballast the universities and colleges, these would become trade and training institutions.[2]

Something very similar could be, and indeed often has been, said of the situation in Canada and Australia. Without the stimulus of external standards, without connections with cultural metropolises abroad, few Commonwealth countries could boast of enough indigenous resources to sustain a robust and creative local culture. Each needs an effective national culture which blends local with external elements, using the English language as either the main medium or a lingua franca through which local elements can be transmitted. To develop a strong local intellectual community another language may be needed, as in Canada, West Africa, and Mauritius. Canada and Mauritius both joined La Francophonie when it was established in 1970 to develop contacts between French-speaking countries. The Commonwealth, an older and more formidable counterpart on which La Francophonie was to some extent modelled,[3] remains symbolic of how a common use of English, through educational and other institutions, has enabled local communities to go beyond their immediate horizons.

Nevertheless, there is still little Commonwealth literature, in the sense of a corpus of writing derived from a variety of Commonwealth sources and read

---

[1] 'A further step towards a West African intellectual community', in J. T. Saunders & M. Duowuna, eds., *The West African intellectual community* (1962), p. 23.

[2] 'The formation of a West African intellectual community', ibid., p. 14.

[3] The Commonwealth secretary-general was represented at the meeting at Niamey, in Niger, in March 1970, at which the body was set up. His *Third Report* (pp. 5–6) says: 'It seems significant that the French-speaking countries have found it necessary to create an association, where none existed before, to carry out basic and practical programmes of co-operation in functional fields such as science, education and law, and that in so doing they have drawn on Commonwealth experience.'

in all parts of the Commonwealth.[1] 'English and American literature' is what is read in the English-speaking world at large. There have been movements towards a common culture to which a wider range of sources would contribute. The very problems of the Commonwealth in the 1960s probably aroused more interest in Britain in such African writers as Achebe, and the presence there of West Indian immigrants may have given some impetus to the publication of Caribbean novelists, including George Lamming and V. S. Naipaul, but it remains true that British and other Commonwealth readers outside Canada do not know what they are missing in Morley Callaghan, and that Australians have still to discover Cyprian Ekwensi, James Ngugi, and other Africans writing in English.

v

Sport has undoubtedly been a common factor between many parts of the Commonwealth. To many people in the overseas Commonwealth, Britain means Lord's or Twickenham or St Andrew's rather than Westminster, Whitehall, or even Stratford-on-Avon. The spread of sport throughout the Empire is a remarkable phenomenon, unjustly neglected by historians.[2]

The British invented many modern sports, such as football, lawn tennis, and cricket, and made popular and formal a number of others which were traditional, including golf and rowing. Some were given special status by being patronized by the British upper classes, like boxing and horse-racing. Of those which remained special preserves of the countries which the British colonized and acquired, cricket is the most obvious.

In some spheres attempts have been made to make the Commonwealth as a whole a venue for particular sports, the most successful being the institution of the British Empire Games in 1930. These have been held every four years, except for 1942 and 1946. The name was changed to British Empire and Commonwealth Games for the Vancouver Games of 1954, and to British Commonwealth Games for those at Edinburgh in 1970. The Games are probably the next most representative after the Olympic Games; this was one reason why the 1970 gathering was threatened with the possibility of boycott by a number of Commonwealth countries if Britain allowed a South African cricket team to play in England in that year. South Africa had not been represented at the Games since 1958.

It was in cricket and rugby that most political controversy, centred on

[1] John Press, ed., *Commonwealth literature* (1965), the record of a conference at Leeds in 1964, is a good introduction to some of the problems discussed here, esp. the papers by R. K. Narayan and Chinua Achebe. A. L. McLeod, ed., *The Commonwealth pen* (1961), is an introduction to literature in Commonwealth countries. See also Walsh, *A manifold voice*.

[2] Vol. 3 of *The Cambridge History of the British Empire*, titled *The Empire-Commonwealth*, has no entries in the index for Sport, Pastimes, Cricket, Football, Tennis, or Literature. Modern historians could learn something from Sir Charles Dilke; see e.g. his shrewd discussion of sport in Victoria in his *Problems of Greater Britain* (1890), pp. 152 ff.

South Africa and Rhodesia, was experienced in the 1960s. The most distressing, in terms of public feeling, was probably the series of arguments in New Zealand about whether rugby teams should be sent to South Africa without Maori members. New Zealand and South Africa are the world's two foremost rugby countries, and the game is taken more seriously there than anywhere else, except perhaps in Wales. In the end South Africa agreed to receive Maoris, but the issue had probably drawn more attention in New Zealand to the policy of apartheid than anything else could have done.

It was in cricket that the full force of anti-apartheid feeling was most directly expressed, and the South African government showed itself most unyielding—perhaps because cricket is played largely by the English-speaking population, whereas rugby has been fully absorbed into the Afrikaner ethos. Expression of this feeling began in 1960, when David (later Bishop) Sheppard refused to play for England against a visiting South African team and demonstrations and protest marches were held, as again in 1965. In 1967–8 the matter became acute because of the possibility that Basil d'Oliveira, of Cape Coloured origin, might be included in an English team touring South Africa in 1968, and that the South African government would refuse to accept him.[1] After conflicting statements by South African ministers, the MCC sought help from Sir Alec Douglas-Home, who had been its president in the previous year and was visiting South Africa. He reported that he thought South Africa would accept whatever team England picked on merit, but that it would be inadvisable for the team to play in Rhodesia (normally part of the South African cricket scene) if the British government were opposed to this—as, understandably, it was. D'Oliveira was first rejected by the England selectors, then included when a selected player proved to be unfit to tour. The South African prime minister stated that d'Oliveira had been included for political reasons, and that the team as constituted was unacceptable. The MCC decided that the tour should not take place.

A South African team was to come to England in 1970, but anti-apartheid demonstrators threatened action which would effectively disrupt the games. The English Cricket Council wished the tour to proceed. As already mentioned, the Commonwealth Games to be held in July were threatened; Harold Wilson describes his own approach to the matter when he appealed to the Council to think again:

It had become clear, through the withdrawal of one Commonwealth country after another, that the Commonwealth games due to be held in the magnificent new sports stadium built . . . in Edinburgh, might be attended by athletes from only a handful of countries. I made a strong appeal that the South African tour be abandoned in the interests of other sports. My warning went wider: 'I hope it won't spread to the point where—but it could you know, if these attitudes persist about South African

---

[1] These and later details are from ch. 41 of Diana Rait Kerr & Ian Peebles, *Lords 1946–70* (1971).

questions and apartheid—where a British Prime Minister is presiding over a Commonwealth Prime Ministers' conference again cut down to just a rump of the Commonwealth. . . .'[1]

This dire prospect was not realized. The Council did not respond, although it did inform the South African cricket authorities that there would be no further tour unless South African teams were selected on a multiracial basis. However, on 22 May, following representations from the Home Secretary, it decided to cancel the tour. The Edinburgh Games went ahead as planned.

Also in 1970 cricket in the West Indies occasioned what the editor of *The West Indies Cricket Annual* called 'the most serious dispute in the English-speaking islands since the West Indies Federation disintegrated in 1962'.[2] It arose from a visit to Rhodesia by Garfield Sobers, the captain of the West Indies test team, the most famous living Barbadian, and regarded by many as the foremost living cricketer in the world. Sobers eventually published an explanation, saying that in accepting the invitation to play in a two-day double-wicket competition in Rhodesia he had been assured that there was no segregation in sport in that country but he was not aware of the deep feelings of the West Indian people. 'I have since learnt of this feeling and the wider international issues involved . . .'. These wider issues had involved a statement by Forbes Burnham, the prime minister of Guyana, to the effect that 'until he recants and apologizes for his foolish and ill-advised stand Sobers will be unwelcome in Guyana', and a reply by the deputy prime minister of Barbados that this was 'an affront to the people of Barbados'. Sobers eventually issued his explanation after consultation with Errol Barrow, the prime minister of Barbados, and after receiving advice from the prime minister of Trinidad, Eric Williams. Williams in turn was in touch with the prime minister of India, Mrs Gandhi, since an impending tour of the West Indies by an Indian team was said to be in jeopardy. Sobers's explanation was, in due course, accepted by all.

Such an amount of political turmoil can be explained partly by the importance of cricket in the Caribbean, where it has been one of the few means of drawing the English-speaking communities together, and partly by the feeling of coloured people throughout the Commonwealth that a man of the eminence of Sobers should not make himself even the apparent and unwitting tool of the Smith regime in Rhodesia. In the 1950s the West Indies had become a great force in test cricket, in comparison with its relative ineffectiveness in earlier years. The agitation against the South African tour in England owed something to the presence there of West Indian and Indian immigrants, to whom cricket was a symbol of national pride. South Africa had never played the West Indies, India or Pakistan. India and Pakistan had themselves played only

[1] *Labour government*, p. 784.
[2] Tony Cozier, ed., *The West Indies cricket annual 1971*, p. 14. The same source applies to the whole of this paragraph.

three series between 1952–3 and 1960–1, and then abandoned the effort: the cricket was said to be wretchedly cautious, since both sides were fully aware of the damage their national prestige might suffer from being beaten. They played twelve successive drawn matches.

It was not a new thing for national pride to be aroused by test cricket: similar things had happened during the 'bodyline' test series between England and Australia in 1932–3, when the Dominions Secretary intervened to counsel caution after Australian tempers had been aroused by some Australian players being hit by the English fast bowlers. But in the 1960s the whole affair had a sharper edge. The players themselves showed a better spirit than the politicians: Indians, South Africans, West Indians, and Pakistanis mingled freely in English county games after the relaxation of residence requirements, and all were included in international sides such as the one which played 'tests' against England in 1970 when the official South African tour was cancelled. South African cricketers in 1971 were trying to rescue their country from cricketing isolation by endorsing the idea of merit, not colour, as the standard by which teams should be picked;[1] but their government was determined that no multiracial side should represent South Africa. This intransigence was bound to breed resentment in countries in which coloured men had shown themselves to be as good as, and lately better than, white cricketers from England and Australia, the countries which had traditionally been supreme. It was a matter of the chicken and the egg, whether the demonstrators in London had 'introduced politics into cricket', or whether South Africa had done so by its refusal to integrate a game which had long been integrated everywhere else. In the ideological climate of the 1960s, with so much attention directed towards racial issues, South Africa's traditional approach could no longer be accepted by all.

International test cricket is governed by the International Cricket Council, the name since 1965 of the Imperial Cricket Council established in 1909. It has traditionally been run from Lord's where the conference meets annually. The original members were England, Australia, and South Africa. India, New Zealand, and the West Indies were added in 1926 and Pakistan in 1952. South Africa left in 1961 when it withdrew from the Commonwealth. It did not return after the change of name, but England and Australia continued to play unofficial tests against it until the upheavals of 1970.[2]

To many people cricket is a symbol of the Commonwealth, the image which comes most readily to mind when they are trying to think of something

---

[1] See, e.g., Peter Pollock, 'South African cricket overshadowed by isolation', *The Cricketer*, June 1971, p. 3.

[2] The 1965 changes allowed countries outside the Commonwealth to be elected as full or associate members of the ICC. None had become a full member up to 1969. As associates (countries which did not yet merit test series), the US and Ceylon were elected in 1965; Bermuda, Holland, Denmark, and East Africa in 1966; Malaysia in 1967; Canada in 1968; and Gibraltar and Hong Kong in 1969 (*Wisden cricketer's almanack 1970*, p. 1053).

distinctive. V. S. Naipaul writes in *The Middle Passage* of the West Indian, at Lord's in 1957 on the day when Sobers scored a century against the MCC, who exclaimed delightedly: 'A century on his first appearance in the Kremlin of cricket, man. *In the Kremlin.*' This is hardly the imagery which English cricket-lovers might choose, but they would recognize the universality of the feeling. Harold Wilson may have been fanciful in suggesting that playing cricket against South Africa might deplete the numbers at a Commonwealth Prime Ministers' Meeting, but a few would probably have made excuses in January 1971 if the South African tour had gone ahead in 1970.

VI

Just as the migrating engineer or accountant took his sports with him to the Commonwealth, so he took his professional qualifications. In 1903 24 per cent of the members of the British Medical Association were in the overseas empire. The same was true of 19 per cent of the Institution of Civil Engineers in 1908 and 5 per cent of the Royal Institute of British Architects. The accountancy bodies had about 6 per cent at the same time, each of the newer ones striving to outdo its older rivals by acquiring members overseas.[1] With the passage of time, the emphasis shifted to native-born professional men with qualifications acquired locally but recognized by the appropriate professional bodies in Britain, some of which set up local branches while others retained their central organization as the body which set requirements. In the countries which had power to set up local qualifications, such as Canada, Australia, New Zealand, and India, there were sometimes departures from the British standards but more often the links within the professions were preserved.

Independence for Asian and African countries meant a change in some respects, but not as much as one might have expected. The guild aspect of the professions has obviously remained influential, even when new sovereign states had the right to legislate on professional qualifications. Sir James Currie, investigating the situation at the end of the 1960s, noted that former affiliations with British institutions had diminished although, as in all professional organizations, there was little uniformity. Actuaries and company secretaries in Australia and New Zealand still had to take the examination of British organizations. In the group of professions connected with land economy, examinations were held by national bodies though their standards were usually still those of Britain. In such professions as medicine, law, and engineering, British or other qualifications or training and experience might not be sufficient to comply with local standards; for instance, in some Canadian provinces, however well qualified a British engineer might be, he required a period of experience there before he could apply for provincial membership and acquire

---

[1] Morris Jones & Johnson, *Round Table*, Nov 1970, p. 387.

the P.Eng. In the reverse direction, not all Commonwealth teachers would be acceptable in Britain.

Dealing with actual qualifications, Currie revealed a good deal of uniformity, even when professional bodies in the overseas Commonwealth had become independent of their British progenitors. In regard to architecture, the Royal Institute of British Architects, through its Board of Architectural Education, influenced the content and determined standards in some seventeen Commonwealth schools of architecture, while the Australian Institute, through its Joint Board, influenced architectural curricula in the states and made its recognition important. 'This is a near approach to the ideal and is wide in its application.' It was also one of the reasons why the Commonwealth Association of Architects was set up to search for uniformity 'or at least discussion on it', to enable an architect in one Commonwealth country to speak the same technical language as another Commonwealth colleague. Other professions, as veterinary medicine, surveying and land economy, insurance, secretarial and actuarial professions, and to a large extent accountancy, had similar common standards, in some cases agreeing in every detail and with identical qualifying examinations; in other cases sufficiently close in general.[1]

Much of the similarity arose from the fact that standards had been set by the requirements of colonial governments, which naturally chose British standards. Often this is said to have led to hardship for local officers striving to obtain qualifications which expatriates had obtained more readily. It also led, in some fields, to inappropriate training for local conditions and to difficulties in setting up local facilities to provide training acceptable to the British professional organizations, e.g. in medicine, engineering, and veterinary work.[2] Problems of this kind accelerated demands for autonomy in various professional fields, although these were balanced by the recognition that if local standards were lower than those in Britain and other Commonwealth countries, this would restrict job mobility. The retention of common standards can also be explained partly in technical terms—i.e. bridges must not fall down— and partly in terms of the wish to take advantage of wider horizons.

Official Commonwealth awareness of professional organizations dates from 1964, when Douglas-Home, as British prime minister, was looking for constructive ideas to put to the Prime Ministers' Meeting in June (see ch. 17). Amongst the ideas brought before a cabinet committee was that of closer Commonwealth links between members of the professions. Such a scheme had been suggested in a book published in 1963 by Lord Casey;[3] Patrick Gordon Walker too had drawn attention to 'the establishment and maintenance of

---

[1] James Currie, *Professional organisations in the Commonwealth* (1970), pp. xiv–xv.

[2] These points are made, with examples from a number of colonial and ex-colonial areas, in Richard Symonds, *The British and their successors* (1966), pp. 238–47.

[3] *The future of the Commonwealth* (1963), pp. 115–16. The extent to which Lord Casey's suggestions about future Commonwealth activity (pp. 135–8) have been followed up by the secretariat and the Foundation is remarkable.

common standards in measurement, research, education and professional qualifications' as part of 'the infrastructure of the Commonwealth' in a book published in 1962.[1] In April 1964 the CRO invited some thirty representatives of professional and voluntary organizations to a meeting at Marlborough House to discuss the whole complex of Commonwealth relations in the unofficial field; another such conference was held by the Royal Commonwealth Society soon afterwards. The outcome was a proposal put to the prime ministers by Douglas-Home and accepted; the communiqué stated:

> It might be desirable to establish a Commonwealth Foundation to administer a fund for increasing interchanges between Commonwealth Organisations in professional fields. This Foundation could be administered by an independent Board; and, while it could be financed by contributions from Commonwealth Governments, it would also welcome support from all quarters, whether public or private.[2]

The Foundation was perhaps fortunate in being coupled with the Commonwealth secretariat as a new creation. This may have given it momentum. The same conference of officials which drafted an Agreed Memorandum on the secretariat drafted one for the Foundation, both being adopted at the Prime Ministers' Meeting of 1965. The Foundation Memorandum[3] showed that the new body was intended to deal with professional organizations, and not, initially, with cultural activities and the press, and was to help in setting up national professional organizations where those did not exist and to promote the growth of regional and Commonwealth-wide associations 'in order to reduce the present centralisation in Britain'. There was to be a director, and a board of trustees nominated by subscribing governments. The chairman was to be 'a distinguished private citizen of a Commonwealth country appointed with the approval of all member Governments'. It was decided that the Foundation would start with an annual income of £250,000, of which Britain would subscribe half and the others varying proportions. John Chadwick, assistant under-secretary in the CRO, who had been much concerned with the idea from the beginning,[4] was appointed director, and the Australian Nobel Prize-winning scientist, Sir Macfarlane Burnet, first chairman.

The Foundation went on to encompass the development of professional bodies in the dependencies as well as in the members of the Commonwealth. In 1971 its annual funds were increased to £350,000 by the Heads of Government Meeting, and the director was confirmed for a further five years. Grants had totalled upwards of £1·5 m., and 28 Commonwealth governments were contributing funds.[5] The Foundation's activities had included helping to

[1] *The Commonwealth*, pp. 226–9.

[2] Commonwealth Foundation, *First Progress Report*, p. 7.

[3] Reprinted ibid., p. 6, from Cmnd 2714.

[4] See his 'Intra-Commonwealth relations: non-governmental associations', in Hamilton & others, pp. 124–47.

[5] *Year Book of the Commonwealth 1972*, p. 657.

bring into being some 12 new Commonwealth-wide professional associations as well as 5 national Professional Centres—suites of offices to be shared by professional bodies. The first two were in Kampala and Port-of-Spain. The Foundation had moved beyond the traditional circle of the professions to include town planners, magistrates, administrators, and those studying language and literature. It had been successful in decentralizing certain Commonwealth associations: the headquarters of the Commonwealth Veterinary Association was in Ottawa, that of the Commonwealth Geographical Bureau in Ceylon. Its grants were subsidizing attendance at conferences in many parts of the Commonwealth, and were enabling regional conferences to take place on a large scale, e.g. in the Caribbean.

The Foundation's philosophy, very much in line with the 'lattice-work' ideas of the Commonwealth secretary-general, was thus stated in its *Second Progress Report*, issued in October 1969, when it said that the value of the Commonwealth-wide professional bodies lay in 'the spread of effort and responsibility' they inspired and in the co-operative educational and training activities they helped to foster. What the Commonwealth Secretariat was now increasingly achieving in political, economic, and educational terms could be supplemented by the professions through their growing network of central secretariats working to benefit national societies and individual practitioners throughout the Commonwealth, although no doctrine of exclusivity was implied. 'It simply remains a fact that, as in other fields of activity, the Commonwealth has an organic plus-mark to its credit. This applies as much to regional as to Commonwealth-wide co-operation.'

VII

One might simply leave the matter at that, pointing out that the Commonwealth's 'organic plus-mark' applied to all the activities considered in this chapter, and not just to the professions. One could go further, indeed, and point to the persistence of British practices in public administration well after British control had ceased,[1] and to the same in the armed services, already remarked on in respect of India, Pakistan, and Nigeria. An even more striking example in the military sphere is Australia. In spite of twenty years of military co-operation with the US following the signing of the Anzus Pact in 1951 (including participation in the Vietnam war), the Australian navy, army, and air force are recognizably British services in terms of rank, appearance, education, organization, ethos and inclination, as well as in awards and honours. Close co-operation with the US in weaponry, communications, and intelligence has not induced either US forms of organization or an American cast of mind. The situation is quite compatible with a strong sense of nationalism and

[1] A. L. Adu, *The civil service in new African states* (1965) is a remarkable testament in this respect.

a determination not to be under a British thumb, both of which were displayed by the Australian forces in World Wars I and II.

Nevertheless, in asserting the existence of a common culture amongst the educated in the Commonwealth, and in noticing the special application of this in professional fields, we need to remain aware that the largest country speaking English is the US. Increasingly, in Britain as much as in any of the overseas Commonwealth countries (apart from Canada), US cultural influences have increased, whether through books and magazines or films and TV programmes, or scholarships to American universities, or comic-strips and advertising. Traditional British institutions cannot remain immune from this sort of influence.

It would be as foolish to assume either that Commonwealth culture was immune from, or that it was always at odds with, American culture as to assume that its common element applied equally to all Commonwealth countries and could be counted on to produce the same response in all. The reality is more complex. Since World War II a wider English-speaking culture, to which all can contribute, has become more common and will grow. Yet within this wider common culture there will be room for diverse strands, not only national or regional, but also traditional; and it is in the sustenance and re-invigoration of traditional connections that the Commonwealth cultural contribution will find a distinctive place.

CHAPTER 22

IMAGES OF THE COMMONWEALTH

THE Commonwealth has been not only a collection of institutions, actions, and policies; it has also been an idea in men's minds. During the period covered by this book that idea was debated at great length and in a variety of circumstances, though not everywhere in the Commonwealth. In some countries, such as Cyprus or Pakistan, the Commonwealth was either accepted as given or seen in a very limited context of particular policies. Elsewhere, especially in Britain, the debate was carried on with feeling at such times as its existence seemed to be threatened or its basic assumptions challenged. Some aspects of the debate have already been described. It was characteristic of each of the occasions we have considered—Suez, the departure of South Africa, the attempt by Britain to enter the EEC, and the Rhodesian imbroglio—that men should set up conflicting images of the Commonwealth in order to justify the lines they were taking, and that others, less convinced of a line to follow, should have been puzzled about whether the Commonwealth was fulfilling the purpose or remaining faithful to the image which they had ascribed to it.

In fact, as suggested in Chapter 2, changing conceptions of what the Commonwealth stood for, especially in racial terms, provided one of the constant themes of the period, though there was nothing new in this. Throughout the heyday of the British Empire and in the period of its transmutation into a Commonwealth, people had asked themselves what it was for. Hancock, writing in 1936 in the first Chatham House Commonwealth *Survey* saw a triad of characteristics—Liberty, Equality, and Unity—as the objective of an emerging British Commonwealth, and 'the government of men by themselves' as the theme on which he was writing. Such a view was natural when the quest for a satisfied nationalism was common to Commonwealth members and to the remaining colonies, and when it was still possible to see the British Commonwealth 'not as part of the British Empire, but as the whole British Empire viewed in the light of this experiment [of the government of men by themselves]'.[1] Thirty years later these objectives looked less relevant to an association of sovereign states in which each was striving for separate national interests, often at variance with other members.

In two ways, however, the triad still mattered. First, its elements were invoked over certain Commonwealth issues, such as those in Southern Africa, since the notions and ideals of the imperial period necessarily outlived the

---

[1] Hancock, *Survey*, i. 60-1.

Empire and coloured the whole discussion. Second, the fact that certain distinctively imperial issues remained for discussion (e.g. Rhodesia and, for some time, British Guiana) reinforced this persistence of notions and ideals which were still as relevant as they had been to the question of Indian self-government in the 1930s. It was natural not to draw a sharp line between 'colonial' and 'Commonwealth' questions; indeed, while scholars normally did so in the 1950s and 1960s, and the Colonial and Commonwealth Relations Offices operated on the basis that the two were quite separate, public opinion did not. Accordingly, in Commonwealth discussions everyone spoke, at some time or another, as if Liberty, Equality, and Unity mattered in a specifically Commonwealth sense, even if interpretations varied.

Hence a chapter on Images of the Commonwealth has a place in a series concerned with networks of association. Images constitute less of a network than do trade, investment, language, and education, but they affected these in all member states and especially in Britain, to whom the Commonwealth was important.

A particular instance was the response to change of certain Commonwealth institutions which were obliged to present a contemporary image of the Commonwealth. Like received doctrine about the Commonwealth, these could not maintain the same face under pressure from the changes in membership, tone, and range of activity; at the same time their history prevented them from making a completely fresh start. Here three such bodies, the Commonwealth Institute, the Royal Commonwealth Society, and the Commonwealth Parliamentary Association, are briefly examined as examples, but first we discuss some of the ideas about the nature and purpose of the Commonwealth published in the 1950s and 1960s.

I

At the start of our period certain broad propositions were widely accepted amongst those who took an interest in the Commonwealth and wished it well. These are exemplified in Mansergh's statement that 'the touch of healing of which Pandit Nehru had spoken' was given a new reality at the Fifth Unofficial Commonwealth Relations Conference at Lahore in March 1954,[1] in an article on the conference by another of the participants, William Clark,[2] and an editorial in *The Times* on the approaching Prime Ministers' Meeting of 1955.[3] Certain common elements in these could be paralleled in many other writings. There is agreement that the arguments of the 1930s about status and common policies are out of date, and that no one's interest will be served by bringing them up again. There is recognition that the Commonwealth imposes no obligations other than discussion, and that if it tried to do so it would lose not

[1] *The multiracial Commonwealth.*
[2] 'Debating the Commonwealth', *Observer*, 28 Mar 1954.
[3] 'The Commonwealth', 13 Jan 1955.

only its Asian members but possibly others as well. There is a strong feeling that the Commonwealth provides a bridge between countries which might otherwise have little to say to one another, especially since they are divided into those which support the United States in world affairs and those which do not. There is a real and growing concern about race relations as a test of whether countries can stay in the Commonwealth. There is also a quest for the common factor which members share, and it is often found in parliamentary institutions. A summing-up from *The Times* epitomizes the consensus between these sources:

> A conference of Ministers in the Commonwealth assumes the existence of no enemy, nor does it assume identity of view, or even the wish of identity of view, among its participants. What it does assume is a common habit of thought, based partly on long mutual familiarity and partly on similar parliamentary institutions, and a degree of forbearance which will always be ready to put the best interpretation on a fellow member's words and actions. The atmosphere of mutual confidence among like-minded if not like-intentioned men is the very substance of Commonwealth unity within the domain of public affairs, and confidence grows in the privacy of these informal meetings.
> ... The disintegration of the Commonwealth is less likely to come about through failure of the machinery than by the renunciation of its unwritten ideals. A country adopting a totalitarian form of government, or committing itself to deliberate racial persecution or persistently bellicose would in the end find the partnership unworkable, whatever its relationship on paper to the rest.

If we make this statement a point of departure, we can see what difficulties were to arise for image-makers in the next decade and a half. Parliamentary institutions were soon to be discarded by Pakistan, and later distorted or set aside by some of the newer members; on a number of critical occasions discussed the best interpretation was not put on fellow members' words and actions. Anyone who knows the history of later Commonwealth events will be aware that neither 'like-minded' nor 'like-intentioned' were the right words to describe Commonwealth leaders in conclave; that privacy was not maintained amongst them; and that the 'unwritten ideals' were renounced, permanently or for the time being, by a number of governments. The accepted image of 1954–5 was to be continually flouted.

The attitudes and ideas which developed in the ensuing years will be analysed here in a general context (that of people writing about the Commonwealth as a whole), and in a national context (i.e. in terms of the writers' own countries' roles and interests). One must of course remember that general and particular motives are normally mixed, and that scholarship and propaganda run into each other without the persons in question being aware of what is happening. The selection of writings we consider are, to a large extent, reflections of the imperatives which seemed to be present at the times in which they were written.

II

In looking over those writings which attempt to place the Commonwealth in a general setting, I can distinguish four sorts of attitude, which one might describe as the scholarly-contemplative, the idealistic-traditional, the idealistic-progressive, and the realistic-optimistic. The first runs through the whole period; the others can be placed, roughly speaking, in a more or less chronological order.

One is tempted to suggest that the scholarly-contemplative is best represented by the two articles on 'Cwthmanship' which *The Economist* published in Christmas weeks in 1958 and 1968, the 'w' being pronounced as in Ebbw Vale, thus allowing constant distinction between the cwth and the uncwth.[1] The first of these, using Stephen Potter's model of Gamesmanship, indicated both the extent of difference within the Commonwealth and the varieties of policy which it was possible to pursue—including the Dublin Gambit, which enabled one 'to get all the advantages of Cwth-membership without actually belonging'. Much of the Commonwealth future development was foreshadowed by this light-hearted but hard-headed article, as the second, ten years later, was able to point out.

The scholarly-contemplative category is represented in a series of books, some of the most notable being by lawyers or written in legal terms. We can instance K. C. Wheare, *The Constitutional Structure of the Commonwealth* (1960), J. E. S. Fawcett, *The British Commonwealth in International Law* (1963), and S. A. de Smith, *The New Commonwealth and its Constitutions* (1964) as books in which the changing character of the Commonwealth was clearly perceived, its transformation from the status-ridden institution of the 1920s and 1930s was described, and the implications of its members' independence fully treated. These books all accepted and elaborated the image of the Commonwealth which had emerged after Indian independence. They explained the characteristic behaviour of a Commonwealth more diplomatic than co-operative, and the limitations which the members appeared to have placed upon themselves. Similarly, the book with which the Canadian Frank Underhill began the series published by the Duke University Commonwealth-Studies Center, *The British Commonwealth* (1956), showed a broad appreciation of the changes resulting from Asian membership and the opportunities which these created for countries like Canada.

In the main, however, the noisy events of the 1960s inhibited reflection by scholars about the Commonwealth at large, and it was not until the end of the decade that the definitive work on Commonwealth history appeared by Mansergh, with its contemplative and just verdict on the flexibility which, in

[1] Cwthmas', 27 Dec 1958, and 'God Rest Ye Merry, Cwthmen', 21 Dec 1968. *The Economist* does not permit the names of its authors to be divulged, but good information suggests that the first article was written by Andrew Boyd and Roy Lewis.

the early 1950s, had seemed so notable a feature and so great a virtue of the post-1947 Commonwealth, in which he noted the fact that

there was bound to be a limit in practice, even if it were not susceptible of theoretic definition, to such flexibility, beyond which meaningful Commonwealth existence ceased for its member-states. That frontier between reality and nothingness was approached in the international and racial policies in the two post-war decades in which, paradoxically as it may seem, the Commonwealth idea acquired content and substance in respect of social, economic and educational cooperation, such as it had not hitherto possessed.[1]

This is a judgment to which we shall return, as also to Hedley Bull's characterization of the Commonwealth in 1959.[2]

The idealistic-traditional category of thought is best represented not by an Englishman, but by Sir Robert Menzies, whose devotion to the Commonwealth was often commended to me in Britain in the 1950s by Conservatives who found their own ministers less satisfactory representatives of traditional thinking. He expressed his views after he became prime minister in 1949 in his lecture *The British Commonwealth in International Affairs* (1950), which can be compared with 'A Critical Examination of the Modern Commonwealth' in his memoirs, *Afternoon Light* (1967). His long-standing bases of assumption were British, monarchical, parliamentary, and related to the common law. Britain was the source of his own country's institutions and culture; the Commonwealth was the later version of the British Empire, in which he saw many virtues and few if any faults; while the Commonwealth adhered to such ideals as those embodied in the monarchy, parliament, and the common law, it would be effective; if it did not, it would become a denial of its origins. He was, for example, greatly affected by the fact that Nkrumah swore a Privy Councillor's oath in London and then went home to declare a republic: 'after that cynical performance, it was not possible for me to have any personal respect for him'.[3] Menzies had no objection to non-white countries becoming Commonwealth members. What he objected to was their disowning or ignoring the British heritage that had brought them into the Commonwealth. He was prepared for differences over policy, and to understand why the newer members felt so strongly about racial discrimination and colonialism, but he believed that the Commonwealth could endure only to the extent that it was true to its British traditions. Throughout his prime ministership (1949–66) he specially emphasized the monarchical element: 'so long as there remains a nucleus of nations who live within the common allegiance to the Crown, there will be a British Commonwealth which will need no documents to maintain it'.[4] In the upshot, it was this assembly of Britain, the old dominions, and such

[1] *The Commonwealth experience*, p. 342.
[2] 'What is the Commonwealth?', *World Politics*, July 1959.
[3] *Afternoon light*, p. 188.   [4] Ibid., p. 227.

of the smaller states as wished to retain the British connection that he felt embodied the Commonwealth relationship.

His position aroused an emotional response in Britain whenever the Commonwealth, as a body, seemed to be moving away from British leadership. His emphasis upon the old dominions was, for example, echoed by the then British Liberal leader, Jo Grimond, after the Suez debacle.[1] Both Macmillan and Wilson found him a useful ally when Britain was being challenged by the newer members, especially the Africans. Indeed, their memoirs suggest that both of them, allowing for differences in temperament and idiom, found him congenial because they were firm British nationalists and could find no other Commonwealth prime minister prepared to take a distinctively British position in the 1960s.

However, to say this is to throw light on two defects in Menzies's position, both arising from his backward-looking view of the Commonwealth: first, in the 1960s no other Commonwealth country was prepared to identify its interests so closely with Britain's; second, even in Australia his heavy emphasis upon Britain as the Commonwealth leader generated opposition among his opponents and even his supporters and his ministers. The stress on Britain seemed to many Australians to be down-grading their own country's interests. His successors showed themselves to be less traditionalist in regard to Britain's role, but no less opposed to the newer developments in the Commonwealth: Menzies's disappointment with the changes of the 1960s soured not only his own attitude but theirs too.

While Macmillan and Wilson may both, in their different ways, have sighed for the traditionalist form of Commonwealth which Menzies evoked, they were forced to adapt to change and to recognize its possible advantages because of problems which could be solved only within a Commonwealth context, i.e. those concerning colonial self-government. Menzies could afford to pass these by, except in terms of freedom slowly broadening down from precedent to precedent, because his own colonial problem, in New Guinea, required little such attention. His standpoint was buttressed by the belief that support of Britain was inextricably linked with general world support for US policy, an attitude not shared by many of the newer Commonwealth leaders. If it was on the whole shared by the leaders of Britain, Canada, and New Zealand, none of them, except perhaps Holyoake, pursued it with the same single-minded devotion as Menzies; they took more notice of the Africans and Asians. It was as if, to Menzies, the newer members of the Commonwealth could largely be written off as diplomatic forces, except for Malaysia and Singapore, which were military associates of Australia. Such a position was seen as unrealistic by most other leaders in the 'white' Commonwealth in the 1960s; but this did not prevent some of them, and their supporters, from sympathizing with Menzies's views, even if they could not, for reasons of

[1] 'Cementing the Commonwealth', *Spectator*, 14 Dec 1956.

state, admit this publicly. It was a declining attitude, becoming more of an anachronism as the permanent changes in the Commonwealth grew more evident. Two features which made it most anachronistic were its monarchism and its lack of emphasis upon multiracialism. The second was the more serious since, as we have seen, monarchy proved capable of adapting itself readily to republican membership.

The strength of the idealistic-progressive attitude lay in its ardent acceptance of multi-racialism. It had many adherents on the radical side of British politics in the 1950s and 1960s and for a time (see ch. 8) it was to some extent shared by the right as well, especially when it was believed in Conservative circles that unless some stand was taken against apartheid, Britain's influence in the world would be diminished through a wholesale renunciation of the Commonwealth by Afro-Asian states. Indeed, the departure of South Africa was said by Gaitskell to show that a change had occurred

which rejects the old idea that this association and grouping of nations need have no special principles and its members no special affinities, except historical ties. It is a change which implies clearly the existence of common ideals—the common ideals of racial equality, political freedom, extending the right of self-government to the rest of the Commonwealth, non-aggression in international affairs, and co-operation and aid between nations. These ideals may be imperfectly realised in many instances, but . . . they . . . give the Commonwealth its real justification today.[1]

Such an attitude is seen at its most sincere and revealing form in Guy Arnold's *Towards Peace and a Multiracial Commonwealth* (1964) and in Derek Ingram's *Partners in Adventure* (1960), with their sense of the Commonwealth as not only the right body for Britain to develop but also the right one for co-operation between races:

In the Commonwealth we have in our hands the instrument to bridge the gulf between East and West, to put meat and vegetables in the mouths of the hungry, to teach a man enough to become another Shakespeare, another Rembrandt, another Leonardo if there be one in the shanties of Sophiatown or Singapore with the latent talents but without the means. We have in our hands the instrument to achieve a world in which black men and white can live together in peace and dignity and equality. We must not let it fall from our grasp.[2]

The same view, expressed in rather more guarded terms after a decade of further experience, is found in Malcolm MacDonald's Ditchley Foundation Lecture, *The Evolving Commonwealth* (1970).

This idealistic-progressive attitude embraced many degrees of fervour and had various points of emphasis. Some laid most stress on economic aid and co-operation, others on promoting racial equality. It varied also with the events of the time: for example, the assertion of racial equality as a Commonwealth principle required different arguments in terms of Rhodesia, of the

---

[1] 637 HC Deb., 22 Mar 1961, col. 457.
[2] *Partners in adventure*, p. 184. Sophiatown was a black urban settlement in South Africa.

Kenyan Asians, and of coloured immigration into Britain. Its supporters would all have said that they were upholding Hancock's triad, Liberty, Equality, and Unity as elements of Commonwealth purpose, especially as those applied to British policy. There is a clear approximation to these in Gaitskell's list of common ideals.

The difficulty with this list is that it did not include the one principle which Commonwealth governments had shown they prized above all others. Lord Salisbury, speaking on the same day as Gaitskell and about the same events (South Africa's withdrawal), expressed his belief that the survival of the Commonwealth would depend on 'one thing only': on whether all the members were able and willing 'to make it a cardinal principle of their association . . . that neither the Commonwealth as a whole nor the member states individually shall interfere in the internal affairs of their fellow members'.[1] Macmillan's view of this statement is illuminating; saying that it was perfectly sound in logic and on the basis of established convention, he added: 'It broke down, however, like so many similar arguments, against the march of events and the force of human feelings'.[2] He meant that it broke down in this particular case; but it was upheld in regard to their own affairs by all Commonwealth members and provided a potential stumbling-block to any effort to apply general principles to Commonwealth behaviour. For example, although the prime ministers declared themselves in favour of multiracialism in 1964, and drove the point further home in their declaration of principles in 1971, they avoided terms which would either force an individual member to mend its ways or enable the remainder to expel it for its existing practices. The kinds of racial inequality practised in communal societies such as Malaysia, Fiji, and Cyprus; the immigration restrictions imposed by Australia, most West Indian countries, Canada, New Zealand, and Britain; the disabilities suffered by untouchables in India, Asians in East Africa, aborigines in Australia, and Indians in Canada— these were rigidly regarded as domestic matters by Commonwealth heads of government, in spite of the insistence that apartheid had become such a world-wide scandal that it had passed beyond the sphere of domestic jurisdiction into that of international action.

What then could one say of Equality as part of the Commonwealth triad? It did not mean absolute equality; it could not be used as a Commonwealth cry, except when political circumstances (as in respect of Rhodesia) made it feasible to mount a campaign against British policy; and even then it could not be enforced. Similarly, while those who saw that Liberty as a Commonwealth principle could demand 'one man one vote' in Rhodesia, they were powerless (and often disinclined) to prevent the long suspension of the electoral process in Pakistan and its debasement in Ghana. Thus, the 'common ideals' of which Gaitskell spoke may well have been characteristic of many people in the Commonwealth, even of certain leaders; but they had to make way before the

[1] 229 HL Deb., 23 Mar 1961, col. 1247.   [2] *Pointing the way*, p. 302.

principle enunciated by Salisbury, which all Commonwealth governments asserted in practice.

Those adhering to the idealistic-progressive attitude would probably have retorted to such a criticism that, while they recognized the force of sovereignty and power politics in the policies of Commonwealth states, they believed that this force could be moderated by public affirmation of Commonwealth ideals, and that in any case, where Britain still had responsibility for colonial change—as in Rhodesia—Britain should be made to put into practice the ideals which it had officially adopted in the past. In effect, the idealistic-progressive view was expressed very largely in terms of British policy. While occasionally a writer might suggest that Australia should be brought to book on Commonwealth grounds for its immigration policy, or India and Pakistan be required to submit their Kashmir quarrel to Commonwealth examination, there was always an uneasy recognition that these governments would not in fact submit, and that others would back them. South Africa was the one case in which the idealistic-progressive attitude triumphed against a Commonwealth member other than Britain; and in this case, as subsequent events showed, the triumph was more apparent than real, since it had no effect on apartheid and did not prevent further economic co-operation between the South African regime and other Commonwealth members. The idealistic-progressive image of the Commonwealth was partial and hopeful rather than realistic, a projection of aims and not a replica of behaviour.

None the less, it rested on foundations which were only gradually and never finally eroded—the sense of past responsibility, the awareness of common experience and often common ideas, the community of opinions arising from the use of English, and the knowledge that, whatever may have been the reasons for acquiring colonies, they had long been administered in terms of certain ideals.

What I have called the realistic-optimistic school consists of writers and thinkers who, after the Commonwealth had settled down in its post-1947 pattern, began to urge that it would have to find new things to do in order to survive. 'If the Commonwealth association is to wax not wane in the next chapter but one, new ties must take the place of the Old Boys Club', wrote *The Economist* on 7 April 1956.

The problem was to find out what new ties would best suit the members, bearing in mind their jealous tradition of not allowing Britain to tell them what to do. The Commonwealth Scholarship and Fellowship Plan of 1958 was a notable step forward, though it was not fully recognized as such at the time. A sense of practical co-operation between Commonwealth states did not seem to count for much until Douglas-Home put forward his new proposals at the 1964 Prime Ministers' Meeting, and did not receive an impetus until the Commonwealth secretariat was set up. While the Commonwealth Agricultural Bureaux continued to function, the Commonwealth Air Transport Council, largely consultative and advisory in character, had declined into quiescence. The Commonwealth of the late 1950s was a body in which joint action had become difficult, if not impossible in many cases, because of divisions between India and Pakistan and between India and the old dominions on the Cold War. These differences could be smoothed over through the mutual forbearance of the Prime Ministers' Meetings, but they were not conducive to joint action. As is usual in such cases, the very lack of action had itself become something of a dogma. It suited all the parties, for the time being, that the Commonwealth's negative qualities should be praised.

An objection was raised by W. H. Morris Jones in an address in New Delhi in March 1960.[1] He was dissatisfied that the Commonwealth had become so negative an association. How far, he asked, could it continue on the basis merely of inertia and agreement to differ? He pointed out how few people had experience of the actual operation of Commonwealth relations, and questioned whether such slight contacts could generate what was needed to keep the association together. It must become 'something which is at once more positive, more public and closer to the people'. The need was for 'constructive work'. He wanted an extension of scholarships, more co-operative economic ventures, and more opportunities for young people to work on community projects in other Commonwealth countries. A growing number of statements from 1960 onwards reflected this kind of concern, especially the detailed list of possible forms of Commonwealth co-operation in Lord Casey's *The Future of the Commonwealth* (1963). As the African members grew in number, it became clear that they were readier to consider joint action than had been India, in particular. By the end of the 1960s emphasis on co-operation had become something of a received doctrine on which the operations of such bodies as the Secretariat and the Foundation depended, and which was given full expression in Derek Ingram's *The Commonwealth at Work* (1969).

It might well be asked how the line is drawn between idealistic-progressive and realistic-optimistic attitudes, since both stress the need for joint action, and the same author (Ingram) has been instanced amongst the writers typical of both. The answer lies in time and temperament. The aims of the idealistic-progressives included 'constructive work', but they often went well beyond this, especially on racial issues. The questions of South Africa and Rhodesia seemed to many of them to call for Commonwealth action at the highest political level—a level at which, as previous chapters have shown, the Commonwealth was neither equipped nor, in its component parts, willing to take. The shift of emphasis to practical co-operation was, in my view, a recognition by many that a demand for high policy led to a dead end within the Commonwealth, whereas 'constructive work' could build on the Commonwealth's past and provide more of a bridge between peoples in the future. The idea of functional co-operation was not, of course new. What was new was a Common-

[1] 'Towards a new Commonwealth', *Foreign Affairs Reports*, May 1960.

wealth membership prepared to consider it as a going concern, as members unexpectedly did when they agreed to the proposal for a Commonwealth secretariat.

One work remains outside the categories used above, Patrick Gordon Walker's *The Commonwealth* (1962), the only extended piece of writing by a politician with experience of working the Commonwealth system. It is certainly realistic-optimistic in its suggestions for co-operation and its belief in the Commonwealth's future, but its realism is vitiated to a certain extent by its overwhelming sense of the Commonwealth as the evolution of a natural unit and by the note of inevitability which such a sense induces from time to time. It has something attaching it to each of the four categories, and remains unusual in blending a variety of elements of analysis and policy.

Each of these groups of writers produced images of the Commonwealth which can be reconciled in some degree with Hancock's triad, although the weight they give to Unity is slight, and they continually stress the limitations which the sovereignty of each member has placed upon Liberty and Equality. The idealistic-traditional and idealistic-progressive both stress Unity as desirable but their interpretations of Liberty and Equality differ so much that this Unity would be put to quite different uses once attained—in the first case to the mutual protection of the sovereignties of the members, almost as if they were still one sovereignty, and in the second to the redress of inequalities, the widening of opportunities, and the creation of some equality of condition between the members, even if this should mean a curtailment of sovereignty. The realistic-optimistic, on the other hand, looks to limited Unity in practical matters to provide extensions of both Liberty and Equality where these can be furthered by constructive work.

III

National images need to be taken into account, since each member's government sees the Commonwealth very much in terms of its own interests and preoccupations. Often this means that its view turns upon relations with Britain rather than upon an association of equals. However, while one can see policy operating in this way, there is little evidence, since there is not that element of national debate and discussion, that mass of polemical literature, which has been so noticeable in Britain. For whereas in the 1950s and 1960s Britain was constantly involved in Commonwealth issues which were constantly discussed, this was not true of any other member. The others were intermittently involved in particular issues. Sometimes these might seem crucial, as immigration and sugar for Jamaica, or the Rhodesian question for Zambia, but there were not enough of them to generate the same discussion. The aftermath of imperial control was more important to those who had controlled than to those who had been controlled: the questions were more numerous, the issues more complex, the difficulties of adjustment greater.

In India the image of the Commonwealth was very much a construct of Nehru's or a replica or counter-image of his. For a long time after independence his opponents in the Lok Sabha raged and stormed about the Commonwealth whenever a difficulty arose with Britain. Nehru answered them on most occasions by saying that the Commonwealth imposed no obligations and gave no other member any opportunity to attack India.[1] He ascribed no positive virtues to the Commonwealth but to the end of his days emphasized its flexible character:

The real value [of the Commonwealth] is its extreme flexibility, which enables people from the four corners of the earth to gather together in a friendly way to discuss matters frankly and yet be able to come to some broad conclusions. I think this type of association . . . is a very good type and far better than the associations which limit the way of each country, and that is why the Commonwealth has succeeded in spite of differing opinions. . . . It is because of its flexibility that it carries on successfully. Rigid things tend to break up when there are vital differences. . . .[2]

Nehru's famous remark that the Commonwealth contributed 'a touch of healing' was so vague as to mean little in practice. His main purpose at Commonwealth meetings appeared to be to expound the doctrine of non-alignment and to ward off Pakistani attempts to entrap India over Kashmir. One of the few occasions on which he seemed to put forward a more positive notion was in December 1958, when he was asked to comment on a statement by Malcolm MacDonald that he saw no reason why a military dictatorship and parliamentary democracies should not coexist within the Commonwealth. He then said that the drift away from elected parliamentary government was a wrong one, and should not be supported.[3] This, of course, was a direct reference to what had happened in Pakistan, and seemed to suggest that only parliamentary regimes should be members. It is tempting to suggest that Nehru's course in respect of the Commonwealth was set by the need to keep Pakistan under surveillance, and that this is the reason for the generally cautious attitude which he and his successors maintained.

Certainly most Indian commentators took a strongly nationalistic view of any Commonwealth action which seemed to favour Pakistan—or rather, of any *British* action which seemed to do so, since relations with Britain remained the touchstone of the Commonwealth for most articulate Indians.[4] Otherwise, the emphasis was on finding reasons why India should not quit the Commonwealth rather than why it should stay and use the Commonwealth to its own advantage; and this was aided by the widespread ignorance of Indians about

[1] The chapter on 'India and the Commonwealth' in Rajan, *India . . . 1954–6*, provides the best account of the Indian debate, which showed little development afterwards.

[2] At a press conference at India House, London, 20 Sept 1962; from COI, *Quotations on the Commonwealth* (1964), p. 7.

[3] *The Times*, 11 Dec 1958.

[4] See the argument in Gangal, *India and the Commonwealth*, ch. 3.

Commonwealth countries other than Britain or those to which Indians had migrated. The attempts of M. S. Rajan to suggest wider possibilities of association seemed to have relatively little effect. After Nehru's death in 1964 events hardly enhanced Indian interest in the Commonwealth. Instead, the tensions over the Indo-Pakistani war, over Indian migrants in Britain, and over Indians in East Africa left India with little relish for Commonwealth connections, especially since, unlike the smaller and newer members, it had little to gain from British economic aid. Other Indian writers followed this trend.[1] In general, Indian images of the Commonwealth have often been incomplete and one-sided.

Despite the fierce quarrels between some African members and Britain, African images of the Commonwealth were more positive. Although Nkrumah was ambivalent and constantly attacked neo-colonialism, he continued to support the Commonwealth, often on what might seem old-fashioned grounds. In denying that the francophone African states could transform the French Community into something like it, he insisted that such a scheme did not 'comprehend the essential uniqueness of the Commonwealth':

The fact is that, in the circumstances of having to dissolve an existing association to replace it with a new one, constitution-making will have to be invoked. This will at once instil a principle which is entirely out of keeping with the whole idea of the Commonwealth, which is not governed by any constitution.[2]

Tom Mboya, in his *Freedom and After* (1963), emphasized that Kenya did not support India against China because it was a Commonwealth member but because 'she has been attacked and there was proof that Chinese troops were encamped on Indian territory',[3] but went on to endorse various ways in which the Commonwealth might prove useful to Kenya and to the Afro-Asian cause. He said that Kenya would leave the Commonwealth if Britain granted independence to Southern Rhodesia, or if the Commonwealth became an obstacle to African unity, but the sense of interest and goodwill which he felt is apparent in his writing.

The two notable African figures in constructing images of the Commonwealth have been Nyerere amongst the political leaders and Mazrui amongst the scholars. Nyerere made his position clear when Tanzania joined the Commonwealth and he adhered to it: there is a consistent progression from his 'Tanganyika and the Commonwealth' of 1961[4] to his pamphlet for the 1971 Heads of Government Meeting, *South Africa and the Commonwealth*. In 1961 he wrote:

... what really matters about the Commonwealth, from our point of view, is its

---

[1] See e.g. B. K. R. Kabad, 'Will the Commonwealth last?', *Times of India*, 11 Jan 1969.
[2] *Africa must unite* (1963), pp. 185–6.   [3] Mboya, p. 243.
[4] First published in the Rl Commonwealth Society's journal, Dec 1961; reprinted in *Freedom and unity*, pp. 135–7.

underlying principles. Each nation interprets these basic principles according to its own circumstances, but it is only renunciation of the basic equality and dignity of mankind which calls for exclusion. . . .

He added that the association's existence and its possibilities as a factor in world peace derived from its flexibility and 'its implied attitude of international friendship based on equality'.

Ten years later, in endorsing Edward Heath's reported statement that 'the Commonwealth has always existed and worked on the basis that members respect each other's interests', he wrote that this implied a mutual responsibility between Commonwealth members, as well as 'the complete national sovereignty of every individual member to pursue his own country's interests'. It was a recognition that, while every Commonwealth member had complete freedom to make its own decisions, each member nation had also 'accepted an obligation to try to the best of its ability to pursue its own interests in such a manner that its actions will not adversely affect the basic interests of other members'. This was 'an important and fundamental part of Commonwealth membership'; there was besides one basic principle implicitly accepted by every member: 'If we are not opposed to racialism, we have no business sitting down together in an association which consists of representatives of all the racial groups in the world.'[1]

This image of the Commonwealth thus went further than that of 1961. Nyerere's new definition was both subtle and realistic: subtle in avoiding the idea that Commonwealth members should pass judgement on each other's actions, but realistic in asserting that the members could hardly hope to stay together if they ignored one another's interests altogether. From Commonwealth practice he was, as it were, distilling a Commonwealth principle. It was akin to Macmillan's warning to the South Africans in 1960: 'Mind your own business, but mind how it affects my business, too.' From a general standpoint, it should have been highly acceptable to the British government, though its application in the context of arms sales to South Africa in 1971 was less so. It is clear from Nyerere's speeches and writings that, like Kaunda and other African leaders, he regarded it as a fundamental principle of British colonial policy not to hand over power to a minority. There is an appealing wholeness about his attitude towards the Commonwealth and his attempt to apply to it principles which he also regarded as applicable to his own domestic politics.

Ali Mazrui's *The Anglo-African Commonwealth* (1967), the first work on the Commonwealth by an African, was also the first book to examine, at some length, the African effect on the Commonwealth. In his view, Nigerian independence in 1960 brought into being a 'Third Commonwealth', in which the balance of racial composition had shifted in favour of the coloured members. The principle of multiracialism was thus strengthened, South

---

[1] *South Africa and the Commonwealth*, p. 1.

Africa's withdrawal being a response to this 'new era of coloured preponderance'. The Third Commonwealth was marked by a decline in British control over Commonwealth affairs, so that by 1964 it could be called an Anglo-African association. There were two centres of influence, one British, the other African, to which the remaining members tended to gravitate, with the Asian members in particular finding themselves sometimes drawn into African anti-colonial militancy and also sometimes towards Britain in urging moderation. He observed that African racial sensitivity by now exceeded Asian, largely because of the existence of South Africa, 'the most blatantly racialistic regime in the world'; however, he also suggested that the African members were more influential precisely because they were the least anglicized, and were deemed to be in greater need of tolerant indulgence from the others than the prime ministers of Jamaica or of India. Britain had to be warier of African sensibilities than of those of the more anglicized members. Yet he acutely noted that to try to 'de-anglicize' the Commonwealth much further would be to 'risk dissipating its sense of fellowship', for 'what could a New Zealander have in common with a Jamaican or a Zambian if not the bonds of a shared British-ness?'[1]

Mazrui's image of the Commonwealth is thus based upon recognition of both new and old forces: it may be a little too sharply focused on the Southern African issue, but it is a valuable reminder of the basis of the African demands and also of some community of background in the Commonwealth. His book epitomizes the most frequent African attitude towards the Commonwealth, which includes a readiness to accept and extend Commonwealth practices, especially on the issues of colonialism and multiracialism, together with what Dennis Austin has called 'a fascinated attachment to Britain and a genuine liking for British ways of behaviour'.[2]

Images of the Commonwealth in Australia in the 1950s and 1960s were too strongly influenced by Menzies to require analysis. They are exemplified in Gordon Greenwood's chapters in the two volumes of *Australia in World Affairs* for 1956–60 and 1961–5, where one feels that the issues are about Menzies and his views on the monarchy, not about the Commonwealth as such—although there was some opposition, both in parliament and press, to his stands on Suez, South Africa, and Rhodesia. There is an ingrained poverty of response by Australian politicians and officials to the Commonwealth as a possible field of diplomatic or social effort, due perhaps to the same causes as Australian suspicion of the UN—a fear that this body might bring Australia to book or interfere in its cherished ways of doing things. The existence of a number of academic works by Australians about the Commonwealth (e.g. Zelman Cowen's *The British Commonwealth of Nations in a Changing World*, 1965) does not alter this basic combination of indifference

[1] *Anglo-African Commonwealth*, p. 41. Earlier quotations are from pp. 1–2, 27–8, 34, 37–9.
[2] 'The Commonwealth turned upside down', *World Today*, Oct 1966, p. 418.

and hostility towards the Commonwealth as an association, coupled with a basic warmth and superficial ambivalence towards Britain.

For Canada, from 1947 until the coming to office of Pierre Trudeau, Commonwealth action and Commonwealth sentiment were part of the official creed, 'an attitude of contentment and satisfaction, mixed with some degree of creator's pride'.[1] Though the Commonwealth somewhat receded as a Canadian official concern when Trudeau became prime minister, it still remained a favoured body, especially since a Canadian was the first Commonwealth secretary-general. The reasons for this continued interest lie mainly in the widespread sense amongst leading Canadians that the Commonwealth association admirably lent itself to the exercise of diplomacy. There was, in fact, a distinctive Canadian image of the Commonwealth. Using a medley of sources, it can be sketched briefly.[2]

Essentially, the image is of Canada reaching out for contacts beyond the North American continent, and finding that the Commonwealth, the product largely of Canadian insistence on autonomy within the British Empire, affords both a link with Britain and a bridge for making contact with Asians, Africans, and others. It also affords a kind of shield against too great US pressure. Canada, as a country of varied ethnic origins, appreciates the diversity of the Commonwealth and sees this as a source of strength, in the sense that it enables contacts to be made and isolationism avoided. While the highly 'British' character of the Empire, and, in its earlier years, of the Commonwealth was a hindrance to full acceptance by French-Canadians, this difficulty has been reduced by the fact that membership has not prevented Canada from giving substantial economic aid to francophone countries in Africa and from joining La Francophonie. Now that the influence of Britain has diminished, that of Canada has increased. The Commonwealth runs counter to no vital Canadian interest, and can foster a variety of such interests, including that of greater Canadian influence amongst the Commonwealth Caribbean states.

Not every Canadian political leader or intellectual would agree with this sketch, yet Canadians have shown a remarkable degree of agreement about the nature of the Commonwealth and its value for their country. New Zealand— not discussed here at any length—perhaps comes closest in this respect, though on occasions its image of the Commonwealth resembled Australia's, if not for long. The distinctive Canadian image came to the fore in the Suez, South African, and Rhodesian affairs, and can be regarded as the most influential, in political terms, of all those constructed outside Britain.

---

[1] From ch. 5, 'Canada in the Commonwealth', a useful summary of opinion in Eayrs, *Canada in world affairs 1955–7*, p. 161.

[2] Among the sources, ibid., and Eayrs, *Minutes of the sixties* (1968), ch. 5; Vincent Massey, *Canadians and their Commonwealth* (1961); Lester Pearson, *Democracy in world politics* (1955); John Holmes, 'A Canadian's Commonwealth', *Round Table*, Oct 1966; and various conversations.

IV

Britain's central position has naturally meant that the literature of the Commonwealth is overwhelmingly British—even though, as James Eayrs has pointed out, much of it has been written by people who came originally from other Commonwealth countries.[1] Here I shall consider first the attitudes expressed in the Labour and Conservative parties, then the changing official consensus, and then the opinions of publicists in what might be designated a nationalist-sceptical vein, i.e. those who actively questioned the value of the Commonwealth to Britain. In considering these attitudes, it is worth bearing in mind that through most of the 1950s and 1960s British people were consistently presented with a favourable image of the Commonwealth by a number of newspapers, including the *Guardian* (notably in the reporting of Patrick Keatley), the *Observer* (in that of Colin Legum), and *The Times* (particularly when Roy Lewis was its Commonwealth correspondent). Others, including *The Economist* and *Financial Times*, were more ambivalent in the later years. The Beaverbrook press consistently over-sold the Commonwealth; after its founder's death it shifted to a critical position akin to that of the *Daily Telegraph*. The sensationalist press was either violently in favour or violently against, depending on the incidence of publicized clashes within the association. By and large, however, the Commonwealth had a good press, except when the African states were vehemently attacking the British position over Rhodesia. There was, for example, little criticism when South Africa was forced out in 1961 or of continued decolonization. It was only during that general disillusionment characteristic of the latter half of the 1960s that the Commonwealth as an institution was subjected to concentrated criticism.

The two major political parties had, throughout the period, their separate visions of the Commonwealth, and almost, one might say, at times their separate Commonwealths.[2] Their backgrounds were different. As the party of Empire, of Disraeli and Joseph Chamberlain, the Conservative ideological background was that of advocacy of an imperial estate, well developed and mutually self-supporting, although this line had normally been more strongly advocated by backbenchers than by ministers. Orderly progress towards self-government, by those who had shown themselves capable of it, was natural from a Conservative standpoint; headlong progress was not. Kinship with the old dominions was natural, but not the same degree of warmth towards the leaders of African and Asian members who until recently had been leading nationalist movements. Conservatives recognized the triad of Liberty, Equality, and Unity, but were inclined to put more emphasis on the third than on the first two.

Labour traditions were of sympathy with the colonial nationalist and

[1] *Minutes of the sixties*, pp. 181–2.
[2] See Gordon Walker's interesting exposition in McKitterick & Younger, pp. 164–70.

suspicion of Conservative plans for the 'imperial estate', although this suspicion probably owed a good deal to earlier free trade attitudes and was not characteristic of Labour governments after 1945. Labour had long experience of dealing with nationalist movements, which were, almost by definition, socialist in outlook, though their ideas of socialism might not tally with those of the British Labour movement. It was to the fringes of the Labour, not the Conservative Party, that movements for 'colonial freedom' naturally gravitated. Labour people thought of themselves as champions of the underdog, as supporters of internationalism, and as opposed to autocracy and the colour bar. They were especially proud of the Attlee government's grant of independence to India. In all these respects it was natural for them to show more interest in the colonial politician than the colonial official, and to be attracted more readily to the newer than the older Commonwealth members.

Such party attitudes resembled those on other questions in being more strongly held by some backbenchers than others, by backbenchers than ministers, and by party supporters outside parliament than party members inside it. In terms of the actions of Conservative and Labour governments, they were vague inclinations, not actual programmes. When either party was in opposition, these attitudes were likely to be more plainly expressed. British governments of the 1950s and 1960s had to deal with the Commonwealth as it was and as it was becoming. As we have seen, the parties did not differ greatly, when in office, over such matters as South Africa, entry into the EEC, and Rhodesia. In particular, the Labour Party showed itself from 1964 onwards to be capable of adopting and adapting much of what its predecessors had done. Since its vocal supporters were often more interested in colonial independence than in relations with ex-colonies after independence, the Commonwealth as an association of states was not of primary concern to them, although they responded to the appeals for multiracialism and 'one man one vote' from African leaders such as Nyerere. They were less for Unity than for Liberty and Equality.

It was rather in the Conservative Party that interesting debate about the Commonwealth took place. This is understandable, since the Conservatives were in office most of the time, and had to take responsibility for Suez, South Africa, the EEC, Commonwealth immigration, and the dissolution of the Federation of Rhodesia and Nyasaland. To the abandonment of traditional policies in most of these cases there was a variety of responses, although the party was in general acquiescent. One can distinguish a group impelled by what Goldsworthy calls 'residual imperialism',[1] to whom the principal issue was Britain's greatness, and who regarded Macmillan's policies, in particular, as leading to perdition. To these, any departure from the imperial tradition of British leadership was regrettable; they were suspicious of the solicitude which British governments showed towards Nehru, for example, and sometimes

---

[1] *Colonial issues*, pp. 287–99.

suspicious of too close connections with the US. Yet there was some overlap between this group and the Expanding Commonwealth Group (see p. 392). Both groups were primarily concerned with British strength, but the Expanding Commonwealth Group settled for a 'Code of Consultation' which would in effect have barred most if not all activities by Commonwealth members which became troublesome to British governments. The last of the Group's pamphlets was written before South Africa's withdrawal; thereafter its members proved much less tolerant towards Commonwealth countries' pressure upon Britain.

Macmillan's premiership was of vital importance in shaping the Conservative image of the Commonwealth. He assured party members that 'the Empire is not breaking up, it is growing up';[1] he continued to proclaim traditional sentiments but at the same time agreed to rapid change. He was actuated by his sense of history and awareness of current political options. For a time he persuaded his party that all was well: the 1960 *Wind of Change* pamphlet by Utley and Udal already quoted reflects the state of mind which he induced at his most successful; Sandys's *The Modern Commonwealth* of 1962 expresses the hopeful side of Macmillan's views.

Thereafter events conspired to make the Commonwealth markedly less popular with Conservatives. Richard Hornby's *The Changing Commonwealth* and the Bow Group's pamphlet on Britain's place in the world,[2] both of 1965, were sober attempts to be realistic while not pessimistic about its value to Britain, but the tone of vocal party feeling in the latter part of the 1960s was set much more by the caustic article of 'A Conservative' in *The Times* in 1964. As we have seen (ch. 15), the image of a co-operative Commonwealth inspired by Macmillan's ebullience was replaced by a harsher one of a Commonwealth asking too much and costing too much. This in turn was modified by the restrained approbation given to the Commonwealth by Heath's ministers after they had settled down to their task. It would be fair to say that, by 1971, old-style Conservative feelings about the Empire and its successor were confined to the old dominions, although there was a sense of post-colonial responsibility for underdeveloped Commonwealth countries. Otherwise the association inspired feelings ranging from indifference to annoyance by way of cautious acceptance. Six years of governmental experience between 1964 and 1970 had produced a somewhat similar range of feeling on the Labour front bench.

If we turn to what might be called official orthodoxy—i.e. to the image of the Commonwealth projected by British government departments and largely constructed by officials—we find it, as we might expect, pitched very much at

---

[1] Goldsworthy (p. 306) attributes this statement to Alan Lennox-Boyd, as colonial secretary, at the 1955 Conservative conference. I am sure he said it and I have a persistent feeling that Macmillan said it quite often. That he did say it is confirmed in a letter from his secretary dated 8 July 1971.

[2] Leon Brittan & others, *A smaller stage* (1965).

the level of ministerial consensus. The COI's pamphlet *What is the Common-wealth?* was, in its 1954 and 1956 editions, a reflection of that Commonwealth harmony of the early 1950s to which we have previously drawn attention. It stressed 'the common heritage', being able to say that all Commonwealth members were parliamentary democracies, that nearly all of them were subject to the Queen, and that they had a 'generally similar attitude on fundamental issues' of world politics. In summing up what was called 'a tested relationship' it was able to hark back to the statements of the 1926 Imperial Conference. The 1962 edition defined the Commonwealth more narrowly, stressed the organs of consultation rather than its spirit, was more circumspect about parliamentary government and about the sovereign, and substituted 'the values which they hold in common' for a 'generally similar attitude on funda-mental issues'. It quoted from Menzies in 1960 rather than Balfour in 1926, to stress the equality of members and their lack of a powerful organic associa-tion. The emphasis was more cautious and there was much more stress on multiracialism.

A similar trend can be found in official publications for schools, though here the lag is perhaps greater. *The Commonwealth of Nations*, prepared by the COI in 1957, followed the earlier pamphlet fairly closely but gave greater prominence to the sovereign and, like most such publications, tended to blur the distinction between colonies and Commonwealth members. Dudley Barker's *The Commonwealth We Live In* (1960) was vague and hopeful, reflect-ing the euphoria of the early Macmillan years. In contrast, a pamphlet for teachers of 1966, *The Commonwealth in Education*, faced all the contemporary criticisms (including that by 'A Conservative'), and resolved them by showing that the Commonwealth was the easiest part of the world for English children to understand, for obvious reasons, and that international understanding is a prime need. The association itself did not receive the same praise as in the other publications described.

Perhaps the most interesting and unusual reflection of official attitudes is *The Future of the Commonwealth: a British view*, the report (by T. P. Soper) of a conference held at Ditchley in 1963 at the instance of the CRO, at which senior officials were slightly outnumbered by businessmen and academics, although the report was very much that of a group of senior British civil servants concerned to advise on policy. The conference was held soon after de Gaulle's rejection of Britain's first attempt to enter the EEC; its report strikingly com-bined realism about difficulties with conviction that the Commonwealth was still of value to Britain. 'No single suggestion was made that it had, in effect, fulfilled its usefulness and could be discarded'; on the contrary, Britain 'should respond to the challenge by herself showing imagination and courage and by encouraging others to do so too'. The strains on the Commonwealth relation-ship arising from the racial problem, differences over defence, uneven econ-omic progress, and divergent conceptions of democracy were not glossed over.

It was agreed that much of the public attitude towards the Commonwealth in Britain 'revealed an ignorance of current developments and an emotionalism that had ceased to accord with the facts'. Even so, it could be said that its existence had proved a shock absorber for British public opinion. Those who had grown up used to seeing the map painted red and to regard a quarter of the globe as 'our Empire' would have found it harder to adjust to Britain's loss of material power and changed position in the world 'had they not been able to cling to the comforting concept of the Commonwealth', although this might be dangerous if it fostered an exaggerated idea of what Britain could or should do.

The main conclusions of the conference were that, although the Commonwealth was not an international entity, its members did 'share a common frame of mind', and Britain's relations with all other members were valuable; their relations with each other should be further encouraged. Countries retaining membership could play 'a constructive role in helping to solve current world problems' and could also assist developing Commonwealth countries (who would also need help from non-members, especially the US). Commonwealth countries 'should stand by the principles in which they believe'. The principles were elaborated as including the rule of law, personal freedom, tolerance and fair play in the international sphere, and racial equality. The summary of discussion ended with a number of suggestions which foreshadowed much of what was soon to be undertaken by the Commonwealth secretariat.

This sober assessment of circumstances and possibilities, coming when it did, in the lull between applications to the EEC and before the hubbub over Rhodesia, was very much in line with what was being put forward in 1970, when entry into the EEC was almost assured and the hubbub had largely died down. A pamphlet published by the Commonwealth Institute in August 1970 (*The Commonwealth at Work*), which concentrated on the aspects which the Ditchley conference had singled out and which the secretariat was stressing, can be taken as representative of this official mood. Its conclusion was:

> The Commonwealth is only one of the instruments available to governments for raising the living standards of their peoples and fighting racial discrimination, but it is a particularly useful instrument for these purposes. It is, after all, a partnership of peoples equipped, through their long association, with well tried machinery for mutual help and with the will to improve and make good use of it.

This modified, qualified, but essentially practical image was the one which appealed to many British officials and ministers once the stormy period of colonial independence and post-colonial argument was over. It did not require emphasis on British leadership or on too great an alleged community of ideals. Its stress on a network of associations inherited from the past and its recognition that the Commonwealth was only one amongst a number of bodies to which its members belonged were congenial, especially in the circumstances of near-entry into the EEC.

The nationalist-sceptical state of mind which was prevalent in the 1960s (see chs 12 and 15) was mainly a reaction against what those holding it regarded as hypocrisy, and was capable of taking more than one form. A hard-hitting early example, Lord Altrincham's 'Is the Commonwealth a Sham?'[1] of 1960, was the utterance of a disappointed believer who discovered 'that an English-speaking but multiracial Commonwealth, with unity of purpose and clearly defined principles, was just as remote from reality as the federated British Empire of which some idealists used to dream'. The article was an attack on those who attempted to use the Commonwealth to foster the cruder sorts of self-deception in Britain. The Commonwealth 'is only a sham to the extent that its members, Britain in particular, fail to see it for what it is'; yet self-deception was rife and led to frequent miscalculation about the extent to which the rest of the Commonwealth would support Britain. The article contained certain phrases worth rescuing,[2] but it ignored diplomatic advantage, and perhaps threw out the baby with the bathwater.

Later similar articles tended to be more critical in financial and military terms, their object often being to show that Britain gained less and less from the Commonwealth while spending more on it, and needed to readjust its sights towards Europe. Neglecting those which were propagandist or narrowly technical, we may glance at two of a representative kind.

The first, by Hugh Seton-Watson—'Commonwealth, Common Market, Common Sense'—originally appeared in *Encounter* in July 1963.[3] The main theme was Altrincham's, but set in the context of Britain's diminished stature and the unwisdom of failing to distinguish between 'polite relationships and political reality'. 'Britain in 1963 was *not* the centre of a great Empire, or of a great world-wide community of high-minded nations of all colours looking to her for moral leadership.' In fact, Britain's closest connections were with the US and the old dominions, and with Europe next: 'an Atlantic Community is desirable for the Americans and Europeans, but vital for the British'. Help for the l.d.c.s should come in part from Britain but even more from the US and Europe; it was in collaboration with these, not locked up in its own Commonwealth, that Britain could act most effectively.

The second and later article, published by Max Beloff in 1970,[4] is stronger and more detailed, and takes account of the troublesome events of the later

---

[1] *National & English R.*, May 1960.

[2] 'The Commonwealth is a strange phenomenon. It has length and breadth, but very little depth.' 'If the United Nations is the R.A.C., the Commonwealth is Brooks's.' 'The "Commonwealth idea" is no more than ectoplasm: it has never lived in the hearts of ordinary people and there is little chance that it ever will.' 'Any ordinary club which tried to maintain itself in such conditions would very soon be out of business.'

[3] Reprinted in his *Nationalism and communism* (1964).

[4] 'The Commonwealth: can it survive?', originally published in *The Times*; reprinted *Canberra Times*, 2 Sept 1970.

1960s. It argues that, while the Commonwealth has certain advantages, in some respects it is a positive disadvantage to Britain. First, it impedes and discredits Britain's commitment to Europe; second, it is misunderstood in the US, where it engenders suspicion; third, it may prevent closer relationships with individual members, such as Australia and New Zealand; fourth, it is an obstacle to the integration into Britain of Commonwealth immigrants already there, since its existence makes it marginally harder for those people to identify themselves wholly with Britain; lastly, its existence encourages pressure for Britain to take sides in disputes simply because they arise in the Commonwealth (such as the Nigerian civil war), and thereby to exhaust its strength on matters which are not in its own interest. Beloff's view is that the advantages of the Commonwealth could be retained and the disadvantages removed if it were recognized that Britain has valuable though differing relationships with the other members, and that these are best pursued on a bilateral basis, not within the mental confines of the Commonwealth as such.

Each of these three critical articles shows, in varying measure, impatience with an attitude of mind, not confined to a single party, which was prevalent during the earlier years of Macmillan's premiership: the view that the Commonwealth gave Britain material and moral stature, enabling it to speak with more authority in world councils, and that this stature would be diminished unless the Commonwealth remained in being. Essentially, this view is criticized on grounds of unreality. None of the authors questions that Britain has special links with Commonwealth countries, but all doubt whether the Commonwealth is the right means to retain these links, and whether, even if it is, it is still a prime interest of Britain's to preserve them at the expense of other links which may prove more vital. In 1970 the debate rested somewhere between the Beloff position and what had been the received official doctrine, as shown in *The Future of the Commonwealth*.

V

Some conclusions can be drawn from these overlapping and sometimes contradictory images of the Commonwealth.

First, it is clear that the discussion has taken a different turn from what was customary before World War II. The legalism, the question of status, and the schemes for unified policy have no longer occupied people's attention. Instead, they have looked to multiracialism and limited functional co-operation as specific Commonwealth attributes. Gradually the notion of fundamental agreement on world problems has receded, to be replaced by the more fragmentary notion that, in spite of their frequently divergent policies, Commonwealth members share a heritage of institutions and culture, which provides a basis for co-operation.

Again, the relationship of Britain to other members, especially the question whether the Commonwealth still represents a balance of advantage to Britain, has been discussed in more vigorous terms than since the debate about the Empire in the mid-nineteenth century temporarily reduced it in public opinion to a set of millstones round Britain's neck. The upshot has been that in Britain, as in many of the other member states, the Commonwealth has emerged as an instrument of limited but distinct value, engaged in minor but sometimes vital enterprises (especially for the smaller members), and especially suited to co-operation in the educational and professional fields.

Thirdly, at each stage of its development, and in respect of nearly all the images of it which men have constructed (except the most sceptical), the Commonwealth has engaged loyalty and idealism in those who had to do with its operation—partly because of its past, partly because of the promise it seemed to hold for the future. One sees Hancock's triad, variously interpreted, as still significant to many people—although the history of actual Commonwealth relations shows how elastic each of its elements has been, and how easily honest men could differ about what it meant in terms of policy. Along with the hopes of high purpose, in fact, has generally gone a rueful, sometimes resentful, awareness of how close at hand political realities were, and how intractable were the problems of relationship, especially in the racial sphere.

No one has ever effectively pinned down the relationship between ideas and action in politics, between the images men construct of the institutions and aims with which they are concerned, and the results which follow from the clash of political forces. Figgis tried to hold the balance in this argument: 'If ideas in politics more than elsewhere are the children of practical needs, none the less is it true, that the actual world is the result of men's thoughts. The existing arrangement of political forces is dependent at least as much upon ideas, as it is upon men's perception of their interests.'[1] Yet men's perceptions of their interests are themselves ideas, since 'practical needs', when formulated in general terms, inevitably require labels which are ideational in character. In the case of the Commonwealth, which grew sometimes imperceptibly and sometimes in a series of jerks out of the British Empire, the images of the past and those of the present have often collided to produce distortions of reality, as well as rationalizations to fit current crises.

The Commonwealth secretary-general robustly maintained in 1967 that there were several false images of the Commonwealth and one proper one.[2] The first false image was the 'kith and kin' one, which proved inadequate for Canada, a country which played a pivotal role in developing the modern Commonwealth. The second was the image 'of the Commonwealth as a sort of ghost or dilution of empire, something to curtsey to'. The third was of it 'as a surrogate, a sort of placebo, for a vanished empire'. A fourth was of it as serving 'to even out the scales of population and power, and to give Britain a

---

[1] J. N. Figgis, *Studies of political thought from Gerson to Grotius* (Cambridge, 1923), p. 1.
[2] Arnold Smith, *Canada and the Commonwealth* (1967), pp. 15–17.

voice as an equal member of the big three world powers in an otherwise hier-archical world of subordinates'. The proper and true image was of the Commonwealth as an instrument 'for all its members to help shape the future'. It had always been 'the product of hard-headed forward-looking calculation' and not 'an automatic product of the dissolution of empire', as many countries formerly ruled by Britain—like Burma, Egypt, Iraq, and the Sudan—had not become members of the Commonwealth. 'Those who did, did so because they were concerned with the future and saw how the . . . association could be constructively used.'

These hard-headed calculations about the future are not merely selfish, any more than Canadian interests in our formative years of concern for the Commonwealth were merely selfish. At this level, idealistic vision for humanity and long-term interest can coincide. The leaders of many National Liberation movements, the fathers of countries, are often, I have found, and it is not really surprising, men of unusual vision, moral courage, and spiritual force.

Perhaps, then, the triad was not so much damaged by the stresses of the 1960s as it seemed to be at the time. Arnold Smith's 'proper' image is not heavily British, but it agrees with much British thinking at the end of the period, about the Commonwealth as one, but only one, of the instruments of policy available to its members. The use of that instrument would still depend, in part, upon the underlying principles which Commonwealth leaders thought applied to it.

VI

The experience of three bodies established long before our period began, which had to adapt to the expansion of the Commonwealth and the disputes within it, especially between Britain and the newer members, is instructive.

The Commonwealth Institute, founded as the Imperial Institute in South Kensington in 1887, was originally a private foundation under royal charter, but in 1902 was vested in the Board of Trade. It was then largely concerned with trade and scientific questions, especially in regard to colonial products. It became increasingly somnolent until the Tweedsmuir Committee, in 1952, recommended a complete reconstitution and its greater use in educational work. Although the Institute remained governmental, it was given an inde-pendent board of governors on which each Commonwealth member was represented. In 1957, by a highly symbolic decision of the Macmillan govern-ment, it was given its present name and a new building; the Commonwealth Institute Act of 1958 provided both. A brilliant new structure arose in another part of Kensington. Although Britain was responsible for building, furnishing, and staffing, each Commonwealth government (and several colonial govern-ments such as Hong Kong) was persuaded to mount a special exhibit illus-trating life in its own country. The formal responsibility for the Institute was transferred from the Ministry of Education to the FCO, but its Common-wealth character was emphasized by a swelling board of high commissioners. It was increasingly used by schools and became one of the most popular museums in London, as well as acting as something of a social centre.

Its undoubted success was due to change, just in time, from its outdated name and building; to the fact that money was available because 'Common-wealth' was then a word of power; to a dynamic staff and co-operation from many Commonwealth governments in what was plainly a non-political enter-prise; to constant adjustment to the new Commonwealth; and to a ready-made clientele in British schoolchildren (not only in London, but also in Scotland, a branch being established in Edinburgh in 1956). It was not affected by the disputes between Commonwealth members.[1]

Somewhat similar success was enjoyed by the Commonwealth Parlia-mentary Association. Founded as the Empire Parliamentary Association in 1911, it had begun with six branches in Britain and the Dominions, and had, by the end of the 1960s, over ninety branches in Commonwealth legislatures. The number is so large because it included the States of Australia, India, and Malaysia, the Canadian Provinces, and legislatures in non-self-governing areas. Only in Nigeria, Pakistan, Lesotho, and Uganda were its branches in abeyance in 1970–1.[2] The Association's activities increased with the enlarge-ment of the Commonwealth, although in many cases the legislatures in question had already been members before their countries gained independence. Its name had been changed in 1948. From 1961 onwards its formerly biennial conferences were held annually, each time in a different Commonwealth capital. These were attended by delegations from a great many countries, representing oppositions as well as governments, and strenuously debated a variety of matters, including economic affairs, migration, and defence. It was traditional not to take votes. The General Council headquarters in London gave help to visiting parliamentarians, organized a variety of conferences, published *The Parliamentarian* (formerly *Journal of the Parliaments of the Commonwealth*), and encouraged the study and discussion of parliamentary procedure and the place of parliaments in modern government. As we have seen (ch. 10), Britain was sometimes strongly criticized at the Association's conferences, but this seems neither to have discouraged British support for it nor to have prevented continued criticism.

There were several reasons for the CPA's continued success. Most politi-cians like to travel, and all parliaments provide money for them to do so. Participants met on a personal basis (often for a short tour beforehand of the country in which a conference was being held), and made friendships of an

---

[1] Material on the Institute is from its annual reports, its pamphlets, and personal dis-cussions.

[2] *Year Book of the Commonwealth, 1972*, p. 664. Details are from this source, the Associa-tion's publications, and personal discussions.

enduring kind. The CPA's officers were constantly looking for ways of stressing the interests which parliamentarians had in common, and had a fertile field in the minutiae of parliamentary procedure. The British heritage of all Commonwealth parliaments is so obvious that it provides a network of association in its own right; and those running the CPA were careful to ensure that control of it was effectively multilateral, and not preserved for the British.

The third body, the Royal Commonwealth Society, was founded in 1868 as the Royal Colonial Institute; it changed its name to Royal Empire Society in 1928 and to the present form in 1964. The comparatively late change in both cases was perhaps symptomatic of its character: it was essentially a meeting-place for colonial officials and for imperially-minded people from the old dominions, especially from Australia, New Zealand, and South Africa. It found it much more difficult to adjust to change in the 1950s and 1960s than had the other two bodies.[1] It was non-governmental and had no public funds, although its building in London and its splendid library were in constant use by those wishing to study or publicize the Commonwealth. Its traditional connection with, and dependence upon, the old dominions was something of a handicap: although its more forward-looking members wanted it to extend its activities in respect of India and the new African states, it was difficult to do so because change was resisted, especially in Australia. It was a critical experience for the Society when South Africa left the Commonwealth in 1961, and the Rhodesia question proved nearly as difficult. Although some zealous members wanted rapid change, the membership was ageing and was not being replaced in sufficient numbers, since colonial officials were a dying race and business people with connections in the newer parts of the Commonwealth did not have the same attachment to the Society as their predecessors.

So firmly rooted in an earlier period, the Royal Commonwealth Society could not respond to the enlargement of the Commonwealth. It had been founded and maintained, in terms of 'kith and kin'; and, whatever one may think of Arnold Smith's description of various images of the Commonwealth, by 1969 that image certainly was false.

[1] See Trevor R. Reese, *The history of the Royal Commonwealth Society 1868–1968* (1968), chs 14, 15, & 16.

PART VII

CHAPTER 23

REVIEW

L OOKING back to what I described in Chapter 2 as the major themes in the evolution of the Commonwealth after 1953, we can now see how significant each of these was in its transformation.

Throughout the 1950s and 1960s a more complex world, with increasing responsibilities in both politics and economics, had been encountered by each former colony as it became independent, and this made more intricate the external relations of the old dominions and the Asian members which had gained their independence immediately after World War II. The ending of the Cold War had complicated matters still further: alignment and non-alignment had both lost significance by 1969, and the Commonwealth had far less unity of approach at the end of the period than at the beginning, despite the protestations of common principles made by its leaders. The Rhodesian issue above all had shown the gulf there could be between members' national interests; so had turmoil in the Indian subcontinent; so had the break-up of the sterling area. There had been a significant growth in new Commonwealth machinery, especially in the creation of the secretariat, but it had been greeted more warmly by the smaller and newer members than by the bigger and older ones. All this led to considerable change in British opinion about the value and purpose of the Commonwealth, and specifically about its racial implications. These implications, while relatively easy to follow in the case of apartheid, were more difficult to accept in respect of Commonwealth immigration, the future of Rhodesia, and the sale of arms to South Africa.

Thus in 1969 the Commonwealth was bigger, looser, more diffuse in many ways though more organized in others, yet more self-conscious (though not necessarily nearer to unanimity) about its principles. It had changed, but it also had continuity. How can we effectively define it, especially in relation to other international bodies?

I

Unfortunately, contemporary study of international organizations does not help us much. Very much the preserve of American scholars, it has produced little or nothing about the Commonwealth or bodies which might be compared with it.[1] During the period covered in this book, studies of international

---

[1] Exception should be made of the incisive treatment of earlier myths about the Commonwealth by Inis L. Claude, Jr., *Swords into plowshares* (1959), pp. 116–20.

organization tended to be preoccupied with four main topics: the UN and its agencies; alliances; the process of integration, or movement towards a 'community' of existing states, notably in Europe; and regional organization, which might involve either alliance or integration or both. None of these is much use in considering the Commonwealth. The UN and its agencies operate in a different manner and against a different background. Alliances provide a different purpose and framework. Regional bodies demand geographical propinquity. Above all, the process of integration, to which most attention has been given, is concerned with states drawing closer to one another and acquiring more commitments, whereas the members of the Commonwealth have been moving in the other direction.[1]

Perhaps the nearest that contemporary theory can offer as a category into which the Commonwealth might fit is that of the 'pluralistic security-community' devised by Karl Deutsch and his colleagues.[2] This is a community in which the legal independence of separate governments is maintained, but in which there is real assurance that the members will not fight each other physically. The US and Canada are said to constitute such a community. However, while the conditions laid down can be regarded as applying to certain groups of states within the Commonwealth—Britain, Australia, New Zealand, and Canada, perhaps—they cannot be made to apply to all. While we recognize that the notion of 'community' is appropriate in some ways to the members of the Commonwealth, especially in regard to those networks of association considered in Part V—though even in relation to these we must be careful not to read too much into transactions which may have no lasting effect[3]—it is clear that the writers on integration have little to offer us in discussing the nature of the Commonwealth. It is not that sort of association.

Those seeking to classify international bodies usually ask first whether they are universal or sectional in membership; if sectional, where their members come from; what kinds of constitution they have; and, most important, what functions they perform. The first three of these questions are easy to answer about the Commonwealth. It is not universal in membership, but sectional. It does not have a constitution, but does have a certain amount of machinery and has even been said to constitute a system, as we saw in Chapters 17 and 18. Its functions, however, require rather more attention and may be the subject of dispute.

---

[1] See Stanley Hoffmann, 'Discord in community', *Int. Org.*, Summer 1963, esp. p. 527, for a good discussion of the differences between these two processes, and the kinds of study they require.

[2] Karl Deutsch & others, *Political community and the North Atlantic area* (1957), pp. 5–7 & 65 ff.

[3] See Bruce M. Russett, 'Transactions, community and international political integration', *J. Common Market Stud.*, Mar 1971, which also has the advantage of distinguishing between the meanings ascribed to 'community' and 'integration' by a number of leading writers on the subject.

II

The Commonwealth, as an organized political unit, seems to me to have performed three separate functions for its overseas members—the former dominions and dependencies—in the 1950s and 1960s. These were not equally performed for each, and were not mutually exclusive.

The first was simply that of something to belong to. In contrast with the old dominions before World War II, which belonged to the League of Nations and little else except the ILO and highly technical bodies such as the Universal Postal Union, members of the Commonwealth in 1969 could belong to 41 bodies of the UN and its specialized agencies, not to speak of a variety of regional bodies and alliances. Commonwealth members varied considerably in their membership of the 41; for example, India belonged to 34, Australia to 28, Ghana to 22, Jamaica to 19, Malta to 11, and the Gambia to 7.[1] These represented deliberate choices, based on a state's sense of its needs and of the effects on others important to it of its decision to join or not.

Membership of the Commonwealth was likewise a matter of deliberate choice, but not to the same extent: for most members it had been as natural as joining the UN itself, an act taken almost automatically by those in a position to do so. The fewer non-Commonwealth bodies states belonged to, the more important the Commonwealth might seem to them as a means of achieving national ends. The smaller members, able to afford membership of relatively few bodies and to establish diplomatic missions in only a few foreign capitals, presumably gave a high priority to the Commonwealth on this account. But it is likely that for the foreign offices of many of the members, a meeting of Commonwealth prime ministers was comparable to a session of the UN General Assembly, a Seato, Anzus, or Asean conference, or the annual OAU conference. Any uniqueness which the Commonwealth had originally been able to claim was probably diminished by this plethora of diplomatic assignments. Moreover, tactics appropriate to other bodies were readily employed in the Commonwealth, as we have seen, in spite of the feeling of older members that the uniqueness of the Commonwealth required certain forms to be maintained. By the end of the period, the Commonwealth probably looked to most member governments more like any other international body than it had at the beginning.

The second function was that of carrying on unfinished business, especially in the official sphere. This applied in particular to the many states which became independent in the 1960s. The former British presence had left behind a great many connections which could not be snapped without loss. Some of these were directly economic (such as the Commonwealth Sugar Agreement and the financial settlements made at independence), while others were military (including the bases in Cyprus, Malta, and Singapore), and others again

[1] *Year Book of the Commonwealth 1969* (1969), pp. 39–42.

educational, cultural, and administrative. For each colony gaining independence, there was bound to be an interval or breathing-space in which former
arrangements were adjusted to the new condition of sovereignty, and such
bodies as armies, central banks, universities, and civil services took on a new
look. It could be argued that Britain would probably have helped ex-colonies
during this interval even if they had not decided to join the Commonwealth;
but the spirit of the time, on both sides, was in favour of membership, and
independence had been predicated on that ground, even if only tacitly. In
addition, the kinds of connection to which we drew attention in Chapter 21,
were influences favouring Commonwealth membership: being themselves
unfinished business, they emphasized the other ways in which a continued
connection with Britain might be necessary and desirable. How long the
breathing-space would be was incalculable, since it depended so much upon
conditions in each country. The pace of change towards a new state of things
in which British norms would no longer be dominant varied with the impact
these norms had had in the past, and with the energy which governments
brought to the task of changing attitudes and institutions. Even if the pace was
rapid, the Commonwealth might still be accommodated within the country's
diplomatic armoury, as an instrument for forwarding policies and gaining
benefits.

The third function was that of serving as a link with history, a tribute to
continuity. Again, its importance varied from member to member. For those
which had very close ties with Britain in blood and sentiment the sense of
continuity was considerable. In Australia, New Zealand, Canada to a lesser
degree, Trinidad, Jamaica, Barbados, Fiji, and some of the smaller African
members such as Sierra Leone, imperial language and symbols were often
still in force: in some cases knighthoods, the Queen's portrait on the wall and
on some of the coins, and the sense of pride in continuing with a parliamentary
system all enabled the Commonwealth to be seen as the flowering of an
imperial tradition. Such attitudes did not prevent members from taking
positions different from the British or from entering into associations of a
highly unBritish character. Rather, they helped to ease the movement towards
full independence by enabling backward-looking rhetoric at one level of public
life to be combined with calculation of national advantage at another.

This third function was obviously of diminishing importance. It was
unfinished business which, in most cases, would be finished before long. The
'frontier between reality and nothingness' to which Nicholas Mansergh thought
the flexibility of Commonwealth relations might be leading the members, was
being neared by several at the end of the 1960s and may well have been
passed by some. Those which continued with imperial symbols would reach it
later than those which had eagerly embraced the symbols of total independence, but even for these, 'meaningful Commonwealth existence' might well
lose much of its reality.

The functions performed by the Commonwealth for Britain are of cardinal importance in assessing its changing character. The nearer Britain approached that frontier, the less vitality the Commonwealth would probably display, since British effort and support had given it most vigour in the past. For British governments the Commonwealth had performed a joint function. It had retained many links of consequence with former colonies, including financial and economic links, and in the process comforted the British public with the thought that the Empire was not breaking up but growing up; moreover the Commonwealth had preserved at least the appearance of British power in the world. Both functions were especially valuable in the 1950s. In the words of *The Economist* of 7 April 1956:

> For Britain, the Commonwealth is a gentle let-down, a featherbed of fine phrases and outward forms, to ease the psychological impact of the loss—now approaching its last phase—of a powerful Empire. Yet the phrases and the forms can still symbolise something positive and valuable that can persist. The new ways of parting friends has prolonged Britain's influence in a way Holland might envy and France may soon sadly miss. It has given a short respite in which the adjustment can be made to the real loss of power, the consequences of which emerge nakedly from time to time, as, for example, at Abadan. It has preserved the friendship of former dependencies. And it has kept up Britain's stock in America, though at times the consequences of Britain's real loss of power have dismayed Americans.

The two functions were much less significant in the latter half of the 1960s. The first was reduced by each new case of decolonization, which brought nearer the time when Britain would have no more colonial problems to solve. It was reduced even more by the Rhodesian affair, in which the Commonwealth appeared to many British people, especially in the government, to be a positive handicap in smoothing the decolonization process. The second, while clearly of much importance to Eden, Macmillan, and Douglas-Home, and to Wilson in his early years as prime minister, had been weakened appreciably by the end of the 1960s, when participation in the Europe of the Six had become a more urgent objective of British policy than the attempt to represent Britain as a major power in its own right.

In the 1950s and early 1960s the prime function of the Commonwealth, so far as British governments were concerned, appears to have been to bolster British power vis-à-vis the US in order to prolong the 'special relationship' of World War II. We have seen how Macmillan, following Eden's example, strove to preserve this situation, yet was aware of the contradictions which it involved in the light of Britain's manifestly reduced strength. We have seen too how Wilson, playing from an even weaker hand, tried to do the same in connection with US intervention in Vietnam.

The fact of the matter, discerned by *The Economist* in 1956 but unheeded by British governments at the political level until much later, was that Britain no longer qualified for the 'top table' of major world powers. Bringing in the Commonwealth to weight the scales was no way of evading this situation, since most members were unsympathetic towards the objectives which British governments were seeking in the 1960s, different though the situation had been in the preceding decade. By the end of the 1960s it had become received doctrine amongst British leaders that the time to seek an independent position at the 'top table' was past, and that British influence would be most effective if exerted as part of a 'Europe' in which Britain's tradition of imperial wisdom was given its due weight. There was still the need to exercise influence upon the US, but this was to be concerted, both economically and politically, with West Germany, France, and the other states of Western Europe, most obviously through membership of the EEC but also in arrangements about currency and defence. The earlier British effort to combine Europeanism in Nato with a specific British effort in currency, trade, investment, migration, and military activity east of Suez was, by the advent of the Heath government in 1970, already declining.

In such a situation the attractions of the Commonwealth understandably waned, especially when they were further reduced by the disturbance of spirit caused in Britain by the issues of Commonwealth immigration and Rhodesia. Britain's abandonment of the system of parallel diplomacy, undertaken (as we saw in ch. 17) with little or no protest in either Britain itself or the overseas members, was a sign that a 'Commonwealth system' was no longer needed to serve British interests. The importance of the Commonwealth countries had waned in comparison with that accorded the European countries. In any case, the Commonwealth was no longer required as a make-weight to increase British importance in the eyes of Washington, since British governments were no longer trying, with the zest of past years, to impress the US with power which Britain did not possess.

Hedley Bull pointed out in 1959 that the Commonwealth's continued existence had constantly been preferred to its serving any special purpose or taking any particular form:

It has been successively judged more important that the Commonwealth should persist unimpaired than that it should be based on the indivisibility of the Crown, than that it should have a common strategy, than that its members should all be parliamentary democracies, than that none of them should practise racial discrimination, than that they should have any distinctive ideals beyond the truisms that are the stock-in-trade of all governments. So far is the Commonwealth from being an association which has consistently pursued any particular purpose that those who write about it often appear, *post hoc*, to cast about for purposes which would provide it with a *raison d'etre*: thus its mission has been discovered to be to provide a prop to the League of Nations, to set an example in race relations, to develop backward countries, to undertake an experiment in international co-operation, to form the nucleus of a Third Force.[1]

Such an account of the diplomatic purposes served by the Commonwealth underlines its significance for Britain, since all these justifications and rationalizations were largely British in origin, put forward when they were most helpful to British policy and opinion. This chameleon-like variation in the purposes which the Commonwealth was supposed to serve was not, of course, a denial of the much more stable connections between peoples in the Commonwealth, which have been described in Part VI. Rather it was variation on the theme of a changeable British attitude towards the Commonwealth, the British being accustomed to regard the body as essentially theirs to order as seemed best for them and the other members—most of which had been quite willing, in the 1950s and sometimes later, for this kind of management to take place. The decisive changes, from 1960 onwards, were that first the newer members turned the machinery of management against Britain over African issues, and then that Britain itself began to lose both faith in, and need for, the Commonwealth as an essential instrument of external policy.

In effect, by 1969 or soon afterwards those who in Britain thought primarily of the Commonwealth as such an instrument had reached Mansergh's frontier and were pushing beyond it. The Commonwealth was still an element in policy, but not an essential or even very useful one, as it had seemed earlier. There might in future be even closer relations with some members on a bilateral basis, freed from the constraints of treating all members equally: immigration and currency were spheres in which this might be fruitfully applied, as it had been applied earlier in military co-operation and economic aid. But there would not be a reversion to the importance which Macmillan, Douglas-Home, and Wilson had assigned to the preservation of the Commonwealth.

IV

Perhaps the Commonwealth is hard to classify in terms of international theory because it has increasingly become a mirror or microcosm of the international system as a whole. True, it does not include any communist state, but otherwise it has approximated more and more to the divisions normally found in world politics. In particular, what has come to be called the 'North–South' division, between rich and poor countries, has been a feature of the Commonwealth since 1947 and especially since the onset of African independence. Whereas the earlier Commonwealth could be regarded as a specifically 'British group' from the 1920s to the end of World War II (and was usually so regarded, for example, by the US Department of State), the appearance first of Indian non-alignment and then of the African members' deliberate use of the Commonwealth as a reinforcement to their efforts at the

[1] In *World Politics*, July 1959, p. 582.

UN meant that British leadership was no longer feasible on major issues and that former talk of 'unity' was quite inapplicable.

In this sense, one can view the attrition of Commonwealth bonds as part of the attrition of consensus in the international community, especially since that community lost its traditional Eurocentric character and became subject to super-power tensions and the demands of the Third World located in Asia, Africa, and Latin America. Europe had of course had its own divisions; so had the 'old Commonwealth' of the 1920s and 1930s. But they were family divisions of a kind different from those which we have seen in the Commonwealth of the 1950s and 1960s, and which were essentially disputes between old and new states. In this respect, Suez was a watershed.

Naturally, the divisions did not express themselves in exactly the same way within the Commonwealth as in the whole community of states. In part, this was because some elements were missing: for example, neither the US nor the Soviet Union was actually present in the Commonwealth context, although their friends sometimes were, especially friends of the US. The main reason, however, lay in the fact that the Commonwealth debate was confined to countries which shared something of a common frame of reference, derived largely from British sources. The members of the Commonwealth never ceased to communicate with one another, even at the times of least consensus over Suez, South Africa, and Rhodesia. The network between them was strained but did not break. This did not mean that they were in a state of 'unity' or were even trying to achieve one. It meant rather that they were speaking something of a common political language, in spite of the close ties of interest which they had outside the Commonwealth—some with the US, some with other African or Asian states, some with Arab or communist states. This language was imperfect and often capable of misconstruction, but it gave the members of the Commonwealth an opportunity to talk.

In a book published in 1958, I tried to find an adequate description of the Commonwealth as it was then.[1] I called it a 'concert of convenience', concert conveying the idea of agreement, though no greater agreement than Commonwealth members had managed to attain, and convenience being what held the Commonwealth together: members had no need to consult anything but their own convenience; they found it convenient to be in, convenient not to be out. Some reviewers accepted this description as adequate for the main outlines of the highly flexible Commonwealth of the time but said that it did not allow for the element of genuine co-operation, of a common habit of mind, which was characteristic of members in their relationships and joint activities. Taking into account what happened in the 1960s, it seems to me that the description will still suffice, but that it needs some addition in terms of the 'lattice-work' of co-operation which grew in that decade, especially after the establishment of the secretariat and the addition of a considerable number of small, poor

[1] *The Commonwealth in the world*, p. 275.

members. Convenience was still the keynote of Commonwealth diplomacy: major unified effort was still absent, and the foreign policies of members directed the tactics they followed and the decisions they reached at the Commonwealth level. To this had been added, however, a more pressing need on the part of the smaller members, and some further acceptance of responsibility by the bigger—though not in any exclusive sense, and not with binding obligation. For most members the Commonwealth was a convenience, for some a necessity.

To provide something to belong to, to deal with unfinished colonial business which in some cases might never end, and to serve as a link with history, especially in the use of a common political language, were functions which, in varying degree, gave the Commonwealth a meaning. With the passage of time, its symbolic and diplomatic importance had declined for Britain. It was still useful to the overseas members' diplomacy, and had gained, in the 1960s, special significance through the help it could muster for their smaller confrères. In the future, it would probably become looser still, its residual significance being found increasingly in cultural and non-political terms, these being the aspects of the relationship least susceptible to attrition.

In recognizing that the diplomatic functions of the Commonwealth were diminishing while its cultural functions were increasing in importance, one is going beyond the immediately political, and acknowledging that the Commonwealth was an association of peoples as well as of governments. All who shared in the priceless gift of the English language, and in what it embodied, had received something more than political advantage or diplomatic convenience. As we saw in Chapter 21, they had inherited a variety of connections which, though sometimes productive of hostility as well as agreement, provided something beyond politics. Affected by politics, the connections were not directly dependent on it. Rather, their life had an independence of its own, based upon ideas and practices which governments might disown but people could still share.

The Commonwealth of the 1970s would be one in which bodies such as the secretariat and the Foundation strove to reinforce the non-political relations which drew Commonwealth members together. They would do so in full realization of political realities and through political means, since governments were the bodies through which co-operation would most obviously and readily be arranged; but they would often be building on foundations laid before Commonwealth members had become independent. It would be an irony, but a reasonable and humane irony, if the Commonwealth and la Francophonie existed amicably side by side as primarily cultural bodies flourishing on what had been taught in the schools of empire.

SELECT BIBLIOGRAPHY

Note: This is a list of works cited in footnotes; it does not pretend to cover the whole ground, especially in relation to official publications and newspapers.

Special mention should be made of two sources which have been used extensively. The first is Nicholas Mansergh's *Documents and Speeches on Commonwealth Affairs 1952–62*, published for Chatham House in 1963. Wherever possible, I have used this rather than original documents, because of its direct relevance to this *Survey*. The second is the publication of the British Central Office of Information, under the successive names of *Commonwealth Survey*, then (from January 1967) *Survey of British Commonwealth Affairs*, and then (from January 1971) *Survey of Current Affairs*. It appeared fortnightly until 1971, when it became monthly. The publications on foreign affairs of the Australian, Canadian, and New Zealand governments—*Current Notes on International Affairs* (Canberra), *External Affairs* (Ottawa), and *External Affairs Review* (Wellington)—have also proved consistently helpful.

A. *British Command Papers*

Cmd 8753. Southern Rhodesia, Northern Rhodesia and Nyasaland: report by the conference on federation. 1953.

Cmd 8754. Southern Rhodesia, Northern Rhodesia and Nyasaland: the federal scheme. 1953.

Statements on Defence: Cmd 8768, 1953; Cmd 9075, 1954; Cmd 9391, 1955; Cmd 9691, 1956. (See also Cmnds 1639 & 2270 below).

Cmnd 124. Defence: outline of future policy. 1957.

Cmnd 237. The United Kingdom's role in Commonwealth development. 1957.

Cmnd 363. Report on defence. 1958.

Cmnd 814. Report of the Nyasaland Commission of Inquiry. 1959.

Cmnd 1148. Report of the Advisory Commission on the Review of the Constitution of Rhodesia and Nyasaland. 1960.

Cmnd 1291. Report of the Southern Rhodesia Constitutional Conference. 1961.

Cmnd 1400. Southern Rhodesia constitution: Part II—detailed provisions. 1961.

Cmnd 1449. Commonwealth consultations on Britain's relations with the European Economic Community. 1961.

Cmnd 1565. The United Kingdom and the European Economic Community. 1961.

Cmnd 1639. Statement on defence: the next five years. 1962.

Cmnd 1805. The United Kingdom and the European Economic Community. 1962.

Cmnd 1836. Commonwealth Prime Ministers' Meeting: final communiqué. 1962.

Cmnd 1948. The Federation of Rhodesia and Nyasaland. 1963.

Cmnd 2073. Southern Rhodesia: correspondence between HM Government and the Government of Southern Rhodesia, April–June 1963. 1963.

Cmnd 2093. Report of the Central Africa Conference. 1963.

Cmnd 2147. Aid to developing countries. 1963.

Cmnd 2270. Statement on defence. 1964.

Cmnd 2276. Report of the Committee on British Representational Services Overseas. 1964.

Cmnd 2441. Commonwealth Prime Ministers' Meeting 1964: final communiqué. 1964.

Cmnd 2592. Statement on the defence estimates. 1965.

Cmnd 2713. Commonwealth Prime Ministers' Meeting 1965: agreed memorandum on the Commonwealth secretariat. July 1965.

Cmnd 2714. Commonwealth Prime Ministers' Meeting 1965: agreed memorandum on the Commonwealth Foundation. 1965.

Cmnd 2739. Immigration from the Commonwealth. 1965.

Cmnd 2807. Southern Rhodesia: documents relating to the negotiations between the United Kingdom and Southern Rhodesian Governments November 1963–November 1965. 1965.

Cmnd 2834. Documents relating to British involvement in the Indo-China conflict 1945–65. 1965.

Cmnd 2890. Commonwealth Prime Ministers' Meeting in Lagos 1966: final communiqueé. 1966.

Cmnd 3115. Commonwealth Prime Ministers' Meeting in London 1966: final communiqué. 1966.

Cmnd 3159. Rhodesia: proposals for a settlement 1966. 1966.

Cmnd 3171. Rhodesia: documents relating to proposals for a settlement 1966. 1966.

Cmnd 3417. The brain drain. 1967.

Cmnd 3547. Commonwealth telecommunications organisation. 1968.

Cmnd 3787. The Basle facility and the sterling area. 1968.

Cmnd 3793. Rhodesia: report on the discussion held on board HMS *Fearless* October 1968. 1968.

Cmnd 3878. Report of the observer team to Nigeria. 1969.

Cmnd 3919. Commonwealth Prime Ministers' Meeting in London 7–15 January 1969: final communiqué. 1969.

Cmnd 4065. Rhodesia: report on exchanges with the regime since the talks held in Salisbury in November 1968. 1969.

Cmnd 4107. Report of the Review Committee on Overseas Representation 1968–9. 1969.

Cmnd 4589. Legal obligations of HM Government arising out of the Simonstown Agreements. 1971.

Cmnd 4715. The United Kingdom and the European Communities. 1971.

Cmnd. 4835. Rhodesia: proposals for a settlement. 1971.

Cmnd 4964. Rhodesia: report of the Commission on Rhodesian Opinion under the chairmanship of the Right Honourable the Lord Pearce. 1972.

B. *Books and Monographs*

Abraham, W. E. *The mind of Africa*. London, 1962.

Abrahams, Peter. *A wreath for Udomo*. London, 1956.

Adu, A. L. *The civil service in new African states*. London, 1965.

Alexander, H. T. *African tightrope: my two years as Nkrumah's chief of staff*. London, 1965.

Allen, Richard. *Malaysia: prospect and retrospect*. London, 1968.

Alport, Lord. *The sudden assignment: being a record of service in Central Africa during the last controversial years of the Federation of Rhodesia and Nyasaland 1961–3*. London, 1965.

Arikpo, Okei. *The development of modern Nigeria*. Harmondsworth, 1967.

Arnold, Guy. *Towards peace and a multiracial Commonwealth*. London, 1964.

—— *Economic co-operation in the Commonwealth*. Oxford, 1967.

Ashby, Eric. *Community of universities: an informal portrait of the Association of Universities of the British Commonwealth 1913–63*. Cambridge 1963.

—— *African universities and Western tradition*. London, 1964.

Austin, Dennis. *Britain and South Africa*. London, 1966.

Ayub Khan, Mohammad. *Friends not masters: a political autobiography*. London, 1967.

Baago, K. *A history of the National Christian Council of India 1914–64*. Nagpur, 1965.

Ball, George W. *The discipline of power*. London, 1968.

Barber, James. *Rhodesia: the road to rebellion*. London, 1967.

Bareau, Paul. *The sterling area: what it is and how it works*. London, 1950.

Barker, Dudley. *The Commonwealth we live in*. London, 1960.

Barnes, William Gorell. *Europe and the developing world: association under part IV of the treaty of Rome*. London, 1967.

Beaton, Leonard, & others. *No tame or minor role*. London, 1963.

Beloff, Max. *Imperial sunset*, i: *Britain's liberal empire 1897–1921*. London, 1969.

Beloff, Nora. *The General says no: Britain's exclusion from Europe*. Harmondsworth, 1963.

Bilgrami, Asghar H. *Britain, the Commonwealth and the European union issue*. Ambilly-Annemasse, 1961.

Bing, Geoffrey. *Reap the whirlwind*. London, 1968.

Birkenhead, Earl of. *The Prof in two worlds: the official life of Professor F. A. Lindemann, Viscount Cherwell*. London, 1961.

Birkenhead, Lord. *Walter Monckton*. London, 1969.

Blood, Sir Hilary. *The smaller territories: problems and future*. London, 1958.

Blundell, Michael. *So rough a wind*. London, 1964.

Boyce, Peter. *Malaysia and Singapore in international diplomacy: documents and commentaries*. Sydney, 1968.

Boyd, Andrew. *Fifteen men on a powder keg: a history of the UN Security Council*. London, 1971.

Brandon, Henry. *Anatomy of error: the secret history of the Vietnam war*. London, 1970.

Branyan, Robert L. & Lawrence H. Larsen. *The Eisenhower administration 1953–61*. New York, 1971. 2 vols.

Brecher, Michael. *India and world politics: Krishna Menon's view of the world*. London, 1968.

Bretton, Henry L. *The rise and fall of Kwame Nkrumah*. New York, 1966.

Brittan, Leon & others. *A smaller stage: Britain's place in the world*. London, 1965.

Brown, Bruce & others. *New Zealand and Australia: foreign policy in the 1970s*. Wellington, 1970.

Brown, George. *In my way: the political memoirs of Lord George-Brown*. London, 1971.

Brown, Neville. *Arms without empire: British defence in the modern world*. Harmondsworth, 1967.

Buchan, Alastair. 'Commonwealth military relations', in W. B. Hamilton & others, eds. *A decade of the Commonwealth 1955–64*. Durham, NC, 1966, pp. 194–207.

Burgess, Anthony. *The long day wanes: a Malayan trilogy*. (*Time for a tiger, The enemy in the blanket*, and *Beds in the east*.) New York, 1966.

Butler, Lord. *The art of the possible: memoirs*. London, 1971.

Butterwick, Michael & Edmund Neville Rolfe. *Food, farming and the Common Market*. London, 1968.

Cairncross, A. K. *Home and foreign investment 1870–1913*. Cambridge, 1953.

Calvocoressi, Peter. *South Africa and world opinion*. London, 1961.

Camps, Miriam. *Britain and the European Community 1955–63*. London, 1964.

—— *What kind of Europe? The Community since de Gaulle's veto*. London, 1965.

Canada, Dept of External Affairs. *Foreign policy for Canadians*. Ottawa, 1970.

Carrington, C. E. *The Commonwealth Relations Conference 1959*. London, 1959.

—— *The Commonwealth in Africa: report of an unofficial study conference held at Lagos, Nigeria, 8–16 January 1962*. London, 1962.

Carr-Saunders, A. M. *New universities overseas*. London, 1961.

Casey, Lord. *The future of the Commonwealth*. London, 1963.

Choudhury, G. W. *Pakistan's relations with India 1947–66*. London, 1968.

Clarkson, Stephen, ed. *An independent foreign policy for Canada?* Toronto, 1968.

Claude, Inis L. *Swords into plowshares: the problems and progress of international organization*. 2nd ed. New York, 1959.

Clegg, Edward. *Race and politics: partnership in the Federation of Rhodesia and Nyasaland*. London, 1960.

Cohen, Andrew. *British policy in changing Africa*. London, 1959.

Commonwealth Parliamentary Association, General Council. *Report of proceedings of 11th Commonwealth Parliamentary Conference held in Wellington December 1965*. London, 1966.

—— *12th Commonwealth Parliamentary Conference, Ottawa, Canada, 28 September–4 October 1966, report of proceedings*. London, 1967.

Commonwealth Secretariat. *Reports of Commonwealth secretary-general:* [First] *report 1966; Second report Sept 1966–Oct 1968; Third report Nov 1968–Nov 1970*.

—— *Report of the Review Committee of Intra-Commonwealth Organisations*. London, 1966.

—— *Flow of intra-Commonwealth aid 1966*. London, 1968. (Also 1968 ed. pub. 1969.)

—— *Commonwealth trade 1968*. London, 1969. (Also for 1966, 1970 etc.)

—— *Commonwealth scholarship and fellowship plan, 9th annual report 1968–9*. London, 1969.

—— *Diplomatic service: formation and operation*. London, 1971.

Commonwealth Treasury (Australia). *Overseas investment in Australia* (Treasury Economic Paper no 1). Canberra, 1972.

Conan, A. R. *The sterling area*. London, 1952.

—— *Capital imports into sterling countries*. London 1960.

—— *The rationale of the sterling area: texts and commentary*. London, 1961.

Conference on the Future of the Commonwealth, Ditchley Park, Apr 1963. *The future of the Commonwealth: a British view; the report* . . . (rapporteur T. P. Soper). London, 1963.

Cook, Ramsay. *Canada and the French-Canadian question*. Toronto, 1966.

Cox, Richard. *Pan-Africanism in practice, an East African study, PAFMECSA 1958–64*. London, 1964.

Cowen, Zelman. *The British Commonwealth of nations in a changing world*. Melbourne, 1965.

Coxill, H. Wakelin & Sir Kenneth Grubb, eds. *World Christian handbook 1962 edition*. London, 1962.

Cozier, Tony, ed. *The West Indies cricket annual 1971*. Bridgetown, 1971.

Crawford, J. G. *Australian trade policy 1942–66*. Canberra, 1968.

Cross, J. A. *Whitehall and the Commonwealth: British departmental organisation for commonwealth relations, 1900–66*. London, 1967.

Currie, Sir James. *Professional organisations in the Commonwealth*. London, 1970.

Dalvi, John. *Himalayan blunder*. Bombay, 1969.

Darby, Phillip. *British defence policy east of Suez 1947–68*. London, 1973.

Davison, R. B. *Commonwealth immigrants*. London, 1964.

Day, John. *International nationalism: the extra-territorial relations of Southern Rhodesian African nationalists*. London, 1967.

Deakin, Nicholas & others. *Colour, citizenship and British society*. London, 1970.

de Smith, S. A. *The new Commonwealth and its constitutions*. London, 1964.

Deutsch, Karl & others. *Political community and the North Atlantic area: international organization in the light of historical experience*. Princeton, NJ, 1957.

Duncan, Andrew. *The reality of monarchy*. London, 1970.

Dutton, Geoffrey, ed. *Australia and the monarchy: a symposium*. Melbourne, 1966.

Eayrs, James. *Canada in world affairs Oct. 1955 to June 1957*. Toronto, 1959.

—— ed. *The Commonwealth and Suez, a documentary survey*. London, 1964.

—— 'The military policies of contemporary Canada', in Richard H. Leach, ed., *Contemporary Canada*. Durham, NC, 1967.

—— *Minutes of the sixties*. Toronto, 1968.

Eden, Anthony (Earl of Avon). *The memoirs of the Rt Hon. Sir Anthony Eden*, ii: *The reckoning*; iii: *Full circle*. London, 1965 & 1960.

Eisenhower, Dwight D. *The White House years*, i: *Mandate for change 1953–6*; ii: *Waging peace 1956–61*. Garden City, 1963 & 1965.

European Economic Community Commission. *Report to the European Parliament on the state of the negotiations with the United Kingdom*. Brussels, 1963.

Expanding Commonwealth Group. *The expanding Commonwealth*. London, 1956.

—— *Expanding opportunity*. London, 1958.

—— *Expanding obligation*. London, 1961.

Fawcett, J. E. S. *The British Commonwealth in international law*. London, 1963.

Feit, Edward. *African opposition in South Africa: the failure of passive resistance*. Stanford, 1967.

Fielden, Lionel. *The natural bent*. London, 1960.

Foot, Sir Hugh. *A start in freedom*. London, 1964.

Foot, Paul. *Immigration and race in British politics*. Harmondsworth, 1965.

—— *The rise of Enoch Powell*. Harmondsworth, 1969.

Franklin, Harry. *Unholy wedlock: the failure of the Central African Federation*. London, 1963.

Franks, Oliver. *Britain and the tide of world affairs*. London, 1955.

Gangal, S. C. *India and the Commonwealth*. Agra, 1970.

Gann, L. H. *A history of Southern Rhodesia: early days to 1934*. London, 1965.

Gelber, H. G. *Australia, Britain and the EEC 1961 to 1963*. Melbourne, 1966.

Ghazali bin Shafie, Dato Muhammad. *Malaysia in Afro-Asia*. Kuala Lumpur, 1964.

Glazebrook, G. de T. 'Canada in world affairs', in Dominion Bureau of Statistics, *Canada one hundred 1867–1967*. Ottawa, 1967, pp. 438–62.

Goldsworthy, David. *Colonial issues in British politics 1945–61: from 'colonial development' to 'wind of change'*. Oxford, 1971.

Gordon Walker, Patrick. 'Policy for the Commonwealth', in T. E. M. McKitterick & Kenneth Younger, eds., *Fabian international essays*. London, 1957, pp. 163–94.

—— *The cabinet*. London, 1970.

—— *The Commonwealth*. London, 1962.

Gray, Richard: *The two nations: aspects of the development of race relations in the Rhodesias and Nyasaland*. London, 1960.

Great Britain, Central Office of Information. *Britain and education in the Commonwealth*. London, 1964.

—— *Britain's external trade and payments*. London, 1972. Ref. pamph. R5529/72.

—— *Britain's international investment position*. London, 1970. Ref. pamph. R5829/70.

—— *Britain's invisible exports*. London, 1969. Ref. pamph. 582/69.

—— *The Commonwealth of nations*. London, 1957.

—— *Commonwealth preference*. London, 1969. Ref. pamph. R5155/69.

—— *Commonwealth tour: quotations from the speeches . . . of the prime minister of the United Kingdom, The Rt Hon. Harold Macmillan, MP*. London, 1958.

—— *The pattern of British exports*. London, 1970. Ref. pamph. R5760/70.

—— *The pattern of Commonwealth trade*. London, 1962. Ref. pamph. R5494.

———— *Political advance in the United Kingdom dependencies.* London, 1959. Ref. pamph. 6.

———— *What is the Commonwealth?* London, 1954, 1956, 1963.

——Dept of Education and Science. *The Commonwealth in education.* London, 1966. Ed. pamph. 51.

—— House of Commons, Select Committee on Estimates. *Third report*, session 1958–9, HC 252; *Fourth report*, session 1959–60, Colonial Office.

—— Treasury. *Britain and the European communities: background to the negotiations.* 1962.

Greenwood, Gordon & Norman Harper, eds. *Australia in world affairs 1956–60* and *1961–5.* Melbourne, 1963 & 1968.

Griffith, J. A. G. & others. *Coloured immigrants in Britain.* London, 1960.

Gullick, J. M. *Malaysia and its neighbours.* London, 1967.

Gupta, Sisir. *Kashmir: a study in India-Pakistan relations.* Bombay, 1966.

Gutteridge, W. F. *The military in African politics.* London, 1969.

Hall, Richard, *Zambia.* London, 1965.

—— *The high price of principles: Kaunda and the white south.* London, 1969.

Hamilton, W. B. & others, eds. *A decade of the Commonwealth 1955–64.* Durham, NC, 1966.

Hancock, W. K. *Survey of British Commonwealth affairs*, i: *Problems of nationality 1918–36*; ii: *Problems of economic policy 1918–39*, pts 1 & 2. London, 1937 & 1940–2.

—— *Argument of empire.* Harmondsworth, 1943.

—— *Colonial self-government.* Nottingham, 1956. (Cust Foundation lecture.)

—— *Smuts: the fields of force 1919–50.* Cambridge, 1968.

Harper, Norman & David Sissons. *Australia and the United Nations.* New York, 1959.

Harvey, Heather J. *Consultation and co-operation in the Commonwealth.* London, 1952.

Hayter, Sir William. *The Kremlin and the embassy.* London, 1966.

Hertzman, Lewis & others. *Alliances and illusions: Canada and the NATO-NORAD question.* Edmonton, 1969.

Hibbert, Christopher. *The British monarchy today.* London, 1968.

Hill, Clifford. *Immigration and integration: a study of the settlement of coloured minorities in Britain.* Oxford, 1970.

Hilsman, Roger. *To move a nation: the politics of foreign policy in the administration of John F. Kennedy.* Garden City, 1967.

Holmes, John W. 'The relationship in alliance and world affairs', in John S. Dickey, *The United States and Canada.* Englewood Cliffs, NJ, 1964, pp. 95–131.

Holyoake, Keith. *A defence policy for New Zealand.* Wellington, 1969.

Hoopes, Townsend. *The limits of intervention.* New York, 1969.

Hornby, Richard. *The changing Commonwealth.* London, 1965.

Hurd, Douglas & Andrew Osmond. *Send him victorious.* London, 1969.

Ingram, Derek. *Partners in adventure.* London, 1960.

—— *The Commonwealth at work.* London, 1969.

Jansen, G. H. *Afro-Asia and non-alignment.* London, 1966.

Jones, A. Creech. 'The Labour party and colonial policy 1945–51', in A. Creech Jones, ed., *New Fabian colonial essays.* London, 1959, pp. 19–37.

Jones, D. B. 'The Commonwealth sugar agreement', in London University, *The changing role of Commonwealth economic connections.* London [1971], pp. 75–86.

Josey, Alex. *Lee Kuan Yew.* Singapore, 1968.

—— *Lee Kuan Yew in London.* Singapore, 1968.

—— *Lee Kuan Yew and the Commonwealth.* Singapore, 1969.

Karanjia, R. K. *The philosophy of Mr Nehru.* London, 1966.

Kaul, B. M. *The untold story.* Bombay, 1967.

Kaunda, Kenneth D. *Zambia shall be free, an autobiography*. London, 1962.
Keatley, Patrick. *The politics of partnership*. Harmondsworth, 1963.
Kerr, Diana Rait & Ian Peebles. *Lord's 1946–70*. London, 1971.
Kilmuir, Earl of. *Political adventure*. London, 1964.
Kirkman, W. P. *Unscrambling an empire: a critique of British colonial policy 1955–66*. London, 1966.
Kitzinger, Uwe. *The challenge of the Common Market*. Oxford, 1962.
—— *The European Common Market and Community*. London, 1967.
—— *The second try: Labour and the EEC*. Oxford, 1968.
Kotelawala, Sir John. *An Asian prime minister's story*. London, 1956.
Kumar, Dharma. *India and the European Economic Community*. Bombay, 1966.
Laird, Dorothy. *How the Queen reigns: an authentic study of the Queen's personality and life work*. London, 1961.
Lardner-Burke, Desmond. *Rhodesia: the story of the crisis*. London, 1966.
Legum, Colin, ed. *Zambia: independence and beyond; the speeches of Kenneth Kaunda*. London, 1966.
Legum, Colin & Margaret. *South Africa: crisis for the west*. London, 1964.
Leistner, G. M. E. *South Africa's development aid to African states*. Pretoria, 1970.
Leys, Colin. *European politics in Southern Rhodesia*. Oxford, 1959.
Lipton, Michael. 'Prospects for Commonwealth co-operation and planning', in Paul Streeten & Hugh Corbet, eds. *Commonwealth policy in a global context*. London, 1971, pp. 198–220.
Listowel, Lord. *Commonwealth future*. London, 1957. (Fabian tract 308.)
Lloyd, Trevor. *Canada in world affairs 1957–9*. Toronto, 1968.
Lockwood, Sir John. 'The transplantation of the university: the case of Africa', in W. B. Hamilton & others, eds. *A decade of the Commonwealth 1955–64*. Durham, NC, 1966.
London University, Inst. of Commonwealth Studies. *The changing role of Commonwealth economic connections*. London, [1971], mimeo.
Lyon, Peyton V. *Canada in world affairs 1961–8*. Toronto, 1968.
Lyttelton, Oliver (Viscount Chandos). *The memoirs of Lord Chandos*. London, 1962.
McDermott, Geoffrey. *The Eden legacy and the decline of British diplomacy*. London, 1969.
MacDonald, Malcolm. *The evolving Commonwealth*. Enstone, 1970. Ditchley Foundation Lecture ix.
Mackenzie, W. J. M. & J. W. Grove. *Central administration in Britain*. London, 1957.
McLeod, A. L., ed. *The Commonwealth pen: an introduction to the literature of the British Commonwealth*. Ithaca, 1961.
McKitterick, T. E. M. & Kenneth Younger, eds. *Fabian international essays*. London, 1957.
Macmillan, Harold. *Britain, the Commonwealth and Europe*. London, 1962.
—— *Tides of fortune 1945–55*. London, 1969.
—— *Riding the storm 1956–9*. London, 1971.
—— *Pointing the way 1959–61*. London, 1972.
Maitland, Patrick. *Task for giants: an expanding Commonwealth*. London, 1957.
Mallaby, George. *From my level: unwritten minutes*. London, 1965.
Mansergh, Nicholas. *The multi-racial Commonwealth*. London, 1955.
—— *Survey of British Commonwealth affairs: problems of wartime co-operation and postwar change 1939–52*. London, 1958.
—— *South Africa 1906–61: the price of magnanimity*. London, 1962.
—— *The Commonwealth experience*. London, [1969].

—— ed. *Documents and speeches on British Commonwealth affairs, 1931–52 & 1952–62.* London, 1953 & 1963.

Mansholt, Sicco. *Agriculture 1980—New Zealand and the EEC.* Wellington, 1969.

Marshall, Charles Burton. *Crisis over Rhodesia: a skeptical view.* Baltimore, 1967.

Marshall, Geoffrey. *Parliamentary sovereignty and the Commonwealth.* Oxford, 1957.

Martin, L. W. *British defence policy: the long recessional.* London, 1969. (Adelphi Papers no. 61.)

Mason, Philip. *The birth of a dilemma: the conquest and settlement of Rhodesia.* London, 1958.

—— *Year of decision.* London, 1960.

Massey, Vincent. *Canadians and their Commonwealth.* Oxford, 1961. (Romanes Lecture, 1961.)

Maxwell, Neville. *India's China war.* London 1970.

Mayhew, Christopher. *Britain's role tomorrow.* London, 1967.

Mazrui, Ali A. *The Anglo-African Commonwealth: political friction and cultural fusion.* Oxford, 1967.

—— *Towards a pax africana: a study of ideology and ambition.* London, 1967.

—— 'Geographical propinquity versus Commonwealth cohesion', in Paul Streeten & Hugh Corbet, eds. *Commonwealth policy in a global context.* London, 1971, pp. 16–31.

Mboya, Tom. *Freedom and after.* London, 1963.

—— 'Pan-Africanism and the Commonwealth: are they in conflict?', in Ali A. Mazrui, *The Anglo-African Commonwealth.* Oxford, 1967, pp. 158–53.

Menzies, R. G. *The British Commonwealth of nations in international affairs.* Sydney, 1950. (Aus. Inst. Int. Aff., Roy Milne Lecture.)

—— *The changing Commonwealth.* Cambridge, 1960. (Smuts Memorial Lecture.)

—— *Afternoon light: some memories of men and events.* London, 1967.

Millar, T. B. *The Commonwealth and the United Nations.* Sydney, 1967.

—— *Australia's defence.* Melbourne, 1969. 2nd ed.

—— *Australia's foreign policy.* Sydney, 1968.

Miller, J. D. B. *The Commonwealth in the world.* London, 1958.

—— 'Commonwealth conferences 1945–55', *Year Book of World Affairs 1956.* London, 1956.

—— 'Britain without Europe', in Coral Bell, ed. *Europe without Britain.* Melbourne, 1963, pp. 27–44.

—— *The politics of the third world.* London, 1966.

Minifie, James M. *Peacemaker or powder-monkey.* Toronto, 1960.

Mitchell, B. R., with Phyllis Deane. *Abstract of British historical statistics.* Cambridge, 1962.

Mitchell, B. R. & H. G. Jones. *Second abstract of British historical statistics.* Cambridge, 1971.

Modelski, George, ed. *The new emerging forces: documents on the ideology of Indonesian foreign policy.* Canberra, 1963.

Moncrieff, Anthony, ed. *Suez ten years after.* London, 1967.

Monroe, Elizabeth. *Britain's moment in the Middle East 1914–56.* London, 1963.

Moran, Lord. *Winston Churchill: the struggle for survival 1940–65.* London, 1966.

Morrah, Dermot. *The work of the Queen.* London, 1958.

Muller, C. J. F., ed. *Five hundred years: a history of South Africa.* Pretoria, 1969.

Munger, Edwin S. *Afrikaner and African nationalism: South African parallels and parameters.* London, 1967.

Murphy, Robert. *Diplomat among warriors.* Garden City, 1964.

McDermott, Geoffrey. *The Eden legacy and the decline of British diplomacy.* London, 1969.

Naipaul, V. S. *The mimic men.* London, 1967.
—— *The middle passage.* Harmondsworth, 1969.
Nehru, Jawaharlal. *India's foreign policy: selected speeches, September 1946–April 1961.* Delhi, 1961.
New Zealand Dept of External Affairs. *New Zealand assistance to the Republic of Vietnam.* Wellington, 1965.
Nicol, Davidson. 'The formation of a West African intellectual community', in J. T. Saunders & M. Duowuna, eds. *The West African intellectual community.* Ibadan, 1962.
Nielsen, Waldemar A. *The great powers and Africa.* New York, 1969.
Nkrumah, Kwame. *The autobiography of Kwame Nkrumah.* London, 1957.
—— *I speak of freedom.* London, 1961.
—— *Africa must unite.* London, 1963.
Nutting, Anthony. *No end of a lesson: the story of Suez.* London, 1967.
Nyerere, Julius K. *Freedom and unity: a selection from writings and speeches 1952–65.* London, 1967.
—— *Freedom and socialism: a selection from writings and speeches 1965–7.* Dar es Salaam, 1968.
—— *South Africa and the Commonwealth.* Dar es Salaam, 1971.
Ojukwu, C. Odumegwu. *Biafra: selected speeches.* New York, 1969.
Okigbo, P. N. C. *Africa and the Common Market.* London, 1967.
Panter-Brick, S. K., ed. *Nigerian politics and military rule.* London, 1970.
Patterson, Sheila. *Immigration and race relations in Britain 1960–7.* London, 1969.
Peach, Ceri. *West Indian migration to Britain: a social geography.* London, 1968.
Pearson, Lester B. *Democracy in world politics.* Princeton, 1955.
—— *Partners in development: report of the Commission on International Development.* London, 1969.
Pelzer, A. N. *Verwoerd speaks: speeches 1948–66.* Johannesburg, 1966.
Perham, Margery. *Colonial sequence 1949 to 1969.* London, 1970.
Phillips, A. A. *The Australian tradition.* Melbourne, 1958.
Pickles, William. *Britain and Europe—how much has changed?* Oxford, 1967.
Pike, John G. *Malawi: a political and economic history.* London, 1968.
Poynton, Sir Hilton, 'A review of the changing role of Commonwealth economic connections', in London University. *The changing role of Commonwealth economic connections.* London, [1971], pp. 1–17.
Press, John ed. *Commonwealth literature: unity and diversity in a common culture.* London, 1965.
Preston, Richard A. *Canada in world affairs 1959–61.* Toronto, 1965.
Rajan, M. S. *The United Nations and domestic jurisdiction.* London, 1961.
—— *India in world affairs 1954–6.* New York, 1964.
—— 'The future of the Commonwealth', in A. Appadorai, ed. *India: social and political developments 1947–67.* Bombay, 1967, pp. 270–302.
Reddy, T. Ramakrishna. *India's policy in the United Nations.* Rutherford, NJ, 1968.
Reese, Trevor R. *The history of the Royal Commonwealth Society 1868–1968.* London, 1968.
—— *Australia, New Zealand and the United States: a survey of international relations 1941–68.* London, 1969.
Rhodesia in the context of Africa. Salisbury, Govt Printer, 1966.
Robertson, Janet. *Liberalism in South Africa 1948–63.* Oxford, 1971.
Robertson, Terence. *Crisis: the inside story of the Suez conspiracy.* London, 1965.
Robinson, Kenneth. 'The intergovernmental machinery of Commonwealth consul-

tation and co-operation', in W. B. Hamilton & others, eds. *A decade of the Commonwealth 1954–64*. Durham, NC, 1966, pp. 89–123.

Rose, E. J. B., ed. *Colour and citizenship*. London, 1969.

Rosecrance, R. N. *Defense of the realm: British strategy in the nuclear epoch*. New York, 1968.

Rosenwater, Irving. 'The South African tour dispute', in *Wisden cricketers' almanac 1971*. London, 1971.

Rothstein, Robert L. *Alliances and small powers*. New York, 1968.

Sandys, Duncan. *The modern Commonwealth*. London, 1962.

Sar Desai, D. R. *Indian foreign policy in Cambodia, Laos and Vietnam 1947–64*. Berkeley, 1968.

Saunders, J. T. & M. Duowuna, eds. *The West African intellectual community*. Ibadan, 1962.

Seton-Watson, Hugh. *Nationalism and communism: essays 1946–63*. London, 1964.

Shils, Edward. 'A further step towards a West African intellectual community', in J. T. Saunders & M. Duowuna, eds. *The West African intellectual community*. Ibadan, 1962.

Shonfield, Andrew. *British economic policy since the war*. Harmondsworth, 1958.

Sinclair, Keith, ed. *Distance looks our way: the effects of remoteness on New Zealand*. Auckland, 1961.

Sithole, Ndabaninghi. *African nationalism*. Cape Town, 1959.

Slimming, John. *Malaysia, death of a democracy*. London, 1969.

Smiley, Donald V. *The Canadian political nationality*. Toronto, 1967.

Smith, Arnold. *Canada and the Commonwealth*. Toronto, 1967. (Centennial Lecture, Toronto Univ.)

Soper, Tom. *Commonwealth and common market*. London, 1962.

Soref, Harold & Ian Greig. *The puppeteers*. London, 1965.

Sorensen, Theodore C. *Kennedy*. London, 1965.

Spearman, Diana. *The sterling area*. London, 1953.

Spence, J. E. *Republic under pressure: a study of South African foreign policy*. London, 1965.

Spender, Sir Percy. *Exercises in diplomacy: the ANZUS treaty and the Colombo plan*. Sydney, 1969.

Starke, J. G. *The ANZUS treaty alliance*. Melbourne, 1965.

Stead, C. K. 'For the hulk of the world's between', in Keith Sinclair, ed. *Distance looks our way*. Auckland, 1961, pp. 79–96.

Stebbins, Richard P. *The United States in world affairs 1963*. New York, 1964.

Strange, Susan. *Sterling and British policy: a political study of an international currency in decline*. London, 1970.

Streeten, Paul & Hugh Corbet eds. *Commonwealth policy in a global context*. London, 1971.

Study Group of the Conservative Commonwealth and Overseas Council. *Policy for the Commonwealth*. London, 1967.

Symonds, Richard. *The British and their successors: a study in the development of the government services in the new states*. Evanston, 1966.

Thomas, Hugh. *The Suez affair*. London, 1967.

Thompson, G. J. *New Zealand's international aid*. Wellington, 1967.

Thompson, W. Scott. *Ghana's foreign policy 1957–66*. Princeton, 1969.

Thomson, Dale C. *Louis St Laurent: Canadian*. New York, 1968.

Trades Union Congress. *Britain and the EEC*. London, 1967.

Underhill, Frank. *The British Commonwealth: an experiment in co-operation among nations*. Durham, NC, 1956.

Uri, Pierre, ed. *From Commonwealth to common market.* Harmondsworth, 1968.
Utley, T. E. & John Udal (rapporteurs). *Wind of change: the challenge of the Common-wealth.* London, 1960.
Walsh, William. *A manifold voice: studies in Commonwealth literature.* London, 1970.
Watt, D. C. *Documents on the Suez crisis, 26 July to 6 November 1956.* London, 1957.
Welensky, Roy. *Welensky's 4000 days: the life and death of the Federation of Rhodesia and Nyasaland.* London, 1964.
Wheare, K. C. *The constitutional structure of the Commonwealth.* Oxford, 1960.
Williams, Geoffrey & Bruce Reed. *Denis Healey and the policies of power.* London, 1971.
Williams, Peter. *Aid in the Commonwealth.* London, 1965.
Wilson, Edmund. *O Canada: an American's notes on Canadian culture.* London, 1967.
Wilson, Harold. *The new Britain: Labour's plan.* Harmondsworth, 1964.
—— *The Labour government 1964–70: a personal record.* London, 1971.
Winks, Robin. 'Malaysia and the Commonwealth: an inquiry into the nature of Commonwealth ties', in Wang Gungwu, ed. *Malaysia: a survey.* London, 1964, pp. 375–99.
Young, Kenneth. *Sir Alec Douglas-Home.* London, 1970.
—— *Rhodesia and independence: a study in British colonial policy.* London, 1967. Revised ed. 1969.

C. Articles*

Altrincham, Lord. Is the Commonwealth a sham? *National & English R.*, May 1960, pp. 156–64.
Anglin, Douglas. Nigeria: political non-alignment and economic alignment. *J. Mod. Afr. Stud.*, 2/2 (1964), pp. 247–63.
Austin, Dennis. The Commonwealth turned upside down. *World Today*, Oct 1966, pp. 418–26.
—— White power? *JCPS*, July 1968, pp. 95–106.
Ball, W. Macmahon. The Australian reaction to the Suez crisis. *Aus. J. Pol. & Hist.*, 2/2, pp. 129–50.
Barber, James. The impact of the Rhodesian crisis on the Commonwealth. *JCPS*, July 1969, pp. 83–95.
Barratt, James. The outward movement in South Africa's foreign relations. *Newsletter* no. 3, S. Afr. Inst. Int. Aff., Aug 1969.
Baxter, G. H. & P. W. Hodgens. The constitutional status of the Federation of Rhodesia and Nyasaland. *Int. Aff.*, Oct 1957.
Beloff, Max. The Commonwealth: can it survive? *Canberra Times*, 2 Sept 1970.
Boyce, Peter. Australian diplomacy in Malaya. *J. Southeast As. Hist.*, Sept 1963, pp. 96–9.
Bull, Hedley. What is the Commonwealth? *World Politics*, July 1959, pp. 577–87.
Carrington, Charles. How to improve the CRO. *The Times*, 18 Dec 1959.
Clark, William. Debating the Commonwealth. *Observer*, 28 Mar 1954.
'Conservative, A.' Patriotism based on reality not on dreams. *The Times*, 2 Apr 1964.
Cowen, Zelman. The contemporary Commonwealth: a general view. *Int. Org.*, Spring 1959, pp. 204–18.
Curtin, T. R. C. Total sanctions and economic development in Rhodesia. *JCPS*, July 1969, pp. 126–31.
'Cwthmas'. *The Economist*, 27 Dec 1958.
Day, A. C. L., & others. What price the sterling area? *The Listener*, 21 & 28 Nov 1957, 2 Jan 1958.

* For abbreviations see p. ix.

Desai, M. J. Commonwealth relations. *J. United Service Inst. of India*, July–Sept 1957, pp. 1–9.

de Smith, S. A. The Commonwealth and South Africa. *Univ. Malaya Law R.*, Dec 1961, pp. 167–90.

—— Fundamental rules—forty years on. *Int. J.*, Spring 1971, pp. 347–60.

Eayrs, James. The overhaul of the Commonwealth. *Round Table*, Jan 1967, pp. 48–56.

Gangal, S. C. The Commonwealth and Indo-Pakistani relations. *Int. Stud.*, July–Oct 1966, pp. 134–49.

God rest ye merry Cwthmen. *The Economist*, 21 Dec 1968.

Gordon Walker, Patrick. Commonwealth secretary. *JCPS*, Nov 1961, pp. 17–28.

—— The British Labour party and the Commonwealth. *Round Table*, Nov 1970, pp. 503–10.

Gupta, Anirudha. The Rhodesian crisis and the Organization of African Unity. *Int. Stud.*, July 1967.

—— The Asians in East Africa: problems and prospects. *Int. Stud.*, Jan 1969, pp. 270–302.

Harnetty, Peter. Canada, South Africa and the Commonwealth. *JCPS*, Nov 1963, pp. 33–44.

Harvey, Heather Joan. The British Commonwealth: a pattern of cooperation. *Int. Conciliation*, Jan 1953, pp. 3–48.

Hoffmann, Stanley. Discord in community. *Int. Org.*, 17 (1963), pp. 521–49.

Holmes, John W. The impact on the Commonwealth of the emergence of Africa. *Int. Org.*, 16 (1962), pp. 291–302.

—— A Canadian's Commonwealth. *Round Table*, Oct 1966, pp. 335–49.

—— The new perspectives of Canadian foreign policy. *World Today*, Oct 1969.

Hoskyns, Catherine. Africa's foreign relations: the case of Tanzania. *Int. Aff.*, July 1968, pp. 446–62.

Howell, John. An analysis of Kenyan foreign policy. *J. Mod. Afr. Stud.*, 6 (1968), pp. 29–48.

Jacobson, Dan. Alienation of a South African. *Guardian*, 18 Mar. 1961.

Jeffries, Sir Charles. Staffing oversea public services. *The Times*, 23 June 1958.

Jennings, Sir Ivor. South Africa and the Commonwealth: constitutional problems in admitting republics. *Optima*, Sept 1960, pp. 117–22.

Johnson, Harry. The Commonwealth preferences: a system in need of analysis. *Round Table*, Oct 1966, pp. 363–76.

Kabad, B. K. R. Will the Commonwealth last? *Times of India*, 11 Jan 1969.

Lawson, Nigel. Should there be another Commonwealth meeting? *FT*, 23 June 1965.

Leach, Richard H. The secretariat. *Int. J.*, Spring 1971, pp. 374–400.

Lewis, Roy. Britain and Biafra: a Commonwealth civil war. *Round Table*, July 1970, pp. 241–8.

Leys, Colin. Power and principle in Central Africa. *The Listener*, 12 Sept 1957.

Lipton, Merle. British arms for South Africa. *World Today*, Oct 1970.

Lipton, Michael & Clive Bell. The fall in Commonwealth trade. *Round Table*, Jan 1970.

Low, D. A. The Buganda mission. *Hist. Stud.* (Melbourne), Oct 1968, pp. 353–80.

Lyon, Peter. The Commonwealth in the 1970s. *World Today*, Apr 1971, pp. 174–85.

Mayall, James. Malawi's foreign policy. *World Today*, Oct 1970, pp. 435–45.

Mazrui, Ali A. African attitudes to the European Economic Community. *Int. Aff.*, Jan 1963.

—— Anti-militarism and political militancy in Tanzania. *J. Conflict Resolution*, Sept 1968, pp. 269–84.

—— Africa, the west and the world. *Aus. Outlook*, Aug 1972.

Menzies, R. G. The ever changing Commonwealth II, need for new forms of consultation. *The Times*, 12 June 1956.

—— Let's have reason on Rhodesia. *Sunday Telegraph*, 24 Apr 1966.

Miller, J. D. B. The CRO and Commonwealth relations. *Int. Stud.*, July 1960, pp. 42–59.

—— The Colonial Office and the Estimates Committee. *Public Administration*, Summer 1961, pp. 173–9.

—— South Africa's departure. *JCPS*, Nov 1961.

—— British interests and the Commonwealth. *JCPS*, Nov 1966, pp. 180–90.

Morris Jones, W. H. Towards a new Commonwealth. *Foreign Affairs Reports* (New Delhi), May 1960, pp. 45–54.

—— & T. J. Johnson. A Commonwealth of learning. *Round Table*, Nov 1970, pp. 385–96.

Nicholson, Sir Godfrey. The Colonial Office and the Estimates Committee. *Public Administration*, Summer 1962, pp. 151–7.

Normanbrook, Lord. Meetings of Commonwealth prime ministers. *J. Parl. of Commonwealth*, 45 (1964), pp. 248–54.

Nyerere, Julius K. The African view on Rhodesia: objections to the *Fearless* proposals. *Round Table*, Apr 1969, pp. 135, 140.

—— A United States of Africa. *J. Mod. Afr. Stud.*, 1/1 (1963).

—— Why we recognized Biafra. *The Observer*, 28 Apr 1968.

O'Connell, James. The inevitability of instability. *J. Mod. Afr. Stud.*, 5/2 (1967), pp. 181–91.

Ojedokun, Olasupo. The Anglo-Nigerian entente and its demise, 1960–2. *JCPS*, Nov 1971, pp. 210–33.

Pollock, Peter. South African cricket overshadowed by isolation. *The Cricketer*, June 1971.

Rajan, M. S. The Indo-Canadian entente. *Int. J.*, 17 (1962).

—— The Tashkent declaration. *Int. Stud.*, July–Oct 1966, pp. 1–26.

Reid, Escott. Canadian foreign policy 1967–77: a second golden decade. *Int. J.*, 22/2 (1967), pp. 171–81.

Rippon, Geoffrey. South Africa and naval strategy. *Round Table*, July 1970, pp. 303–10.

Russett, Bruce M. Transactions, community and international political integration. *J. Common Market Stud.*, Mar 1971, pp. 224–45.

Smith, Arnold. The need for Commonwealth. *Round Table*, July 1966, pp. 219–27.

—— The modern Commonwealth. *New Commonwealth*, 9 (1970), pp. 3–5.

Smith, William Edgett. Profiles of Julius K. Nyerere. *New Yorker*, 16, 23 & 30 Oct 1971.

Spence, J. E. South Africa's 'new look' foreign policy. *World Today*, Apr 1968, pp. 137–45.

Springer, Hugh. Problems of aid in education in the Commonwealth. *Round Table*, July 1970.

Sutcliffe, R. B. The political economy of Rhodesian sanctions. *JCPS*, July 1969, pp. 113–25.

Trethowan, Ian. Africa in the Commons. *New Commonwealth*, 9 Nov 1953, pp. 490–2.

Vivekanandan, B. The Commonwealth secretariat. *Int. Stud.*, Jan 1968, pp. 301–31.

Younger, Kenneth. Reflections on Africa and the Commonwealth. *World Today*, Mar 1962, pp. 121–9.

INDEX